Historical Dictionaries of Asia, Oceania, and the Middle East

Edited by Jon Woronoff

Asia

1. *Vietnam*, by William J. Duiker. 1989. *Out of print. See No. 27.*
2. *Bangladesh*, 2nd ed., by Craig Baxter and Syedur Rahman. 1996. *Out of print. See No. 48.*
3. *Pakistan*, by Shahid Javed Burki. 1991. *Out of print. See No. 33.*
4. *Jordan*, by Peter Gubser. 1991.
5. *Afghanistan*, by Ludwig W. Adamec. 1991. *Out of print. See No. 47.*
6. *Laos*, by Martin Stuart-Fox and Mary Kooyman. 1992. *Out of print. See No. 35.*
7. *Singapore*, by K. Mulliner and Lian The-Mulliner. 1991.
8. *Israel*, by Bernard Reich. 1992.
9. *Indonesia*, by Robert Cribb. 1992. *Out of print. See No. 51.*
10. *Hong Kong and Macau*, by Elfed Vaughan Roberts, Sum Ngai Ling, and Peter Bradshaw. 1992.
11. *Korea*, by Andrew C. Nahm. 1993. *Out of print. See No. 52.*
12. *Taiwan*, by John F. Copper. 1993. *Out of print. See No. 34.*
13. *Malaysia*, by Amarjit Kaur. 1993. *Out of print. See No. 36.*
14. *Saudi Arabia*, by J. E. Peterson. 1993. *Out of print. See No. 45.*
15. *Myanmar*, by Jan Becka. 1995. *Out of print. See No. 59.*
16. *Iran*, by John H. Lorentz. 1995. *Out of print. See No. 62.*
17. *Yemen*, by Robert D. Burrowes. 1995.
18. *Thailand*, by May Kyi Win and Harold Smith. 1995. *Out of print. See No. 55.*
19. *Mongolia*, by Alan J. K. Sanders. 1996. *Out of print. See No. 42.*
20. *India*, by Surjit Mansingh. 1996. *Out of print. See No. 58.*
21. *Gulf Arab States*, by Malcolm C. Peck. 1996.
22. *Syria*, by David Commins. 1996. *Out of print. See No. 50.*
23. *Palestine*, by Nafez Y. Nazzal and Laila A. Nazzal. 1997.
24. *Philippines*, by Artemio R. Guillermo and May Kyi Win. 1997. *Out of print. See No. 54.*

Oceania

1. *Australia*, by James C. Docherty. 1992. *Out of print. See No. 32.*
2. *Polynesia*, by Robert D. Craig. 1993. *Out of print. See No. 39.*

3. *Guam and Micronesia*, by William Wuerch and Dirk Ballendorf. 1994.
4. *Papua New Guinea*, by Ann Turner. 1994. *Out of print. See No. 37.*
5. *New Zealand*, by Keith Jackson and Alan McRobie. 1996. *Out of print. See No. 56.*

New Combined Series
25. *Brunei Darussalam*, by D. S. Ranjit Singh and Jatswan S. Sidhu. 1997.
26. *Sri Lanka*, by S. W. R. de A. Samarasinghe and Vidyamali Samarasinghe. 1998.
27. *Vietnam*, 2nd ed., by William J. Duiker. 1998. *Out of print. See No. 57.*
28. *People's Republic of China: 1949–1997*, by Lawrence R. Sullivan, with the assistance of Nancy Hearst. 1998. *Out of print. See No. 63.*
29. *Afghanistan*, 2nd ed., by Ludwig W. Adamec. 1997. *Out of print. See No. 47.*
30. *Lebanon*, by As'ad AbuKhalil. 1998.
31. *Azerbaijan*, by Tadeusz Swietochowski and Brian C. Collins. 1999.
32. *Australia*, 2nd ed., by James C. Docherty. 1999. *Out of print. See No. 65.*
33. *Pakistan*, 2nd ed., by Shahid Javed Burki. 1999. *Out of print. See No. 61.*
34. *Taiwan (Republic of China)*, 2nd ed., by John F. Copper. 2000. *Out of print. See No. 64.*
35. *Laos*, 2nd ed., by Martin Stuart-Fox. 2001.
36. *Malaysia*, 2nd ed., by Amarjit Kaur. 2001.
37. *Papua New Guinea*, 2nd ed., by Ann Turner. 2001.
38. *Tajikistan*, by Kamoludin Abdullaev and Shahram Akbarzedeh. 2002.
39. *Polynesia*, 2nd ed., by Robert D. Craig. 2002.
40. *North Korea*, by Ilpyong J. Kim. 2003.
41. *Armenia*, by Rouben Paul Adalian. 2002.
42. *Mongolia*, 2nd ed., by Alan J. K. Sanders. 2003.
43. *Cambodia*, by Justin Corfield and Laura Summers. 2003.
44. *Iraq*, by Edmund A. Ghareeb with the assistance of Beth K. Dougherty. 2004.
45. *Saudi Arabia*, 2nd ed., by J. E. Peterson. 2003.
46. *Nepal*, by Nanda R. Shrestha and Keshav Bhattarai. 2003.

Historical Dictionary of Iran

Second Edition

John H. Lorentz

Historical Dictionaries of Asia, Oceania, and the Middle East, No. 62

The Scarecrow Press, Inc.

Lanham, Maryland • Toronto • Plymouth, UK

2007

SCARECROW PRESS, INC.

Published in the United States of America
by Scarecrow Press, Inc.
A wholly owned subsidary of
The Rowman & Littlefield Publishing Group, Inc.
4501 Forbes Boulevard, Suite 200, Lanham, Maryland 20706
www.scarecrowpress.com

Estover Road
Plymouth PL6 7PY
United Kingdom

British Library Cataloguing in Publication Information Available

Library of Congress Cataloging-in-Publication Data

Lorentz, John H. (John Henry), 1940–
  Historical dictionary of Iran / John H. Lorentz. — 2nd ed.
    p. cm. — (Historical dictionaries of Asia, Oceania, and the Middle East ;
no. 62)
  Includes bibliographical references and index.
  ISBN-13: 978-0-8108-5330-0 (hardcover : alk. paper)
  ISBN-10: 0-8108-5330-2 (hardcover : alk. paper)
  1. Iran—History—Dictionaries. I. Title. II. Series

DS270.L67 2006
955.003—dc22   2006028034

CONTENTS

FIGURES AND TABLES

EDITOR'S FOREWORD

Many countries are reputed to have a strategic geographic location. But there are few of which this is truer than Iran, known in earlier times as Persia. Located between Europe and Asia, astride the Middle East, its location is unique. Yet, while this should have brought benefits, and sometimes did, it has more often been a disadvantage due to invasions or domination by other countries, whether the earlier Great Powers or the United States and Soviet Union during the Cold War. This will doubtlessly explain its fear of foreign influence, which has become particularly noticeable under the Islamic Republic. Yet, while it can be an irritant for some other countries, and what its government and clerical rulers do is not even always appreciated at home, Iran is far too important—with its abundant oil resources, large population and political and religious dynamic—to ignore, let alone keep on the margins of the international community.

It is obviously much easier to understand what is going on in present-day Iran by looking into its long history, the periods of glory and those of disaster, to see how it was shaped. That is certainly facilitated by this second edition of the *Historical Dictionary of Iran*. The long view is provided, first, by a rather extensive chronology, from the earliest times to the present day. The big picture then emerges from the introduction, reflecting on the past and the present. Countless details are then described in some 320 dictionary entries on important persons, places and events, institutions and major features of its politics, economy, society, culture, and religion. Other sources of information are then listed in the bibliography. So this is an excellent place to start, before referring to other sources, but also one to which readers can return to elucidate specific aspects.

This new, updated, and considerably expanded edition was written by the same author as the first, John H. Lorentz, who not only knows Iran well but obviously has a deep affection for the country. He first visited it in the early 1960s as a Peace Corps volunteer and has returned a number of times, including a stint as a Senior Fulbright-Hays Fellow. Dr. Lorentz has penned monographs and articles on Iran and the Iranians and has taught about the Middle East at Portland State University, Willamette University, and presently Shawnee State University, where he is both Professor of History and Director of the Center for International Programs and Activities. This long experience has contributed strongly to a handy guide that is not only well researched, but easy to read.

Jon Woronoff
Series Editor

PREFACE

This work deals with all historical periods and considers history in the widest definition of the term. There is, however, a concentration on the modern period, defined here as the turn of the 18th century (1800 A.D.) to the present. And, the primary focus is on political history. Some narrowing was a necessity given the enormous length and depth of Iranian history. Nonetheless, there are a goodly number of entries that could be categorized as cultural, literary, economic, social, or geographic. Furthermore, much attention is paid to American involvement in Iran in the 19th and 20th centuries and to Americans with attachment to Iran. This is particularly evident in the large number of American biographical entries. Iranian biographies, of course, are considerably more, amounting to over 30 percent of the entries spread evenly across kings and princes, prime ministers, political figures, religious figures, particularly of the Islamic Revolution, literati, and other cultural figures. Of the biographical listings, two-thirds are political figures. Of these, about half are centrally connected to the Islamic Revolution of Iran. Thus, if there is a bias in numbers, very recent Iranian history holds sway. Approximately one-third of the biographical listings are cultural figures equally divided between literary figures and representatives of other cultural forms.

About 10 percent of the total entries are geographical terms. The significantly large number here reflects the belief of the author that historical understanding is only attainable with an appreciation of the stage upon which history occurs. Another category with about 10 percent of the total listings is political groups, parties, and constitutions. Iranian organizations and companies make up another 10 percent. Other categories contain approximately five percent each of the total number of listings. These include colleges and universities, foreign organizations and instrumentalities, treaties and wars, titles and names, religions and religious movements, tribes, women, film directors, economic sectors, and various foreign nationals other than Americans.

This second edition of the *Historical Dictionary of Iran* appears a full decade after the first edition. Much of historical significance has happened in the intervening years, particularly in the cultural and political arenas. In the former case, Iranian film has blossomed into a world-class cinema. On the surface, this would seem an oddity in light of the stringent political limitations dictated by the conservative Islamic government of Iran. Nonetheless, Iran since the **Islamic Revolution** ranks highly in the artistic quality of its filmic output. The reason is two-fold. First, while the artist must be sensitive to the ever-shifting demands of propriety, there is considerably more freedom of expression in Iran than popularly believed in the West. Second, Iranians are masters at finding ways to creatively express themselves by indirect means. Satire and its cousins are alive and well in Iran. A good example in film is the frequent use of children to explore some very adult themes.

Filmmakers in contemporary Iran are constantly pushing the boundaries of censorship and have achieved remarkable creative output in the past decade. This circumstance is reflected in this edition, which contains a number of new film-related entries. Ten such entries have been added, including an overview entry on **cinema** and separate entries on nine film directors.

With regard to politics, in the past decade there have been three presidential elections in Iran. The country has swayed from a conservative Islamic political persuasion to a liberal one with the election of President **Muhammad Khatami** in 1997, and then back towards a conservative mode with the election of President **Mahmud Amadinejad** in June of 2005. In the course of this time, the debates over the relationship between religion and politics have been abundant and intense. The rise and fall of numerous politicians, a number of whom are also religious scholars, has occurred. Intellectuals, both secular and religious, have also been buffeted by the varying political winds. The political scene in Iran has been, is, and will surely continue to be a lively one. Tracking key characters gives some sense of the dynamic and evolving political scene. Thus, this edition contains a large number of new entries on contemporary political and intellectual figures. More than 20 such individuals have been added. Likewise, a considerably increased number of political organizations and movements have found their way into the book as entries.

Another feature of this second edition is that whole new categories of entries have been added. Economics, for instance, was sparsely covered in the first edition, but has a considerable number of entries in this edition. Similarly, only a handful of cities were in the first edition, whereas the second has entries on every Iranian city of 200,000 persons or more according to the latest census data (1996). Beyond that benchmark, other cities are included because they are deemed of such historical importance that inclusion was a must. Thus, there are 18 entries on individual cities, and several more if one takes into account ancient cities that are now archaeological sites.

Full entries on Iranian **tribes** have been added. As well, an overview entry on **women** in Iran and 11 separate entries on various women of importance in Iranian history and in contemporary times have been added.

New entries written for the second edition of the *Historical Dictionary* number 146. Most of the entries in the first edition of the *Historical Dictionary* were retained, though many were either added to or updated. The new total of entries is 320.

This second edition is, in light of the information above, considerably more comprehensive than the first. Care has been devoted to choosing entries and writing them in such a way that they are integrated, both in the nature of the content and organizationally. The hoped for result is that a fuller picture will emerge for the reader who chooses to go beyond individual entries and trace the components of a larger picture via the cross-referencing indicators, as discussed in the section entitled "Reader's Notes". Like pieces of a puzzle, the reader can look at any single piece, or put pieces together to form a more complete understanding of related issues, persons, concepts, and the like.

The choice of entries has been determined, in part, by the dictates of the point above. Most, of course, are worthy in their own right apart from considerations of integration. However, some entries are included to give a more complete picture of certain events and trends, whereas certain other entries were not included because space was limited. Thus, there are judgment calls. And, while not all may agree with what is included and not included, it is hoped that the reader's forbearance be forthcoming.

As indicated in the acknowledgments, I asked the advice of specialists in fields not my own and made choices in accordance with the principles that governed the overall work. Oversights and errors of judgment are, of course, the fault of the author alone. The reader is enjoined to recall that this work is not an encyclopedia. It is not intended to be all inclusive. If successful, the book will provide a helpful and balanced, though not exhaustive, guide to pertinent names, places, and events of Iranian history. By design, the work should provide information in an easily accessible manner useful to both the informed and general audience. To find a proper balance between specialized and general knowledge was often vexing. The degree to which success has been achieved is a determination to be made by individual readers. To each, I can only promise that I did my best.

ACKNOWLEDGMENTS

The ultimate responsibility for the contents of this work rests with the author alone. As with all books, however, there are many who shared in one aspect or another in the production and without whom the final product would be considerably lessened. Sometimes in mechanical ways, sometimes in spiritual ways, the author owes a debt of gratitude to the following: Cinda St. John, Bill Holmes, Angel Ginn Reed, Lois Webster and, especially, Golriz, my wife, who endured as the months turned into years. My thanks are extended also to Laura Day who did an outstanding job of typing, and to Jon Woronoff, Series Editor, whose patience was sorely tried, but never exhausted.

For the second edition, I am indebted to a number of scholars on Iran who enlightened me with their expertise and suggestions. Above all, Farhang Rajaee deserves special mention for his constant encouragement and advice. Thanks also belong to Houchang Chehabi, Mark Gasiorowski, Muhammad Ghanoonparvar, Ali Akbar Mahdi, and Farzin Vahdat.

Valuable support for the second edition was provided by several research assistants: Melissa Hoople, Jynx Jenkins, Bruce Rankin, and in particular, Brian and Crystal Gilliam. Shawnee State University also supported this endeavor. The assistance of all mentioned above contributed greatly to this work, as did the ever-present hand of Jon Woronoff, and I am grateful. The greatest debt of gratitude, however, continues to belong to Golriz, who good-heartedly suffered the loss of time that this book snatched from her.

READER'S NOTES

GENERAL

Writing this book brought home an important lesson. It is much more difficult to be concise, yet meaningful, than to be expansive. The need to be brief often proved frustrating, especially when attempting to do justice in several pages to historically complex episodes, such as the Islamic Revolution of Iran. I have strived to include adequate detail so as to convey the historical significance of each subject while also imparting sufficient general information to provide contextual meaning. This is where the publisher's system of cross-referencing came in handy. In the text, the first mention in all entries of any other entry is indicated by bolding. In this manner, the reader is invited to consult the referenced entry for more background and context on any particular name, term, person, event, organization, or place. In addition, at the end of some entries the reader is enjoined to "see" other entries which the author feels are particularly relevant for additional background information or detail, yet are not referenced via bolding in the entry itself.

In several instances I have used words interchangeably in the text. The word *ulama*, a collective term used to designate the body of Islamic religious scholars, or those trained in the religious sciences, is sometimes translated as clergy or clerics. While this translation is not altogether accurate, since it implies a religious hierarchy which is lacking in Islam, it is commonly utilized in the literature. In this work, I use one word or the other depending upon the context and my own judgement of whether the more "technical" word ulama or the more "popular" word clergy was the most appropriate. In addition, I have used the words *Iran* and *Persia* interchangeably. Generally, for historical periods except the 20th century, *Persia/Persian* has been used with the occasional use of the term *Iran/Iranian*, depending upon whether there is a cultural or historical reference. In any event, the terms mean one and the same as explained in the introduction.

ALPHABETIZATION

Entries are arranged alphabetically. Multi-word entries are treated in letter order, word by word. For instance, Imam Ali precedes Imam Hussein, and Islamic Republic of Iran precedes Islamic Republican Party. Honorifics are included as part of entry headings. For example, Ayatollah is attached to the names of Khomeini, Shari'at-Madari, Taleqani, and others who are claimants to that title. Likewise, Shah is attached to the names of kings after the historical time that the title was routinely added to the first name of the reigning monarch. Some entries are alphabetized under the title of an individual. Such is the case with the title Mirza, under which three entries are listed. The justification is that in usage the title has become incorporated into the full name to such an extent that it is virtually a single unit. Examples are the entries Mirza Malkom Khan, Mirza Saleh Shirazi, and Mirza Taqi Khan Amir Kabir. Some Iranian family names include appellations or titles in a hyphenated form. Such double family names, for instance Hashemi-Rafsanjani and Sharif-Emami, are hyphenated in this work and appear under the first part of the name.

TRANSLITERATION

The system of transliteration utilized in this work is a slightly modified version of that introduced by Farideh Tehrani in *Negligence and Chaos: Bibliographical Access to Persian-Language Materials in the United States* (Scarecrow Press, 1991). The only exception to that scheme is the substitution of "ei" instead of "ey" to represent the diphthong consisting of short vowel "e" and long vowel "i." Thus, the name of the prime minister during most of the 1960s and 1970s is spelled *Hoveida* rather than *Hoveyda*. The choice of the system proposed by Tehrani was dictated primarily by its simplicity in contrast to the many other versions of transliteration in the marketplace. There are no diacritical marks for either consonants or vowels and, in the opinion of this author, the system nicely approximates the actual Persian pronunciation of the words. A linguistic purist would argue that the idea of reversibility into the original Arabic script is lost with this system, and it is. However, I doubt that the specialist will be bothered since the proper pronunciation will be readily recognizable and the advantages to the general reader are considerable, not the least of which is that words on the page are more pleasing to the eye.

Not all Persian words and names or place-names are transliterated. Many have an accepted English form and are familiar to English-speakers accordingly. Examples would include the town *Qum*, instead of *Qom*; the term *Shiah* instead of *Shi'ah*; and the name *Muhammad*, instead of *Mohammad*. The standard I have used in this work is *Webster's Third New International Dictionary*. Words of Persian origin which appear in this dictionary are used in their English form rather than being transliterated.

DATES

All dates, not otherwise specified, are given in the A.D. calendar. Dates prior to year one are designated as B.C. Most dates had to be converted from either the lunar or solar A.H. calendars which in many cases presented problems of exact equivalencies. (For a more detailed consideration of such problems, the reader might wish to consult the **calendars** entry in the text.) Consequently, despite a great deal of care devoted to the determination of the correct A.D. dates, there may be a few calculation errors. For instance, depending upon the month in which they occurred, some birth and death dates might be off by one year. In a few cases, dates might differ more significantly with one or more other sources. This is because of discrepancies among sources. Such is the case with the birth date of Muhammad Mossadeq which is variously recorded. In such cases, I have made the best determination possible after consulting multiple sources. In one case, the entry on Mirza Saleh Shirazi, there are no birth or death dates recorded because not a single source specifies a date. In several other entries only a death date is listed for lack of historical records.

ACRONYMS AND ABBREVIATIONS

ABCFM	American Board of Commissioners for Foreign Missions
AIOC	Anglo-Iranian Oil Company
APOC	Anglo-Persian Oil Company
CIA	Central Intelligence Agency (U.S.)
EEC	European Economic Community
IAEA	International Atomic Energy Agency
IRP	Islamic Republican Party
IUST	Iran University of Science and Technology
JRM	Jameh-yi Ruhaniyyat-i Mobarez (Militant Clergy Association)
LMI	Liberation Movement of Iran
MPRP	Muslim People's Republican Party
MRM	Majma-yi Ruhaniyyun-i Mobarez (Militant Clerics Association)
NIOC	National Iranian Oil Company
NRM	National Resistance Movement
NSC	National Security Council
OPEC	Organization of Petroleum Exporting Countries
OSS	Office of Strategic Services (U.S.)
SAVAK	Sazman-i Amniyyat va Ettele'at-i Keshvar (State Intelligence and Security Organization)
SAVAMA	Sazman-i Ettele'at va Amniyyat-i Mihan (Homeland Information and Security Organization)
WOI	Women's Organization of Iran

ACRONYMS AND ABBREVIATIONS

CHRONOLOGY

8th-10th Century B.C. Iranian peoples migrate onto the Iranian Plateau and into the Zagros Mountains.

8th Century Median Confederacy is established.

550-530 Reign of Cyrus the Great and foundation of the Achaemenian Empire.

522-486 Darius the Great reigns; Persepolis is built.

334-330 Alexander the Great conquers the Achaemenian Empire and places it under Hellenistic rule.

323 Death of Alexander the Great and division of his empire; eastern province falls to Alexander's chief general Seleucus.

305 Seleucus establishes his capital, Seleucia-on-the-Tigris, from which he controls Mesopotamia and most of Iran.

373-247 Seleucids rule Iran; infusion of Hellenistic influences into Persian culture.

ca. 247 Araces revolts against the Seleucids and founds the Parthian royal house.

247 B.C.-224 A.D. The Parthian Dynasty is in primary power in Mesopotamia and Western Iran.

ca. 171-138 B.C. Mithridates I reigns; Parthians establish firm control over Iranian Plateau and Mesopotamia.

1st Century A.D. Indecisive conflicts arise between the Roman and Parthian Empire.

53 The Parthians are victorious over the Romans at the Battle of Carrhae.

63 Armenia is created as a buffer state between the Roman and Parthian Empires.

2nd Century Parthian decline and Roman capture of Selucia in the Mesopotamian campaigns.

224 Ardashir ends the Parthian Empire and establishes the Sassanian Dynasty.

260 Shapur is victorious against the Romans and captures Emperor Valerian.

274 Death of Mani, founder of Manichaeism.

224-651 Sassanian rule; expansion of the state and adoption of Zoroastrianism as the state religion.

309-379 Shapur II reigns 70 years and restores the power and prestige of the Sassanian Dynasty.

524 Mazdak is executed and Mazdakites massacred in ensuing years.

488-531 Kavad reigns and is indulgent towards the communistic Mazdakite Movement which rises in revolt.

531-579 Khosrow Anushiravan reins; height of Sassanian splendor and glory.

632-651 The last Sassanian ruler, Yazdagerd III, reigns.

ISLAMIC PERIOD

570 The prophet of Islam, Muhammad, is born.

610 Muhammad begins his teachings in Mecca.

622 Year of the Hegirae (flight from Mecca); Muhammad establishes Islamic state in Medina.

630 Islam is accepted by the Meccans and Muhammad returns to Mecca.

632 Muhammad dies.

634 Arab conquests erupt into territory outside of Arabia.

637 Arabs defeat the Sassanians at the Battle of Qadisiya and occupy the capital, Ctesiphon.

641 Arabs defeat the Sassanians at Nahavand, effectively ending resistance to the Muslims; the Sassanian Empire is effectively dissolved and placed under the rule of the Caliphate.

651 Yazdagerd III, the last Sassanian ruler, is murdered.

7th-8th Centuries Islamic Caliphate rules Iran.

747 Abu Muslim begins a revolt in Khorasan against the Umayyad Caliphate.

750 The Abbasids defeat the Umayyads at the Battle of the Great Zab and Abu al-Abbas is named first Caliph in the Abbasid line.

775-778 Revolt of the Veiled Prophet in Khorasan.

9th-10th Centuries Decline of the Islamic Caliphate; independent Iranian dynasties are established.

816-833 Revolt of Babak.

820-872 Reign of the Tahirid Dynasty in the area of Khorasan.

867-903 The Saffarids control most of the Iranian Plateau.

872-999 Reign of the Samanid Dynasty in Transoxiana and Khorasan.

932 The Buyid Dynasty arises in western Persia.

945 Buyid armies occupy Baghdad and hold the Caliph prisoner.

962-1186 Establishment of the Ghaznavid Dynasty in Khorasan and spread of rule eastward.

1000-1030 Reign of the Ghaznavid Prince Mahmud, who invades India.

1011 *Shahnameh* is completed by Ferdowsi and is dedicated to Prince Mahmud.

1040 Seljuk Turks are victorious over the Ghaznavids and seize control of Khorasan.

1055 Seljuk Turks occupy Baghdad and Tughril Beg becomes Sultan.

12th Century Iran is ruled by local Turkish dynasties of the Khwarazm and Seljuk Turks.

1220 Ghengis Khan defeats the Khwarazm Turks and seizes Khorasan.

1221 Mongol armies under the command of Ghengis Khan cross the Oxus; the cities of Marv, Nishapur, and Herat are destroyed.

1258 Mongols plunder Baghdad, kill the last Abbasid Caliph and establish the Ilkhanid Dynasty.

1335 Last Ilkhanid ruler dies and Iran is split into two provincial states.

1370 Timur conquers Khorasan and Transoxiana.

1370-1405 Timur extends his rule from India to Mediterranean until his death in Herat.

1378-1469 Reign of the Black Sheep Turkoman Dynasty in Azerbaijan and Armenia.

1387-1502 Reign of the White Sheep Turkoman Dynasty in portions of Iran and Azerbaijan.

1405-1477 Reign of Shah Rokh in Herat; the Timurid Empire shrinks to Khorasan base.

SAFAVID PERIOD

1501 Shah Ismail Safavi crowned at Tabriz; Twelver Shi'ism is declared state religion.

1507-1622 Portugal controls the Straits of Hormoz.

1514 The Ottoman Empire is victorious at Chaldiran over the Safavids.

1587-1628 Shah Abbas I (the Great) reigns during the high point of Safavid power; Isfahan becomes capital.

1616 The British East India Company begins trade with Persia.

1722 The Afghans capture Isfahan; end of Safavid rule.

AFSHARID AND ZAND PERIOD

1736 Nader Shah seizes the Persian throne.

1739 Nader Shah extends control and captures Delhi.

1747 Assassination of Nader Shah; a period of anarchy ensues.

1750-1794 Reign of the Zand Dynasty which restores order.

QAJAR PERIOD

1796 Agha Muhammad Khan Qajar crowns himself and establishes the Qajar Dynasty; Tehran is named the new capital.

1807 Treaty of Finkenstein establishes a relationship between France and Persia.

1808-1813 The first war between Czarist Russia and Persia.

1812 Definitive Treaty of Friendship and Alliance is signed between the British Empire and Persia.

1813 Treaty of Gulistan ends the First Russo-Persian War; Iran renounces claims to Caucasian territories.

1827 Beginning of the second war with Czarist Russia.

1828 Treaty of Turkmanchai ends the Second Russo-Persian War; Iran pays Czarist Russia a war indeminity, cedes territory, and grants Russia commercial privileges.

1844 Babi Movement begins in Persia.

1850 The leader of the Babis is executed.

1852 Attempt to assassinate Naser al-Din Shah by followers of the Babi Movement; subsequent heavy persecution of Babis.

1890 The British citizen Talbot is given sole rights to the Persian tobacco market.

1891-1892 The Tobacco Revolt; the Tobacco Concession given to Talbot is revoked due to nationwide boycott.

1896 Assassination of Naser al-Din Shah.

1901 A British company, called the Anglo-Iranian Oil Company, is given a concession to explore for oil in southwest Persia.

1905 Constitutional Revolution; constitution granted in August 1906.

1907 Anglo-Russian Convention of 1907 divides Iran into spheres of influence that buffer Imperial Russia from British India.

1908 First oil strike by the Anglo-Iranian Oil Company.

1911 Under Russian pressure, Morgan Shuster's financial reform mission to Persia fails.

1921 The nationalist Reza Khan takes power in a bloodless coup.

1925 Ahmad Shah is deposed and the Qajar Dynasty comes to an end.

PAHLAVI PERIOD

1925 Reza Khan is crowned Reza Shah Pahlavi initiating a new dynasty; Persia is renamed Iran.

1925-1941 Reza Shah reigns with a program of centralization and modernization.

1933 New Anglo-Persian oil agreement.

1941 Great Britain and the Soviet Union invade Iran, forcing the non-aligned Reza Shah to abdicate the throne to his young son, Muhammad Reza.

1946 Azerbaijan crisis; separatist movements in Azerbaijan and Kurdistan collapse; Tehran reasserts central control.

1949 National Front political party is formed and is led by Muhammad Mossadeq.

1950-1953 Oil crisis with Great Britain.

1951 Mossadeq becomes prime minister and nationalizes the Anglo-Iranian Oil Company.

1953 Mossadeq is overthrown by a royalist group with U.S. and British support.

1954 A foreign oil consortium is given the right to manage Iranian oil resources.

1961-1962 Prime Minister Ali Amini tries to establish economic reform measures and is forced to resign.

1963 January: The White Revolution reform program is instituted. **June:** Ayatollah Khomeini attacks the Shah and the White Revolution; hundreds die in rioting.

1964 October: The Shah exiles Khomeini to Iraq.

1966 Founding of the *Mojahedin-i Khalq-i Iran* (Iranian Peoples' Freedom Fighters).

1971 The Maoist *Feda'iyan-i Islam* political group attacks a gendarmerie post in the north, beginning a period of armed opposition to the Shah's rule.

1973 Oil prices rise and lead to an economic boom.

1975 International Border and Good Neighborly Relations Treaty (Algiers Agreement) is signed in Algiers between Iran and Iraq.

1976 May: The United States supplies 226 kg of depleted uranium to Iran for aircraft wing ballast. **July:** The Atomic Energy Organization of Iran (ATEOI) signs an agreement with Germany for the construction of a nuclear power plant at Bushehr. German contractors were reportedly paid $7.8 billion. **August:** Talks between the U.S. and Iran on nuclear cooperation are suspended after disagreement on safeguards. **October:** French President Valery Giscard d' Estaing signs an agreement for Iran to purchase two nuclear reactors immediately and six more at a later date. **November:** The British Aircraft Company agrees to accept Iranian crude oil in payment for a $640-million deal to supply the Iranian Imperial Army with the Rapier short-range anti-aircraft missile system.

1977 August: Jamshid Amuzegar replaces Amir Abbas Hoveida as prime minister and institutes an austerity program; the economic boom slows. **December:** U.S. President Jimmy Carter visits Iran and toasts the Shah and his government as an island of stability.

1978 January: A state newspaper runs a scathing editorial attack on Ayatollah Khomeini leading to violence between protestors and police in Qum and the deaths of many of the assembled protestors. **February:** Demonstrations lead to violence in Tabriz and the Iranian government briefly loses control of the city. **May:** Large demonstrations take place in Tehran and Qum. **August:** Fire rages through a theater in Abadan and kills over 400; anti-government opposition links security agency SAVAK to the fire. **September:** Martial law is declared immediately before a scheduled demonstration in Tehran's Zhaleh Square and the military kills several hundred demonstrators. **October:** Khomeini is forced to leave Iraq. **December:** Huge Muharram processions fill the streets of Tehran in defiance of martial law and in nonviolent protest against the Shah.

THE ISLAMIC REPUBLIC

1979 January: The Shah leaves Iran and Shapur Bakhtiar becomes the new prime minister. **February:** Khomeini returns and the Iranian monarchy is dissolved; Mehdi Bazargan is declared prime minister of the Provisional Government. **March:** Through a referendum the Islamic Republic is established; Kurdish, Baluchi, and Turkoman tribesman clash with Iranian troops over minority rights. **April:** Khomeini declares the establishment of a "government of God;" former Prime Minister Amir Abbas Hoveida is executed. **May:** Establishment of the Revolutionary Guards. **July:** Khomeini declares a general amnesty for offenses committed during the Shah's reign; four leading mullah's join Mehdi Bazargan's cabinet, beginning the process of a clerical takeover of the state. **August:** The first Assembly of Experts meets to work on the constitution of the Islamic Republic; 20 opposition newspapers are ordered to close; Khomeini appoints himself commander-in-chief and orders a general mobilization against the Kurds. **October:** Muhammad Reza Shah enters a U.S. hospital for cancer treatment. **November:** The U.S. Embassy is seized and its staff held hostage by Iranian students who demanded in exchange the forced return of the Shah to Iran; the Bazargan government falls and the Revolutionary Council takes control; the U.S. freezes Iranian assets in the United States. **De-**

cember: The Constitution of the Islamic Republic is ratified by referendum; disorder in Tabriz.

1980 January: Abol Hasan Bani-Sadr is elected the first president of the Islamic Republic. February: Bani-Sadr is appointed commander-in-chief of the military. March: The first parliamentary elections since the 1979 revolution are held. April: An attempt by the U.S. military to rescue the Tehran embassy hostages fails. May: The first parliament of the Islamic Republic convenes; the European Economic Community and Japan impose economic embargoes on Iran. The Iranian government ignores a unanimous UN ruling to end the hostage situation. July: Muhammad Reza Shah Pahlavi dies in Egypt; Ali Akbar Hashemi-Rafsanjani is elected speaker of parliament and Bani-Sadr is officially sworn in as president. August: Amnesty International appeals to Iran to end executions and imprisonments based on beliefs and ethnic origins. September: Iraq invades Iran to regain control of the Shatt al-Arab lost as a result of the 1975 Algiers Agreement. October: Assembly of Experts approves a constitutional provision for Khomeini to become Iran's supreme jurist (*Faqih*), giving him ultimate veto power over selection of all candidates for government offices. Pahlavi Crown Prince Reza proclaims himself Shah Reza II in exile.

1981 January: The American hostages are released after 444 days of captivity. February: Iranian intellectuals charge the government with torture of political prisoners and attacks on democratic rights and civil liberties. March: Clashes between supporters and opponents of BaniSadr break out; Revolutionary Courts investigate charges of treason against the president. June: Bani-Sadr is removed as president; the Islamic Republican Party leadership is decimated by an explosion in party headquarters; the *Mojahedin-i Khalq-i* Iran Party clashes with the new government; Amnesty International reports that over 1,000 executions have occurred since the revolution. July: Elections are held for the presidency and the parliamentary seats left vacant by the June bombing; Muhammad Ali Raja'i is elected president and Muhammad Javad Bahonar is selected as prime minister. Au-

gust: President Raja'i and Prime Minster Bahonar are assassinated; 23 Iranians are executed for sedition. **September:** Ali Khamene'i and Muhammad Reza Mahdavi-Kani are appointed interim president and prime minister respectively. **October:** Khamene'i is elected president and Mir-Hussein Mosavi is appointed prime minister; radical Islamic groups consolidate control of Iran. **November:** Iran rejects an Iraqi cease-fire offer; *Mojahedin-i Khalq-i Iran* increases attacks on Islamic government officials. **December:** In a wave of arrests, more than 170 members of the *Mojahedin-i Khalq-i* Iran and other leftist dissident groups are detained.

1982 January: Six Bahai leaders are executed for collaboration with the former Shah. **March:** Over 10,000 prisoners are pardoned on the third anniversary of the revolution; 40 members of the *Feda'iyan-i Islam* are killed in a raid by the Revolutionary Guards. **April:** Sadeq Qotbzadeh, a former supporter and confidant of Ayatollah Khomeini, is arrested; the Iranian government initiates a campaign to discredit Ayatollah Muhammad Kazem Shari'at-Madari. **May:** Iran recaptures Khorramshahr in the largest offensive of the war; 50 *Mojahedin-i Khalq-i* Iran leaders are killed in the course of Revolutionary Guard raids. **June:** Iran sends 1,000 Revolutionary Guardsmen to Lebanon following the Israeli invasion. **July:** Iran rejects a UN cease-fire resolution. **August:** More than 65 *Mojahedin-i Khalq-i Iran* members are killed in Tehran raids; 25 Jews in Mashhad are arrested for smuggling. **December:** Elections are held for a new Assembly of Experts to determine the succession procedures after Khomeini dies.

1983 January: The government imprisons Tudeh Party leaders; a purge of the revolutionary tribunals commences. **February:** A general amnesty frees more than 8,000 prisoners. **May:** The government dissolves the Tudeh Party and detains more than 1,000 Tudeh members. **July:** Prime Minster Mir-Hussein Mosavi condemns illegal bazaar activities; new regulations are issued to prevent hoarding and profiteering and 13 merchants are arrested for violations. **September:** All Bahai groups in Iran are banned.

1984 February: The "war of the cities" escalates; Iran tentatively accepts an Iraqi cease-fire offer. **March:** Iran charges Iraq with the use of chemical weapons. **May:** Parliamentary elections are held and Ali Akbar Hashemi-Rafsanjani is reelected speaker of the house. **November:** Iran is accused by the International Red Cross of serious violations in the treatment of Iraqi POWs.

1985 February: Over 150 shops are shut down in Tehran for spreading "decadent Western culture." **March:** Over 40 Bahais are executed and others are imprisoned and tortured; in return for accepting a UN peace proposal, Iran demands $350 billion in war reparations, the ouster of the Iraqi regime, and the return of Iraqi refugees to Iraq. **August:** The presidential elections are boycotted by Liberation Movement members after Mehdi Bazargan's candidacy is not approved by the Council of Guardians; outbreaks of civil disorder in Tehran follow. **November:** Ayatollah Hussein Ali Montezari is selected as Khomeini's successor as Supreme Leader by the Assembly of Experts.

1986 March: Khomeini extends to women the opportunity to participate in public life and the military. **April:** Ayatollah Muhammad Kazem Shari'at-Madari dies following five years of house arrest; the first revelations of Israeli involvement in the arms-for-hostages deal appear. **September:** In a clandestine broadcast on Iranian television, Shah Reza II declares himself ruler of Iran and calls for the overthrow of Khomeini's government. **October:** The Iran-Contra Affair is revealed; the "war of the cities" escalates with Tehran and Baghdad the major targets. **December:** Iran launches "Kerbala," a major offensive aimed at the southern front; civilian residential areas are targeted in both Iran and Iraq.

1987 February: Khomeini calls for "war until victory" against Iraq. **May:** The UN confirms Iraqi use of chemical weapons on Iranian civilian targets; following a decision by the International

Court of Justice (World Court), the United States returns $450 billion in Iranian assets frozen since the 1981 Algerian Accords. **June:** The Islamic Republican Party is dissolved in order to promote national unity; *Mojahedin-i Khalq-i Iran* leader Massoud Rajavi announces the formation of the Iranian National Liberation Army to overthrow the Tehran government. **July:** The UN passes cease-fire Resolution 598 which Iraq accepts and Iran disavows; Iranian Hajj pilgrims in Saudi Arabia hold demonstrations which result in the deaths of 400 pilgrims. **October:** Iran and Iraq officially sever diplomatic ties and close their respective embassies in Baghdad and Tehran.

1988 February: The "war of the cities" and the tanker war in the Gulf escalate to the highest levels of the war period. **April:** In parliamentary elections, only one-quarter of the seats are won by clerics, compared to one-half in the previous elections. **June:** The USS *Vincennes* shoots down an Iranian civilian airliner; Iran accepts UN cease-fire resolution 598. **August:** Iran and Iraq officially declare a cease-fire. **December:** The government approves the establishment of a limited number of political parties.

1989 February: Khomeini issues a religious edict calling for the execution of Salman Rushdie, author of *The Satanic Verses*; over 3,000 prisoners are pardoned during the 10th anniversary celebration of Khomeini's return to Iran. **March:** Ayatollah Hussein Ali Montezari resigns as successor to Khomeini; the Combatant Clergymen and the Women's Society of the Islamic Republic are permitted to be political parties. **June:** Ayatollah Ruhollah Khomeini dies; Ayatollah Ali Hussein Khamene'i becomes Supreme Jurist. **July:** Ali Akbar Hashemi-Rafsanjani is elected president; voters approve an amendment to abolish the office of the prime minister. **September:** Khamene'i takes over as commander-in-chief of the military. **October:** The Majlis decrees that all future Majlis candidates must hold a bachelor's degree or be a graduate of a theological school. **November:** Over 15,000 Iranians participate in demonstrations marking the 10th anniversary of the takeover of the U.S. Embassy in Tehran. **December:**

Disturbances break out in Soviet Azerbaijan; Moscow accuses Iran of supplying ammunition to the Azerbaijan Shiah Muslims.

1990 January: Iran rejects an Iraqi request for resumption of peace talks. **April:** One person is killed and 65 arrested during an anti-government demonstration in Tehran; the Majlis introduces the death penalty for hoarding and black marketeering. **May:** Iranians boycott the Hajj pilgrimage for the third year. **June:** The government bans the Liberation Movement and arrests eight of its members for subversive activities; an earthquake in the Caspian Sea region kills an estimated 30,000 and injures over 100,000. **July:** In Geneva, Iran and Iraq hold the first direct talks since the 1988 cease-fire. **September:** Iran and Great Britain restore diplomatic relations severed during the Salman Rushdie affair. **October:** Khamene'i is accused of rigging elections against radical candidates; the European Economic Community lifts sanctions against Iran. **December:** Rushdie emerges from hiding and issues a statement in support of Islam and in opposition to a paperback edition of *The Satanic Verses.*

1991 January: Iranian university students continue the strike for improved education, the release of detained students, and the closure of campus Islamic societies. **June:** Intellectuals and businessmen who had fled Iran in 1979 are advised that investment and travel restrictions have been lifted. **August:** Former Prime Minister Shapur Bakhtiar is assassinated in Paris. **September:** Widespread demonstrations and strikes erupt in protest of economic and working conditions. **October:** Iran purchases nuclear technology from China for "peaceful purposes."

1992 March: The government orders all non-Iranian Red Cross workers to leave the country following public reports regarding extensive civil rights violations. **May:** In national elections, the Combatant Clergymen win more than 75 percent of the seats; nine women are elected deputies. **June:** The government orders severe measures to curtail riots and demonstrations in Arak and Marshad. **August:** The *Mojahedin-i Khalq-i Iran* takes responsi-

bility for a bomb explosion near the grave of Khomeini in Tehran. **November:** The government decrees that men and women
should ride separately on Tehran buses.

1993 February: Iranian authorities reiterate the edict calling for
the death of Rushdie and condemn Britain and other countries
for rejecting the decree. **March:** Ayatollah Montezari is arrested
after denouncing the country's spiritual leader, Ayatollah
Khamene'i. **May:** Attacking from bases in Iraq, the *Mohjahedin-
i Khalq-i Iran* severely damages several oil pipelines in Khuzistan. **June:** Hashemi-Rafsanjani is reelected president with 63
percent of the vote. **July:** Agreement concluded with China to
buy a 300-megawatt nuclear power station. **October:** Eight of 22
retired military officers are released after arrests for signing an
open letter critical of spiritual leader Ali Khamene'i; the Majlis
restricts contact between government employees and foreigners.
November: Demonstrations in Tehran mark the 14th anniversary of the seizure of the U.S. Embassy and Khamene'i restates
the impossibility of resuming diplomatic relations with the
United States; U.S. President Bill Clinton meets with Salman
Rushdie, who as author of *The Satanic Verses* provoked the
fatwa issued by Khomeini in 1989. **December:** United Nations
moves to condemn Iran for the executions of dissidents and the
continuing threat on Rushdie's life; the Majlis enacts legislation
implementing capital punishment for producers and distributors
of pornographic videos; Iran refuses to negotiate with the United
Arab Emirates regarding sovereignty over the Greater and Lesser
Tumbs and Abu Musa islands; Pakistan and Iran reach agreement on a gas supply pipeline to Pakistan.

1994 January: Superintendent of the Assemblies of God
Churches Bishop Haik Hovsepian Meir found dead. **February:**
Gunshots erupt at speech by President Rafsanjani commemorat-
ing 15th anniversary of the Islamic Revolution. Gunman
Kourosh Nikakhtar is charged with attempted assassination of
the president. **April:** Government bans television satellite dishes
and orders their seizure on grounds that they undermine Iranian
and Islamic culture. **June:** Private banks allowed for first time

since 1979; after 25 killed, 70 injured in bombing of Imam Reza Shrine, government claims *Mojahedin-i Khalq-i Iran* responsible, and kill alleged member Mehdi Nahvi the next month in attempt to arrest him. **July:** Protestant clergymen Tedhis Mikhailyan and Mehdi Dibaj found murdered. Alleged *Mojahedin-i Khalq-i Iran* member Farahnaz Amani arrested in connection with the murders. **August:** Qazvin erupts into riots after Majlis rejects a bill to create a new provincial government allowing Qazvin to retain agricultural profits. Qazvin is separated from Zanjan Province, and absorbed into Tehran Province. Further riots lead to 37 deaths, 386 injuries, and 745 arrests. **September:** Iranian Foreign Minister Ali Akbar Velayati proposes at the UN a Gulf Security Pact to curb proliferation of conventional weapons and to outlaw weapons of mass destruction. **October:** Open letter of 134 novelists, publishers, and translators published calling for end to censorship. **1 November:** Majlis passes bill permitting police to shoot to kill demonstrators. **18 November:** Special council in Iranian judiciary passes new law allowing women divorced by their husbands up to half the property accumulated during marriage. **29 November:** Grand Ayatollah Muhammad Ali Araki dies at age 100. **6 December:** Government appoints Ayatollah Ali Khamene'i as grand ayatollah and sole *marja'*. Khamene'i rejects role of sole *marja'*. **26 December:** Majlis reiterates ban on television satellite equipment, banning sale, manufacture, and distribution. Interior Ministry insists on seizure of existing equipment.

1995 4 January: U.S. and Israel claim Iran is five years away from developing a nuclear weapon. **8 January:** Russia agrees to complete nuclear power plant, begun by Germany in 1974 at Bushehr, for a cost of $800 million. **16 January:** Norway recalls ambassador to Iran after a disagreement over Salman Rushdie's death sentence and the 1993 wounding of his publisher. **20 January:** Mehdi Bazargan dies of heart attack in Switzerland. **1 February:** Norway downgrades diplomatic relations and expels Iranian diplomats over their dispute regarding Salman Rushdie. **11 February:** President Rafsanjani addresses 150,000 in Tehran to mark 16th anniversary of the Islamic Revolution. **12 Febru-**

ary: Brother of Ayatollah Ali Khamene'i, Hadi Khamene'i has his publication, *Jahan-i Islam,* banned for violating law prohibiting anti-Islamic publications. **22 February:** Germany lifts trade restrictions on Iran. **14 March:** Agreement between U.S. company Conoco and the National Iranian Oil Company for developing and exporting gas and oil is announced. This is the first such agreement since the U.S. severed diplomatic ties with Iran. **15 March:** American government blocks Conoco-NIOC agreement by announcing ban on U.S.-Iranian oil-development agreements. **16 March:** Greece and Iran agree to cooperate in law enforcement, narcotics interdiction, and security. **May:** American government bans all trade between U.S. companies and Iran. **July:** Weekly newspaper, *Peyam-i Daneshju,* is banned by Ministry of Culture for violating press laws.

1996 February: U.S. and Iran agree to $131.8-million settlement for the 1988 downing of Iran Air Flight 655 by the USS *Vincennes* in the Strait of Hormoz. **August:** Iran files lawsuit against the U.S. in the International Court claiming the Americans had violated the 1981 Algerian Accords by passing laws aimed at funding covert anti-Iranian actions and putting sanctions on non-U.S. trade with Iran. **October:** During visit, South African Trade Minister Alec Erwin and Iranian President Rafsanjani sign trade agreement between the two countries. **November:** Sadra Azam-Nuri is appointed mayor of seventh district of Tehran, becoming the first woman in the Islamic Republic to hold such a position.

1997 April: German court implicates Iranian government and religious officials—including President Rafsanjani—in the 1992 murders in Berlin of four members of the Iranian opposition. Germany and Iran both expel four diplomats of the other's nation, and recall their ambassadors. Consequently, the EU suspends state of "critical dialogue" with Iran and urges members to withdraw their ambassadors. The EU soon agrees to return diplomats to Iran, but takes measures to prevent future bilateral visits, block Iranian intelligence officials from Europe, and ban weapon sales to Iran. Iran refuses the return of the German and

Danish ambassadors. **10 May:** Massive earthquake kills 2,400 and injures 6,000 in northeast Iran. **22 May:** Muhammad Khatami is elected Iranian president with 69 percent of the vote. **July:** U.S. has paid $32.5 million to families of victims of downed Iran Air Flight 655. **7 September:** Foreign Minister Kamal Kharrazi announces European Union ambassadors can return to Iran. **20 September:** Iranian journalist Faraj Sarkuhi sentenced to one year in prison for spying for European nations and participating in anti-state propaganda. **4 October:** Russia and Iran sign agreement recognizing need for economic, industrial, and trade cooperation, initiating a string of subsequent agreements. **November:** Outrage over Ayatollah Hussein Ali Montezari's comments questioning the clergy's legitimacy to rule sparks days of violent protests on both sides of the issue. Ayatollah Ali Khamene'i threatens prosecution of opposition to his rule, and calls for charges of treason against Montezari.

1998 January: President Khatami appears on America's Cable News Network (CNN) calling for cultural exchange between the U.S. and Iran. Both Khatami and Ayatollah Khamene'i agree that no direct relations with the U.S. would be possible, but even Khamene'i praises the idea of cultural exchanges. By the end of the month, U.S. President Clinton expresses hope in a holiday address to Muslims that the exchanges could encourage closer relations between the nations. **February:** U.S. announces easing of visa restrictions on Iranian visitors. **6 March:** Russia announces plans to sell nuclear reactors to Iran. **8 March:** Large pro-democracy rallies at Tehran University end in several arrests after authorities object to slogans. **4 April:** Tehran mayor, Gholam Hussein Karbaschi, is arrested for connection to an embezzlement case. **14 April:** Over 2,000 students at Tehran University protest Karbaschi's arrest. Tear gas is used to break up the demonstrations. **17 June:** U.S. Secretary of State, Madeline Albright, suggests Iran support a "road map" for normalizing relations. Iran says U.S. must show "good will" first. **21 June:** Abdollah Nouri dismissed as minister of interior by Majlis. President Khatami immediately appoints him a vice president. **23 July:** Mayor Karbaschi is convicted on corruption charges and sentenced to five years imprisonment, 20 years ban on holding public office, $330,000 fine, and 60 lashes. **25 July:** Iran confirms test of medium-range missile for "deterrent" purposes. **31 July:** In Qum 4,000 protest against the publication of offensive newspapers. They call for the resignation of Minister for Islamic Culture and Guidance Ata'ollah Mohajerani. **1 August:** The daily *Tus* is ordered to stop publication. Editors of *Tus* begin publishing a new daily, *Aftab-i Emruz*, the next day. **8 August:** Hashemi-Rafsanjani's daughter, Fa'ezeh Hashemi, begins publishing *Zan*, the first daily concerning women's issues. While seizing Mazar-i Sharif, Taliban forces murder Iranian diplomats. **1 September:** Iran begins military exercises on Afghan border in response to the murders by the Taliban of Iranian diplomats. **4 September:** Abdollah Nouri and Ata'ollah Mohajerani assaulted at a rally for Iranian soldiers killed in the Iran-Iraq War. **18 September:** Funeral for the diplomats slain by the Taliban draws massive crowds. Anti-Taliban demonstrations take place across Iran. **22 September:** President Khatami announces in New York that the Salman Rushdie question was "completely finished." **24 September:** Foreign Minister Kharrazi denounces death threat against Rushdie, prompting Britain to restore diplomatic relations with Iran. **27 September:** The Foreign Ministry says it can not rescind the *fatwa* demanding Rushdie's death. **October:** The 15th of Khordad Foundation increases bounty against Rushdie, raising the total to $2.5 million. **3 November:** Iran recalls its ambassador to the Czech Republic due to Farsi broadcasts from Prague of the U.S.-supported Radio Free Europe/Radio Liberty. **22 November:** Daryush Foruhar, a vocal critic of the Iranian government, and his wife Parvaneh found murdered in their Tehran home. **December:** Dissident writers Muhammad Ja'far Puyandeh, Majid Sharif, and Muhammad Mokhtiari are found murdered. Journalists' organizations demand protection, and demonstrators take to the streets. At Daryush and Parvaneh Foruhar's 40th day funeral observance, opponents to Khatami's reforms attack some of the 2,000 mourners, prompting riot police intervention.

1999 5 January: Interior Ministry announces rogue intelligence officers were responsible for the murders of the dissident writers, and that arrests had been made. **13 January:** The U.S. places economic sanctions on Russian Institutes accused of aiding Iran's nuclear weapons program. **9 February:** Intelligence Minister Qorbanali Dorri-Najafabadi resigns due to his department's involvement in the dissident murders. **22 Februrary:** Election board disqualifies 50 candidates from upcoming local election due to lax loyalty to Ayatollah Khamene'i. **26 Februrary:** First local elections since the Islamic Revolution take place as 300,000 candidates vie for 200,000 local council seats. **28 February:** Mohsen Kadivar is arrested by the Special Court for the Clergy for "disturbing public opinion." Students protest outside Kadivar's Shiraz home. **March:** Khatami makes first state visit to the West in Italy, meeting with Italian Prime Minister Massimo d'Alema and Pope John Paul II. **7 April:** *Zan* magazine banned after an offensive cartoon and New Year's greeting from the former Iranian Empress Farah appeared in the publication. **21 April:** Mohsen Kadivar sentenced to 18 months imprisonment. Proposal to Majlis calls for impeachment of Islamic Culture and Guidance Minister Ata'ollah Mohajerani for not adequately controlling the press. **27 April:** Five reformist candidates—including Abdollah Nouri—elected on 26 February to Tehran's Municipal Council are disqualified by the electoral supervisory committee. **May:** Mohajerani narrowly survives a vote-of-no-confidence in the Majlis. **7 June:** Thirteen Jewish Iranians are arrested, charged with spying for Israel and the U.S. **23 June:** Iran sets up fund to compensate industrialists, including exiles, whose assets were seized in the revolution. Pahlavi family members and associates are not eligible for compensation, however. **July:** Protests against the closing of the newspaper *Salaam* erupt into nationwide student protests; Tehran University students beat by police after barricading themselves in their dormitories. Tens of thousands of students protest and riot throughout the middle of the month, bringing criticism from conservatives towards the reformist attitudes of Khatami and his supporters. **4 August:** The Special Court of the Clergy bans *Salaam* for five years, and bans publisher Muhammad Musavi-Khoiniha from journalism for three years due to its publishing of confidential Intelligence Ministry documents. **10 August:** Arrest of 98 police officers for their role in the 9 July student dorm raids. **25 August:** Police Chief Lotfian is dismissed and is to be prosecuted for his role in the 9 July Tehran University dorm raids. **September:** Khatami announces a five-year plan calling for drastic economic changes, including privatizing the communications, post, railway, and tobacco industries. **3 November:** On the anniversary of the seizure of the American Embassy in Tehran, some of those involved hold rally to encourage improved U.S.-Iranian relations. **11 November:** Special Court of the Clergy votes to convict Abdollah Nouri due to offenses appearing in his publication *Khordad*. **27 November:** Abdollah Nouri sentenced to five years imprisonment and barred from publishing and writing for five years. His publication *Khordad* is ordered closed.

2000 January: Supreme Leader Ayatollah Khamene'i pardons Gholam Hussein Karbaschi. **5 February:** A bomb intended for Ayatollah Khamene'i's residence kills three and injures six in Tehran. **15 February:** Former hostage in Lebanon, Terry Anderson, files a $100-million lawsuit against Iran in a U.S. federal court, claiming the Iranian government was responsible for his abduction. **19 February:** Khatami supporters win 188 seats in the Sixth Majlis. The announcement sparks riots in Shush, where two die. **8 March:** Deputy Foreign Minister for Europe and the Americas Morteza Sarmadi announces Iran's intent to buy U.S. wheat and medicine in return for eased sanctions on Iranian carpets, pistachios, and caviar. Washington responds positively and does ease these sanctions later in the month. **24 March:** Terry Anderson is awarded a settlement of $341 million in his case against Iran. **17 April:** The outgoing Fifth Majlis passes bill expanding the press law to ban criticism of the Constitution, to increase penalties of offenders of the press law, to allow courts greater suspension powers over publications, and to prevent suspended publications from reprinting under new names. **22 April:** Journalist Akbar Ganji is arrested for violating the press laws. **6 May:** Khatami supporters pick up 56 of 66 remaining Majlis seats in runoff election. **7 May:** Council of Guardians calls for recount of votes, alleging election tampering. **16 May:** A Tehran Public Court forces closure of former Mayor Karbaschi's publication *Ham Mihan* on charges of "advocating lies and suspicion." **18 May:** Ayatollah Khamene'i halts recount of Majlis election votes. World Bank grants first loan in seven years to Iran. **30 May:** Soheila Jelodar-Zadeh is elected to the temporary presiding board of the Majlis, the first woman to hold the position since the revolution. **18 June:** Sixth Majlis eases restrictions on the press passed by the Fifth Majlis in April. **1 July:** Ten of 13 Iranian Jews accused of spying for Israel and the U.S. are convicted, and sentenced to between four and 13 years imprisonment. Two Muslims are also convicted for aiding the alleged Jewish spies. **1 August:** Iran's Islamic Republic News Agency (IRNA) announces six religious leaders had issued a *fatwa* allowing women to lead groups of women in congregational prayer. **28 August:** Violence between *Ansar-i Hizballah* and students in Khorramabad result in many injuries, and the death of a policeman. **29 August:** Rioters attack the funeral of the slain policeman in Khorramabad, injuring Nurollah Abedi, the governor general of Luristan Province. A student dies in further violence between *Ansar-i Hizballah* and the students. **September:** Farah Khosrati announces her intention to run for president in 2001, becoming the first female presidential candidate. **2 October:** Majlis forces Ata'ollah Mohajerani to resign his position as Islamic Culture and Guidance Minister. **29 October:** The Majlis drafts legislation to reverse allowing the judiciary to suspend newspapers. **30 November:** Journalist Akbar Ganji, while on trial before the Revolutionary Court, implicates high-level officials and clerics in a series of political murders throughout the 1980s. He names, amongst others, former Intelligence Minister Ali Fallahian, head of the Special Court of the Clergy, Moshemi Ejei, and Ayatollah Mesbah Yazdi. **14 December:** President Khatami accepts Mohajerani's resignation, and appoints him chairman of the International Center for Dialogue among Civilizations.

2001 7 January: Italian Interior Minister Enzo Bianco makes first post-revolution visit to Iran by a European interior minister.

13 January: At least eight, including Akbar Ganji, are convicted and sentenced to varying prison terms for attending an alleged "un-Islamic" conference in Berlin in 2000. Ganji receives a harsh 10-year prison sentence, with an additional five years exile following his release. **11 March:** A meeting of the Iran Freedom Movement is raided at the behest of the Revolutionary Court, resulting in 21 arrests. **12 March:** Iranian President Khatami and Russian President Vladimir Putin sign agreement opening door to Russian sales of conventional weapons to Iran. **18 March:** All activities of the Iran Freedom Movement are banned along with those of the Religious Nationalist Alliance. **17 May:** Plane crash kills 29, including Iranian Transportation Minister Rahman Dadman and seven Majlis members. Akbar Ganji's sentence is reduced to six months by a court of appeals, resulting in his immediate release. **24 May:** Iran executes alleged U.S. Central Intelligence Agency spy Muhammad Reza Pedram. **30 May:** Majlis passes a bill prohibiting secret trials of dissidents. It also seeks to improve prisoner's rights. **10 June:** President Khatami is reelected by a landslide. **16 June:** Iranian appellate court increases Akbar Ganji's sentence to six years. **19 June:** Preparations are made for Iran's first private bank since the revolution, to be called *Bank-i Eqtesad-i Novin*, or the Modern Economic Bank. **5 August:** Ayatollah Khamene'i prevents President Khatami's inauguration due to the Majlis's rejection of conservatives to a Constitutional oversight board by the Majlis. **7 August:** Majlis confirms two conservatives to the Constitutional oversight panel to ensure Khatami's inauguration. **18 August:** Iranian Supreme Court orders the retrial of 15 intelligence officers allegedly involved in the murders of dissident writers in 1998. Their original trial was before a military court. **18 September:** Candlelight vigil for victims of the 9/11 terror attacks in the U.S. is broken up by security forces. **25 September:** Foreign Minister Jack Straw makes first visit of a high-ranking British official to Iran since 1979. **10 October:** The U.S. blocks Iran's entry into the World Trade Organization. **11 November:** Members of the Iran Freedom Movement go on trial for plotting the overthrow of the Islamic Republic. The trial is closed to the public. Iranian television station preempts its regular programming with a CNN broadcast covering a plane crash in a residential area of New York City. It is the first Western broadcast on Iranian official media since the revolution.

2002 14 January: President Khatami personally pledges support to Afghani Interim President Hamid Karzai. Khatami denies that Iran is aiding Taliban forces fleeing from the American invasion of Afghanistan. **30 January:** Iran outraged by American President George W. Bush's labeling of Iran as part of an "Axis of Evil" during his State of the Union address. **6 February:** Iran denies plans to acquire nuclear weapons in response to Washington's allegations to the contrary. **11 February:** Anti-Americanism, fueled by Bush's State of the Union address, is apparent in celebrations marking the anniversary of the Islamic Revolution. **April:** Chinese President Jiang Zemin makes the first visit by a Chinese leader to Iran since the revolution. **June:** Large earthquake kills 500 in northwest Iran. **23 September:** Iran accepts new British ambassador after restoring diplomatic ties with the U.K. **24 September:** President Khatami requests more power from the Majlis to circumvent the closing of publications by the clergy, as well as to investigate acts contrary to the constitution by members of the Revolutionary Court. **12 October:** Shiah clerics are angered by American televangelist Jerry Falwell's characterization of the Prophet Muhammad as a terrorist. **23 November:** Two weeks of student protests over the death sentence of the academic Aghajari come to an end. Hashem Aghajari made a speech in June 2002 harshly criticizing the legitimacy of clerical rule. **26 November:** Students are banned from protesting in support of Aghajari. **3 December:** Hashem Aghajari appeals his sentence. **7 December:** In reaction to a U.S. policy of photographing and fingerprinting all Iranians entering the United States, the Ministry of Culture and Islamic Guidance announces it will do the same to all American journalists entering Iran. **8 December:** Tear gas disperses an assembly of thousands of students at Tehran University protesting Aghajari's death sentence. **11 December:** Hossein Mir-Muhammad Sadeghi resigns from the judiciary in protest over Aghajari's death sentence. **12 December:** Several university students are arrested for illegal demonstrations in support of Aghajari. They appeal to President Khatami and the Majlis, comparing themselves to the revolutionaries in 1978. **13 December:** Iran rebukes claims by the U.S. that two new nuclear power plants will be used in the production of nuclear weapons. Iran insists the plants will be for power only. **18 December:** The Majlis lifts many restrictions on television satellite dish technology.

2003 21 January: Conservative daily *Resalat* encourages the release of Ayatollah Hussein Ali Montezari from house arrest due to his failing health, arguing that his continued imprisonment could prove problematic for the conservative cause. **15 February:** The Revolutionary Guards reaffirm Salman Rushdie's death sentence. **10 March:** Some 120 members of the Majlis present an open letter against the university expulsion of students who protested the death sentence of Hashem Aghajari. **28 March:** Many thousands march through Tehran to protest the U.S.-led war against Iraq. **1 April:** A pickup truck with a makeshift petroleum bomb explodes when it hits a curtain wall at the British embassy in Tehran. No injuries to the embassy personnel or serious damage to the compound are reported. **12 April:** Iraqis ransack the Iraqi embassy in Tehran, destroying vestiges of the Saddam Hussein regime. **12 May:** The Iranian government compiles a list of at least 15,000 "pornographic" websites to be banned for their content and anti-government dissent. **13 May:** President Khatami visits Lebanon to meet with Lebanese President Emile Lahoud to discuss Hizbollah and other internal matters. Hassan Nasrallah, leader of the Shiah Hizbollah, was also present. **3 June:** U.S. Central Command reports that Iranian officials detained a number of U.S. citizens for interrogations as their ship traveled up the Shatt al-Arab. They were released after several hours. **6 June:** Iran's Atomic Energy Organization announces that Iran had not violated the non-nuclear weapons proliferation treaty and has no plans to develop nuclear weapons. **10 June:** Student riots lasting for 10 days begin in Tehran and quickly spread to cities throughout Iran. Protestors charge that reforms are too slow. **19 June:** U.S. President Bush states that the world community would not tolerate Iranian nuclear capability. He also encourages opponents of the Iranian government and comments that they had the support of his administration. **29 June:** In a joint press conference with British Foreign Minister Jack Straw, Iranian Foreign Minister Kamal Kharrazi indicates that Iran is ready for "talk and cooperation" regarding the nation's nuclear plan. **15 July:** Iran announces the discovery of a 38-billion-barrel oilfield near the southern port of Bushehr—one of the largest oil fields in Iran. **20 July:** Iran publicly arms its Revolutionary Guards with the Shahab-3 ballistic missile, in response to international pressure to stop its controversial missile program. **21 July:** The European Union warns Iran against failing to sign the International Atomic Energy Agency's (IAEA) enhanced nuclear inspections protocol. **13 August:** Iran's hardline Council of Guardians rejects two bills aimed at eliminating torture and discrimination against women. **17 August:** According to senior Iranian officials the government successfully foiled several attacks against Iran planned by the al-Qaeda terrorist network. **19 August:** Tehran issues a statement claiming that Israel "will pay dearly," in response to Israeli threats to attack Iranian nuclear facilities. **23 August:** Iran extradites to Riyadh a number of Saudi al-Qaeda members who were arrested in Iran following the U.S.-led invasion of Afghanistan. **21 September:** The IAEA unanimously approves a 31 October, 2003 deadline for Iran to prove that it is not secretly developing nuclear weapons. **25 September:** IAEA inspectors find traces of highly enriched uranium at an Electric Company on the outskirts of Tehran. **13 October:** Russia's Atomic Energy Ministry announces a one-year delay for the startup of Iran's Bushehr nuclear reactor. **21 October:** Tehran announces the suspension of its nuclear enrichment program and invites the IAEA to inspect its nuclear program. **29 October:** The Iranian government rejects U.S. request for information regarding al-Qaeda and demands that the White House take "practical steps" before resuming the dialogue on security. **30 October:** Iran meets the IAEA deadline to provide documents demonstrating the peaceful nature of its nuclear program. **3 November:** Supreme Leader Ayatollah Ali Khamene'i endorses the agreement opening the Iranian nuclear program to tougher inspections by the IAEA, but warns inspections would be terminated if national interests are threatened. **11 November:** An official IAEA report indicates that evidence did not indicate Iran was trying to manufacture nuclear weapons, but it was unclear if Iran's nuclear program was strictly for peaceful purposes. **26 November:** The UN, Germany, Great Britain, and France all agree to warn Iran to stop violating nuclear nonproliferation safeguards. **7 December:** Nearly a thousand students rally in Tehran to observe "Student Day," demanding free speech and the release of all political prisoners. **18 December:** Iran agrees to sign an additional protocol of the Nuclear Nonproliferation Treaty in response to months of mounting pressure related to alleged secret nuclear programs. The agreement permits intrusive snap inspections of nuclear facilities. **19 December:** An earthquake with a 6.3-6.7 magnitude on the Richter scale strikes the southeastern city of Bam, killing tens of thousands, destroying 70 to 90 percent of the residential areas, including the 2,000-year-old Bam citadel. **29 December:** Supreme religious leader Ayatollah Ali Khamene'i and President Khatami visit the earthquake survivors in Bam. **31 December:** The U.S. eases restrictions on aid to Iran in wake of the Bam quake.

2004 2 January: Iran turns down an American offer to send a delegation to Bam to assist in relief efforts for earthquake victims. **11 January:** The Council of Guardians bars more than 80 incumbent members of the Majlis from seeking reelection, mostly leftist reformers. **14 January:** Ayatollah Ali Khamene'i recommends that the Council of Guardians reconsider their decision to disqualify 2,000 candidates, including 83 incumbents, from the 20 February elections for the Majlis. **20 January:** Following permission from Ayatollah Ali Khamene'i, the Council of Guardians agrees to reinstate 200 disqualified candidates for 20 February elections. **21 January:** Many of the 24 ministers and six vice presidents hand in their resignations following the decision of the Council of Guardians. **23 January:** The Iranian government announces that it would place al-Qaeda suspects on trial. **24 January:** The IAEA requests that Iran suspend more of its uranium-enriching activities. **25 January:** The Council of Guardians rejects a bill passed by the Majlis requesting that most of the disqualified candidates, including 83 incumbents, be reinstated on the election ballot. **30 January:** The Council of Guardians rejects another request to reinstate disqualified candidates, increasing the number of rejected incumbent candidates from 83 to 87. **1 February:** More than 100 members of the Majlis resign over the Council of Guardians' refusal to reinstate reform party members to the election ballot. **2 February:** Iran's largest pro-reform party, the Islamic Participation Front, vows to boycott the upcoming elections due to the Council of Guardians refusal to reinstate disqualified candidates. **4 February:** In response to a boycott threat, Ayatollah Ali Khamene'i orders that the February elections go ahead as scheduled. **6 February:** The Council of Guardians finishes its review of the disqualified candidates, reinstating an additional 200. **12 February:** The Iranian government admits to possessing a previously undisclosed design for a high-speed centrifuge to enrich uranium after UN inspectors found evidence of the plan. **20 February:** Iranian officials extend the voting time for Majlis elections in order to increase the number of voters. Supreme religious leader Ayatollah Ali Khamene'i calls those boycotting the elections "enemies." **22 February:** Violence breaks out in several locales over initial results of the Majlis elections. Seven protestors and one police officer are killed in protests. **23 February:** IAEA inspectors find evidence of Iranian experiments involving polonium, an element used in nuclear weapons. Iranian officials declare that the polonium was to be used for electricity generation. **24 February:** Iran's Interior Ministry declares that conservatives won 156 of the 290 available Majlis seats. However, an estimated 60 seats remain undecided as voting entered a second round. **13 March:** Hours after the IAEA negotiated a resolution praising Iran for its cooperation with nuclear inspectors, but condemning Iran's failure to disclose all nuclear-related activities, the Iranian government bans inspectors from entering the country. **14 March:** U.S. and Iranian forces exchange fire along the Iraq-Iran border. The United States had increased the number of troops patrolling the border in order to prevent infiltrations that might assist the Iraqi insurgency. **15 March:** Iranian officials announce that they would readmit IAEA nuclear inspectors by the end of

March. **31 March:** The German, French, and British foreign ministers criticize Iran's decision to construct a uranium conversion plant in Isfahan. **6 April:** Iran pledges to increase cooperation with the IAEA's efforts to inspect nuclear sites throughout the country, but pushes for completion of inspections by June 2004. **7 April:** Diplomats announce Iranian plans to begin building a nuclear reactor in June that could produce weapons-grade plutonium. Officials insist the reactor would be for research only. **12 April:** UN nuclear inspectors arrive in Iran to verify that it had stopped uranium-enriching work. **14 April:** Iranian diplomats arrive in Baghdad to mediate between Muqtada al-Sadr's forces and the Coalition Provision Authority. **5 May:** Iranian authorities announce intentions to build a nuclear fuel cycle despite U.S. demands to halt nuclear activity. **8 May:** The Council of Guardians passes legislation from the Majlis banning torture, after previously rejecting the measure three times, claiming it violated Islamic law. **29 May:** The Majlis elects Gholam Ali Haddad-Adel Speaker of the Parliament, the first non-cleric speaker since the 1979 Revolution. **1 June:** A confidential IAEA report indicts Iran for pursuing uranium enrichment technology more aggressively than had been admitted. **6 June:** Human Rights Watch releases a report on Iran documenting thousands of illegal arrests and beatings, as well as other forms of torture. **18 June:** President Khatami threatens to renew Iran's uranium enrichment program if his government disagrees with the UN report to be issued following an IAEA meeting in Vienna. **21 June:** Iran's Revolutionary Guard Corps arrests eight members of the British Royal Navy and seizes three vessels in Iranian waters. London says the boats were meant to be delivered to Iraq to assist with the Iraqi Riverine Patrol Service. **24 June:** Iran frees all British service personnel. **27 June:** Iran announces that it would resume building centrifuges to be used in its nuclear program. **18 July:** Iranian officials announce that some al-Qaeda operatives blamed for the 9/11 attacks may have illegally passed through Iran from Afghanistan, but deny U.S. claims that Iran may have helped in the assault. **31 July:** Iranian officials reverse an October pledge to Britain, France, and Germany that it would suspend all nuclear enrichment-related activities. **1 September:**

Iran informs the IAEA of intentions to convert 37 tons of "yellowcake" uranium into uranium hexafluoride. **12 September:** Iran rejects European demands to halt its pursuit of nuclear technology, but reiterates that it would not use this technology to manufacture weapons. **19 September:** Iran rejects demand from the IAEA to freeze its uranium enrichment program and threatens to refuse last-minute atomic facilities checks if its case is sent before the UN Security Council. **12 October:** Iranian Vice President Muhammad Ali Abtahi, an outspoken liberal cleric, resigns his position, saying that religious hardliners were preventing him from carrying out his duties. **20 October:** Iran test-fires an improved version of the Shahab-3 ballistic missile. **3 November:** Thousands of Iranians gather outside the former U.S. Embassy in Tehran to mark the 25th anniversary of the hostage crisis in 1979. **14 November:** Iran agrees to suspend its nuclear programs immediately in exchange for European guarantees that it would not face UN Security Council sanctions. **30 November:** Iran's chief nuclear negotiator says that Iran would suspend its uranium enrichment activities for only a few months pending negotiation, but reiterates that Iran would never fully abandon the program. **23 December:** The Iranian intelligence minister announces the arrest of 10 Iranians on charges of spying for the United States and Israel.

2005 14 February: Iran protests U.S. intelligence surveillance flights over Iranian airspace. **15 February:** At least 59 people killed, and 210 injured, by a fire that raged through a crowded mosque in Tehran. **22 February:** A strong earthquake, measuring 6.4 on the Richter scale, kills 500 and injures many more outside of Zarand in Kerman Province. **27 February:** Iran and Russia sign a nuclear fuel agreement. The plan calls for Russia to supply nuclear fuel to Iran, and to take back the spent fuel to ensure that it cannot be diverted into a weapons program. The agreement is a key step towards bringing Iran's first nuclear reactor online by mid-2006. **2 March:** Iran denies a request by IAEA monitors to visit the Parchin military complex. **29 March:** Rafat Bayat, a female lawmaker, announces that she will stand in Iran's presidential election in June, challenging the Council of

Guardians' declaration that only men could be president. **17 June:** The first round of the ninth Iranian Presidential Elections takes place with the frontrunners being Ali Akbar Hashemi-Rafsanjani and Tehran Mayor Mahmud Ahmadinejad. Rafat Bayat, a female lawmaker, was denied the right to stand in the elections by the Council of Guardians. **24 June:** The second round of elections takes place in the form of a run off. Ahmadinejad is declared the winner with 19.48 percent in the first round of voting and 61.69 percent in the second round, with over 60 percent of the registered population voting. **27 June:** Oil prices in world market escalate to over 60 dollars a barrel, reflecting high demand and concerns over Iran's presidential elections. **30 June:** The U.S. government said that it was examining reports that Iranian President elect Mahmud Ahmadinejad took part in the 1979 hostage taking at the U.S. Embassy in Tehran. Ahmadinejad denies these actions. Three Iranians who were involved in the action substantiate his claim. **22 August:** Iran oil exports are estimated to exceed 59 billion dollars by the end of fiscal year 2005. **1 October:** Iranian officials present opposing views to the European Union's attempt to get Russia to change its position on Iran's nuclear program. **3 October:** Iranian officials attempt diplomacy with EU officials with respect to Iran's nuclear program, but are unsuccessful. **8 October:** India's prime minister declares that his vote at the IAEA council was not against Iran. **15 October:** John Bolton, U.S. ambassador to the United Nations, accuses Iranian officials of conspiring to manufacture nuclear weapons. **31 October:** Iranian officials warn that oil could reach $150 per barrel if the UN should establish stringent sanctions against Iran. **2 November:** Iran agrees to let UN nuclear inspectors have access to a military site. **6 November:** Iran announces plans to convert more uranium at an undisclosed site near Isfahan. **8 November:** Iran rejects the EU demand to halt nuclear activities. **11 November:** Iran announces intentions to enrich uranium on Iranian soil. **13 November:** Chief of the IAEA announces a plan to have Iranian officials move their nuclear enrichment operations to Russia; Iranian officials reject U.S. accusations that Iran is enriching uranium to manufacture nuclear weapons. **30 November:** Iran announces that it has no plans to talk with U.S. officials concerning security in Iraq. **2 December:** Russia announces plans to sell Iran more than one billion dollars worth of missile technology. **4 December:** U.S. officials announce possible non-UN-endorsed sanctions against Iran; Iranian officials announce plans to launch a counterstrike offensive in response to any Israeli hostile action regarding Iran's nuclear program. **6 December:** An Iranian military plane crashes into a Tehran suburb, killing at least 128 people. **7 December:** Norsk Hydro, a Norwegian energy specialist group, announces a major discovery of oil reserves along the Iran/Iraq border. **8 December:** Iranian President Mahmud Ahamadinejad speculates that Holocaust is a myth, and suggests that if Western nations are concerned about retribution for the Holocaust, then maybe Israel should be moved to Europe. **9 December:** Iranian officials announce large-scale naval maneuvers to take place in the Indian Ocean and the Sea of Oman. **10 December:** Iran's supreme religious ruler, Ayatollah Ali Khamene'i, supports President Ahmadinejad's comments on Israel. His statement suggests that the occurrence of the Holocaust in Europe does not justify the Israeli occupation of the "Palestinian Homeland." Speculation abounds that Israeli Prime Minister Ariel Sharon may order a military strike against Iranian nuclear enrichment facilities by March 2006. **11 December:** Israeli Major General Amos Gilad, head of the Defense Ministry's foreign policy department, rescinds earlier suggestions that a major military offensive against Iran may begin in March. However, he did not rule out a future military campaign. **12 December:** Iran successfully tests surface-to-sea missiles with a range of 68 miles. **14 December:** Iranian and Russian officials announce the completion of the Bushehr Nuclear Facility. **16 December:** German Intelligence warns that Iran has purchased long-range missiles from North Korea. Iran denies these allegations.

2006 7 January: Police seize over two tons of illegal narcotics in Kerman province. Iranian social reform leaders acknowledge the rise in illegal narcotics entering Iranian borders. **8 January:** Iranian officials announce the removal of UN seals from all of their nuclear facilities. Iran announces intention to reestablish nuclear fuel research; Iran, India, and Pakistan announce plans to collaborate on a gas pipeline connecting the three countries. **7 February:** Supreme Leader Ayatollah Ali Khamene'i states that Iran will continue its efforts to gain dignity, national power and independence without yielding to any threats. **17 February:** U.S. Secretary of State Condoleeza Rice urges Arab nations to isolate Iran for its refusal to compromise on demands to halt its pursuit of nuclear technology. **28 February:** Iranian official states that the United States and other Western countries can no longer claim the ideals of human rights as tools to advance their interests in light of the negligent treatment of prisoners held in U.S. captivity at Guantanamo and Abu Gharib prisons. **4 March:** Iran guarantees Arab nations that the Bushehr nuclear power plant is operationally safe. Iranian officials also take the opportunity to deny U.S. allegations that Iran is pursuing nuclear technology for the purpose of manufacturing weapons. Iranian officials maintain that their pursuit of nuclear technology is limited to the production of nuclear power only. **5 March:** U.S. President George W. Bush declares that Iranian people are being "held captive by clerical elitists, who deny basic liberties, sponsor terrorism, and pursue nuclear weapons." **6 March:** President Bush takes the opportunity to maintain his position that Iran is still a member of "The Axis of Evil," previously stated in a 2002 speech.

INTRODUCTION

Iran is a country with a deep and complex history. Over several thousand years, Iran has been the source of numerous creative contributions to the spiritual and literary world, and the site of many remarkable manifestations of material culture. It is a land and a people full of fascination for both the specialist and the more casual observer. This book is aimed at both readers.

The historical uniqueness of the country is rationale enough to write about Iran. The special place that Iran has come to hold in contemporary historical events, most recently as a center stage actor in the unfolding and interconnected drama of worldwide nuclear arms proliferation and terrorism, is all the more reason to explore the characters and personality of Iran and Iranians. The first edition of the *Historical Dictionary of Iran* was published 11 years ago. The 2006 second edition is considerably revised and expanded. There is nearly double the number of entries. While a handful of earlier entries were dropped, most of the first edition entries have been retained, though a number have been added to and expanded. Of the new entries, the majority fall within the time of the Islamic Revolution and Islamic Republic of Iran, or the past quarter century. Throughout, entry choices centered around the interrelationships of persons and historically significant events.

The book is designed to give the reader a quick and understandable overview of specific events, movements, people, political and social groups, places, and trends. With its system of extensive cross-referencing and intentional choice of entries that complement and supplement one another, the work also allows for considerable exploration of a number of historical and contemporary topics and issues. In particular, the modern period, defined as 1800-present, is covered extensively.

LAND AND PEOPLE

The name of the country that this book is about has an unusual history of its own. Iran, known also as Persia in the English language, derives its name from the ancient term *Aryan* which has a meaning in the Indo-European family of languages of "noble" or "aristocratic." Aryan tribes migrated onto the Iranian Plateau, or what became the heartland of Iran, towards the middle of the second millennium B.C. and, in time, referred to themselves as Iranian and the area they inhabited as Iran. These terms have remained constant to the present day. However, in the fifth century B.C. and for the next several hundred years, the Greek encounter with Iran produced a variation based upon the word *Pars* or *Fars*. Though referring more specifically to the locale of the ruling Achaemenid clan, the term passed into Latin and eventually English to become the word *Persian*. Thus, *Persia* is a foreign designation for the technically more correct term *Iran*. So common, however, was the European terminology that even the official stance of the Iranian government came to allow either term to be used interchangeably. Thus *Iran/Persia* are the same entity, and *Iranian/Persian* refer to the same people.

As an historical concept, perhaps *Iran Zamin* best captures the idea of cultural identity and the relationship between a highly diverse people and their land. There are no exact boundaries of the area termed *Iran Zamin*. Roughly, it is the area where Iranian political and cultural influence predominated in the past two and a half millennia. This would include all of today's nation-state of Iran, but also areas extending far beyond current-day political boundaries, from the Persian Gulf in the south well north of either side of the Caspian Sea into the Caucasus and Central Asia, and from approximately the current Iraq-Iran border in the west to all of Afghanistan and well into Pakistan and India in the east.

CULTURE

Part of the fascination of Iran is the uniqueness of its history. It is difficult to summarize the multitude of accomplishments and contributions nurtured by Iranian civilization, notable for the historical and cultural role it has played throughout the centuries. It is one of a handful of civilizations that traces an unbroken cultural thread back thousands of years. Without a doubt, the key element in the continuous sense of cultural identity in the face of multiple forces of fragmentation has been the Persian language. This is true less in the sense of language as a linguistic entity than as a vehicle for the transmission of a cultural heritage. (For additional detail, see the entry on **Persian language**.) Indeed, one of the curiosities of Iranian history is the lack of a truly indigenous alphabet for any historical stage of language development. Persian language always borrowed an alphabet from other languages. In the most recent reincarnation, the Arabic alphabet was borrowed in the ninth century A.D.

Persian language provided the bond of common identity for people living on the Iranian Plateau since the beginning of recorded history, despite a bewildering parade of different tribes, peoples, and subcultures that over time passed through and inhabited this area. Repeated invasions by non-Iranian peoples and long periods, often centuries, of political domination by outsiders did little to diminish the luster of Iranian culture. Quite the opposite. Foreign influences were incorporated into and made part of Iranian culture which continued to thrive and to develop while retaining a uniquely Iranian character.

An equally important component of the glue which held Iranian culture in place and provided a sense of continuity and destiny was the idea of charismatic kingship. Sometimes designated in the literature as "divine kingship," I prefer charismatic in the pre-modern sense of the term, referring to a supernatural grace. Albeit, such grace was mostly divine in origin, but the distinction is nonetheless important since it takes away the often assumed extension of "divine kingship" to the idea of a sacred or divine king. The royal aura was not the same as divinity and such had never been the case, despite attempts of various kings throughout Iranian history to cloud the issue.

The divination of kings was not what formed the basis of rulership. Rather, legitimacy resided with kings only so long as they fulfilled the obligation inherent in their charismatic role. The concept is variously referred to in the literature as Divine Glory, Royal Glory, or the Arabic/Persian word *farr*. Not entirely unlike the idea of the "social contract" in Western culture, Iranian kings were sanctioned in their "divine" authority, but were obliged to rule in accord with culturally determined standards. Justice, for instance, not in a legal sense, but in a humanistic sense, was one such standard. Thus, the divinely sanctioned king was required to be a "just king." Overall, as an abstract concept, the Iranian idea of kingship formed a basis for continuity in rulership and contributed to the maintenance of cultural continuity.

The wedding of language and cultural identity is found in the Iranian epic, the *Shahnameh*. (For details see the entries on **Abol Qasem Ferdowsi**, *Shahnameh,* and **Characters of the Shahnameh**.) The epic formed the continuing basis of a sense of national identity throughout the centuries, whatever the vagaries of the political situation. It need be remembered that for most Iranians the epic was not merely adventure stories and episodic tales, but the very essence of history itself. More than any other single element, the epic formed the historical consciousness of Iranian peoples. It has served as a collective memory in widely divergent social, economic, and political circumstances, and so, transcended the physical to provide a sense of community. This identity was cultural rather than political, what I would call a "cultural nationalism" to distinguish it from the modern-day concept of political nationalism associated with the idea of a nation-state. Boundaries were not at issue. Thus, Iranianness was defined culturally and extended wherever Iranian language and literature held sway.

HISTORICAL PERIODS

A sketch of Iranian history by period reveals an historical continuity of over 2,500 years. This work contains details of various historical periods in entries specific to those periods. Here the barest outline is provided to give the reader a sense of the scope and flow of Iranian history.

Mention should be made of the prehistoric period of events on the Iranian plateau. Less is known of this period than the fifth century B.C. on since it predates historical records. However, abundant archeological evidence has given us a partial picture of events and cultural developments over a very long period of time, thousands of years. Above all, we know that the Iranians were not the original peoples of the Iranian plateau. Rather, Aryan people migrated onto the plateau from the Siberian steppes in a long, drawn-out migration which was a part of a massive displacement and movement of Aryans westward and southward into Europe, the Iranian plateau, Afghanistan, and the Indian subcontinent. The original inhabitants of the Iranian plateau were gradually absorbed and disappeared as separate entities in a process of assimilation seen elsewhere in world history. An Iranification of the plateau occurred. It is this area which has constituted the heartland of Iranian political entities since and which now forms the major geographical part of the modern nation-state of Iran.

The unification of the plateau politically, and the first well-documented historical period is the Achaemenid period which began with Cyrus the Great in the fifth century B.C. Sometimes referred to as the first world empire, the Achaemenid period left a profound stamp on subsequent Iranian history. Indeed, most of the later resurgent political entities that encompassed the Iranian plateau made conscious attempts to recreate the glories of the Achaemenid Empire. In this sense, it was the touchstone of all subsequent Iranian history. One could, however, make a case that the current Islamic Republic of Iran is the antithesis to this point, seeking as it does a legitimacy grounded in the Islamic religion versus a glorious pre-Islamic past rooted in the charisma of kingship.

The Achaemenid period lasted from 550 B.C. to the sacking of the grand imperial center of Persepolis in 330 B.C. by Alexander the Great. Upon the death of Alexander in 323 B.C., his vast empire was divided amongst his generals and the Iranian portion fell to his chief general, Selucus. The ensuing historic period is known as the Seleucid Dynasty, which was characterized by a marked infusion of Hellenism. This dynasty lasted, however, for less than a century and was supplanted by the Parthians. For nearly a half a millennium, from 247 B.C. to 224 A.D., the Parthian Dynasty prevailed at a time known also as the Arascid Period after Arasces, the founder of the dynasty who revolted against the Seleucids.

Weakened by centuries of conflict with the Roman Empire, Parthian rule ended in 224 A.D. with the advent of the king-to-be Ardashir, who established the Sassanian Dynasty. The Sassanians adopted Zoroastrianism as the state religion and reigned supreme for over 400 years, definitively blocking any further eastward expansion of the Roman Empire. In the sixth century A.D. the Sassanians were perhaps the most splenderous and powerful empire in the world.

All came crashing down in the seventh century A.D. with the advent of Islam and the subsequent Arab conquest which enveloped Iran. Successive defeats of Sassanian armies by the Muslims led to the establishment of Islamic Caliphate rule in Iran in the seventh and eighth centuries.

By the ninth century and into the 10th century, the power of the Caliphate had declined and a number of independent dynasties emerged, including the Tahirids, the Saffarids, the Samanids, the Buyids, and the Ghaznavids. The following several centuries were marked by successive waves of Turkic migration onto the Iranian plateau from Central Asia. The rule of the Seljuk Turks beginning in the 11th century, and later the Khwarazm Turks, mark the period.

In the early 13th century Iran was caught up in the eastward movement of the Mongols. Ghengis Khan himself seized Khorasan in 1220 A.D. For over a century the Mongols held sway in the successor period known as the IlKhanid Dynasty. The IlKhanids gave way to a new world-conqueror named Timur, or Tamerlane as he is popularly known in the English language. The Timurid period was short, lasting only from 1370 to the death of Timur in 1405 A.D.

The Iranian plateau in the 15th century was split into competing minor dynasties including a successor, though highly attenuated, Tirmurid Empire. In 1501, however, a new and powerful force emerged in the form of the Safavid Dynasty. Founded by Shah Ismail, the Safavids extended control over the entire Iranian plateau and beyond, and served for the next several centuries as a counterbalance to the vast and powerful Ottoman Empire to the west. European emissaries made their way to the Safavid capital of Isfahan to seek the support of what was truly a world power of the time. Adorned by Shah Abbas the Great, the incredible sight and grandeur of Isfahan led to the coining of the phrase "Isfahan is Half of the World," by English travelers. This is a phrase which endures to the present day, the applicability of which is evident in the magnificent architecture of the city even now.

The Safavid Dynasty lasted from 1501 to 1722 A.D. The remainder of the 18th century was marked primarily by the political competition of contenders for control of the Iranian plateau. Several short-term successes were the fleeting glory of yet another world-conqueror, Nader Shah, and the brief seizure of control resulting in the Afsharid Period, and the partial restoration of centralized control in the latter half of the 18th century imposed by Karim Khan Zand and his successor. The Zand Period, however, was more of a regional rather than national dynasty.

The modern period begins with the establishment of the Qajar Dynasty by Agha Muhammad Khan Qajar in 1796 A.D. In step with such prior dynasties as the Sassanians and the Safavids, the Qajars attempted to expand Iranian control beyond the plateau and into areas where the Achaemenid Dynasty had previously dominated. In the process, the first Qajar ruler quickly clashed, in the Caucaus region, with the expanded empire of Czarist Russia which had gradually extended its sway southward over the previous century. The ensuing Russo-Persian War dragged on for decades, the Russians unable to devote focused attention and resources to this front due to preoccupation with continental European politics, in particular the expansionist ambitions of Napoleonic France. However, all came to a head with the crushing military defeats of the Qajar forces which led to two disastrous treaties for Iran, the Treaty of Gulistan (1813) and the Treaty of Turkmanchai (1828).

The Persian encounter with the Russians was the Iranian version, psychologically and politically, of Napoleon's invasion and occupation of Egypt at the turn of the century. It marked a new relationship with the West, one in which power had shifted dramatically and various political entities in the Middle East found themselves in inferior positions. The impact of the West and response to that impact through various reform efforts became a common theme of Iranian history throughout the 19th and early 20th centuries.

Ultimately, the turmoil of the 19th century led to a Constitutional Movement which resulted in the granting of a constitution in 1906. Propelled, in part, by nationalist sentiment, the grand experiment in democratic government failed as Iran continued to be caught up in the vagaries of European power politics and the events leading up to and resulting in the First World War.

After WWI, the fatally weakened Qajar monarchy came to an end, in actuality long before its official demise with the establishment of the Pahlavi Dynasty in 1925. Reza Khan crowned himself Reza Shah and embarked on a path of modernization somewhat akin to what was occurring simultaneously in Turkey under Ataturk. In both cases, strong nationalist sentiments propelled the emergence of a modern nation-state.

However, though their purposes were similar in desiring to modernize their countries and there were many policy similarities in the economic and social realms, the political paths that Ataturk and Reza Shah chose were divergent. The former attempted to lay the groundwork for an emerging secular democratic system of government. The latter established a secular autocratic system harking back to the pre-Islamic Iranian past and seeking its legitimacy in the charisma of kingship, as opposed to the democratic will of the people.

The reign of Reza Shah came to an abrupt end in 1941 when Iran was invaded by England and Russia and the king abdicated in favor of his son. Again, Iran was a victim of Great Power conflicts, this time with a new power player, Germany. As the nation was caught up in the sweeping events of WWII and its aftermath, the monarch who ascended the throne, the young and inexperienced Muhammad Reza Shah Pahlavi, was not much of a factor. In time, he became a political presence. However, he never emerged entirely from the domineering shadow of his father, partly due to personality and in part due to circumstances.

Much of the Muhammad Reza Shah period was influenced by the Cold War, the new game of Great Power Politics with a shift in the primary power players. The United States and Stalinist Russia both considered Iran a vital interest. Indeed, the Azerbaijan Crisis in 1946 was the opening shot in the Cold War.

A growing nationalist movement led by Muhammad Mossadeq forced Muhammad Reza Shah to leave the country in 1953. However, the United States reacted to the oil nationalization crisis with an unfounded fear of a communist takeover of Iran and sponsored a military coup engineered by the CIA. The result was a temporary triumph for American Cold War interests. But, after 1953, Muhammad Reza Shah was perceived by the greater Iranian public as beholden to Western interests. The impeccable Iranist credentials of his father were tainted and, try as he did, Muhammad Reza Shah never quite attained a nationalist pedigree to go along with his repeated attempts to hearken back to the roots of Iranian monarchical legitimacy. In the end, despite a long reign (1941-1979), Muhammad Reza Shah left a legacy marked more by tragedy than triumph.

By the mid-1970s, the building pressure for political change began to be palpable. Ironically, a heavy contributing factor was the very success of the Iranian economy in the late 1960s and early 1970s which was arguably the fastest growing economy in the world. The indecisiveness of the Shah in times of crisis contributed to the growing malaise. Some attributed the vacillation of the Shah in 1978 to the closely guarded secret of his declining health. Others placed more emphasis on the flaws of his character. In any event, in 1978 the Pahlavi world began crumbling in the events leading to the Islamic Revolution. In January 1979 the Shah went into exile, never to return, as the Pahlavi Dynasty was swept aside and replaced with the Islamic Republic of Iran.

The Islamic Republic continues to the present day. Much of this book covers the period. By following the cross-references in the text, the reader can attain a thorough picture of the Islamic Republic. To mention a few highlights, the towering presence of the commonly considered father of the Islamic Revolution, Ayatollah Khomeini, stands out. Significant events include the adoption of a new basis of government in the Constitution of the Islamic Republic of Iran, the U.S. Embassy hostage crisis, and the Iran-Iraq War. Furthermore, the cause of a considerable number of noteworthy political events and struggles since 1979 deserves mention. The ongoing internal political debate over the nature of the relationship between politics and religion has been and continues to be an active intellectual and political exercise.

ECONOMY

The economy of Iran was historically tied to agriculture and trade. However, with the discovery of oil in large commercial quantities in the 20th century, the Iranian economy became dependent on oil income. So significant was this trend that by the 1970s economic scholars warned of the dangers of dualistic economic conditions. There was an unbalanced growth of the economy resulting from huge sums of oil-generated revenue, lagging capital formation in non-oil sectors of the economy, and ineffective coordination of the constituent elements of national development.

The reliance of Iran on oil for economic well-being has led to other problems. The lion's share of the nation's revenue comes from oil. In fact, 80 percent of the overall export revenue comes from oil exports. With such reliance on one sector, the Iranian economy is subject to fluctuations in the world energy markets. A downturn in world demand results in an inordinate negative impact on Iran, a happenstance that has occurred several times in the modern history of the country. An interesting paradox is that in order to diversify its economy Iran must use income from its oil industry and that is what the various economic development plans instituted by the Iranian government were designed to do. In the Pahlavi period under Muhammad Reza Shah, there were no less than five long-term plans from 1949 to 1979, ranging in length from five to seven years. These plans were developed and implemented by a cabinet ministry entitled Plan Organization. The government of the Islamic Republic has attempted to continue along the same path. Despite such efforts, the Iranian economy today is still overly dependent on oil income.

CURRENT AFFAIRS

In light of the 1979 Islamic Revolution of Iran and subsequent events, it is well to question whether the sense of historical Iranian national identity outlined above is intact and well today. Certainly, the adoption of a different concept of legitimate rule, institutionalized in the Constitution of the Islamic Republic of Iran with the notion of *Velayat-i Faqih*, would seem to indicate a dramatic departure. (For specifics, see the entries on Assembly of Experts, Constitution of the Islamic Republic of Iran, Council of Guardians, *Faqih*, Islamic Republic of Iran, Ayatollah Ruhollah Khomeini, and *Velayat-i Faqih*.) It is beyond the scope of this discussion to explore this issue. And, in any event, the outcome is yet to be empirically determined. Suffice it to say that the historical capacity of Iranian cultural themes to rebound and live on in ever-revitalized forms is well documented. The history of Iran in coming decades is likely to be a fascinating one.

Politically, in the past decade there have been three presidential elections in Iran. The country has swayed from a conservative Islamic political persuasion to a liberal one with the election of President Muhammad Khatami in 1997, and then back towards a conservative mode with the election of President Mahmud Ahmadinejad in June of 2005. In the course of this time, the debates over the relationship between religion and politics have been abundant and intense. The rise and fall of numerous politicians, a number of whom are also religious scholars, has occurred. Intellectuals, both secular and religious, have also been buffeted by the varying political winds. The political scene in Iran has been, is, and will surely continue to be a lively one. Tracking key characters gives some sense of the dynamic and evolving political scene. Thus, this edition contains a large number of new entries on contemporary political and intellectual figures. More than 20 such individuals have been added. Likewise, a considerably increased number of political organizations and movements have found their way into the book as entries.

In 2005 Iran became the focus of a major controversy on the world political scene over charges that the country was developing a nuclear arms capability. The charges were not new. Over a period of years, intermittent concerns surfaced regarding attempts by the Islamic Republic to reenergize the program of peaceful nuclear energy development begun under Muhammad Reza Shah in the latter years of the Pahlavi Dynasty. Billions of dollars had already been invested in nuclear power capability. Western powers, including the United States, supported those efforts and, indeed, profited handsomely. Occasionally, questions arose as to why a country, which at the time was near the top of world ranking in both oil reserves and oil production, needed to develop nuclear power capability. But, any such concern was subdued as the Shah was considered a Western ally. After the 1979 Islamic Revolution of Iran, the attentions of the nation were focused throughout the 1980s on internal power struggles and the Iran-Iraq War. Thus, it was not until the 1990s that the nuclear power issue reemerged.

The terms of the debate are clear. Iran claims that the nuclear intentions of the nation are entirely peaceful. Indeed, Iran is a signatory to the UN-sponsored Nuclear Non-Proliferation Treaty and over the years has opened its nuclear sites to UN inspection teams under the terms of that treaty. Critics claim that the Iranians have not been entirely forthcoming and have developed a secret nuclear capability aimed at the eventual production of nuclear arms.

The debate has intensified in the early years of the 21st century, particularly since the American invasion of Iraq in 2003, an incursion that was justified on what proved to be the false grounds of Iraqi development of weapons of mass destruction. By 2006, the focus of such charges had shifted dramatically to Iran, despite the fact that Iran has consistently maintained that its nuclear program is for peaceful purposes and that the country wishes to operate its program under the supervision of the International Atomic Energy Agency (IAEA).

In significant ways, the ongoing crisis of nuclear arms capability has taken on the dimension of an American-Iranian standoff, part of the continuing negative dynamic of U.S.-Iranian relations since the Islamic Revolution. As such, the European powers have generally acted as intermediate brokers, toning down the crisis. In the early months of 2006, however, the crisis has come to the brink as the combination of exertive American pressure on the international community and the intransigence of the Iranian government with respect to international inspections have pushed the Europeans more toward the American side of the controversy. The election of President Mahmud Ahmadinejad in June 2005 and his subsequent actions and public statements have intensified the distrust of Iranian intentions and complicated the matter. The possibility of UN sanctions on Iran is impending in the spring of 2006, though negotiations continue. Eventual resolution of the nuclear Iran issue will not likely occur anytime soon.

Provinces and Provincial Capitals

Figure 1

THE DICTIONARY

-A-

ABADAN. The city of Abadan was founded by a holy man named Abbad sometime in the eighth or ninth century A.D. The name of the city was originally spelled Abbadan. However, due to **Reza Shah**'s policy of Persianizing Arabic names, the spelling was changed to Abadan in 1935. The city is located on the southwest side of an island also named Abadan. The island is situated between the **Shatt al-Arab** River to the west and the Bahmanshir River to the east. During the Abbasid Dynasty, Abadan was a thriving port city along the Persian Gulf coast of Iran. However, silt from the Shatt al-Arab has expanded the delta to the point where Abadan is now located 30 miles inland.

When the Shatt al-Arab emerged as the boundary between the Persian and Ottoman Empires in the middle of the 17th century, Abadan became disputed territory. In the 1847 **Treaty of Erzerum** the island was formally given to Iran. After the early 20th century discovery of **oil** in **Khuzistan** province, the city prospered along with the growth of the oil industry. By 1951, the population of the city was nearly 200,000 and it had the largest oil refinery in the world. As oil production soared over the next three decades, Abadan gained ever-greater importance as an economic and strategic asset. The city suffered accordingly in the **Iran-Iraq War** (1980-1988). During the war, the refinery was destroyed as well as over 50 percent of the city.

After the Iran-Iraq War, both the city and the oil refinery were rebuilt. However, Abadan has yet to attain its prior status. The 1996 census population of the city was 206,073, only

1

slightly more than the population a half a century earlier. Additionally, the lack of a permanent settlement between Iran and Iraq with regard to the issue of sovereignty over the Shatt al-Arab continues to cloud the future of Abadan.

ABBAS MIRZA (1789-1833). Abbas Mirza was the eldest son of **Fath Ali Shah**. He was appointed governor of the province of **Azerbaijan** where he ruled as crown prince and heir apparent to the **Qajar** throne. In 1805, at the age of 16, the Crown Prince was given command of the Persian Army. He led a disastrous campaign against the Russians from 1805 to 1813, pitting his woefully inadequate army against the Russian veterans of the Napoleonic Wars. The result was a bitter loss for Iran, confirmed in the **Treaty of Gulistan** (1813). The humiliation of this overwhelming defeat gave rise to Abbas Mirza's passion and obsession for modernization in Iran.

As part of his campaign for progress, Abbas Mirza sent students abroad for study and training. In 1811, he sent two young men to England with the returning British envoy, Sir Harford Jones. In 1815, Abbas Mirza sent five more students to London for technical and professional training in such areas as gunsmithing, artillery, and engineering. Among this group was **Mirza Saleh Shirazi** who would bring back a printing press and later publish Iran's first newspaper. Abbas Mirza's internal efforts to bring the country up to par with Europe and Russia were met with indifference from the Shah and contempt from court ministers. His reforms were opposed by his political rivals and failed to take root.

Though Abbas Mirza continued to fight for the modernization of his army, he went into battle against the Russians in 1827 as ill equipped as he had been in the earlier battles. His army was thoroughly routed and the defeat led to the **Treaty of Turkman-chai** (1828) in which Iran was forced to yield numerous costly concessions to the Russians. He accepted responsibility for the outcome and retired to **Mashhad** where he died in 1833, predeceasing his father, and thereby never succeeding to the throne. His pleas for modernization were later taken up by like-minded Iranians, such as **Mirza Taqi Khan Amir Kabir**, and some of the progressive changes Abbas Mirza initiated began to occur more successfully during the middle of the 19th century.

ABDI, ABBAS (1956-). Abbas Abdi was only 23 years old when he helped to orchestrate the 4 November, 1979 takeover of the American Embassy in **Tehran**. Abdi met with the 300 students who would later be known as the **Students Following the Imam's Line** on the morning of the event, which was intended to last three to seven days, but evolved into 444 days of holding **American Hostages in Iran**. According to Abdi, Washington's refusal to meet demands and pressures from other facets of the **Islamic Revolution** forced the students to continue the occupation and holding of 52 American hostages.

In 1980, Abdi attained a prominent position in the new government of the **Islamic Republic** in the prosecutor general's office where he served for several years. After the death of **Ayatollah Ruhollah Khomeini** in 1989, Abdi voiced his opposition to the ruling clergy and was imprisoned for eight months. He later supported the election of President **Muhammad Khatami** in 1997 and began speaking out for a more democratic Iran as editor of the **reformist press** newspaper *Salaam*. The Iranian government ordered the newspaper closed in 1999 for its outspoken advocacy of openness and reform. The banning of the newspaper ignited demonstrations of angry Iranian students at **Tehran University** which were brutally suppressed in the affair known as the **Student Dormitory Attacks**.

In 1998 Abdi traveled to UNESCO headquarters in Paris where he met with former embassy hostage Barry Rosen in a spirit of reconciliation. Abdi spoke at the event, not in apology of the actions in 1979, but in hopes of better relations with the U.S. Abdi's decision to meet with the former hostage, which he called a "personal initiative," prompted mixed responses from Iranians and Americans, and has failed to bring about the intended reconciliation. It, nonetheless, served as an important symbolic gesture. *See also* ASGHARZADEH, IBRAHIM; EBTEKAR, MASSOUMEH.

ABU ALI IBN SINA (980-1037). Abu Ali Ibn Sina, known to the West as Avicenna, was one of the most important and influential Persian intellectuals of all time. Born in Bokhara, Turkestan in 980, he lived in a great number of places before his death in **Hamadan** in 1037.

Ibn Sina lived in a turbulent time and was driven from place to place by the threat of political instability. Given the towering nature of his intellect it was not surprising that he was drafted into the field of politics. Once settled in Hamadan, he became grand vizier, the second most powerful state position, to the Buyid ruler. His interests, however, were clearly more in the intellectual realm to which he devoted himself continually, even during the time of his short-lived political career.

The writings of Ibn Sina were many and covered a wide variety of fields. He was a noted physician, philosopher, and poet. His extensive travels throughout the Middle East sparked his development of a new theory of social class, based on an individual's position within society rather than the traditional hereditary basis.

His writings are rooted in the teachings of the Greek philosophers, a mix of Aristotelian and neo-Platonist philosophies. A thinker of great originality, he had a tremendous impact on both Middle Eastern and Western thought. His major work, *The Canon*, is a detailed book describing his theories on medicine, physics, astronomy, and numerous other scientific subjects.

Avicenna's medical knowledge was incredible for a man of his time. He wrote about diseases, explained bodily functions, and described varied uses for drugs in medical treatment. As a compendium of known medical knowledge, *The Canon* was perhaps the most important and influential medical book ever written. It served as the standard medical text in the major schools of medicine in Europe for nearly seven centuries, and the medical treatises of Ibn Sina were used by European physicians even into the 20th century.

ACHAEMENID DYNASTY. The Achaemenid Dynasty, a term synonymous with the "Persian Empire," was the first of the great world empires. Many of the developments of the Achaemenids, such as the king's absolute power being legitimated by religion, would resonate in many other empires throughout history.

The Achaemenid Dynasty was founded by **Cyrus the Great** in 550 B.C. after his tribe, the Parsi, successfully revolted against the Medes. In 546 B.C., Cyrus conquered Babylon after a long siege by diverting the Euphrates River away from the city. The Hebrews immortalized this event in the scripture, honoring Cyrus as the liberator who allowed their return to Jerusalem. Achaemenid Persia would eventually come to cover most of the Middle East, including Egypt. The expeditions of **Darius I** and Xerxes into Greece became legendary, although Persia never fully subdued all of the Greek city-states, which would result in the future destruction of the Achaemenid Empire. King Darius III (ruled 336-330 B.C.) was the last Achaemenid king. After his murder in the midst of war, the Achaemenid Empire was conquered by Alexander the Great.

While the cities of Babylon, Ecbatana (present-day **Hamadan**), and **Susa** were important **trade** and administrative centers, **Persepolis** was both the spiritual center and the capital of the empire. Overlooking a wide fertile plain near the present-day city of **Shiraz**, construction on the city was begun by King Darius and finished by King Artaxerxes III. Most histories relate that when Alexander the Great conquered the empire, he sought revenge for the Persian burning of the Athenian Acropolis by burning Persepolis to the ground. Some scholars say the burning, shortly before the death of Darius III in 330 B.C., was accidental. Ironically, the ashes from the timber roof formed a protective covering over the city, preserving it and the records contained in the treasury for posterity. After the **Islamic Revolution** certain elements of the **Islamic Republic** sought to destroy the remains, viewing them as a symbol of monarchy, but the ruins were saved by local townspeople who made a living giving tours of it.

The state religion of the Achaemenids was **Zoroastrianism**. In fact, the absolute authority of Achaemenid rulers, known as "ShahanShah" ("King of Kings"), derived legitimacy from the religion. The concept of justifying absolute power via religion would be borrowed by future empires and dynasties throughout the world, and especially in the West. Zoroastrianism also gave a cohesiveness to the core of the empire, while its tolerant attitude allowed conquered peoples to more contentedly become part of the new empire, losing relatively little cultural autonomy. The Achaemenid Dynasty's legacy to the Iranian people has been great. Throughout history, Iranian rulers have referred to the Achaemenids, claiming a place of continuity in an ancient tradition. The Iranian people look with pride to the Achaemenids, feeling part of one of the oldest and most influential groups in history. In this way, the dynasty's influence continues to the present day.

AFKHAMI, MAHNAZ (1941-). Mahnaz Afkhami was born in Kerman, Iran. She has distinguished herself with a life of activism in the field of **women**'s rights. Afkhami founded the Association of Iranian University Women, served as the minister of state for women's affairs in the latter years of the **Pahlavi Dynasty**, and held the position of secretary general of the **Women's Organization of Iran (WOI)** prior to the **Islamic Revolution**.

In October 1978, Afkhami came to the United States from Iran. She was finishing negotiations with the United Nations to set up the International Research and Training Institute for the Advancement of Women in Tehran. While still in the U.S. she received a call from her husband in Iran telling her about the deteriorating political situation. Since she was the most visible representative of the women's movement in Iran and because of her close association with the Pahlavi regime, return was fraught with danger. She chose to remain in the U.S. and shortly thereafter, the Islamic Revolution occurred.

In exile, Afkhami began to feel a loss of identity which sent her on a search to find herself. Everything that had constituted her identity—her country, home, job, colleagues, friends, and language—were all abruptly gone. She has written a book about her experiences entitled *Women in Exile*. In the book, she tells about being a woman in exile from her own personal view. She writes not only of herself, but of 12 other women who came into exile to the United States with her.

In the U.S., she has continued to work with women's rights groups and organizations. For her work over three decades she has attained a reputation as one of the leading advocates of women's rights, not only in Iran, but worldwide. She is the founder and the president of the Women's Learning Partnership (WLP), which began operations in spring of 1999, and focuses on the leadership roles of women and their participation in civil society. She is also the executive director of the Foundation for Iranian Studies, a U.S.-based organization devoted to encouraging and aiding both Iranians and non-Iranians in the interdisciplinary study of Iranian culture.

Afkhami has written numerous publications. Many of these have been translated and distributed internationally. She is widely known and respected as an authority on women's rights and issues, particularly as pertaining to the Middle East and North Africa.

AFSHAR. The Afshar have their origins in the 11th century under the rule of the Mongols and are considered to be a blend of **Turkoman** tribes forced from Asia by the Mongols and certain Iranian **tribes** that immigrated to southeast Iran after the invasion of the **Arabs**. The Afshar might best be described by the comment of one scholar who writes of Iranian tribes that they are sometimes "fortuitous conglomerations" of people and groups with disparate origins. The Afshar speak mostly Turkish, but have incorporated many words from the **Persian language**, and religiously, the majority adheres to **Shiah** Islam.

The Afshar are centered in the **Kerman** province and in their transhumant nomadic existence roam cyclically from winter to summer pasturages. They survive through means of animal husbandry and selling of artisan items. The tribe has been known throughout history for its carpets, weavings, wools, and household tools.

Not particularly large in number, probably less than 100,000, the Afshar did not usually play a major role in Iranian history unless allied in a larger confederacy. However, the Afshar did enjoy the power of establishing one of the dynasties which ruled Iran after the Mongols. Nader Qoli Beg was born to the tribe on 22 October, 1688. He became Iran's most well-known military strategist, driving the Afghans from the country and conquering far-flung lands. He ascended to the throne in 1736, as **Nader Shah**, and ruled until 1747, followed by three Afshar rulers, in the brief 18th century Afsharid period of Iranian history.

AGHA MUHAMMAD KHAN QAJAR (Ruled 1787-1797). The first of the **Qajar** line of Shahs, Agha Muhammad Khan established **Tehran** as the capital of Persia in 1788. He established his claim to the throne by first dominating rivals on the **Iranian Plateau**, and then by asserting control over areas that had formerly been part of the previous great Persian Empires. His reign was marked by continual warfare in the attempt to reunite the greater Persia of **Nader Shah**. He refused to be crowned until he controlled Georgia and restored Persian hegemony in the Caucasus. Agha Muhammad Khan was a eunuch and some historians have attributed his renowned cruelty to that fact. He was greatly feared, and the stories are legion of his iron hand and lack of compassion, not only for foe, but towards his own kin. It was this character trait that led directly to his death at the hands of his own servants. Agha Muhammad Khan had condemned them to death for disturbing his rest with a quarrel, but they acted first. Agha Muhammad Khan was assassinated in 1797, appropriately enough in the course of a war campaign. Thanks to the foresight of Agha Muhammad Khan, the Qajar line continued. Long before his own coronation, he had arranged for his nephew, Fath Ali Khan, who was coronated **Fath Ali Shah**, to succeed to the throne.

AGRICULTURE. Agriculture is important in many developing countries and Iran is no exception. While not nearly as large a source of revenue as **oil**, agriculture does represent a significant sector of the **economy**. The agriculture sector is the second largest employer of Iranians; second only to the service **industry** (45 percent). However, despite its large number of laborers, agriculture contributed only 11.2 percent of the gross domestic product in 2004. This figure has fluctuated both higher and lower since the **Islamic Revolution** due to such contributing factors as the **Iran-Iraq War**, variable rainfall, inconsistent government investment, and land reform.

Post-revolutionary attempts at land reform led to intense internal debate and tension, and while some land distribution took place under a Land Reform Bill enacted by the **Revolutionary Council**, in 1983 the bill was cancelled by the **Council of Guardians**. Previous land reform efforts under the **Pahlavi Dynasty**, notably the land distribution provisions of the **White Revolution**, were partially successful and, likewise, stirred emotions and entailed political consequences.

Some products deriving from Iranian agriculture are wheat, sugar beets, nuts, fruits, wool, caviar, dairy products, and rice. In particular, fruits and nuts are important for export, as is wool in the form of carpets. Nearly all caviar is exported, and while the value is high, the volume is low. The local vegetable oil and sugar refining industries depend upon Iranian agricultural products for a significant portion of their raw materials.

Iran has sometimes been called a land of villages with estimations of over 40,000 rural settlements in existence. Until the 20th century and the discovery of oil, its wealth as a nation was always intertwined with its agricultural well-being. While the status of Iranian agriculture in the 20th century was relegated to a secondary position, in the 21st century it is still a key element of the economy.

AHMADINEJAD, MAHMUD (1956-). Mahmud Ahmadinejad was elected to be the sixth president of Iran on 24 June, 2005, in a landslide victory over the popular moderate candidate and former president, **Ali Akbar Hashemi-Rafsanjani**. In the first round of the election over 1,000 candidates were rejected by the Iranian **Council of Guardians**, leaving seven official candidates. That round was dominated by Rafsanjani, with Ahmadinejad receiving only 19.5 percent of the votes. However, in the second run off round, with a 60 percent turn out, Ahmadinejad's appeal to the religious rural poor of Iran, reinforced by his simple lifestyle and populist stance, secured nearly 62 percent of the votes, taking Rafsanjani, and much of the world, by surprise.

Ahmadinejad, who served as mayor of **Tehran** from May 2003 until his election to the presidency, was born in Aradan near Garmsar in 1956, and moved with his family to Tehran as an infant. He studied civil engineering at Iran University of Science and Technology (IUST) starting in 1976, continuing into graduate studies. During his studies, Ahmadinejad became a representative of the university, attending meetings with **Ayatollah Ruhollah Khomeini** that would eventually spawn the Office for the Strengthening of Unity, created by the students calling themselves **Students Following the Imam's Line** who would seize the American Embassy at Tehran in 1979. While earning a master's degree in 1986, Ahmadinejad was prompted by the Iran-Iraq War to join the Islamic **Revolutionary Guards** Corps, eventually becoming the head engineer of the sixth army of the Revolutionary Guards as well as the head of the Corps' western province staff. After the war Ahmadinejad served as an advisor to the Ministry of Culture and Islamic Guidance and upon earning a Ph.D., became a professor in the civil engineering department at IUST.

Until his election to the office of mayor of Tehran, Ahmadinejad was a relatively unfamiliar figure in Iranian politics. However, his replacement of many previous mayoral decisions with religiously rooted alternatives brought him attention. More focus landed on Ahmadinejad when he began to publicly criticize and quarrel with then President **Muhammad Khatami**. Despite his controversial positions, Ahmadinejad was named to a list of 65 finalists, out of 550, for the title of World Mayor 2005, of which only nine were from Asia.

Ahmadinejad was officially installed as president of the **Islamic Republic** on 3 August, 2005, during a celebration where the new president kissed the hand of **Ayatollah Ali Khamene'i**, becoming only the second president to give tribute to a supreme leader (*Faqih*) upon taking office. Ahmadinejad submitted his ministry candidates for approval to the **Majlis** on 14 August and 10 days later most were approved. However, four appointees were rejected, making his the first cabinet not to receive blanket approval since the **Islamic Revolution**. Such resistance was an indication of the significant splits in the Iranian body politic over the political direction the new President wished to move the country.

The presidency of Ahmadinejad to date has featured considerable controversy. Shortly after his election, allegations began to surface regarding Ahmadinejad's role in the 1979 American Embassy siege by the Students Following the Imam's Line. The publicity surrounding Ahmadinejad's victory prompted several former U.S. Embassy hostages to claim recognition of Ahmadinejad as one of their captors during the 444 days of **American Hostages in Iran**. The Western media embraced the accusations leading to admonitions by certain U.S leaders. Five former hostages claimed to explicitly remember Ahmadinejad as an interrogator and guard. However, three other former hostages expressed that they could not specifically recall Ahmadinejad as one of the embassy guards or interrogators. Several former hostage-takers disavowed the allegation entirely, including the siege spokesperson to the West, **Massoumeh "Mary" Ebtekar**, who served as vice president under Khatami. Also, **Abbas Abdi**, one of the students who initiated the siege and a political opponent of Ahmadinejad, stated that Ahmadinejad played no role in the takeover and was certainly not responsible for any security during the embassy occupation as was alleged. Ahmadinejad himself declared that while he publicly expressed support for the embassy siege and hostage taking, after it was praised by Khomeini, he was never actually involved in the events.

This story was shaped considerably by a photo, first published by *Iran Focus*, and quickly picked up by Western media agencies, including the Associated Press and Reuters, which seemed to show a young Ahmadinejad leading a blindfolded hostage during the siege. The unexamined photo was so quickly introduced to the media that its validity was just as rapidly questioned. Shortly after it first appeared, the *Los Angeles Times* reported that an unnamed U.S. official involved in an investigation of Ahmadinejad's behavior during the Islamic Revolution claimed that there were "serious discrepancies" between the photo in question and photos of Ahmadinejad at the time, including dissimilarity in facial structures and features. Following this, Reuters and the AP also reported that there were "discrepancies" in the identification of the man in the 1979 photo and that it had been reported by **Sa'id Hajjerian**, a reformist politician in Iran and former presidential advisor, as well as a critic of Ahmadinejad, that the man shown in the photo was a student named Taqi Muhammadi.

At the same time, allegations of political impropriety were being made against the president-elect claiming that Ahmadinejad had used a network of mosques, the Islamic Revolutionary Guards Corps, and the **Basij** to illegally mobilize and enforce support for his candidacy. Ahmadinejad's popular opponent, Rafsanjani, even alleged that underhanded tricks had been used to win Ahmadinejad the presidency, though he later urged support of the new president. However, claims of election fraud may not be entirely unfounded as Iran's Interior Ministry received more than 300 complaints of electoral and polling place violations in Tehran alone.

Since taking office, Ahmadinejad has made no qualms about his belief, expressed during his campaign, that improved ties with the West are unnecessary. He has also stressed that Iranian nuclear research, as strictly technological, energy-related research, will continue regardless of opposition by the United States or the United Nations. He has lived up to his assertions. In the waning months of 2005 and the early months of 2006, Ahmadinejad has led a very hardline approach towards the enrichment of uranium on Iranian soil in defiance of the International Atomic Energy Agency (IAEA) and the Western powers, particularly the United States. Ahmadinejad has further alarmed the international community by making outrageous claims, such as the denial of the Holocaust. His steadfast insistence of Western deceit concerning the Holocaust and persistent verbal attacks against Israel and the United States have fueled a climate of mistrust, further complicating the nuclear issue. Negotiations have produced little in the way of settlement. As of this writing, the matter of Iranian enrichment has been referred to the UN Security Council and resolution appears slim as almost daily the rhetoric intensifies. In early 2006, whether by intention or circumstance, Ahmadinejad has taken the spotlight on the world stage.

AHVAZ. Located in southwest Iran, the city of Ahvaz is positioned on the **Karun River** and serves as the administrative center for the **Khuzistan** province. The city is effectively divided by the Karun into an east-bank residential district and a west-bank industrial district. A substantial industrial presence, combined with significant rail and highway **transportation** hubs, has allowed Ahvaz to serve as a major shipping and distribution center. The river itself has also served as a transportation link historically since the Karun was navigable by steamer up to Ahvaz where the river is about 100 meters wide.

An ancient city, Ahvaz was known by the **Achaemenids** as Tareiana, and as Hormozd-Ardashir under the **Sassanid** ruler King Ardashir I. At this time Ahvaz first excelled economically due to the commencement of irrigation and the construction of a river-damming system. After the Arab conquest in the seventh century A.D., the city was renamed Suq al-Ahvaz and served as an important trading center until the 13th century. However, disrepair of the damming and irrigation systems so vital to the city led to severe flooding of the commercial district, and subsequent economic decline.

In the early 20th century, the discovery of **oil** reserves in the vicinity of Ahvaz led to a restructuring period and substantial economic growth for the city. Given the centrality of its location between Masjed-i Soleiman and **Abadan**, Ahvaz prospered as the oil industry blossomed in Iran. Investment in the 1960s in the restoration of irrigation systems led to the development of agribusinesses in the area. However, the **Islamic Revolution** and subsequent events seriously disrupted the city. Several battles of the **Iran-Iraq War** impacted Ahvaz, destroying many of the city's historical landmarks.

After the war Ahvaz resumed growth. The city remained tied into the oil **industry** and began to develop an industrial focus on the manufacturing of textiles, pottery, and processed foods. As of 1996, Ahvaz had a population of nearly one million, double that of only a decade earlier in the midst of the Iran-Iraq war, and was home to Shahid **Chamran** University, as well as several other educational and technical institutions. The city has continued to prosper into the 21st century.

AIRBUS INCIDENT. On 3 July, 1988 an American Aegis Class Cruiser, the USS *Vincennes*, mistakenly shot down an Iranian commercial airliner, Iran Air Flight 655, killing all 290 passengers and crew on board the airbus. The incident occurred in the Persian Gulf near the **Hormoz Strait**, a vulnerable chokepoint for maritime traffic carrying **oil** to the world market. Tensions in the Gulf were especially high at this time due to the ongoing **Iran-Iraq War**, which resulted in various hostile engagements and the flagging, for purposes of protection, of foreign oil tankers by the American military in Operation Earnest Will.

Flight 655 was making its weekly **Tehran**-Bandar Abbas-Dubai flight when the radar of the American naval vessel began tracking it from Bandar Abbas on its way to Dubai. At the same time, the USS *Vincennes* was engaged in a skirmish with multiple Iranian gunboats, which had just fired at a U.S. Navy helicopter in the area. A consequent series of mistakes and misjudgments led to the ship's captain to determine that Flight 655 was a hostile Iranian F-14 aircraft poised to strike at the USS *Vincennes*, requiring defensive action to save the ship and its crew. The following missile salvo led to a tragic international incident and loss of innocent lives, the result of which still reverberates today in **U.S.-Iranian Relations.**

Controversy still surrounds the event as the U.S. government maintains the commander of the USS *Vincennes*, Captain William C. Rogers, was only taking defensive action in accordance with established rules of engagement against an airplane his advanced Aegis radar had determined to be hostile. It seemed logical in this situation that an unidentified aircraft departing from Iran and not responding to radio warnings might seek to attack the American ship as it engaged Iranian gunboats. The aggressive defensive posture taken by the Americans was further compounded by an Iraqi attack a year earlier on the USS *Stark* while patrolling the Persian Gulf, in which an Iraqi military jet fired an Exocet missile at the ship, killing 37 Americans on board, and because U.S. Intelligence was predicting an attack in the area on or about July 4th. The combination of circumstances proved deadly.

Iranians maintained that the egregious attack could easily have been avoided, unless of course the U.S. had intentionally shot down the aircraft. Arguments abounded that the USS *Vincennes* failed to follow international protocol by making radio contact on established civilian frequencies to warn the aircraft of the approaching danger. Also, Flight 655 was following the same route it had flown every week since the early 1960s, and the U.S. military should have been aware of civilian air traffic in the area. The situation was further aggravated because the U.S. government not only failed to issue an official apology, but also offered only token compensation to the victims' families, while at the same time admitting no responsibility for the event. And as if to add insult to injury, at the end of his cruise, Captain Rogers was awarded the Legion of Merit, one of the military's highest awards.

Many American military documents surrounding the downing of Flight 655 are still highly classified, and the public may not know the true nature of the attack for many years to come. In the meantime, even with the passage of 18 years, the Airbus Incident remains fresh in the minds of Iranians and continues to add to the air of mistrust between Iran and the United States.

AL-AFGHANI, JAMAL AL-DIN (1839-1897). Jamal al-Din al-Afghani was born in 1839 in a small village outside **Hamadan**. An original and unorthodox thinker, Jamal al-Din left Iran at a young age and traveled throughout the Middle East and Europe. He studied and wrote about the relationship between religion and political action, expressing the view that the Middle East could prevent imperialism only by adopting Western technology, and by using the revolutionary tenets of **Islam** to mobilize the masses against foreign influence. His writing and thought were instrumental in the forging of a religious-radical alliance in **Qajar** Iran. His letters to **Shiah** clerics in the late 19th century helped fuel the **Tobacco Revolt**, a forerunner to the **Constitutional Revolution** in 1906 which resulted in the granting of the first Iranian Constitution.

A pan-Islamist and noted philosopher, Jamal al-Din remains a controversial figure within the pan-Islamic movement. In his extensive travels, he adopted the persona which would be most beneficial in his current situation. He was Persian, but claimed to be an Afghan, hence the sobriquet "al-Afghani." He could be Sunni or Shiah Muslim, pro-imperialism or an active protestor against foreign influence—depending upon his immediate environment. Many critics tend to dismiss him as a self-serving, paranoiac political agitator, but others recognize his profound impact on 19th century Muslim thought, and continue to study this unorthodox writer who is still widely quoted in Iran today.

AL-BIRUNI, ABU REIHAN (973-1048). Respected as one of the world's greatest scholars, al-Biruni was known to have masterful proficiency in mathematics, physics, metaphysics, philosophy, history, and geography, as well as advanced knowledge in geology and astronomy.

Al-Biruni was born around 973 A.D. in Khiva (then part of Iran) and was taken into the court of Sultan Mahmud Ghaznavi as a prodigy at an early age. For 20 years al-Biruni traveled through India with the Sultan learning Hindu philosophy, geography, and mathematical sciences. During his time in India al-Biruni also translated into Arabic several Sanskrit texts pertaining to cosmology and metaphysics. He recorded his observations in such detail that they were still used for study over 600 years later.

Upon returning from India, al-Biruni began to write books based upon his observations and theories, the first of which, *Qanun-i Masud*, discussed al-Biruni's theories on solar, lunar and planetary motions, trigonometry, and related topics, and was dedicated to Sultan Masud. Later writings approached such subjects as geography and the ancient history of nations, including accurate values of latitude and longitude, the exact positioning of several known stars, the specific weight of various elements and precious stones, and the workings of natural springs using the hydrostatics principle of communicating vessels. An index alone of al-Biruni's written contributions to science could be compiled which would contain no less than 60 pages of text.

In addition to his writings, al-Biruni conducted research in his various fields of interest that contributed directly to the founding of modern sciences and the modern scientific method. His elaborate experiments related to astronomy were the first of their kind, allowing the scientist to describe the nature of nebulous stars and document the solar eclipse of 8 April, 1019 and the lunar eclipse of 17 September, 1019. Through his research, al-Biruni first documented that the speed of light was of an immense nature compared to the speed of sound, that there were seven ways to find the directions of north and south, and that mathematical formulas could be used to calculate the exact beginning of any given season. Additionally, al-Biruni initiated the first simplified method of stereographic projection, first studied the phenomenon of conjoined twins, and first noted that flowers have either three, four, five, six, or eight petals, but never seven or nine.

Both Persian and **Shiah** by birth, al-Biruni expressed somewhat agnostic tendencies throughout his studies. He held a deep sense of Persian identity and anti-Arabism. He died in 1048 at age 75 in Ghazna (Afghanistan). His legacy was such that scholars attribute the development of modern scientific study to al-Biruni.

AL-E AHMAD, JALAL (1923-1969). Jalal Al-e Ahmad was born into a traditional urban **Shiah** family in **Tehran**, where his father served as a religious elder and prayer leader in the local mosque. He worked in the **bazaar** by day and attended classes at the **Dar al-Fonun** at night. He taught for a short period, then became involved with the **Tudeh**, serving on the central committee in Tehran. He also wrote for and edited several publications, including *Mardom* and *Rahbar*. The last two decades of his life, Al-e Ahmad was married to the important writer, **Simin Daneshvar**. The two of them, together and repeatedly, exerted enormous influence in the intellectual life of 20th century Iran and the field of Persian **literature**.

The work of Al-e Ahmad includes short stories, translations, essays, and social and literary criticism. Al-e Ahmad maintained unequivocal positions on foreign affairs, modernization and westernization, the American presence in Iran, the importance of religion in society, and Iranian nationalism. A not so subtle critic of the **Pahlavi Dynasty**, his writings reflect the many critical cultural and social issues that he and other Iranians confronted during the reign of **Muhammad Reza Shah**. He used a blend of realism and irony, and a touch of Persian folklore as well, to convey the essence of anti-Pahlavi intelligentsia thought.

Much of his work was banned in Iran during the 1970s as the Pahlavi regime struggled to maintain authority in the face of growing opposition. Not until the 1980s, after the **Islamic Revolution**, were the majority of his critical writings available to the public; though, there had long been an active underground distribution. Al-e Ahmad is, perhaps, the most translated (into English) contemporary Iranian writer. Among his translated major works are *Lost in the Crowd, By the Pen,* and *The School Principal.* His most translated book is *Westruckness* (also translated under the titles *Occidentosis* and *Plagued by the West*), in which he denounces the disruption of foreign influence and portrays the West as a dehumanizing force in Iranian society.

The Persian title of the book, **Gharbzadegi**, has entered the lexicon of the **Persian language** as a term to describe the state of being enamored by all things Western. Al-e Ahmad favored a government with Islamic law as a foundation, though not so religiously extreme a government as the **Islamic Republic** which emerged following the Islamic Revolution in 1979.

Officially, Al-e Ahmad died of a heart atack in 1969 in Tehran. However, his friends report several threats on his life by **SAVAK** and attribute his untimely death at the age of 46 to unnatural causes. Al-e Ahmad left a valuable legacy in the body of literature and social commentary he produced in his short lifetime. He ranks as one of the major voices in modern Persian literature, equally renowned as a writer of fiction and nonfiction.

ALAM, ASADOLLAH (1911-1978). Asadollah Alam was a longtime associate and close confidant of **Muhammad Reza Shah**, and played an influential role in Iranian public life until his death in 1978. In 1957, he took office as the leader of the **Hezb-i Mardom (People's Party)**, which was established by royal decree to serve as "loyal opposition" to the majority **Hezb-i Melliyun (National Party)**. In July 1962, he replaced the controversial Dr. **Ali Amini** as prime minister and effectively ended major challenges to the Shah's authority with repressive measures. Alam was in favor of pursuing the execution of **Ayatollah Ruhollah Khomeini** in 1963, in the wake of Khomeini's role in fomenting the June demonstrations against the Shah's regime, advice the Shah later regretted ignoring. Alam himself accepted responsibility for the brutality involved in suppressing the 1963 riots. Though he resigned from the premiership in 1964, he remained in close contact with the Shah. Alam continually exercised considerable power in the Iranian political system thanks to his proximity as one of the three most trusted allies of the Shah, along with **Eqbal** and **Sharif-Emami**.

Alam also served in a variety of other governmental capacities. He was minister of interior, a governor-general, **Majlis** deputy, chancellor of **Pahlavi University**, and lastly served as the Shah's minister of court. He was one of the very few who dared to question or contradict the Shah on any matter, and was extremely influential and persuasive in determining governmental policy during the critical period of the 1970s. His death in April 1978 coincided with the beginning of a downward spiral for the **Pahlavi** regime, as opposition movements gained momentum against the ineffective suppressive tactics of the government.

ALAVI FOUNDATION. The Alavi Foundation is the current name for a philanthropic organization created by **Muhammad Reza Shah** in 1958. Originally named the Pahlavi Foundation, it was one among several shadowy royal foundations in Iran which were ostensibly formed to provide a variety of charitable services for the public. Among the major stated causes of the foundation were study abroad programs for students and assistance to orphans, the poor, the disabled, and other disadvantaged groups. From the beginning, the foundation utilized a mixture of both the Shah's personal wealth and state resources by investing them in a consortium of business ventures. The foundation also financed American-style universities inside Iran, offering grants to several major American universities for educational development. For instance, the University of Pennsylvania was contracted to revamp the existing **Shiraz** University along American educational lines in conjunction with its change of name to **Pahlavi University**. Later, Harvard University was contracted to establish a new business school in **Tehran**.

The foundation's financing came from sometimes controversial investment revenues it earned as a large business conglomerate, with control over factories, luxury hotel chains, book and newspaper publishing firms, and the like. While the foundation no doubt made significant contributions to the disadvantaged, critics claim it was little more than a racket for the **Pahlavi Dynasty**, adding to the royal purse and controlling far too much of the national economy through its vast economic networks.

After the **Islamic Revolution** of 1979, the Pahlavi Foundation assets were seized by the revolutionaries and reorganized under a new title, the Foundation for the Disinherited (*Bonyad-i Mostazafin*). **Ayatollah Ruhollah Khomeini** considered the workings of the former Pahlavi Foundation to have been corrupted by serving the Shah and his elites, and wanted the new foundation to truly reflect Islamic values of charity and alms.

The Foundation for the Disinherited was one among several newly formed "Reconstruction Units" that were tasked with building new government housing units and schools in Iran, and providing many other types of social welfare for the citizens. Like the Pahlavi Foundation, the new organization has maintained deep business ties that are highly lucrative and provide a steady flow of income. The foundation is directed by clerics, but because of its complexity and its secretive nature, there is no transparency. And, like its predecessor, it has suffered from persistent charges of corruption.

There was also an American branch of the Pahlavi Foundation, the crown jewel of which was a newly constructed office building located on Fifth Avenue in Manhattan, New York on a site purchased in 1973. After the Revolution, this building was seized by the new Iranian government. Renamed at first the Mostazafin Foundation of New York, it changed its name to the Alavi Foundation in 1992, whereas the parent counterpart in Iran retained the name Foundation for the Disinherited. The foundation operates as a nonprofit organization under American law and uses its American assets to provide funding for Iranians studying in the United States and to provide financial assistance to organizations that teach the Persian language and Islamic culture. A number of American universities have received grant assistance for such purposes, most recently Portland State University in 2005. Among the stated aims of the foundation is the promotion of understanding and harmony among people of different religions. Another basic aim is to advance the study of the humanities, arts, and pure and applied sciences. Critics of the foundation consider it a cover for more sinister political aims, not an unexpected claim given the highly charged negative climate occasioned by the nature of **U.S.-Iranian Relations** of the post-**Islamic Revolution** period. However, careful scrutiny, including close monitoring by the U.S. government, has failed to substantiate extra-legal activity.

ALBORZ COLLEGE. Alborz College is the outgrowth of the American High School for boys in **Tehran**. The College was founded in 1925 and received a permanent charter from the Board of Regents of the University of the State of New York in 1932. Originally called the American College, it was renamed Alborz College in 1935 as the movement toward nationalism in Iranian **education** gained momentum.

The development of the college was the lifework of **Samuel Jordan**, an American missionary and educator. After his arrival in Iran in 1898, Jordan served first as both a teacher and principal of the former high school, and then as president of the college until his retirement in 1941. The mission of Alborz College was to enable Iranian students to receive a comprehensive, "Western style" education without the socially corrupting influence of foreign societies. The graduates of Alborz College distinguished themselves with many firsts in the developments leading towards a modernized Iran during the reigns of the two **Pahlavi** kings. The college was closed in 1940 when all mission schools in Iran were nationalized. Though the nationalization policy was later rescinded, the school never returned to mission status. It reopened in 1943 under public control.

ALBORZ MOUNTAINS. The Alborz Mountains, narrow and steep, provide a stunning panorama along Iran's northern border. The range runs along northern Iran, separating the **Caspian Sea** coast from the interior plateau. They contain **Mount Damavand**, one of the world's highest mountains at over 5,486 meters. The Alborz range is penetrated by few passages, constituting a formidable barrier to the establishment of an efficient communication system between the northern coastal and interior regions.

The sheer size of the range contributes to the striking contrast in climate between the northern and southern faces. The moisture from the Caspian Sea, on the northern face, provides plentiful annual rainfall for the region and the mountain growth is lush. Temperate weather allows year-round cultivation of fruits, vegetables, and grains along the narrow littoral between the mountains and the sea.

In contrast, the southern face picks up the features of the arid **Iranian Plateau**, presenting a stark landscape in which sparse steppe-like vegetation grows and human habitation is minimal. Habitation in the interior Alborz region is limited to the broader valleys where farmers, though heavily dependent on irrigation systems, are able to produce limited cereal and fruit crops. Some grazing is available at higher elevations, but settlements are generally confined to the less steep areas. Outside the valley areas, the landscape ranges from barren desert to grassy scrub with an occasional stand of poplar trees.

Economically, the Alborz region contains major hydroelectric projects on the mountain rivers that have bolstered the area's declining populations. Many of the residents who had fled to large cities as modernization progressed are now willing to return to the area. The mountains also provide limited coal and iron ore mining. The more hospitable climate of the Caspian Sea side of the Alborz has proven favorable for the establishment of tourist-oriented facilities to boost the regional **economy**.

ALGERIAN ACCORDS. The Algerian Accords of January 1981 are a peculiar set of agreements made indirectly between Iran and the United States through the intermediary of Algeria. The accords brought an end to the crisis of the **American Hostages**

in Iran by addressing grievances the two nations could not effectively resolve without diplomatic ties. Following the **Islamic Revolution** of 1979, relations between the new **Islamic Republic** and the United States deteriorated, eventually resulting in the official breaking of diplomatic ties between the nations.

The revolution was steeped in anti-Americanism due to U.S. involvement in the overthrow of **Muhammad Mossadeq** in 1953 and support for the reinstalled **Muhammad Reza Shah** that persisted from that point. After the revolution, continuing *faux pas* on both sides further weakened relations between Iran and America. The final blow came with the taking of the American Embassy in Tehran and the ensuing hostage crisis. Although carried out by the purportedly independent **Students Following the Imam's Line**, the action gained **Ayatollah Ruhollah Khomeini**'s approval after the fact. This resulted in the end of formal relations between the nations.

Still, the nations needed to resolve the situation. Iran had become an international pariah in the wake of the hostage crisis and it was suffering from the freezing of assets and sanctions imposed by the United States. The U.S. needed to free its citizens, both for the hostages' sake and for the pride of the nation (and President Jimmy Carter) in general. After much wrangling behind the scenes on both sides, the Iranians announced in November 1980 that they would negotiate through Algeria so as to avoid direct contact with the "Great Satan," that is, the U.S. This turn of events, born of indirect talks in Germany in September of 1980, allowed the two nations to finally work at resolution of the crisis. Through the special "Nabavi Committee," the Iranian **Majlis** represented Iran in the negotiations, while U.S. Deputy Secretary of State Warren Christopher led a team representing America. Through Algerian diplomats who would relay the demands of each of the parties to one another, Iran and the U.S. came to a compromise.

For its part, Iran wanted to claim the assets of the Shah, estimated at several billion dollars, as well as to free up other Iranian financial assets frozen by the United States. Iran was also concerned about legal action against the Islamic Republic by American citizens, and looked for protection against this. Washington on the other hand had many legalistic qualms with the nature of the Iranian demands. For instance, Iran wanted the Shah's assets, but the U.S. felt it could do nothing unless the Islamic Republic went to court to claim the **Pahlavi** wealth. The U.S. was also adamantly opposed to preventing citizens from exercising their right to sue the Islamic Republic for damages.

President Carter was defeated by Ronald Reagan in the November election and Christopher could provide no guarantees as to how the Reagan administration would deal with the situation. Though early on the Iranians made enormously extravagant claims, at one point as high as $24 billion, the need to finish before the Carter administration lapsed brought Iranian claims downward.

Eventually, Iran agreed to free the hostages when just under $8 billion would be put in escrow with the Bank of England. However, to pay previous outstanding loans to the Shah's government, only $2.2 billion would transfer to Iran upon release of the hostages, with the rest covering the loans and any litigation against Iran. The United States also agreed to facilitate the Islamic Republic in litigation to claim the Shah's wealth, as well as to remain clear of Iran's internal affairs. Even with the accords in place, problems at the various banks prevented immediate transfer of the money and delayed the hostage release. As well, the Iranians had their own sense of timing. The hostage release came only shortly after Ronald Reagan's inauguration: a purposeful last jab at the Carter administration from the Islamic Republic.

AMERICAN BOARD OF COMMISSIONS FOR FOREIGN MISSIONS (ABCFM). The American Board of Commissions for Foreign Missions (ABCFM) was an interdenominational Protestant board established in 1819 to send missionaries to the countries of the Mediterranean. In 1831, the ABCFM decided to extend its mission to Persia and dispatched the first American missionary to Iran to found the Persia Mission. **Justin Perkins** arrived in **Tabriz** in 1834, and subsequently moved to **Urmieh** to work among the Nestorian Christians there. In 1835, Perkins was joined by a medical doctor, **Asahel Grant**. The ABCFM continued to operate until 1870, when it split up and left the American Protestant mission field in Iran to the Presbyterians. The Presbyterians extended their work among the **Armenians** and Muslims, and in May 1870, changed the name of their organization to the **Iran Mission**.

AMERICAN HOSTAGES IN IRAN. On 4 November, 1979, over 300 radical Iranian students, supporters of the new revolutionary government and calling themselves **Students Following the Imam's Line**, seized control of the American Embassy in **Tehran**. The event was triggered by the admission of the deposed **Muhammad Reza Shah** to the United States for medical treatment. Iranian extremists viewed the American action as part of a plot to weaken and ultimately overturn the newly formed **Islamic Republic**. Demands from the students for the return of the Shah and $24 billion of Iranian funds deposited in U.S. banks were ignored by the American government, and counter demands from the United States for the immediate release of the 52 hostages were unavailing. The students, with the tacit approval of **Ayatollah Ruhollah Khomeini** and the overwhelming support of the Iranian people, were motivated to disregard overtures and proceeded with the captivity which would last for 444 days.

As worldwide attention focused on the events unfolding in Tehran, President Jimmy Carter and the U.S. government began employing diplomatic tactics to secure the release of the Americans. When this approach failed, economic pressures were applied. Iranian assets in U.S. banks were frozen and embargoes on Iranian products were enforced. Military threats followed, and an ill-fated rescue attempt in April 1980 caused the deaths of eight American servicemen. The students justified the continuation of the hostage situation by revealing the contents of sensitive documents recovered from the embassy files. These were interpreted as evidence of a movement involving the United States, the Soviet Union, and several leaders in the revolutionary government of Iran to undermine and overturn the **Islamic Revolution** of 1979. Reminders of the involvement of the United States in the overthrow of **Mossadeq** and the return of the Shah in 1953 stiffened their resolve to prevent such a reoccurrence by retaining the hostages as security.

Massive public support in Iran for the embassy takeover contrasted sharply with the pressure applied by the American public for U.S. government action to secure the return of the hostages. President Carter's economic and military initiatives had failed and relations between the two countries were almost nonexistent. Senator Edmund Muskie was sent quietly to propose a settlement which would resolve the situation. The negotiations produced the **Algerian Accords** of January 1981, a complex document brokered by Algeria, which involved political and economic concessions by the United States. The hostages were to be released on 20 January, 1981. As a final gesture of defiance aimed at the Carter administration, the announcement of the release was exquisitely timed to coincide with the inauguration celebrations for Ronald Reagan.

Though the American people celebrated the return of the hostages, the episode and its conclusion were considered a serious defeat for American foreign policy. Deeply rooted negative attitudes toward Iran were formed and would strongly affect future efforts for rapprochement between the two countries. *See also* HOSTAGE RESCUE MISSION.

AMINI, ALI (1904-1992). Amini was a member of the Iranian aristocracy with a personal pedigree extending back to **Qajar** roots. His mother was the daughter of **Mozaffar al-Din Shah**. He was educated in France as an economist and began his political career as an elected Democrat party member of the 15 Majlis in 1947. A relative of **Muhammad Mossadeq**, he held several positions during that prime minister's reformist administration, including finance minister. In 1954, Amini was the chief Iranian negotiator with the foreign **oil** companies during the restructuring process which followed the Mossadeq period and resulted in a significant role for the **National Iranian Oil Company**. As Iran's ambassador to the United States in the late 1950s, he developed solid, trusted relationships within the U.S. State Department.Growing public dissatisfaction with the **Pahlavi** regime was apparent as the 1960s began. Faced with internal pressure from opposition groups and external pressure from the administration of John F. Kennedy in Washington, **Muhammad Reza Shah** replaced Prime Minister **Ja'far Sharif-Emami** with Amini. Though distrusted by the Shah, who feared political and economic reform, Amini was preferred over the **National Front** contender.

As prime minister, Amini immediately dissolved the 20th Majlis and replaced the unpopular head of **SAVAK**. He appointed opposition members to head ministries, and carried out land reform and International Monetary Fund directives.

Amini's administration was to last for only 14 months due to the public's dislike of his stringent measures. He faced opposition from the National Front, and the **Tudeh** perceived him as an agent of the United States. The Shah, on the other hand, considered Amini too independent of the personal control the monarch wished to exercise. He was succeeded by **Asadollah Alam** in July 1962.

Amini was politically quiescent for the next decade and a half. He reemerged in the period of revolutionary activity in the latter part of 1978. He offered to act as a go-between for the palace and the opposition, even offering to negotiate directly with **Ayatollah Ruhollah Khomeini** on behalf of the Shah. However, despite his record of independent thought and action, Amini was so discredited from his past association with the Pahlavi regime that Khomeini refused to meet with him. *See also* WHITE REVOLUTION.

AMUZEGAR, JAMSHID (1923-). Jamshid Amuzegar graduated from **Tehran University** in 1943 and for seven years attended graduate school in the United States. He returned to Iran and accepted a position with the U.S. Agency for International Development. Over the years, he also served as Minister of Finance and headed Iran's delegation to the Organization of Petroleum Exporting Countries (OPEC). Considered a supreme technocrat, he was chosen to lead the liberal Progressive wing of the **Rastakhiz Party**.

In August 1977, in the midst of an economic crisis and growing political unrest, **Muhammad Reza Shah** appointed

Amuzegar to replace **Amir Abbas Hoveida** as prime minister. Amuzegar proved to be politically clumsy. He was criticized for fence-sitting on sensitive political issues and also for his close ties with the United States. Those ties, and his alienation from the Iranian masses, damaged his credibility. The Shah dismissed him after little more than a year in office as the political crisis that led to the **Islamic Revolution** deepened.

ANGLO-IRANIAN OIL COMPANY (AIOC). In 1901, William Knox D'Arcy, a wealthy Englishman, got permission from **Mozzafar al-Din Shah** of Persia to explore the country's **oil** resources. In 1908, oil was discovered at Masjed-i Suleiman in **Khuzistan** in southwestern Iran, and soon after the Anglo-Persian Oil Company (APOC) was formed in order to develop this new source of oil. Pipelines were built from the mountainous source to a sea outlet on the **Shatt al-Arab** at **Abadan** where the largest refinery in the world at the time was also built.

By the 1920s, APOC had secured its position as one of the world's largest oil companies. The high demand for oil in World War I enabled APOC to expand into an integrated oil business. In 1925, the **Qajar Dynasty** gave way to the **Pahlavi Dynasty** of **Reza Shah**. In accord with his assertion of Iranian national interests and attempts to economically develop the nation, Reza Shah pressured the British to change the terms of the concession. Changes were made in 1933 though the terms were still highly favorable to the British which set the stage for a later confrontation of interests. In 1935, Reza Shah changed the name of the country from Persia to Iran. Subsequently, the name of the oil company became the Anglo-Iranian Oil Company.

In the post-World War II period, the nature of oil company concessions in the Middle East was undergoing drastic shifts which affected Anglo-Iranian Oil Company operations in Iran. It also led to one of the most important events in modern Iranian history, the nationalization of oil in 1951 by the government of **Muhammad Mossadeq.** This act led to an embargo on Iranian oil and the eventual collapse of the **National Front** coalition led by Mossadeq, and the direct involvement of the United States in Iranian affairs.

The business of the Anglo-Iranian oil company was brought to a halt by the act of nationalization by Mossadeq. Only after the return of **Muhammad Reza Shah** to the throne was a new agreement signed in 1954 which substantially altered the nearly exclusive British position regarding oil operations in Iran in the first half of the 20th century. Amongst the changes was the creation of the **National Iranian Oil Company (NIOC)**, a new government-controlled entity which gave Iran more of a voice in the exploitation of its vital natural resource.

ANGLO-RUSSIAN CONVENTION OF 1907. The Convention of 1907, also termed the Anglo-Russian Agreement, was an accord between Great Britain and Russia. The two powers sought to resolve the conflict which resulted from their escalating political battle for economic control of Iran, along with Afghanistan and Tibet. Each side was driven by its unique interests in Iran.

In 1901, the British had been granted a 60-year petroleum concession in Persia's southern territory. In particular, the southeastern region was considered by the British a strategic location for control and regulation of **trade** in the Persian Gulf. The area was also considered important as a barrier between Britain's Indian Empire and the expansion-minded Russian Empire.

The Russians were interested in economic control of the more populated northern section of Iran. A customs agreement in 1901 lowered tariff rates on commerce between the two countries. Russia made generous loans to the ruling monarch, **Mozaffar al-Din Shah**, to support his opulent international lifestyle, and used his indebtedness to secure favorable political and economic concessions from the Iranian government. Russia was permitted to move troops and advisors into **Khorasan** and **Azerbaijan** Provinces. Implement ation of new policies, including loans from other foreign nations, required Russian approval. By the 20th century, as a result of the relentless battle between Russia and Britain, Iran had become virtually powerless.

In the first decade of the 20th century, the growing strength and imperialistic tendencies of Germany became increasingly apparent to Russia and Britain. War clouds were forming over Europe, and Russia experienced military defeat at the hands of the Japanese in 1907. The Convention of 1907 was designed to protect the interests of the two powers, and limit their sustained rivalry in Iran in light of a new common enemy.

Zones of Influence Established by Anglo-Russian Convention of 1907

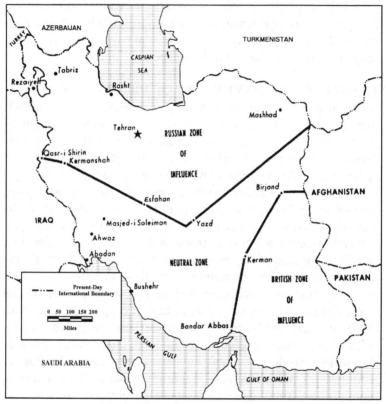

Figure 2

The country was divided into spheres of influence, with Russia retaining control in the north and Britain holding sway in the southeast. A neutral zone in the central "dead heart" region ostensibly remained under exclusive Iranian control. This agreement was intended to protect Russian and British interests while maintaining the "integrity" and "independence" of Iran, although Iran was never consulted about the details of the arrangement.

The Anglo-Russian Convention caused great anguish among the democratic liberals of the Iranian Constitutional Movement who had looked to Great Britain for inspiration in their nationalistic struggle. Following the Russian Revolution in 1917, the Anglo-Russian Convention was renounced by the Bolshevik government, which effectively ended its provisions. However, to the present day, Iranians have not forgotten the blatant carving up of their country by the imperial powers of Russia and Britain. *See also* QAJAR DYNASTY.

ANJOMANHA-YI ISLAMI (ISLAMIC ASSOCIATIONS). The Anjomanha-yi Islami, or Islamic Associations, were formed and established throughout Iran in the 1940s by pious lower middle-class Muslims, who were mainly members of the older guilds or fraternal groups. Their goal was to promote the compatibility of **Islam** with changes being made during the attempts of **Muhammad Reza Shah** at modernization. In the 1940s, they focused on educated professional men in order to promote Islamic values as being consistent with contemporary standards. Eventually, these organizations expanded their social base and became effective instruments of socio-religious integration for rural migrants who were fueling an urban population boom in the 1960s and 1970s. They also became increasingly politicized as the secular agenda of the Shah became ever more apparent. However, the associations were not highly visible until the beginning of Islamic revolutionary activity leading up to the collapse of the **Pahlavi Dynasty**.

The organizational networks of these informal associations were crucial to the success of the Islamic Revolutionary Movement. The distribution of information, in particular the taped messages of **Ayatollah Ruhollah Khomeini** during 1978, and the planning and oversight of the massive demonstrations which brought down the Shah, were impressive accomplishments of these organizations. Following the **Islamic Revolution** of 1979, they remained active politically, recruiting new members from factories, universities, and business offices, to ensure and sustain conformity with the new Islamic ideology and to combat the influence of possible subversives or resistance groups.

ARABS. Arab **tribes** arrived in Iran in the early centuries of **Islam** from the Arabian Peninsula, dispersing in the area to the east of the **Shatt al-Arab**. Though the Arab territory is to the west of the **Bakhtiari** tribal land, some groups cooperate and intermingle with the Bakhtiari. The Arab tribes have been successful in keeping their Arabic language and customs, and are mostly **Shiah**.

The largest group of Arab tribes is Bani-Kaab, whose members live on Minoo Island, around **Khorramshahr** and along the **Karun River**. Other sub-tribes include Bani-Lam, Bani-Saleh, Bani-Tamim, and Al-Khamiss. While the groups originally settled in the **Khuzistan** region, many were forced to other regions of Iran during the Iraqi invasion in 1980 and the subsequent **Iran-Iraq War**. The last census of Arab tribes took place before the **Islamic Revolution** and counted 300,000 Arab tribespeople living in Iran.

ARASCID DYNASTY *See* PARTHIAN PERIOD.

ARMENIANS IN IRAN. Historically located to the northwest of Iran and east of Turkey, Armenia has been the focus of many military campaigns due to its position as a passageway between Europe and Asia. Rarely masters of their own identity, Armenians have often been reduced to refugees. At such times they often fled into the Iranian-occupied area of **Azerbaijan**, settling in cities to the west of the **Caspian Sea** such as **Tabriz**.

Under **Safavid** rule, Armenia and most of Transcaucasia would be united under Iranian control, posing a major threat to the Ottomans. The harsh climate and insufficient means of communications to Constantinople from Armenia allowed it to remain in Safavid hands until a peace agreement was signed in 1555 splitting Armenia into a western Ottoman portion and an eastern Iranian portion. During the struggle for territory, each side deported native Armenians into territories under their own control, replacing them with Kurdish populations and disrupting the population balance of Armenia.

In 1590, **Shah Abbas the Great** saw the deficiency of the Iranian military and signed a second treaty with the Ottomans relinquishing eastern Armenia and a portion of Iranian Azerbaijan. He broke the treaty 13 years later, appearing as a savior to the Ottoman-oppressed Armenians. The military conquests of 1603 brought several Ottoman lands into Abbas' rule including the area of Julfa, an Armenian town with a successful merchant and trading class. Abbas then deported 25,000 to 30,000 Armenians to Iran and particularly to **Isfahan**, his new capital, in an attempt to destroy the economic viability of the Armenian region, and to enhance the **economy** of the capital.

The wealthier Armenians of Julfa were settled on the banks of the Zayandeh-Rud, opposite of Isfahan where they were permitted to build a new settlement called New Julfa. The district was given many rights not afforded to other minorities of the time, including an elected mayor, public religious processions, and their own churches and courts. Additionally, the population of New Julfa, which was entirely Armenian, was not required to comply with restrictions on clothing or wine that applied to their Muslim neighbors in Isfahan. Soon the population grew to 50,000 and New Julfa was granted trading privileges, which were focused on the silk **trade**. Trade between Iran and Europe began to center in New Julfa and the town became increasingly wealthy. Armenians were also instrumental in expanding trade with Russia and India while holding a monopoly on silk.

The Armenians of New Julfa formed trading companies that competed with the East India and Muscovy companies and established Western connections that helped secure diplomatic ties for the Shah. Also, ties to the West allowed one prominent Armenian priest to travel to Italy where he learned the art of printing and returned with Iran's first printing press in 1638. The first printed book in Iran was an Armenian translation of the Book of Psalms. This trend continued from the 17th century onward, allowing the Armenians to become one of the key transmitters of western technology to Iran.

As the 20th century approached, 100,000 Armenians lived in Iran. The political turmoil at the turn of the century in Turkey and Russia affected the Armenian community and brought even more refugees into Iran. This is said to have influenced the movement which led to the **Constitutional Revolution of 1906**.

The **Pahlavi Dynasty** undertook modernization that greatly benefited the Armenian population and allowed advancement in many sectors including arts and sciences, the **oil** and caviar industries, and many specialized professions. The population continued to increase by taking in refugees, though increasingly from Russia through World War II. The population reached over 250,000 by the 1970s.

The Armenian community was heavily impacted by the **Islamic Revolution** in Iran. The country's economic isolation, combined with **Ayatollah Ruhollah Khomeini**'s restrictions, forced the emigration of nearly 100,000 Armenians. Currently, the government of the **Islamic Republic of Iran** accommodates the Christian Armenian population allowing Armenian schools and social activities, as well as some churches. Under the **Constitution of the Islamic Republic,** Armenians have two parliamentary deputies in the **Majlis,** one from the northern part of the country and one representing Armenians in southern Iran, still concentrated in New Julfa.

ARYAN. The word Aryan is a term used to describe a race of fair-complexioned people who are thought to have originated in Central Asia. Scattered throughout the broad plains of South Persia, north of the Himalayan and Hindu Kush Mountains, Aryans were also known in later history by the tribal and linguistic designation of Indo-European. Some 7,000 years ago these people began migration to the north, west, and south for reasons that have been variously speculated upon. Eventually, Indo-Europeans settled and peopled lands far from their origins including Northern Europe, the **Iranian Plateau**, and India. The common origin of these widely spread peoples is deduced mainly from linguistic evidence.

The term Iran itself derives from the word Aryan, which literally means "noble people." The land of Iran was peopled by non-Aryans prior to the third millennium B.C., but by the end of the millennium came to be known as "the land of the Aryans," the indigenous peoples having been displaced or absorbed by migrating Indo-Europeans. Thus, in recorded history, the peoples inhabiting the geographical area that came to be termed the Iranian Plateau knew their land as Iran, though a unified political dynasty did not come into existence until the middle of the first millennium B.C. with the establishment of the **Achaemenid Dynasty** by **Cyrus** in 550 B.C. It was during this dynasty that some parts of the original homeland came under the political sway of one of the first great world empires, including the area known as Bactria and Sogdiana.

Through a linguistic process dating back to contact with the Greeks during the Achaemenid period, the name Persia came into common usage in European languages to designate the country that Iranians had always referred to as Iran. It was even adopted by Iranians, in a reverse influence, as the name of their nation-state in the modern period. The term Iran, derived from Aryan, always remained, however, as perhaps the most dominant territorial designation in the consciousness of the people who inhabited the land.

Physically and linguistically, the Iranian people have much in common with their ancestral cousins in Europe and elsewhere. Despite considerable intermixture with other races, particularly Semitic and Turkic peoples, and despite historical and cultural interconnections and influences with other peoples in the region of the Middle East, Iranians have retained a distinct identity with their Aryan past. This connection was magnified in the 20th century in the service of mobilizing war support for Iranian nationalism and in advancing the political notion of the nation-state of Iran.

On 12 March, 1934, during the reign of **Reza Shah**, the name Persia was officially changed to Iran. The Aryan past was glorified and found expression in many politically encouraged outlets in fields such as **literature** and architecture. An attempt was even made to purify the national language, Farsi, with the creation of an Iranian Academy in 1935 charged with purging Turkish and Arabic words and substituting them with old and sometimes newly contrived Persian words. Such forced purification failed to permeate Iranian society and was less intense after the abdication of Reza Shah. His son, **Muhammad Reza Shah**, was not as insistent. Nonetheless, a glorification of an Aryan past and identity continued to be a persistent policy of the **Pahlavi** monarchy until its overthrow by the **Islamic Revolution** of 1979. An excellent example of such a policy was the trappings of the ceremonies surrounding the coronation of Muhammad Reza Shah. *See also* PERSIAN LANGUAGE.

ASGHARZADEH, IBRAHIM (1955-). Ibrahim Asgharzadeh was 24 years old and studying engineering in **Tehran** when he planned the 1979 American Embassy siege which resulted in the capture and holding of 52 American diplomats. These **American Hostages in Iran** were held for 444 days by the group known as **Students Following the Imam's Line.** Asgharzadeh admits to having planned the takeover, which he estimated would last three to seven days, in response to American support of **Muhammad Reza Shah.** It was Asgharzadeh's voice that the world heard reading out the first shocking communiqué regarding the hostage situation at the embassy.

After the establishment of the revolutionary government of **Ayatollah Ruhollah Khomeini,** Asgharzadeh served in the **Majlis,** only to be removed from his parliamentary post after Khomeini's death in 1989, a pattern visible in the careers of some other Iranian student hostage-takers. Like other former revolutionaries, Asgharzadeh found himself in opposition to the conservative ruling clergy in the **Islamic Republic** and faced prison for his disagreement.

Later, Asgharzadeh served as a member of the Tehran Municipal Council in the government of moderate President **Khatami,** a victory at the time for the pro-reform pragmatists in whose camp he had firmly settled. Asgharzadeh told a *Time* magazine reporter in 1999 that he is a hostage-taker turned democrat, saying "There is no need to change the world anymore." *See also* ABDI, ABBAS; EBTEKAR, MASSOUMEH.

ASSEMBLY OF EXPERTS. The Assembly of Experts was convened by the **Revolutionary Council** in lieu of the large constituent body agreed upon by various factions during the Iranian Revolution. Its purpose was to draft a constitution for the new **Islamic Republic of Iran.** An early draft of a constitution had been promulgated after the plebiscite which declared Iran an Islamic Republic, but it was considered too secular by the Islamists and too religious in orientation by secular modernists. Most of the latter called for an inclusive constitutional assembly. The Assembly of Experts was the compromise that **Ayatollah Ruhollah Khomeini** promoted to offset pressure for a secular constitution. It was overwhelmingly dominated by Islamic clergy and committed Muslims. Under the guidance of **Ayatollah Muhammad Hussein Beheshti**, the original Assembly consisted of 73 members, 66 of whom were high-ranking members of the ulama, or members of the **Islamic Republican Party**. Its Islamic orientation was apparent in its Persian name—*Majles-i Khobregan*—which implies religious expertise, and in the selection of 73 members, the number of persons involved in the events in Karbala, where **Imam Hussein** and his followers were massacred.

The formation of the Assembly was vehemently protested by **Mehdi Bazargan** and others in the **Provisional Government**, as well as by intellectuals and middle-class merchants in the private sector. They objected on the grounds that it violated popular sovereignty and made the Islamic clergy a virtual ruling class in Iran.

The Assembly survived these attacks and proceeded to produce an amended constitution which cemented **Islam** as the overriding authority in governmental affairs. The extraordinarily controversial concept of *Velayat-i Faqih* was included in the final document. The **Majlis**, or the legal constituent body, was given the power to confirm one person, or alternatively a council of three to five members, to replace Ayatollah Khomeini as *Faqih*. This individual or council would have absolute authority over all three branches of government.

Strong opposition to the proposed constitution was ineffective against the appeals from the charismatic Khomeini and his widespread network of committed supporters. The Assembly of Experts met first in August, 1979 and finished its work in short order. The **Constitution of the Islamic Republic** was submitted to the voters in December 1979, and was accepted by an overwhelming majority.

The concept of the Assembly of Experts continued to live on in the form of a constitutional provision whereby the succession to the position of *Faqih* would be determined by a new elected Assembly of Experts. This provision was activated in 1982 and deliberations on who was to succeed Khomeini began in 1983. These deliberations continued sporadically until 1985 when **Ayatollah Hussein Ali Montezari** was selected as the successor. However, Montezari's outspoken criticism of Khomeini and *Velayat-i Faqih* led to his resignation as successor at the urging of Khomeini in March 1989. One day after Khomeini's death on 3 June, 1989, the Assembly of Experts elected **Ayatollah Ali Khamene'i** as *Faqih*. In a possible effort to save face, the Assembly of Experts contended that it, as a body, had not elected Montezari in 1985, but that its vote was simply a reflection of the will of the people.

ATTAR, FARID AL-DIN (1142-1221). Known as one of the greatest Sufi poets, Attar was born in the northeastern Iranian city of Nishapur. Attar's father was a wealthy pharmacy-owner, allowing the young poet to attain higher **education** in medicine, theosophy, and Arabic from a school at the shrine of Imam Reza at **Mashhad**. Attar worked in his father's pharmacy preparing drugs and tending to the ill and became the owner, upon his father's death.

After an unsettling visit in the pharmacy of a wandering fakir who challenged Attar's ability and freedom to see the world, weighed down as he was by his prosperous shop, Attar closed the pharmacy and set out to travel. Over several years, the poet visited and explored Damascus, Mecca, Kufa, Turkistan, and India where he met and studied with **Sufi** sheiks and learned the *tariqah*, exercises devised by the Sufis to help the worshipers come closer to God and feel contented and elated while carrying out the faith.

Feeling fulfilled by his travels, Attar returned to his pharmacy and began writing what would become some of the greatest contributions to Sufi thought. His first writing was entitled *Tadkhirat al-Auliya* (Memorial of the Saints) in which Attar compiled the sayings and messages of those Sufi saints who had not written their own texts. The poet went on to write about Sufi thought in *Asrar Nameh* (Book of Secrets) and *Elahi Nameh* (Divine Book). Attar's most impressive, and best known, work is called *Manteq al-Tayr* (Conference of the Birds) in which the birds of the world travel to meet their king through seven valleys, undergoing a series of trials which require them to free themselves of possessions and change their state of mind.

Scholars believe that the poet lived for one hundred years producing from 114 to nearly 200 books of **poetry** as well as countless other works. According to legend, Attar died in 1221, beheaded by invading Mongols.

AVICENNA. *See* ABU ALI IBN SINA.

AYATOLLAH. With the onset of **Islam**, men of religious learning assumed the role of spiritual leadership within the community. These men were not clergy in the sense of Western religions. There was no church hierarchy and men of religious learning had not necessarily completed a formal course of religious study. They were shopkeepers, merchants, landlords, craftsmen, and jurists. A man of religious learning earned the title "mullah" from the community he served, and because Islam had no formal clerical hierarchy, mullahs are "promoted" only by consensus of the community, based on their piety, learning, and the regard of the people. Among the **Shiah**, such promotions were more pronounced than among the Sunni. The continuing existence in Shi'ism of allowing the most learned to exercise independent judgement in interpreting the sources of law was a key contributing factor. The term *mujtahid*, or jurisconsult, refers to a religious scholar who has attained this high status. As a mullah's reputation grew, he could be given the title jurisconsult only by another jurisconsult, the first of whom had received their titles from the infallible Imams themselves.

Ultimately, an informal ranking of Shiah religious scholars developed. Thus, certain terms came into usage among the Shiah to reflect the relative "rank" of men of religious learning, such as Hojjat al-Islam and Ayatollah. The former was a lesser title than the more elevated term Ayatollah.

Nineteenth century Iran was, in general, a land of lofty rhetoric. This inflation struck religious titles. Ayatollah, meaning "miraculous sign of God," was an exalted title conferred on a few of the very greatest jurisconsults. At the turn of the century, only a handful of ayatollahs existed, but the title was less discriminately granted to many during the following period. A system of hereditary titles also developed and the number of ayatollahs increased proportionately.

Nonetheless, only the more learned and prestigious religious scholars attained the title and any who carried it also commanded a significant following. The title, thus, while not formalized in an office, carried with it considerable power. The person holding it was both an articulator and molder of public opinion. The most significant example of the latent political power which an ayatollah could activate was the role of **Ayatollah Ruhollah Khomeini** in guiding the **Islamic Revolution** of 1979.

AZERBAIJAN. Historically, the geographical entity known as Azerbaijan covered a much larger area than the present-day Iranian provinces of the same name, extending to the north and to the west across the boundaries of several contemporary nation-states. For most of the history of modern Iran there has been a single Azerbaijan Province situated along the **Zagros Mountain** range in the plateau region of northwestern Iran. Only in recent times has the current political subdivision into East and West Azerbaijan Provinces occurred with their respective administrative centers in **Tabriz** and **Urmieh**. For all practical purposes the two can be discussed as a single entity.

Azerbaijan is a major crossroad for **trade** and communication, particularly with the states of Turkey and Russia. Active trade and **industry**, combined with a relatively prosperous **agricultural** market, have resulted in a dense population of about six million people. Azerbaijan's farming **economy** can be attributed to the availability of water from year-round precipitation as farmers need not rely exclusively on irrigation systems to support their crops of wheat, barley, tobacco, and cotton. For this reason, Azerbaijan is sometimes referred to as the "breadbasket" of Iran. Industry in Azerbaijan consists of carpetmaking, tanning, textile manufacturing, and copper mining.

The major city of Azerbaijan is Tabriz, which is connected by road and by rail with the national capital, **Tehran**. Tabriz today has a population approaching one and a quarter million and is the fourth-largest city in the country. A system of hard and dirt surfaced roads connects other cities within Azerbaijan and facilitates trade between pastoralists from the upland regions and the farmers of the lowland. The majority of Azerbaijan inhabitants are Azeri-speaking Turks, with a scattering of **Kurdish** and **Armenian** settlements, and most are **Shiah** Muslims. *See also* AZERBAIJAN CRISIS.

AZERBAIJAN CRISIS. The **Azerbaijan** Crisis, as it has become known, was the result of European power politics projected in the Middle East during World War II, and was the catalyst for the opening shots of the subsequent Cold War between the United States and the Soviet Union. As World War II raged in Europe during 1941, the Soviet Union and Great Britain invaded Iran and used it as a supply route to deliver desperately needed war materiel to help save the Soviet Union from Nazi annihilation, while at the same time allowing Great Britain to maintain control of its Iranian **oil** supplies. The Tripartite Treaty of 1942 made guarantees to Iran that the occupiers would withdraw their forces no later than six months after the end of the war, and that Iran would receive economic aid as a consequence of the occupation. As the U.S. entered the war, it also sent troops to Iran to facilitate the massive resupply of the Soviet Union. At the **Tehran Conference**, the Tripartite Treaty pledges were reaffirmed by the Allies in the Tehran Declaration of December 1943.

As World War II ended and the 2 March, 1946 deadline for troop withdrawal from Iran passed, the Soviet Union maintained its military presence, much to the shock of Iran and the United States. To make matters worse, the Soviets had been fomenting a separatist movement in Iran's Azerbaijan province, utilizing the **Tudeh** Party as its political tool, and preventing the troops of **Muhammad Reza Shah** from entering the area to put down the rebellion.

Fearing Soviet expansion, the U.S. was quick to bring the matter before the United Nations, which ordered the Soviets and Iranians to negotiate a settlement over the matter. As a result, the Iranian government of Qavvam Al-Saltaneh skillfully (though some Iranians viewed the matter as a treacherous betrayal of Iranian interests) offered the Soviets an oil concession in return for the Soviet troop withdrawal. Once the Soviet troops left in May 1946, the Iranian **Majlis** voted against the concessions and implementation never occurred. With its new political momentum and strong American approval, Iran sent troops to the Azerbaijan province to reestablish control. Upon arrival, the Tudeh Party seemed to evaporate, and there was an outpouring of pro-American sentiment from the Azerbaijan locals.

Though the oil concession offered by Iran no doubt encouraged Joseph Stalin to pull his forces out of Iran, the threat of American intervention was the true catalyst of Soviet submission during the crisis, as Washington had a nuclear monopoly and the proven will to use it. U.S. policy-makers had clearly begun to view the Soviet Union as the new strategic enemy. This U.S.-Soviet standoff is significant not only as a Cold War marker, but because Iranians began to view the U.S. as its benign liberator, a view which only a few years later would be reversed, in the events which surrounded the rise and fall of Prime Minister **Muhammad Mossadeq**. See also ROOSEVELT, KERMIT; U.S.-IRANIAN RELATIONS AFTER THE ISLAMIC REVOLUTION.

-B-

BABI MOVEMENT. In Twelver Shi'ism, the Bab is the precursor to the **Hidden Imam**. This person is to serve as the "gateway" between the worlds of flesh and spirit and communicate with the divine. The true Bab will appear on earth at the end of time to prepare for the return of the Mahdi (Hidden Imam) on Judgement Day.

In 1848, a man named Mirza Ali Muhammad Shirazi proclaimed himself the Bab. He called for social and economic reform, focusing on governmental corruption. His message was entirely Iranian in content and held great appeal among those discontented with the Islamic clergy and social conditions in general. He attracted a large following which cut across all social classes. In his book, *Bayan*, Shirazi went so far as to imply that he was the Hidden Imam who had returned to purify and restore **Islam** to its original state. Babism encouraged a call to arms to effect revolutionary change in society. The Babis became the target of rigorous persecution, first by the ulama and later, after a series of prolonged Babi-inspired social and political uprisings throughout the country, by the government. In 1850, the Bab was executed by firing squad in **Tabriz**, but faithful followers continued the movement. After the attempted assassination of **Naser al-Din Shah** in 1852 by members of the Babi Movement, over 40,000 adherents were arrested, many were massacred, and Babism was effectively halted. It continued to exist, but never again flourished. However, an offshoot transformed itself into a universalistic religion and is known today as **Bahaism**.

BAHAISM. The Bahai Movement arose from the ashes of Babism with a radically transformed message. Following the collapse of the **Babi Movement**, Mirza Hussein Ali Nuri declared himself to be the messiah of a religious divine spirit, or the "Baha'ullah" (the Splendor of God), and acquired a following called the Bahais. Bahaism promoted spiritual unity, pacifism, and social evolution rather than the militant revolutionary reform of the Babis. The world vision of the Bahais was liberal, cosmopolitan, and humanitarian, combining elements of Judaism, Christianity, and **Islam**. Thus, unlike the Babi Movement from which Bahaism sprang, the latter was more universalistic and less tied to an Islamic context. Like the Babis before them, the Bahais were considered apostates from Islam by the **Shiah** ulama who accused them of "modernism" and perceived them as a direct threat to their power.

In the 1950s, Shiah religious scholars sponsored unsuccessful legislation to have Bahaism suppressed. However, following the **Islamic Revolution** of 1979, the Bahais were subject to persecution by the reigning religious government. Bahaism was declared illegal, adherents were arrested, and their property was confiscated for "political reasons." Some Bahai leaders were executed. There are still a considerable number of Bahai adherents in Iran today, though totally quiescent. Accurate numbers are impossible to calculate and the source of wild speculation. Bahaism is still practiced openly outside Iran today. Its universal message and lack of formal ritual or sacraments hold wide appeal for adherents, as does its pacifist orientation toward social change. These factors have contributed to significant worldwide growth.

BAHONAR, MUHAMMAD JAVAD (1933-1981). Bahonar was born in **Kerman** to an upper-class merchant family. He studied in **Qum**, a student of **Ayatollah Ruhollah Khomeini**, and later taught theology at **Tehran University**. An associate of **Ayatollah Morteza Mottahari**, one of the leading intellects among Islamic revolutionaries, Bahonar became a member of the speaker's bureau associated with the **Husseiniyeh-i Ershad**, a religious lecture hall in Tehran. An outspoken critic of the **Pahlavi** regime, he was jailed in 1964 and again in 1975 during crackdowns of prominent dissident clerics.

Bahonar was an influential member of Khomeini's Iranian support network during the long period of his mentor's exile. Following the **Islamic Revolution** in 1979, he was appointed to serve on the **Revolutionary Council** and was also a founding member of the **Islamic Republican Party (IRP)**. He held various positions in the newly formed **Islamic Republic** including minister of **education**, member of the **Assembly of Experts** which drafted the **Constitution of the Islamic Republic**, and secretary-general of the IRP.

In June 1981 he was elected prime minister, but his term of service was very brief, as he and President **Muhammad Ali Raja'i** were killed in the bombing of the Prime Ministry in August 1981.

BAKHTARAN. *See* KERMAN.

BAKHTIAR, SHAPUR (1914-1991). Shapur Bakhtiar received his **education** at the University of Paris, earning a doctorate in law. He returned to Iran in 1946 and worked for the **Khuzistan** Labor Office before becoming deputy minister of labor in **Muhammad Mossadeq**'s cabinet. Bakhtiar was a key member of the **National Front** party during the politically turbulent 1950s, pushing for liberal constitutional reforms and democratic government.

Bakhtiar was an ambitious politician who was distrusted even by his closest associates. His unmistakable Western demeanor in dress and speech attracted U.S. politicians and diplomats, but detracted from his support in Iran. Despite his membership in the National Front, he was appointed prime minister by **Muhammad Reza Shah** on 29 December, 1978, at a time when the Shah was desperate to find any political solution to a deteriorating situation. The National Front was outraged by his acceptance and dismissed him from its membership. He did persuade the Shah to leave the country on an extended "vacation" and assume a "reign not rule" position. After the Shah's departure, Bakhtiar set up the Regency Council to carry out constitutional functions. When his policies met with further resistance, he threatened the opposition with an abandonment of constitutional government and the establishment of a military dictatorship.

Despite the Shah's absence and Bakhtiar's threats, the National Front and the Khomeini-inspired masses continued the strikes and protests against the government. When **Ayatollah Ruhollah Khomeini** returned to Iran on 1 February, 1979, Bakhtiar was soon forced from office to make way for the new Islamic revolutionary government. Bakhtiar went into exile in France where he became heavily involved in political opposition to the **Islamic Republic**. On 6 August, 1991, he was assassinated in Paris, allegedly by operatives of the Iranian government. *See also* ISLAMIC REVOLUTION.

BAKHTIARI. One of a number of distinct pastoral nomadic **tribes** of Iran, the Bakhtiaris live primarily in the central and southern **Zagros Mountains** region. The largest concentrations are in the eastern provinces of Lorestan and **Khuzistan** extending to **Isfahan**, within 160 kilometers of the Iraqi border. Bakhtiari are **Shiah** Muslim and speak the Lur Bozorg dialect, similar to the dialect spoken by the **Lurs** and closely related to the **Persian language**. Bakhtiari are divided into two main tribal groups—the Chahar Lang in the north and the Haft Lang in the south. While the Chahar Lang have historically been the leaders of all Bakhtiari until the mid-19th century, the Haft Lang have been known for their role in Iran's modern political sphere.

Records of a pastoral tribal group called Bakhtiari exist from the late 1300s; however the modern bi-tribal group dates only from the late 18th century. From 1870 until 1930, the Bakhtiari exercised significant political influence, even on the national scene. They were an instrumental military force, for instance, in defense of the **Constitutional Revolution of 1906**. They stormed **Tehran** in 1909 after **Muhammad Ali Shah** attempted to suspend the constitution resulting in the restoration of the **Majlis**. Known for military expertise, the **tribes** ruled villages of Arabic, Persian, and Turkic-speaking people in their geographic area, resulting in a wide use of the word Bakhtiari.

During the 1900s, **Reza Shah** began the forced settlement of all of Iran's nomadic peoples, and as a result, the esteem and power of the Bakhtiaris began to decline. Unlike other groups, those Bakhtiari who settled in villages and urban areas tended to receive **education** and easily assimilated into Persian culture. By 1979, use of the term Bakhtiari had been limited to identifying the approximately 250,000 tribes—people who still practiced pastoral nomadic ways.

BALUCHI. The Baluchi make up the majority population of the Sistan and **Baluchistan** province in western Iran, bordering the Baluchistan province of Pakistan. In Iran, the Baluchi reside mostly in the desolate Makran highland region and speak an Indo-Iranian language that more closely resembles the Pashtu language of Afghanistan and Pakistan than the **Persian language**. The Baluchi are divided into several principal tribes including the Saravan, Lashari and Yarahmadzai, as well as the Sadozai and Barazani who live along the coast of the Gulf of

Oman. The majority of Baluchi are Sunni Muslims as opposed to the **Shiah** Muslim majority of Iran. At various times this has produced religious tensions, particularly since the **Islamic Revolution** and most severely in the Sistan and Baluchistan capital of **Zahedan**. The remote location of the Baluchi, and the subsequent lack of control and monitoring by the Iranian government, has allowed half of the estimated total population of over half a million to remain nomadic, following tribal organization and authority, while the other half have become settled farmers or villagers. However, the neglect of the region has also established the Baluchi as one of the most poverty stricken and under-educated peoples in Iran.

BALUCHISTAN. Baluchistan is a provincial area in the southeastern region of Iran, with a topography which ranges from barren deserts and rugged mountain ranges to fertile valleys and pleasant coastal areas. The climate is temperate in the southern coastal regions, in sharp contrast to the major seasonal swings in temperature in the interior, which are aggravated by dust storms during dry windy periods and flash floods following sudden heavy rains. Little farming is done outside the valley regions. Nomadic and semi-nomadic pastoralism is an economic adaptation in the area though the harshness of the climate does not allow for great herds such as those that occur in the central **Zagros Mountains**.

The most promising area of the province is the coastal region along the Arabian Sea. The availability of water and the mild climate make the area attractive for the development of industries requiring access to shipping routes. On the other hand, there are no major urban centers or markets in the general vicinity and internal communications are severely limited. The coast also sustains scattered date groves that produce an important staple of the Baluchi diet. The mountainous configuration of the province has hampered road construction and kept rail service minimal, leaving most towns rather isolated. Most of the one million plus Iranian Baluchi live in the large towns of Khash, IranShahr, Sarawan, and Chah Behar, and speak Baluchi, one of the oldest living languages. The majority of the Baluchi are Sunni Muslims though they also retain and observe many ancient tribal traditions.

The inhabitants of Baluchistan are mostly Baluchi tribesmen. Fellow Baluchi live in the adjacent countries of Afghanistan and Pakistan, inhabiting large contiguous areas which form a greater geographical entity also termed Baluchistan. In this area, the national borders are essentially meaningless.

BANI-ETEMAD, RAKHSHAN (1954-). Rakhshan Bani-Etemad is known as the leading female contemporary film director in Iran and is called the "First Lady of Iranian **Cinema**." She was born in **Tehran**, and studied film at the University of Dramatic Arts there. After her schooling, she worked as an assistant director in commercial filmmaking and made several documentaries between the years 1981 and 1987. Her first three feature films were all dark comedies with strong overtones of social satire.

A consistent characteristic of Bani-Etemad's filmmaking is the combination of feature film and documentary style. She has referred to her genre as the social documentary. At first Bani-Etemad was reluctant about dealing with **women**'s issues. Thus in the beginning of her career women were only in her films as backdrops, not prominent characters. In the 1990s, Bani-Etemad began to work more with women's issues within her films. Instead of focusing on the lead characters as individuals, she would focus on the harsh circumstances and situations that would have to be faced and worked through by women. Rather than producing entertainment films, she worked more on producing epics from a human interest angle. She made three successive films about women's struggles: *Narges*, *The Blue-Veiled*, and *May Lady*.

Narges was produced in 1992. The first of a trilogy, this was a courageous film on the part of Bani-Etemad because it could either have made her career or broken it. It featured a strong-willed young woman, and contrary to taboos of the time, the film marked the first time in the cinema experience of the **Islamic Republic** that a love triangle served as the central theme.

The Blue-Veiled was produced in 1994. It is about a farm worker who responds to the affectionate interests of her rich older boss. The movie theme is centered on love defying the social strata of class and social structure.

May Lady was produced in 1998. This was one of Bani-Etemad's most personal films. In this film, she features a middle-class female Iranian filmmaker. The protagonist deals with the hardship of trying to balance a demanding job and a rebellious teenager while simultaneously serving as the object of her unseen lovers object of affection.

Her film *Under the Skin of the City*, produced in 2001, is by far the most popular film she has directed. At the Tehran Fajir Film Festival, its first screening, the film won five awards and continued to have a presence in over 40 festivals all over the world, including the 2001 Moscow International Film Festival in Russia where it was winner of the Grand Jury Prize. *Under the Skin of the City* was also selected by Iranian Film Critics as Best Film of Year 2001.

Continuing her remarkable success, and following her familiar theme of subtle social and political criticism, Bani-Etemad premiered a widely popular documentary entitled *Ruzegar-i Ma* (*Our Times*) in 2002. The film features two sets of women participating in the presidential elections of the time. The first set are young women, essentially teenagers, who set up a **Muhammad Khatami** campaign headquarters and personify the hope of progressive change. The second set is a group of female candidates who had presented themselves as presidential candidates. The film follows one of these women in detail as she demands to be heard. The result is an uneasy balance of hope and despair. As an accurate portrayer of the tenor of early 21st century Iran, Bani-Etemad added to her credentials as the foremost woman film director of Iran. *See also* CINEMA; MAKHMALBAF, SAMIRA.

BANI-SADR, ABOL HASAN (1933-). Bani-Sadr became active in the movement in opposition to the **Pahlavi** regime of **Muhammad Reza Shah** in his early student days. In the 1960s at **Tehran University**, he was a supporter of the **National Front**. He obtained his higher **education** in France where he began to refine his political ideas in lecture form. These were collected into a book which has been translated into English under the title of *The Fundamental Principles and Precepts of Islamic Government*. The contents provide clear insight into his thoughts on the role of **Islam** in government and reflect his background. Rooted in a family of religious scholars, he had a firm commitment to Islamic political ideals which he synthesized with the principles of democratic nationalism.

Bani-Sadr was elected the first president of the **Islamic Republic of Iran** in January 1980, and in June 1981 he was dismissed from his post. The reasons for his short term in office stemmed mainly from his failure to cooperate with the **Islamic Republican Party (IRP)** and the **Revolutionary Council**. Bani-Sadr's experience as president illustrates the complex power structure of the Islamic government, and **Ayatollah Ruhollah Khomeini**'s absolute control in that government.

A former student of Khomeini, Bani-Sadr was a staunch advocate of his ideas. While Khomeini was in exile in Paris, Bani-Sadr remained close to him and provided constant support. He was one of the drafters of the new Islamic Constitution. However, when Bani-Sadr became president, his opinions about Khomeini and the Islamic Republic changed. He soon discovered that as president he did not have much power, and that a select group of fundamentalist clerics controlling the Revolutionary Council and the IRP were the true rulers. He felt that Khomeini had become a dictator, and had abandoned the ideas that had sparked the revolution. Bani-Sadr constantly clashed with clerical leaders like **Ayatollah Ali Khamene'i**, **Ali Akbar Hashemi-Rafsanjani**, and **Ayatollah Muhammad Hussein Beheshti**, and his appeals to Khomeini for support were rejected.

Bani-Sadr believed that the religious scholars should only have an indirect role in government, and that technocrats should actually govern. Since this was not the case, he searched for power in other ways. Because of his post, Bani-Sadr was head of the army. Soon he found himself spending more and more time reorganizing and strengthening the Iranian military, a necessity when war with Iraq ensued in September 1980.

He also tried to appeal to the public by writing a column called "The President's Diary." In this column he talked about his philosophies of government, his war plans, and his disappointment with the present Islamic government. He spoke out against the arbitrary terror of various revolutionary groups pursuing their own agendas outside of a governmental process, and called for human rights. Bani-Sadr's column was his way of trying to gain power through a direct appeal for public support. The rift between Bani-Sadr and Khomeini and the IRP widened, and in June 1981, he was removed from office and forced to flee the country. He continues to speak out against the current regime in Iran from his exile in France. In 1989, Bani-Sadr published a book in French about his political experiences which subsequently appeared in a 1991 English-language edition entitled *My Turn to Speak*.

BARZANI, MULLA MUSTAFA (1903-1979). Mulla Mustafa Barzani was born into the Barzani tribe in the Kurdish region of northwestern Iraq. While his brother Shaikh Ahmad was the spiritual leader of the Barzanis, Mulla Mustafa was the political and military leader. He effectively assumed leadership of an endemic Kurdish revolt aimed minimally at autonomy and ideally at independence for the **Kurds**. His operations were focused primarily in northern Iraq, but events brought Mustafa Barzani and his forces into a central role in modern Iranian history.

In 1935, the Barzanis ambushed Iraqi ground forces in punitive expeditions against the Kurds supported by the British Royal Air Force bombing of their villages. Shaikh Ahmad was forced to flee to Turkey; however, Mulla Mustafa was captured. For the next seven years he was imprisoned in the town of Sulaimaniya.

In 1943, he escaped and traveled by foot to Iran. Within a short time, he returned to Iraq and began to build an army and an arsenal. In 1945, following yet another Kurdish revolt against Iraqi overlordship, Mulla Mustafa returned to Iran with substantial military forces. Once there, he united with other Kurds who supported the Kurdish nationalist movement led by Qazi Muhammad of Mahabad. Mulla Mustafa quickly pledged his support to the autonomous **Kurdish Republic** and brought his men into Mahabad. He believed that with the support of the Soviet Union the Kurdish Republic would endure. However, Soviet support waned with the forced withdrawal of occupying Russian troops from northern Iran after the Allied Powers invoked the terms of the 1943 **Tehran Conference** Agreement. This left the nascent Kurdish Republic in direct confrontation with the central government in **Tehran** which quickly pushed to reestablish **Pahlavi Dynasty** control. When tribal leaders were unable to cooperate with one another, the Kurdish Republic began to unravel. On 15 December, 1946, the Iranian army peacefully conquered the Kurdish Republic. Mulla Mustafa and his forces moved back to Iraq. A short time later he was forced to flee with some of his men to the Soviet Union some 320 kilometers away. He passed through Iran pursued unsuccessfully by the armed forces of **Muhammad Reza Shah**, who pressed hard for the capture of Mulla Mustafa. Mulla Mustafa was unable to return to his homeland for over 11 years.

When the Iraqi monarchy was overthrown in July 1958, the new leader invited Mulla Mustafa to return. In 1961, the Barzani forces, known as the Peshmergas (guerillas), under the command of Mulla Mustafa revolted. During the long, drawn-out revolt, the forces of Mulla Mustafa often found support from the same monarch who had recently pursued him decades before. The Iranian government was now at odds with the Republic of Iraq over a number of issues, including the boundary dispute over the **Shatt al-Arab** and a struggle for predominant political power in the Persian Gulf region. A political rapprochement between Iran and Iraq in 1975 led to withdrawal of support for the Kurdish revolt. The forces of Mulla Mustafa were defeated and he went into exile for what would be the rest of his life. In 1979, Mulla Mustafa Barzani died in Washington, D.C.

BASIJ. The Basij (also called Basij Mustazafin or Mobilization of the Oppressed) were created in 1980 by **Ayatollah Ruhollah Khomeini** and formally became an auxiliary force under the authority of the **Revolutionary Guards** in January 1981. The force came into being primarily due to the manpower demands of the **Iran-Iraq War** and the lack of means of the Iranian armed forces to prosecute the war in the fashion of a well-equipped modern military force. In particular, the cutoff of Iran from its primary source of weaponry and ammunition, the United States, during the **Pahlavi** period created a significant hardship. The isolation of Iran from the world community as a result of the **American Hostage Crisis** and the break-off of **U.S.-Iranian Relations** forced Iran into unusual and, quite often, innovative military measures.

Membership within the Basij typically consisted of the very young (under the age of 17 and not old enough for regular military service) or the elderly above the age of 50. Basij were generally voluntary militia groups that came mainly from rural towns and villages. These volunteers typically enlisted for three-month terms, corresponding to fall and winter months when their fields lay fallow. Though many of its membership were recruited from rural areas, and subsequently were poorly educated, the Basij also recruited in high schools, universities, and factories.

Each Basij unit trained in small arms tactics and the ideology of the **Islamic Revolution**. Basij commanders (always recruited from the Revolutionary Guards), with the help of political clerics, concentrated more on ideology than tactics. Consequently, the Basij remained a poorly armed yet highly motivated force whose common tactic was the "human wave" during the Iran-Iraq War.

In the war, the Basij were sometimes used as "cannon fodder," clearing the way for the Revolutionary Guards. One example was at the battle for Bustan, where 100 young Basij walked deliberately into a minefield to clear it for attacking troops. There were also known instances in which young Basij members strapped on explosive bomb harnesses and hurled themselves at Iraqi tanks. This was not simply a matter of compulsion. It stemmed from a deep-seated belief and a determination to be victorious. In fact, many Basij wore keys around their neck to symbolize the fact that if they died a martyr they would enter immediately into the kingdom of heaven.

Even though the Basij were poorly equipped, in part relying on captured Iraqi weapons and equipment scrounged from the battlefield, they were an effective weapon during the Iran-Iraq War. However, the nature of their tactics brought victory at great cost in human lives. These losses were compounded as the Iraqis began to use chemical weaponry towards the end of the bloody eight-year-long war.

After the Iran-Iraq War the Basij changed considerably. Whereas once they fought with a sense of purpose and necessity to protect the very life of the **Islamic Republic**, they became reduced to the role of being heavy-handed policemen. Whereas once many poor and patriotic Iranians flocked to the Basij, the organization has declined in prestige, even though members often enjoy preferential treatment in educational and employment opportunities. The primary role of the Basij in Iran today is to protect the nation's morality as opposed to its security. The Basij concentrate on daily patrol activities, combating what they view from a conservative religious perspective as vice, including mixed sex parties, alcohol use, and public violations of female dress codes and veiling.

The Basij either from a sense of duty or for better public relations have also served in other more positive roles. For instance, they have been used extensively to offer assistance to civilians after floods and earthquakes. In addition, the Basij have been used to organize inoculation campaigns among Iranian children. But even so, the Basij are having problems recruiting, and the average urban Iranian views the members, who are still heavily recruited from conservative rural communities, as petty thugs and bullies. This holds especially true among Iranian youth who were born after the Iranian Revolution and are chaffing under the oppressive nature of the Basij and religious fundamentalism. To many, the Basij are no longer viewed as the "mobilization of the oppressed," but as the "mobilization of the oppressors."

BASKERVILLE, HOWARD (1885-1909). Baskerville was an American missionary and educator. A graduate of Princeton Theological Seminary, he arrived in Persia in 1907 to teach at the American Memorial School in Tabriz. He became involved in the **Constitutional Revolution of 1906** and was killed fighting along with the revolutionaries in 1906. Baskerville was sometimes referred to as "the American Lafayette in Iran" and became a national hero to many Iranians.

BAST (SANCTUARY). *Bast* is the traditional form of Persian sanctuary, surviving into modern-day Iran. Refuge has customarily been sought in a shrine, mosque, or foreign embassy. Many individuals have sought sanctuary for political reasons, while at times large groups have taken sanctuary to protest government policy. During the **Constitutional Revolution of 1906**, large numbers of protesters took sanctuary against arbitrary government policy, and threatened to leave the country en masse unless their demands were met.

BAZAAR. The bazaar is a very important sociopolitical force in Iran. At its base level it is merely any of the country's informal market places. However, these also serve as gathering places and distribute not only goods but disseminate information as well. The markets are often run and frequented by the poorer citizens of the country. This allows not only a source of employment for citizens, but also provides a source of a large variety of cheap goods.

The bazaar, however, is a much more powerful force than a simple marketplace. It serves as a meeting place for individuals with varying motivations, including politics. The bazaar merchants and customers have been a source of political unrest in several periods. Throughout Iranian history, and most certainly in the 19th and 20th centuries, the bazaar has been a key element in political developments. The **Tobacco Revolt** in the early 1890s and the subsequent **Constitutional Revolution of 1906**, for instance, were both heavily influenced and partly driven by the economic interests of the bazaar. The bazaar merchants were a large portion of the coalition that brought the first **Majlis** and they had a large number of seats within the newly formed body.

Since the bazaar is on the front lines of the **economy** of the nation, it is a place in which economic unrest is felt by the everyday citizen. This can generate dissatisfaction with an administration's economic policies. This dissatisfaction can lead to large protests of the young and the urban poor against the government. Most recently, the **Islamic Revolution** of 1979, resulting in the overthrow of the **Pahlavi Dynasty** and the formation of the **Islamic Republic** of Iran, was an example of how key a role in both the mobilization and finance of social and political protest the bazaar can play.

The bazaar is also a strong cultural force. The marketplace becomes a source of foreign goods and ideas to enter the country. These ideas and products spread from the markets to everyday citizens. Often these products and ideas are from vastly different cultures and are sometimes at odds with what the ruling forces say and value. This can also create unrest and political demonstrations. Thus, though the bazaar has mostly been a crucible of traditional social and political forces, there are deeper and more complex elements to its role in Iranian society. It has served as a vehicle for both the defense of tradition and progressive enlightenment. Above all, the bazaar has been the focused center of urban existence and the economic engine of society. Even today, it is a very important institution for the people of Iran and for the economic success of the state.

BAZARGAN, MEHDI (1907-1995). Educated in France as an engineer, Bazargan returned to Iran and taught at **Tehran University.** He was a political moderate who combined Islamic concerns for social justice with the notion of democratic values. He was a founder of the Iran Party, one of the most significant of the parties which joined under the leadership of **Muhammad Mossadeq** to form the **National Front** in 1949.

Bazargan established strong nationalist credentials through his political activity in association with the National Front. However, unlike the secular orientation of the National Front, Bazargan was more of an Islamic activist and supported close ties with anti-regime clerics. In 1961, in conjunction with the "leftist" cleric **Mahmud Taleqani**, he founded a moderate religious party called the **Liberation Movement of Iran.** Never a very effective political force, the movement emerged as one of the many elements forming the revolutionary coalition in 1978-1979 that toppled the **Pahlavi** regime. Four days after **Ayatollah Ruhollah Khomeini**'s triumphal return to Iran on 1 February, 1979, Bazargan was asked by Khomeini to form a **Provisional Government.** On 11 February, the government of **Shapur Bakhtiar** collapsed, and Bazargan became prime minister. He remained head of the largely ineffective and powerless provisional government until forced to resign in November 1979.

Since the 1950s, Bazargan had strongly opposed **Muhammad Reza Shah** and sought a change in government. However, he desired a democratic **Islamic Republic**, not the clerical rule that developed after the revolution. He felt that clerics lacked the skills needed to govern effectively. The cabinet of his provisional government illustrates this point. It was made up almost entirely of moderate technocrats.

The increasingly powerful **Islamic Republican Party (IRP)** opposed Bazargan, and constantly challenged his authority while he was prime minister. Bazargan had no control over the **Revolutionary Guards** that were rampaging and terrorizing the country. He was unable to prevent arrests or executions. As head of government, Bazargan had virtually no power. He appealed to Khomeini for support which was never fully forthcoming.

Bazargan wished to maintain an open foreign policy, which included reserved relations with the United States. This ultimately led to his downfall. He was forced from office because of a meeting abroad, which led to the accusation of collaborating with the United States about the fate of the Shah. Actually, Bazargan had met with an American official about improving relations between the two countries, but his enemies played it in public as an agreement to allow the Shah to enter the United States for cancer treatment. The resulting storm of protest culminated in the takeover of the American Embassy in **Tehran** by radical students, the holding of **American hostages**, and the collapse of Bazargan's provisional government.

BEHBAHANI, SIMIN (1927-). Simin Behbahani was born in **Tehran** into a family that was highly literate and financially secure. Behbahani's family encouraged her to become educated and independent. Her father, Abbas Khalili, was at one time a highly controversial writer through the 1920s and continued to write during the **Pahlavi Dynasty** until about 1960. He was one of the early Iranian writers to write in a Western style and published several books in addition to editing the journal *Eghdam* (*Action*).

As with the fathers of some other important 20th century female poets, such as **Parvin E'tesami** and **Forugh Farrokhzad**, Simin's father acted as a catalyst in encouraging her emerging talent. What is unique is that her mother, Fakhr Adl Khalatbari, was also very well educated and the equal to her husband. She studied such diverse topics as Persian **literature**, Islamic jurisprudence, astronomy, Arabic, philosophy, history, and geography. Her parents jointly encouraged Simin's **education** even though they officially separated by the time she was two years old.

When she was a teenager, Simin was already writing her own publishable **poetry**. In fact, her first poem was published at age 14 in the journal *Nou Bahar*, published by Malik al-Shuara Bahar. Simin was a very good student and finished six years of middle school in four by taking extra classes. Later she enrolled in a **trade** school for midwifery where her independent streak quickly brought her into conflict with the dean of the school. Simin's political leanings—she had become a member of the **Tudeh Party**—and her poetry offended the school administration and led to her expulsion.

Several months after being expelled, and at the age of 17 she married Hassan Behbahani. Her husband taught high school English, and though they were together for 20 years and had three children together, Simin described themselves as being "incompatible," and the two eventually divorced. During the latter part of their marriage Simin had started law school. There, she met a man whom she later married, Manouchehr Koushiyar. The two finished law school together, Simin taught high school literature and wrote poetry. Simin and Manouchehr remained married for 14 years until he died of a heart attack.

Poetically, Simin Behbahani is considered to have produced some of the more significant work of 20th century Persian literature. Her balance of artful expression and shocking realism distinguished her voice in a lifelong struggle for freedom of expression. As such, much of her work reflects cultural and political experiences that have shaped late 20th century Iranian history. This is particularly true in her 1999 poem "Banu, Our Lady" which makes a powerful statement reflective of the **Student**

Dormitory Attacks by soldiers and vigilantes at **Tehran University** who were protesting government limitation on freedom of expression.

The efforts of Simin Behbahani in advancing the cause of human rights have found international recognition with several awards and grants. Her literary talents were recognized in 1997 when she was nominated for a Nobel Prize in literature.

BEHESHTI, AYATOLLAH MUHAMMAD HUSSEIN (1928-1981). Ayatollah Beheshti was a former student and loyal disciple of **Ayatollah Ruhollah Khomeini.** He graduated from an influential religious school in **Qum,** pursued advanced studies in Europe, and worked for the Ministry of **Education** in the early 1970s as a religious advisor. As the opposition movement against **Muhammad Reza Shah** gained momentum, he became the coordinator of the clerical opposition group which formed Khomeini's active underground network in Iran in the prerevolutionary period. During this period he was arrested and imprisoned by government police, along with several other prominent clerics.

Following the **Islamic Revolution** of 1979, he assumed leadership of the newly formed **Islamic Republican Party (IRP).** As the most politically astute member of Khomeini's **Revolutionary Council,** he played an influential role in the formation of the constitution for the nascent **Islamic Republic.** He served as secretary of the Revolutionary Council, president of the Supreme Court, and as a member of the **Assembly of Experts** which shaped the **Constitution of the Islamic Republic.** These positions gave Beheshti varying degrees of control over the legislative, executive, and judicial branches of the government. Beheshti managed to consolidate extraordinary power within the IRP, thereby exerting considerable influence in formulating government policy during the early days of the Republic. He and President **Abol Hasan Bani-Sadr** carried on a bitter rivalry which resulted in Bani-Sadr's dismissal in June 1981. Later that same month, on June 28, Beheshti was among those killed when a bomb exploded at the IRP headquarters.

BEIZA'I, BAHRAM (1938-). Perhaps best known for his socially conscious work in film as a producer, director, editor, and screenwriter, Bahram Beiza'i is also well regarded for his work in the theater, especially as a researcher. Born in **Tehran**, Beiza'i early found his interest in the theatrical arts, creating several Iranian historical plays while still in high school. Though in 1973 he would become a professor at the Fine Arts College at **Tehran University**—only to be removed from his position after the establishment of the **Islamic Republic**—his own stint as a student at said university was brief. Beiza'i dropped out before completing his studies.

Largely self-taught, Beiza'i's independent studies would propel him to a career at once highly lauded, yet at the same time largely controversial. During the 1970s, he became labeled as part of a movement in Iranian **cinema** known as the "New Wave," which was constituted of the more artistically inclined filmmakers. His own works in film generally criticize contemporary social issues—as well as Iranian history and culture—often through the lens of classical Iranian theater and literature. This emphasis is doubtlessly thanks to his in-depth research on the subject that began soon after he left college. Though the social critique aspect of his filmmaking aroused the ire of both the regime of **Muhammad Reza Shah** and the Islamic Republic, even more controversy derived from Beiza'i's focus on the roles women played in his films. Often taking leading roles, women in his films not only traverse an Iranian culture that Beiza'i portrays as oppressive to them, but they also persevere through their own will, transcending the bounds of society.

Though Beiza'i's subject matter and style have caused him difficulty in receiving support for his films, both before and after production, he is becoming known throughout the world as one of Iran's premiere filmmakers. Films such as *Tara's Ballad* (1978) and *Yazdgerd's Death* (1980) are unable to receive screening permits from the Islamic Republic, but moviegoers around the world experience his films on home video or on the international film festival circuit. Perhaps his best known film abroad is *Bashu, the Little Stranger* produced in the mid-1980s, but barred from screening in Iran until after the **Iran-Iraq War** as the subject matter was about a boy's loss of family and home to the war. With work on over a dozen films, authorship of several books—including the well-regarded resource, *Theater in Iran*—and his professorship at Tehran University, Bahram Beiza'i has contributed, and continues to contribute, much to the output of today's Iranian artistic intelligentsia.

BENJAMIN, SAMUEL GREENE WHEELER (1837-1914). Benjamin was an author and diplomat, born in Greece and educated in the United States. He traveled extensively and published several books about Greece. In 1883, he was appointed as the first American minister to Persia, and drafted the diplomatic code used by the American Legation in Persia.

BERLIN CONFERENCE. Following the overwhelming reformist victory in Iran's parliamentary elections of February 2000, the Heinrich Boll Foundation, in cooperation with the *Haus der Kulturen der Welt* (House of World Cultures), held the controversial conference "Iran after the Elections" in April of 2000. The conference was intended to encourage cultural and economic ties between Iranian reformers, Iranian exiles, and the general German public, as well as provide information on the status of Iran. Seventeen speakers were from Iranian reformists parties, both religious and secular.

The Iranian press filmed the conference and broadcast it in Iran several weeks later, causing an uproar. The Berlin Conference came under attack by conservative elements who considered the proceedings defamation of the **Islamic Republic of Iran**. All of the Iranian speakers were prosecuted by **Tehran** officials on charges such as harming "national security," "propaganda against the state," and "insulting Islam." Notable defendants included the lawyer **Mehrangiz Kar**, publisher Shahla Lahiji, student leader Ali Afshari, researcher Hojjat al-Islam Hassan Yousefi Eshkevari, politician **Ezzatollah Sahabi**, and journalist **Akbar Ganji**.

Mehrangiz Kar and Shahla Lahiji—both women's rights defenders—and Ali Afshari were detained without charge for over two months. Kar and Lahiji were both denied the legal right to a public trial and tried on 31 October, 2000 behind closed doors.

Upon his return from Europe in August of 2000, Hojjat al-Islam Hassan Yousefi Eshkevari was arrested on vague charges of defamation, heresy, being a threat to national security, being at war with God, and corruption on earth—a charge punishable by death. He was convicted in October in a disputable trial by the Special Court for the Clergy. Eshkevari was released after serving four years of a seven-year sentence.

Ezzatollah Sahabi was arrested in late April 2000 and then released on bail in late August of that year with a trial pending in November. Sahabi faced charges that were not made known, but were believed to be in connection with his statements at the Berlin Conference. He was rearrested and released on bail several times for related statements in other arenas, until finally in May 2003 he was convicted and sentenced to 11 years in prison. Suffering ill health, he was released in 2005.

Most notably involved was Akbar Ganji. Arrested and charged with similar offenses as his peers, Ganji used his trial to controversially speak out. He made claims against **Ali Akbar Hashemi-Rafsanjani** and went on to accuse Ali Fallahian, who Ganji referred to as the "Master Key," of ordering murders while he was the intelligence minister. Many others fell under scrutiny due to Ganji's testimony which publicly revealed corruption. Expectedly, he was convicted and then sentenced to 11 years in prison, the longest sentence received in connection with the conference. As of 2006, Ganji is still serving his sentence.

BLACK FRIDAY. By 8 September, 1978, the environment in **Tehran** had become heated with anti-Shah protest. **Muhammad Reza Shah** was known for his political autocracy, attempts at Westernizing Iran by turning the country's landed nobility into capitalist investors through the **White Revolution**, and encouragement of secularism. Reactions led to open protests in 1963 fomented by certain clerical leaders ultimately resulting in the exiling of **Ayatollah Ruhollah Khomeini** in 1964. The intervening years marked the growth of opposition to the policies of the

Pahlavi regime and resulted in the late 1970s in public defiance as the events of the **Islamic Revolution** unfolded.

The week of 8 September marked the end of the Muslim fasting month of Ramadan and more than 100,000 Iranians took part in public prayers which soon became a visible venue for anti-government demonstrations. In response, the Shah declared martial law in Tehran and 11 other cities during the night of 7 September, too late to significantly affect a planned demonstration the following morning. Troops were ordered to fire into the demonstrators at Tehran's Jaleh Square killing hundreds and wounding thousands. Though the official count tallied only 87 deaths, independent observers confirm hundreds. Many of those killed and injured were university students, who were demonstrating peacefully.

This day, which would become known as "Black Friday," destroyed any remaining support for the Shah and radicalized the government opposition led by an exiled Khomeini. A key event in the development of the Islamic Revolution, it marked a point of no return. The coming months saw revolting, burning of shops and banks, and other construed symbols of Western "corruption" brought by the Shah, as well as eventually a military rebellion in which Iranian soldiers attacked officers of the Shah's Imperial Guard. These events, triggered by the Black Friday massacre, led ultimately to the flight of the Shah from Iran in January 1979, and the subsequent collapse of the Pahlavi regime and its replacement by the **Islamic Republic of Iran**.

BROWNE, EDWARD GRANVILLE (1862-1925). Edward G. Browne was a British scholar who specialized in Persian studies. At a young age he was attracted to the Persian culture, particularly the elements of **Sufi** mysticism in **literature**. He spent a year in Persia and became a staunch advocate of the country and its people. He deplored the negative aspects of British and Russian influence which permeated so much of 19th century Persian history, and wrote controversial essays in defense of the **Constitutional Revolution of 1906**. Browne led the drive to form the Persia Committee in Great Britain, enlisting many influential members of Parliament to provide positive support for pro-Persian policies.

Browne was a prolific writer on Persian subjects. His first book, *A Year Amongst the Persians*, described his travels in Persia and his contacts with people from all classes and walks of life. Browne also wrote the monumental *A Literary History of Persia*, a comprehensive four-volume study of Persian literature ranging from the earliest times to the date of its publication in the early 1920s. Even today, Browne is considered one of the greatest champions of Persian life and letters, by Persians and non-Persians alike.

-C-

CALENDARS. In recent history, various calendars have found usage in Iran, including the lunar A.H., solar A.H., A.D., and the ShahanShahi. The Christian calendar designates the year as A.D. (anno Domini) while the Muslim calendar is designated A.H. (anno hegirae). In the A.H. calendar the year "one" begins with the day the Prophet Muhammad left Mecca for Medina. This corresponds to 622 A.D.

The Muslim A.H. calendar is lunar, consisting of 12 28-day months based on the cycles of the moon. The A.H. calendar has 336 days per year compared to 365+ for the A.D. calendar. Thus, the dates of the A.H. calendar vary from year to year, the same A.H. date falling earlier from one year to the next with respect to the solar A.D. calendar. For example, Ramadan, the month of fasting for Muslims, may fall in the summer season one year, and some years later be observed in the winter season. Exact conversion from one system to the other is complicated. For instance, elements that need to be considered in converting from the Muslim to the Christian calendar are the day the Muslim year started, how many Christian calendar days have passed, if the year was a common year or a leap year, and if the Christian year was Gregorian or Julian Old Style.

In addition to Muslim lunar and Christian solar dating, there is an Iranian solar calendar which was adopted by **Reza Shah** in

1925. Sometimes referred to as the Iranian civil calendar, it is derived from a pre-Islamic **Zoroastrian** calendar. This calendar is also termed A.H., since the year "one" begins with Muhammad's flight to Medina. Like the A.D. solar calendar, the Iranian A.H. solar calendar has fixed seasonal dates with a leap year

Equivalents: Iranian and A.D. Solar Months

Farvardin	21 March to 20 April
Ordibehest	21 April to 21 May
Khordad	22 May to 21 June
Tir	22 June to 22 July
Mordad	23 July to 22 August
Shahrivar	23 August to 22 September
Mehr	23 September to 22 October
Aban	23 October to 21 November
Azar	22 November to 21 December
Dei	22 December to 20 January
Bahman	21 January to 19 February
Esfand	20 February to 20 March

Table 1

every fourth year. Both the A.D. and the Iranian A.H. solar calendars represent 365 and one-quarter days, unlike the 336-day lunar A.H. calendar. The Iranian A.H. solar calendar begins the new year on 21 March, or the spring equinox, in contrast to the January 1 New Year's Day of the A.D. calendar.

In the Iranian A.H. solar calendar, six months have 31 days, five months have 30 days, and one month has 29 days (30 days in leap years). New Year's Day is on the first of Farvardin correlating to the spring equinox. The months of the Iranian solar calendar and their corresponding A.D. dates are listed in Table 1.

In Iran today, all three of the calendars mentioned above are used. Most Iranians adhere to the A.H. solar seasonal system and most Iranian holidays fall in that calendar. However, Muslim religious events are observed according to the A.H. lunar calendar. Most **Christians in Iran** and some segments of the Iranian business community prefer the solar A.D. calendar which corresponds to the dating system used in Western countries. A fourth calendar had a short-lived existence from 1976 to 1978. The ShahanShahi, or royal calendar, was introduced by **Muhammad Reza Shah** Pahlavi. Similar to the Iranian A.H. calendar, this was a solar calendar with the new year set at the spring equinox. However, the calendar's beginning date was based on the establishment of **Achaemenid** rule, calculated to be 559 B.C. The underlying presumption was a calendar to mark the years of continuous Iranian monarchy. Thus, the year of introduction, 1976, converted to the Royalist year 2535, whereas the corresponding Iranian A.H. solar year stood at 1355. Unpopular from its inception, the ShahanShahi calendar aroused a storm of controversy and was never fully incorporated into Iranian life. The masses of Iran were opposed to the new Royalist calendar, as were the ulama. The Shah himself agreed to scrap the calendar in 1978, only two years after its inception, as part of an unsuccessful attempt to stem the tide of protest which culminated in the **Islamic Revolution of 1979**.

CARTER DOCTRINE. The collapse of the **Muhammad Reza Shah** regime in Iran, along with the Soviet invasion of Afghanistan, prompted the issuance of the Carter Doctrine in January 1980. It promised U.S. intervention to protect Western interests in the Middle East, which were now at risk with a hostile government in Iran, as well as intervention against blatant Soviet aggression into the area.

The **Iran-Iraq War** intensified the interest of those countries critically dependent on Persian Gulf **oil** supplies. The spread of hostilities between Iran and Iraq prompted the entry of U.S. naval forces into the Persian Gulf to protect shipments from Kuwait. Such intervention was anticipated in the Carter Doctrine which provided the immediate justification. Subsequent clashes between Iranian and U.S. military forces in the Persian Gulf further damaged the already frigid relations between the two countries and led to the **Airbus Incident** in which an Iranian civilian airliner was shot down by the USS *Vincennes* in July 1988. *See also* IRAN AIR.

CASPIAN SEA. The Caspian Sea is actually a lake and not a sea. It is the world's largest inland body of water and is located between southeastern Europe and southwestern Asia, to the north of Iran. The surface of the lake covers an area of 231,745 square kilometers with a maximum depth of 975 meters at its southern end, and a depth of only 5 meters at its shallow end to the north. The Caspian Sea is located approximately 92 feet below sea level.

The Caspian Sea is bordered by Kazakhstan to the northeast, Turkmenistan to the southeast, Iran to the south, **Azerbaijan** to the southwest, and Russia to the northwest, and is one of the principal drainage basins for those countries. Thirteen rivers flow into the Caspian, the most important ones being the Volga, Ural, Embra, Kura, and Terex rivers. Since the construction of a dam on the Volga River, which supplied over 75 percent of the Caspian's water, the water level has decreased. The evaporation rate is high in the eastern part of the Caspian, which allows for the harvesting of salt.

While the Caspian Sea is a saline lake, its salt content is lower than that of the world's oceans, allowing it to have abundant fish, while at the same time it is salty enough to result in poor flora along the coast. The lower courses of the rivers that flow into the Caspian allow for the production of fine caviar, sturgeon fishing, and important fisheries. Caviar has long been a key export product of Iran, and economically important to the Caspian region and the state. Villages in Iran located in the littoral between the sea and the **Alborz Mountains** experience high humidity and rainfall. In stark contrast with the **Iranian Plateau**, the Caspian area of Iran is tropical in nature and extremely fertile, producing abundant supplies of rice, tea, and citrus fruits.

The Caspian Sea is rich in **oil** reserves, with Azerbaijan, Iran, Kazakhstan, Russia, Turkmenistan, and Uzbekistan each having disputed areas of control. Since the fall of the Soviet Union, international companies have been attracted to the area hoping to profit from the production of oil. This has led to an increase in investment in the area, as well as the introduction of new technologies and commerce. While Uzbekistan does not surround the sea, it benefits from oil exporting routes that it shares with other countries.

In previous times, the Caspian Sea has also been known as the Mare Sapium, Mare Hyrcanium, and the Sea of Baku.

CHAMRAN, MUSTAFA (1933-1981). One of the founding members of the **Liberation Movement of Iran (LMI)**, Mustafa Chamran became an important figure in the nascent **Islamic Republic**. Born in **Tehran**, Chamran would focus on his **education**, proving especially adept in academic pursuits. Also a devout Muslim, he supplemented his studies with participation in Islamic student groups, as well as with visits to **Ayatollah Mahmud Taleqani**'s mosque. His dedication led him to study electrical engineering at **Tehran University**. It was there that he became involved in the **National Resistance Movement**, a forerunner to the LMI.

After briefly teaching at Tehran University in 1959, Chamran traveled to the United States for graduate school, studying at Texas A&M and the University of California at Berkeley before receiving his Ph.D. Though he worked for a short time with Bell Laboratories, he soon abandoned his engineering career.

By this time, he was already part of a contingent of LMI members abroad (referred to as the Liberation Movement of Iran Abroad), a list which also included **Ibrahim Yazdi** and **Ali Shari'ati**. This wing of the LMI, which often operated autonomously of LMI proper, took the stance that armed resistance would be needed to overthrow **Muhammad Reza Shah**, and thus set out to train young Iranians in leftist-inspired guerilla tactics. Chamran and the LMI Abroad formed the Special Organization for Unity and Action in Egypt with Chamran as its head. This group sought to train Iranians in warfare, and operated until 1966 when tensions with Gamal Abdol Nasser forced the group's exodus from Egypt.

With the **Islamic Revolution** of 1979, Chamran returned to Iran. His experience as a guerilla trainer led to his appointment first as a commander of the **Revolutionary Guards**, and ultimately as the minister of defense. During the period of the **Provisional Government**, Chamran—along with **Mehdi Bazargan** and Ibrahim Yazdi—had their fateful meeting with U.S. National Security Adviser Zbigniew Brzezinski in Algeria. Word of the meeting reached Iran at the same time that news of Muhammad Reza Shah's admittance to the U.S. occurred, events which would lead Bazargan to resign. Still, Chamran maintained his official standing.

With the outbreak of the **Iran-Iraq War**, Chamran's position put him on the front. In June 1981, while in the village of Dehlaviyeh, Mustafa Chamran was ostensibly killed by shrapnel, although reports are varied. Speculation includes hints at Chamran's death as a murder by elements within the government which had become hostile to the LMI. To this day, the exact details are unclear.

CHRISTIANS IN IRAN. Christianity has had a presence in Iran since the earliest days of Christian history. When Constantine I ruled Christianity to be the state religion of the Roman Empire in 313 A.D., the **Sassanid** rulers of bordering Persia began persecution of those practicing the faith. Double taxes were instituted and suspicion of Christians as disloyal citizens was prevalent. In the mid-fifth century, persecution lessened and the church was recognized by the King Hormizd III.

After the Arab conquest in the seventh century, Christians were given "protected" status under the Code of Omar. This status gave way to religious tensions that deepened throughout the Crusades and the Mongol invasion.

Christians in Iran were divided in the mid-15th century when part of the Aramaic-speaking community entered into communion with the Roman Catholic Church. This group would become the Chaldean Catholic Church, while the remaining independent group would become the Assyrian Church of the East. By the 19th century, Western Christian missionaries had begun work in Iran, mostly in support of existing Christian churches and populations, the largest of which was, and still is, the Armenian Apostolic (Orthodox) Church. Missionaries also attempted to convert Iranian Muslims, though with little success.

Currently, Iran is home to between 200,000 and 250,000 Christians, down from 300,000 prior to the **Islamic Revolution** of 1979. While the **Constitution of the Islamic Republic** recognizes the Armenian and Assyro-Chaldean churches as official minorities, there are also Protestant and Evangelical churches active in the country. In recent years, the Iranian government has actively closed Evangelical churches, in addition to performing identity checks outside of services and requiring reports to the Ministry of Information regarding new converts or members. Although worship is generally permitted among the recognized groups, Christians in Iran are required to pass Islamic theology tests during schooling, for admittance to university, and to hold public sector jobs.

According to the Center for International Development and Conflict Mangagement's "Minorities at Risk" project, Iranian courts regularly award lesser settlements and larger penalties to Christians, and while Christian texts are legal, they are seldom given the necessary government approval for publication. According to the U.S. State Department, Christians are currently emigrating from Iran at a rate of 15,000 to 20,000 per year, and, thus, the community is dwindling.

CHUBAQ, SADEK (1916-1998). Author Sadeq Chubak was born in Bushehr where his father was a well-known **bazaar** merchant. After his schooling in Bushehr and **Shiraz**, Chubak attended **Alborz College** which prepared him for work as a teacher for the Ministry of **Education**. He spent time in the later 1930s in the army, where he worked in English translation.

In 1945, Chubak took the position of librarian for the **National Iranian Oil Company** and began his writing career with the publication of a collection of short stories called *Kheymeh Shab Bazi* (*The Puppet Show*). The collection, which detailed Chubak's observations of human motivation, was well received. Three more collections and two novels, *Tang Sir* (1963) and *Sang-i Sabur* (1966), were published before Chubak's retirement in 1974. The latter, translated into English as *The Patient Stone*, is considered to be one of the most important novels in the **Persian language**.

With the coming of the **Islamic Revolution**, Chubak was uncomfortable. The author's writing had been critical of the **Shiah** institution in Iran, and Chubak felt living under the revolutionary government of the **Islamic Republic** stifling and moved to London, later relocating with his wife to San Francisco.

In addition to his original writing, Chubak translated William Shakespeare's *Othello*, Romain Rolland's *La Fin du Voyage*, Carlo Collobi's *Pinocchio*, and Honore de Balzac's *Le Pere Goriot* into Persian for Iranian audiences.

Chubak was considered a key figure in the modernist literary school of fiction. He followed in the footsteps of **Muhammad Ali Jamalzadeh**, along with his close friend, **Sadeq Hedayat**. Elements of Chubak's writing carry somewhat anti-Semitic and anti-Arab undertones, as shown by his novel *The Patient Stone* and the short story "The Last Offering," respectively. The writings of Chubak are most remembered, however, for their keen insight into human nature. Renowned for his minimalist language when detailing complex events or ideas, Chubak made elegant use of the colloquial language of Iran's southern provinces. His writings have been likened to many of those he quoted as inspirations, including Ernest Hemmingway, Sadeq Hedayat, Henry James, and William Faulkner.

One of a number of important literary figures of 20th century Iran to go into exile from his native country, like many others he never returned. Sadeq Chubak died in July of 1998 in a hospital in Berkeley, California. *See also* LITERATURE.

CINEMA. The public screening of films in Iran began in 1904 in the backroom of a small antique shop in **Tehran**, though nobles and members of the royal family had been viewing silent films and newsreels privately since 1900. The following year the shop owner, Mirza Ibrahim Khan Shahaf Bashi, opened the first public theater in Tehran only to see it destroyed soon after for political reasons. However, by the mid-1920s, 25 theaters were operating in Iran.

Iranian screens showed mostly news footage and royal coronation ceremonies, until in 1926 an **Armenian**-Iranian named

Ovanes Ohanian returned to Iran from studying cinema in Moscow and opened the Cinema Artist Educational Centre, a school focusing on acting and performances in film. During the late 1920s and early 1930s, a few silent comedies based on foreign models were produced in Iran. In 1934, the first Iranian "talkie," a comedy called *The Lur Girls* by Abdul Hussein Sepenta, was filmed in India.

World War II kept Iranian film production stagnant from 1937 until 1949, when the first Iranian films began to be produced within the country. From this time until the mid-1960s, Iran's film industry ballooned, producing nearly 325 films shown in over 200 domestic theaters. However, commercial cinema was mainly composed of low-quality, slapstick-style comedies based on American and European films. It was not until Siamak Yasami's 1965 film *Ganj-i Qarun*, an exploration of the depth of morals among the poor in contrast to the upper class, that deeper subjects began to surface. This film was an enormous success, grossing today's equivalent of $1 million at the time.

The success of this film was followed by **Daryush Mehrjui**'s *The Cow* in 1969, a groundbreaking film which combined with the success of *Ganj-i Qarun* began a reformation of Iranian film. *The Cow* was initially banned by the **Pahlavi** regime of **Mohammad Reza Shah**. The feeling was its portrayal of rural Iranian life and one man's insanity gave the wrong impression to outsiders. However, the film was smuggled out of the country and entered in the Venice Film Festival where it won several awards, earning it a conditional permit for showing in Iran. A preface was added stating the time frame depicted in the film was 50 years earlier, placing it during the time of the previous **Qajar Dynasty**. Though popular among viewers, cinema was regarded as corrupt by the majority of clerics until the exiled **Ayatollah Ruhollah Khomeini** saw Mehrjui's film on French television and subsequently gave a speech on the educational value of film.

Ten years later, the **Islamic Revolution** threatened the blossoming film industry. Over 200 theaters were burned by Islamic zealots who saw cinema as a vehicle of Westernization. Film production and content were put under the control of the government while several directors and actors were charged with corrupting society and over 2,000 domestic and foreign films were banned. Regulations were established including a four-phase censorship system. The first phase of this system included rejecting film scripts showing feminine clothing, physical contact or tenderness between man and woman, jokes on the army or police, negative characters wearing beards, the favoring of a solitary character, and badly dressed or disagreeable soldiers. Also, it was deemed desirable for films to include a prayer scene and exalt heroism in war (the **Iran-Iraq War** was in full swing) and the defiance of Western influence. The following phases included approval of cast and crew, post-production screening by a censorship board (and making subsequent changes), and applying for a screening permit based on a quality rating system. A prospective film could be permanently halted at any phase in this process.

In the 1980s, then Minister of Islamic Culture and Guidance **Muhammad Khatami** challenged Iran's official film policy by declaring, "Cinema is not the mosque," which brought his forced resignation from the post. At the same time Iranian filmmakers had begun to experiment with language and images that allowed them to circumvent unremitting censorship regulations. A new leader emerged in this era of Iranian cinema in **Abbas Kiarostami**, who in late 1979 made a film called *Case No. 1, Case No. 2* which addressed questions of loyalty and betrayal at a time when these very issues were confronting all Iranians directly in the aftermath of post-revolutionary Iranian society. Though the film was not approved for release, it marked the beginning of a new phase of modern Iranian cinema. Government restrictions were often circumvented in the representation of daily life by uniquely coalescing documentary forms and fiction.

With a sense of mission, filmmakers began to embrace the idea of capturing Iranian life by way of metaphor and symbolism, heavily relying on children to represent forbidden emotions of desire and rebellion. With *The Runner* (1985), Amir Naderi became the first director to cast children in leading roles since the start of the revolution, starting a trend. As illustrated in **Bahram Beiza'i**'s *Bashu, The Little Stranger* (1987), a condemnation of the nearly decade-long holy war against Iraq, children and metaphor became a formidable opponent to the stringent laws guarding criticism of the Islamic government. Film became a way of contemplating society and **Islam** for many Iranians, including directors. Renowned Iranian filmmaker **Mohsen Makhmalbaf**, for instance, committed himself entirely to the removal of the Shah and to the new revolutionary government. After the establishment of the **Islamic Republic of Iran**, Makhmalbaf was director of the Islamic Artistic Theater Centre, a government propaganda organization, when he began to explore cinema through which he reflected on his country's situation. In 1987, with complete support of the regime, Makhmalbaf directed *The Peddler*, which proved to be a harsh and obvious criticism of the ruling establishment and warned of the "lies of the mosque." When questioned about his reversal of opinion, the director commented that cinema had "changed the way [he] looked at the world."

Kiarostami would also continue to challenge the religious hold on Iranian society by attacking the brainwashing of children in *Homework* (1997), and casting doubt on the afterlife in *The Wind Will Carry Us* (1999).

While Khatami's landslide victory in the 1997 presidential election meant more moderate enforcement of film censorship, independent Iranian filmmakers, including an increasing number of **women** directors, were enjoying international success for their honest format and symbolic portrayal of life in Iran. In 1995, **Ja'far Panahi**'s *The White Balloon* won the Camera d'Or at the Cannes Film Festival and Best Foreign Film from the New York Film Critics Circle. Kiarostami was awarded the *Palme d'Or*, or Golden Palm, at the 1997 Cannes Film Festival for *Taste of Cherry* (1997), and in the year 2000, 19-year-old **Samira Makhmalbaf**, daughter of director Mohsen Makhmalbaf, was the youngest award winner in the history of the Cannes Film Festival for her film *Blackboard* (1999).

In the past decade, Iranian films have won nearly 300 awards at international festivals and the country continues to produce films rich in image and truth. Limits are continually tested by modern films, like Panahi's *The Circle* (2000), which portrays prostitution, a topic previously forbidden in Iran.

While mainstream, government-produced films exist in Iran, 20 talented directors, including the aforementioned, produce 15 percent of Iranian films each year. Annual production numbers are growing with more than 400 Iranian directors producing over 80 films each year. *See also* BANI-ETEMAD, RAKHSAN; MAJIDI, MAJID; SAYYAD, PARVIZ.

CONSTITUTION OF THE ISLAMIC REPUBLIC OF IRAN. Following the overthrow of **Muhammad Reza Shah** in 1979, a clerically dominated **Assembly of Experts** proposed a draft for a new constitution based on **Ayatollah Ruhollah Khomeini**'s theocratic ideology for a modern Islamic nation-state. Many groups opposed the draft, however anti-American sentiment, fanned by Khomeini, united his followers and assured passage in a national referendum held in December 1979. The constitution established the **Islamic Republic of Iran** and proclaimed the sovereignty of the people. In actuality, Khomeini retained absolute power.

The constitution provided for a president, but ultimate power rested with the **Faqih**, the supreme religious leader of Iran, ruling on behalf of the **Hidden Imam** of **Shiah** Islam. The constitution assured clerical dominance over the institutions of state, as **Islam** became the foundation for the legal system and all facets of the government. The constitution established a 12-member **Council of Guardians**, with half chosen by the Faqih, to decide whether laws conform to religious principles. The veto power of the Council of Guardians over all actions of Parliament assured that legislation would be Islamically correct. Overall, the constitution transformed the judiciary system, placing it under the complete control of religious jurists. It also gave Khomeini, and his successors in the role of Faqih, complete power, themselves responsible only to God.

CONSTITUTIONAL MOVEMENT. *See* CONSTITUTIONAL REVOLUTION OF 1906.

CONSTITUTIONAL REVOLUTION OF 1906. An organized movement in Iran began in 1905 in protest of autocratic government, economic insecurity, and pervasive foreign influence throughout the country. Reformers resented British and Russian dominance and the costly economic concessions they received from the **Qajar** Shahs, who directed the financial benefits into questionable projects and personal use. By 1905, Great Britain had been granted **oil** concessions in the southern region, and Russia militarily controlled the north. Many foreigners had been employed to oversee government affairs, and were considered an affront and a threat to Iranian autonomy and its religious and social traditions.

In 1905, a coalition of clergymen, landlords, and intellectuals presented demands to the government. The monarchy ignored the demands and began to suppress the opposition. When government troops opened fire on the participants in the funeral procession of a protester, public outrage intensified and massive demonstrations and general strikes paralyzed the country. Great Britain and Russia took opposing stances in the movement, with Britain publicly supporting the protest while Russia worked to maintain the status quo. The demonstrations, coupled with British influence, persuaded the king to accept the demand for the first Persian constitution and parliament, both of which limited the monarchy's powers.

The Constitution of 1906 was signed by the ailing **Mozaffar al-Din Shah** in August 1906. The constitution provided for separate legislative, executive, and judicial governmental branches. The Iranian Parliament, or **Majlis**, would formulate new laws and decrees. More importantly, treaties, economic concessions, and monopolies would be determined by the legislators. The constitution guaranteed the rights of private property and freedom of speech, press, and assembly. Secular aspects of the constitution restricted the power of the clergy, but also acknowledged **Islam** in important ways. In clauses which were never implemented, the constitution guaranteed that legislation would be reviewed by a panel of five learned, religious scholars to ensure that new laws and educational curriculum would meet Islamic requirements, and the king, ministers, and judges were required to be adherents of the Twelver sect of **Shiah Islam**. These clauses were a precursor of the similar, and far more effective, measures adopted by the **Islamic Republic of Iran** which constitutionally established a **Council of Guardians** to protect Islamic interests. The adoption of the constitution and institution of a parliament failed to produce effective changes, due mostly to Russo-British interference, and a rift in the alliance of diverse groups which had made the changes possible. By 1911, the revolutionary movement had dissipated as key religious elements had defected and economic problems grew. As World War I approached, both Britain and Russia increased their military presence in Iran.

Though the constitution was unsuccessful in effecting significant change, it remained in place throughout the remainder of Qajar rule and through the **Pahlavi Dynasty** as well, a symbol of the united efforts of the Iranians toward the goal of representative government. The 1906 Constitution was superseded by the new Constitution of the Islamic Republic of Iran which went into effect in December 1979.

COUNCIL OF GUARDIANS. The Council of Guardians was established following the **Islamic Revolution** of 1979. It was institutionalized in the **Constitution of the Islamic Republic of Iran** and has played a vital and powerful role in the political proceedings and legislative process of the Islamic Republic ever since. The 12-member panel is responsible for ensuring that all legislation passed by the **Majlis** conforms to the principles of **Islam**. In addition, Majlis candidates must be screened by the Council prior to being placed on the ballot, and elections for the office of president, as well as parliamentary elections, are supervised by the Council. Six of the Council's members are appointed by the **Faqih** and the remaining six by the Supreme Judicial Council, both effective sources for assuring Islamic control over the content of legislation passed in the Majlis.

In its history, the Council of Guardians has asserted itself a number of times. For instance, the Council has rejected significant reform measures, such as nationalization of industries and land reform, as contrary to Islamic standards, and has also invalidated several parliamentary elections. Most recently, the Council has come under fire from reformists for banning over 2,500 candidates, many of whom were reformers, in the 2004 Majlis elections. The Council also barred all but six out of over 100 candidates for the 2005 presidential election.

CYRUS THE GREAT (Ruled 550-530 B.C.). Cyrus II, usually known as Cyrus the Great, was the first king of the **Achaemenid Dynasty.** He united the Medes and Persians under his rule and initiated one of the most prosperous empires in history. His first conquest on the road to establishing a world empire was the defeat of the fabled King Croesus of Lydia in 546 B.C. He proceeded to attach Asia Minor, Armenia, several Greek colonies, Parthia, Chorasnia, Bactria, and Babylon to his empire. Cyrus established his first capital at Ecbatana (present-day **Hamadan**) and later built another imperial center at Pasargadae in Fars Province.

Cyrus the Great was born in Persia and descended from a long line of kings. He was a fearless battlefield warrior and a tolerant, benevolent ruler of his own people and those he conquered. He established a new pattern of conquest by treating the populations of defeated nations humanely, winning them over to his side rather than destroying them. Cyrus is mentioned in the Old Testament as the king who released the **Jews** from Babylonian captivity and enabled them to return to Jerusalem to rebuild their temple. He also freed many other captive groups in the lands he conquered. After securing Babylon, he left his son Cambyses II to oversee preparations for the conquest of Egypt and moved eastward to deal with restless nomadic **tribes.** He died in battle in 530 B.C. His body was returned to Pasargadae, north of today's **Shiraz** in Fars Province, and buried in a tomb which still stands today. Cyrus II earned his designation as "The Great" through bravery in battle, benevolent leadership, and innovative policies of administration.

-D-

DAMAVAND, MOUNT. Snow-capped Mt. Damavand is the most striking feature of the **Alborz Mountain** range. Located 64 kilometers northeast of **Tehran**, it rises in a majestic, symmetrical cone to a height of 5,604 meters. It is the highest peak in Iran and higher than any other summit to the west of it in Asia or Europe. Once an active volcano, it has been dormant for a millennium. The presence of sulphur gas reported by modern mountain climbers indicates a possibility that the mountain could erupt again.

Though nomads have occupied the lower regions of Mt. Damavand throughout Persian history, the lava flow from the active volcanic period has limited cultivation to small patches of usable soil even beyond its base, thereby restricting population of the area. Some small villages are situated on its ledges, but the steep slope of the peak has kept them in the lower regions of the foothills.

The sheer magnitude and isolation of Mt. Damavand have contributed to its recurrent appearance in Persian **literature** and lore. The inaccessibility of its upper regions made it the perfect dwelling place for the heroes, demons, and mythical creatures which abound in Persian literature. The *Shahnameh* of the famed Persian poet **Abol Qasem Ferdowsi** recounts the imprisonment of the evil king Zahhak on the peak after being dethroned by the noble Faridun. The Simorgh, Ferdowsi's immortal magical bird, nested there. According to legend, Zal, the son of the warrior Sam, was abandoned on Mt. Damavand by his father when it was discovered that he was an albino. Rescued and nurtured by the Simorgh, Zal was protected until Sam appeared to reclaim him. Zal went on to become a great warrior and father of Rostam, the greatest of the Iranian heroes. *See also* RAYY.

DANESHVAR, SIMIN (1921-). Daneshvar was born in **Shiraz**, where she attended a missionary school and became fluent in English. The young Daneshvar started writing at the age of 15, publishing an article in her local newspaper. While studying Persian **literature** at **Tehran University** in 1941, the new writer's father died, forcing her to find employment at Radio Tehran in order to support her family. Daneshvar's grasp of English allowed her to rise to assistant director of foreign news, which combined with the relaxed social and political atmosphere of the time led her to rely on journalism as a source of income.

During this time, Daneshvar began writing fiction without any formal training in technique or style. Despite her amateur status, Daneshvar wrote *Atesh-i Khamush* (*The Quenched Fire*), a collection of 16 short stories, at the age of 27. The stories were heavily inspired by O. Henry, who Daneshvar had became familiar with during her studies. She dwelled on issues of basic humanity in Iranian society, with a focus on the contrasts between rich and poor, and right and wrong.

Daneshvar earned her Ph.D. in Persian literature from Tehran University and met her future husband, the well-known contemporary writer and social critic **Jalal Al-e Ahmad**, to whom she was married in 1950. In 1952, Daneshvar received a Fulbright scholarship and traveled to Stanford University in the U.S. where she studied for two years. After her return to Iran, Daneshvar became an associate professor of art history at Tehran University and taught for 20 years. During her tenure, Daneshvar never advanced to full professor as the university was under pressure from **SAVAK** to keep the outspoken writer from influencing students.

Her second collection of short stories, *Shahri Chun Behesht* (A City of Paradise), was published in 1961 and at the same time Daneshvar began translating foreign works into Persian. Though Daneshvar lived in the shadow of her famous husband she continued to write culminating in her masterpiece work, *Savushun*. This was the first novel written by an Iranian woman from the perspective of **women**. Sadly, Jalal Al-e Ahmad died in 1969, two months before the successful publication of *Savushun*.

Daneshvar is known for a style of writing that vividly reflects reality, as opposed to a fictional fantasy, exploring issues from childbirth, death, adultery, and marriage to treason, profiteering, poverty, and disease. At the height of her career in the

1960s and 1970s, issues like these saturated Iranian society and addressing them established immediate credibility for a writer. Daneshvar retired from Tehran University in 1979 and began working on a book called *Al-e Ahmad, Ghorub-i Jalal* (The Loss of Jalal), a descriptive tribute to the personality and life of her late husband. This piece is known as her most intimate and moving and she details the last days spent with Al-e Ahmad, one of Iran's great literary figures.

DAR AL-FONUN. Among several prominent reformers of the 19th century, perhaps the most notable was **Mirza Taqi Khan Amir Kabir**. He was among the first Iranians to advocate "modernization" programs. As chief minister to **Naser al-Din Shah**, one of his primary concerns was military reform, and he advocated an instructional program utilizing European-style **education** and training for Iranian troops.

In 1851, with royal approval and support, he founded the first school of higher learning in **Tehran**, the Dar al-Fonun, which offered technical, scientific, and military instruction. The institution was established within a Western-oriented framework, and most classes were instructed by European teachers with the aid of local translators. The school housed the State Printing Press and offered an impressive curriculum in European languages.

For many years, the Dar al-Fonun was the only modern school of higher education in Iran and had a fundamental influence on the thinking of the young men from the upper class who were fortunate enough to be enrolled there. Instructors such as the pro-Western reformer **Mirza Malkom Khan** taught at the Dar al-Fonun in its earliest years. Exposure to a European curriculum and international faculty brought a new dimension of Iranian thought into existence and changed the course of the country's cultural development. This mode of education produced a cosmopolitan outlook in its students who later would become the diplomats and advisors for the **Qajar** Shahs. The Dar al-Fonun survived through the century and was the predecessor of **Tehran University**, the first comprehensive university opened in Iran in 1934.

DARIUS (Ruled 522-486 B.C.). Darius is considered the greatest leader of the **Achaemenid** Period. He seized control of the empire following the death of Cambyses II, the son of **Cyrus the Great**, and ruled from 522-486 B.C. He devoted the first years of his reign to quelling rebellions within the empire, and then turned to organizing his territory into satrapies, a revolutionary system of central government which allowed semi-independent provincial lords to exist within a monarchial structure. He also introduced a revolutionary coinage system, standardizing the precious metal content by degree of purity, which facilitated **trade** in the empire.

Darius supported the development of high culture in art, **literature**, and architecture. His palace at **Susa** was constructed by craftsmen drawn from all areas of his widespread kingdom, who incorporated their ideas and materials into an eclectic style which still remained entirely Persian. The magnificent imperial capital of **Persepolis** was built initially as a spiritual center for the empire by Darius. He also implemented plans to dig a canal from the Nile River to the Red Sea to facilitate movement on the waterways.

Darius suffered his first military defeat at the hands of the Greeks during the Battle of Marathon in 490 B.C. He died four years later. It was his wish, gleaned from inscriptions which remain in the ruins of Susa, that he be remembered as a just lawgiver and authority. He is remembered as this and more. Through his abilities as an administrator, military strategist, and humanist, Darius secured an exalted position in Persian history.

DASHT-I KAVIR. *See* IRANIAN PLATEAU.

DASHT-I LUT. *See* IRANIAN PLATEAU.

DEFINITIVE TREATY OF 1812. The Definitive Treaty, also known as the Treaty of Friendship and Alliance as well as the **Tehran** Treaty of 1812, was a military alliance between Persia and Great Britain. It was a sharp departure from the terms of the 1807 **Treaty of Finkenstein** between Persia and France. This treaty was negotiated by Sir Gore Ouseley and signed on 17 March, 1812. It upheld, in essence, the articles found in the **Preliminary Treaty** negotiated in March 1809, by Sir Harford Jones, the first official British envoy to the **Qajar** Court. It continued provisions for financial aid or troop reinforcements from the India Corps if a European power attempted to invade Persia. It also made provision for the training of Persian soldiers by British officers, and for the building of a Persian naval presence on the **Caspian Sea**. In addition, the treaty included a pledge by Britain to remain out of the conflicts between Persia and Afghanistan, unless England was called on to mediate by both sides. For her part, Persia committed to block any European force that might attempt to cross her territory to reach India, a clear reference to Napoleonic France.

A significant problem with the treaty involved clauses which promised military aid in the amount of 150,000 pounds if Britain was unable to send Indian forces to aid in repelling any European nation invading Persia's territorial integrity. When Russia attacked Persia, Britain faced a dilemma due to its alliance with Russia against France. When British officers assisted Persian soldiers in repelling a Russian invasion, a diplomatic *faux pas* occurred, and hastened the renegotiation of the Definitive Treaty. The result was a new treaty known as the **Tehran Treaty of 1814**.

DEKHODA, ALI AKBAR (1879-1956). Born in **Tehran**, Ali Akbar Dekhoda was to become one of Iran's most important literary scholars and social critics of the 20th century. He spent his early life in study, spending time at the newly founded School of Political Science in Tehran. Later, Dekhoda became secretary to the **Qajar** ambassador to the Balkans, Moaven al-Doleh Ghaffari. Through this position, Dekhoda traveled with Ghaffari to Europe for two years, most of which was spent in Vienna, Austria. There, Dekhoda not only improved his French skills, but also became acquainted with the liberal democratic ideas prevalent in European circles at the time.

Dekhoda returned to Iran in 1905 on the eve of the **Constitutional Revolution of 1906**. It was during this period, as the author of the "Charand Parand" ("Balderdash") segment of the socialist newspaper *Sur-i Esrafil* (*Trumpet Call of Esrafil*) that Dekhoda began his public literary career. Writing under the pseudonym "Dakhow" (a dialectic form of *dekhoda*, or "village head"), he satirically lambasted hypocrisies and injustices amongst the ruling and religious elites. He even attacked the tradition of women's veiling. The serial was hugely popular with the common people of Iran—as well as praised by the world's literary elite—partly because Dekhoda used the common speech of the Iranians, with all its colloquialisms and proverbs. It was this that earned Dekhoda the distinction as one of the progenitors of modern Iranian literature.

Authorites stopped *Sur-i Esrafil*'s printing on several occasions. The staff was even threatened with death by the ulama on one occasion. Printing came to a final halt following the bombardment of the **Majlis** in 1908. The paper's editor, Mirza Jahangir Khan, was executed, but Dekhoda managed to escape. He was even able to publish several issues of *Sur-i Esrafil* from Switzerland. Financial pressures, however, proved too daunting. Dekhoda often sought new locations of exile, including Istanbul, and even amidst the **Bakhtiari** tribe. Not until after World War I was Dekhoda able to return to Tehran.

With the price of political activism too high, Dekhoda focused his strength on literary pursuits, though he did once again become politically active during **Muhammad Mossadeq**'s brief tenure. With the forced return of **Muhammad Reza Shah** to the throne, he retired again from politics.

Continuing in the vein of his work with *Sur-i Esrafil*, Dekhoda studied the vernacular language of Iran and its history. In addition to writing masterful works of **poetry** and prose, his research also led him to compile expansive information on the **Persian language** he loved. In 1932, he published *Amsal va Hekam* (*Proverbs and Wise Sayings*), which was a collection of idioms, metaphors, and traditional and religious stories, amongst other things.

The contributions of Dekhoda to the Persian linguistic and literary world are massive, and nothing more so than what will doubtlessly be the most enduring of all, his encyclopedic dictionary. Dekhoda's work on defining the collected terms and meanings of a whole history of a language became the basis of his *Lughat Nameh*, also known as the *Great Lexicon*. Work on this historically monumental project took up most of his later life, and work on the voluminous achievement was continued by others well beyond his death in 1956. *See also* LITERATURE.

DOWLATABADI, MAHMUD (1940-). Famous as a short-story writer and novelist, Mahmud Dowlatabadi was born in the village of Dowlatabad in **Khorasan** in northeastern Iran. Exposure to village storytellers and religious dramas in his youth encouraged his creativity and his reading. Although his only formal **education** was through primary school, Dowlatabadi educated himself. To earn money, he worked jobs ranging from sheepherding to hairdressing. He finally arrived in **Tehran**, where he attended theater school before becoming a stage actor.

Dowlatabadi's writing career began in the early 1960s. He focused on prose, eventually writing several novels, short-story collections, and film scripts. The title of his first short-story collection, 1969's *Desert Strata,* hints at his Marxist conception of class, making a clever play on the concept of strata as both layers of desert earth and layers of hierarchical classes. His stories often focus on the peasants or urban poor and small business classes in a struggle with capitalistic forces backed by the government.

Though he published many popular novels throughout his career, including *The Legend of Baba Sobhan* (1970) and *Solomon's Emigration* (1974), his multivolume novel *Klidar* (1983) is widely considered his premiere work. The work details the story of a peasant who gets caught up in an armed revolution, and finally unfolds in the tragic death of the protagonist at the hands of government forces. Though Marxist in its view of classes, *Klidar* does not denigrate **Islam**. In fact, it utilizes a metaphor between the slaying of the main character and his forces with the martyrdom of **Imam Hussein**. By drawing such obvious parallels and refraining from attacking Islam, Dowlatabadi leaves open the door for the support of the religious in a possible future revolution.

Dowlatabadi's activist writing often attracted the attention of the authorities, both during **Muhammad Reza Shah Pahlavi**'s rule as well as the after the rise of the **Islamic Republic of Iran**. He was arrested several times throughout his career, once simply for the fact that his books were often read by dissidents. In 2000, Dowlatabadi attended the infamous **Berlin Conference**. This conference featured discussion about the future of the reform movement in Iran, but anti-reform forces in Iran quickly labeled it anti-Islamic and accused the participants of threatening Iranian national security. Along with many other high-profile artists, politicians, and businesspeople, Dowlatabadi was arrested. However, although some of the participants were found guilty, including **Akbar Ganji** who received a 10-year sentence, Dowlatabadi was acquitted. *See also* LITERATURE.

-E-

EBADI, SHIRIN (1947-). Shirin Ebadi studied law at **Tehran University**, eventually leading to her becoming Iran's first female judge. From 1975 to 1979, she even served as the president of the city court of **Tehran**. After the **Islamic Revolution** of 1979, however, she (along with all female judges) was removed from her position by the new **Islamic Republic of Iran**.

Ebadi remained in Iran, continuing to practice law and to lecture at Tehran University. Over time, she became one of Iran's most outspoken voices for reform, calling for stricter adherence to civil rights, more religious freedom (especially for the **Bahai**), and less censorship. She advocated improvements in family law as regards the status of **women** and children in divorce and inheritance. All of her arguments were based on Islamic principles, giving a level of legitimacy to her pleas that hardline **Shiah** elements in the government could not so easily refute as they could secularist claims.

In her professional career, Ebadi became involved in some of the most public internal Iranian events of the late 20th century and early 21st century. In 1998, her client list included Daryush and Parvaneh Foruhar who were slain that autumn in a series of activist writers' murders, perpetrated by renegade elements of the Intelligence Ministry. Following the **Student Dormitory Attacks** at Tehran University in the summer of 1999, Ebadi fought to bring those responsible for the deadly attacks to light. For this, the courts convicted her on charges stemming from her alleged distribution of a taped confession by a conservative official that implicated others. She received a suspended sentence and a five-year ban on practicing law.

For her long and successful involvement in Iranian reform activism, Shirin Ebadi received the Nobel Peace Prize in October 2003. She was the first Iranian—as well as the first Muslim woman—to be recognized as such. Though there was some opposition by Iranian ultra-conservatives, epitomized by a statement from a group of ulama and theological students in **Qum** denouncing the award as part of a Western conspiracy against the Islamic Republic, many recognized it as a source of Iranian pride. Thousands participated in jubilant demonstrations of support, including in Tehran, where upon the return of Ebadi from the award ceremony women wore white scarves and threw white flowers in a gesture of peace.

EBTEKAR, MASSOUMEH (MARY) (1960-). Ebtekar was educated in the United States where she lived for several years as a child. She completed her schooling in **Tehran** where she attended Shahid Beheshti University earning a degree in laboratory science, and then Tarbiat Modrares University where she earned both an M.S. and a Ph.D. in immunology.

Primarily known in the West for her role as the spokesperson for **Students Following the Imam's Line**, she was dubbed "Mary" by the foreign media and in her role as press secretary she became, under her pseudonym, a household name over the 444 days of the holding of **American Hostages in Iran**. She rarely speaks of her involvement in the siege though she has published a book detailing the ordeal from the inside in which she attempts to clarify the American media misconception of the goals of the students involved.

Like many of the other hostage-takers, Ebtekar took a prominent role in the ensuing society and government of the **Is-**

lamic Republic. She acted as editor of the English-language newspaper *Kayhan International* from 1980 to 1981, a post handed to her by future Iranian President **Muhammad Khatami**. In 1985, Ebtekar presided as head of the National Committee of the fourth World Conference on **Women**. In 1990, she joined the academic staff of Tarbiat Modares University where she continues to teach.

In 1997 President Khatami named Ebtekar vice president and head of Iran's Environmental Protection Organization, making her the first woman to hold such a position, a move lauded as a breakthrough for women in Iran. Ebtekar is also known, along with several other prominent Iranian women, as a founding member of the Women's Party of Iran, a branch of the Islamic Iran Participation Front.

Today, Ebtekar acts as managing editor of *Farzaneh*, a bilingual women's studies quarterly, and is an advocate for women's rights and environmental preservation and restoration, as well as a leader of Iran's reform movement.

ECONOMY. Historically, the economy of Iran was rooted in **agriculture**. Possessed of sufficiently extensive fertile land and the technology to irrigate it through the use of *Qanats*, there were riches to support successions of empires and allow for the flowering of both material and intellectual culture. The Iranian economy also benefited throughout history from the fruits of its geo-strategic location. The country sat astride major international trading routes.

Dramatic changes occurred in the 20th century during which time the Iranian economy became intertwined with fossil fuels, especially **oil**. Throughout the century, Iran was a vital cog in the head long rush of the world's economy into petroleum dependency. Oil was first discovered in commercial quantities in the Middle East in Iran, in 1908 at Masjed-i Soleiman, which led to the creation of the **Anglo-Iranian Oil Company**. Oil has played a dominant role in the Iranian economy ever since.

In early 21st century Iran, the economy is highly dependent upon the fossil fuel **industry**. The country has 133.3 billion barrels of oil in reserve (9 percent of global reserves) and relies on oil for its economic well-being. Oil income makes up 40 percent of government revenue and 80 percent of export earnings, with four million plus barrels of oil produced each day. Iran consumes 1.4 million barrels and exports 2.7 million barrels per day. Prior to the 1979 **Islamic Revolution**, which brought production to a near halt, Iran was the world's second leading exporter of oil. It has since recovered and is now the sixth leading producer of the world's oil supplies.

Natural gas is another fossil fuel found in abundant supply. Following only Russia, Iran has the second-largest reserve of natural gas in the world (26.7 trillion cubic meters). Sadly, this large reserve is under-utilized by the nation, coming in at only 26th in the world exporting market. Production is at 79 billion cubic meters per year and the national consumption nearly equals that at 72.4 billion cubic meters.

The fossil fuel industry employs 25 percent of working Iranians, which translates into about six million workers who greatly depend on this industry. The overall economy of Iran, and the financial security of its citizens, shifts dramatically with the varying price and supply of oil. Greater stability could be brought to the economy with steady foreign investment into the oil and natural gas industries, but political uncertainties continue to haunt the **Islamic Republic of Iran** and foreign investors are hesitant to get involved. The instability is further compounded by the now quarter of a century rift in **U.S.-Iranian relations** following the 1979 Islamic Revolution.

For the fiscal year 2005, some key economic indicators are as follows: GNP $551.6 billion, GNP growth rate 4.8 percent, per capita income $8,100, labor force 23.68 million, unemployment rate 11.2 percent, inflation rate 16 percent, and a budget deficit of $11.58 billion (revenues of $48.82 billion against expenditures of $60.4 billion). Oil retains its position as the primary sector of the economy. Other industries are not nearly as influential, but have been growing by a 3.5 percent annual rate. These industries include textiles, construction materials, food processing, metals, and weapons manufacture. However, oil accounts for the majority of export **trade** and provides a disproportionate amount of the national income. Without oil the Iranian economy would experience a soaring trade deficit. Thus, despite decades of government efforts at economic diversification, Iran still remains economically tied to a single commodity.

EDUCATION. Secular education in Iran began in the **Qajar** period with the establishment of schools based upon a Western pattern of education. The first such school was the polytechnic **Dar al-Fonun**, founded in 1851 by direction of the early modernizing reformer, **Mirza Taqi Khan Amir Kabir**. Following soon, a Ministry of Science was conceived, established by E'tezad al-Saltaneh. He was appointed the first minister of science in 1858. Prior to the 1850s religious education was the only attainable schooling available in Iran. However, earlier in the 19th century the practice of sending students abroad, both privately and under government auspices, commenced. Throughout the century, numerous students were sent to Europe for higher education. Among the more prominent returnees who made important contributions to Iranian society were **Mirza Saleh Shirazi**, introducer of the printing press and founder of the first newspaper, and the reformer **Mirza Malkom Khan**.

Gradually, after the 1850s, more government schools began opening at all levels. It was a slow process, but by 1925 there were 110,000 students enrolled nationwide. Beginning in 1925, and throughout the reign of **Reza Shah**, the first king of the **Pahlavi Dynasty**, Iran underwent a modernization which included a strong emphasis on educational development. In 1934, **Tehran University** was formed. It was the first facility of comprehensive education that allowed Iran to train students in medicine, theology, law, engineering, literature and science. At this time, women were traditionally only permitted to study in schools of teaching or midwifery. However, one year after the opening of Tehran University, the drive toward modernization prompted Iran to open university doors to women and to enforce a more Western dress code at the schools. Other universities were created. Several additional medical faculties were added in the 1960s as part of **Pahlavi University** (established in 1962, and renamed in 1979 to **Shiraz** University) and Shahid **Beheshti**

University, established in 1960 as **Melli University**, then renamed in 1986.

Iran continued to grow educationally throughout the Pahlavi period and under the **Islamic Republic**. Universal education, though mandated early on, became more practical and widespread as the 20th century progressed. And, the needs of modern society demanded a more educated populace. There have even been attempts to address the educational needs of rural society. A prime example was the 1960s establishment of the **Literary Corps**, a national program to provide rural teachers by substituting teaching service in the corps for mandatory military conscription.

Today, an exceptionally high percentage of Iran's population is of student age. Over 50 percent of the population is under the age of 25 and demands on the educational system are high. General education in Iran is free and compulsory·from the age of six for five years of primary training. Following completion, Iranian children attend three years of lower secondary, three years of upper secondary, and one year of pre-university education. Both the upper secondary and pre-university levels may require tuition depending on the location and institution. The first day of school is traditionally 22 September (Mehr 1). While the curriculum has been transformed repeatedly in recent history, the current model includes a developed vocational education system.

As of 2002, Iran was home to 54 public universities and institutes of higher education, operating under the Ministry of Science, Research and Technology, as well as over 33 private institutions offering both undergraduate and postgraduate courses, many in both sectors operating on multiple campuses. In the academic year 1998-1999, 1,308,150 students were attending institutions of higher learning in Iran, with 52 percent enrolled in private sector programs. In both public and private schools, the proportion of university-level female students averages 43 percent. In 1998, 246,437 students were awarded diplomas from Iranian universities, with 64 percent graduating from private institutions. **Tehran** remains the center of higher academic study in Iran with over 45 facilities for advanced study in a variety of fields within the city. *See also* ALBORZ COLLEGE; FEIZIYEH SEMINARY; HAQQANI SCHOOL; JORDAN, SAMUEL.

ENTEZAM, ABBAS AMIR (1933-). Abbas Amir Entezam, the longest-serving political prisoner in Iran, was born into a middle-class family in **Tehran**. Early on, Entezam began an association with politics. In 1955, at age 22, he became a representative of the **Liberation Movement of Iran (LMI)**, charged with attempting to make contact between the LMI and the U.S. Embassy. However, his service in this function was short lived, and by the following year he left for France to attend the Sorbonne. His **education** concluded in the United States with a postgraduate degree from the University of California, Berkeley. He would remain in the United States, establishing himself as a successful businessman, until the 1970s, when he returned to Iran to be with his ailing mother.

The **Pahlavi** regime prevented Entezam from leaving Iran because of his earlier position with the LMI, so he settled in Iran. In addition to beginning a family, Entezam also regrouped with LMI founder **Mehdi Bazargan**, creating a business partnership. Entezam's engineering company would prove to be quite a successful venture.

After the **Islamic Revolution** and the creation of the **Provisional Government**, Prime Minister Bazargan appointed Entezam as deputy prime minister. Reprising the role he held with the LMI as a liaison with the United States, Entezam attempted to slow the deterioration of relations between **Tehran** and Washington. Still, with the growing power of the radical religious elements, Entezam's position in Iran was precarious. As a means of protection, Bazargan appointed Entezam ambassador to Sweden, and in August 1979, sent him out of the country.

By December 1979, Entezam had returned to Iran, purportedly enticed by a letter of dubious origins. While in the process of returning, the **Students Following the Imam's Line**, the group responsible for the taking of the U.S. Embassy in the Hostage Crisis in November, announced it had found secret documents revealing clandestine connections between Iranians and

U.S. "spies" at the embassy. Among those implicated was Entezam, who was arrested for treason shortly after his arrival in Tehran. It was not until early 1981 that Entezam was finally brought to court, and even then he was not to be allowed legal representation or given a chance to review the so-called incriminating evidence. In June 1981, Entezam was sentenced to life imprisonment.

Entezam spent over 15 years in prison, claiming to have endured both physical and psychological torture. International pressure against his imprisonment increased, including Amnesty International naming him "Prisoner of the Year" in 1991. This pressure combined with recurring health problems led to his release in 1996. However, Entezam became quite outspoken against the government. For instance, in 1998 he gave an interview to the U.S. foreign radio broadcast "Voice of America" in which he claimed the recently deceased head of Evin prison had allowed the torture of Entezam as well as perpetuating deplorable prison conditions. Actions such as this resulted in Entezam being regularly returned to prison for a time before rerelease. In 2005, he was still imprisoned for his latest perceived infringement.

EQBAL, MANUCHEHR (1909-1977). Manuchehr Eqbal was a devoted **Pahlavi** government official who served **Muhammad Reza Shah** in various capacities. Trained in France as a medical doctor, he served first in various health-related capacities, but upon attaining the trust of the Shah, moved into many important political and economic positions extending for over 30 years. Until his death Eqbal remained a close confidant of the Shah, one of a handful which included **Asadollah Alam** and **Ja'far Sharif-Emami**.

Eqbal was appointed as prime minister in 1954 at a time when the **Majlis** was reformed following the disruption of the **Mossadeq** period. His "rubber stamp" Majlis supported the Shah's progressive programs with little or no dissenting opinion. This period was marked by evidence of substantial material progress, along with growing social tension. In 1957, Eqbal accepted the leadership of the newly formed **Hezb-i Melliyun (Na-**

tional Party), one of the two parties formed by the Shah to consolidate his authority. Following the disputatious elections of 1960, Eqbal and his cabinet were forced to resign when the Shah dissolved the Majlis. The post Eqbal held the longest (15 years) and through which he wielded great power and influence was as chairman and managing director of the **National Iranian Oil Company (NIOC)**.

E'TESAMI, PARVIN (1907-1941). Iranian poet Parvin E'tesami was born in the city of **Tabriz** where she lived until her family relocated to **Tehran** in 1912. E'tesami attended primary school in Tehran, though her father and closest companion, Mirza Yusef E'tesami, had begun teaching her Arabic and Persian literature from the age of six while traveling through Iran and Europe. This training led Parvin to compose her first classical style work at the age of eight.

After years of home and public classroom instruction, Yusef E'tesami desired a broader education for his daughter and entered her in the American College for Girls in Tehran. Parvin excelled at the school where she learned English language and Western culture. After her graduation in 1924, Parvin remained at the college for three years as an instructor, until deciding to dedicate all of her time to Persian **poetry**.

Near this time, Yusef E'tesami founded a literary publication called *Bahar* which became the means of distribution for Parvin's poetry among the male-dominated academic and literary circles of early 20th century Iran. Often Parvin participated in gatherings held at the home of her father, reading her works and contributing to discussions of political issues of the day, regularly arriving at the topics of poverty, **women**'s rights and education, and the oppressive regime of **Reza Shah**. In this setting Parvin began to cultivate a strong sense of social justice while being described as an exemplary Muslim woman by her peers.

This sense of justice and a growing resentment toward the Shah's regime prompted Parvin to refuse a position in the court as tutor to the Queen in 1927, and later to refuse a medal honoring her contribution to Persian literature.

In 1934, Parvin married, only to divorce within three months, a setback that could not compare to the death of her father four years later. The death of Yusef E'tesami crushed Parvin, causing her to separate from her literary peers, as well as to lose means of distribution to predominantly male literary circles. Only three years later, at the age of 35, Parvin succumbed to typhoid fever and was buried next to her father in **Qum**.

During her life, Parvin E'tesami's 210 poetic works were known throughout Iran for focusing on education of the masses, the plight of the destitute and orphaned, and later in her writing, on Iranian women and their lack of education and social access. In the world of literature, E'tesami is known for the style of *monazere*, or debate, in her works. In this technique she used imagery to present two counterarguments, finishing with E'tesami's own observation as the conclusion to the debate.

While Parvin E'tesami's first collection of poetry was published in 1935, her completed works would not be published until 1954, well after her death. Time did not diminish the popularity of the *Divan-i Parvin* which was reprinted six times over the next 20 years. Her legacy was substantial. Once referred to as "A Queen of a Poetess," many a modern Iranian poet found inspiration in the life and works of Parvin E'tesami.

EXPEDIENCY COUNCIL. From its inception, the **Council of Guardians**, charged with ensuring that legislation conformed to Sharia, was constantly at odds with the **Majlis**. Able to veto legislation by the Majlis, the Council of Guardians regularly thwarted reforms attempted by the Majlis. In an attempt to overcome some of these deadlocks, on 6 February, 1988, **Ayatollah Ruhollah Khomeini** formed the Expediency Council (*Majma'i Tashkhis-i Maslahat-i Nezam*). This body's main purpose was to override vetoes issued by the Council of Guardians.

Though not in the **Constitution of the Islamic Republic** at the time, Khomeini exerted his power as *Faqih* to form the Expediency Council. As first constituted, the Expediency Council consisted of 13 members: six members of the Council of Guardians, six parliamentary deputies, and the cabinet minister directly concerned with the issue at hand. With the relevant minister as a temporary member, the members of the Council of Guardians (religious power) were outnumbered by politicians.

With the revision of the Constitution in 1989, the Expediency Council was provided for by Article 112, though in a slightly modified form. In addition to the relevant minister being a temporary member on a case-by-case basis, the chair of the involved parliamentary committee was also included, ostensibly putting the Council of Guardian members in a definite minority.

Despite this seeming slant towards the political sphere, some have criticized the Expediency Council as a symbol of the *Faqih*'s autocratic power. The Council in its form before being solidified in the revamped 1989 Constitution could not only override vetoes, but could—under the letter of Khomeini's pronouncement—actually formulate its own legislation. Even after this power was removed by the Constitution, the practice continued.

The Expediency Council also has other functions in addition to its primary one of reconciling disputes between the Majlis and Council of Guardians. The Expediency Council can also be presented various issues by the *Faqih*, in a consultative function. In the occurrence that the Supreme Leader dies, resigns, or is dismissed, the Expediency Council appoints a member of the Council of Guardians to the Leadership Council—also consisting of the president and the head of judiciary—to perform the functions of the *Faqih* in the interim between the loss of the *Faqih* and the appointment of a new *Faqih* by the **Assembly of Experts**.

In March 1997, Supreme Leader **Ayatollah Ali Khamene'i** revamped the Expediency Council in an attempt to solidify its central power. He expanded its membership to 25 members, as appointed by the *Faqih* (in this case himself), and placed former President **Ali Akbar Hashemi-Rafsanjani** as the body's new head. Each of the appointees serves a five-year term. Five years later, the balance of power had definitely shifted. In 2002, Khamene'i appointed new members, drawing the ire of reformists after increasing the number of religiously conservative members.

-F-

FAQIH. A *faqih* is a legal expert or jurisprudent who is regarded by Muslims as capable of interpreting Islamic law (Sharia). The term took on a peculiar twist with the establishment of the **Islamic Republic of Iran** in conjunction with the concept of **Velayat-i Faqih**, which refers to government by the jurist-scholar. In this form of theocratic government, articulated in the book *Velayat-i Faqih* (*Guardianship of the Jurist*) written by **Ayatollah Ruhollah Khomeini** long before the revolution, the Faqih is the foremost religious authority and serves as both judge and leader for the **Shiah** community. Political legitimacy belongs to the Faqih and though he holds no formal political office, his capacity to intervene in state affairs is unlimited. He is considered to be the representative or trustee of the **Hidden Imam** and he possesses all power regarding religious, political, social, or legal matters. Though several men may hold the designation of Faqih concurrently, they are enjoined to settle legal questions by consensus and present a unified decision. *See also* ISLAM.

FARDUST, HUSSEIN (1919-1988). Hussein Fardust was the son of an Army lieutenant. He was hand picked by **Reza Shah** to be a classmate of the crown prince, completing his schooling in Switzerland with **Muhammad Reza Shah**. Rising quickly in the military ranks, as a colonel, he was an instructor at the Military College in **Tehran**. Fardust headed the Shah's Imperial Inspectorate, and ironically later headed **Ayatollah Ruhollah Khomeini**'s secret police.

Fardust long held the post of inspector general and was considered to be a close confidant of the Shah. Operating independently of **SAVAK**, the Imperial Inspectorate was a feared security agency. Fardust reported only to the Shah and was very loyal to him. He discreetly checked information that he had received from other officials. He made unpublicized trips around the country investigating military matters as well as civilian governmental activities. His reports could easily result in the termination of a career or even in criminal action that brought corrupt officials into disrepute.

Major General Hussein Fardust was deputy director of SAVAK until the early 1970s when the Shah promoted him to the directorship of the Special Intelligence Bureau. SAVAK was formed under the guidance of U.S. and Israeli intelligence officers in 1957. The CIA trained SAVAK until 1961. This was halted as an attempt to reduce Iran's dependency on the United States, and SAVAK began to develop its own training program under the direction of Fardust. By 1966, SAVAK had developed the capability to train all its personnel in the fundamentals of intelligence work.

Despite his long-standing priviledged position and presumed loyalty to the Shah, Fardust turned against the **Pahlavi** regime. Some attribute a pivotal role to Fardust in the paralyzing of the military forces at a key point in the **Islamic Revolution** of 1979. He is said to have instructed the withholding of reinforcements on 10 February, 1979 for the embattled Imperial Guard, the most important force supporting the **Shapur Bakhtiar** government. Fardust had himself been a long-time major player in the Shah's patrimonial control of the Iranian military and was positioned to exercise decisive influence over the wavering generals the Shah left in command when he left the country only days before. He is known to have been in secret dialogue with **Mehdi Bazargan** and **Ayatollah Muhammad Hussein Beheshti** and may well have cut a deal. It is, perhaps, indicative that upon the collapse of the Pahlavi regime, he was appointed the first director of SAVAK's successor agency SAVAMA, the secret police of the new **Islamic Republic**.

The turncoat act of Fardust did not make him immune to the revolution turning on its own children. He was accused of being a Soviet informer, and was arrested as such in 1985. In a 1988 television "confession," Fardust "exposed" the inner secrets of the Pahlavi royal palace, the very palace to which he was previously so loyal. In a paranoid-like rambling he charged that Reza Shah was a closet **Bahai** and accused Muhammad Reza Shah of having secret connections with British organizations and British royalty. He died a few weeks after the airing of these confessions. Three years later, Fardust's more detailed memoirs were released in both English and Persian. They included, amongst other things, a slander against Ernest Perron, a childhood friend of the Shah in Le Rosey School in Switzerland that was also attended by Fardust. He claimed that Perron had been planted by the British to seduce the young crown prince. In addition, he accused Perron of heading a royal court-based homosexual clique.

The full impact of the twisted career of Major General Hussein Fardust is yet to be revealed. It is known that he lived the majority of his life in the loyal service of the Shah. Ironically, he died in the service of Khomeini, and was successful in tarnishing the reputation of the order he had served since childhood.

FARROKHZAD, FORUGH (1935-1967). One of relatively few women in Iran who have been recognized for their achievements outside the home is modern poet Forugh Farrokhzad. One of seven children, Farrokhzad was born into a middle class family in **Tehran**. She attended public school through the ninth grade, and also received training in sewing and painting. At the age of 16 she married. Within a year of that union, Farrokhzad had her only son, who she addressed in "A Poem for You." Several years later Farrokhzad filed for divorce and relinquished her son to her ex-husband's family in order to pursue poetry and the independent lifestyle she had desired. However, this new stage of liberation was not an easy transition for Farrokhzad and is reflected in poems such as "The Deserted Home," in which she admits that leaving her husband and child had deprived their home of "the happiness of life." By the mid-1950s she was clearly voicing her opinion about conventional marriage and the plight of independently minded women living in Iran with poems such as *"The Captive," "Call to Arms,"* and *"The Wedding Band."*

Farrokhzad published five books of poems, *The Captive, The Wall, Rebellion, Another Birth,* and *Let Us Believe in the Beginning of the Cold Season.* She was influenced in her poetic life by such poets as **Nader Naderpour**, Nosrat Rahmani, **Nima Yushij** and, later, Yadollah Roya'i. While Farrokhzad had largely followed the "New Poetry" style of Nima Yushij in her earlier works, her outspoken rebellion against tradition and norms gave her the freedom to experiment and develop her own style. Rather than simply writing poems that describe the unhappiness of women she began to use her poetry to discuss societal issues, and erotic subjects that had not traditionally been discussed. The most powerful virtue of her poetic vision was her insistence on the sacredness of women and the beauty of sex.

Farrokhzad's independent lifestyle, erotic tone, and outspoken criticism of various social customs elicited considerable disapproval inside Iran. She participated in several short-term relationships with men, one of which she describes in "The Sin," stating, "I sinned a sin of full pleasure." In 1958, Farrokhzad met her life partner, controversial filmmaker and writer, Ibrahim Gulistan. In the 1960s, Farrokhzad made a short documentary movie about a leper colony entitled *The House Is Black*. The film was acclaimed internationally and won several prizes.

On 14 February, 1967, about four years after the publication of *Another Birth*, Farrokhzad was involved in a fatal car accident. In 1975 her last collection, *Let Us Believe in the Beginning of the Cold Season*, was published. The strength of her last two books granted her a place among the greatest contemporary poets, those who have played an important role in the development of modern Persian poetry.

Of particular note has been the influence of Farrokhzad's poetry on many modern female poets and, as well, the impact that her emotional insights into the feminine world have had across the modern Iranian literary world and in the field of literary criticism. Her own self-transformation, evident in the evolution of her poetry, produced a body of work that demanded a reexamination of traditional social conventions. As a consequence, Farrokhzad is sometimes referred to as a "social poet," in the same vein as such poets as **Mehdi Akhavan Sales** and **Ahmad Shamlu**. From an historical perspective, despite the few productive years of this brilliant talent whose life was tragically cut short, Farrokhzad endures as a paragon of social and psychological commentary and critique. *See also* BEHBAHANI, SIMIN; E'TESAMI, PARVIN.

FARSI. *See* PERSIAN LANGUAGE.

FATH ALI SHAH (Ruled 1797-1834). Fath Ali Shah, uncle to **Agha Muhammad Khan Qajar**, was the second king of the **Qajar Dynasty**. He was noted for his long black beard and several hundred wives and children. His successors inherited many problems related to the size of the idle aristocracy he created. During the reign of Fath Ali Shah, there was a significant increase in clerical influence in the state. A pious king who also fancied himself somewhat of a religious scholar, Fath Ali Shah bestowed the largesse of the state on mosques, shrines, religious schools, and gifts to leading members of the ulama. He also cultivated personal relationships with the most learned and influential religious figures, deferring often to their advice. This policy, and the long reign of Fath Ali Shah, led to a revival of religious learning in Iran during the early decades of the 19th century. It also resulted in a pattern of intervention in the political realm by the formal religious establishment which has characterized clergy-state relations in Iran from that time forward.

While religious **education** received a boost thanks to the reigning monarch's religious policy, the reign of Fath Ali Shah also witnessed the first development towards a Western-style educational system. Crown Prince **Abbas Mirza** sent the first Iranian students for study abroad. He sent two students to England in 1811. In 1815, he sent five more students to England. Several of these students were later to make important contributions to Iranian society. Of particular note was the career of **Mirza Saleh Shirazi**, who introduced the first printing press to Iran and later edited and published the first official newspaper of Iran in 1837.

Under the reign of Fath Ali Shah, the initial contacts in what was to quickly become a "new" relationship between Iran and the West occurred. In 1801, a military alliance was agreed upon by a representative of British India and Persia. Both sides saw the alliance as mutually beneficial against what at the time were their common threats: the French, the Russians, and the Afghans. However, after Great Britain and Russia had a warming of relations, this alliance became strained. Britain was reluctant to aid the Persians against the expansionism of the Russian Empire in the Caucasus. Fath Ali Shah turned to the French. In 1807, a pact with Napoleon, the **Treaty of Finkenstein**, was signed, and the agreement with the British was negated. The French sent a military mission and began an attempt to modernize the Persian Army under the leadership of General Gardane. Little resulted as the Franco-Persian Alliance was short lived. Napoleon lost interest after his defeat in Russia.

The Irano-Russian conflict continued in the Caucasus, and Fath Ali Shah once again turned to the British for an ally. The British responded this time by sending a representative directly from London. The result was the **Preliminary Treaty** of 1809, the first in a succession of Anglo-Persian treaties that established diplomatic relations between the two countries, and placed Iran firmly within the orbit of European power politics. As the French had before them, the British sent a military mission to Iran to reform the army on a Western model.

The sporadic reform attempts of Fath Ali Shah, or more precisely, by the Crown Prince Abbas Mirza who spearheaded the effort to modernize the military, failed to achieve any power balance and, perhaps, even weakened the ability of Iran to resist foreign encroachment. Indeed, the outcome of hostilities with Russia in the Caucasus was the disastrous **Treaty of Gulistan** (1813) in which Iran ceded territory and granted concessions. Iran fared even worse when hostilities broke out again and a second war was waged against Russia. The result was the **Treaty of Turkmanchai** (1828) which weakened Iran to such an extent that it all but destroyed Persian sovereignty.

The sorry episode of military reform during the Fath Ali Shah period illustrated well the "new relationship" that Iran had entered with the West. The stage was set for the pattern which held for the following century. Iran was presumably independent, but rival imperialisms dominated events and left little room for Iran to maneuver between the interests of the Great European Powers. *See also* DEFINITIVE TREATY OF 1812; TEHRAN TREATY OF 1814.

FEDA'IYAN-I ISLAM. The Feda'iyan-i **Islam** (Devotees of Islam) was a religiously oriented group established in 1946 by Seyyid Navab Safavi to fight secular elements in society and foreign influences in Iran. This conservative right-wing party had a limited, traditional middle-class membership composed mainly of lower echelon **bazaar** merchants. It was dogmatically committed to the reinstatement of fundamentalist Islam in all areas of Iranian life. The Feda'iyan-i Islam was essentially a fringe political group that nonetheless represented the concerns of an important traditional middle-class constituency.

The group resorted to extremist tactics and was responsible for the assassination of many influential Iranians. The first organized act of the Feda'iyan-i Islam was the assassination in 1946 of **Ahmad Kasravi**, a noted essayist and historian accused of anti-Islamic themes in his writings. The assassins were acquitted by a military court which was reportedly influenced by the lobbying efforts of religious leaders. Five years later the group was implicated in the assassination of Prime Minister Ali Razmara.

Despite being repressed, the membership continued its activities alone and in concert with **Ayatollah Abol Qasem Mostafavi Kashani**'s Society of Muslim Warriors, a **National Front** offshoot. In the early 1950s, the Feda'iyan-i Islam cooperated with **Muhammad Mossadeq** during the movement to nationalize the Iranian **oil** industry, but never formally became a part of the National Front. Though most widely known for their assassinations, the Feda'iyan-i Islam also organized bazaar strikes, encouraged public support for the Palestinians, and staged violent demonstrations against the **Pahlavi** regime. However, even Kashani, who sympathized with the political views of the group, broke with them in 1951 over the tactics of political terrorism.

Following the departure of Mossadeq and the subsequent suppression of all militant opposition parties, the membership of the Feda'iyan-i Islam dwindled, and its activities were later taken over by the new guerilla organizations which emerged in the early 1960s. Remnants of the group reappeared during the late 1970s to take part in **Ayatollah Ruhollah Khomeini**'s Islamic revolutionary movement.

FEIZIYEH SEMINARY. Located in the holy center of **Qum,** approximately 140 kilometers south of **Tehran,** the Feiziyeh Seminary is one of the largest and most famous **Shiah** schools of religious sciences in the world. The Feiziyeh Seminary is regarded by many to be the ideological epicenter of the **Islamic Revolution** of 1979, led by the seminary's most famous student and teacher, **Ayatollah Ruhollah Khomeini.** Khomeini developed his thoughts on the concept of *Vilayat-i Faqih,* the God-given authority of a supreme leader to govern the affairs of both religion and politics, while at the seminary. His version of the *Vilayat-i Faqih,* adopted after the Islamic Revolution in the **Constitution of the Islamic Republic,** is what dominates Iranian government to this day.

Not only known as an important theological school of Twelver Shi'ism, the Feiziyeh Seminary is also renowned for its beauty. The actual structure was originally built in the 13th century under the command of the **Safavid** king Shah Tahmasb the First. Originally known as the Astaneh School, the name was later changed to Feiziyeh after one of its famous teachers, Mohsen Feiz Kashani. During the **Qajar** era the structure was expanded and beautifully reembellished. The large rectangular courtyard features lush gardens with a pool in the center. From the courtyard students can see the inner walls covered with beautiful yellow, blue, and turquoise mosaics. Each side of the courtyard is patterned with high arches standing two stories high. Another striking feature of the seminary is that it is adjoined to the famous Shrine of Hazrat Massoumeh. A gateway from Feiziyeh leads directly to the courtyard of the holy shrine, which houses the Tomb of Fatima, the sister of Imam Reza, sixth in the **Shiah** line of imams. The shrine complex also houses the tombs of a number of Safavid kings and Muslim saints, and is the object of pilgrimage for many Shiah muslims.

In contemporary times, among the most notable students and teachers of the Feiziyeh Seminary were Hojjat Al-Islam **Ali Akbar Hashemi-Rafsanjani, Ayatollah Mahmud Taleqani,** and **Ayatollah Hussein Ali Montezari,** all of whom were connected in their stance against the **Pahlavi** regime and active during the Islamic Revolution. But most famous is Ayatollah Ruhollah

Khomeini, the father of the Islamic Revolution. It was there in 1963 that Khomeini made a series of anti-Shah speeches in opposition to the **White Revolution**, which prompted **Muhammad Reza Shah** to respond militarily, killing a number of students and damaging the seminary. Further, the Shah exiled Khomeini and closed the seminary. Later reopened, the seminary served as a base for students who acted as a bulwark in opposition to the Shah and his policies.

In 1975, the seminary was closed once again. From exile in Najaf, Iraq, Ayatollah Khomeini made a series of subversive speeches against the Shah's newly formed **Rastakhiz Party**, which further served to spread unrest, particularly among religious students. In another show of solidarity against the Shah, students at the Feiziyeh held demonstrations within the seminary on the anniversary of the murderous siege of 1963. A crowd of demonstrators also gathered outside the seminary in protest. After three days, government troops once again attacked the seminary, ransacking it and arresting over 250 students. Many were injured and at least one was killed during the episode. A second time, the seminary was closed, and it was not until after the Islamic Revolution that Feiziyeh was reopened.

Today, the seminary attracts students from all over the world, who study there because of its reputation in religious sciences and knowledge. It houses about 500 students and accepts others who do not live on site. It has become somewhat modernized, with an updated library boasting over 120,000 titles and an electronic book index. Political instability in the Shiah holy city of Najaf, Iraq, during the 1980s caused a large exodus of clerics from that city to Qum, adding to the status of the Feiziyeh Seminary as one of the world's preeminent Shiah religious schools.

FERDOWSI, ABOL QASEM (d. 1025). Ferdowsi is considered among the greatest poets of Persia. He was the compiler of the *Shahnameh*, or *The Book of Kings*. He was born in **Khorasan** in the village of Tus, an area which was a bastion of traditional Persian culture. The ancient heritage of Persia, before **Islam**, was still warm in the memories of the people, which probably influenced his enthusiasm towards the past grandeur of the Persian Empires. Ferdowsi composed the *Shahnameh* in 50,000 rhymed couplets. It is a compilation of mythical and historical stories that compose the Iranian national epic. Prior to Ferdowsi, the *Shahnameh* had remained an oral tradition, although there was at least one earlier prose work composed in Pahlavi or Middle Persian to which Ferdowsi had access. Ferdowsi began serious work on the *Shahnameh* after the death of the eminent poet Daqiqi in 980. Daqiqi had been commissioned by monarchs of the Samanid Dynasty to turn prose versions of the national epic into **poetry**, but he died before accomplishing much. Ferdowsi picked up the task and labored for 35 years to produce what came to be the definitive *Shahnameh*. Other versions of stories in the *Shahnameh* were in circulation both before and after Ferdowsi, but these largely disappeared due to the monumental success of Ferdowsi's version.

After finishing the work, Ferdowsi presented it to Sultan Mahmud of Ghazna, ruler of Khorasan at the time. Sultan Mahmud paid Ferdowsi only a fraction of what had been promised, prompting a bitter response from Ferdowsi in the form of a satire placed within the preface of the *Shahnameh*. Eventually, Sultan Mahmud reconsidered and sent full payment, but too late to rescue Ferdowsi from a life of impoverishment. Though born into wealth, Ferdowsi had exhausted his resources writing the *Shahnameh* and died poor and ill, just as his literary fame began to dawn. To the present day, Ferdowsi's name and his recounting of the tales of the Iranian epic are alive and very much current on the lips of the vast majority of Iranians. See also POETRY; *SHAHNAMEH*, CHARACTERS OF.

FREEDOM MOVEMENT OF IRAN. *See* LIBERATION MOVEMENT OF IRAN.

FRYE, RICHARD NELSON (1920-). Frye is a scholar and educator specializing in ancient Near Eastern studies. He is a prolific writer on pre-Islamic Iran. Appointed to an endowed chair at Harvard University, he has enjoyed a long and distinguished academic career. Educated at Harvard and in London, Frye served as a research analyst for the Office of Strategic Services (OSS) in World War II. He later served as the executive secretary of the Near East Committee of the American Council of Learned Societies from 1948 to 1950. He served as director of the Asia Institute at the **Pahlavi University** in **Shiraz** from 1969 to 1974. Among his more important works are *Heritage of Persia* and *The Golden Age of Persia: The Arabs in the East*. Most recently, Frye has written an account of his own career in the book *Greater Iran: A 20th Century Odyssey*.

-G-

GANJI, AKBAR (1959-). A one-time member of the **Revolutionary Guards** and official within the Ministry of Islamic Culture and Guidance, Akbar Ganji electrified the Iranian reformist movement and enraged the hardliners with his investigative journalism in the late 1990s and into 2000. From a modest upbringing, Ganji eventually attained a university degree in sociology, as well as became well versed in Western philosophy. He was also devoutly Muslim, and with this combination of both social theory and religious devotion, the ideals of the **Islamic Revolution** and **Ayatollah Ruhollah Khomeini** held great appeal to the young Ganji. In addition to honing his rhetorical skills as a propagandist for the **Islamic Republic**, Ganji even served for a time as one of Khomeini's bodyguards.

As the Republic progressed, Ganji began to feel disillusioned by the oppressive means some of the conservative elements within the government used to protect the system. By the 1990s, he had become decidedly pro-reform in his outlook, and he used the skills he had developed in his **education** and within the government to become an activist journalist. Several **reformist press** newspapers published his articles, most notably *Sobh-i Emruz* (*This Morning*), published by his close friend **Sa'id Hajjerian**.

It was his investigation of the murder of four reformists in 1998 that elevated Akbar Ganji to folk hero status. In a series of articles, in *Sobh-i Emruz*, he revealed evidence of government and clerical involvement in these murders, as well as the system of cover-ups employed to protect those involved. Much of his information was suspected to have been supplied by Sa'id Hajjerian, who had been a member of the Ministry of Intelligence and still had connections. Though the articles were cryptic at first, not directly naming individuals, Ganji soon fingered **Ali Akbar Hashemi-Rafsanjani** for having known about these types of murderous practices dating all the way back to his presidency. Ganji had broken an unwritten rule of journalists in the Islamic Republic, namely to never criticize government officials. His accusations led not only to much personal popularity amongst the Iranian public, but also dealt a harsh blow to Hashemi-Rafsanjani's 2000 bid for a seat in the **Majlis**.

Angered and likely fearful of more accusations, hardliners searched for a way to silence Ganji. When he attended the infamous **Berlin Conference** in 2000, which was labeled "anti-Islamic," Ganji was arrested along with other notable attendees, including **Liberation Movement of Iran (LMI)** leader **Ezzatollah Sahabi** and celebrated writer **Mahmud Dowlatabadi**. Ganji used his trial to make new shocking revelations. He reiterated his claims against Hashemi-Rafsanjani, but also claimed Ali Fallahian, whom Ganji had only referred to as "Master Key" in articles, had ordered the murders while intelligence minister. He blamed the powerful judge Mohseni Ejei for ordering the murder of Piruz Davani, a Marxist who vanished after the murders in question. He also lambasted Ayatollah Taqi Mesbah Yazdi, and the **Haqqani School** to which he was attached, not only for advocating the murder of "apostates" (read reformists), but also for installing themselves in appointed governmental positions which allowed the perpetuation of such heinous crimes.

Not surprisingly, Akbar Ganji received an 11-year sentence, the longest of any of those convicted in connection with the **Berlin Conference**. He regularly staged hunger strikes to protest conditions at Evin Prison, where he was incarcerated. By 2005, his lawyer, Nobel Laureate **Shirin Ebadi**, argued Ganji was in need of better health care, and possibly an amnesty, due to his deteriorating health, exacerbated by his hunger strikes and prison conditions. As of 2006, he is still imprisoned.

GHARBZADEGI (WESTRUCKNESS). The concept of *gharbzadegi*, or "Weststruckness," is most simply described as the process of detrimental Western principles and conduct being purposefully inflicted upon an unassuming or mesmerized East. The term was originally coined by the Persian intellectual Ahmad Fardid, who likened the effect of Western modernization on the East to a destructive force wreaking havoc on an ecosystem. The term was rescued from obscurity by the modern Iranian writer, **Jalal Al-e Ahmad**, who used it to title his 1962 treatise which outlined the impact of *gharbzadegi* on Iran in particular. He likened the effect to symptoms of a poisoning illness.

The basis of Al-e Ahmad's claim was that Western imperialist capitalists had taken advantage of the collapse of the Ottoman Empire to incite nationalism within the newly created separate states, thereby destroying the cohesive unity of the Middle East with **Islam** as its core. Al-e Ahmad also contended that the world was split into two "blocks"—the producers of the machine and the buyers of the machine—with the West (Europe, Japan, South Africa, Israel and the United States) owning the machine and the East, or the developing countries (Asia, Africa, and Latin America), needing the machine. In particular, Al-e Ahmad saw Iran as falling prey to the plot by the embracing of the vague concept of modernization espoused by the regime of **Reza Shah**.

Focusing on Iran, the author felt the installation of a Western-approved leader (**Muhammad Reza Shah**) who pushed modernization, and dependence and interaction with the United States, was the culmination of the *gharbzadegi* "infection" and the end of Iranian national identity. Al-e Ahmad contended that Western-style **education** pushed by the **Pahlavi** regime, based on Christianity, alienated Iran from its religion, culture, and social structure. Next, the machine of "modernization" began a premature urbanization of Iran, destroying villages and **agriculture**, and forcing Iranians to become reliant on consuming Western food, grains, and other products, eventually ruining the Iranian **economy**. Additionally, the **women** of Iran were superficially liberated in the name of modernization, argued Al-e Ahmad, without any sort of rationalization of the social significance, leaving them to fall into the trap of Western sexuality and, in reality, a deeper form of oppression.

In his writing Al-e Ahmad argued that *gharbzadegi* is a disease to be feared and fought. He maintained that the people of Iran have been blinded by the allure of Western life. Many have argued that *gharbzadegi* was only curbed by the **Islamic Revolution** in Iran which used the concept as a driving force. Some would argue that the youngest generation of Iranians, not remembering the forces that fueled the revolution and led to the establishment of an **Islamic Republic** in 1979, has already been infected by a new strain of "Weststruckness." It is not at all clear that Al-e Ahmad himself, deceased in 1969 and not witness to the revolution, would have approved of the instrumental use of his concept in the fashion that prevailed. His solution to "Weststruckness" was not likely to have been a substitution of one form of despotism for another.

GOLSHIRI, HUSHANG (1937-2000). For over a period of 30 years, Hushang Golshiri created some of the finest contemporary Iranian **literature**. He was born into a middle-class Iranian family in the city of **Isfahan**. He began showing interest in literature after falling in love with a British teacher of English language and literature, and meeting a group of young people who were fascinated by the postwar French literature of the 1920s. Another important literary influence was his wife, Farzaneh Taheri, herself a literary critic and translator.

The works of Golshiri found favor with both the literary elite and common readers due to his ability to use modern writing techniques coupled with his excellent command of the **Persian language** and sound grounding in classical literature. His writing exhibits great storytelling abilities. The first collection of short stories by Golshiri was about the monotonous lives of small-town office workers, published in 1968 under the title *As Always*.

He is best known, however, as a novelist. The novel that Golshiri is most famous for is *Prince Ehtejab*, published in 1968. It was later turned into a film which was distributed abroad and achieved some international acclaim. Golshiri used his books and writing abilities to question the integrity of those who served under **Muhammad Reza Shah**'s command, as evident in the 1975 short story collection, *My Little Prayer Room*. This is the primary reason most of Golshiri's literature was banned from Iran during the **Pahlavi** period. Nor did the situation change under the government of the **Islamic Republic** since Golshiri continued to champion freedom of expression and promoted democracy and human rights. In the 1990s, Golshiri smuggled his book, *King of the Benighted*, to the United States to be published in English under a pen name (Ardeshir Mohasses). Confirmation that Golshiri was the author only surfaced after his death. His book depicted religious fanatics who wished to revert back to the Middle Ages. For his last great work, *The Book of Genies*, Golshiri left Iran several times in order to complete it because of the constant harassment of the press and authorities.

In 1998, two of Iran's secular authors paid with their lives for public advocacy of freedom and human rights when security agents murdered them. At their funeral, Golshiri gave a moving speech that was labeled the "most defiant statement by an Iranian writer in recent years." In Germany, he was awarded the Erich Maria Remarque Peace Prize in 1999 for his consistent efforts in defiance of oppression and human rights advocacy. Though his writings clearly had a sharp edge of social and political critique, Golshiri always kept a sense of humor and never allowed his literary genius to degenerate into polemics. Instead, he set the focus of his work on the condition of humanity and drove his point home through allegories.

GOOGOOSH (1950–). Born Fa'eqeh Atashin, the girl who would come to be known worldwide as a famous entertainment icon, Googoosh got an early start in the entertainment world of Iran. Googoosh's father, an entertainer himself, raised Googoosh in **Tehran**, early on encouraging her to perform. By the time she was three years old Googoosh was already amazing audiences in the bars and clubs of Tehran with her singing. When she was seven, she appeared in her first film *Bim Va Omid*, with subsequent roles following.

Her fame seemed only to accelerate. Her movie roles and performances attracted the attention of Iranian songwriters and record producers, and by the 1960s, Googoosh began a recording career that would not only make her an Iranian pop culture icon, but an internationally renowned artist as well. Throughout the 1960s and 1970s, Googoosh recorded over 200 songs in Farsi, not to mention countless projects in other languages.

Googoosh's popularity had an impact on Iranian youth and pop culture not unlike the pop stars of the West. Young people filled large venues throughout Iran to see her performances. Her films were very popular with the people, if not the critics (although the 1970s avant-garde film *Bita* did achieve for Googoosh an acting award). The streets of Iran's cities were filled with young **women** imitating Googoosh's fashions and hairstyles. She was, perhaps, the most recognized face in Iran in the 1970s.

However, as is often the case in the entertainment industry, the business behind Googoosh's fame was not as positive as public appearances indicated. Googoosh was unavoidably involved with the unscrupulous forces that controlled certain sectors of the performance world. A club owner named Parviz Ghorbani manipulated Googoosh's finances to ensure she would be irrecoverably indebted to him. He exploited this situation to force a marriage upon her in 1973. Though the marriage resulted in a son, it did not last long and by 1976 Googoosh had already moved onto another short-lived marriage with Iranian superstar actor Behrooz Vosoughi.

Though tribulations like this did not stall Googoosh's career, the **Islamic Revolution** did. The **Islamic Republic** banned female solo recording artists, as well as the types of movie roles for which Googoosh was known. Rather than go into exile from her homeland to continue her career, Googoosh went into a de facto retirement, becoming nearly reclusive throughout the years following the revolution. Still, her music was not forgotten and a large black market in illicitly produced Googoosh recordings flourished in Iran. Though she had not publicly performed or recorded anything in years, by the 1990s youth of a new generation were still discovering her music. With the growing power of reformists and **Muhammad Khatami**'s election in 1997, Googoosh's music could be heard more openly, although still not legally.

In the midst of this new atmosphere of relative openness, Googoosh left Iran to resume her music career. Iranian expatriates and fans around the world welcomed her triumphal return to music in 2000. She not only toured North America, Europe, and the Middle East, but also released her first new album since the Islamic Revolution. The album, *Zoroaster*, set the stage for a return that would also include a subsequent album, *Khabar*, which set a record for most sales of a Farsi-language album. Thanks to a massive Iranian audience in exile, longing for reminiscences of a culture gone astray, Googoosh's return to show business was in some ways more successful than her pre-revolution work. For those in exile, Googoosh not only reminded them of a long lost youth, but of a place that no longer existed.

GRANT, ASAHEL (1807-1844). Dr. Grant was a medical doctor turned missionary who served under the auspices of the **American Board of Commissioners for Foreign Missions**. He was the second American Protestant missionary to arrive in Iran, joining **Justin Perkins** in **Azerbaijan**. There the two established a mission in **Urmieh** which was to remain a center of the Protestant mission for nearly 100 years.

Grant believed that the Nestorians were remnants of the lost tribes of Israel and wrote a book entitled *The Nestorians or the Lost Tribes*. From 1835 to 1844 he worked with the **Christian** Nestorians and the Muslim **Kurds**. Respected by the two communities, though they were enemies and uneasy neighbors, Grant carried on his medical work with both. He died of typhus in 1844 while caring for the victims of an epidemic.

GROSECLOSE, ELGIN EARL (1899-1983). Groseclose was an economist and author who taught at the American mission school in **Tehran** and was secretary of the Persian Relief Commission. He was a special assistant to **Arthur Millspaugh's** economic mission and was appointed treasurer-general of Iran by the Iranian Parliament, or **Majlis**, in 1943. Groseclose wrote a history entitled *Introduction to Iran*, as well as novels based on his experiences in Persia.

-H-

HAFEZ (1320-1391). Hafez, the "sweet singer of **Shiraz**," was born in that city in 1320. He perfected the ghazal form of Persian **poetry** in his writing and within it he celebrates the human nature of man rather than the divine. Though his poetry is composed in the **Sufi** mystical tradition, doubt exists as to whether he was actually a true Sufi. Hafez's poems maintain a skeptical balance between the religious and the profane—the divine and the sensual—which lends more realism than mysticism to his work, exhibiting an earthier character than traditional Sufi poetry. He acknowledges normal human needs and, unlike those who would ignore or consider them sinful, he accepts the inadequacies of this world and dwells on the sweetness of it. He lyricizes the beauty of roses without avoiding the inevitability of thorns.

For many years, Hafez wrote under the patronage of princes and noblemen in Shiraz, but complaints from religious authorities forced him to be temporarily banished from his beloved city. The clergy disapproved of his irregular lifestyle and accused him of using his verse to encourage dissolute practices and unorthodox opinions among the common people. His writings found more favor with the German poet Johann Wolfgang von Goethe, who credits Hafez with inspiring lyrical works of his own. It is believed that many of Hafez's works contain veiled political commentary or allusions to social conflict, but many of the allusions have been lost in time, and what remains is the music and the charm of the verses he composed. The simple **Persian language** and style he utilized in his poetry continue to make him popular among Persians to this day, both poetically and for purposes of divination. The collected poetry of Hafez is often used by the common person to foretell the future by randomly opening the work and pointing to a verse, which when read augurs whatever question fills the mind of the seeker.

HAJJERIAN, SA'ID. (1954-). A former Ministry of Intelligence official and Islamic revolutionary activist (he had participated in the taking of the **American Hostages in Iran** in 1979), Sa'id Hajjerian became a centerpiece of the reform movement in Iran that would emerge in the early 1990s. Like many others, Hajjerian felt concerned over the loss of voice of the left in Iranian politics. After **Ayatollah Ruhollah Khomeini**'s death in 1989, conservatives solidified their hold on the **Islamic Republic**, leading much of the left wing of the government to search for new avenues of political voice. Thus, Hajjerian thrust himself into the political landscape, developing an ideology of pro-democratic reform soon after he left the Ministry of Intelligence in the late 1980s.

Hajjerian's views would become more accepted as the 1990s progressed. As varying views within the emerging reformist camp came into conflict, Hajjerian expertly worked at compromise, helping make the reform movement more cohesive and thus effective. He worked with his friend **Muhammad Khatami** to develop a political strategy that would raise Khatami to the presidency in 1997. With the burst of energy from the reformers that followed, Hajjerian and several others, including Muhammad Reza Khatami—President Khatami's brother—created the Islamic Iran Participation Front (IIPF), a new reformist political party. Through the efforts of Hajjerian, who was also serving as one of President Khatami's chief advisers and political strategists, IIPF reformists won massive victories in the 1999 local elections and the 2000 **Majlis** elections. In fact, Hajjerian himself was elected to the **Tehran** City Council in the 1999 election, the first local-level election since the **Islamic Revolution** in 1979.

Hajjerian also contributed to the reform agenda by publishing the newspaper *Sobh-i Emruz* (*This Morning*). Amongst its pro-reform articles, *Sobh-i Emruz* also published the articles of investigative journalist **Akbar Ganji**. Ganji aroused the ire of hardliners with his investigations into the murders of four dissidents in 1998, which he tied to government figures, most prominently **Ali Akbar Hashemi-Rafsanjani**. Not only were these articles published in *Sobh-i Emruz*, but the nature of the information suggested that Hajjerian provided Ganji much of the source material, drawing on his connections with the Ministry of Intelligence.

In 2000, Hajjerian suffered two gunshot wounds to the head in an attempted assassination in Tehran. Although a lone university student, Said Asgar, was charged and convicted of the crime, speculation abounded of government involvement. Witness reports indicated the use of powerful motorcycles banned to the general Iranian public but used by Iranian security forces in the getaway. While recovering, Hajjerian could not continue his publishing or political duties. Opponents capitalized on the situation, citing a rule in the publishing code that requires a publisher to be actively publishing to be eligible for a license. Using this as well as other trumped-up charges, *Sobh-i Emruz* was banned, another victim of the rash of bans following the reform victories in the 2000 elections.

Hajjerian continued to speak out for the reform movement as the dwindling days of Khatami's presidency approached. He became both a soft critic and apologist for the Khatami administration, realizing that more should have been done to achieve reformist goals, but also accepting the fact that hardliners, institutionalized with power, had prevented these goals. Compared with his activities before the assassination attempt, Hajjerian was much less visible. Still, Hajjerian had popularized ideas that continued to resonate with the Iranian public in the face of the reform movement's institutional ineffectiveness. His role in the development of reform ideology and strategy has been a crucial factor in the politics of the Islamic Republic and the tensions between moderates and conservatives. His full legacy is yet to be determined.

HAMADAN. Hamadan, the oldest extant Iranian city, is located in western Iran about 375 kilometers from **Tehran**. It has a large central roundabout (named after **Ayatollah Ruhollah Khomeini**) with six avenues running into it. Hamadan is linked by roads to Tehran, Qazvin, **KermanShah**, Malayer, Borujerd, and Saveh. To the southwest and east of the city is a great mountainous area with the Alvands running northwest to southeast.

The geography features numerous caves, the largest being the unique nearby cave of Ali Sadr, which contains a lake that can be sailed many miles. At an altitude of 1,800 meters, the climate of Hamadan is temperate mountainous. The city has cold winters and mild temperatures from May to October, the ideal time for tourism and when many Iranians flock to Hamadan.

The city has a rich history and is credited with being a contributor to human civilization. Its origins date back far into the Iranian past, well before the establishment of the **Achaemenid Dynasty** founded by **Cyrus the Great** in 550 B.C. According to legend and the poet **Ferdowsi**, Hamadan was built by King Jamshid.

Hamadan used to be known as Ecbatana. This was the capital of the Medes before they were united with the Persians under Cyrus. The name, Ecbatana, meant a place of assembly. The city became the summer capital of the Acaemenid Empire.

Hamadan was subject to many invasions over the centuries because of its coveted natural position lying astride the storied "Silk Road" from Baghdad to China. It was a meeting place of many highways and thus instrumental in both **trade** and politics. The Assyrians and Mongols both destroyed Hamadan and it was rebuilt both times. The Ottomans tried to take control in the 12th century, but the city held despite heavy damage.

The city also served as a political center at various times, not only in Median and Achaemenid times, but in later Islamic periods. It was, for instance, the capital of the Buyids in the 10th and 11th centuries under whose patronage the great Persian philosopher and world intellectual **Abu Ali Ibn Sina** and the important mystic poet Baba Taher flourished. The tombs of both are in Hamadan.

Today, Hamadan is capital of Hamadan Province which has a population of about 1,650,000 people of various ethnic origins. The province has an almost even distribution of urban and city living with a quarter of the population centered in Hamadan. The city itself has a population of 401,281 (according to the 1996 census). Almost all of the population is Muslim, and the **Persian language** is dominant. The city once had a significant Jewish population. The tombs of two Old Testament figures, the

Achaemenid Queen Esther and her uncle, Mordachai, are situated in Hamadan. Thus, the city retains significance for Judaism as a whole, as well as for **Jews in Iran**. Economically, the area is well known for handicrafts like leather and ceramic work. Carpet weaving is also an important industry. A prominent monument is the Stone Lion which was carved out as a **Parthian** monument in the **Arascid** era. It stands as the symbol of the city of Hamadan. Early people assigned it magical healing powers. Another famous attraction is the Ganjnameh Tabloids (written in cuneiform and ancient Persian) which contain King **Darius**'s words for the preservation of the country. A famous contemporary native is **Shirin Ebadi**, winner of the 2003 Nobel Peace Prize.

HAQQANI SCHOOL. Reputed to be a school espousing extremist and violent brands of **Islam**, the Haqqani Seminary in **Qum** has produced many high-ranking officials in the non-elected facets of the **Islamic Republic**. The school was founded as the Manzarieh School in 1964 amidst **Pahlavi** restrictions on religious learning centers, such as the **Feiziyeh Seminary**, and the government crackdown on outspoken religious scholars which resulted in the expulsion of **Ayatollah Ruholla Khomeini** from Iran. The building was originally funded by a trader named Haqqani-Zanjani, after whom the school was named, though financial responsibilities for the administration of the school changed hands until a leather trader named Hajj Mirza Abdollah Tavasoli took over the financial reins. Tavasoli had contacts with extreme conservatives, which led to a break with some of the previous benefactors. **Ayatollah Muhammad Hussein Beheshti**'s views greatly influenced the intellectual tone of the school, as did those of Ayatollah Muhammad Taq Meshbah-Yazdi, who served on the school's board of directors.

Though the early influence of the school was primarily cultural, after the formation of the **Islamic Republic** in 1979 many of Haqqani's graduates took appointed positions of power. These appointees tended towards favoritism and often hired their own friends from the seminary, creating a solid network of Haqqani graduates within the government. High-ranking Haqqani figures included Ayatollah Beheshti, who headed the judiciary, and former Haqqani director Ayatollah Qoddusi, who became head of the Revolutionary Courts. Haqqani figures have been deployed throughout power positions in the government since the **Islamic Revolution**, with particularly strong representation in the judiciary, the intelligence services, and the **Revolutionary Guards**. Some have argued that these political figures have conspired to promote the goals of the extremist Haqqanis. For instance, when **Akbar Ganji**, a controversial journalist, looked into the high-profile murders of four reformist figures in 1998, he warned that the network of Haqqani graduates was working to reinforce their views, and circumvent justice to protect their own and like-minded individuals. Whatever the case, figures involved with the Haqqani Seminary continue to occupy many powerful positions in the government into the year 2006.

HASHEMI-RAFSANJANI, ALI AKBAR (1934-). Hashemi-Rafsanjani is one of the most powerful politicians of the **Islamic Republic of Iran**. Elected president of the Republic in the summer of 1989, he had previously held the influential position of speaker of the Islamic Consultative Assembly (**Majlis**) since the convening of the first assembly of the Islamic Republic in 1980.

Born in the area of Rafsanjan near **Kerman**, Hashemi-Rafsanjani departed for **Qum** at the age of 14 to undertake a religious education. There he came under the influence of **Ayatollah Ruhollah Khomeini**, with whom he studied. He did not complete a high level of formal religious education, a factor which accounts for his religious title at the level of Hojjat al-Islam, a ranking of religious respect below that of **Ayatollah**. Nonetheless, his association with Khomeini and the credentials he attained through his long record of anti-**Pahlavi** political activity, which landed him in prison on four separate occasions (1963-1964, 1967, 1972, 1975-1977), qualified him to be a member of Khomeini's inner circle. As the main organizer of a militant group of clerics with connections to Khomeini in exile, Hashemi-Rafsanjani played a key role in the revolutionary activity which brought down the regime of **Muhammad Reza Shah**. He was even more instrumental in the political infighting after the revolution, which culminated in an Islamic government dominated by radical clerical influences.

Hashemi-Rafsanjani was a founding member of the **Islamic Republican Party (IRP)** and a member of the **Revolutionary Council** which assumed de facto political control upon the collapse of the Pahlavi Dynasty. In addition to the positions of influence previously cited, Hashemi-Rafsanjani also served the Islamic Republic as provisional Friday prayer leader of **Tehran**, deputy minister of interior in the **Provisional Government** of **Mehdi Bazargan**, deputy secretary-general of the IRP, and representative of Ayatollah Khomeini on the Supreme Defense Council.

Throughout his two-term presidency, Hashemi-Rafsanjani was generally considered a radical due to his politico-religious views, even though he often acted moderately, giving pragmatic justifications for the disparity between his belief and his actions. Making political concessions to appease a growing reformist sentiment in Iran would not help him develop a firm support base amongst the restless public and the reformist politicians. His hardline ideology and his political connections led his opposition to view him with distrust throughout his time in office. On the whole, however, Hashemi-Rafsanjani maintained a diverse power base owing to this dichotomy between his thoughts on the one hand and his practice on the other. He was elected to two consecutive terms as president, the limit under the **Constitution of the Islamic Republic** (although more nonconsecutive terms are permitted).

With the rise of the reformist movement both publicly and politically, Hashemi-Rafsanjani faced a popular opposition which would hinder his political ambitions. In light of his announcement to run for Majlis in hopes of becoming speaker of the house, controversial investigative journalist **Akbar Ganji** announced that Hashemi-Rafsanjani was well aware during his presidency of murderous actions taken by elements within the hardliner community to eliminate opposition. Immensely popular, Ganji's articles dashed Hashemi-Rafsanjani's hopes of assuming the speaker's position.

Still, Hashemi-Rafsanjani remained in the public spotlight, espousing pragmatic views on the issues of the day. By the spring 2005 Presidential Election, he was ready to make another bid for his former position. During the campaign, his promises were almost uncharacteristically reformist in nature. Political analysts figured Hashemi-Rafsanji to be the favorite due to the combination of his own liberal pragmatic campaign promises and the weakness of the reformist camp. (The reformists suffered from internal struggles and the ban of all viable candidates by the hardline-controlled **Council of Guardians**.) Remarkably, after winning the first-place position in the first round of elections, a determining runoff election between Hashemi-Rafsanjani and Tehran Mayor **Mahmud Ahmadinejad** brought the latter to the presidency. Though the results that brought the ultra-conservative Ahmadinejad to office were initially questioned by many, Hashemi-Rafsanjani rather quickly retracted his early comments questioning the results. Instead, he called upon Iran to support its new president in hopes of maintaining order.

In the forging of the **Islamic Revolution**, through the creation of the Islamic Republic, and its evolution for over two and a half decades, Hashemi-Rafsanjani has played a vital, if often understated role. A remarkable political tactician, he will undoubtedly also influence future developments.

HEDAYAT, SADEQ (1903-1951). Sadeq Hedayat is considered to be the preeminent figure of modern Persian **literature**, and the father of the modern Persian short story. Born to an aristocratic **Qajar** family in **Tehran**, he was educated at the prestigious **Dar al-Fonun** and continued his studies in Europe during the 1920s. He was attracted to the teachings of **Zoroastrianism** and Buddhism and his works reflect that interest.

Besides short fiction, Hedayat's work also includes drama, translations, criticism, folklore, and travel. He is best known for *The Blind Owl*, a deeply Iranian novel composed of the fictional notes of a neurotic, opium-addicted man. The book contains barely concealed criticism of Iranian society, and caused extreme reactions, both positive and negative, upon publication in 1941. In other works, Hedayat wrote of the dangers of imperialism and stressed the obvious dichotomy of the social class structure in Iran.

Though he continued to write until his death, much of his later work was published and translated posthumously. A natural introvert, Hedayat withdrew into seclusion and alcoholism to escape the notoriety associated with his writing. At the age of 48, he committed suicide in his Paris apartment where he had taken refuge from society.

HELMAND RIVER. The Helmand River begins its course in the mountainous central region of Afghanistan and flows southwesterly until it nears the Sistan province of Iran. The Helmand then changes to a northerly course, creating a natural border between Iran and Afghanistan before disappearing into shallow lakes and sandy marshes. The river's journey of 1,127 kilometers ends in the basin of Sistan, providing the low-lying area with the largest source of water in the **Iranian Plateau.** The basin lake reaches its maximum size in May after the seasonal rains and melted snow from the surrounding area drain into the river. However, the annual "Wind of 120 Days" from May through October causes significant evaporation, shrinking the basin lake to three smaller lakes surrounded by marshes and swamps covering approximately 483 square kilometers. After the water levels of the lakes have been reduced by evaporation, about 724 square kilometers of vegetation grows in sufficient amounts to be used for animal grazing. Because of the availability of fresh water from the Helmand River, parts of the Sistan area have some potential for development, despite the current isolation of this eastern province from the rest of the country.

HENDERSON, LOY WESLEY (1892-1986). Henderson was an American diplomat. He served in Russia, Iraq, and India before his appointment as ambassador to Iran in 1951, a post which he held until 1955. He was a key player in the volatile Iranian political arena in the early 1950s and was instrumental in forging close Iranian-American ties. Henderson worked closely with **Kermit Roosevelt** and other officials to coordinate the coup which ousted **Muhammad Mossadeq** as prime minister and returned **Muhammad Reza Shah** to power in 1953.

HEZB-I MARDOM (PEOPLE'S PARTY). *See* HEZB-I MELLI-YUN (NATIONAL PARTY).

HEZB-I MELLIYUN (NATIONAL PARTY). The Hezb-i Melliyun (National Party) and the Hezb-i Mardom (People's Party) were both established by **Muhammad Reza Shah** in 1957. It is difficult to separate the two parties, sometimes referred to as the "Tweedledee and Tweedledum" of the political party system. The Melliyun party was designated as the majority voice in the **Majlis**, while the Mardom party represented the loyal opposition, actively criticizing internal policies and actions of the government while solidly supporting foreign policy. Both parties worked to enlist broad public participation in the political process by holding congresses and party celebrations and maintaining scores of branches around the country. Two longtime friends and supporters of the Shah were chosen to lead the parties. Prime Minister **Manuchehr Eqbal** headed the Melliyun majority, and **Asadollah Alam** represented the opposition Mardom Party. The new two-party Majlis instituted a series of constitutional reforms aimed at reducing the incidence of future opposition and increasing the powers of the Shah. A change in the party composition of the Majlis occurred in 1964 with the replacement of the Melliyun party by the **Iran Novin (New Iran Party)**, a group composed of young economists and social scientists who could more fully understand and efficiently promote the Shah's reform program, called the **White Revolution**, which had been announced the prior year.

The two-party system remained in place until the Shah's decision in 1975 to dissolve the existing parties and create a single-party system represented by the **Rastakhiz Party**.

HIDDEN IMAM. Belief in the Hidden Imam is a fundamental tenet of the **Shiah** Muslim sect known as the Imami Shiah, or Twelvers. They believe in the divinely inspired, infallible leadership of the first 12 imams in a direct line. While all Shiah Muslims acknowledge that the leader of the religious community (an imam) should be a direct descendant of the Prophet Muhammad beginning with **Imam Ali**, the Twelvers believe that the imam should extend through the bloodline of Musa al-Kazem, the Seventh Imam. Some followers of the Imamate broke at various points to follow other lines. The Seveners, known as the Isma'ilis, for instance, followed the younger brother of the seventh imam and recognize a living imam to the present day. Thus, instead of the Hidden Imam, the Seveners recognize the current Agha Khan as the leader of their sect.

The Twelvers continued to recognize the sovereignty of the Imams up to the Twelfth Imam. In 874, the Twelfth Imam, Muhammad al-Montazer, disappeared and was said to be in hiding. In the first stage of concealment, termed the Lesser Occultation, he was able to fulfill the essential functions of the Imamate by granting four chosen representatives the authority to speak on his behalf. Following the death of the fourth deputy, the Imam was said to have gone into a second stage, the Greater Occultation. This seclusion of the Twelfth Imam ended the Imamate for the Imami Shiah, hence the title of the Twelvers.

The Twelvers believe that the imam, who disappeared as a child, will return at the end of time as a savior, or Mahdi, to destroy evil and cleanse the earth of wickedness. Until his return, Twelvers acknowledge the leadership of the ulama, or religious scholars, and a special group amongst them entitled the mujtahids, or interpreters of Islamic law, for social and spiritual guidance. Belief in the Hidden Imam legitimizes the functions of the ulama as agents of the Imamate. They are considered, however, to be temporary, imperfect intermediaries who will yield to the imam when he is messianicly revealed. In the modern period, however, an important intermediate step was introduced in the concept of the *Velayat-i Faqih* as elucidated by **Ayatollah Ruhollah Khomeini** and institutionalized in the **Constitution of the Islamic Republic of Iran**. No one knows when the Hidden Imam will return, but Twelvers faithfully await his reappearance as the redeemer of his people. *See also* FAQIH; IMAM HUSSEIN.

HOJJATIYEH SOCIETY. Formed in the 1950s as a **Shiah** reactionary movement based in opposition to both communism and especially **Bahaism**, the Hojjatiyeh Society enjoyed a relative level of freedom—and unofficial support—from the **Pahlavi** regime in an era in which many religious opposition groups experienced government suppression. From a base in **Mashhad**, the founder of the movement, known as Sheikh Mahmud Halaby, issued orders that would create a nationwide movement, all the while never making any public appearances. His message combined vitriolic attacks against the Bahai with a traditionalist reading of Twelver Shi'ism. The Hojjatiyeh's campaign of propaganda, surveillance, and violence in an effort to convert or eliminate Bahai or other infidels received tacit approval from **Muhammad Reza Shah**, and purportedly some covert aid from **SAVAK**. This was because the Hojjatiyeh adhered to a decidedly Twelver Shiah conception of government as illegitimate until the return of the **Hidden Imam**, which implied that the clergy should not participate in government affairs. Hoping to encourage the spread of this nonparticipatory ideology—as many religious groups opposed the government quite harshly—the Shah overlooked the Hojjatiyeh oppression of the Bahai, regardless of his public stance of tolerance for religious minorities.

Following the **Islamic Revolution** of 1979 and the inception of the **Islamic Republic of Iran**, however, the Hojjatiyeh's ideology came into direct conflict with the concept of *Velayat-i Faqih*. With a government based on Shi'ism with religious figures institutionalized in key positions, the Hojjatiyeh ideal of clerical nonparticipation stood in fundamental opposition. Now, the Islamic Republic subjected the Hojjatiyeh to the same type of suppression the Shah's regime allowed against the Bahai. Government propaganda labeled the Hojjatiyeh heretics intent on forcing a return of the Hidden Imam, amongst other public derisions. No longer effective in the face of stringent opposition, including direct denunciation by **Ayatollah Ruhollah Khomeini**, Sheikh Mahmoud Halaby discontinued the official activities of the Hojjatiyeh Society in 1983. Occasional accounts surface of oppositional activity by former associates of the Hojjatiyeh Society, hinting at one of the society's core tenets, namely that the Hojjatiyeh would not dissolve until the Hidden Imam's return.

HORMOZ STRAIT. The Hormoz Strait is the channel linking the Persian Gulf to the west, with the Gulf of Oman and the Arabian Sea to the southeast. The strait varies in width from 56 to 97 kilometers and separates Iran on its northern boundary from the Arabian Peninsula to the south. The larger islands of **Qeshm**, Hormoz, and Hengam are located within its waters, along with several smaller but strategically important isles.

The critical location of the Hormoz Strait has been exploited since the British seized control of the area in 1622 in order to secure its shipping routes to India. Iran seized the Hormoz Strait islands of Abu Musa and the Greater and Lesser Tumbs in 1971. The takeover was, in part, a territorial dispute, but related also to the strategic concern of monitoring traffic in and out of the Persian Gulf. Even though the construction of **oil** pipelines has lessened reliance on shipment by sea, a substantial percentage of the world's supply of crude petroleum still passes through the strait every day. The Western powers are vitally interested in protecting this passage since their economic foundation rests on the supply of Persian Gulf oil.

The critical importance of the Hormoz Strait has not lessened with recent world events. The political volatility of Persian Gulf nations keeps the powerful industrialized nations keenly aware of potential developments which might alter the existing situation in the area. *See also* CARTER DOCTRINE.

HOSTAGE RESCUE MISSION. On 4 November, 1979, 66 Americans were seized by student protestors calling themselves **Students Following the Imam's Line**, and held hostage in the U.S. Embassy in **Tehran**. Fourteen black and women hostages were quickly released. After months of negotiations had failed to secure the release of the 52 captives still being held, the administration of President Jimmy Carter, facing a flood of negative public opinion in a crucial election year, decided on a plan of direct military intervention to rescue the hostages. Hastily devised, dozens of mistakes were made both in planning and execution. On 24 April, 1980, eight helicopters entered Iranian airspace and a bizarre series of accidents occurred which forced the exercise to be called off. Three helicopters were rendered inoperable. One crashed with a refueling plane in a planned rendezvous and eight American servicemen died in the Iranian desert (*Dasht-i Kavir*). The survivors made a hasty departure and were forced to abandon helicopters, weapons, maps, and secret documents. Had the operation reached Tehran, it is almost certain that it would have been met by massive resistance, and the lives of the hostages would have been in serious danger. The Carter administration avoided further overt action, and through the resumption of negotiations secured the release of the captives in January 1981, after 444 days of captivity. *See also* ABDI, ABBAS; ALGERIAN ACCORDS; AMERICAN HOSTAGES IN IRAN; ASGHARZADEH, IBRAHIM; EBTEKAR, MASSOUMEH.

HOVEIDA, AMIR ABBAS (1919-1979). Amir Abbas Hoveida was prime minister under **Muhammad Reza Shah**, serving longer in that capacity than any other prime minister in the history of modern Iran. Appointed in 1965, he served continuously until August 1977, when due to a growing economic crisis, he was replaced by **Jamshid Amuzegar**, an economist. Despite undeniably loyal service, Hoveida was abandoned by the Shah as revolutionary pressures built. In November 1978, under orders from the Shah, he was arrested, along with 131 other government officials, in order to quell the protests of the public. When the Shah was forced to leave the country in January 1979, Hoveida was still in jail. Soon after the Revolutionary Courts were set up by **Ayatollah Ruhollah Khomeini**, Hoveida was tried, convicted, and executed, all within a matter of hours. He died on 7 April, 1979, a hapless victim of the fervor of the **Islamic Revolution**.

HUSSEINIYEH-I ERSHAD. The Husseiniyeh-i Ershad, founded in 1964, was conceived as an institute to contain a mosque, a library, and a lecture hall. Work began in that same year in northern **Tehran**. Building was completed in 1967 and it was officially registered as the Husseiniyeh-i Ershad Research and Educational Institute (*Mo'aseseh-ye Taqiqati va Ta' limati-ye Husseiniyeh-i Ershad*).

From the beginning, the Husseiniyeh-i Ershad was intended as a forum for the teaching of religious modernism. Initially, the regime of **Muhammad Reza Shah** supported the Husseiniyeh-i Ershad and hoped the religious intellectuals that lectured there would serve to weaken the hold of the more traditionally minded clerics, or to at least create a liberalizing tendency within the ranks of the religious scholars towards a more secular modernism. In addition, the government hoped, by promoting Muslim student associations and the Husseiniyeh-i Ershad, to attract the more modern-minded youth away from the **Tudeh** party that was actively recruiting in the universities. These hopes initially left a taint upon the Husseiniyeh-i Ershad that caused many to be skeptical about the openness of its forum. Matters developed quite differently, in large part due to the role that **Ali Shari'ati** played.

Ayatollah Morteza Mottahari, a religious scholar who had close ties to **Mehdi Bazargan** and **Ayatollah Mahmud Taleqani**, though not himself a member of the **Liberation Movement of Iran (LMI)**, was co-founder and chief intellectual architect of the Husseiniyeh-i Ershad. Mottahari invited Ali Shari'ati to speak at the Husseiniyeh-i Ershad. He quickly eclipsed Mottahari by rapidly becoming the most popular and controversial speaker. Prolific in his output, the lectures of Shari'ati were later collected and published in more than 50 volumes. During his speeches, Shari'ati sketched a prophetic picture of the Islamic nature of the revolution which was to grip Iran in the near future. However, his opposition to many of the traditional clergy (and to the views of Mottahari) and open embrace of leftist elements of modernism served as a source of alienation between them. Similarities between his speeches and the ideology of various leftist groups such as the **Mojahedin-i Khalq** and its Marxist elements (which openly recruited at the Husseiniyeh-i Ershad) only served to exacerbate this alienation.

It was perhaps inevitable that the brand of nationalism espoused at the Husseiniyeh-i Ershad would lead to both its closure in 1972 and the arrest of many of those associated with it, including Shari'ati. However, the ideological seeds planted at the Husseiniyeh-i Ershad bore fruit a decade later in the unfolding of the **Islamic Revolution** of 1979.

HUYSER MISSION. General Robert Huyser of the American Army was sent to Iran in January 1979 in an attempt to stabilize the Iranian military and prepare it to support the existing government in the event that revolutionaries attempted to overthrow **Muhammad Reza Shah.** Huyser's analysis of positive support for the regime on the part of the Iranian military was vastly overestimated. His reports were widely accepted by the American government despite contradictory reports from embassy officials in **Tehran.** Huyser later authored a work entitled *Mission to Tehran,* detailing his experiences and recollections. *See also* SULLIVAN, WILLIAM H.

-I-

IMAM ALI. Following the death of the Prophet Muhammad, a dispute arose over the determination of his successor to lead the nascent Muslim community. Two opposing groups emerged from the fight: the Sunni, the People of the Community; and the **Shiah,** the Partisans of Ali.

The Sunni believed that the preservation of the community depended on the allegiance and loyalty of all believers (umma). Leadership of the community should, therefore, be a matter of the consensus of that community as to the qualifications of the chosen leader. The Shiah claimed that only a charismatic leader like Muhammad could ensure the rule that **Islam** envisaged—a spiritual leader who would also hold temporal rule. The Shiah believed that the lineal descendants of Muhammad would be most qualified to rule as they would inherit these charismatic traits. As the cousin, son-in-law, and closest companion to the Prophet, Ali was considered to be the only choice for the Caliphate.

The Sunni prevailed and selected the first three Caliphs to guide Islam. The Shiah rejected them and continued to support the legitimacy of Ali, who was elected as the fourth Caliph by the Sunni method of consensus.

Ali was murdered by the Kharijites, a splinter group which disagreed with Ali over the nature of leadership of the community of believers. Ali died in 661, providing the first martyr for the Shiah community. He is revered for his courage, knowledge, humility, and wisdom. Devotion to Ali forms the spiritual foundation for Shiah belief. Though his martyrdom was tragic, it was the murder of Ali's son, **Imam Hussein**, at **Kerbala**, which provided the Shiah with a quintessential martyr and a cause, and decisively separated the followers of Ali from the main body of Islam to form a religio-political community of their own. From this basis, various Shiah sects evolved, including the Imami, or Twelver Shiah, the sect which has been the state religion of Iran since the beginning of the **Safavid Dynasty** in 1501. *See also* HIDDEN IMAM.

IMAM HUSSEIN. The **Shiah** sect of **Islam**, including the Imami branch prevalent in Iran, acknowledges Hussein as the third in a direct line of descendants from the Prophet Muhammad who embody divine leadership and are titled Imam. Hussein and most of his family were murdered in 680 near what is today the Iraqi city of **Kerbala** by the army of the reigning Umayyad Caliph, Yazid. His death, following the murders of his father, **Imam Ali**, and brother, Hasan, cemented the Sunni/Shiah split within Islam, and has given Shi'ism a tragic cast and a proclivity toward the veneration of martyrdom. Hussein's life and death are vividly and dramatically recreated each year during the Moharram celebrations which occur during the first 10 days of the Muslim calendar month of the same name. Parades, emotional readings (*rowzeh-khani*), and dramatic passion plays (*taziyeh*) commemorate the events on the plains of Kerbala in the seventh century. Numerous times in history, unpopular current leaders and governments have been reviled by being associated in the plays with the foes of Hussein. The power of this metaphor was vividly demonstrated in 1978-1979 in the **Islamic Revolution** of Iran which toppled the **Pahlavi** regime. *See also* HIDDEN IMAM.

IMAMI SHIAH. *See* HIDDEN IMAM; IMAM ALI; IMAM HUSSEIN.

IMBRIE, ROBERT WHITNEY (1883-1924). Robert Whitney Imbrie was an American attorney who held diplomatic posts in Russia and Finland before being appointed as vice consul in **Tehran** in 1923. He served less than a year before he was killed by a group of Muslim worshippers for taking pictures of a religious celebration, a notorious incident which momentarily damaged **U.S.-Iranian Relations** and scuttled negotiations involving the exploitation of northern Iranian **oil** by American oil interests.

INDUSTRY. Industry in Iran is largely centered upon the **oil** sector. Oil is the principle export of Iran and as such the industry to support its development is quite important. Two major industries are the petroleum and petrochemical industries. The oil industry has current production numbers of nearly four million barrels per day.

Other industries in Iran include textiles, construction materials, metals, and weaponry. These industries, together with the petroleum-based industries, employ one-quarter of the nation's 23 million workers. Excluding oil, industry is growing at a 3.5 percent annual rate.

The industry of Iran is closely linked to the volatile world oil market. With the inevitable variation in price and supply, Iran's **economy** can shift wildly with a minor variation in oil prices. This, combined with the high level of inefficient state control, has led to the industrial sector being an uncertain sector of the economy. This uncertainty prevents substantial foreign investment from coming in which, in turn, is what is needed to break the dependence on oil. The only industry many foreign investors are interested in is the oil industry. This leads to a paradox. To break from oil dependence Iran must depend on oil. Even this sector suffers, however, from the political policies of the **Islamic Republic** which have hindered the reintegration of Iran into the world market. In particular, the failure of **U.S.-Iranian Relations** to warm after the **Islamic Revolution** and the holding of **American Hostages in Iran** in 1979 has had a dampening influence, above all in the fossil fuels segment of the economy. Foreign investment is also limited by the extent of state control over the economy.

While traditional industries such as carpet weaving do still provide jobs and find an export market, the underdeveloped modern industrial sector leaves Iran economically vulnerable. According to 2004 figures, 40 percent of the population lives below the poverty line. Another unfortunate fact is the rate of inflation, a very high 15.5 percent. This is likely exacerbated by inefficiency due to the state-dominated economy. *See also* TRADE.

IRAN AIR. Iran Air is the country's national airline. It was formed in 1962 as a government corporation, whose full name is the Iranian National Airways Corporation. The symbol of the airline, after which it is sometimes named, is a mythical bird from Iranian legend called *Homa*.

Along with other public sector enterprises, Iran Air joined the general strike against the rule of **Muhammad Reza Shah** in 1978. On 3 July, 1988, following a battle with Iranian gunboats, an American destroyer, the USS *Vincennes*, shot down an Iran Air passenger plane—mistaking it for an attack jet. In this tragic encounter, the **Airbus Incident**, all 290 passengers on the plane were killed. Iran immediately condemned the action as "barbarism," but took no retaliatory measures. The United States, while expressing regret for the loss of civilian life, placed the blame for the disaster squarely on Iran. No apology or compensation was immediately offered, though compensation to families was later forthcoming. *See also* AMERICAN HOSTAGES IN IRAN.

IRAN-CONTRA ARMS AFFAIR. In 1985, Iran was experiencing isolation in its war with Iraq. The United States had thrown its support toward protecting the integrity of other Middle Eastern nations, and the Soviets were involved with their own war in Afghanistan. Furthermore, the **Iran-Iraq** War had taken an enormous toll on Iran and left the supplies of the largely U.S.-equipped army seriously depleted. With supplies for the war effort running low, the Iranians were amenable to the secret

American plan formulated by the National Security Council (NSC) and the Central Intelligence Agency (CIA).

The United States was looking for a way to secure the release of American hostages in Lebanon and to provide financial support for the Contra revolutionary movement in Nicaragua. Iran had influence with the Hezbollah leaders in Lebanon who were controlling the hostages. In return for the supply of military arms and spare parts, the plan called for the Iranians to intercede on behalf of the American hostages in Lebanon.

With the tacit approval of **Ayatollah Ruhollah Khomeini** and President Ronald Reagan, the deal was concluded in May 1986. Military supplies were sold to Iran, three hostages were released in Lebanon, intelligence information was provided to Iran from the Israelis (who were looking for a means to disrupt the Arab alliance against Iran), and money from the weapons sale to Iran was used to secretly support the Contra movement in Nicaragua. The stringent U.S. policy of securing Congressional approval for such agreements was bypassed. When the details became public in November 1986, the Irangate scandal unfolded. Lt. Colonel Oliver North and John Poindexter of the NSC were charged and forced to testify in Congressional hearings.

The affair was defended by the highest government officials involved, who argued that the best interests of the United States were being upheld even though extraconstitutional means were utilized. Public sentiment was still extremely negative toward Iran, and no arrangements would have been possible had the issue been presented for Congressional approval. Expert analysis of the factors involved suggest that political interests (deterring Soviet intervention in Iran), as well as economic factors (**oil** investments), were the prime motivating factors for the original plan which evolved into a national scandal involving the highest officials of government in the United States, Israel, and Iran.

IRAN-IRAQ WAR. The Iran-Iraq War was a prolonged conflict between the two nations during the 1980s. On 22 September, 1980, Iraqi troops invaded the southwestern Iranian province of **Khuzistan**. Iraq, under the leadership of Saddam Hussein, was seeking control of the **oil**-producing fields of southwest Iran, along with the right to control the **Shatt al-Arab**, the strategic waterway forming part of the Iran-Iraq border. Saddam Hussein was also retaliating for Iran's incitement of Iraq's **Shiah** Muslim population to revolt against his government. Iraq was counting on the internal disorder and military breakdown in Iran following the 1979 **Islamic Revolution** to allow an easy victory.

The invasion took Iran by surprise. Iraqi troops captured the city of **Khorramshahr**, but were held up at **Abadan**. By December, the offensive had been stopped by the unexpectedly fierce resistance of Iranian forces. Utilizing the militia and the **Revolutionary Guards**, along with regular armed forces, the Iranians began pushing the Iraqis back in 1981. Khorramshahr was recaptured in 1982, and later that year the Iraqis voluntarily withdrew from all occupied Iranian territory and sought a peace agreement. However, the antagonism of **Ayatollah Ruhollah Khomeini** toward Iraq thwarted any settlement, and Iran pressed on with the war, seeking to overthrow Saddam Hussein's government.

The Iraqis strengthened their position defensively, and a stalemate occurred. Prolonged fighting ensued just within Iraq's borders. Waves of Iranian troops, many of them young boys who were members of a para-military organization called *Basij*, failed to push back the Iraqis who were equipped with superior weaponry. Sporadic air and missile attacks were launched by both sides at enemy cities, oil installations, and tankers in the Persian Gulf. The United States, along with several European nations, sent warships to the Gulf to protect oil tankers after repeated Iranian attacks on the ships of Kuwait and other neutral Gulf countries.The loss of oil revenues in both countries arrested economic development and made it difficult to sustain war expenditures which mounted into billions of dollars by the war's end. Iraq received considerable support from Saudi Arabia and Kuwait, along with some aid from other moderate Arab states, the United States, and the Soviet Union. Iran's foreign support was more limited, consisting primarily of political support from the governments of Syria and Libya. Later in the war, world opinion turned against Iraq because of the documented use of chemical weapons. Iraq continued to seek peace through the 1980s, but

Iran refused to negotiate while seeking the total capitulation of Saddam Hussein's government.

Finally, Iran's economic problems, coupled with Iraqi military gains including missile attacks on such cities as **Tehran** and **Isfahan**, pushed Iran to accept a United Nations negotiated cease-fire on 18 July, 1988. A year before, in July 1987, UN Security Council Resolution 598 had been accepted by Iraq. UN Resolution 598 provided the framework for a cease-fire and negotiated settlement. Since 1988 the cease-fire has held, but formal peace has yet to be concluded between the two countries. *See also* IRAN AIR.

IRAN MISSION. The Iran Mission was established in 1870 by the U.S. Presbyterian Board of Missions to take over the work of the **American Board of Commissioners for Foreign Missions**. Under its auspices, hundreds of missionaries arrived in Iran to spread Christianity among the "heathens." Many of the missionary volunteers were able to accept the depth of Muslim resistance to conversion and turned instead to establishing schools and hospitals. To help staff these institutions, they trained Iranians as teachers, doctors, and nurses.

The Iran Mission continued to serve in Iran until its functions were transferred to the Evangelical Church of Iran in 1965. Some dedicated volunteers remained and continued their work until all American missionaries were expelled from the country in 1969. Many firsts were recorded in the fields of **education** and medicine by the Christian missionaries, and to this day, many Iranians warmly associate individual Americans with the humanitarian efforts of the Iran Mission. *See also* ALBORZ COLLEGE; JORDAN, SAMUEL; PERKINS, JUSTIN.

IRAN NOVIN (NEW IRAN PARTY). Following a period of disturbance over the implementation of land reform programs inspired by the **White Revolution** in the early 1960s, **Muhammad Reza Shah** dissolved the **Majlis** in May 1961. He then proceeded to enact laws by royal decree or referendum, bypassing the legislative process entirely. He allowed new elections in 1964, but strictly controlled the results through the formation of a new majority party called the Iran Novin (New Iran) which replaced the **Hezb-i Melliyun (National Party)** in December 1963. This move was made in order to provide representation for, and to serve as, the voice of a new pro-Western generation of technocratic politicians. It was originally led by **Hasan Ali Mansur**, who was assassinated in January, 1965, after serving only 10 months as prime minister. Mansur was succeeded as party head and prime minister by **Amir Abbas Hoveida**, who made Iran Novin almost the sole party contesting elections. The party continued to control the Majlis until 1975, when it was abolished by the establishment of the Shah's monolithic **Rastakhiz Party**.

IRANIAN PLATEAU. The topography of Iran consists of a vast desert plateau with the perimeter of the country bordered by two mountain ranges. Encircling the plateau are the **Alborz Mountains** to the north, along the **Caspian Sea**, and the **Zagros Mountains** that border Iran from the northwest running southeast to the Persian Gulf coast. The central plateau covers approximately one-half the land area of the country and varies in elevation from about 2,500 meters to as low as 305 meters in the basins.

The basins are a unique feature of the plateau, because the water from the mountains drains inward and eventually evaporates in the arid climate or disappears into the Dasht-i Lut or the Dasht-i Kavir. The Dasht-i Kavir is a vast salt marsh covering almost one quarter of central Iran. Located southeast of **Tehran**, the Dasht-i Kavir is uninhabited due to the jagged crust of salt which forms atop the slimy marshland, and the impenetrable winter fogs which envelop the region. The Dasht-i Lut, a desert of sand and rock, is also largely uninhabited. Temperatures in the plateau region fluctuate between 45 degrees centigrade in the summer and four degrees centigrade in the winter. The area receives minimal precipitation, and frequent high-velocity wind storms intensify seasonal temperatures.

Population is largely confined to the outer edges of the two deserts which form the "dead heart" that comprises much of the plateau. A population density map (Figure 3) illustrates the emptiness of the deserts and the concentration of population in areas where plateau and mountains intersect.

Population Density of Iran

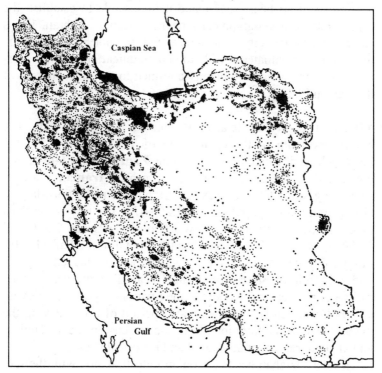

Source: Interior Ministry, Tehran.

Figure 3

In some areas on the outer rim of the plateau, a more temperate climate, along with access to a water supply, often provided by means of a *Qanat*, allows limited **agricultural** settlements and animal herding. Farmers raise cash crops of cotton and olives, along with indigo, henna, and saffron—the dye plants necessary for the production of colorful Persian carpets. Other notable products of agriculture include grain, fruits, nuts, and a wide variety of vegetables. Pastoralism, particularly the output of nomadic **tribes**, provides the plateau inhabitants with meat, milk, hair, and wool from the flocks of sheep and goats. The discovery of mineral deposits of iron ore, coal, and copper has led to the development of mining industries in towns such as **Kerman** and Bafq.

Iran's "dead heart" has made it impossible to establish the capital city in a geographically central location. Tehran, Iran's capital and largest city, is located within the north central "rim" of the country, situated astride the communication and transportation systems which are mainly confined to the outer margin of the Iranian Plateau.

ISFAHAN. The city of Isfahan is located in central Iran, 414 kilometers south of the capital city of **Tehran** and along the Zayandeh-Rud, which originates in the **Zagros Mountains** flowing inland as the largest river of the central **Iranian Plateau**. According to the latest census (1996), Isfahan is the third-largest city in Iran with a population of 1,266,072. The city is the third oldest in Iran, settled by a Jewish colony between 2,500 and 2,700 years ago. Isfahan served as the capital of the **Safavid Dynasty** from 1598 to 1722, during which the city reached its glory under the rule of **Shah Abbas the Great**. The city was historically a grand center for **trade** among nations, as well as serving as a political center for an extended period of time, leaving the modern city with a tradition of diverse art, customs, and religion, and also impressive architectural and historical sites.

Modern Isfahan has taken on an industrial side with the second-largest number of industrial workers in the country and ranks second nationwide also, only to Tehran, in terms of value added when all categories of **industry** are grouped together. Perhaps the most important of the Isfahan industries is the Steel Mill Company established in the mid-1960s in cooperation with the then Soviet Union. A wide variety of traditional arts and crafts, most notably carpet weaving, also form an important part of the local **economy**.

Historically, during the **Sassanian Dynasty**, Isfahan was overseen by the "Espoohrans," members of seven noble Iranian families who resided in the city which served as a military center. After the coming of **Islam**, the city was ruled by Arabs, like much of Iran, and in the 10th century, the Abbasid Caliph Mansour selected it as the provincial capital until its capture and subsequent decline at the hand of the Mongols in the 13th century.

Isfahan rose to prominence again when Shah Abbas chose the city as his capital in 1598 and developed it as a showpiece for the dignitaries of Europe. During this time, Isfahan was dubbed *Nesf-i Jahan*, or "half the world," as contemporaries thought that to see this bustling and modern city was to see half of the entire world. It is said that at its pinnacle in the 16th and 17th centuries, Isfahan possessed 163 mosques, 48 religious schools, 1,801 shops, and 263 public baths, along with a population of some 600,000. Even to the present day, Isfahan remains artistically and architecturally one of the most interesting and beautiful cities in the world.

One Iranian scholar (Brian Spooner) asserts that Isfahan may reasonably claim to have been the most important city on the Iranian Plateau. Most would agree, certainly from an architectural point of view. The greatest collection of historical buildings in Iran is in Isfahan. Among these are such monuments as the Imperial Mosque, the mosque of Sheikh Lotfallah, the Ali Qapu Gateway and Royal Administrative Center, and the monumental entrance to the covered **bazaar**. All these are located on the Imperial Square built as the centerpiece for a new imperial city, adjacent to the ancient city, by Shah Abbas. Further, and still existent additions of Shah Abbas, are the remnants of extensive gardens and pavilions highlighted by the palace known as *Chehel Sotun*, or "Forty Columns," and the *Chahar Bagh*, or "Four Gardens," which is a broad, 55-meter-wide avenue intended as a place of promenade. The latter, full of trees, flowers, and fountains extended for nearly a kilometer down to the river and across a grand bridge, the Allah Verdi Khan, to the new town of Julfa. Julfa, or New Julfa as it came to be called, was founded by a large community of **Armenians** who were transplanted from Julfa in **Azerbaijan** by Shah Abbas for their craft and artistic skills. They enjoyed royal protection and themselves built a notable cathedral and several churches which are still standing and worthy of visiting.

Other significant historical sites in Isfahan are the Congregational Mosque which is an architectural archive, having been erected over many centuries and thus consisting of a variety of architectural types and styles, and the religious school of the Mother of the Shah which dates back to 1714. Overall, it is fair to say that Isfahan is one of Iran's most historical, attractive, and charming cities, which accounts for its UNESCO designation as a World Heritage Site.

ISLAM. One of the world's three monotheistic **religions**, along with Christianity and Judaism, Islam is the majority religion of most countries in the Middle East. Originating in the Arabian Peninsula in the seventh century A.D. with the prophet Muhammad, Islam quickly spread and eventually extended its politico-religious sway throughout all of the Middle East, across North Africa to the Atlantic, into Central Asia up to the Oxus River, and as far east as India. The **Sassanian Dynasty** in Iran was quickly overwhelmed by the Arab invasion of the seventh century under the banner of Islam and, in time, the **Zoroastrianism** of the Iranians was almost entirely supplanted by Islam as the religion of Iranians.

Islam divided into two major sects, the Sunni and the **Shiah**. The Sunni were the majority and established major dynasties, most notably the Umayyad Dynasty centered on Damascus and the Abbasid Dynasty centered on Baghdad. Much of Iran came under the nominal political overlordship of these two dynasties until the final collapse of the Abbasid Dynasty at the hands of the Mongols in 1258. During this time, Iranians contributed greatly to a new cultural synthesis composed of a wide variety of cultural inputs into what came to be referred to as Islamic culture and civilization. Thus, Iranians helped mold and influence the development of Islam as they began to adopt it as their own.

The marriage was never entirely a comfortable one as deep in the Iranian psyche there is a sense of cultural superiority over the Arabs and a feeling that Islam was a foreign imposition. Nonetheless, Islam became the dominant religion in Iran which it is to the present day.

The Islam of Iran today is Twelver Shi'ism which became the state religion of Iran with the establishment of the **Safavid Dynasty** in 1501. There are several branches of Shi'ism within Islam as a whole, but the Twelvers predominate in Iran. The vast majority of Iranians are of the Twelver Shiah persuasion though there are smaller communities of other religions in Iran and some significantly large Sunni communities. A number of **tribes**, for instance, are Sunni.

The unique characteristics of Twelver Shi'ism are intertwined with the Iranian body politic, especially in the events leading up to the **Islamic Revolution** and the establishment of the **Islamic Republic of Iran**. Since the Safavid period the relationship between religion and state has consistently been a part of the political dynamic. And, that relationship has always been weighted by the issue of political legitimacy in light of the inherent millennial aspiration in Twelver Shi'ism. The concept of the **Hidden Imam** plays a crucial role. Even the two constitutions which have served as the basis for institutional governance over the past century, the 1906 Constitution and the **Constitution of the Islamic Republic of Iran**, both reflect the legitimizing role of religion and, as well, acknowledge the ultimate return of the only legitimate authority over the community of believers, the Hidden Imam.

Secular state power and the religious scholars of Twelver Shi'ism have long interacted in an uneasy equilibrium, complicated by the fact that religious scholars have been unable to agree among themselves on a single interpretation of the relationship. Now, the government of Iran is dominated by the vision of a particular interpretation crafted by **Ayatollah Ruhollah Khomeini**. However, the debate continues over how and to what extent Islam should intrude in the governance of individual lives as versus serving as a moral code. There is no unanimity amongst religious scholars and even less among secular politicians and intellectuals over the proper role of religion. The interplay of these elements in a world increasingly influenced by secularism is one of the more fascinating aspects of the current "Government of God" represented in the Islamic Republic.

ISLAMIC REPUBLIC OF IRAN. The Islamic Republic of Iran was formed following the **Islamic Revolution** of 1979. Massive demonstrations were held almost daily in the latter part of 1978 in opposition to the economic policies of **Muhammad Reza Shah** and perceived subservience to foreign influences. Hundreds of deaths resulted from the brutal suppressive tactics of the Iranian military. From exile in France, **Ayatollah Ruhollah Khomeini**, Iran's predominant religious leader, urged continuation and escalation of the protests. As the situation grew more volatile, the increasing pressure forced the Shah to flee the country on 16 January, 1979. A reform government under the leadership of Prime Minister **Shapur Bakhtiar** assumed control. In the wake of the Shah's departure, the military and political structure of Iran crumbled. Demonstrators flooded the streets demanding the return of Khomeini. The Bakhtiar government acquiesced, and Khomeini returned to Iran on 1 February, 1979.

His return signaled the beginning of a new revolutionary government for Iran. Bakhtiar was dismissed, and **Mehdi Bazargan** became prime minister of the new **Provisional Government**. Following an overwhelming victory in a national referendum held in March 1979, Khomeini proclaimed the Islamic Republic of Iran. A new constitution was ratified giving Khomeini, as *Faqih*, unlimited power in all aspects of Iranian religious, political, economic, and social life. The clergy became dominant political players, reflecting Khomeini's views regarding traditional **Islam** as the guideline for government policy. Within this framework, church and state were combined, and traditional Islamic customs and laws were soon revived, while Western influences were suppressed.

The transition from monarchy to theocracy was not without problems. A group of middle-class moderates, as well as remnants of various radical secular groups, opposed strict Islamic fundamentalism as the constitutional base. Regional disturbances broke out among the **Kurds**, the **Turkoman**, and **Arabs** as they sought greater autonomy from central authority. The strength of the opposition forced Khomeini to reactivate the **Revolutionary Guards** and the secret police, SAVAMA, modeled ironically after the hated **SAVAK** of the Shah.

In November 1979, the **American Hostage** crisis at the U.S. Embassy in **Tehran** and the accompanying internal political struggle created the conditions which finally secured Khomeini's interpretation of Islamic government. By actively supporting the **Students Following the Imam's Line** responsible for the takeover and ignoring American demands for the release of the hostages, Khomeini rallied massive support to his side and was able to begin implementing his Islamization program throughout Iran. *See also* CONSTITUTION OF THE ISLAMIC REPUBLIC OF IRAN; REVOLUTIONARY COUNCIL; VELAYAT-I FAQIH.

ISLAMIC REPUBLICAN PARTY (IRP). The Islamic Republican Party was founded 17 February, 1979, one week after the establishment of the Islamic revolutionary **Provisional Government**. It was formed by fundamentalist clerics, led by **Ayatollah Muhammad Hussein Beheshti**, who represented a politically militant group of clergy supporting **Ayatollah Ruhollah Khomeini**. The IRP advocated a return to pure Islamic principles and culture, and also called for the nationalization of major industries, an Islamic university system, and programs to aid the poor. Its members denounced liberalism and secular parties and were opposed to establishing relations with the United States and the Soviet Union.

The IRP was instrumental in shaping the new **Constitution of the Islamic Republic**, and stood in direct opposition to the more moderate members of the Provisional Government. In the more than a year transitional period to constitutional Islamic government, the IRP, along with the **Revolutionary Council** was the most important wielder of political influence and power. Not surprisingly, there was considerable overlap in the membership of these two organizations.

In 1980, the party lost its presidential bid, but gained the majority of seats in the **Majlis**. With its power established, the IRP extended its influence into Islamic Associations and mosques. The most militant faction of the IRP utilized street gangs, entitled Hezbollah, to break up opponents' political meetings and attack university students. Employing political finesse, and in conjunction with brute force and intimidation, the IRP largely succeeded in eliminating the opposition and took control of state institutions, mosques, the media, and even local political associations.

The IRP, under the guidance of Beheshti, brought about the overthrow of the constitutionally elected president, **Abdol Hasan Bani-Sadr**, in June 1981. Through a systematic campaign, the IRP isolated Bani-Sadr and pressured the previously neutral Khomeini to replace him. Resentment of the IRP's authoritarianism and repressive tactics began to build. It ran particularly high amongst moderate middle-class politicians and those of the radical left, both of whom had gradually been cut out of the political process. On 28 June, 1981, an explosion at the IRP's headquarters killed 74 of its leaders, including Beheshti. The act was blamed on the left-wing Islamic Socialist group, the **Mojahedin-i Khalq**. Open warfare ensued between the IRP-dominated government and the Mojahedin-i Khalq, resulting eventually in the total dominance of the IRP in the revolutionary regime.

With its external enemies eliminated, however, the IRP began to lose internal cohesiveness. Radical and pragmatic elements clashed within the party and eventually the former began to lose sway. By 1985, the influence of the party within the government had eroded to such an extent that some branches were eliminated and others restricted. Once the primary organization of mass mobilization in support of the regime, the role of the IRP was further reduced until, on 1 June, 1987, it was dissolved by order of Ayatollah Khomeini. Ironically, the dissolution came at the request of President **Ayatollah Ali Khamene'i** and speaker of the Majlis, **Ali Akbar Hashemi-Rafsanjani**, both founders of the IRP, who now saw its activities as divisive in light of an institutionalized Islamic Republic.

ISLAMIC REVOLUTION. The Islamic Revolution in Iran was the culmination of a movement which brought together disparate elements that had long advocated the overthrow of the regime of **Muhammad Reza Shah**. Its proponents worked to generate discontent with the Shah's economic policies and the pervasive foreign influence in all areas of Iranian society. A coalition of clerics, merchants, and intellectuals, with political ideologies ranging from right-wing religious conservatism to Marxism, succeeded in creating a political atmosphere which ultimately led to the demise of the **Pahlavi Dynasty**. The Shah was denounced for human rights violations, media censorship, and disregard for constitutional rights.

In 1978, general strikes throughout the country paralyzed commerce, and massive demonstrations erupted daily in protest against the regime. Attacks by government troops on demonstrators resulted in hundreds of deaths. The participants in these protests, though representing diverse groups, were united by their loyalty to **Ayatollah Ruhollah Khomeini**—a key religious leader of the Iranian **Shiah** Muslims and the figure ultimately seen by most Iranians as the father of the revolution. He had directed the movement from exile in France through an extensive network of dedicated followers within Iran.

In the face of overwhelming opposition, the Shah fled Iran on 16 January, 1979. A reformist government under the leadership of Prime Minister **Shapur Bakhtiar** took control. Conditions continued to deteriorate, and on the first of February, Khomeini triumphantly returned from exile. He proposed a **Provisional Government** to replace Bakhtiar's, and proceeded to set up a **Revolutionary Council**. By February, the revolutionaries had overcome the last resistance from the Iranian Army and the Imperial Guard, and secured complete control of **Tehran**. **Mehdi Bazargan**, a middle-class moderate politician, was appointed prime minister to replace Bakhtiar. Bazargan, however, was unable to establish control. Though the revolution succeeded thanks to a coalition of widely differing political interests, the traditional religious party of Khomeini quickly established dominance during the confusion and disorder which developed in the aftermath of the revolution. This was symbolized by the referendum held in March, 1979, which established the **Islamic Republic of Iran** on terms dictated by Khomeini.

-J-

JACKSON, A.V.W. (1862-1937). A.V.W. Jackson was an Oriental-
ist and philologist and an authority on ancient Iranian religion, in
particular Zoroastrianism. He traveled throughout Iran and India,
and in 1918 served as a member of the American Persian Relief
Committee helping to organize famine relief in war-torn Iran.
Jackson taught Indo-Iranian languages at Columbia University
from 1886-1935, and authored a number of books, both scholarly
works and travel books, about his experiences in the Middle
East. His most well-known work is *Persia, Past and Present: A
Book of Travel and Research.*

JAMALZADEH, MUHAMMAD ALI (1892-1997). Although
Sadeq Hedayat became recognized as the major pioneer of the
Persian short story, the honor of being the first Iranian to publish
a collection of short stories belongs to Muhammad Ali Jamalzadeh. Born to a progressive mullah father who was arrested due
to anti-government speeches and murdered in prison, Jamalzadeh
left Iran in his early teens. He may have left at a young age, but
his connection with and concern for his native land remained.
Studying law in Lebanon, France, and Switzerland, he eventually
settled in Berlin, working for Iran's embassy in Germany. It was
in Berlin that Jamalzadeh would join other Iranians in publishing
an Iranian nationalist journal named *Kaveh*. This journal—as
well as the group that published it—criticized the perceived deg-
radation of Iranian culture and autonomy at the hands of foreign
influences.

   In 1921, Jamalzadeh published the groundbreaking *Yeki Bud
Yeki Nabud* (*Once Upon a Time*), which was the first collection
of short stories in Farsi ever published. Drawing on a precedent
set by **Ali Akbar Dehkhoda** years before, the subject matter of
Jamalzadeh's writing consisted of a focus on social issues as
well as local colloquialisms. Reiterating the concern the journal
Kaveh expressed, the stories within *Yeki Bud Yeki Nabud* called
into question both the supplanting tendency of Western influence
as well as the repressiveness of some within the clergy. While it

was celebrated outside Iran, Jamalzadeh's masterpiece was initially reviled in his homeland, mainly due to its unflattering portrayal of the **Shiah** clergy. Jamalzadeh was devastated by the unfavorable reception in Iran, and, although *Yeki Bud Yeki Nabud* eventually achieved Iranian acclaim, he published no new fictional works throughout the rest of the 1920s or 1930s. Jamalzadeh's career shifted to working for the International Employment Office in Geneva, Switzerland, from which he would retire in 1956. In the 1940s, he began publishing fiction once again. However, critics claimed his new works were less innovative and quite pretentious. Despite this, he continued to produce works regularly into the 1970s. Still, when Jamalzadeh died in 1997, at well over 100, his initial work—the first of its kind and revolutionary in its own right—was also his best known. Jamalzadeh and *Yeki Bud Yeki Nabud* introduced a form perfected by Hedayat, and carried on in form and spirit by such writers as **Gholam Hussein Sa'edi** and **Mahmud Dowlatabadi**. *See also* LITERATURE.

JAMI (1414-1492). Known as one of the great mystical poets of Iran, Jami was born in **Khorasan** in the district of Jame, near modern Herat, Afghanistan. He is most known as a **Sufi** scholar and mystic, as well as a man of deep intelligence. He studied mathematics and philosophy, but wrote extensively across fields including **poetry**, grammar, mysticism, music, and theology. Jami is said to have bragged about his knowledge, insisting that finally achieving humility was only another way of boasting of one's success.

Jami is credited with writing over 100 works, including a poetic collection called *Haft Aurang* (*Seven Thrones*), which consisted of some 25,000 couplets. Amongst this collection were the well-known allegory "Salaman and Absal," a version of the story of Joseph and Potiphar's wife, and what most consider the masterpiece of Jami, the love story "Yusef and Zuleikha," said to have been written when the author was in his seventies. His poetic style was direct and unadorned, in sharp contrast to the classical Persian poetry of later ages.

Additionally, Jami successfully explored other forms of literature and completed a selection of short stories called *Baharistan* (*Abode of Spring*). His most famous work, however, is *Lavayeh* (*Flashes of Light*), in which the poet precisely explains Sufi doctrines and gives accounts of the lives of other Sufi mystics.

Aside from two brief trips to **Mashhad** and the Hejaz, Jami remained near his birthplace his entire life. He died in Herat two days after his 78th birthday. *See also* LITERATURE.

JEWS IN IRAN. The Jewish community in Iran is ancient with its roots in the sixth century B.C. It was at this time, after **Cyrus'** defeat of Babylonia, that the ruler decreed that the exiled Jews could return to Judea. However, many had established themselves in what had become Persia and chose to remain, though the official religion was **Zoroastrianism**. These former exiles would become the source of the Jewish community in Iran and were met with a tolerant attitude by early rulers.

After the overthrow of the **Achaemenid Dynasty** by Alexander the Great, the subsequent **Sassanid Dynasty** saw significant growth in the Jewish population. The defeat of the Sassanids by the Arabs in 642 A.D. brought Persia into the Arabo-Islamic body where Arabic seeped into the **Persian language** and **Islam** was established as the state religion. Under Arab rule and through the special laws of the Dhimmi, or the "protected," non-Muslims were essentially rendered second-class citizens.

After the 10th century, Iranian Jews became active in banking and money lending, as these routes allowed for some social advancement when the Jewish community was forbidden from government service. Moderate progress was made until the Mongol invasion in the 13th century.

During the **Safavid Dynasty** of the 16th and 17th centuries, the **Shiah** sect of Islam became the state religion. With Shi'ism came the belief that non-Muslims were unclean, forcing Jews to choose between persecution or conversion as synagogues were closed down. Iranian Jews were forced to publicly declare Islam upon conversion, but it was common practice to continue Jewish worship in secret. In 1661 this practice was mercifully ended with the decree that Jews could openly practice their faith.

As the 20th century approached, a Constitutional Movement swept Iran culminating in the **Constitutional Revolution of 1906** and the adoption of a constituion which granted rights to **Christians**, Jews, and Zoroastrians in Iran, and allowed each to elect a government representative. Until this time the Jewish population had been forced to live within restricted areas of towns, and Jews were limited to particular fields of work that allowed for only minimal upward mobility.

In 1925, the **Pahlavi Dynasty** was established, bringing the ideas of secularization and Westernization to Iran. While controversial, the change served the Jewish community well, allowing Jews to participate in all walks of life and work without the hindrance of religious discrimination.

With the succession of **Muhammad Reza Shah**, son of **Reza Shah**, in 1941, the **economy** began a boom that benefited the Jews, most of whom were previously peddlers and moneylenders.

By the 1979 overthrow of the Shah in the **Islamic Revolution**, there were 85,000 Jews living in Iran. This number would plummet by tens of thousands after the establishment of the anti-Israeli **Islamic Republic of Iran** by **Ayatollah Ruhollah Khomeini**, despite the *fatwa* issued by Khomeini that "People of the Book" (Christians and Jews) should be protected and allowed freedom of religion. Khomeini also stressed that the Iranian government could differentiate between the Zionists of Israel and the Jews of Iran. Nonetheless, the population of the Jewish community in Iran dropped from 85,000 in 1978 to 50,000 in 1986.

Currently, the number of Jews living in Iran is debated, with estimates ranging from 25,000 to 35,000. The American Jewish Committee estimated the number at only 11,000 in 2003, though most agree this number is low and contend that Iran has the largest Jewish population of any Muslim country. However, Jews remain a focus of suspicion by the Iranian government. Phone contact and mail communications to Israel have often been cited since 1979 as evidence of "spying." Over 45,000 Iranian Jews have emigrated to Israel since 1948, many leaving family behind.

Iranian Jews are allotted a parliamentary deputy under the **Constitution of the Islamic Republic**. Though the status of the Jewish community remains in accordance with the 1979 Constitution, instances of suspicion and even arrest add to the feeling of insecurity among the Jewish population in Iran and contribute to the trend of emigration. To date, the majority of Jews leaving Iran since 1979 have settled in the United States, with the largest numbers concentrated in Los Angeles and New York.

JORDAN, SAMUEL (1871-1952). Samuel Jordan was one of the most famous and respected Americans to be involved in Iran. He is often referred to as the "father of modern education in Iran." As a missionary connected with the Presbyterian Church Board of Foreign Missions, he devoted his life to the establishment of sound **education** with Christian principles for the young men of Iran. His career began with his arrival in Iran in 1898. Jordan served first as a teacher, and then as principal, of the American High School for Boys in **Tehran** which he later developed into the American College, also known as **Alborz College**.

His principles of education rested on the belief that men would be better educated within the element of their own society, rather than being sent to foreign countries. He incorporated the dignity and value of physical labor with high academic standards, and his school produced some of Iran's finest 20th century intellectuals. Evidence of the appreciation of his contributions to Iran—Jordan Hall, Jordan Boulevard, and a statue erected in his memory—still remains today. *See also* AMERICAN BOARD OF COMMISSIONERS FOR FOREIGN MISSIONS; IRAN MISSION.

-K-

KADIVAR, MOHSEN (1959-). Mohsen Kadivar was born in Farsa, near **Shiraz**. His family has been active in the politics of Iran. His grandfather was a dissident under **Reza Shah**. His father was a dissident under **Muhammad Reza Shah**. The political activism has continued. Both Mohsen and his sister are outspoken critics of the current regime.

Kadivar studied electronics engineering at **Pahlavi University** prior to the revolutionary events of 1978, but later changed his studies to religious **education**. He went to **Qum** in 1981 where he studied Islamic philosophy under the tuteledge of **Ayatollah Hussein Ali Montezari**. He received the highest degree of **Shiah** learning and taught at at Qum Seminary for 14 years. In 1997, he moved to **Tehran**.

From 1991 to 1999, Kadivar was the director of the Department of Islamic Thought, Center for Strategic Research. He has a long record of research, writing, and teaching in the field of Islamic theology and philosophy and political thought in **Islam**, having published 12 books and over 100 papers in numerous Iranian journals.

Part of the younger generation of reform-minded clerics, Kadivar has come under fire from the conservative factions of the **Islamic Republic** for his views. His sister, Jamileh, is also a critic of the ideology of the **Islamic Revolution**, and is married to reformist and former President **Muhammad Khatami**'s cabinet member **Ata'ollah Mohajerani**.

Kadivar's most controversial view is on the concept of *Velayat-i Faqih*. Not only did Kadivar claim that the concept is not universally supported by most important religious scholars, but he also claimed that it is not self-evident in the Shariah or Shiah *fiqh*. Kadivar argued that it presupposes individuals were incapable of handling their own affairs. However, in *fiqh*, people are supposed to be inalienably in charge of their own destinies. Thus, in the view of Kadivar, the inherently nondemocratic nature of *Velayat-i Faqih* is not in accord with the realities of the modern day, which required an acceptably different interpretation of Islam.

Instead, Kadivar suggested that government should be based on democratic principles. Though a critic of the current form of the Islamic Republic, the primary quest of his thought is to reconcile Islam and modernity, particularly the democratic rights of the individual in a civic society. He uses Ayatollah Montezari's view that the *Faqih* must be selected by, and accountable to, the people. He argues that because people must be in charge of their own affairs, and because the line of divine appointment in the Infallible Imams would not be present until the return of the **Hidden Imam**, it is required that the people themselves choose their representation in government, and even the *Faqih*. According to Kadivar, no form of government that violates this would be legitimate under Shiah Islam.

Opposition to Kadivar was fierce from the conservatives. In 1999, he was brought before the Special Court of the Clergy and convicted of spreading anti-Islamic Republic propaganda and of spreading lies and rumors. He was sentenced to 18 months in jail, which he served. This has not quieted Kadivar's reformist thoughts, as he continues to express his views unequivocally. The lectures of Kadivar are packed and his books are popular. His arrest and imprisonment has led, ironically, to a spreading of his ideas and a wider engagement of the issues he has addressed as a clerical critic of the Islamic Republic.

KAR, MEHRANGIZ (1944-). Future attorney and human rights activist Mehrangiz Kar was born in the southern Iranian city of **Ahvaz**. As a young woman she relocated to **Tehran** where she attended the College of Law and Political Science at **Tehran University**. Upon completion of her **education**, Kar worked for the Institute of Social Security and acted as a public defender in Iran's civil and criminal courts. During her legal career, Kar became active in writing and speaking on the status of **women** and children in Iran, working toward the improvement of conditions and legal status for both.

Kar has been published regularly in Iranian and international journals, contributing over 100 articles and 14 books. Her writing includes *Quest for Identity: The Image of Iranian Women in Prehistory and History, Vols. I and II* (co-edited with Shahla Lahiji, Iran's first woman publisher and founder of the Iranian Society for the Defense of Human Rights) and *Angel of Justice and Patches of Hell*, a collection of essays examining the status of women before and after the **Islamic Revolution**.

Kar was arrested in 2000 along with 19 other writers, academics, and leading reformist figures, and tried for participating in the cultural and academic "Iran after the Election" **Berlin Conference** (7-9 April, 2000). She was sentenced to six months in prison, four weeks of which was to be spent in solitary confinement. Kar has labeled the Berlin Conference, described by the Revolutionary Court of the **Islamic Republic** as "anti-Islamic," as a major turning point in the limitations of freedom in Iran. The same year (2000), the activist was diagnosed with breast cancer which required major treatment, forcing her to move to the Netherlands and then the United States for health care in 2001. She has continued her outspoken ways abroad. Because of her highly vocal civil and women's rights activism, and his own outspokeness, Kar's 73-year-old husband, still located in Tehran, was kidnapped, questioned, and finally jailed for endangering national security.

Kar has been recognized for her women's advocacy and legal service by several individual countries, and by Amnesty International. She has also been awarded the respected French Ludovic Trarieux Human Rights Prize. *See also* EBADI, SHIRIN.

KARBASCHI, GHOLAM HUSSEIN (1954-). Appointed in 1989, Gholam Hussein Karbaschi spent almost a decade as the mayor of **Tehran**. During his tenure in office, Karbaschi angered many conservatives by building libraries, sporting facilities, modern art galleries, and recreation centers in the city. Both the symbolism and the resultant tax burden were sources of wrath. He also helped to build supermarkets in the city, which impacted the traditional **bazaar**, and also replaced revolutionary graffiti with Western advertisements.

A strong supporter of President **Muhammad Khatami** and former President **Ali Akbar Hashemi-Rafsanjani**, he helped to found the reformist political group *Kargozaran-i Sazandegi-ye Iran* (Servants of Reconstruction) in 1996. He founded and edited the municipal newspaper *Hamshahri* as well as the popular daily *Ham-mihan*, which was banned in May 2000, along with 12 other dailies in a massive crackdown on the **reformist press**.

Ham-mihan had only begun publication in January 2000 after Karbaschi's release from prison.

Karbaschi was arrested in April 1998, partly because he had angered Islamic hardliners with his attempts to modernize the city, but mostly due to his reform-minded views and activities. He was accused of mismanagement, embezzlement, and misconduct by his opponents. In July, he was sentenced to five years imprisonment, 60 lashes, a substantial fine, and a 20-year ban from holding an elected office. The sentence of 60 lashes was suspended. Karbaschi appealed his sentence and, in December 1998, his sentence was reduced to two years imprisonment, a 10-year ban on holding an elected office, and a lesser fine. He began his sentence in May 1999. Notedly, Karbaschi's televised trial had ratings in Iran second only to the World Cup.

In 2003, Karbaschi's critics accused him of trying to begin yet another newspaper as well as trying to run in the Tehran City Council elections, both of which he denied. It was also rumored that he intended to set up a private bank. Whatever his intentions and despite his maverick status with the more radical elements of the **Islamic Republic**, Karbaschi remains a force in Iranian politics.

KARGOZARAN-I SAZANDEGI. *Kargozaran-i Sazandegi*, variously translated as "Servants of Reconstruction" or "Executives of Iran's Reconstruction" was a political grouping founded in 1996. It consisted mainly of technocratic supporters of the then President **Ali Akbar Hashemi-Rafsanjani** who compiled a list of candidates for the upcoming 1996 **Majlis** elections. Amongst the 16 founders were such figures as Vice President **Ata'ollah Mohajerani** and eight cabinet ministers of the Rafsanjani government. Another key figure was the mayor of **Tehran, Gholam Hussein Karbaschi**, who played an active role in both the formation of this new pragmatic political camp and in the election success of their approved candidates in the parliamentary elections of 1996. Karbaschi and the Kargozaran were also instrumental in the electoral victory a year later of President **Muhammad Khatami** (Rafsanjani was barred Constitutionally from running for a third consecutive term.)

The Kargozaran were sometimes referred to as the "modern right," as opposed to the radically religious conservative right, best represented by the political grouping known as the *Jame'eh-yi Ruhaniyyat-i Mobarez* (League of Militant Clergy). Whereas the latter was more concerned with the ideological purity of the **Islamic Revolution**, the Kargozaran placed greater emphasis on economic development, favoring a free market **economy**, and more open social reform, or "enduring reconstruction," as one of their slogans stressed. By extension, this also meant rejoining the global community of nations in cooperative economic ventures, which was only possible by relaxing the more strident aspects of foreign policy. In particular, the possible breaking of the iconic taboo of relations with the United States, while not a part of the platform of the Kargozaran, was implied. Several Kargozaran members said as much publicly.

The electoral success of the Kargozaran indicated a major shift in the mood of the country. Even the ranks of the conservative right had been split with the breakoff of a group of radical-populist clergy from the *Ruhaniyyat-i Mobarez* to form the *Majma'i Ruhaniyyun-i Mobarez* (Union of Militant Clergy) prior to the 1988 Majlis elections. The latter generally supported the Kargozaran candidates in the 1996 elections. President Khatami appointed a cabinet consisting mainly of young technocrats with pragmatic leaning. There were 17 newcomers and many of the new ministers were originators of the Kargozaran.

The backlash was not long in coming. The conservative clergy mounted a sustained campaign to block new initiatives and smear the more outspoken pragmatic politicians. These included such figures as Mohajerani, who was forced to resign his cabinet position, and Karbaschi, who was charged, tried, and jailed on charges of corruption. In a wider sense, the battle in the late 1990s and into the 21st century was for control over the fate of the revolution. The result was a series of setbacks for the pragmatist camp. These included the shutdown of many newspapers of the **reformist press**, the jailing of intellectuals and journalists, most notably **Akbar Ganji**, and attacks on student supporters of a more open society, such as the **Student Dormitory Attacks** at **Tehran University**.

While the conservatives "won" the first round, the contest lingers, and continues unresolved in a less acute fashion. The Kargozaran, in their call to address in new ways social and economic problems, unleashed significant forces that are still much a part of the Iranian domestic political dynamic.

KARIM KHAN ZAND (Ruled 1750-1779). Muhammad Karim Khan Zand of the **Lur tribe** founded the Zand Dynasty in 1750. He had served as a general under the great conqueror and ruler **Nader Shah**. In the chaotic aftermath of the assassination of Nader Shah in 1747, Karim Khan took control of the central and southern parts of Iran. He left in place in **Isfahan** a figurehead, Shah Ismail III, the grandson of the last reigning monarch of the **Safavid Dynasty**. Actual rule lay in the hands of Karim Khan under the title of *Vakil* (Deputy). Eventually, he did away with the facade and became the singular ruler of most of the **Iranian Plateau** with the exception of **Khorasan** and parts of the north.

Though the founder of a new dynasty, Karim Khan never took on the title of *ShahanShah* (King of Kings), but retained his self-designated title of *Vakil*. He is remembered as a beneficent and compassionate ruler. He made **Shiraz** his capital where he reorganized the fiscal system and became a patron of the arts. Karim Khan also adorned the city with several enduring architectural features, the *Vakil* Mosque and the large covered **bazaar** which also carries his name.

The kingdom prospered under the reign of Karim Khan with political stability and the expansion of **trade**. In 1763, he allowed the British East India Company to establish a trading post in Bushehr. In 1775-1776, he attacked and captured the port city of Basra. The period of prosperity under Karim Khan was short lived, an interlude in an 18th century Iran fraught with frequent upheavals and anarchy. Upon the death of Karim Khan in 1779, his weak and rivaling relatives failed to maintain control. Ensuing civil war led to the final collapse of the Zands at the hands of **Agha Muhammad Khan Qajar** in 1794 and the establishment of the **Qajar Dynasty** with its new capital of **Tehran** in 1796.

KARROUBI, MEHDI (1937-). Born in the village of Behrin in the southern Chahar Mahal Bakhtiari Province, Karroubi was the son of Mullah Ahmad Karroubi. His father insisted on his **education** in the Quranic schools at Najaf, Iraq until he began study at the seminary in **Qum**, where he focused on Islamic studies. From early in his studies, Karroubi developed an anti-Shah disposition, fighting alongside his politically active father opposing the **Pahlavi** reign. After the 1963 uprising in Qum which resulted in an attack by government troops on **Feiziyeh Seminary**, Karroubi was arrested for the first of several times and quickly rose in the ranks of the **SAVAK**'s watch list. After his release from prison in 1976, Karroubi began living quietly, under the watch of the secret police, all the while studying the writings and speeches of **Ayatollah Ruhollah Khomeini** and distributing them among the poor and rural areas of Iran.

In 1979, after the **Islamic Revolution**, Karroubi became the head of the Imam Khomeini Relief Committee, until moving to the position of director of the Martyr's Foundation in 1980, where he remained until 1989. In 1990, Karroubi was elected Speaker of the Third **Majlis**, which proved a challenge as the internal discord between religious hard liners and left-wing officials nearly caused the assembly to be dissolved. During the controversy, Karroubi and several others formed a militant organization called the MRM (Union of Militant Clergy) to create a force of a radical solidarity in the assembly. Again, Karroubi was elected speaker in 2000, this time for the Sixth Majlis, a position in which he served until 2004. In the intervening years between 1990 and 2004, Karroubi gradually migrated from a leading radical position to a more reformist agenda, one of several such transformations among key revolutionary personalities.

In 2005, he entered the race for president. Though he was favored from the start, in the first round of voting Karroubi received just 17.28 percent of the votes, placing him third behind former president **Ali Akbar Hashemi-Rafsanjani** and **Tehran** mayor **Mahmud Ahmadinejad**, which removed him from the final runoff voting.

KARUN RIVER. The Karun River originates in the **Zagros Mountains** and is an important transportation resource as well as a water supply for the inhabitants of the southwestern **Khuzistan** Province. It is Iran's largest and only navigable river, but navigation is limited to the length between Shushtar and **Khorramshahr** (renamed Khuninshahr in the 1980s as a result of the **Iran-Iraq War**), due to the rapids and swamps which interrupt its flow. The river is about 724 kilometers long, and runs through deep gorges, pasturelands, woodlands, and valleys.

The Karun supports diverse lifestyles along its length. Seminomadic pastoralist groups, most notably the **Bakhtiari**, live in the meadowlands and grassy valleys. Others cultivate vegetables, fruit, and grains, utilizing the river for irrigation needs. Employment opportunities related to the recent development of the **oil** industry in the southwest have led to a sharp rise in the population of the Karun valley.

The Karun joins with the waters of the Tigris and Euphrates Rivers after they have lost their separate identities and formed the **Shatt al-Arab**. Approximately 40 percent of the waters flowing into the Persian Gulf from the Shatt al-Arab are provided by the Karun.

KASHAN. Kashan is located in the north of the province of **Isfahan** in west central Iran. Current (1996) population estimates list the city proper at 201,372. It is 258 kilometers south of the capital of Iran, **Tehran**. Located to its east is the township of Ardestan and to its south are the townships of Natanz and Isfahan. It sits on the high **Iranian Plateau** that makes up the majority of inner Iran. To its east is the Dasht-i Kavir, one of the several great deserts of the country which is also one of the driest areas of Iran. The **Zagros Mountains** stretch to the west. Thus, Kashan is situated between natural barriers, the mountains and the desert.

The climate of Kashan is dry. The farmers of the region depend heavily on the use of irrigation. The mulberry tree, which is used for silk production, grows widely in Kashan. The city has long been known throughout the world for its silk and its production of carpets and silk textiles. Other noted economic activities include the production of ceramics, copperware, rose water, velvets, and porcelain tile. The last was particularly celebrated in the **Safavid** period, during which time Kashan served briefly as the capital of the dynasty under Shah Abbas II. The **Persian language** term for mosaic tile (*kashi*) is indicative of Kashan's significance in tile production.

Kashan is one of the oldest cities of Iran. The findings of archaeologists in the Siyalk Hillocks suggested that the area was one of the centers of prehistoric ages. This area is part of greater Kashan lying only four kilometers west of the current city. Another noted regional attraction is *Bagh-i Fin*, an extensive and lovely garden estate not far from Kashan. A royal retreat during the **Qajar** period, *Fin* achieved some notoriety as the location of **Mirza Taqi Khan Amir Kabir**'s forced suicide in the mid-19th century.

In Kashan, there was a large **Babi** community. In 1844, the message of the Bab first came to Kashan. Later, there was also a large **Bahai** community in Kashan. Reportedly, there was a large conversion of Kashani **Jews** to the Bahai faith. Kashan played an important role in the dispersion of the Bahai. Consequently, when attacks against Bahais occured throughout the country, there was heavy persecution of Bahai followers in Kashan.

The region thrived in the **Sassanid** and Safavid periods. In the intervening periods Kashan was less prominent and was damaged heavily during the Seljuk and Mongol eras. The town and its nearby villages were laid to waste by major earthquakes occurring in the 19th century. Social and political turmoil also negatively impacted the economics of the city. More recently, things have been quieter and the city has prospered.

Kashan, as a 21st century city, possesses a number of historical and architecturally interesting sites. In general, it is considered one of the more attractive cities of Iran.

KASHANI, AYATOLLAH ABOL QASEM MOSTAFAVI (1885-1961). **Ayatollah** Kashani was born in **Tehran**, the son of a prominent **Shiah** cleric who insisted on his training in Quranic studies from an early age. At age 16, Kashani began seminary study focusing on Arabic language and literature, logic, and Is-

lamic jurisprudence, continuing at a seminary in Najaf, Iraq where he received a jurisprudence degree at the age of 25.

Kashani held deep political beliefs regarding the extensive power of the **Pahlavi** Monarchy and what he saw as failures of government policy. Kashani was persistently outspoken against British influence in Iran and elsewhere in the Middle East. He was also particularly concerned about growing secularism in Iran and the lack of independence from foreign control, especially in the lucrative **oil** sector. Kashani became a well-known figure for his support of **Muhammad Mossadeq**'s oil nationalization plan. In 1952 Ahmad Qavam was appointed by **Muhammad Reza Shah** to replace Mossadeq. Soon after, the new prime minister renounced Mossadeq's oil plan. In response, Kashani led the Mojahedin-i Islam, a group made up of multiple political parties espousing rejection of the Shah, oil nationalization, and the sovereignty of Iran to govern according to **Islam**, in massive protests of the new administration. These protests forced the Shah to reinstate Mossadeq.

During this time Kashani's popularity grew, especially among a growing devout segment of the middle class who believed wholly in governance by Islamic Law (shariah), administered by the ulama alone. While Kashani, in his role as leader of the Mojahedin-i Islam, did not see this idea come to fruition, his political views on the role of **religion** in society would be an important forerunner of **Ayatollah Ruhollah Khomeini**'s ideology which powered the 1979 **Islamic Revolution** in Iran.

KASRAVI, AHMAD (1890-1946). Ahmad Kasravi was a prolific writer and reformer in 20th century Iran. A native of **Tabriz**, he was a self-educated intellectual, influenced by Western ideas. He served for a brief period in several government ministries before turning to a career as an iconoclastic historian and writer. His work also ranges through geography, **literature**, and philology. The sum of his works numbers in the hundreds, including more than 80 book-length volumes.

It is for his work in the social criticism genre that Kasravi is best known. He began publishing a monthly journal entitled *Peiman* in 1933, which he used as a vehicle for developing and disseminating his controversial ideas. Many of the articles were lengthened into book form following the demise of the journal in 1942. Kasravi was also a founding member of an informal political party formed after **Reza Shah**'s abdication, which consistently attacked religious, government, and educational institutions.

He continually challenged the Iranian political and social system, particularly the influence of **Shiah** Islam and the clergy. Though critical of the **Pahlavi** regime, he cited the emergence of a religio-political system as the most potent danger to the country. He promoted social solidarity, not in the communistic sense, but as a means of maintaining and fostering individual rights. Polemic writings directed at the **Tudeh** underscored his attitude toward socialist/communist ideologies.

Kasravi's influence was at its height in the 1940s, at the same time that an Islamic fundamentalist movement was gaining momentum. The biting anti-clerical views of Kasravi provoked a strong reaction in religious circles. Nine books authored by clerics appeared in response. In 1943, he came under attack in **Ayatollah Ruhollah Khomeini**'s book, *Revelation of Secrets*. Kasravi's critical writings continued unabated. In the mid-1940s, he published such works as *What Do We Want, What Will Be the Fate of Iran*, and *Let the Government Respond to Us*, presenting clear analyses of the existing social situation and outlining his own solutions to what he considered grave problems confronting Iran during this period of political and social flux.

In 1946, at the height of his productivity, he was assassinated by members of the fundamentalist **Islamic** organization **Feda'iyan-i Islam** for his persistent attacks on Shiah clergy and **religion** in general.

KERBALA. Kerbala is a significant site to **Shiah** Muslims and is a key center of pilgrimage for the Shiite sect. Located in central Iraq, this holy city is the capital of Kerbala Province and is on the edge of the Syrian Desert. Kerbala owes its importance and growth as a city to the presence of the shrine of the third in the line of Shiah leaders, **Imam Hussein**. As both a burial ground and a destination for pilgrimage, over the centuries Kerbala has sprouted from a dusty plain into a modern-day city of nearly 300,000 people.

Hussein was born in Al-Medina, Arabia, the son of **Imam Ali**. He was martyred at age 57, as was most of his family, at Kerbala. The martyrdom of Imam Hussein and his followers at Kerbala embodies to Shiites the pinnacle of humanity's struggle against injustice and serves as a symbol that Shiah believers should strive to heighten their spiritual senses until they reach the magnitude exhibited by Hussein.

The impact of Kerbala cannot be overestimated. Even today, clay from the ground is pressed into tablets and exported to Shiites around the world to use in prayer. They place the tablet on the ground and press their forehead against it when they bow in prayer.

Imam Hussein and a band of followers were massacred at Kerbala as an offshoot of differences within the Community of Believers over the legitimacy of rulership within Islam. Two competing principles were embodied in the Sunni and Shiah positions. The Sunni had prevailed as the majority. The Shiah position maintained that the Caliph was a usurper and that true authority lay with the Imam. The departure of Hussein from Mecca was seen as an act of sedition by the ruling Sunni Caliph. An army was dispatched to intercept and caught up with Hussein at Kerbala, killing the Imam and most of his followers. Seemingly broken, like a Phoenix, Shiism arose and became a vital force in the Islamic world.

By his sacrifice at Kerbala, Hussein had revitalized the Islamic spirit of righteous struggle. A religious festival featuring a dramatic reenactment, the *Taziyeh*, commemorates the martyrdom of Imam Hussein each year on the anniversary of the event. And thus, the memory of Kerbala is refreshed and renewed in the minds of all Shiah. **Ayatollah Ruhollah Khomeini** effectively harnessed the emotion of this event in his resistance to the rulership of **Muhammad Reza Shah** and the **Pahlavi Dynasty**, which led to the eventual establishment of the **Islamic Republic of Iran**. Even after the establishment of the Republic, Kerbala was invoked as a symbolic rallying cry in the naming of various military offensives during the **Iran-Iraq War**.

KERMAN. The city of Kerman is located in south-central Iran, 1,064 kilometers from the capital city of **Tehran**, at an altitude of 1,860 meters above sea level. Separated from the Dasht-i Lut by mountains, the city's location affords hot summers and heavy, sometimes violent, springtime sand storms. The weather is relatively cool the remainder of the year. Historically, the Kerman area has long been famous for the abundance and length of its *Qanats*, the underground water channels, a testament to the engineering genius of the ancient world.

Kerman is considered one of Iran's oldest cities. Constructed during the third century in the **Sassanid** period by Ardashir I, the new city was called "Ardashir Khoreh" and was referred to as "Karamani" by the Greeks. Since the seventh century, Kerman has been ruled at different times by the **Arabs**, the Buyids, the Seljuks, the **Turkomans**, and the Mongols, but prospered most under the **Safavid Dynasty** in the sixth and seventh centuries. The city was mentioned for its leather workers, silk trading, and embroidery by Marco Polo in his 13th century travel records. While parts of the ancient city remain, many of Kerman's historical sites were destroyed by a devastating earthquake in 1794. One of the best-known sites to survive into modern times is the Masjed-i Jameh of the 14th century.

Modern Kerman has a population of 384, 991 (1996) and is famous for its fine carpets as well as other cotton and wool textiles. The Rafsanjan-Kerman area is known for its pistachio production. These enterprises are aided by the still developing **transportation** system which connects Kerman to cities like Tehran, Bandar Abbas, and **Zahedan** by air, ground, and rail. In particular, the city has benefited in recent decades by the extension of the Iranian **railroad** system from Bafq to Kerman. Even greater benefit will soon be forthcoming with the anticipated 2007 completion of the final link to connect the Indian subcontinent to Europe by rail. This link will extend from Kerman to Zahedan, adjacent to the Pakistani border, where it will connect to the rail system of Pakistan via an already existing link from Zahedan to the border.

In addition, the relatively close copper mining **industry** in Sarcheshmeh has been an economic boon to Kerman since its development in the 1960s. The continuing prosperity of the city seems assured.

KERMANI, MIRZA AGHA KHAN (1853-1896). Mirza Agha Khan Kermani, born Abdul Hussein Khan in the village of Mashiz, just outside **Kerman**, became an important figure in the tumult that characterized the end of the **Qajar Dynasty**. His father was a wealthy landowner, which allowed Kermani to receive extensive, traditional religious **education**. He was also exposed to other educational influences. In addition to his parents, who were **Sufis**, Kermani's early education introduced him to both **Babism**—a precursor to **Bahaism**—and **Zoroastrianism**.

He also came into contact with modern European philosophy, which Kermani latched onto with vigor. As his interest in the field grew, his disenchantment with the facets of traditional Iran also grew. In his profuse—and sometimes contradictory—writings, Kermani lambasted **Islam**, Twelver Shiism, Sufism, Babism (even though he considered himself a Babi at one time), the **Sassanid Empire**, and other staples of Iranian society. Kermani especially detested the **Arabs**, whom he felt had supplanted a glorious Persian heritage following the Islamic defeat of the Sassanian Empire. According to Kermani, Islam was an attempt to raise a barbaric people to some semblance of civility, and when applied to an advanced civilization such as Persia, it only denigrated and subjugated that culture with its unfamiliar and sub-level concepts. Kermani tapped into Iran's Indo-European (**Aryan**) heritage to claim that, along with the Europeans, Iranians were somehow superior to the Semitic Arabs and **Jews**. He envisioned a return to the "golden age" of the Zoroastrian **Achaemenid Empire** as ideal.

Kermani spent much of his life in exile: first from Kerman, where he had angered a governor, and later from Iran itself. In 1886, Kermani found his way to Istanbul. There, he became acquainted with **Jamal al-Din al-Afghani**, and with his friend Shaikh Ahmad Ruhi, took part in a pan-Islamic circle. Despite his antipathy to Islam, Kermani sought an alliance with Iranian ulama to bring about the fall of the Qajar Dynasty. He wrote for and edited the Persian newspaper *Akhtar*, which angered **Naser**

al-Din Shah with its anti-regime stance, such that the king pressured the Ottoman government to suppress it in 1895. He participated in a letter-writing campaign to Iranian clergy to garner their support, becoming a harbinger for a tradition of secular and religious cooperative opposition to the status quo in both the **Constitutional Revolution of 1906** and the **Islamic Revolution of 1979**.

Kermani wrote extensively (some 20 books and treatises), calling consistently for a modernized Iran which he saw as only possible by overthrowing the old order by revolutionary means and establishing a new rationalist social and political structure. His persistant antipathy to Naser al-Din Shah and the Qajar Dynasty led the monarch to call upon the Ottomans to extradite both Kermani and Ruhi, but Afghani's intervention prevented this. Unfortunately, outrage over the Shah's assassination a short time later forced the Ottomans to extradite them to Iran, and both were soon executed.

KHAMENE'I, AYATOLLAH ALI (1939-). Khamene'i was elected the third president of the **Islamic Republic** in October 1981, and held this powerful position throughout the turbulent 1980s. After **Ayatollah Ruhollah Khomeini**'s death in June 1989, Khamene'i was named to take his place as the supreme *Faqih*, a keystone position in the Islamic Republic which derived from Khomeini's elaboration of the concept of **Velayat-i Faqih**.

Khamene'i had a long association with Khomeini. He was a former student of Khomeini in **Qum** where he also held a position of junior lecturer in a theological school. He maintained connections with Khomeini after the latter's exile in the early 1960s. In the 1960s and 1970s, Khamene'i worked as a preacher in both **Mashhad**, his birthplace, and Iran shahr. He was arrested frequently for his participation in protests against the government of **Muhammad Reza Shah**, the last time in 1975. He also authored books on Muslims in India and on the Western threat to **Islam**. He was the youngest of a group of militant clerics linked under the leadership of Khomeini in outspoken opposition to the

Shah's regime, all of whom later filled important positions in the **Islamic Republic**.

Along with **Morteza Mottahari, Mehdi Bazargan, Mahmud Taleqani**, and others, Khamene'i was involved with a pre-revolutionary committee that developed the ideology for an Islamic government. As a populist, his intent was to create the theocratic state outlined in Khomeini's writings.

In addition to serving as president of the Islamic Republic, Khamene'i held other positions of influence in the formative early period of the Republic. Following Khomeini's return to Iran in February 1979, he was appointed to the **Revolutionary Council**. He was the Friday prayer leader in **Tehran** and Khomeini's representative on the Supreme Defense Council, which he later chaired. Khamene'i was also one of the founding members of the **Islamic Republican Party** and served as secretary-general of the party.

In recent Iranian history, as *Faqih*, Khamene'i became the figurehead of one side of a contentious coexistence of two forces in Iranian politics. With the emergence of the reformist movement in the mid-1990s and the subsequent electoral popularity of reformist politicians following the election of **Muhammad Khatami** to the presidency in 1997, conservative elements within the government used their institutional power to circumvent the political and social reform the new ideology demanded. As per the **Constitution of the Islamic Republic of Iran**, important positions within the government, including the *Faqih* and the judiciary, were set up to provide a religious check to the more democratic institutions of the presidency and the **Majlis**. In the late 1990s, these offices were almost exclusively dominated by religious conservatives, and their oversight power essentially rendered the executive and legislative branches, which were both dominated by reformists after the 2000 Majlis elections, ineffective. As the most visible and the most powerful example of this element of the government, Khamene'i came to symbolize the reactionary conservative side of government in direct opposition to the symbol President Khatami became for the reformists. Still, Khamene'i was a shrewd politician who recognized the tone of Iranian society. Thus, although many times he supported hardliner efforts to stifle reformists—such as bans on reformist candidacies or newspaper closings—he also tolerated some reformist inroads, such as his refusal to overturn the results of the 2000 elections in which reformist candidates won the majority of the seats in Majlis.

The offices he has held suggest the degree of his importance in the Islamic Republic. Khamene'i was involved in most significant political developments in the Islamic Republic, including the dismissal of the first president, **Abol Hasan Bani-Sadr**, and the downfall of Khomeini's clerical rival, **Ayatollah Shari'at-Madari**. It is no exaggeration to conclude that, as one of a handful of Khomeini's confidants, Khamene'i played a critical role in engineering the **Islamic Revolution** and influencing the course of the Islamic Republic.

KHARG ISLAND. This continental island is situated in the Persian Gulf, 25 kilometers from the coast of Iran and 483 kilometers (300 miles) north of the **Hormoz Strait**. The island is under the administration of the Bushehr Province, which is the mainland Iranian province adjacent to Kharg Island.

The makeup of the island is unique to islands in the Persian Gulf in that its porous limestone rock collects freshwater, supporting significant numbers of gazelles and terns. The island was designated as a Protected Region in 1960 along with the smaller nearby island of Khargu, and then upgraded to a Wildlife Refuge in the early 1970s.

With the rapid expansion of **oil** production in Iran during the 1950s and 1960s Kharg became a beehive of industrial activity. In a marvel of engineering ingenuity, an oil pipeline was pulled along the seafloor to connect the mainland with Kharg and provide an outlet for the Gach Saran oilfield located in the **Zagros Mountains**. Extensive storage and offshore loading facilities were built and Kharg quickly became transformed from a sleepy island to a major economic asset, further enhanced by offshore discovery of oil within sight of Kharg. The island has served as Iran's chief oil export terminal in the Persian Gulf and was the world's largest off shore facility of its type until it was rendered nonfunctional in 1986. The island's position in the center of the

Darius Oilfield made it a primary target for bombing during the **Iran-Iraq War** from 1982 until its near destruction in 1986. Though repairs commenced when the war ended in 1988, progress was slow, periodically disrupted by conflicts such as the Persian Gulf War of January 1991. Even into 2005, Kharg has yet to regain its former prominence in a continuing atmosphere of political and economic uncertainty.

KHATAMI, MUHAMMAD (1943-). Serving as a symbol for Iran's reform movement after his surprise presidential election victory in 1997, Muhammad Khatami would become torn between his implicit promise of change and the powerful hardliner establishment that hindered his effectiveness throughout his administration. Khatami was born in Ardakan into a religious teacher's family, which shaped the direction of Khatami's **education**. Beginning with clerical training at **Qum** and **Isfahan**, he eventually attained the status of Hojjat al-Islam, the title of a middle-ranking clergyman. Intellectually astute, his studies of philosophy and education—the fields in which he has a university degree—informed not only his views on the needs of the **Islamic Republic**, but also his methodology for disseminating these views.

Although more left leaning than many in the pre-**Islamic Revolution** religious opposition to **Muhammad Reza Shah**, Khatami still provided his voice to the growing dissent against the **Pahlavi Dynasty**, speaking and writing against the regime. Following the revolution, Khatami served as a member of parliament in the Republic's **Majlis**, but his most important position was as the head of the Ministry of Culture and Islamic Guidance, a position he would hold for a decade. A harbinger for his future presidency, he was known for his leaning towards anti-censorship, a fact which would lead to his resignation in 1992 after conservative elements took control of the Majlis, promising not only ineffectuality in his ministry work, but also a likely vote-of-no-confidence.

Despite this early 1990s hardliner sweep, the call for reform progressively became stronger. By the middle of the 1990s, factors such as a large youth population and continuing economic hardships led to questions about the course of the revolution, and a regime of democracy and civil rights beckoned as an attractive alternative. With the help of aides, such as **Sa'id Hajjerian**, and the support of **reformist press** newspapers, such as *Salaam*, Khatami emerged from a five-year stint as an administrator at the National Library as the reform movement's presidential hopeful. His message resonated with the new cultural landscape of Iran, and he won an astounding victory over Ali Akbar Nateq-Nouri in the 1997 election.

In addition to a pro-democratic reform stance, Khatami also opted for Iran to become a more open nation, no longer a pariah state. Not only did he become the first Iranian president to make an official visit to a Western nation, but he also put forth the idea of the "Dialogue of Civilizations." In an effort towards rapprochement with the world, he urged a first-step engagement in cultural and intellectual exchanges between nations, including the United States. In 1998, he even gave an interview to Christiane Amanpour, a CNN reporter of Iranian descent, in which he directly addressed the American public on the subject.

Khatami's election energized the reform movement, resulting in stunning reform victories in local-level elections in 1999 (the first since the Islamic Revolution) and the Majlis elections of 2000, not to mention his own reelection in 2001. However, the structure of Iran's governmental institutions placed hardliner-controlled offices—namely the judiciary and the Supreme Leader **Ayatollah Ali Khamene'i**—above the executive and legislative branches dominated by the reformists. With Khamene'i and Khatami becoming like the opposing pillars of the ideologies they represented, it soon became evident that Khamene'i's power was greatly hindering Khatami's effectiveness. This created disillusionment amongst the supporters of reform towards the hope for change that Khatami represented. As hardliners became more reactionary—closing newspapers, arresting vocal critics, and even participating in the **Student Dormitory Attacks** at **Tehran University**—the fervor of the reform minded amongst the public increased, only giving the reactionaries more justification for crackdown. Khatami was unable to stem the conservative backlash and lost the luster of his original appeal.

By the end of his second and final term, Khatami became more a figurehead of an ideology, as opposed to a harbinger of democratic reform. In 2004, the **Council of Guardians** banned over 2,000 reform candidates from running in the Majlis elections, ensuring a return to a more conservative national legislature. Still, even though official means to change became increasingly difficult to achieve, Khatami's presidency stood as a demonstration of the will of a growing segment of the Iranian population. Combining reform and religion, President Hojjat al-Islam Muhammad Khatami seemed to exemplify a new dynamic of the people of the Islamic Republic at the beginning of the 21st century. However, as he ended his eight years of presidency with the June 2005 elections, the dynamic that Khatami represented drifted even further away from realization with the election victory of the conservative candidate **Mahmud Ahmadinejad**.

KHAYYAM, OMAR (d. 1122). Omar Khayyam was a noted 12th century Persian poet and scholar, excelling in mathematics, astronomy, physics, and philosophy. Though considered an intellect of great merit, Khayyam is not counted as a major poet by Iranians. In the West, however, he has become known primarily as a poet, thanks to Edward Fitzgerald's translation of his **poetry** into English in the 19th century. Pessimistic by nature and strongly influenced by **Sufi** mysticism, the poems of Khayyam reflect this outlook by stressing the helplessness of man on earth and his uncertainties about the next world.

Khayyam composed *The Rubaiyat* in rhymed quatrains. Fitzgerald's translation does little justice to the original Persian. The translator took great liberties in putting the sentiments of Khayyam into good English verse. In the process, Fitzgerald left an enduring Khayyam legacy in the West. More than a century later, *The Rubaiyat* is still published in a variety of English editions and remains a coffee-table staple.

KHOINIHA, MUHAMMAD MUSAVI (1938-). Outside Iran, the life of Muhammad Musavi Khoiniha may seem impossibly contradictory. He studied under the exiled **Ayatollah Ruhollah Khomeini** in Najaf, Iraq. He was directly involved in the taking of the U.S. Embassy and the holding of the **American Hostages in Iran,** and served in various governmental positions immediately following the **Islamic Revolution**. Yet, Khoiniha also helped form the reformist religious political faction, Ruhaniyyun-i Mobarez; published one of the most important pro-democratic **reform newspapers,** *Salaam*; and advocated a degree of rapprochement with the United States. In Iran's distinctive dynamic between religion, politics, and society however, this clergyman-cum-political animal is hardly peculiar.

Before the Islamic Revolution, Khoiniha pursued a religious path, which would eventually lead to his rank of Hojjat al-Islam. Deeply offended by **Muhammad Reza Shah**'s attempts to secularize not only Iranian government but also Iranian society, he spoke out against the **Pahlavi** regime during sermons and speeches in **Tehran** mosques. By the mid-1970s, Khoiniha's activism finally incited **SAVAK** to directly confront him; he found himself interrogated about his views and about other notables in the religious opposition, including **Ali Akbar Hashemi-Rafsanjani, Ayatollah Morteza Mottahari,** and **Ayatollah Muhammad Hussein Beheshti**. He downplayed the anti-regime elements of his views and those of other future revolutionary figures during these interviews.

However, Khoiniha was in contact with and in support of the movement and its spiritual leader, Khomeini, whom he had studied with briefly in the mid-1960s. Thus, following the revolution, he became not only Khomeini's public spokesperson, but also the overseer to the first presidential election for the **Islamic Republic**. He was even part of the **Majlis,** his famed speech on the floor of this body denouncing President **Abol Hasan Bani-Sadr** helping intensify the furor that led to the removal of said president. Khoiniha's politics leaned towards the left, and he became an important link between Khomeini and the cadre of the religious left.

The most enduring remembrance of Khoiniha during the early period of the Republic was his direct involvement with the **Students Following the Imam's Line** in their taking of the U.S.

Embassy in Tehran in 1979. Khoiniha not only aided the students after the fact, he also knew of the takeover prior to its occurrence and participated in the planning. Though Khomeini would offer his approval of the act after it happened, Khoiniha prevented any advance warning of the situation reaching Khomeini to prevent any loss of political capital in the event the public did not react positively to the takeover. However, the public did receive the news enthusiastically, and Khoiniha gained some political capital of his own, parlaying his newfound fame into a successful bid for a Majlis seat. In fact, he received so much acclaim that his party elected him vice speaker of the Majlis.

Throughout the first decade of the Islamic Republic, Khoiniha continued his political career, eventually even becoming one of the initial members of the **Expediency Council** established in 1987. In that same year, Khoiniha and **Mehdi Karroubi**, amongst others, created the Ruhaniyyun-i Mobarez, a splinter group from the older Ruhaniyyat-i Mobarez, consisting of left-leaning religious political figures uncomfortable with the growing differences with the conservative elements of the original faction. It was because of this group's lack of a public voice that Khoiniha joined with former members of the Students Following the Imam's˙ Line, **Ibrahim Asgharzadeh** and **Abbas Abdi**, to begin publishing the daily newspaper *Salaam*.

Though *Salaam* began as a mouthpiece for the mainstream left, as the political climate began to shift throughout the 1990s, and a call for pro-democratic reform emerged, Khoiniha and *Salaam* began to shift as well. In fact, *Salaam* is credited as having had a major role in the election of President **Muhammad Khatami** in 1997, which drew the ire of hardliners. Despite Khoiniha's past with the embassy takeover, the paper even expressed a view supporting a moderate rapprochement towards the United States. Views like these eventually led the hardliners to close down *Salaam* in 1999. A Special Clerical Court banned its publication for five years, and though it had originally sentenced Khoiniha to a three and a half-year prison sentence and a flogging for spreading lies, disturbing public opinion, and publishing classified documents, his status as a revolutionary figure led to his sentence being reduced to a fine and a three-year suspension from publishing. Though the ban ended in 2004, and Khoiniha had been mentioned on numerous occasions as a possibility for future public office, he has remained relatively quiet after this trouble compared to his earlier politicking and activism. His eventual reentry into the political arena is not at all unlikely, however.

KHOMEINI, AYATOLLAH RUHOLLAH (1902-1989). No man had more impact on Iranian politics in the last half of the 20th century than Ayatollah Khomeini, the driving force behind the **Islamic Revolution** of 1979. Ruhollah Khomeini was born in the village of Khomein in 1902 and pursued religious studies at Arak and **Qum**. His dynamic and inspirational speeches on ethics and Islamic values attracted a faithful following and his reputation spread throughout Iran. His speeches were highly critical of the government's violations of, and disregard for, Islamic law. Because of his outspoken criticism of the **Pahlavi** regime, he was arrested in 1963 and ultimately banished from Iran in 1964. He fled first to Iraq, where he continued anti-Shah activities and where he remained in exile for over a decade. A rapprochement between Iran and Iraq forced Khomeini to move once again and in 1978 he alighted in Paris, where he continued his activism via critical writing and speeches channeled through his network of supporters in Iran.

Ironically, Khomeini stepped into greater prominence and public presence in France than was possible in Iraq thanks to the ultra-modern communications network the Iranian government had installed linking the major capitals of the world. Instant communication links between Khomeini and his followers in Iran were certainly a factor in the speed with which the Islamic Revolution developed. This fact led to the quip that the Islamic Revolution was the first revolution in history that can be dubbed a "cassette revolution." As quickly as events unfolded, Khomeini communicated responses that were recorded, copied, and distributed in Iran through a network of mosques, shrines, and religious groups.

The timing of the Iranian revolution was unexpected, but the entire concept of a revolution based on Islamic traditions had been expounded by Khomeini years earlier. In his book, *Velayat-i Faqih*, he condemned the corruption and dictatorial practices of **Muhammad Reza Shah**, and proposed an Islamic state headed by theologians as the most satisfactory form of government. He continually called for revolutionary activism directed at ousting the monarchy and re-forming the government with its basis in Islamic ideology. Massive demonstrations and riots erupted in the late 1970s condemning the Shah's administration and calling for a new order. Brutal attempts by **SAVAK** to quell the disturbances only fueled revolutionary fervor.

In January 1979, Khomeini surged to international prominence as the Pahlavi Dynasty crumbled, and an Islamic government headed by Khomeini and his supporters emerged from the chaos. The first months following the installation of the new regime were disorganized and bloody. Former government officials were executed. Intellectuals fled the country and violent riots erupted. The **Revolutionary Guards**, Revolutionary Committees, and Revolutionary Courts stepped in to restore order. These organizations were not unified or under direct government control, and concentrated on terrorizing or executing those in opposition to the new regime. To the extent that there was coordinating policy, the **Revolutionary Council**, the members of which were appointed by Khomeini, played far more of a role than the **Provisional Government** of **Mehdi Bazargan**.

As the guiding light of the new government, Khomeini was cast in the role of supreme political and religious authority. This position was institutionalized in the **Constitution of the Islamic Republic of Iran** with the adoption of the concept of *Velayat-i Faqih* and its incorporation in the office of *Faqih*, or supreme jurist. Khomeini controlled both the presidency and parliament and concentrated his influence by mediating and maintaining a balance of power between the two. Khomeini was reluctant to place any real authority in the hands of an elected president. The first presidents of the government were frustrated by the lack of power accorded the position and served only short terms before resigning or being forced from office.

Several significant events occurred during Khomeini's tenure. In November 1979, rioting students captured the U.S. Embassy in **Tehran** and held the occupants hostage for more than a year, causing a deep rift in the already deteriorating Iran-United States relationship. The **Iran-Iraq War** began in September 1980, and continued until a cease-fire was arranged in mid-1988. Though the war devastated Iranian resources, Khomeini used it as a political device to promote national unity, and to deal with factionalism within the **Islamic Republican Party**.

Khomeini died on 3 June, 1989, a decade after the revolution. His death left many questions and uncertainties concerning the viability of the government he established and its future course without his charismatic leadership. Subsequent years have seen much debate over the actual meaning and intent of Khomeini's vision. Clearly, however, the legacy of Khomeini is secure as the father of the **Islamic Republic of Iran**. *See also* AMERICAN HOSTAGES IN IRAN; STUDENTS FOLLOWING THE IMAN'S LINE; U.S.-IRANIAN RELATIONS.

KHORASAN. Today a northeastern provincial area of the nation-state of Iran, the historic geographical region of Khorasan was much larger, encompassing parts of Afghanistan and Central Asia. The ethnically diverse population of Iranians, **Turkoman**, **Kurds**, **Baluchi**, and **Arabs** are descendants of warriors and kings who battled fiercely for control of the region, but also valued cultural achievements. At the beginning of the ninth century, Khorasan became a center of art and literature, and one school of Sunni Islamic law developed here. **Sufism**, the mystic element of **Islam**, was heavily influenced by Khorasani thought and culture, as this was the area where many of the early mystics were born. The first poetry composed in the new **Persian language** called Farsi originated in Khorasan late in the ninth century. Until the devastation of the Mongol invasion in the 13th century, Khorasan was considered to be the cultural center of Persia. In later centuries, Khorasan was largely converted to the **Shiah** sect of Islam under the influence of the **Safavid Dynasty**, and became a prime target for Czarist Russian expansionism and exploitation in the 18th and 19th centuries. Present-day provincial

Khorasan only took shape in the 19th century with the increasing definition of borders that accompanied the creation of the nation-state of Iran. A single province for most of modern history, a 21st century (2004) political subdivision has divided the area into three provinces: North Khorasan, Razavi Khorasan, and South Khorasan.

The terrain of Khorasan ranges from mountain peaks to deep gorges, from the green of the broad valleys to the stark landscape of the plateau region. In the northern section, plentiful rainfall allows communities of settled farmers to raise cereal crops, fruits, and vegetables. The higher elevations are occupied by semi-nomadic pastoralists who raise herds of sheep and goats. The more arid southern region is given over mainly to pastoralism, though scattered agricultural communities survive. In the Atrak Valley, communication lines have given rise to a few market towns which provide opportunity for agricultural-pastoral exchange, while offering a small number of manufactured goods for sale.

Industrial development is minimal in the region, though large reserves of natural gas are available for exploitation. Trace amounts of copper, coal, and iron ore exist, but are not considered sufficient for industrial mining investment.

Mashhad, the spiritual and economic hub of Khorasan, is connected with **Tehran** via air, road, and the railroad. It is the most densely settled city of the area with an estimated population of nearly two million, the second-largest city in the country.

Reflecting its history, the population of Khorasan remains ethnically diverse. Most are Shiah Muslims, though adherents of other religions are also found.

KHORRAMSHAHR. Khorramshahr is located in **Khuzistan** Province in southwest Iran, near the Persian Gulf, at the junction of the **Karun** and **Shatt al-Arab Rivers**. The name Khorramshahr was adopted during the time of **Reza Shah** in the 1920s and means "a joyful city." After the **Iran-Iraq War** the name Khuninshahr was substituted, which meant "city of blood." This sobriquet was in honor of the bitter and bloody fighting which engulfed Khorramshahr during the war and the devastating losses which occurred. Prior to the 1920s, the city had been named Mohammerah, a name adopted in 750 A.D. after the city fell under the control of the Abbasid Dynasty. Prior to this time, the city existed as a small port since the time of Alexander the Great who invaded Iran in 331 B.C.

Never a particularly important city until the modern period, Khorramshahr's development dates back to the late 19th century when steam navigation of the Karun River started. Khorramshahr became the main commercial port of Iran and remained so in the 20th century until 1980. The city took on vital importance during the 20th century because it was very close to **Abadan**, where the world's largest **oil** refinery was located on a nearby river island. Oil was discovered in Iran in 1908, and after the discovery, both Abadan and Khorramshahr grew rapidly.

In 1928, after completion of the **Tehran**-Khorramshahr highway, the port gained greater prominence as sea trade began to expand in conjunction with the rapid economic development of the country. By the end of the 1930s, the two cities of Abadan and Khorramshahr were connected by air, rail, and road routes to the administrative center and capital of the country, Tehran. Despite the development of alternative ports on the Persian Gulf, Khorramshahr remained the major commercial port of Iran and flourished until captured by Iraq during the first weeks of the Iran-Iraq War, 1980-1988. Bearing the brunt of the Iraqi attack, the port of Khorramshahr was closed in 1980 along with Abadan. The city was occupied by Iraq from the beginning of the war until 1982. In battles for control of the port it was almost completely destroyed.

The population of Khorramshahr before the war was 146,709 and the count in 1996 was approximately 50,000. After the war, the port was partially restored and the economy has been somewhat revitalized, though it is unlikely the city will ever recapture its former glory. Although the port has been reopened since 1992 and is functioning, it is not fully rebuilt or cleaned up. Along the Karun River, rusty boats line the shore and masts of boats are sticking out of the water. The bottom of the river is still covered with sunken boats from the war. The vulnerability of the port due to its location, amply demonstrated in the Iran-Iraq War, will encourage the continuing development of alternative outlets to the sea. This trend was already evident by the 1980s and is now in full swing at such port cities as Bandar Abbas and Bushehr which have taken on added importance.

KHUZISTAN. The Khuzistan Province of Iran is strategically located in the southwestern region of the country. Most of the population consists of Arabic-speaking members of the **Shiah** sect of **Islam**. Prior to the 1980s, Khuzistan's cities of **Abadan** and **Khorramshahr** served as major ports for Iranian oil refineries and commercial trade. The **Iran-Iraq War** devastated the two cities, particularly the city of Khorramshahr which was the scene of such bloody fighting that it was renamed Khuninshahr, or City of Blood. The war temporarily halted the economic prosperity of the province, but the abundance of resources, particularly **oil** and natural gas, has led to rapid restoration and assures a full economic recovery in time. Such recovery is ultimately dependent upon the fate of the **Shatt al-Arab**, which is in turn subject to political vicissitudes.

Khuzistan has several major oil fields contributing to the development of oil-related technology and **industry**. Pipelines and roads connect towns such as Masjed-i Soleiman and Abadan, and the **Trans-Iranian Railway** passes through **Ahvaz** and Bandar Shahpur, connecting to Khuninshahr. Besides an abundance of oil and natural gas, the province benefits from **agriculture** with large areas of fertile land enhanced by irrigation systems. The availability of water from the **Karun River** allows inhabitants to cultivate sugar cane, rice, and wheat. The area exports dates, milk products, and wool. Cotton is also an important commercial crop. Khuzistan's abundance of natural resources and its prime location make this province a promising area for further industrial development. *See also* INDUSTRY.

KIAROSTAMI, ABBAS (1940-). By the 1990s, Iranian **cinema** had become renowned on the international scene for its unique vision and its unparalleled innovation. Abbas Kiarostami, perhaps more than any other Iranian filmmaker, exemplifies this trend. Born in **Tehran**, Kiarostami would go on to earn a degree in fine arts and painting from **Tehran University**, utilizing his developed skills in such endeavors as graphic design and book illustration. Although Kiarostami is now best known on the world stage for his film directing, he also creates in myriad other artistic spheres, including painting, poetry, prose, and still photography. This is reflected in his versatile position within the film industry, also being a well-known screenwriter, editor, and producer, his skills honed due to his early eclecticism in artistic training and learning.

In the late 1960s, Kiarostami developed and filmed commercials—his first real experience with film. In 1970, he became a key figure in the development of a film division of the Institute for Intellectual Development of Children and Young Adults. During his stint with the Institute, he worked on many educational film projects developing techniques which would later play prominently in his work. He also directed his first film, *The Bread and Alley* (1970), while at the Institute.

Kiarostami directed short films throughout the 1970s—many of which received awards within Iran—before tackling his first feature film, *The Report*, in 1977. This film began Kiarostami's emergence as a unique light on the international film scene, although widespread recognition would not come until well after the **Islamic Revolution** of 1979. During the 1980s, Kiarostami formulated his peculiar and novel style, which borrowed heavily from the "New Wave" of Iranian film represented by such filmmakers as **Bahram Beiza'i** and **Parviz Sayyad**. Many of his works, such as *First Graders* (1985) and *Homework* (1990), could be considered traditional feature documentaries, but Kiarostami brilliantly blended documentary and drama in many of his films—a technique which would become a Kiarostami hallmark.

This technique was evident in what has become known as (though he himself does not label it as such) a trilogy of films, *Where Is the Friend's House?* (1990), *Life and Nothing More* (1992), and *Through the Olive Trees* (1994). These films elevated Kiarostami into international consciousness. Following the filming of *Where Is the Friend's House?*, a massive earthquake devastated Gilan, killing tens of thousands. Ostensibly, *Life and Nothing More* follows the filmmaker and his son on a search for the young actors in the original movie. However, in *Through the Olive Trees*, which contains elements of both fact and fiction, the story is told of the filming of *Life and Nothing More*, revealing its dramatic—as opposed to documentary—nature. Through this process, Kiarostami forces the audience to question what is real and what is fantasy. Kiarostami courageously deconstructs and reconstructs the audience's ability to suspend disbelief, making the viewers active participants in the creation of meaning for his films.

Kiarostami also utilizes ambiguity, or outright omission, to bring the audience into an active role. In *Life and Nothing More*, the search for the whereabouts of the young actors is left unfulfilled to the viewers, leaving them to decide for themselves what happened following the earthquake. Kiarostami's landmark film, *Taste of Cherry* (1997), also allows for the same audience participation. *Taste of Cherry* follows the course of a man who wants to commit suicide, asking numerous people for their assistance in the act. However, Kiarostami omits vital pieces of information, including what has driven the protagonist to want to end his life. The audience is thus encouraged to determine this on their own.

Although his films of the early 1990s, including those of the aforementioned trilogy, gained Kiarostami international recognition, it was *Taste of Cherry* that brought him his highest honor. The film received the award for Best Film at the 1997 Cannes Film Festival, the *Palme d'Or*. The award was a confirmation not only of Kiarostami's unparalleled genius, but also of the nascent prominence of Iranian cinema generally in the world's eye.

Despite the praises given to Kiarostami's work, it was not without criticism. One major criticism is his lack of well-defined female characters. However, beginning with *The Wind Will Carry Us* (1999) and culminating with *10* (2002), Kiarostami has featured an increased importance of **women**. In fact, *10* features the daily routine of a woman as experienced through the lens of a camera mounted on her car's dashboard; the title refers to the film's being divided into 10 segments. Even if Kiarostami is simply addressing criticism, this does not denude the fact that these films with strong female characters are further examples of

Kiarostami's progressing art. Like so many of his films, *10* has been praised by critics around the world.

Kiarostami represents for many the explosion of Iran's film industry onto the international scene. He has created a style which has garnered the praise of critics and fellow filmmakers alike. A new generation of Iranian filmmakers has looked to his example for inspiration, including **Ja'far Panahi**, who directly sought and received the aid of Kiarostami in launching his own career. In addition to being a representative of a wonderfully diverse and active Iranian film scene, Kiarostami's brilliance ensures that his importance will transcend geographical boundaries. As Martin Scorcese said of Kiarostami, "Kiarostami represents the highest level of artistry in the cinema." The world has taken notice.

KURDISH DEMOCRATIC REPUBLIC OF IRAN. Following invasions by the Arabs in the seventh century, a strong Kurdish identity began to emerge. For the next 12 centuries, the Kurds developed a cultural identity and a desire for self-government. This desire clashed with **Reza Shah**'s efforts to instill a new Iranian nationalism. In his efforts to create a sense of nationalism, the Shah persecuted the Kurdish minority in Iran, even going so far as to ban the Kurdish language. This persecution did not let up until 25 August, 1941, when the Soviet Union and Great Britain invaded Iran and forced the Shah to abdicate in favor of his son, **Muhammad Reza Shah**.

On 16 September, 1942, a group of 15 Kurds met to discuss the formation of a Kurdish political party. This new political party became known as Komala, which means the "Committee of Life of Kurdistan." The governing body of the Komala was the Central Committee, which was officially elected in April 1943. It is important to note that while the Soviet Union supported the Komala, it was not a puppet of the Soviet Union. In October 1944, Qazi Muhammad was asked to join the Komala.

Qazi Muhammad was a well-respected local Islamic judge in the city of Mahabad. A conservative, he quickly became one of the leading figures in the Komala. It soon became clear that the Kurds could not be free while under the rule of **Tehran**, so on 22

January, 1945, Kurdish autonomy was formally proclaimed. Qazi Muhammad was the first president of the Kurdish Republic. Soon, fighting broke out between the Kurdish Republic and **Azerbaijan**. This led the Soviets to impose the Treaty of Friendship and Alliance, which was signed on 23 April, 1946.

Knowing the Kurdish people could not always depend on the Russians to protect them from Iran, Qazi Muhammad tried unsuccessfully to gain recognition of the Kurdish Republic from the United States. Under intense international pressure, the Soviet Union was forced to withdraw its troops from Iran on 6 May, 1946, a direct result of the declaration of the three powers regarding Iran that came out of the **Tehran Conference** of 1943. The Iranian army invaded the Kurdish Republic on 15 December, 1946 and peacefully reconquered the territory. As the short-lived Kurdish Republic collapsed, rather than flee the country, Qazi Muhammad chose to remain in Mahabad. He was publicly hanged in March 1947 by the Iranian government.

KURDS. The over four million Kurds residing in Iran make up what is considered the third most important ethnic group in Iran, behind the Persians and **Azerbaijanis**, and constitute about seven percent of the country's population. The Kurds reside primarily in the area of the **Zagros Mountains** along the borders of Iraq and Turkey, adjacent and contiguous to the Kurdish population of those two countries. Several related dialects are spoken among the Kurds in Iran, often varying from valley to valley, known collectively as "Kirmanji." In the larger cities of the Kurdish region, educated Kurds speak both their Kurdish dialect and **Persian language**.

Kurds in Iran have been known as both urban and rural, with half of the latter practicing nomadism. However, by the late 1970s, only 15 percent of the Kurdish population of Iran were nomadic. Kurds are found throughout Iran, from **Khorasan** to Sistan and Baluchistan, due to periods of major migration spurred by government removal of Kurds from the western region of Iran. At the time of the **Islamic Revolution** 40 Kurdish tribes were recognized, all which maintained a tribal organization and authority, which included a feudal-type system of cash dues signifying allegiance to the tribal chief.

The majority of Kurds are Sunni Muslim, though the southern Kurdish areas see more diversity with some villagers following **Shiah** beliefs and smaller breakaway sects such as the Ahl-i Haqq and Yazdis, both considered heretical by mainstream Shiah. Iranian governments have repeatedly curbed Kurdish uprisings throughout history; the most recent followed the Islamic Revolution and was not put down until 1982. Following this conflict, the Kurdish population has been tightly controlled by the government of the **Islamic Republic**.

-L-

LIBERATION MOVEMENT OF IRAN (LMI). The Liberation Movement of Iran was founded as a moderate politico-religious group in May, 1961. The formation of the LMI was initiated by the Islamic activists **Mehdi Bazargan** and **Ayatollah Mahmud Taleqani**. The 12 founders of the LMI believed that countering imperialism through the combination of nationalism and Islam would lead Iran to a just government. The party considered itself a part of the Second **National Front** which, in the early 1960s, was an uneasy and short-lived alliance of various secular pro-**Mossadeq** groups and the more religiously oriented nationalists who formed the LMI.

The LMI failed as a singular political force. It lasted as a formal organization for only 19 months. In January 1963, with the arrest of nearly all of its top leadership, the LMI ceased to exist as an organized political party. There was a hiatus from 1963 to 1977, though the combination of religious and nationalist sentiments that the movement represented continued to percolate. Indeed, young activists who had originally been under the umbrella of the LMI broke away in 1965 and founded a separate organization known as the **Mojahedin-i Khalq-i Iran**, which opted for armed guerrilla opposition in response to the repression of **Muhammad Reza Shah**'s regime.

In 1977, the LMI revived as part of the explosion of political activity which culminated in the **Islamic Revolution** of 1979. Again, Bazargan and Taleqani played key roles in the reconstitution of the party.

After the Islamic Revolution and the triumph of **Ayatollah Ruhollah Khomeini**'s interpretation of the revolution, Bazargan and the LMI began to see in the Ayatollah Khomeini the same autocratic power that had characterized the Shah. The party argued against Khomeini's claim to divine rule, and the concept of *Velayat-i Faqih*, and fought for the sovereignty of the people through the parliamentary process. On 2 June, 1988, the **Islamic Republic of Iran** moved against the LMI. **Revolutionary Guards** raided the LMI headquarters and captured 31 people, including several former cabinet ministers in Bazargan's **Provisional Government**. The former minister of health in Bazargan's provisional government, Dr. Kazem Sami, was found stabbed to death in his office. However, these tactics of intimidation failed, and the LMI has continued to function openly for some time.

Ironically, in a time typified by progressive aspects in leadership roles in the Islamic Republic, the LMI found itself repressed, and ultimately banned, with many of its members sentenced to imprisonment. Following **Muhammad Khatami**'s election in 1997 and the election of many reformist candidates in the parliamentary and municipal elections (the first municipal elections since the revolution) in 1999 and 2000, conservatives began to fear the dwindling of their power. The conservative judiciary found a justification for a crackdown in the actions of the United States. In Washington's outspoken support for dissidents in Iran, the conservatives were able to play upon anti-American sentiment to move against reformist groups and media, including the LMI. Following student unrest in 1999 (which led to the **Student Dormitory Attacks** at **Tehran University**), the LMI was blamed for instigating the uprising, leading to 60 members being imprisoned in March 2000. By 2002, given the furor over being labeled a member of an "Axis of Evil" (along with Iraq and North Korea) by the George Bush administration, and the continued American vocal support of Iranian dissent, the conservatives were emboldened to act decisively. In July 2002, the LMI was disbanded by the Iranian Revolutionary Courts. The court also sentenced 33 members of the party to varying terms of imprisonment (ranging from four months to ten years) and fines (all over $1,200) for such various crimes as seeking to overthrow the Islamic Republic; spreading rumors and lies in lectures and interviews; and having connections with foreigners. Twenty-one members were also banned from political activity for 10 years. **Ibrahim Yazdi**, the secretary general of the LMI, was out of Iran at the time of the arrests receiving treatment for prostate cancer in the U.S., but did return soon after to face the charges. He was never convicted.

Despite the official disbanding, the LMI continued to operate, citing clauses in the **Constitution of the Islamic Republic** which state a political party only needs a license for official recognition purposes. Nothing forbade a group to function as a de facto party without recognition. The LMI continued to function, although its members were consistently banned from running in both the 2003 municipal elections and the 2004 **Majlis** elections. This led the group to officially boycott the 2004 Majlis elections in protest of the bans.

In 2005, the LMI announced that Secretary General Ibrahim Yazdi would run for president, but only if certain conditions were met. These were the resignation or removal of members of the **Council of Guardians** as well as the end of extra-legal activities by officials. The demands, and Yazdi's candidacy, were meant to send a message of protest against what the LMI saw as unconstitutional and undemocratic practices. It was just one more reiteration of the LMI's long-held activist democratic stance, and will likely not be the last.

LITERACY CORPS. The Literacy Corps was one component of the reforms that came to be called the **White Revolution**, initiated by **Muhammad Reza Shah** in 1963. This national program utilized educated youth as part of a countrywide service to increase literacy, particularly in the rural areas of Iran. Recruits were secondary school graduates of conscription age who would receive credit for military duty through service in the Corps.

Academics and teaching methods, along with military training, were part of the four-month training period. Corps members were then assigned by the Ministry of Education to villages, in their native districts if possible, to serve for a required term of 20 months. A remarkable 80 percent stayed on as teachers after their mandatory service time had expired.

Most of the recruits lived in villages, although some traveled in circuits to fill needed positions. They were accorded the traditional Iranian respect for teachers by the villagers they served. Their program included reading curricula for both children and adults, and they also helped with rural community development in the areas of health service, agriculture, and self-government. Many filled in as primary-level teachers in order to alleviate the shortage of trained instructors, and also helped build schools and small libraries.

At the onset of the program, members were usually men, or on occasion a husband/wife team. As an increasing number of **women** sought admission to the program, the Women's Literacy Corps was created in 1968 and began actively recruiting female high school and university graduates. In 1970, the membership of the Corps had grown to 60,000 and 4,300 of them were women.

The government used the Literacy Corps as a tool to combat superstition and ignorance as well as illiteracy. Many Muslim clerics viewed the Corps as a threat to their role as village teachers, but vocal protest was limited due to the popularity and obvious success of the program with the people. The importance and effectiveness of the Literacy Corps enabled it to survive the **Islamic Revolution** in 1979, despite the political and religious misgivings of the new government. *See also* EDUCATION.

LITERATURE. Persian literature is generally described as literature written in the modern **Persian language** of the Islamic era, and written in Arabic script. The vast collection of Persian literature, dominated by poetry but including other literary forms, is not limited to the borders of modern-day Iran. It was also nurtured in the wider Persian cultural arena which would include today Turkey, Afghanistan, Pakistan, and parts of Caucasia, Central Asia, and northern India. Composed by saints, kings, beggars, and professional poets alike, Persian literature has poetically evolved from a rigidly defined form and metric system, to the free verse style of today. Prose has existed from the earliest of days, but has developed as a full-blown literary genre primarily in the modern period.

Fragments of pre-Islamic Persian literature do still remain, written in Old and Middle Persian between 650 B.C. and 650 A.D. They consist mainly of religious texts. The most ancient collection of pre-Islamic literature remaining is the Avesta or Zend-Avesta, the prayer book of **Zoroastrianism**. It forms the sacred scriptures of the present-day Zoroastrians, known as Parsis, who live in small communities in Iran, India, and Pakistan. Avestan and Old Persian, the language of the Avesta, was probably spoken in the northeast of ancient Persia. Except for scriptural use, Avestan died out centuries before the Islamic invasion.

In the centuries following the Muslim invasion of the seventh century, Modern Persian (Farsi) emerged as the literary language. The language incorporated a large Arabic vocabulary and adopted Arabic script. Under the Samanids, who established at Bokhara the first of many dazzling courts that were to patronize learning and letters (9th-10th centuries), a new literary era began, and the ancient customs of Persia merged with the culture of **Islam**.

The emerging literature was strongly influenced by **Sufism**, the mystical, ascetic element of the Islamic religion which evolved in response to the perceived loss of spirituality. Its influence can be found over many subsequent centuries in the strong mystical content beneath the literal meaning of Persian writings. Most of the great poets of classical Persian literature were professionals who worked for courts and produced poetry as works on demand for the ruler. The craft of poetry was not entered into lightly and was thought to require years of apprenticeship and preparation. The fine craftsmanship expected is evident in the versatile work of the poet Rudaki, known as the father of Persian poetry.

Persian **poetry** is generally composed within four main genres: the epic, qasida (purpose poem), masnavi (long narrative poem), and the ghazal (lyric). The epic has a special place in Persian literature and history. The Persian epic is epitomized in the **Shahnameh**, composed by **Abol Qasem Ferdowsi** around the beginning of the 11th century. Ferdowsi, considered to the present day among the greatest poets in Perisia, devoted some 35 years to this monumental work of 50,000 rhymed couplets. The *Shanameh* is the history of Persian kings from the earliest times to the death of the last **Sassanian** king in 651. The **characters of the *Shahnameh*** are those of giants and heroes.

A different form of the epic is the qasida, a form first introduced by Rudaki. The majority of qasidas are panegyrics, but they occasionally deal with philosophical or biographical literature. One of the most esteemed writers of philosophical qasidas, Naser-i Khosrow, was also influential in the modest beginnings of Persian prose. The *Safarnameh*, composed by Naser-i Khosrow in 1088 relates his pilgrimage to Mecca and his journeys in Syria, Egypt, and Arabia. One of the masters of *rubaiyyat* was **Omar Khayyam**.

The second half of the 13th century through the first part of the 14th century is often referred to as the golden age of Persian poetry. During this period lived three of the greatest Persian poets, Sa'di, Rumi, and Hafez. The ghazal, a sometimes mystical lyric form, excelled above all others in the poetry of Hafez.

A number of significant poets utilized the masnavi form, particularly for mystical and philosophical themes or romantic stories. The first reported mystic masnavi was written by Sanai. He was followed by a number of significant mystics, such as **Farid Al-Din Attar** and Rumi, the acknowledged master of the masnavi. Rumi's *Masnavi-ye Ma'navi*, consisting of six books containing over 25,000 couplets, is considered the most profound and the greatest work of Persian literature. Of the romantic masnavis, the most well known is *Khosrow o-Shirin* (Khosrow and Shirin), which is one of the five poems in the *Khamseh* (Quintet) of **Nezami Ganjavi**.

A popular genre of prose writing was that of "Mirrors of Princes," books of practical wisdom and rules of conduct. Such works flourished under the Seljuks in the 11th-12th centuries. Among this early prose, the **Qabus Nameh** written by the ruler of Gurgan, Kaikavus ibn Iskandar, is the most striking. In later didactic writing, the most respected prose writer was Sa'di, author of the famous book of maxims the *Gulistan* (Rose Garden) written in 1218.

By the 15th century a period of poetic decline began. The last great classical poet was **Jami**, whose work in both poetry and prose was of remarkable quality and quantity. He is acredited with writing over 100 works, including a poetic collection called *Haft Aurang* (Seven Thrones), and his masterpiece, the love story of *Yusef and Zuleikha.*

By the 16th century many Persian poets were attracted to the court of the great Indian moguls. The style of the Indian court, known as *Sabk-i Hindi* or the Indian style, became the dominant mode during the **Safavid Dynasty** between the 16th and 18th centuries.

A literary revival began during the 19th century and has continued into the present. Various influences, such as the political and religious turmoil of the 19th century and the impact of European literature, led to substantial changes in the form and content of Persian literature. By the end of the 19th century the ornate style of Persian prose began to be simplified and shifted its subject matter toward social and political issues in Iran. By the turn of the century an enthusiastic press had developed and a few pioneering serious dramas on patriotic and nationalistic themes were produced. This new literary activity contributed to the national awareness that led to the **Constitutional Revolution of 1906**.

Drama, in its Western form, was enjoyed for the first time as a separate genre in the late 19th and into the 20th century. Although not constituting a genre in classical Persian literature, there was an important traditional form of drama. The *Taziyeh*—passion plays centering on the lives of Shiah martyrs—was, and is today, deeply rooted in the national consciousness. There plays reached a peak of popularity in the late 19th century. In modern drama, perhaps the most notable Persian playwrite is **Gholam Hussein Sa'edi**. In 1919 the first collection of short stories appeared and a considerable number of 20th century writers excelled in this genre which took precedence over the novel.

Best known are **Muhammad Ali Jamalzadeh, Sadeq Hedayat,** Bozorq Alavi, **Sadeq Chubak,** and **Jalal Al-e Ahmad.** Hedayat is considered by many as the finest composer in modern Persian literature. Besides short stories, Hedayat is also recognized for his work in drama, translations, criticism, and folklore.

The turmoil of the early 20th century brought forth numerous women who began expressing themselves through literature. Many women published poetry and prose via magazines. By the 1930s, 14 women's magazines discussing issues such as rights, veiling, and education were being distributed. Various women authors emerged such as **Parvin E'tesami** who founded a literary publication called *Bahar*.

Since World War II, Persian literature has gained a new vitality, particularly in poetry. Many modern poets, using **Nima Yushij** as their model, left tradition and began experimenting in the "New Poetry" or free verse style. Rather than restricting his poetry to a set form, Yushij allowed the subject matter to dictate the flow of words. The "New Poetry" format was vigorously promoted by important literary figures of the 20th century including **Nader Naderpour** and **Mehdi Akhavan Sales,** also known by his pen name, M. Omid.

Also in the 20th century, **Ali Akbar Dekhoda** revolutionized Iranian prose. Fiction emerged as a new and important genre. Various modern Iranian writers including Mashid Amir Shahi, **Simin Daneshvar,** Ismail Fassih, **Hushang Golshiri,** and **Mohsen Makhmalbaf** (also a director of films) have composed and continue to develop the area of prose.

Since the 1979 **Islamic Revolution,** Persian writers have expanded their range of themes even further. Persian literature today encompasses the full range of social, political, and religious aspects of the Persian culture. Works that are deemed antireligious are banned in the **Islamic Republic.** Nonetheless, as occurred over the long history of Persian literature, the creative genius of writers continues to challenge authority and add to the existing deep and rich literary tradition.

LURS. Closely related to the **Bakhtiari**, the Lurs also reside in the **Zagros Mountains** region, specifically in the areas to the northwest, southeast, and west of the Bakhtiari. The Lurs speak Lur Kucheck dialect, a sister tongue to the Bakhtiaris' Lur Bozorg, and are divided into two main groups: the Posht-i Kuhi and the Pisht-i Kuhi. Each of these groups is subdivided into more than 60 individual tribes, the most prominent of which are the Kuhgiluyeh, the Mamasani, and the Boir Ahmadi.

Historically, the Lurs had a reputation for being fierce warriors, plundering villages in the region including other Lur settlements. Prior to the 20th century the Lurs were pastoral nomads, though they are known for having a significant urban population located in Khorramabad in Lorestan province. While a large number of Lurs were urbanized during **Reza Shah**'s forcible settlement attempts of the early 20th century, upon his abdication in 1941, many returned to the nomadic life. However, by the time of the **Islamic Revolution** the majority of the 500,000 Lurs had, through a gradual process of sedentariazation, settled in villages and towns or had moved to urban centers.

-M-

MAHDAVI-KANI, AYATOLLAH MUHAMMAD REZA (1931-). **Ayatollah** Mahdavi-Kani was born in Kan, a village northwest of **Tehran**. As a youth he studied in Kan and Tehran in the Sepahsalar and Lurzadeh schools. At age 18 he moved to **Qum** and studied under some of the most prominent clerics, including Ayatollah Boroujerdi and **Ayatollah Ruhollah Khomeini**.

In 1961, Mahdavi-Kani moved back to Tehran to teach at a religious school. At this time, a considerable underground intellectual movement of conservative clerics was speaking out in protest against **Muhammad Reza Shah** who was termed the "Taghoot," or tyrannical Shah. Mahdavi-Kani was among them, forming alliances and courting the favor of his old teacher, Ayatollah Khomeini.

In the initial stages of Iran's **Islamic Revolution**, Mahdavi-Kani was appointed to the **Revolutionary Council**, and subsequently would become a key power player in the world of post-revolutionary Iranian politics. In 1981, he became the minister of the interior, and later that same year was confirmed as prime minister for a short interim period. Among the other governmental positions he has held the following: chief of the Islamic Revolution Committees (*komitehs*); interior minister in the **Muhammad Ali Raja'i** and **Muhammad Javad Bahonar** cabinets; member of the Constitution Amendment Assembly; member of the **Council of Guardians**; and member of the **Expediency Council**.

Although initially considered a moderate conservative, Mahdavi-Kani became known as a hardliner in response to the reformist ideologies of Iran's various political factions, which were, in his mind, leading Iranian society away from the conservative platform of the Revolution by opening up society and making it vulnerable to Western influences. In 1998, this conservative-reformist conflict finally caused a split in one of the Revolution's oldest anti-Shah movements, the Tehran Militant Clergy Association (Jameh-yi Ruhaniyyat-i Mobarez-i Tehran, or JRM), of which Mahdavi-Kani is currently the secretary general. The rival splinter group is the reformist Union of Militant Clergy (Majma-yi Ruhaniyyun-i Mobarez, or MRM). The JRM advocates a market economy and a conservative Islamic social structure, while the MRM is more reformist in its platform.

During 2005 and into 2006, the International Atomic Energy Agency (IAEA), backed by the European Union and especially the United States, is applying pressure to allow international inspections of Iran's nuclear facilities. It is suspected that Iran might be developing nuclear weapons, rather than simply generating electricity with its nuclear technology, as it claims. Mahdavi-Kani has been quite outspoken on the issue, maintaining that Iran would never develop nuclear weapons because such weapons violate the tenets of **Islam**. Consistent with the hardline stance of other clerics and government officials, his position is that the United States is once again trying to interfere with Iran's internal affairs and that Iran has a legitimate right to pursue nuclear technology for peaceful purposes.

Mahdavi-Kani is currently the president of both Imam Sadeq University and Tehran's Marvi religious school. Some of his published works include, *The Beginning Points in Practical Eth-*

ics, *The Origins and Basis of Islamic Economy*, and *The Book of 20 Sayings*.

MAJIDI, MAJID (1952-). Majidi is one of the most outstanding contemporary Iranian film directors, in the same class as **Abbas Kiarostami** and **Mohsen Makhmalbaf**. He was born in **Tehran** to a middle-class family. When he was 14 he started acting in amateur groups. He later studied at the Institute of Dramatic Arts in Tehran. While studying, he played small parts in local productions, including parts in several films. His first significant screen role was in the post-**Islamic Revolution** production of a Mohsen Makhmalbaf film entitled *Boycott* (1985). Thus, Majidi had a strong background of performing in front of the lens before he switched roles and moved to the director's chair. This significant dramatic experience is evident in the strong performances he is able to elicit on the set of his own productions.

In common with many other filmmakers in the **Islamic Republic**, Majidi frequently uses children and families metaphorically. In this fashion, larger political and social issues that could not be directly confronted are nonetheless addressed, and more powerfully so in the hands of gifted filmmakers. Majidi's films characteristically operate at several levels, but nearly always in the genre of humanistic **cinema**. *The Children of Heaven* (1997) illustrates these themes well. Splendidly produced and acted, the film garnered a nomination for Best Foreign Language Film in Hollywood's Academy Awards.

Several years later Majidi directed another masterpiece, *The Color of Paradise* (1999). (The title is poorly translated in its English subtitle release as the more exact translation would be *The Color of God*.) Majidi has established a reputation for captivating cinematography and this feature is never more evident than in this production. The film is shot by the **Caspian Sea** and the scenery is breathtaking. He starts the film off at a blind children's school and weaves family life into a story about a blind child and a self-indulgent father to thematically express the concept that one does not really know what he/she has until it is lost. This film also gained widespread recognition at home and abroad. In the U.S., it set a box office record for Asian films.

Majidi has continued to produce praiseworthy films. His film *Baran* (2001) was a critical success. This film dealt with the emotional issue of Afghan refugee camps in Iran. Majidi followed with a 2002 film documentary on his travel to refugee camps in Afghanistan entitled *Barefoot to Herat*.

In common with some other prominent Iranian filmmakers of recent decades, Majidi has acted, written, edited, produced, and directed films. In the process he has produced over a dozen films, several of which are world class. He has contributed in multifaceted ways to the film industry in contemporary Iran and at a relatively young age has already joined an elite group of Iran's best filmmakers.

MAJLIS. The term Majlis most commonly refers to the Iranian Parliament, though the original attribution was to the popularly elected lower house of the Parliament. The first Majlis convened on 7 October, 1906. The formation of the Majlis was the culmination of the agitation of nationalists, merchants, and religious leaders regarding reform in the selection of government officials and legislative procedures. First granted as a monarchial concession resulting from the **Constitutional Revolution of 1906**, the Majlis has continued in existence to the present day.

The members of the Majlis, called deputies, are elected officials of the various districts within Iran, with the number of seats for each district determined by district population. Each deputy serves a four-year term and may be reelected indefinitely. Requirements for election as a deputy stipulate that the candidate be an Iranian citizen, educated, free from criminal conviction, and between 30 and 70 years of age. Candidates must also be Muslim. However, as specified in the constitution, there are two representatives from the **Christian** community and one seat each from the **Zoroastrian** and **Jewish** communities. The Majlis meets in **Tehran** and is presided over by a speaker who is selected from among the deputies.

During the time of the **Pahlavi Dynasty**, the Majlis, also called the National Consultative Assembly, passed legislative bills introduced by the Shah, the prime minister, Parliament deputies, or cabinet members. Once the bill received a simple majority, it was passed on to the upper house of the Parliament, the Senate, and if approved, the bill became law. The Senate was composed of nominees of the ruling monarch. After the **Islamic Revolution**, a new constitution did away with the Senate.

Historically, the Majlis had been strictly controlled by the two kings of the Pahlavi Dynasty. A striking exception occurred during the early 1950s, when the **National Front Party** of Prime Minister **Muhammad Mossadeq** managed to gain control of the Majlis and implement the Nationalization Law, resulting in the transfer of the Iranian **oil** industry from foreign control into Iranian hands. The assertion of Majlis authority was only temporary and died with the return of **Muhammad Reza Shah** from exile. Any trend toward undermining the authority of the Shah was reversed in the mid-1950s by the establishment of a tightly controlled two-party system which would present the majority of candidates for office. The **Iran Novin** party was instituted in 1963 to provide the Shah with a representative number of young technocrats in the Majlis, who would enthusiastically support his **White Revolution** reform program with appropriate legislation.

After the demise of the Pahlavi regime in 1979, the new constitution of the **Islamic Republic of Iran** retained the concept of the Majlis along similar lines of organization. However, there was no longer a monarchial role. Instead, a key new constitutional element relative to the functioning of the Majlis was introduced, the concept of the *Velayat-i Faqih*. The Islamic Revolution also changed the social composition of the Majlis, and the number of Western-oriented delegates declined dramatically. Increasingly, the **Islamic Republican Party** dominated the new Majlis and began to implement Islamic reform. *See also* FAQIH; HASHEMI-RAFSANJANI, ALI AKBAR.

MAJLISI, MUHAMMAD BAQIR (1627-1699). Born in **Isfahan**, Muhammad Baqir Majlisi would become one of the most important theologians and most prolific writers in Twelver Shiah history. His father, Mullah Muhammad Taqi Majlisi, was also an important theologian, though his views were much different than his son's. Muhammad Taqi adhered to many concepts of **Sufism**, which his son would later come to persecute. Still, Baqir studied under his father and like-minded theologians throughout his early years. Soon, however, his focus would shift away from the esoteric nature of his father's Sufism, and he began to study the *hadith* of the Prophet Muhammad and the Imams as his primary focus.

Majlisi's theology emphasized the power of God's justice (*adl*), and thus the requirement of all Muslims to actively oppose evil in the pursuit of God's Will. To provide a primary example for the fulfillment of this goal, Majlisi worked to compile the traditions, or *hadith*, of the Prophet Muhammad and the Shiah Imams. Much of Majlisi's writing, including the still influential multivolume work *Bihar al-Anwar*, includes these examples of *hadith* along with his own commentary. His writing did much to solidify the position of Twelver Shi'ism in Iran, owing much to his use of the vernacular language (Farsi), as opposed to Arabic, in order to be accessible to more of the general population. In practical terms, Majlisi's theology resulted in a more hardline adherence to Shiah precepts, which not only meant stricter attitudes towards things such as **women**'s roles and alcohol consumption, but also greater intolerance towards non-Muslims and non-Shiah—including Sunnis and Sufis.

Majlisi developed his theological position at a time when the Iranian ulama were finally becoming a major factor in Iranian politics. As a prime example of this trend, Shah Soleiman appointed Majlisi Shaikh al-Islam in 1686—a position he would keep through Soleiman's reign and into Shah Hussein's reign. These kings, Shah Hussein especially, allowed Majlisi unprecendented power, not only taking most of Majlisi's suggestions into advisement, but in fact acting on much of his instruction. In many cases, Majlisi was the de facto ruler of Iran in both secular and religious terms in the latter years of the **Safavid Dynasty**.

Majlisi's direct political power persisted until his death in 1699 during Hussein's reign. His body of work, however, left a lasting imprint on the nature of Iran and Shi'ism in general. His works, numbering somewhere near 100, continue to influence Shiah theologians and everyday actual practices in Iran to this day. Majlisi, perhaps more than any other religious figure of the

Safavid period, can be credited with much of the shaping of Twelver Shi'ism into its contemporary form.

MAKHMALBAF, MOHSEN (1951-). Born in **Tehran**, Mohsen Makhmalbaf is a prime example of the complex and never-ending struggles within the **Islamic Republic of Iran**. He was raised in a poor neighborhood and was strictly religious as a youth. He never went to the **cinema** or viewed anything that conflicted with his stringent Islamic outlook or that of an Islamic fundamentalist society. He would not view a film until he was 23. When he reached his teenage years, he dropped out of school and became the leader of a religious group that opposed **Muhammad Reza Shah**. At the age of 17, he was arrested for stabbing a police officer, and was sentenced to five years in prison, narrowly escaping the death penalty because of his age.

Makhmalbaf was imprisoned during the unfolding of the **Islamic Revolution** and at the time of the **American Hostage Crisis**. The new government of the Islamic Republic was responsible for his release. The release inspired him to create, and gave him direction. He began to write novels and screenplays, and in 1982, directed his first film *Nasouh (Repentance)*. He directed several films fashioned in a religious style and became popular during the early 1980s. However, his style changed during the later part of the 1980s and he questioned his earlier films. He began to address social issues and concerns, relying on a more subtle religious tone. The government began to relax their rigid censorship policies, and Makhmalbaf gained even more popularity. In the 1990s his style again transformed and he began to deal with sensitive issues that caused an uproar amongst conservative elements in Iran. Two films he directed in 1991, *A Time for Love* and *The Nights of the Zayandeh Rud*, assaulted conservative sensibilities which led to the banning of their showing in Iran. Showing his work became increasingly difficult, and he grew frustrated; so in 1998, in order to avoid the censorship of his homeland, he filmed *The Silence* in Tajikistan.

Makhmalbaf is generally acknowledged as one of Iran's most gifted filmmakers. He is one of the creators of the cinematic revolution of the past 25 years that has engulfed the country. He is difficult to categorize because his cinematic style is both unique and highly varied. In his almost frenetic output (18 films from 1982 to 1996) over the past two decades he has utilized a multiplicity of styles. The most distinctive of these styles has been described as docu-drama, a mixture of documentary and fiction, or fiction and reality. Also described as poetic, his style might best be summed up in his own words as "poetic realism." His films often have a surrealistic quality to them. These themes are evident in some of his better-known films such as the semi-autobiographical *A Moment of Innocence* and *Gabbeh*, both initially screened in 1996 but prevented from distribution in Iran for years.

In addition to his own film career, Makhmalbaf has also assisted his daughter, **Samira Makhmalbaf**, in her film-directing career. For instance, he played a key role in the creation of *The Apple* (1998), her award-winning film directing debut. He has also collaborated with a fellow pioneer in Iranian cinema, **Abbas Kiarostami**, in the film *Close-Up* (1990). In this film, Kiarostami used Makhmalbaf to play himself. The film is about the true story of an imposter who impersonated Makhmalbaf as a film director and is now confronted by the true director, Makhmalbaf himself. There is an interesting interface between reality and cinema suitable to the complex themes that both directors excel in exploring.

Addressing such issues as arranged marriage, love, and politics, Makhmalbaf continues to be a controversial director in his homeland. He is admired and respected by many, but viewed as a potential threat to social and political stability by others. It might be said that Makhmalbaf's frequent shifts in film style are not only a trademark of the popular director, but also a parallel of the continuous changes engulfing Iran over the last 30 years.

MAKHMALBAF, SAMIRA (1980-). It is said that "the apple does not fall far from the tree." This is the case with Samira Makhmalbaf, the 25-year-old daughter of noted film director **Mohsen Makhmalbaf**. As a child she was exposed to the art of film by watching her father, and by the time she was in her early teens, she asked her father to teach her about film. She dropped out of school and was tutored by her father in the art of filmmaking and **cinema**. Because much of her father's work was conducted at home, she was given the opportunity to learn from some of the most talented artists of Iran.

Samira herself describes her genre of film as social documentary and she has produced outstanding work in her chosen focus. At the age of 17, while watching television, she became aware of a family whose 12-year-old twin daughters had been secluded from the world. The idea for a film developed based upon the girls' lives, and she immediately drew it to the attention of her father. She borrowed her father's equipment, but was restricted in time because he was due to film *The Silence* (1998) in approximately one month. She completed the filming in 11 days, but was unable to do the editing until her father completed his film. Her father helped her throughout the film, encouraging his daughter to pursue a passion he himself understood. His influence was obvious when Samira chose to use an actual family instead of professional actors. Titled *The Apple* (1998), the film gained international attention, and was shown at Cannes in 1999. With her appearance at the International Cannes Film Festival, Samira Makhmalbaf attained distinction at the age of 18 as the youngest filmmaker to have shown (though not in competition) at the prestigious festival.

Only a year later, Samira completed her second film, *Blackboards*, the story of teachers traveling along the Iran-Iraq border in search of students. The story is a complex tale with a great deal of hidden meanings and symbolism, taking the teachers down various paths. This film also found critical acclaim and Samira made history again in 2000 when *Blackboards* (1999) competed for the *Palme d'Or* award at Cannes. She was the youngest director ever to be included in this most prestigious of film competitions. The film won the Jury Prize that year in Cannes. This feat was repeated a few years later when the Jury Prize was awarded in 2003 to her written and directed film, *At Five in the Afternoon*. Samira is sure to continue making films that inspire not only her country of Iran, but also the world. *See also* BANI-ENTEMAD, RAKHSHAN.

MANSUR, HASAN ALI (? -1965). Hasan Ali Mansur was the son of Ali Mansour (Mansour al-Saltaneh), a former prime minister. He completed his university **education** in political science and economics, and trained as a diplomat in the Ministry of Foreign Affairs. He spoke several Western languages and was a gifted public speaker. Mansur held many posts in his career before becoming prime minister in 1964. His posts included chief of staff of Prime Minister Hussein Ala, secretary of the High Economic Council, managing director of the Iran Insurance Company, minister of labor (1959-1960), minister of commerce, founder of the Progressive Association from which the **Iran Novin** party was formed, and 21st **Majlis** deputy from **Tehran**.

The largest block in the 21st Majlis, with 40 seats, was a group called the Progressive Center. In 1961, Mansur had established the Center, an exclusive club of senior civil servants and technocrats, to study and make policy recommendations on economic and social issues. In June 1963, **Muhammad Reza Shah** chose the Center to be his personal research bureau. When the new Majlis convened in October, 100 deputies joined the Center and several months later, Mansur turned the Progressive Center into a political party, the Iran Novin. In March 1964, **Asadollah Alam** resigned his post as prime minister. Public opinion was in favor of Mansur. The general mood was that the country needed a younger leader who would run it along technical and economic lines. The Shah appointed Mansur prime minister at the head of the Iran Novin-led government.

The events leading to the creation of the Iran Novin and the appointment of Mansur as prime minister represented a renewed attempt by the Shah and his advisors to create a political organization that would be loyal to the Crown, attract the support of the educated classes and the technocratic elite, and strengthen the administration and the **economy**. The Iran Novin drew its membership almost exclusively from a younger generation of senior civil servants, Western-educated technocrats, and business leaders. Initially, membership was limited to 500 handpicked persons. It was allowed to grow slowly, but full membership was limited to a very elite group.

The Mansur government enjoyed a comfortable majority in the Majlis with nominal opposition. One exception to this was a response to the Status of Forces Bill, a measure that granted diplomatic immunity to United States personnel serving in Iran for crimes committed on Iranian soil. This measure aroused strong feelings amongst Iranians. On 13 October, 1964, the Majlis approved this bill and, simultaneously, a loan of $200 million to reequip Iranian armed forces was granted by the United States, and submitted to the Majlis for approval. Mansur hailed the loan as a vote of confidence of the United States in the future stability of Iran. **Ayatollah Ruhollah Khomeini** thought differently. He is quoted as saying, "The Government has sold our independence, reduced us to the level of a colony, and made the Muslim nation of Iran appear more backward than savages in the eyes of the world." Convinced that Khomeini could not be silenced, the **Pahlavi** regime decided to exile him. Turkey accepted him on 4 November. Later, he moved to Iraq where he remained until 1978.

Hasan Ali Mansur, the prime minister responsible for Khomeini's exile, was shot outside of Parliament in January 1965. He lived for five days until 26 January, the anniversary of the Shah's **White Revolution**, the event that brought the opposition leadership of Khomeini to the forefront. This assassination was linked to a radical Islamic group. Evidence made available after the **Islamic Revolution** revealed that the group had affiliations with clerics close to Khomeini. On 10 April, 1965, the same party made an attempt on the Shah's life. Four of the participants were sentenced to death, and nine others were sentenced to prison terms. One of the men sentenced to life in prison became the minister of commerce in the post-revolution government of **Muhammad Ali Raja'i**.

Mansur was replaced as prime minister by **Amir Abbas Hoveida**, a former diplomat and an executive of the **National Iranian Oil Company**. Hoveida was the brother-in-law and a close friend and associate of Mansur, and had helped him found the Progressive Center and the Iran Novin.

MASHHAD. The capital of the eastern province of Rezavi **Khorasan**, Mashhad is situated 850 kilometers from **Tehran** in northestern Iran. The city is referred to as Iran's holiest city as its name means "place of the martyr," signifying the burial place of the martyred Imam Reza, eighth in the line of **Shiah** Imams.

Before the death of the Imam, the city was a small village known as Sanabad. The far more important city of the region prior to this time was nearby Nishapur, the home and burial site of **Omar Khayyam**. However, the death caused an influx of pilgrims, many of whom stayed in Mashhad to be near the shrine which developed around the tomb of Imam Reza. It is this growth impetus which gives Mashhad its distinctive bull's-eye profile when viewed from the air. It developed in concentric circles outward from the Imam's tomb. The shrine is also what led to large accumulations of wealth in the city, further enhanced by being sited along an important historic east-west trade route. These factors made Mashhad a favorite target for plunder which occured several times in its history. One of the most devastating of these was the Mongol invasion during the 13th century, nearly destroying the shrine and the city itself.

During the 16th century, the **Safavid Dynasty** established Twelver Shi'ism as the state religion and restored the shrine and the city. Mashhad served as the principal commercial center of eastern Iran throughout the 19th century. The greatest concentration of population growth, however, has occurred in the 20th century, mostly since 1950. In 1986, Mashhad had a population of over one million, a 110 percent increase over the population of 1976, the growth being attributed to an influx of more than 450,000 Afghani refugees to the city.

The tomb of Imam Reza remains a sacred place of pilgrimage for millions of Shiah Muslims each year, bolstering the city's **economy** as well as **transportation** and tourism. The heavily adorned shrine of Imam Reza and the associated shrine complex, including an important library and a theological school, are the key architectural sites of Mashhad. The tomb of the famous poet **Abol Qasem Ferdowsi** is located nearby in the town of Tus. Additionally, Mashhad has developed considerable textile, carpet, and food processing industries in recent decades, and is now home to nearly two million Iranians (1,887,405 according to the 1996 census). This ranks Mashhad as the second-largest city in Iran behind Tehran.

MEHRJUI, DARYUSH (1939-). Daryush Mehrjui was born in **Tehran**. His came from a middle-class family and, as a youth, he was very religious and musically inclined. During this time, he took it upon himself to learn English, which allowed him to obtain a job managing a hotel in Tehran. Working at this job for a couple years, he finally managed to save enough money to travel to the United States.

In 1959, he traveled to California to study **cinema**. Mehrjui enrolled at the University of California, Los Angeles to do graduate work in cinema, but he soon became disillusioned with the program and changed his major to philosophy, from which he graduated in 1964.

Upon graduating from UCLA, he and some other Iranians who felt the West needed further exposure to modern Persian **literature** published a literary magazine called the *Pars Review*. During this time he wrote his first script, a love story based on an ancient Persian tale, and in 1965, he traveled back to Iran with the intent of turning it into a film. He was never able to bring his plan to fruition, however, and during that year he found work as a journalist and a television scriptwriter. From 1966 to 1968, Mehrjui taught English language and literature at the Tehran Center for Language Studies, where he lectured on screenwriting, film aesthetics, films, and novels.

In 1966, Mehrjui produced his first film, *Diamond 33*. The film was a spoof of Western James Bond movies, and while it was well produced, it did not do well commercially. In 1970, he released his second film, *The Cow*. The story itself was based on a short story by **Gholam Hussein Sa'edi** who collaborated on the screenplay. *The Cow* symbolized individual alienation in the face of modernity and for Iranians the film took on added meaning beyond the psychological. It was viewed as a political statement. The film was originally completed in 1969, and even though it was the first Iranian film to receive state funding, it was banned by **Muhammad Reza Shah**'s Ministry of Culture because of its bleak depiction of rural society. The film was finally released in 1970 with a statement that the film took place 50 years prior and not during the time of the **Pahlavi Dynasty**. A copy was smuggled out of Iran and showed at the 1971 Venice Film Festival, where it received the Critics' Award. The film was greeted by both national and international recognition. This film is one of two (along with *Qaysar*, or *Caesar*, by Mas'ud Kimia'i) that marks the emergence of New Iranian Cinema. So important was *The Cow* that it took on the status of a cult film.

The critical success of *The Cow* was followed by the third film of Mehrjui entitled *Mr. Naïve* (1970), a work of light social criticism. This hilarious film also found praise both domestically and abroad, and launched Mehrjui on a highly productive and influential film career. He has gone on to produce many more quality Iranian films, both prior to and following the **Islamic Revolution**, and has earned 49 national and international awards. His controversial film, *Hammon* (1990), marked a shift from social issues to films of more personal cinema. And, beginning in 1992, he produced a series of films focused on female characters, films such as *Banou* (1992), *Sara* (1993), *Pari* (1994), and *Leila* (1996).

Daryush Mehrjui has been a prolific filmmaker, producing 15 films from 1966 to 1998. His impact on the film world in Iran over the past four decades has been profound.

MELLI UNIVERSITY. Melli University (National University) was organized in 1960, within the private educational sector. It is located in Evin, northwest of **Tehran**. Programs of study include architecture, economics, political science, law, medicine and dentistry, literature and humanities, and the natural sciences. A little over a decade after its founding, more than 6,000 students were enrolled at the rapidly growing university. In the 1970s, it became the second-largest university in the country after **Tehran University**. Its programs attracted the noted **Sufi** philosopher, Seyyid Hussein Nasr, to accept the chancellorship in the mid-1970s.

After the **Islamic Revolution**, the name of the university was changed to the University of Shahid (Martyr University), a

reflection of the Islamization process that began to occur generally in Iranian **education**. *See also* PAHLAVI UNIVERSITY.

MILLSPAUGH, ARTHUR C. (1883-1955). Millspaugh was a
political scientist in the U.S. State Department. He was in charge
of a financial mission to Persia from 1922 to 1927 and served as
the administrator general of finances in Persia. His department
controlled all government expenditures and rebuilt the country's
entire financial and tax structures. The first Millspaugh mission
was generally successful. Millspaugh returned on a similar mission for a short period in 1943, though the second mission accomplished little due to widespread opposition to economic reform. He wrote extensively of his experiences and that of
American involvement with Iran in *The American Task in Persia*
and *Americans in Persia*.

MINORSKY, VLADIMIR (1877-1966). Vladimir Minorsky was a
Russian-born scholar considered by many to be the premier
Iranist of all time. He was educated in Moscow, specializing in
law and Oriental languages. Following his education he accepted
a position with the Russian Ministry of Foreign Affairs serving
in Persia, Central Asia, and Turkey. It was during this period of
government service that his lifelong interest in Irano-Turkish
Islamic cultures developed. In his travels throughout Persia and
Turkey he accumulated a vast reservoir of knowledge relating to
these peoples as well as the geographical regions they inhabited.

Minorsky emigrated to France in the aftermath of the Russian Revolution of 1917. While living in Paris, he taught Persian
literature, along with Turkish and Islamic history. He settled in
England in 1932, accepting a position at the University of London as lecturer in Persian. He attained the position of professor
of Persian in 1937. Minorsky retired from active teaching in
1944, though he continued to travel and accept visiting profes-
sorships at various foreign universities. His visit to Russia at the
invitation of the Soviet Academy of Sciences in 1960 was a triumph for this expatriate who retained his love for his homeland
and left his vast library of Oriental holdings to the city of Lenin-
grad. His widow returned his ashes for burial in Russia in 1969.

The writings of Minorsky are varied and equally renowned. Covering a range of historical, geographical, and cultural subjects, he explored aspects of Iran from an insightful and scholarly position. Minorsky continued to write until his death at the age of 89 and two of his works were published posthumously. A prolific writer, the scholary publications of Minorsky number over 200. His multilingual ability enabled him to write in English, French, Russian, and Persian, and he left an unsurpassed and invaluable legacy in the many scholarly works he authored.

MIRZA MALKOM KHAN (1833-1908). Mirza Malkom Khan was an enigmatic, determined reformist deeply involved in the 19th-century Iranian politics of the **Qajar Dynasty**. Born in Armenia in 1833, he was educated in Europe where he developed an interest in the works of socio-political philosophers such as Comte and Mill. As an active proponent of Westernization for Iran, he set an energetic, often contradictory, course toward that end.

After completion of his studies, he returned to Iran and taught at the **Dar al-Fonun**. He introduced freemasonry (*Faramush Khaneh*) into Iran with the approval of **Naser al-Din Shah**, though it was later banned as heretical. He went on to establish the League of Humanity, a group of humanistic, theistically-oriented societies, which Malkom Khan intended to use to form a nucleus of highly placed men to implement his social and political reform program. Although politically suspect, the societies attracted over 300 influential members, including many of the ulama. These individuals later became active in reform movements, such as the **Tobacco Revolt** and the Constitutional Movement which paved the way for the granting of a constitution in 1906.

Beginning in 1881, Malkom Khan spent many years abroad as the representative of Naser al-Din Shah. While serving as the Iranian ambassador in London, he was involved in a fraudulent lottery concession scheme and was dismissed from his post. At odds with the Shah, Malkom Khan remained in Europe and began publication of the *Qanun* newspaper, along with pamphlets endorsing social and political change in Iran. He variously represented himself as a Muslim or a **Christian**, though he believed all religions to be identical.

Malkom Khan's writings, essentially secular in nature, advocated a systematic reform program, which would ultimately undermine clerical power. However, recognizing the need for the support of the ulama, he offered a revised version of his program which was couched in Islamic terms. He curried favor with the most prominent religious leaders, encouraging them in their efforts to regain the power lost to the authoritarian and foreign-influenced Qajar monarchy.

The successes of the Tobacco Revolt of 1891-1892 and the **Constitutional Revolution of 1906** marked a change in attitude for the Iranian people—from the powerless acceptance of authoritarian rule to a demand for representation in policymaking. Though he was unable to actively participate in the revolutionary reform movements, Malkom Khan's publications, along with those of other 19th century reformists, were responsible for the introduction of a climate of thought which influenced the development of these popular uprisings against established authority.

MIRZA SALEH SHIRAZI. The birth and death dates of Mirza Saleh Shirazi are unrecorded. It is probable that he was born in the late 1780s or early 1790s. The only available reference to his death states that he lived into the 1840s.

In the early 19th century, Crown Prince **Abbas Mirza** initiated a sponsorship program for young men to receive technical and professional training in Europe. Among the first group of five students sent to London in 1815 was Mirza Saleh Shirazi. Mirza Saleh was a scholar interested in foreign languages, and was the first Persian admitted to Oxford University. While completing his studies, he used his spare time to learn how to run a printing press, and when he returned to **Tabriz** in 1819, he brought along the equipment he would need to introduce modern printing into Iran.At the request of Abbas Mirza, Mirza Saleh's first mission in Tabriz was to instruct the children of the nobility in European sciences and languages. He never lost his interest in printing and, in 1837, he published the first Iranian newspaper in Tabriz. As a student in London, he was impressed by foreign political regimes and the parliamentary system and used his paper as a forum for discussion of change in the structure of Iranian government. Mirza Saleh's overall goal was to introduce readers to the news and innovations of the outside world and keep them informed of progress within Iran. He promoted the westernization of the country and consistently denounced the religious scholars for obstructing reform and modernization programs, yet his press made a substantial number of **Persian-language** books on Islamic themes available to Iranians for the first time.

His printing career ended in the early 1840s at the bidding of **Muhammad Mirza Shah** who did not encourage literary or cultural advances. Mirza Saleh went to work as an assistant in the Finance Ministry. Before his press shut down, the man who had described himself as "hopelessly inept" in technical matters had introduced Iran to a new and lasting forum for the discussion and dissemination of information from all parts of the world.

MIRZA TAQI KHAN AMIR KABIR (1806-1852). Mirza Taqi Khan was the son of a steward in the royal household, and through this proximity to people in authority, he was accepted for government work and rose steadily through the bureaucracy. He traveled in Russia and worked for an extended period of time in Turkey. His position in the royal household also brought him into extensive contact with foreigners, broadening his outlook regarding Western innovations.

When **Muhammad Mirza Shah** died in 1848, his 16-year-old son **Naser al-Din Shah** succeeded to the throne. His first official act was the appointment of Mirza Taqi Khan as his chief minister. Escorted safely from **Tabriz**, the seat of the crown prince, to **Tehran** by his new chief minister, the monarch gave the title Amir Kabir to Mirza Taqi Khan which proclaimed him "first man of the realm." As regent for the teenaged Naser al-Din Shah, Amir Kabir retained complete authority from 1848-1851, a period marked by fundamental policy changes which set the course Persia and the government would follow for the next 40 years.

During his earlier travel experiences, Amir Kabir began to visualize a modern Iran developing independently of British and

Russian influence. He began his reform campaign by increasing the size and strength of the Persian Army, endeavoring to create an entity which could defend the country with no allied troops. He continued in the tradition of **Abbas Mirza** by sending young men to Europe for technical and scientific training, and put the financial affairs of the country in order which stabilized the economy. The first regularly published newspaper was founded with his support, and the groundwork was laid for the development of a postal system. The most enduring accomplishment of Amir Kabir's regency was the establishment of the **Dar al-Fonun** polytechnic school in 1851, the first Western-oriented institute of higher learning in Iran and the forerunner of the country's university system.

Amir Kabir maintained complete authority to guide the country on its progressive path. When the controversial **Babi Movement** began to cause civil disturbances, he stepped in and ordered the execution of the Bab in 1850, more to restore the order of the state than as an act of Islamic piety. The total control that Amir Kabir exerted from 1848-1851 turned the young Naser al-Din Shah into a virtual cipher. The power and position of Amir Kabir was cemented with his marriage to the sister of the new king. However, through a sinister blend of court conspiracies, foreign interference, and the immaturity of Naser al-Din Shah, the "first man of the realm" was dismissed from his powerful position in 1851. Kept under house arrest for almost a year, Amir Kabir was executed at *Bagh-i Fin* near **Kashan** by order of the Shah in 1852. His death slowed the change process and brought independent initiatives to a halt.

MOHAJERANI, ATA'OLLAH (1957-). Recognized as a reformer, Ata'ollah Mohajerani's views brought him into constant opposition with the conservative elements of the **Islamic Republic**. Mohajerani was recognized as a proponent of free speech and press, which helped a temporary flourishing of a **reformist press** before **Ayatollah Ali Khamene'i** in his role as *Faqih* approved a crackdown soon after President **Muhammad Khatami**'s election in 1997. He also spoke about the possibility of renewed diplomatic ties with the United States.

Mohajerani served as vice president under President **Ali Akbar Hashemi-Rafsanjani**, and came under fire for a 1990 article in the newspaper *Ettela'at* in which he was quoted as saying that relations with the United States would be in Iran's best interest. The backlash caused the Rafsanjani administration to publicly declare that Mohajerani's views were not those of the administration. Additionally, Mohajerani supported a constitutional amendment to remove the two-term limit for the office of president, which would have allowed Rafsanjani to run for a third consecutive term in 1997. This was seen by conservatives as an attack against Nateq-Nuri, who at the time was a likely prospect for the next president, and the candidate backed by conservative hard line clerics.

Both of these past "offenses" came to the fore after newly elected President Khatami appointed Mohajerani as Minister of Islamic Guidance in 1997. Mohajerani was approved by a very slim margin, and the conservative forces in the **Majlis** later attempted to impeach him. Mohajerani was forced to answer for the 1990 article. He claimed that he did not support renewed relations with the U.S., and whatever the case, he argued the situation had definitely changed to the point that diplomatic ties were, at present, impossible.

Mohajerani was a strong proponent of liberal cultural reforms. Backed by Khatami, Mohajerani repeatedly tried to liberalize intellectual and cultural activities, but came under attack from conservatives who accused him of encouraging moral decadence and allowing the "erosion of cultural purity."

The harassment continued, eventually frustrating Mohajerani to the point that he resigned from his prominent ministry post. Khatami then appointed him as head of the Organization for the Dialogue of Civilizations, a body Khatami had created to promote understanding between cultures. Mohajerani stepped down from this position in 2002, another victim of the gradual victory of **Islam**'s traditionalist interpretations of the **Islamic Revolution** over the liberal moderate view.

MOJAHEDIN-I KHALQ-I IRAN (IRANIAN PEOPLES' FREEDOM FIGHTERS). The Mojahedin-i Khalq-i Iran grew out of the brutal **SAVAK** suppression of the older opposition groups, such as the **National Front** and **Feda'iyan-I Islam** in the early 1960s. It evolved from the religious wing of the National Front, and became a formal organization in 1965 under the leadership of six **Tehran University** graduates who were members of the **Liberation Movement of Iran**. From this small nucleus in **Tehran**, the organization expanded into the provinces, recruiting most of its membership from among young **Shiah** Muslim students in **Shiraz, Isfahan,** and **Tabriz.**

Independently, the Mojahedin formed conclusions on the reinterpretation of **Islam** similar to the Marxist-based ideology of **Ali Shari'ati.** Using their belief in Islam as their inspiration, ideology, and cultural base, they urged Muslims to struggle to create a classless society and destroy oppression—classic Marxism in an Islamic frame.

A sharp split in the Mojahedin occurred in 1975 when Marxism, rather than Islamism, was promoted as the major goal of the membership. Both factions continued subversive activities including bombings, robberies, and strikes. The Marxist faction also concentrated efforts on industrial sabotage, while the Islamic group worked on the university campuses to spread Shari'ati's message throughout Iran, and among students attending North American and European universities.

The Mojahedin was one of several guerilla groups which played a significant role during the final days of the 1979 **Islamic Revolution**. Answering **Ayatollah Ruhollah Khomeini**'s call to end the regime of **Muhammad Reza Shah**, the Mojahadin engaged in street combat with government troops and helped deliver the final blow to the last remnants of the **Pahlavi** military structure.

MONTEZARI, AYATOLLAH HUSSEIN ALI (1922-). One of the key players in the **Islamic Revolution** was Hussein Ali Montezari, a Grand **Ayatollah** closely allied with **Ayatollah Ruhollah Khomeini**. Montezari pursued religious studies at **Qum**, and it was there that he met Khomeini and became an ardent supporter of his ideals. He was a founder of the Iran Freedom Movement and organized public protests against **Muhammad**

Reza Shah's regime. During Khomeini's exile in Paris, Montezari was a key figure in the network which delivered Khomeini's messages to the Iranian people. When the **Pahlavi Dynasty** fell, Montezari became active in the new government, holding positions in the **Islamic Republican Party**, the **Assembly of Experts**, and the Friday Mosque Prayer Leaders. His stature was such that, in 1985, the Assembly of Experts designated him the successor to Khomeini, as the *Faqih*, in accordance with the provisions of the new **Constitution of the Islamic Republic of Iran**.

Montezari was a radical, promoting land reform, revolutionary organizations, and the export of the revolution to other Islamic countries. He fell from favor as successor to Khomeini when it was decided that he lacked the charisma and leadership skills necessary to fulfill the obligations of *Velayat-i Faqih*, and was encouraged by Khomeini to resign from government affairs. Though still a force to be contended with, the power of Montezari was severely eroded and he never recovered his former political prominence.

MOSSADEQ, MUHAMMAD (1882-1967). Muhammad Mossadeq was a member of the **National Front** and an advocate of a strong and independent Iran, free from the corrupt and foreign-influenced political administration of **Muhammad Reza Shah**. Long active in Iranian politics, he served as a government official, a deputy to the **Majlis**, and a cabinet minister. In 1951, he was named prime minister and began to assert more control over government affairs. His primary goals were the nationalization of the **oil industry** and independence from the influence and rivalry of Great Britain and the Soviet Union. His position won the support of the Majlis and the people as his policies began to restore a faded national self-confidence. Within a short time he controlled almost all aspects of government, including the military.

While in office he enforced stringent martial law, prohibited strikes by government employees, suspended the Senate and Majlis elections, and curtailed the freedom of the press. He used the profits from the oil industry to improve domestic economic conditions and attempted to end foreign intervention in Iranian affairs.

In 1953, Muhammad Reza Shah left Iran under pressure from Mossadeq. Aided by an American-sponsored military coup, the infamous Central Intelligence Agency operation known as Ajax, the Shah was quickly returned to the throne. Mossadeq was arrested and his government dismantled. Though he held power for only two years, his successful challenge of the **Pahlavi Dynasty** underscored the ongoing and growing dissatisfaction of the Iranian people with the corrupt leadership of the Shah. *See also* ROOSEVELT, KERMIT.

MOTTAHARI, AYATOLLAH MORTEZA (1919-1979). Morteza Mottahari was born in **Mashhad** and pursued religious studies at **Qum** as a favored student of **Ayatollah Ruhollah Khomeini**. He taught theology at **Tehran University** where his outspoken views with respect to the **Pahlavi** regime led to imprisonment in 1964 and again in 1975. Mottahari also authored books stressing the relevance of **Islam** in today's world.

He was a prominent member of the "Society of Monthly Talks for the Propagation of the True Path of Religion," a speaker's bureau which sought to combine Islamic values with modern society. In the mid-1960s, Mottahari was instrumental in the establishment of the **Husseiniyeh-i Er-shad**, a lecture hall in **Tehran** devoted to the ideas of religious modernism. He remained its leading speaker until displaced by the sociologist **Ali Shari'ati**. His disapproval of Shari'ati's anticlerical views was strong enough for Mottahari to acquiesce in the government's closure of the hall in the 1970s.

He was a close associate of **Mehdi Bazargan** and **Mahmud Taleqani** and was a highly influential member of a secret pre-Revolutionary group working to establish the fundamentals of Islamic ideology, further confirming his role as an intellectual force among Islamic revolutionaries. His clerical credentials were impeccable, though when his earliest views were criticized by conservative clergy members, Mottahari moved toward a more populist stance.

As a trusted disciple of Khomeini, he assumed leadership of the newly formed **Revolutionary Council** in February 1979. Though his participation in the formation of the new government was cut short by his assassination in May 1979 by members of the religiously oriented terrorist group Forqan, Mottahari's work had a significant impact on the ideology of the emerging **Islamic Republic**. As such, Mottahari is considered one of the founders of the new republic.

Ironically, and perhaps indicative of the degree to which a quarter of a century later the internal dispute among revolutionaries over the nature of sovereignty is still unresolved, the son of Mottahari attacked conservative clerics for their governmental intervention in 2005. Ali Mottahari, a philosophy professor at Tehran University, is himself a conservative academic with impeccable revolutionary credentials and thus not easily dismissed. He has followed the populist footsteps of his father, but extended them in a more secularist direction.

MOZAFFAR AL-DIN SHAH (Ruled 1896-1907). Mozaffar al-Din Shah was an ailing, sickly man when he succeeded to the throne in 1896. His travels to Europe, seeking medical treatment for the various illnesses that plagued him, put a severe drain on the Crown's resources. In an attempt to raise customs revenues, the Shah turned over the collection of custom duties in Iran's primary exporting provinces of **Azerbaijan** and **Kermanshah** to three Belgian businessmen. This was only one of numerous concessions granted to foreign interests by the Iranian government, often in return for loans to the Crown. In 1901, Great Britain gained petroleum exploration rights in southwest Iran, and in 1908, the company that would evolve into the **Anglo-Iranian Oil Company** hit the first commercial strike of **oil** in the Middle East at Masjed-i Soleiman.

Russia was granted a 75-year loan of 2.4 million pounds which was guaranteed by 5 percent of Iran's customs receipts, excluding duties from those provinces already under the control of the Belgians. As one of the terms of the loan, Russia insisted that Iran repay the British Imperial Bank the indemnity occurred with the cancellation of the Tobacco Concession, a result of the

Tobacco Revolt. This placed Russia in the position of Iran's sole creditor, and allowed the exercise of considerable financial and political control.

In 1903, rioters spurred by the ulama filled the streets, openly protesting the Shah's policies. In 1904, over 2,000 Persians participated in the *bast* (sanctuary) against the Shah, marking a resurgence of the religious-radical alliance first seen in the Tobacco Revolt of 1891-1892. To put an end to the public protests, the Shah verbally agreed to the demands of the demonstrators for political liberalization and national integrity.

However, it took a sustained and concerted protest effort to induce the Shah to give in on the constitution issue. On his birthday, 5 August, 1906, the Shah agreed to substitute the rule of law for unlimited monarchial power, and allowed the establishment of an elected legislative body known as the **Majlis**. The first major act of the Majlis against the Shah was to stop a proposed Russian loan of 400,000 pounds. The Majlis quickly proceeded to draft the Fundamental Law which served as the core of the new constitution. It was signed by Mozaffar al-Din Shah on 30 December, 1906, only five days before his death. *See also* CONSTITUTIONAL REVOLUTION OF 1906; QAJAR DYNASTY.

MUHAMMAD ALI SHAH (Ruled 1907-1909). The successor to **Mozaffar al-Din Shah**, Muhammad Ali Shah was an extreme reactionary who wanted the newly formed Persian Constitution of 1906 abolished. He resented the powers of the **Majlis** that interfered with his absolute authority as monarch, and was susceptible to the influence of Russian advisers who advocated direct action against the constitution. Muhammad Ali Shah continually pledged to uphold the constitution and respect the authority of the Majlis, but this proved to be a stalling tactic. On 3 June, 1908, the Shah dissolved Parliament, and ordered a Russian Cossack force led by Colonel Liakhoff to bombard the Majlis building. Thirty to 40 liberals and nationalists, including the most prominent leader of the Democratic Liberals, Seyyid Hasan Taqizadeh, sought refuge in the British Legation. The Russians encircled the building and threatened to use force if the *bast* (sanctuary) was not terminated. Ultimately, no action resulted, probably due to the reluctance of the Russians to provoke war with the British.

A popular resistance movement, centered in **Tabriz**, arose quickly and called for the restoration of the constitution. Following numerous clashes with government troops, the resistance force encircled **Tehran**, and forced Muhammad Ali Shah to flee to the Russian Legation on 16 July, 1909. A renascent constituent body deposed Muhammad Ali Shah and chose his 12-year old son Ahmad to succeed him. *See also* BASKERVILLE, HOWARD; CONSTITUTIONAL REVOLUTION OF 1906; QAJAR DYNASTY.

MUHAMMAD MIRZA SHAH (Ruled 1834-1848). Muhammad Mirza Shah Qajar was the son of Crown Prince **Abbas Mirza**. Preceded in death by his father, he succeeded to the Persian throne following the death of his uncle, **Fath Ali Shah**. The ascension of Muhammad Shah was aided by the British military mission in **Azerbaijan**, as well as by agents of Imperial Russia. This foreign intervention in the changeover of Shahs set a precedent which would be followed until the **Constitutional Revolution of 1906**. From his predecessor, Muhammad Shah inherited a massive, dependent aristocracy including over 300 ambitious heirs to the throne. These nobles contributed to an unstable political environment, marked by intrigue and corruption, as they competed for important government positions and favored status with the Shah.

Muhammad Shah was led into **Sufi** mysticism by his prime minister, Hajji Mirza Aghasi. The prime minister was responsible for the death of Qa'im Maqam, who was the talented and able adviser of the Shah early in his reign. Historians have speculated that had Qa'im Maqam survived, the history of the period might have been radically different. As it was, the Muhammad Shah reign was marked by a series of fiascoes that seriously weakened Iran. It was a time of rapid economic and social change caused in part by a growing foreign presence and the increasing integration of the Iranian economy into world markets. The resulting social unrest was poorly handled by the "two dervishes," as the Shah and his prime minister came to be called. In fact, Muhammad Shah's religious unorthodoxy was seen by the ulama as a threat to their political influence and power, and they reacted by stirring up popular emotions against the monarch. It was during the Muhammad Shah reign that the **Babi Movement** took root, yet another indication of the turmoil that characterized the period. The legacy of Muhammad Shah was a state in disarray, internally weakened and incapable of resisting the external pressures caused by the persistent encroachments of the European powers. *See also* QAJAR DYNASTY.

MUHAMMAD REZA SHAH (Ruled 1941-1979). On 17 September, 1941, Muhammad Reza Shah was sworn in as the new Shah of Iran and the second king of the **Pahlavi Dynasty**. His father, **Reza Shah**, had been forced to abdicate the throne by the Allied invasion of Iran in 1941.

Muhammad Reza Shah remained in power for almost 40 years, and his reign was marked by attempts at social and economic reforms through a series of economic development plans, and the cultivation of close ties with the West, in particular the United States. Unlike his father, he was not averse to using foreigners to organize and run Iran's young **oil industry**, and was influenced by the West in the formulation of foreign and domestic policy. Along with Saudi Arabia, Iran became one of the United States' "Twin Pillars" in the Middle East. In return for friendly relations and a strong voice in Iranian affairs, Washington provided all of the military and economic aid that Iran desired. Hostility toward the Shah accelerated because foreign influences were once again manipulating Iranian society.

One of the most significant policies imposed by his government was an attempt at land reform, part of a larger reform package entitled the **White Revolution**. The government confiscated many large estates and redistributed the property among the landless farmers. Though socially popular, the programs were poorly designed and executed, and repercussions are still being felt today in Iranian **agriculture**.

Muhammad Reza Shah's reign was marked by domestic unrest. In 1953, he fled Iran under pressure from Prime Minister **Muhammed Mossadeq**'s government. After a brief absence, he returned to the throne with the aid of American intervention, but never acquired the support or respect of the Iranian people. They were angered by the pervasiveness of foreign influence in government, his irresponsible economic policies, and his dictatorial rule. The Shah, his family, and many high-ranking government officials acquired vast personal wealth while the people suffered from high unemployment rates and poverty. Near the end of his reign, he set the country on a disastrous economic course which significantly contributed to the collapse of his regime.

Under growing pressure from the **Islamic Revolution**, on 16 January, 1979, Muhammad Reza Shah fled the country. Only weeks later, **Ayatollah Ruhollah Khomeini** returned to **Tehran** from exile in France. The following month the Pahlavi Dynasty came to an end with the dissolution of the government the Shah had left in place and the successful takeover of power by an Islamic **Provisional Government**. The Shah lived the balance of his life in exile, sick with cancer and repudiated by his people. He died in Egypt on 27 July, 1980. *See also* BAKHTIAR, SHAPUR; ROOSEVELT, KERMIT.

MULLA SADRA (1571-1640). Considered by many to be one of the most important philosophers of Iran, Mulla Sadra's work encouraged a revitalization of philosophy during the **Safavid Dynasty**. Born in **Shiraz** into a notable family, Mulla Sadra went on to study under philosophers in **Isfahan** as well as to take on an almost ascetic mystical life in **Qum**. His understanding of the intricacies of the philosophical and religious tradition in Iran allowed him to develop, amongst other innovations, two groundbreaking concepts. First, he merged several disparate schools of thought under one paradigm. This "metaphilosophy" brought together the major threads of thinking—including **Shiah** theology and **Sufi** mysticism—into one system, allowing a richer understanding of many problems philosophy had been ineffectual at answering before. Second, and most importantly, he made the shift from essences (things-in-themselves beyond sense perception) being the primary foundation of reality to existence itself being primary. Amongst the implications of such a shift was the ability to answer many religious statements which before seemed to be unfathomable. Mulla Sadra published over 40 major works, including the nine-volume *Asfar* (*Journey*) which explains much of his system. He died in 1640 during a pilgrimage to Mecca. His philosophical work formed the basis for modern developments in philosophical Shi'ism.

MUSLIM PEOPLE'S REPUBLICAN PARTY. *See* AYATOL-LAH MUHAMMAD KAZEM SHARI'AT-MADARI.

-N-

NADER SHAH (Ruled 1736-1747). In 1722, Afghan tribesmen invaded Persia and captured the capital city of **Isfahan**, dealing a fatal blow to the once glorious but now faltering **Safavid Dynasty**. Simultaneous incursions into Persia, by Ottoman Turkey in the west and the Russians from the north, fragmented the nation. National recovery seemed unlikely. Yet, only seven years later, from the vestiges of the Persian Army, rose a common **Afshar** tribesman who would restore, at least temporarily, a period of national power and prestige. Nader Qoli Beg was born in the city of **Mashhad**. In 1729, he took command of the faltering Persian Army and expelled the Afghans from Persian territory, recapturing **Tabriz**, **Hamadan**, and Darband, along with the **Caspian** provinces. He then engaged the Turkish troops in the western area in a fierce, bloody conflict and drove them back across their own frontier, retrieving Armenia and Georgia in the process. The Russians were thus induced to withdraw from the northern regions without a battle.

In 1736, upon the death of Abbas III, the last of the Safavid monarchs, Nader Qoli ascended to the vacant throne and assumed the title of Nader Shah, thereby initiating the Afshar Dynasty. His reign was notable for continual military campaigning throughout the region, as well as economic and religious chaos within Iran.

Nader Shah first alienated the **Shiah** Muslims in Persia by the indiscriminate plundering of religiously endowed property (*vaqf*) and ill treatment of the ulama. His attempt to "adapt" Shiah doctrine to align more closely with the four Sunni schools of Islamic law met with fierce resistance. This new school, to be named for Jafar al-Sadeq, the sixth Shiah Imam, required that the central doctrine of Shi'ism regarding the divinity of the Imams be suspended. The total rejection of his plans underscored the deep commitment of Persians to their "national" religion and the episode amounted to no more than a brief interlude of disruption for the Shiah adherents.

He was more successful in military pursuits. A brilliant military strategist, Nader Shah captured vast amounts of territory for his Persian Empire. He also attempted to establish a fleet in the Persian Gulf and annexed the island of Bahrein in 1738 to secure the region. In 1740, he invaded India, marching into the capital city of Delhi where his army plundered priceless national treasures, including the famous Peacock Throne. His exploits were widely reported in the West and he was often referred to as the "second Alexander."

Though his conquests managed to restore a semblance of national pride to the Persians, they were also a costly drain on the country's resources. Heavy taxes were levied to support the military and little advantage was gained by the average Persian through the expansion of territory. His strict methods of discipline alienated his troops and he was assassinated by one of his own bodyguards in 1747. His son, Shah Rokh, ascended to the throne, but internal conflicts, combined with indifferent leadership, led to the steady decline of the Afshar Dynasty. In the last half of the 18th century, most of Nader Shah's hard-won territory fell under the sway of other political entities, most importantly the Zands and the **Qajars**. *See also* KARIM KHAN ZAND, MUHAMMAD.

NADERPOUR, NADER (1929-2000). One of the most important figures of the 20th century movement in Persian **poetry** known as "New Poetry," and a noted social critic, Nader Naderpour was born in **Tehran** to a well-educated and progressively minded family with aristocratic ties ("Naderpour") means "son of Nader," and ostensibly refers to an ancestry traced to the 18th century **Afshar** ruler **Nader Shah** Afshar). His father, who died when Naderpour was 14, encouraged young Nader to read the classical poetry of Iran, and by his teens, Naderpour had not only read the major works, but was also writing his own classic-style poetry. Some of this early poetry even saw publication in **Jalal Al-e Ahmad**'s journal *Mardom*. Al-e Ahmad actually lived with the Naderpour family for several years in the late 1940s, becoming an influence on Naderpour's creativity as well as his worldview in general. Naderpour's social criticism began early, as he joined the **Tudeh Party**'s youth organization while in high school, although he left in disillusionment following the Soviet Union's actions during the **Azerbaijan Crisis**.

Naderpour left for Europe in 1950 after completing his secondary **education**, studying French **literature** at the *Sorbonne* in Paris. While in Paris, he absorbed many of the ideas of the European modernist poets, which would influence his own experimentation with Persian poetry. During his time at the *Sorbonne*, Naderpour wrote for several publications. Some of his early writing was for publications run by Khalil Maleki, founder of the Third Party Force, which was one of the several nationalist groups under the umbrella of the **National Front** organization of **Muhammad Mossadeq**.

Returning to Iran following completion of his bachelor's degree, Naderpour soon became fully enmeshed in his creative output. His poetry and his theoretical stance on poetry became one of the most important foundations of New Poetry in Iran. Naderpour not only published volumes of poetry, beginning with *Eyes and Hands* in 1954, but he also wrote and spoke on his theories about the state of Persian poetry. He believed that New Poetry was not haphazardly violating stylistic rules rather, it was having a progressive perspective that still referenced its inevitable roots in poetic traditions. Therefore, Naderpour's poetry is more moderate, often maintaining elements of the classic poetry which he loved as a child. He received some criticism from elements within the New Poetry movement, devotees of **Nima Yushij**, for not being radical enough in both style and substance. Nonetheless, his stance as a pioneer is secure. Naderpour's 10 volumes of poetry—including *Collyrium of the Sun* (1960), the simultaneously published *Not Plant and Stone, But Fire* (1978) and *From the Sublime to the Ridiculous* (1978), and *The Last Supper* (1978)—became recognized as perhaps the most important examples of the moderate style of Iranian New Poetry.

Although a moderate in style, Naderpour did much beyond his writing to advance the emerging revolution in style. In 1960, he organized the first modernist poetry reading in Iran. For a time, he also took the editor position with the magazine *Namayesh*. In 1968, Naderpour, along with other important figures, became a founding member and manifesto signatory of the Association of Writers in Iran, even serving several terms on its executive committee before he finally left the organization due to differences in 1977. Throughout the 1970s, he also produced the show "Goruh-i Adab-i Emruz" for Iranian National Radio and Television which focused on contemporary Iranian writers and artists.

Following the **Islamic Revolution**, Naderpour left Iran becoming in exile a heated critic of the **Islamic Republic**. Originally settling in Paris, he joined the anti-regime National Resistance Movement (not to be confused with the earlier **National Resistance Movement** against the **Pahlavi Regime**) which had begun there under the leadership of **Shapur Bakhtiar** and which published one of Naderpour's most well known works, *False Dawn* (1982). In 1986, Naderpour immigrated to the United States, where he continued his writing as well as becoming a highly sought after lecturer on the academic scene, teaching and speaking on Persian poetry and society. He lectured at Harvard and Georgetown, among other major universities. His time at University of California at Los Angeles and University of California at Irvine were especially important as they became a way of connecting for many of the extensive Persian exile community of Los Angeles, where Naderpour finally settled. His *lectures* and writing continued to lambaste the Islamic Republic late into his life, even criticizing the emerging reformist movement and **Muhammad Khatami**'s election. However, soon after this new chapter in Iranian history began, Naderpour died in his adopted home of Los Angeles in 2000.

NASER AL-DIN SHAH (Ruled 1848-1896). Upon the death of **Muhammad Mirza Shah** in 1848, Naser al-Din Shah succeeded to the monarchy at age 17. In the early years of his reign, the affairs of state were controlled by his prime minister, **Mirza Taqi Khan Amir Kabir**. Considered by countless Iranians to be the most capable statesman of the **Qajar** period, Amir Kabir skillfully dealt with the numerous problems of state inherited from the Muhammad Mirza Shah period and initiated major reforms. These covered virtually every aspect of Iranian society, and included the establishment of the first Western-style state institution of higher **education**, called the **Dar al-Fonun**. Unfortunately for Iran, Amir Kabir met a fate similar to that dealt his mentor, Qa'im Maqam, by Muhammad Mirza Shah. Naser al-Din Shah dismissed Amir Kabir and after a period of house arrest ordered his execution in 1852.

In the 1850s, Naser al-Din Shah launched a military campaign into the Herat region of Afghanistan, causing the governor-general of India to declare war on Iran. When anticipated Russian military support failed to materialize, Iran opted to end the occupation of Herat and negotiate a peace agreement. The Treaty of Paris of 1857 was signed, and under its terms Iran recognized the sovereignty of Afghanistan and granted commercial concessions to the British. This was a precursor to the "era of concessions" when many Iranian assets were mortgaged to European powers. A significant consequence of foreign economic penetration was the fashioning of what came to be known as the religious-radical alliance. This coalition of **bazaar** merchants, liberal democrats, and religious scholars first succeeded in the **Tobacco Revolt** of 1891-1892 when organized protests forced the cancellation of an exclusive tobacco concession, which had been granted to a British merchant. This same alliance emerged again to lead the successful **Constitutional Revolution of 1906**.

Naser al-Din Shah ruled for nearly 50 years, and made several half-hearted attempts at modernizing reform programs, but never sustained the effort. As the century came to a close, the aging Naser al-Din Shah became increasingly conservative and allowed foreign political and economic interests to dominate Iranian affairs. He died in 1896, struck down by an assassin's bullet. *See also* AL-AFGHANI, JAMAL AL-DIN; KERMANI, MIRZA AGHA KHAN; MIRZA MALKOM KHAN.

NATIONAL FRONT. The forerunner of the National Front was the Democratic Party of Iran which formed during the movement which led to the **Constitutional Revolution of 1906**. Its membership was composed of liberal intellectuals who were seeking the establishment of a representative secular political system to limit the authority of the monarchy and the clergy. The party was influential in securing a constitution which created the **Majlis**, but both internal and external forces prevented significant party development. When the **Pahlavi Dynasty** was established in 1925, the group was brutally suppressed causing it to fragment into a number of smaller associations.

Under the leadership of **Muhammad Mossadeq** following World War II, these small groups were reorganized into a new political party known as the National Front. The main objective of the National Front was the nationalization of Iran's **oil** industry. With the support of the public and the Majlis, the National Front was able to spearhead a drive that culminated in the seizure of the **Anglo-Iranian Oil Company** facilities in 1951.

Mossadeq became the new prime minister, and with his National Front partisans in control of the Majlis, directed his efforts toward the destruction of the monarchy. Under pressure, **Muhammad Reza Shah** was forced to flee the country in 1953, which left Mossadeq in complete authority. But the monarchy was shortly restored through British and American intervention. Mossadeq was arrested and barred from further political participation. The National Front was suppressed, accused of being an instrument of the **Tudeh** (Communist) Party, and faded from preeminence in government affairs.

Over the next two decades the National Front continued to fight for liberalism in government. However, the party never recovered its prominence of the Mossadeq era. A short-lived Second National Front in the early 1960s quickly faded over differences in the main thrust of nationalist thought, a more secularist or Islamist approach. The latter view was represented by the newly formed **Liberation Movement of Iran** which at first considered itself as under the umbrella of the National Front. The difference in focus was a key element in the continuing weakness of liberal nationalism, the very strength of earlier National Front activities. Generally, secular nationalists were increasingly marginalized in the realm of opposition politics, despite a continuing presence and even occasional heroic acts. When the Shah announced the creation of a single-party system in 1975, the **Rastakhiz Party**, National Front members refused to join. Enduring imprisonment, torture, and sometimes death at the hands of the **SAVAK**, party members still called for constitutional reforms.

As the Pahlavi Dynasty crumbled in 1979, the National Front was asked to help form a new government. Recalling the suppression following the ousting of Mossadeq and lacking strong leadership, the party was reluctant to become involved. This left most of the post-revolutionary power and influence in the hands of the Islamic activists. Although National Front member **Mehdi Bazargan** served as the first prime minister of the **Provisional Government**, his removal in the wake of the **American hostage** crisis in November 1979 signaled an end to the influence of the National Front in the Islamic government of Iran. *See also* NATIONAL IRANIAN OIL COMPANY; ROOSEVELT, KERMIT; SANJABI, KARIM.

NATIONAL IRANIAN OIL COMPANY (NIOC). The National Iranian **Oil** Company (NIOC) emerged from the battle between the **National Front** organization headed by **Muhammad Mossadeq** and the British-controlled **Anglo-Iranian Oil Company**. In the late 1940s, the movement for the nationalization of Iran's oil **industry** was fueled by the efforts of dissident groups which wanted Iranian control of the country's vast and lucrative oil deposits and an end to exploitation by foreign ownership. Led by Mossadeq, the movement was stalled until his selection as prime minister in 1951. With the **Majlis** dominated by his National Front partisans, Mossadeq was able to secure the necessary vote to implement the Nationalization Law passed earlier that year. In June 1951, he took over the British oil installations in **Khuzis-**

tan, and a long and bitter battle with the British ensued. Massive demonstrations and bloodshed in July 1952 proved that Mossadeq's "national mission" had captured the support of the masses. The battle resulted in an international oil embargo against Iran, a huge drop in oil production, a debilitating economic crisis, and the temporary removal of **Muhammad Reza Shah** from power. Having fled the country, the Shah quickly returned to the throne, thanks to a military coup inspired by the U.S. Central Intelligence Agency.

In the aftermath, a team headed by **Ali Amini** negotiated the terms of oil exploration and production on Iranian soil. After a protracted series of negotiations and concessions, the Iranians finally regained control of their most productive industry. With the creation of the NIOC in 1954 and within the framework of the Nationalization Law, control of the oil industry reverted to the Iranian government. Provisions were made for contracting rights to subsidiary companies and all subsequent oil discoveries were to be controlled by Iran. In 1957, the Petroleum Act allowed Iranians to form independent companies or become involved in joint ventures in which they would retain at least 30 percent of ownership. The first such venture was concluded in August 1957 with an Italian oil company in which NIOC attained a 75/25 percent split agreement in its favor, the most favorable agreement for an oil-producing nation with a foreign oil company ever attained to that date. Thus, overall, the establishment of the National Iranian Oil Company marked a successful move for Iran against foreign economic control of the nation's key industry. In particular, under the 15-year managing directorship of **Muhammad Eqbal** the company was a vital player in Iranian economic development plans. *See also* ROOSEVELT, KERMIT.

NATIONAL RESISTANCE MOVEMENT (NRM). The National Resistance Movement (NRM) represents a turning point in the history of nationalistic opposition to **Muhammad Reza Shah**'s regime. Formed in 1953 following the coup which ousted **Muhammad Mossadeq** and reinstated the Shah, the NRM would eventually consist of a conglomeration of individuals—such as

Mehdi Bazargan, **Ezzatollah Sahabi**, and **Ali Shari'ati**—and groups—such as the **Party of the Iranian People**, the **Party of the Iranian Nation**, and the **Iran Party**—with a stronger leaning towards religion than previously established groups, such as the **National Front**. However, even with a large number of high-ranking members coming from religious and **bazaar** backgrounds, the aims of the NRM were generally expressed in nationalistic terms only. The NRM did not assimilate religiousness into its nationalism as future organizations such as the **Liberation Movement of Iran** would.

As an opposition group, the NRM required secrecy. Therefore, its organizational structure was cellular, in that there were numerous cells which, although they had connections with higher levels of the NRM, had no knowledge of the other cells that made up the group. These cells were spread throughout Iran's cities, with one member maintaining contact with NRM leadership. The leadership itself met in informal councils at various members' homes to discuss reactions to the government's latest actions.

The NRM participated in numerous anti-regime activities. For instance, the NRM collaborated with the **Tudeh Party** in organizing a general strike in support of Mossadeq, who was on trial in November 1953. While the NRM was successful in closing the Bazaar and **Tehran University**, the Tudeh failed on their part to hinder transportation and production. As a result of the strike and accompanying demonstrations, the government arrested or exiled thousands. The NRM also participated in oppositional activities to the 1953 visit of U.S. President Richard Nixon with the Shah, the rigged 1954 elections, and the 1954 oil agreements with Western companies. In this last case, the NRM released an open letter signed by many NRM members as well as prominent Iranians such as **Ali Akbar Dekhoda**. The NRM claimed the agreements negated any gains made by nationalizing Iran's oil production. The NRM also attempted to publish a newspaper, but it only appeared infrequently due to difficulties in producing an underground paper in an oppressive regime.

By 1955, the NRM began to unravel. Membership dwindled after the 1955 imprisonment of Bazargan and Ezzatollah Sahabi.

Even the Iran Party had left by the time these NRM leaders were freed five months later. The final blow was dealt in 1957 after the government discovered the NRM's **Mashhad** cell. The leaders of this cell were jailed, and after harsh interrogation, the prisoners revealed the **Tehran** leadership of the NRM. With its leadership imprisoned for eight months as a final result, the NRM dissolved.

Still, the NRM marks a point in a linear chain of Iranian opposition which would eventually lead to the **Islamic Revolution** of 1979. Although the NRM did not incorporate religion directly into its politics, the makeup of the group consisted largely of religious nationalists. By the time the Liberation Movement of Iran emerged in the early 1960s, its leadership—many of whom were central to the NRM—did take a decidedly religious approach to Iranian nationalism. The NRM may not have achieved many successes in its own time, but it is part of a progression towards an end that would achieve the overthrow of the **Pahlavi Dynasty**.

NATURAL GAS. *See* OIL.

NEAR EAST FOUNDATION. The Near East Foundation is a nonprofit organization established in 1930 to continue the work of **Near East Relief**. Members of the foundation worked to improve the economic and **agricultural** systems among the rural populations of the Middle East. Educational programs, demonstrations, and training were provided by technical experts to establish agricultural extension, improve public health, and develop rural recreation programs and services. The Near East Foundation was active in Iran, particularly in the area of agricultural education. From 1962-1964, the organization was the in-country administrative agency for the first group of volunteers who served in Iran with the American Peace Corps.

NEAR EAST RELIEF. Near East Relief was organized by James Barton and incorporated by Congress in 1917 to provide relief and assistance for the repatriation and relocation of refugees in the Middle East. The organization was very active in Iran, particularly in **Azerbaijan**. The group provided food, shelter, and medical care, along with social and educational programs, during and after World War I. It continued to operate orphanages and provide disaster relief until replaced by the **Near East Foundation** in 1930.

NEHZAT-I AZADI. *See* LIBERATION MOVEMENT OF IRAN.

NEWSPAPERS—*ETTELE'AT* AND *KAYHAN*. The *Ettele'at* newspaper was founded in 1925 by Abbas Masudi in **Tehran** during the early years of the **Pahlavi Dynasty**. The *Kayhan* began circulation in the 1930s, and the two papers became intense rivals, as well as the giants of the daily press in Iran. Both published afternoon editions, as well as an English language morning paper and airmail editions for international delivery. In the mid-1950s the *Ettele'at* and the *Kayhan* organizations merged to become a publishing empire without precedent in Iran. Both continued as separate printed entities, although the editorial policies merged. This caused a loss in circulation which was offset by the economic advantages of the partnership.

The papers have continued their separate existence. Each provides coverage of local and international events, offers political commentaries, economic news, social criticism, essays, prose and **poetry**, and a calendar of events. Criticism of government policies or officials is banned, along with "false" news, military secrets, and obscenity. Reporters must be accredited by the Ministry of Information. Circulation figures compared to the literacy rate are high compared to other nations. *See also* REFORMIST PRESS.

NEZAM AL-MOLK (1020-1092). Nezam al-Molk was a highly regarded vizier of 11th century Persia. A capable and enlightened government administrator, he feared the deterioration of the Persian way of life following the successful invasion by the Seljuk Turks in 1055. As advisor to the new rulers, Nezam al-Molk encouraged them in the pursuit of such time-consuming activities as wars, hunts, and royal audiences, while he himself effectively conducted the day-to-day affairs of government according to Persian custom.

During this period of Seljuk sovereignty, Persia experienced a cultural and scientific renaissance, largely attributed to the efforts of Nezam al-Molk. Though firmly supportive of the theocratic nature of Persian government, he established a series of schools which were the first essentially civil, rather than religious, educational establishments. These were termed Nezamiyeh. The first school opened in Baghdad in 1065 and eventually expanded to include schools in Amol, Nishapur, Herat, Merv, Balkh, and Damascus.

His most remarkable accomplishment was the *Siyasatnameh*, or *Book of Politics*, which was to serve as a guidebook for the "barbaric" **Turkoman** rulers who controlled Islamic Persia. In it he provided serious professional advice on political, religious, and ethical issues, essentially aiming to turn the nomadic Turks into city gentlemen capable of conducting government business in the Persian tradition. That such a book was written at all points out the disparity in culture between the Persians and the conquering Turks.

In prose of remarkable strength and anecdotal style, the *Siyasatnameh* outlines the organization of the government, its offices and general welfare. It advises against allowing "heretics" to participate in government in that their loyalties would be suspect. Nezam al-Molk believed that some high-ranking officers of state belonged to a faction of **Shiah Islam** called the Ismai'li, who would become better known as the notorious Assassins. Ironically, his warnings incited the Assassins to murder him in 1092.

Though Nezam al-Molk died before the guidelines he proposed in the *Siyasatnameh* could be put into use, his book left a singularly valuable portrait of Persia, colored by the Islamic theocratic society of his time. With no pretense or apology, he presented an exceptionally clear picture of the role of a government strictly bound by the dogma of Islam. His work ethnocentrically defined and defended the constraints placed on society by adherence to one true faith, one right way of life, and one justly dominant sex. Though the *Siyasatnameh* has been criticized for its culture-bound outlook, Persians recognize and honor Nezam al-Molk's efforts to "conquer the conqueror" in order that their more civilized way of life would endure.

NEZAMI GANJAVI (1140-1209). Persian poet Abu Muhammad Ilyas ibn Yusef ibn Zaki Mu'ayyad, known by his pen name Nezami of Ganja, or Ganjavi, was born around 1140 in Ganja, the capital of the Arran province of Transcaucasian **Azerbaijan**. His parents migrated from the city of **Qum** in northern central Iran, but died early in Nezami's life, leaving him to be raised by an uncle who educated him in the arts, sciences, and thought of the time. Though legends have accumulated, little is known about the poet's life apart from his writing and role in establishing the lyrical "Azerbaijani" style of Persian **poetry**.

Nezami refused to use his talents in court writing, instead writing for patrons regarding man's destiny and social, political, and moral-ethical questions of the time. His writing is known for its lyrical and sensual components, and for often lamenting the loss of each of his three wives and offering advice and lecture to his only son, Muhammad. Nezami Ganjavi is most remembered for his five extensive narrative poems called *Khamseh* (Quintet), which included "Treasury of Mysteries," "Khosrow and Shirin," "Leili and Majnun," "Seven Beauties," and "Iskandar Nameh." These poems contrasted with the **Khorasani** (Eastern) style of Persian poetry as they displayed the Azerbaijani style's rhetorical sophistication, innovative forms of metaphor, and technical language of the many fields and subjects the poet had mastered. Through Nezami's poetry, one can see the political and social strife of the time, as well as the topics of interest that captivated 12th century Persia, which included everything from ethics, religion, and law to medicine, astronomy, and mathematics.

Beyond his command of the sciences of his time, the elegance and richness of Nezami's poetry has had an unparalleled influence on literary production in Iran and other parts of the **Persian language**-speaking world. His magnificent command of the art of speech led Nezami to be widely emulated, even to the present day. Though a classical 12th century poet, evaluation and interpretation of his work continue into contemporary times with invigorated energy.

NOURI, ABDOLLAH (1948-). Recognized as a radical cleric during the early days of the **Islamic Republic**, Abdollah Nouri would later become an outspoken voice for reform in Iranian government. Through his early involvement with the revolution, Nouri served in many appointed posts in government, including a position with the **Revolutionary Guards** as appointed by **Ayatollah Ruhollah Khomeini**, and a position on the **Expediency Council** as appointed by **Ayatollah Ali Khamene'i**. In addition to these appointments by supreme leaders, Nouri also served for a time as interior minister under President **Ali Akbar Hashemi-Rafsanjani**.

By the late 1990s, however, Nouri became increasingly associated with the push for reform in government. His ability to use Khomeini's own statements and policies to justify reformist arguments made his positions quite formidable. Fearing another popular revolt if the Islamic Republic failed to address the concerns of the public, Nouri spoke against such things as the consolidation of governmental power into a group with a particular, hardline agenda, as well as the claim to an objective interpretation of **Islam** by a governmental apparatus. Interpretation, Nouri believed, was relative. As such, the government required an open discourse amongst differing viewpoints, since none could claim absolute truth in how to apply Islam to government. Nouri also openly discussed the possibility of an Iranian rapprochement with the United States, as well as criticizing the Iranian government for lambasting Palestine for negotiating with Israel. Effectively, Nouri's association with the hardliners had ended.

Just as Nouri's perceived stance shifted, so too did the Iranian political landscape. With the emergence of the reformers as a viable political force and the subsequent election of President **Mohammad Khatami** in 1997, Khatami appointed Nouri—who had been serving in the **Majlis**—as interior minister, a position he had also held under President Rafsanjani. At the time, elements within the Majlis opposed to Nouri's views were strong enough to block the appointment. Not deterred, Khatami immediately appointed Nouri as a vice president, a position Nouri would soon turn down to run in the first local-level elections in the history of the Islamic Republic. In 1999, along with the election of reformists across the country, Nouri was elected as head of the **Tehran** City Council, capturing a majority of the vote. Again, Nouri held the position for only a short time, stepping down in anticipation of a run in Iran's upcoming general election.

It was Nouri's daily newspaper *Khordad* that finally gave his opposition the opportunity to act against him. Beginning its publication run in 1998, *Khordad* became Nouri's sounding board for criticism against the government. Its pages provided fodder for his enemies, who used it as justification for action. Hardliners not only shut down *Khordad*, but also brought Nouri before a special clerical tribunal. The trial allowed Nouri to express his concerns with the government in a new venue, making claims that the government undermined revolutionary principles by preventing public sovereignty in favor of an autocracy controlled by the *Faqih*, the supreme leader. According to Nouri, *Velayat-i Faqih* was only viable within the confines of the **Constitution of the Islamic Republic**, and never from above it. Nouri's words at trial saw publication as the book *Hemlock for the Advocates of Reform*, gaining him even more credibility with the public as a force for reform. However, the tribunal eventually found Nouri guilty on several counts, and sentenced him to five years imprisonment.

Nouri remained active from jail, continuing to advocate his reform agenda. His reputation continued to grow, and soon Iran recognized Nouri as one of the premiere voices in the quest for governmental reform. Pressure from internal forces, as well as the international community, to release this "prisoner of conscience" mounted. Ali Khamene'i pardoned Nouri in November 2002, following Nouri's highly publicized health problems and the death of Nouri's brother, Member of Parliament Ali Reza Nouri. At the time of his release, many Iranians believed Nouri would be a perfect successor to President Khatami, whose term would end in 2005. However, up to the month before the June

2005 election, Nouri had shown no intent to run, although his views continue to inform the reformist movement.

NOW RUZ. Now Ruz is the Iranian New Year which corresponds to the spring equinox, the first day of spring in the solar calculation of the number of days in a year. The **Persian language** word translates as "new day." A number of ancient kingdoms and cultures of the Mesopotamian region celebrated some form of spring rites as a passage of renewal, and the beginning of Now Ruz celebrations is undoubtedly connected. However, though ancient in origin, the modern celebration of Now Ruz has unique characteristics that have been molded in the Iranian experience. Most significantly, the beliefs of **Zoroastrianism** have influenced Now Ruz. The renewal of natural life blended symbolically with the struggle between the dual Gods of Lightness and Darkness. Now Ruz marked a turning point, the triumph of hope over despair, as the forces of darkness (winter) began to give way to the goodness represented by light (spring).

Now Ruz has been throughout Iranian history a time of great celebration. Though the actual New Year's Day is March 21st, the celebration of Now Ruz continues over several weeks with a number of customary symbolic rituals relating to the concept of renewal. Among these are the setting up of a household table which contains seven items (Haft Sin), the names of which each begin with the letter of the Persian alphabet "sin" (S in English). Each item represents some aspect of renewal, such as fertility, beauty, love, health, and the like. Other rituals involve cleansing of the house and going on a picnic on the 13th day of Now Ruz to both enjoy the renewal of nature and to toss out the lentil or wheat sprouts that have been part of the Haft Sin, thus symbolically ridding the household of "evil spirits." Another symbolic, and fun, ritual is the building of a bonfire on a certain day of Now Ruz and jumping over the flames.

Now Ruz in modern-day Iranian society has its secular trappings. It is the major holiday of the year, a time of two weeks vacation from school and the closing, or skeleton operation, of government offices. It is also a time of personal renewal, ex-

changing of gifts, and a general celebratory atmosphere. *See also*
CALENDARS.

-O-

OIL. With documented reserves of 130.8 billion barrels of oil in
reserve (nine percent of global reserves) Iran is an important
world energy source. The country itself relies heavily on oil production for its economic well-being. In the early 21st century, oil
exports provide 40 percent of national revenue and 80 percent of
export earnings. Iran is currently the sixth leading exporter of oil
in the global market. However, before the **Islamic Revolution** of
1979, Iran was the second leading exporter of oil. The revolution
brought oil exports to a complete stop. The exports have since
recovered to their current levels of just under four million barrels
per day. With additional foreign investment Iran could greatly
increase its share of the global energy market. However, the continuing estrangement in **U.S.-Iranian Relations** and the reluctance of Western capital markets to fully embrace Iran have
slowed the pace of development in the oil sector. American oil
technology, for instance, as well as the participation of American
oil companies in developing the resource, has been denied Iran.

Iran also has a significant petrochemical industry. Beginning
in 1965 with its establishment of the **Shiraz** Fertilizer Plant, both
the **Pahlavi** government of **Muhammad Reza Shah** and the
government of the **Islamic Republic** of Iran have made concerted efforts to develop this sector of the **economy** using Iran's
abundant fossil fuels as feedstock. Though now an important part
of the domestic Iranian economy, programs have been sporadic
due to the destructive impact of the **Iran-Iraq War** (many of the
operations were located in the war zone) and the continuing isolation of Iran from global markets.

In addition to its great oil reserves Iran also possesses the
second-largest reserve of natural gas in the world (26.7 trillion
cubic meters) behind only Russia. These reserves remain largely
underutilized as Iran is only the 26th leading exporter of natural

gas. Overall, both domestically and in foreign export there is a low level of development of this high-potential resource.

With its huge reserves of both natural gas and petroleum, Iran has the possibility to be an energy leader in the world. Thus far, a quarter of a century into the Islamic Republic period of history, Iran has failed to realize this potential. *See also* INDUS-TRY.

-P-

PAHLAVI DYNASTY. In 1925, the mastermind behind the coup d'etat which led to the demise of **Qajar** rule became the first Shah of the Pahlavi Dynasty. Reza Khan, a Cossack colonel, took control and proceeded to change the course of Iranian history as **Reza Shah**.

A major thrust of the Pahlavi Dynasty centered on the rapid industrialization and modernization of Iran, based on Western societies but dictating its own terms. The Pahlavi designation with its connection to an historic pre-Islamic past was deliberately chosen to underscore both Iranian nationalism and the new regime's attitude toward foreign intervention. Foreign influence was diminished in government affairs, though many highly skilled foreign workers were employed in nationalized industries. Marked changes in the social structure were felt as the traditional landed nobility lost rank and prestige, the power of the clergy declined, the position of **women** improved, and private industries were nationalized.

In the pre-World War II period, society as a whole suffered from the concentration of resources on **industrialization**. **Agricultural** and irrigation projects were neglected and social programs (except **education**) were abandoned. The authoritative nature of the Shah encouraged rampant political and social propaganda and the curtailment of the freedoms of speech and the press. In response, there were numerous industrial strikes and the **Kurdish** peasants revolted.

Suspected of pro-Nazi sympathies, Reza Shah was forced to flee Iran when Russian and British troops invaded in 1941. His son, **Muhammad Reza Shah**, succeeded to the throne and co-operated with the Allies' war effort. Iran became a major supply route for war material to the Soviet Union and hosted the **Tehran Conference**, though the effects of the war were devastating to the general populace.

Dissatisfaction with the Shah's regime led to a takeover in 1951 in which the Shah's prime minister, **Muhammad Mossadeq**, seized control of the government until ousted in 1953 by supporters of the Shah, encouraged and backed by the American Central Intelligence Agency. In the 1960s, Muhammed Reza Shah began the **White Revolution** reform program which far outdistanced the modernization plans of his father. He instituted programs for land reform, privatization of industry, literacy, and women's rights, while maintaining an authoritarian style of government.

In imitation of the West, secularization was encouraged at the expense of the socially powerful ulama. The Shah's secret police (**SAVAK**) terrorized the population into following the new dictates. An internal resistance movement gained momentum in the early 1960s, and under the leadership of **Shiah** clergy, in particular **Ayatollah Ruhollah Khomeini**, the Pahlavi Dynasty was overthrown in 1979 and the new **Islamic Republic** was established.

PAHLAVI FOUNDATION. *See* ALAVI FOUNDATION.

PAHLAVI UNIVERSITY. Pahlavi University was founded in 1962 in **Shiraz**. It was modeled after American universities with the intent of introducing the American system of instruction, a new development in Iranian **education**. Senator Isa Sadeq Alam, an American-educated former minister of education, guided its establishment. Foreign instructors filled a number of positions and many courses were taught in English. The university offered such diverse programs as literature, natural sciences, medicine, **agriculture**, and engineering. Later, an institute of agricultural technology and a nursing college were added. The university complex included the Sa'di Hospital, Khalili Clinic for Ophthalmology, and the Nemazi Hospital with a nuclear medicine center. Boarding facilities were built to accommodate over 8,000 students, though by the mid-1970s the enrollment had reached only 5,000. Originally superimposed on the structure of the old Shiraz University, after the **Islamic Revolution** the name of the institution reverted back to Shiraz University. *See also* MELLI UNIVERSITY; TEHRAN UNIVERSITY.

PANAHI, JA'FAR (1960-). Ja'far Panahi was born in the city of Mianeh in **Azerbaijan** and grew up as an Azeri speaker. He served in the army for several years and was even taken prisoner for 76 days by **Kurdish** rebels battling the newly formed **Islamic Republic**. After his discharge, he studied in **Tehran** at the College of **Cinema** and TV.

Once Panahi decided he wanted to work in the cinema, his first step was to contact the well-known Iranian film director **Abbas Kiarostami**. Kiarostami allowed him to assist on the shoot of *Through the Olive Trees*. Out of this grew Panahi's first directoral movie, *The White Balloon*. Panahi told Kiarostami about his plans to make such a movie, and Kiarostami agreed to help him write the script. Kiarostami was the leading contemporary Iranian filmmaker and his help was an auspicious beginning for the aspiring young Panahi and his film. *The White Balloon* won four prizes in Iran and was extensively shown in special theaters, designed specifically for children's films, throughout Iran. The film also attracted international attention. *The White Balloon* won two of the top prizes—the *Camera d'Or* for the best first film and the International Critic's prize at the Cannes Film Festival in 1995. The film went on to win the Tokyo Gold Prize for the best feature, with a cash bonus of $150,000, and the Best Film Award at the Sao Paolo Festival.

Panahi has continued to produce critically acclaimed work such as *The Mirror* (1997) and *The Circle* (2000). He has collaborated on other scripts with Kiarostami, such as on the film *Crimson Gold* (2003) which Panahi produced and directed. His wide-ranging efforts in the film industry of the Islamic Republic of Iran have extended across every aspect of filmmaking. He has acted, written scripts, produced, directed, and edited films. In the process, Panahi has distinguished himself as one of the premiere filmmakers of Iran, and established also an international reputation of note.

PARTHIAN PERIOD. In the middle of the third century B.C., a nomadic tribe known as the Parni established a small kingdom in the Parthava region of the Seleucid Empire—one of several Greek empires left upon the death of Alexander the Great who split his empire between his generals. From this grew an empire that would at its height span from India to Armenia and last well into the third century A.D. Although the early Parthians, as the Parni came to be known, deferred to the Seleucids as superiors even after the first Parthian king Arasces I had established his kingdom in 247 B.C., the power of the Parthians became such that the Seleucids could not resist. Faced with the Roman Empire expanding eastward and the Parthian expanding westward, the Seleucids were finally conquered by the first century B.C.

Now the expansionistic empires of the Romans and the Parthian were faced with each other, roughly along the Euphrates River. For several hundred years, the two empires fought numerous wars, with lands passing back and forth between them often. The Parthians lost and reclaimed their capital city, Ctesiphon, on numerous occasions throughout these years of fighting, but never did the Romans fully defeat the Parthians (nor did they ever completely vanquish any of the Persian empires they faced throughout history). Still, the Romans almost always had the advantage, with most of the Parthian victories simply reclaiming lands lost to the Romans.

The Parthian Empire's decentralized nature may have helped it weather such defeats. Although the capital was Ctesiphon—which is along the Tigris River just south of present-day Baghdad—the Arascid Dynasty, which the kingdom came to be known as, held hegemony over numerous regional, or vassal, kings. Rather than being tied directly into a centralized government, these vassal kingdoms simply paid tribute to the ruling dynasty, whose kings very fittingly took on the ancient title began with the **Achaemenid Dynasty**, "King of Kings." In this way, subordinate kings still functioned when the empire lost its official seat of power, allowing them to levy troops for future defenses.

Although by nature this sort of organization lends itself to cultural diversity, and the Parthians were tolerant, the Parthian Empire went through two distinct cultural phases: Hellenistic and Persian. When the Arascid kings first began to conquer Seleucid lands, they had to accede to the established Greek customs of the aristocratic and bureaucratic classes to be able to solidify their power. Thus, Greek language and script were used in official documents and on coinage. However, by the first century A.D., the Parthians were well on their way to a cultural revitalization of Persian heritage. The historically Persian **Zoroastrianism** became the official religion of the Parthians, and a shift to the use of Pahlavi script used during Achaemenid times and to the speaking of Middle **Persian language** further exemplified the growing Persian element amongst the Parthians. Although the Parthians made few cultural innovations, they did set the stage for the subsequent **Sassanian Dynasty** to reassert a dynamic and progressive Persian culture.

Even with its resilience in empire organization and culture, the Roman attacks continued to exact heavy costs on the Parthians. Although also extremely costly to the Romans, they persisted since they coveted the **trade** routes with India and China which made the Parthian Empire so wealthy. In the year 193, yet another sacking of Ctesiphon resulted in enormous financial hardships and internal unrest amongst the Parthians. Finally, in 224, a vassal of the Parthian rulers revolted, and went on to achieve something the Romans could not. By the second year of the revolt, King Ardashir I captured Ctesiphon and overthrew the final Parthian king. This act established the Sassanian Dynasty.

PARTY OF THE IRANIAN NATION (PIN). A young law student, the son of an army officer, Daryush Foruhar, founded the PIN. He began his political activities during World War II, soon after the 1943 arrest of his father by the occupying British forces on the suspicion of having German contacts. Foruhar began to organize the PIN while he was a student at **Tehran Uni-**

versity. The PIN was ideologically anti-court and anti-clerical and wished to assert a strong national identity.

The PIN members were a pro-**Mossadeq** group of nationalists, and an element of his **National Front**, composed mostly of high school and college students. They seemingly specialized in brawling with the **Tudeh** sympathizers. This gave PIN a greater presence than their limited numbers should have indicated.

After the 1953 royalist coup which toppled Muhammad Mossadeq, nationalistic elements gathered to attempt to assert some sort of opposition to **Muhammad Reza Shah**'s newly reconstituted regime. The PIN was a part of this coalition of opposition and advised what became known as the **National Resistance Movement (NRM)** to be cautious in its opposition. The PIN membership left the NRM in 1955.

In 1960, Daryush Foruhar, and PIN members, were part of a coalition to revive the now defunct National Front. As a member group of the Second National Front, the PIN organized student opposition groups, such as Student Organization of the National Front (organized on campuses during the 1960-1961 academic year) and Student Supporters of the National Front. The PIN also took a role in a further revival of the National Front in 1964-1965. However, by that time, the Shah brooked very little political opposition and National Front participation was by and large ineffectual.

For a brief time, the PIN participated in dialogue with the **Liberation Movement of Iran (LMI)**. However, the religiously tinted dialogue of most of the LMI members was such that there was little cooperation by PIN members. Consequently, in 1977, the PIN sought to revive the again defunct National Front under the name of the Union of National Front Forces. Daryush Foruhar became the spokesman for the group whose membership included the Iran Party, the PIN, and the Society of Iranian Socialists.

As events led inexorably to the **Islamic Revolution** and the establishment of the **Islamic Republic of Iran**, Foruhar and his party played a role. He was arrested after the events of **Black Friday** on 8 September, 1978. Despite a common enemy in the Shah, however, it could be argued that the reluctance of the PIN, and its colleagues, to cooperate with religiously motivated nationalists (such as the LMI) contributed to the inability of nationalists and religious modernists to cope with rapidly changing events during the revolution. Even though Foruhar flew to France to meet with **Ayatollah Ruhollah Khomeini** prior to his return to Iran, the inability of groups such as the PIN to compromise with more religious elements may have contributed to the later victory of more conservative elements.

Foruhar was chosen by **Mehdi Bazargan** to be the minister of labor and social affairs in the **Provisional Government** installed after the collapse of the **Pahlavi Dynasty**. Appointed in February, differences again emerged with his nationalist colleagues, and he was replaced in September, 1979. In early 1980, Foruhar ran for the presidency in the first election held under the newly drafted **Constitution of the Islamic Republic**, but despite his long record of anti-Shah activity, he garnered little support. He was one of eight candidates in the election won handily by **Abol Hassan Bani-Sadr**. Continually at odds with the emergent conservative clerical rule of the Islamic Republic, Daryush and his wife Parvaneh were found murdered in their home in 1998.

PARTY OF THE IRANIAN PEOPLE (PIP). The Party of the Iranian People (PIP), or *Hezb-i Mardom-i Iran*, operated as a political entity within both the **National Front** and the **National Resistance Movement** (NRM). Founded by the **Islamic** socialist Muhammad Nakhshab, the PIP was just one of many groups to support **Muhammad Mossadeq**. Leaving the Iranian Party in 1949 due to discomfort with its support of the atheistic **Tudeh Party**, Nakhshab sought to create a group that could not only incorporate socialism, but also Islam. In 1952, he approached **Mehdi Bazargan** in regards to forming such a group, and although Bazargan did not become involved, Nakhshab proceeded anyway. Originally called the Society for the Freedom of the People of Iran, the group became known as the Party of the Iranian People in 1953.

With the reinstatement of **Muhammad Reza Shah** in 1953, many groups in opposition to the **Pahlavi Dynasty**, including the PIP, joined under the umbrella of the National Resistance

Movement. At this time, many of the younger members became acquainted with **Ali Shari'ati**, who was—like Nakhshab—also interested in combining Islam with nationalism. In fact, Shariati had been part of one of Nakhshab's PIP precursor groups, the Society of God-Worshipping Socialists. This link would prove quite helpful in the formation of future groups based along similar premises to the PIP.

In 1957, the Shah crushed the National Resistance Movement, placing much of its leadership under arrest. The PIP, in common with some other groups within the NRM, tried futilely to reform new incarnations of the National Front. However, as time passed, the membership of the PIP became more restless, and conflict over the question whether to use outright violence against the Shah fragmented the group. In 1962, the PIP had both its first and its last party congress. The legacy of the PIP, however, is a shift from purely or largely nationalistic forms of socialism into more religiously oriented organizations. With the demise of the PIP, many members went on to other groups, such as the **Liberation Movement of Iran**, which carried this concept of both leftist and religious opposition all the way through the **Islamic Revolution** of 1979.

PASDARAN. *See* REVOLUTIONARY GUARDS.

PERKINS, JUSTIN (1805-1869). Perkins was the first American missionary to Iran. He served in Persia for the **American Board of Commissioners for Foreign Missions** from 1835 to 1869. He established the Nestorian Mission at **Urmieh** and translated the Bible into Syriac. He wrote a book about his experiences entitled *A Residence of Eight Years in Persia.*

PERSEPOLIS. The city of Persepolis was the creation of **Darius**, one of the greatest kings of the **Achaemenid Dynasty**, who ruled from 521 to 486 B.C. Located in the remote and mountainous region of Fars Province, it lies in ruins approximately 48 kilometers north of the present-day city of **Shiraz**. Persepolis was constructed to serve as the spiritual center of the empire and Darius brought craftsmen from throughout the known world to fashion the new city. Persepolis served as a monument to the greatness of the Achaemenid Dynasty.

The finished city was a work of architectural genius with all the grandeur of a cosmopolitan city. Built upon a huge terrace with one side up against a mountain, the city overlooked a large plain. Huge columns supported the massive buildings constructed from the dark mountain stone taken from behind the city. Long stairways climbed to the buildings with artistic relief carvings gracing the way. Elaborate tombs were constructed in nearby mountainsides as monuments to the kings who would inherit the glory of the dynasty through the ages.

The ruins of Persepolis are an invaluable source for modern scholars seeking to unravel the history of the early Persians. The city served primarily as a cultural and ceremonial center, while most government business was carried on in the more centrally located imperial cities of **Susa**, Ecbatana (modern-day **Hamadan**), and Babylon. Persepolis was the site of the spring equinox Iranian New Year celebrations during which all ruling kings of the Achaemenid satrapies would arrive to pay homage to Darius, and other Achaemenid rulers who fashioned themselves the King of Kings. Darius' penchant for memorializing his reign has provided a wealth of information about ancient Persian culture. The royal archives of Persepolis, for instance, contained inscriptions written in Elamite script which have furnished clues to the development of the **Persian language** through this time.

The name of the city itself has long been a subject of controversy. A commonly accepted interpretation of the name is that it derives from the Greek term "Perseptolis," which means "destroyer of cities," and was a title bestowed by the Greeks to symbolize their view of the Persians who wrought much destruction on Greek cities. The Persians themselves have always known the place as *Takhti-i Jamshid*, or throne of Jamshid, a mythological king in the Iranian epic, the ***Shahnameh***. *See also* SHAHNAMEH, CHARACTERS OF.

PERSIAN GULF COMMAND. The Persian Gulf Command was established in 1942 to supervise and implement, for the duration of World War II, the movement of American Lend-Lease material and supplies to the Soviet Union via the Persian Gulf and land routes through Iran. The organization constructed and maintained roads, operated the **Trans-Iranian Railway** and port facilities, and built assembly plants. This operation was the first major American presence in Iran with over 30,000 non-combat personnel assigned to the command.

PERSIAN LANGUAGE. In Persia, language has been the most important symbol of identity for its people. It is the common unbroken thread of Persian identity connecting the modern Iranian with the ancients throughout the vicissitudes of history. When viewing the history of the **Persian language**, it is important to remember that much of what has survived from ancient times has been retrieved from the folk stories and myths passed on from generation to generation. The most significant example of this connection is the Iranian national epic, the *Shahnameh*, which was passed on as an oral tradition and not formally written down until the 11th century A.D.

Scholars have been able to identify three stages of development in the Persian language: Old Persian dating back 4000 years, Middle Persian which arose around the third century B.C., and New Persian, the forerunner of Farsi, the language of modern Iran which emerged in the ninth century A.D.

Remnants of Old Persian are found written in Elamite and Akkadian script, but the oral tradition and time have provided sparse clues for translation. It is believed to be an offshoot of the Indo-European language group and dates of origin have been established directly to 2,700 years ago and indirectly to 4,000 years ago. Changes in the composition of the population due to conquest and migration infused elements of Parthian, Soghdian, and various other languages. Such mixture was intensified during the historical period of the **Achaemenids**, led by the great kings **Cyrus** and **Darius**, whose benevolent ruling style helped maintain and spread the language throughout their vast empire.

Old Persian endured until the third century B.C. when the **Sassanians** raised the Persian dialect of Fars to an imperial language, generally referred to as **Pahlavi**. This period is marked by limited vocabulary and a cumbersome Aramaic script. Dari, a simpler, less ornate form of the language, arose in the Sassanian period and soon replaced Pahlavi in Sassanian writing. This Middle Persian period lasted until the ninth century A.D. when, as a consequence of the Arab invasion, there began a process of change in the structure of the Persian language.

Following the Islamic-Arab conquest of Persia, the language underwent a period of significant change. The influx of Arabic elements of grammar, rhetoric, and extensive vocabulary marked a turning point in the composition of Persian **literature**, both oral and written. The simpler Arabic forms replaced the cumbersome and limited Pahlavi formations, and in the ninth century A.D. the work flowing from Persia seems to indicate that the natural poetic inclinations of the Persians were waiting for this opportunity. Literature flourished. Works in the scientific and scholarly fields poured forth as the vocabulary of the Arabic language provided the means for the learned to express their thoughts. And although Arabic elements profoundly influenced literature, Farsi, or New Persian, remained the spoken language. It contained some elements of Arabic but retained its own singular Persian identity.

Resistance to the Arabic influence persisted and periodic movements erupted in Iran to expunge Arabic elements from the language. All have been remarkably unsuccessful. Far from eliminating Persian as a language, many of the finer elements of Arabic were incorporated into its structure and became wholly Persian. From the simplified forms, to the Arabic script, to vocabulary that enables poets endless flight and scholars the means to produce extraordinary works, the Persian language is itself a history of a people who have been conquered only to convert the conquerors to their cultural style, a people who have maintained the unbroken thread of a common language which connects the Persians of today with the ancient kings of old. The language is as rich and diverse, as dynamic and durable as the Persian people who still speak of the great kings and write of their glorious accomplishments. *See also* FERDOWSI, ABOL QASEM; POETRY.

PLAN ORGANIZATION. The Plan Organization (also known as Plan and Budget Organization) was established by the **Majlis** in 1949. A semi-autonomous group reporting to the prime minister, it was the government agency charged with the planning and execution of development and modernization plans. The Plan Organization controlled and allocated a large segment of national income (particularly **oil** revenues) to the various projects in the programs it designed. The original plan was called the Seven Year Development Plan, but it was renamed and reorganized following the disruptions caused by the oil nationalization movement in the early 1950s. Later plans were organized on a five-year cycle.

The bureau was composed of budget experts, technocrats, and social planners, supported by foreign experts, who were to devise the intricate plans necessary to carry out the development programs desired by **Muhammad Reza Shah**. Under the long-term leadership of Abol Hasan Ebtehaj, the group organized the building of dams, improvements to the infrastructure, and the revitalization of domestic **industry** and **agriculture**.

Though composed primarily of supremely able young technocrats, the efforts of the Plan Organization were hampered by the intrusion of various ministries jealously guarding their territory. In the 1960s, the Shah abandoned a moderate supervisory role and assumed the central decision-making position in the Plan Organization as his "Great Civilization" plan was announced. This plan would presumably enable Iran to reach very ambitious economic, social, and cultural goals by the end of the 20th century. The consequence was total subordination of rational economic planning to political aims, with disastrous results in the mid-1970s. What was hailed as an economic miracle of development in the 1960s, a time when the Iranian **economy** was fueled by increasing oil revenues and rational planning, turned into an economic morass by 1976. In such fashion was the stage set for the **Islamic Revolution**, which forced the Shah to leave Iran in 1979 and ended the **Pahlavi Dynasty**.

PLATEAU. *See* IRANIAN PLATEAU.

POETRY. Persian language and poetry go together like lock and key. The language seems to lend itself to poetic expression, and Persians are seemingly born poets. Rare is the Persian who can not recite a significant number of poetic lines from the enormous store of inherited **literature**. Composition of poetry is so common that, if one were to count oral expression on top of written forms, it comes close to qualifying as a national pastime.

Persian classical poetry differs from the Western genre mainly in its extreme unity in structure and theme. Poets followed traditional guidelines or "rules" which emerged during the time of royal or noble patronage of the arts. A major theme was patron glorification. Accomplishments and virtues were embellished and enemies vilified with little regard to factual reliability. Poets outdid one another in their playful word manipulation within strict structural constraints.

Until the modern period, Persian poets were not encouraged to experiment with new styles. Poetic license was, for the most part, frowned upon. Compositions generally followed the prescribed patterns of meter and rhyme developed by past master poets and the themes remained in line with those of older works.

In the 20th century a new style of poetry emerged called "New **Poetry**." **Nima Yushij** is generally acknowledged as the father of this new poetic tradition. Basically akin to the Western genre of free verse, this style was resisted after its introduction in the 1920s and became the source of much controversy. Eventually, however, New Poetry found a place in the repertoire of Iranian poets and is today a common mode of poetic expression.

Most Persian poems in the classical mode are moralistic and abstract and deal with such diverse concepts as religion, history, love, mysticism, philosophy, and lament. The poetic form was used even when the subject matter was mundane and seemed better suited to prose. The works of each poet were often collected in a book form called a "divan."

Classical poetry was composed in a variety of forms and styles. Amongst these were the epic, the *ruba'i*, the *masnavi*, and various forms of lyrical poetry including the ghazal and the qasida, each briefly described below with the name of at least one classical master.

The epic is a long metrical poem written in elevated language and appearing in three different forms: heroic (historical), romantic (moralistic, allegorical), or didactic (instructional). These works were composed to be recited before enthusiastic audiences and the stiffness and repetition of the work—apparent to a reader—disappear in the oral rendering. The most famous epic poem is **Abol Qasem Ferdowsi**'s *Shahnameh*, a huge work which recreates the glorious history of Persia and its people, the central theme of most of the poems of this style. Many Persian epics were connected with mythology and originated from Old and Middle Persian language texts.

Ruba'is are quatrains that are complete poems. This form was popular with the **Sufi** poets who used the *ruba'i* to compose works with a mystical meaning beneath the obvious. **Omar Khayyam** is best known in the West for his collection of these poems entitled *Rubaiyat*.

Masnavis are expansive narrative poems varying in theme. Many epics, didactic poems, and Sufi teachings appeared in *masnavi* style. The mystic poet **Rumi** excelled in this verse form.

The lyrical poem is composed of three parts: the prologue, panegyric, and the conclusion. The many subcategories of lyrical poetry follow strict traditional structures. Ghazals are lyric poems that have a single rhyme and various meters. The most common theme was love, mystical as well as human, but poets utilized any subject capable of stirring emotion. **Sa'di** and **Hafez** are most renowned for their work in this style.

Qasidas are lyric purpose poems—panegyrics, elegies, or lamentations. Qasidas were often didactic in nature in that the form lent itself to entertainment with an element of instruction. Most contained 12 to 50 couplets, a length which was conducive to oral presentation. Little is known about the individual composers of the older qasidas which survived through oral transmission. Among the acknowledged masters are **Rudaki**, Anvari, and Khaqani. *See also* NEZAMI GANJAVI; SHAHNAMEH, CHARACTERS OF.

PRELIMINARY TREATY OF FRIENDSHIP AND ALLIANCE (1809). The Preliminary Treaty of Friendship and Alliance was signed in March 1809 by Sir Harford Jones of the British East India Company and **Fath Ali Shah**. The treaty is also called the Treaty of **Tehran**. This new treaty nullified the **Treaty of Finkenstein** of 1807 which had allied Persia with France. That alliance severed relationships between Persia and Great Britain and fueled British fears of an invasion by Napoleon into India through Persia.

The stated purpose of the treaty was to create a "sincere and everlasting" alliance between the two nations. The Shah pledged to disregard all treaties previously signed with other European nations (with special emphasis accorded to the Finkenstein treaty), to refuse access into Iran to these same nations, and agreed not to enter into any future agreements which would be damaging to the British Crown or its interests in India. In return, Britain pledged military assistance, either with troops or in the form of a subsidy, if any European nation invaded Persia, and also promised to stay out of the affairs of Persia and Afghanistan unless both sides called Britain to conduct negotiations. As a response to the perceived French threat to India via Persia, the treaty ended ebate between opposing British factions—those who wanted to seize Persia by force and those who favored a more liberal diplomatic settlement. It also set the stage for the later **Definitive Treaty** which in 1812 established permanent British diplomatic representation to the **Qajar** court.

PROVISIONAL GOVERNMENT. The Provisional Government of Iran originated in a meeting between the **Ayatollah Ruhollah Khomeini**, **Mehdi Bazargan**, and **Ibrahim Yazdi**, which took place in Paris, France in October 1978. During this meeting, Khomeini asked Bazargan and Yazdi to draw up a list of men who could act as his consultants. The job of these men would be to propose suitable candidates to fill cabinet positions and run for parliamentary elections at a later date. A number of those on this list, including Bazargan, were closely associated and members of either the **National Front** or the **Liberation Movement of Iran (LMI)**. This list was reconstructed as the **Revolutionary Council**, virtually unchanged, in January 1979. Khomeini returned to Iran on 31 January, and within a few days named Bazargan as his prime minister even though the **Shapur Bakhtiar** government, the caretaker government **Muhammad Reza Shah** left in place upon his departure, had not completely collapsed. On 3 February, Khomeini asked the Revolutionary Council to nominate a prime minister. For several days there were actually two prime ministers in the revolutionary turmoil of the time, representing incoming and outgoing governments. On 11 February, when the monarchy did collapse, Bazargan became the first prime minister of the Provisional Government of the **Islamic Republic**.

The Provisional Government of Bazargan was short-lived, lasting from February 1979 to 6 November of the same year, only two days after the takeover of the American Embassy in **Tehran** and the onset of the 444-day holding Bazargan wasted no time in choosing his cabinet from the membership of the Revolutionary Council. Khomeini approved all of Bazargan's choices except one, and appointed new members to fill the empty positions in the Council. Among Bazargan's cabinet members were the following:

Minister of Foreign Affairs, **Karim Sanjabi**, former National Front leader (resigned 16 April and replaced by Ibrahim Yazdi);
Minister of **Economy**, Ali Ardalan;
Minister of Labor, Daryush Foruhar, leader of the **Party of the Iranian Nation (PIN)**;
Minister for Revolutionary Projects, **Yadollah Sahabi**;
Deputy Prime Minister for Revolutionary Affairs, **Abbas Amir Entezam**;
Minister of Interior, Sadr Hajj-Seyyed-Javadi;
Minister of Health, Kazem Sami;
Minister of National Guidance, Naser Minachi;
Minister of Defense, General Valiollah Qarani.

Officials changed frequently when they were unable to gain full authority over their ministry's area of responsibility. The Ministry of Defense changed hands four times. The only secular nationalist minister who held his position during the entire nine-month period of the Provisional Government was Minister of **Economy** Ali Ardalan.

The Provisional Government was intended to be an interim government formed to restore some semblance of order after the chaos of the previous year of revolution. This proved to be very problematic. The Bazargan government was initially popular, but the deliberate and meticulous style of Bazargan, and the inability of the government to bring about immediate change quickly undermined its popularity. The Provisional Government seemed forever plagued by its inability to centralize or consolidate its power. Competing centers of power, such as the Revolutionary Council and the Revolutionary *Komitehs*, sought immediate changes and often undermined the efforts of the Provisional Government.

As Bazargan formed his Cabinet mostly from the liberal religious modernists among the Revolutionary Council and Ayatollah Khomeini appointed replacements, gradually the Council took on a more radical and clerical character. Any action of appointment which Bazargan initiated had to first be approved by the Council and, because of the differing makeup of the Provisional Government and the Council, it became increasingly harder for Bazargan to take any action. Many of the Council's members belonged to the **Islamic Republican Party**, a clerical party that quickly found itself in opposition to Bazargan and the Provisional Government. In July, Bazargan tried to more closely integrate his cabinet and the Revolutionary Council to bring about greater cooperation. This coalescence, however, merely gave his clerical opposition greater confidence in their own management capabilities and more opportunities to work towards the consolidation of their own power.

As the monarchy collapsed, the former apparatuses of power were abandoned and quickly fell into the hands of the people. All over Iran, the people took control of government offices, police stations, and military barracks. Most of the 300,000 weapons seized from military arsenals fell into the hands of young revolutionaries. These revolutionary youths lacked the patience to wait for the Provisional Government to affect change and address past grievances. All over the country, they began to form local *Ko-*

mitehs. These *Komitehs*, and the revolutionary tribunals set up by them, took it upon themselves to arrest anyone suspected of having ties to **SAVAK** or the monarchy and to confiscate property. Often these *Komitehs* would arrest or harass petty bureaucrats simply because they had held office under the monarchy. This was often true even when the Provisional Government felt it preferable for many of them to retain their positions under the new regime to provide some bureaucratic expertise and continuity.

Many of these *Komitehs* were attached to local clerics and were motivated largely by revolutionary zeal, and since they were all armed, it was, despite attempts by the Provisional Government to ban or organize them, impossible to rein them in. Attempts to organize and control these committees led to the formation of the *Pasdaran-i Inqelab*, or the **Revolutionary Guards**, which eventually became a militant arm for the radical clerics and another stumbling block. The job of centralizing government functions under the Provisional Government became impossible. On 6 November, 1979, Bazargan submitted his resignation. Though not the first time Bazargan had submitted his resignation (it was the fourth time, in fact) this time it was accepted by Ayatollah Khomeini.

The Provisional Government officially came to an end in November, but for all intents and purposes it continued as a rump government for several more months until the adoption of the **Constitution of the Islamic Republic** in December 1979 provided the means for a replacement government. A new government was formed in early 1980 by **Abol Hassan Bani-Sadr**, the newly elected president of the Islamic Republic.

-Q-

QABUS NAMEH. Known as both the *Qabus Nameh* (Book of Qabus) and *Andarz Nameh* (Book of Counsel), this text written by 11th century Ziyarid King Kai Kaus ibn Iskandar iln qalus iln Washmgir outlines a father's advice for his son. The author uses the format of the "Mirror for Princes" **literature**, popular at the time as a means to inform Turko-Mongolian rulers of royal Iranian concepts, to instruct his son in matters of ruling and living as a king, or as a member of various other occupations. Kai Kaus ruled the areas along the **Caspian** shore and felt a responsibility to his son to inform and train him in his own experiences as nobility. The work provides instruction on dealing with bureaucracy and exhorts living a life in moderation with regard to drinking, gaming, and **women**. The author focused on both a possible future in politics for his son, who did not succeed his father to the throne, and the possibility of living as a musician, judge, physician, or merchant.

The major theme of the text, regardless of the specificity of the advice, is to stand firm against the winds of political change, and change in general, and to enjoy life as it comes, and neither take fortune for granted nor allow it to stagnate.

While many other "Mirrors for Princes" exist in 11th century Persian literature and later, Kaus' text is one of the most studied and researched of the genre. The writings of Kai Kaus to his son not only shaped the practices and images of the time, but have molded the modern image of Iran's early ruling classes. His words capture the essence of matters ranging from the fashion of the times, to daily pastimes of the Persian elite, to marketplace transactions, capturing a vivid glimpse of life in 11th century Iran.

QAJAR DYNASTY. The Qajars, a **tribe** of Turkish origin, ruled Iran from 1779 until 1925. The first ruler of the dynasty was the fierce tribal leader **Agha Muhammad Khan** who conquered the Zands and established Qajar hegemony on the **Iranian Plateau**. Agha Muhammad Khan Qajar had great strength of character, but his kingly successors were less spirited and quickly became enmeshed in the web of European Great Power politics. The next century and a half was a period of pervasive foreign influence which changed the face and focus of Iranian society.

Only several decades into the 19th century the **Babi Movement** sprung up as a result of widespread social unrest, attributable to the disrupting socio-economic transformation which Iran was undergoing in response to the impact of the West. This religious movement, with its roots in **Sufism** and **Shiah** political thought, was started by Mirza Ali Muhammad, who in 1844 declared himself the forerunner of the **Hidden Imam**. The movement later evolved into **Bahaism** which established itself first in Iran and eventually attained international influence as a universalistic religion. It was during the Qajar period that the influence of the Islamic clergy began to be more pronounced in secular matters, a shift which would have a profound impact on future political administrations.

Iran was considered a "backward" nation by the standards of the rapidly industrializing Western countries. It was underdeveloped, economically weak, and easily manipulated by the great powers which recognized its enormous potential. Russia and Great Britain competed to exploit Iran and its resources for their own benefit. Through a series of agreements and treaties the Qajar kings seriously compromised Iranian sovereignty. In return for large loans, many spurious in nature, they virtually turned internal development over to these two Great European Powers.

Russia made inroads into Iran after the **Treaty of Gulistan** and the **Treaty of Turkmanchai**. They annexed territory in the Caucasus and secured navigation rights on the **Caspian Sea**, as well as favorable **trade** and tariff agreements, and even extraterritorial privileges. They further infiltrated Iran by annexing the formerly Iranian territories of Tashkent, Samarkand, Bokhara, and Khiva east of the Caspian Sea.

Great Britain focused on securing access to Iranian markets and raw materials. Following negotiations with the British financier, Baron Reuter, in 1872 Britain was granted the railroad concession and the right to manage the **oil** and mineral **industry**. Russia protested this agreement and Iran attempted to void the arrangement. Great Britain persisted and continued to wield considerable economic influence. The **Tobacco Revolt** in 1891-1892, protesting the British tobacco monopoly, was the first indication that the Iranian people were willing to stand as a nation and take control of their own affairs.

The imperialistic influence of Russia and Great Britain was not easily displaced. Following the **Constitutional Revolution of 1906** and the adoption of the first ever Iranian Constitution, these two countries signed the **Anglo-Russian Convention of 1907** which split Iran into two zones of influence. Though nominally independent, Iran was effectively controlled by these two nations. Dissatisfaction with the direction the country was taking caused internal disturbances and dissident groups began to protest government policy. The growing unrest, spurred by the ulama and diverse secular factions within society, hastened the downfall of the Qajars as **Sultan Ahmad Shah** yielded in 1925 to **Reza Shah** who founded the **Pahlavi Dynasty**. *See also* ABBAS MIRZA; AL-AFGHANI, JAMAL AL-DIN; DEFINITIVE TREATY OF 1812; FATH ALI SHAH; MIRZA MALKOM KHAN; MIRZA SALEH SHIRAZI; MIRZA TAQI KHAN AMIR KABIR; MUHAMMAD ALI SHAH; MUHAMMAD MIRZA SHAH; NASER AL-DIN SHAH; PRELIMINARY TREATY OF FRIENDSHIP AND ALLIANCE; TEHRAN TREATY OF 1814; TREATY OF FINKENSTEIN.

QANATS. *Qanats* are a form of irrigation used extensively in Iran. A qanat is an underground channel waterway that collects groundwater at the skirts of mountains, at an alluvial fan, and carries it through a tunnel to settlements located at a lower level and usually in a plain. From the air, *Qanats* appear as a line of craters. *Qanats* have a powerful role in determining where settlements are established on the **Iranian Plateau**. The site of a *Qanat* is determined by the slope of the land, topographical conditions, and variations of vegetation, because this indicates where water is evident and what land needs to be irrigated. The *Qanats* are dug by teams of men who often pass on this job to their heirs. The *Qanats* start with a mother well at the alluvial fan. It taps into the water table which is generally closer to the surface than on the plain. The mother well is usually about a meter in diameter. The size depends on the length of the *Qanat*, and how large a gradient there is from the alluvial fan to the settlement on the plain. Once a steady flow of water is hit, the alignment and slope must be determined. If the slope is too steep, the water flow will be too strong and may damage the *Qanat*. Gravity moves the water from the mother well to the settlement.

From a point above the village, after locating the mother well, a trench is started towards the well. When it reaches a certain depth, the trench becomes a tunnel. As the tunnel is being dug, vertical shafts to the surface are dug for air and so that dirt can be lifted in a bucket by a rope and windlass. Tunnels are sometimes dug from two different shafts that are located about 50 to 100 meters apart, towards each other. Tunnels can also be started from the mother well, but the workers have to watch out for water flows that can drown them. To help support the tunnel when loose soils are encountered, baked clay or tile rings are used. The tunnel size is characteristically a meter wide and about one and a half meters deep. The tops of the vertical shafts are in craters shaped from dirt from the tunnels. These craters help protect the *Qanats* from debris, wind, and floods. The *Qanats* also need to be maintained to make sure that there are no tunnel collapses and to clean out debris from the tunnels and shafts.

The length of *Qanats* varies from place to place. Where they surface also differs. Some surface outside a village in open trenches. This can cause problems due to evaporation and contamination. Some *Qanats* surface inside the perimeters of a village. There is an order to the placement of houses and structures around the *Qanats*. The more prosperous villagers will be housed near the upper part where the water from the *Qanat* comes out, and their fields will be watered first. The poorer people will live farther down the line where the water is no longer fresh. Not only is there a social hierarchy, but there is a hierarchy of usage. Drinking water is obtained early in the day and at the head of the *Qanat*. Some villages have downstream structures built where **women** can wash clothes, dishes, and sometimes themselves. A village latrine may exist even farther downstream.

The flow of water is regulated by foremen. They control the water and set up a rotation of irrigation for the crops. Since the flow is determined by the previous winter's snowfall and rainfall, if there is a dry season, smaller crops are planted to match the water flow. The water is distributed in different ways. Most often, it is divided into shares, by turn, by damming, and by opening of outlets. Crop lands are shaped into rectangular plots that are surrounded by a dyke of earth about a foot in height.

When it is time for the plot to be watered, water is diverted to it, and the plot is flooded with an inch or two of water.

Qanats are found throughout Iran. They vary in length, though commonly *Qanats* of eight to 16 kilometers are found. However, the cities of **Kerman** and Yazd are famous for the length of *Qanats* in their respective regions. Some of these extend to incredible lengths, 32 or more kilometers and in one case at Yazd to over 64 kilometers.

Even at the present time, *Qanats* play an important role in the water distribution of the Iranian nation. Ancient in origin and time tested, they provide a steady source of water in a manner not yet supplanted by more modern technologies. However, new *Qanats* are not being built and gradually dams, deep wells, and other means of water access are diminishing the number of functioning *Qanats*. Though many are still operating today, the days of the qanat are numbered. Historically, however, it is no exaggeration to say that settled existence was made possible in many arid areas of Iran by the ancient technological marvel of the *Qanat*.

QASHQAI. The Qashqai are a federation of several Turkic-speaking **tribes** totaling just over 250,000 people in the Fars province of Iran, the vast majority of whom are **Shiah** Muslims. The Qashqai are a nomadic people rotating their herds of sheep and goats between cooler, higher elevations in the **Zagros Mountains** during the summer months, and the lower elevation winter pastures to the north of **Shiraz**, their chief market town. This migration route has been documented and studied for its complexity and difficulty of execution.

During the late 1800s, the Qashqai dominated as the most powerful tribal organization in Iran, even defeating British-led troops. However, in the early 1900s during **Reza Shah**'s attempt to settle the nomadic people of Iran, the Qashqai were defeated when their only passage from the summer pastures to the winter pastures was blocked, forcing the Qashqai into surrender. Like many tribes however, the Qashqai returned to their nomadic practices upon the abdication of the Shah in 1941.

From 1962 to 1964, the Qashqai revolted against the government when an attempt was made to take away their pastures as part of the land reform program of the **White Revolution**. The government launched a full military campaign on the Qashqai, who were again defeated, forcing many to settle in villages and towns. By the mid-1980s, over 100,000 Qashqai were settled, a process that in all likelihood will gradually continue.

QESHM. Qeshm is an island which lies off the southern coast of Iran in the Persian Gulf. It is 120 kilometers long stretching east to west and about 10 to 30 kilometers in width, which makes it the largest island in the Persian Gulf. In 1991, the estimated population was 60,117. Situated adjacent to the **Hormoz Strait**, it is considered the gateway to the Persian Gulf. With this excellent vantage point, the southern coast of Qeshm is passed by a huge number of ships, mostly **oil** tankers, traveling to the many shoreline states of the Persian Gulf. These states include Qatar, Kuwait, United Arab Emirates, Iraq, Saudi Arabia, Bahrain, Iran, and Oman. Qeshm's air space is also traversed by aircraft traveling to and from these Persian Gulf states. Thus, Qeshm acts as a watchdog over the passage through which a large percentage of the world's fossil fuels moves, and has assumed a strategic importance far beyond the merits of its own resources.

Agriculture is restricted on Qeshm, due mainly to a lack of fresh water. Nonetheless, 80 percent of the land is under some sort of cultivation. Milk, dairy products, meat, and manure generate most of Qeshm's agricultural revenue. Technology could improve Qeshm's agriculture since it now depends so heavily on animal labor.

Fishing is a large part of Qeshm's economic structure. Shrimp is a prime asset of the island. Other fish, mollusks, and crustaceans are also part of the fishery in Qeshm. The building of fishing boats and launch yards are also an important element of Qeshm's **economy**.

In August 1990, Iran created a "free area" for economic development on the island, termed the Qeshm Free Zone (QFA). Intended to attract the international business community, various incentives were offered, including a variety of tax concessions, natural gas available at competitive prices, plus currency and monetary agreements. In the QFA, there is no restriction on the conversion of foreign monies and its distribution.

In the past, Qeshm has been in a state of poverty with a low level of economic development. Fortunately, unemployment rates are on the decline due to the increase in economic growth. Qeshm has many advantages working in its favor. With its ideal geographic location, it can serve as a commercial, financial, and industrial center in the Persian Gulf. The island possesses a large amount of energy resources (considerable gas reserves) and has made advances in its economic atmosphere. And, Iranian national economic strategy has created the potential for the development of **industry**. Tourism in Qeshm has also increased and proven to be vital in the island's economic growth.

The future of Qeshm looks bright. A key location and the attraction of international capital have led to a flourishing environment throughout the 1990s and into the 21st century, more so than nearly any other area of Iran.

QOTBZADEH, SADEQ (1936-1982). Sadeq Qotbzadeh was an active supporter of **Ayatollah Ruhollah Khomeini** and an outspoken critic of the **Pahlavi** regime of **Muhammad Reza Shah**. He attended Georgetown University and in the 1960s carried on a high-profile anti-Shah campaign in Washington, D.C. He moved to Paris and was instrumental, along with **Abol Hasan Bani-Sadr**, in organizing the French branch of the **Liberation Movement**, a key anti-Pahlavi group rooted in the **National Front**, but with links to Khomeini. Qotbzadeh was one of the handful of advisors comfortable and well acquainted with the West who clustered around Khomeini in his French exile and provided liaison with Western governments.

After the return of Khomeini to Iran, Qotbzadeh was appointed head of National Iranian Radio and television in the **Provisional Government** of **Mehdi Bazargan**. Being highly suspicious of foreign influence in Iran (and equally opposed), he refused to meet with American officials in Iran. He saw the invasion of Iran by Iraqi troops as part of a plot by the Soviet Union and the United States to isolate Iran and eventually divide the country into Russian and American spheres of influence. Qotbzadeh served as the Iranian foreign minister during much of the time Americans were held hostage in the **Tehran** Embassy.

Eventually, in common with other Islamic nationalists who resisted the increasing anti-democratism of radical Islamic forces, Qotbzadeh was leveraged out of office and politically isolated. He was accused of plotting the overthrow of the government, arrested, and executed. In short order, Qotbzadeh had gone from close advisor to Khomeini and key participant in the **Islamic Revolution** and early governments of the **Islamic Republic** to disgrace and death at the hands of the Revolution—a prime example of a revolution devouring its children. *See also* AMERICAN HOSTAGES IN IRAN.

QUM. Located in central Iran, to the east of the Dasht-i Kavir, the city of Qum is 130 kilometers south of **Tehran**. It is situated along the Qum River which flows from the **Zagros Mountains**, though the river is dry a good part of the year. The city is located in a semi-arid basin region of the **Iranian Plateau** and is dependent on subterranean water sources supplied by *Qanats*. Still, droughts and water shortages have plagued the city throughout history. Currently, the city is the capital of the Qum Province, though until the 1990s the city was a part of the Markazi province. The split from the central province, which for Qum resulted in a provincial identity of its own apart from Tehran, was in part a function of its rise in importance in the politics of the **Islamic Republic of Iran** as a key religious center, as well as its rapid growth.

Previous to the coming of **Islam** in the seventh century, Qum served as a regional nucleus for the ancient **Zoroastrian** faith. In 816, Fatima, the sister of Reza, the eighth Imam, was buried in Qum. A gold-domed shrine was erected in her honor creating a pilgrimage site and securing Qum as one of **Shiah** Islam's most sacred cities. This status opened the path for Qum to develop into a massive gravesite as the faithful sought proximity to a revered saint. The cemetery **industry** is a huge economic generator for the city, along with pilgrim expenditures.

The city remained a center for religious activity throughout historical times and became the burial place for over 10 kings and 400 Shiah saints. Iran's largest and most influential theological college, **Feiziyeh**, is located in Qum which has become a key center of Twelver Shi'ism in recent decades. Qum was the educational center for a young **Ayatollah Ruhollah Khomeini** who would lead the **Islamic Revolution** in Iran. The opening shot of that revolution occurred in January 1978 in Qum with the deaths of demonstrating theological students who were protesting the slanderous attack on Khomeini by the regime of **Muhammad Reza Shah** and were fired upon by government troops.

Modern Qum has marginal food production due to minimal water supply, though the region adequately produces for local consumption oilseeds, grain, some vegetables, cotton and opium poppies. Qum's industries have grown in recent decades focusing on the production of cotton textiles, shoes, pottery, and glass, though a large percentage of the city's livelihood depends on profits from religious pilgrimages and religion-centered products and services. While **oil** and natural gas have been discovered in the area, the accessibility and quality of the fossil fuel supply has limited its value. The most recent growth to take place in Qum stems from expansion of the city's **transportation** links, through rail, highways, and pipeline, to the north and south. This development has contributed to the economic expansion of the city in recent decades and a population increase from 424,048 in 1986 to a listed figure of 777,677 in the 1996 census. According to some estimates, in only five years the population had further increased by nearly 100,000 to over 873,000 in 2001.

-R-

RAILROADS. Throughout history, Iran's strategic location has allowed the country to serve as a **transportation** and communication crossroads between Europe and Asia. While regional conflicts, along with the modern-age appearance of new nations on the northern border, have caused gaps in access, Iran has begun to rebuild its role as a trans-continental link for goods, services, and **industry**.

Iranian Railroads

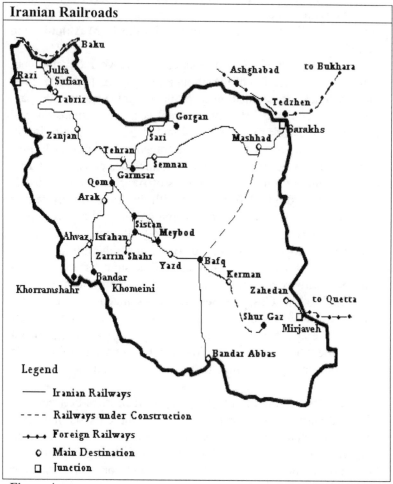

Figure 4

As of 2002, the national railway company of Iran, RAI (*Rah Ahan-i Iran*), reported that the country possessed 7,160 kilometers of main rail lines throughout Iran, with 2,097 kilometers additional industrial or commercial secondary lines, and a length of rail line from Julfa to **Tabriz** (148 kilometers) working as an electrified line. In total, RAI routes 16,330 freight wagons and 1,192 passenger coaches, pulled by 565 locomotives to 363 main stations within the RAI network including international zone stations at Tabriz, Julfa, **Tehran**, **Isfahan**, **Mashhad**, and Sarakhs.

In January 2005, RAI announced a five-year development plan for modernization of the Iranian rail system. The 2005-2010 plan includes the acquisition of 8,800 freight wagons, 500 passenger coaches, and 180 new locomotives. This expansion will enable the network to increase its annual freight capacity by 50 million tons and allow the system to transport as many as 36 million passengers per year. The plan also includes construction of a new line linking Iran to the countries of **Azerbaijan** and Russia, to be completed by 2010. Linkage with the Iraqi Rail System is also planned. In May 2005, it was announced by the government of Iraq that work would begin on a 60 kilometer line linking **Khorramshahr** to the port city of Basra in southern Iraq.

The backbone of the Iranian rail system is the **Trans-Iranian Railway** built in the 1930s and extending from the Persian Gulf to the **Caspian Sea**. Since its inception the Trans-Iranian Railway has been a vital link in the transportation network of the country. This route also played a highly significant role on the world stage during WWII while serving as the single most important supply link to the Soviet Union in the Allied cause.

Currently, in addition to the double track lines between Tehran and Garmsar and Tehran and **Qum**, there exists main line connections between a large number of major Iranian cities (see map of Iranian Railroads). Several lines are being expanded to link into neighboring rail networks. In addition to the existing Sufian-Razi line which links Iran to the Turkish and European networks, and the Mashhad-Sarakhs line which links Iran to the Central Asian rail network (Turkmenistan), a line being constructed between **Kerman** and **Zahedan** will link the Iranian system with the Indian subcontinental network. This final link in a European-Indian Subcontinent rail linkage is due to be completed in 2007. In addition, a new line is being built to connect

Bafq with Mashhad which will more directly link Central Asia with the Persian Gulf.

RAJA'I, MUHAMMAD ALI (1933-1981). Muhammad Ali Raja'i became the prime minister of Iran during the presidency of **Abol Hasan Bani-Sadr**. He emerged from a poverty-stricken background, barely managing to graduate from **Tehran** Teachers' College. His persistence and determination propelled him into leadership positions despite the objections of many who considered him to be nearly illiterate.

Raja'i acquired the position of prime minister through the support of his patrons in the **Islamic Republican Party (IRP)**. President Bani-Sadr and Raja'i were contemptuous of one another's policies, and Raja'i used his position in the IRP-dominated **Majlis** to blunt Bani-Sadr's political ambitions. When Bani-Sadr was driven from office in June 1981, Raja'i took over the presidency, further extending IRP dominance of state offices and marking an ensuing period of open warfare between the IRP and opposition groups.

Raja'i was one of a number of IRP leaders to die violently in 1981 in the course of the internal struggle for control of the **Islamic Revolution**. On 30 August, 1981, President Raja'i was killed, along with Prime Minister **Muhammad Javad Bahonar**, in the bombing of the Prime Ministry. The assassinations prompted **Ayatollah Ruhollah Khomeini** to authorize repressive measures by the **Revolutionary Guards** to stem the escalating violence and destroy groups in opposition to the regime.

RASHT. Located in the northwestern section of Iran near the **Caspian Sea**, the city Rasht is the capital and principal city of Gilan Province. An important commercial center, the city sits along the Rudbar, a channel of the *Safid Rud* (White River). According to the 1996 census, the population of Rasht stands at 417,748 people, a considerable increase over the estimated 1972 population of 162,000. It is the planned site of a Research Center for **Agricultural** Biotechnology, similar to ones in **Isfahan** and **Tabriz**.

Due to its location near the Caspian Sea, the area around Rasht is very fertile and is home to rice and tobacco crops. What was once marshland and lagoons have been turned into rice paddies by all-weather roads. Housing is not like that found throughout most of Iran. Because of rich vegetation and heavy rainfall in the area, most houses are built out of lumber and have sharply sloped tiled roofs. Barns and storage buildings are elevated to keep them dry. The city has a small-scale steel-processing **industry** and a jute-processing plant. It is also a center of **trade** between Russia and Iran, and is home to a thriving silk industry.

Since the city is not mentioned in early texts, it is believed that the city of Rasht was not settled until the 13th century. For a short time in its history (late 14th century and into the 15th century), the city of Rasht was the seat of a minor dynasty known as the Ishakids. In 1557, the city became the administrative and economic center of the Muscovite Company, beginning its long association with Russia.

Thanks to its key location, Rasht has long been a cog in the trans-Caspian trade via its associated port of Enzeli (formerly known during the **Pahlavi Dynasty** as Bandar-Pahlavi). In the early years of the 20th century, the Russians built one of the first modern roads in Iran from Rasht to **Tehran**. It was 322 kilometers long over the **Alborz Mountains** via Qazvin to Tehran. Various hotels were built by the Russians along this route which became an important 20th century commercial link and further enhanced the already well-established Russian trade link through Rasht to the **Iranian Plateau**.

From 1722-1734 the city of Rasht was occupied by the Russians who later restored it to Persia in a treaty. Russian forces at the end of both World War I and World War II again occupied Rasht. Today, Rasht retains its importance as a key strategic center for **transportation** and commerce.

RASTAKHIZ PARTY. Muhammad Reza Shah created the Rastakhiz, or Resurgence, Party in March 1975, declaring it to be Iran's single legal political party. Earlier, the official majority and minority parties, **Iran Novin** and **Hezb-i Mardom**, had been abolished. The restructuring of the party system was brought about by the Shah's desire to strengthen central authority and to increase popular political participation in support of his economic and political policies. It was an effort that failed miserably since few Iranians took the party seriously, despite considerable pressures to join.

The decree of the Shah reversed the stance he had taken in his book, *Mission for My Country*, in which he disparagingly referred to one-party systems as "totalitarian," comparing them to Adolf Hitler's Nazi Party and the Communist Party of Soviet-bloc nations. In announcing this reversal on the issue, he claimed that a multi-party system made losers of the minority parties, despite the fact that they were entirely loyal to the nation. In the new system, minority politicians would be given the opportunity for full participation and cooperation within the governing body.

The Shah delineated the basic ideology of the Rastakhiz Party as retention of the principles of the Constitution of 1906, the legitimacy of the Shah's authority, and sustainment of the programs instituted by the 1963 **White Revolution**.

In structure, the Rastakhiz Party was an element of the executive branch of the central government. It was headed by a secretary-general and consisted of a congress, a central council, an executive board, and a political bureau. The party was declared by the Shah as an umbrella party, under which two political wings would exist: a Liberal wing and a Progressive wing.

The leaders of these branches emerged from the most powerful civilian ministries, Interior and Finance, and both were leading candidates for the position of prime minister. The Progressive wing was headed by Hushang Ansary of the Finance Ministry and favored rapid progression in the modernization process, focusing on long-term benefits regardless of short-term consequences. The Liberal wing, headed by the Interior Ministry's **Jamshid Amuzegar**, favored a slower pace toward long-term goals to prevent problems in the short run. Despite these differences in outlook, conflict was minimal as both leaders worked to appease the Shah and present his policies in a positive light.

The Rastakhiz Party lacked significant power due to the Shah's determination to eliminate any force that might challenge his own supremacy. The split in the party weakened its effectiveness, but the separation was hailed as "democracy" because it provided two opposing viewpoints. The **Majlis** was stimulated into debate but generally on trivial issues rather than those which would challenge the Shah's undisputed authority within the government. In fact, the Shah intended the party as a means to depoliticize debate in the Majlis. However, when the 1977 Majlis convened, it became evident that anti-government sentiment was creeping into Parliament in the form of questions and criticisms regarding the policies of the regime. As the Shah's dictatorship began to collapse in 1978, the headquarters of the Rastakhiz Party was attacked, marking the end of the short-lived single-party experiment of Muhammad Reza Shah.

RAYY. The ancient city of Rayy had a long and eventful past and was known by many names, including Rhaga, Ragae, Ray, Rae, Ragha, Raga, Europos, and Muhammadiya. One of the oldest and most important towns of early Iranian history, the city sat astride major **trade** and communication routes. Ideally situated between mountain and desert, roads of commerce and communication intersected Rayy both north-south and especially east-west, as the city was a waystop on what came to be known as the Silk Route from Baghdad to China. Rayy was also situated in the shadow of **Mt. Damavand**, important in the mythology of Iranian identity. It was an important **Zoroastrian** holy city. Rayy was considered by some accounts as a homeland of Zoroaster and his activity, though this is almost certainly more myth than historical truth. Nonetheless, Rayy was an important center of Zoroastrian religious activity for many centuries and is mentioned as a religiously significant site in many **Christian** and Muslim sources. It was, for example, the see of bishops of the Eastern Syrian Church in the fifth and sixth centuries A.D.

During the Abbasid Caliphate, Rayy is described by a great literateur of the ninth century, al-Jahiz, as one of the 10 major cities of the dynasty, though it is also mentioned as being known for perfidy, perhaps an indication of a lingering Zoroastrian identity. In the Abbasid period, Rayy was greatly expanded with new quarters and became a city of some size. Commensurate with its status and size, the city housed a great library in the early Abbasid Caliphate.

As a commercial and religious center, Rayy was also of political importance and its history reflected such status. The passing of power was often accomplished with some destruction, rebuilding, and expansion. The city passed through many turbulent times as evidenced in the earliest historical records to the final blow dealt by the Mongols in the 13th century. The ancient city never quite recovered from the Mongol period and fell into ruin.

Over the centuries, the ruins of ancient Rayy were built adjacent to, incorporated by, or encompassed by a continuing community which exists today. In the 19th century, Rayy was a separate town some eight kilometers south of the newly designated capital of **Tehran**. Today, Rayy has become a suburb of Tehran. An indication of a continuing link with the past, Rayy is the site of several important shrines, the sanctuary of Shah Abdul Azim, at which site **Naser al-Din Shah** was assassinated in the late 19th century, the tomb of **Reza Shah**, and most recently, the tomb of **Ayatollah Ruhollah Khomeini**.

REFORMIST PRESS—*SALAAM* and *SOBH-I EMRUZ*. An important factor in the popularization of pro-democratic reform and the electoral victories of reform candidates in Iran was the press which expounded the reformist viewpoint. Two of the most important of these newspapers were *Salaam* and *Sobh-i Emruz*. These two papers not only exemplify the tone of the reformist press, but also illustrate the lengths to which hardline elements within the **Islamic Republic** would go to silence these voices for change.

Salaam (*Hello*) began as a mouthpiece for the *Ruhaniyyun-i Mobarez* (Assembly of Combatant Clerics), espousing the views of this left-`leaning religious political faction. *Ruhaniyyun-i Mobarez* founding member **Muhammad Musavi Khoiniha**, along with **Abbas Abdi** and **Ibrahim Asgharzadeh**—both members of the **Students Following the Imam's Line**—began publishing the newspaper in 1991. Though politically left, *Salaam* did not become reformist until the middle of the 1990s. It vocally supported **Muhammad Khatami** in his bid for the presidency, some claiming it was instrumental in his 1997 victory. However, as the reformist camp began to achieve massive success in elections, both in the 1999 local-level elections and the 2000 **Majlis** elections, the conservatives institutionalized in the judiciary began to crack down on the popular reform newspapers. In the summer of 1999, a Special Clerical Court charged with upholding press laws banned *Salaam* on trumped-up charges. Not only did this signal a rash of closings, but it also spurred student unrest that led to the **Student Dormitory Attacks** on 9 July, 1999.

Sobh-i Emruz (*This Morning*) was published by Muhammad Khatami confidant **Sa'id Hajjerian**, and was also an important and popular publication of the reformist period. In addition to advocating the expansion of Iranian democracy, the newspaper became most well known following the investigative journalism of **Akbar Ganji**. Ganji was using the investigation of four reformists in 1998 as a springboard to reveal that conservative elements, largely from the judiciary, were willing to resort to murder to silence voices for democracy and civil rights. Though much of the Iranian public came to view Ganji as a populist hero making the newspaper hugely successful, *Sobh-i Emruz*'s success would come to a halt in 2000. Akbar Ganji was jailed after he attended the infamous **Berlin Conference**, and even more shockingly, Sa'id Hajjerian suffered an assassination attempt. While recuperating, the courts determined that since Hajjerian could not effectively publish his paper while convalescing, they could revoke his publishing license under an obscure provision in the press codes. This, along with the usual barrage of charges, such as being "anti-Islamic," effectively banned *Sobh-i Emruz* during a spate of newspaper closures following the massive electoral victories amongst reformists in the 2000 Majlis elections.

The life cycles of these two newspapers, the most visible of all the reformist papers of the late 1990s, reflected the growing fear among the conservative camp within the Islamic Republic as pro-democratic forces gained popular momentum. So long as the threat was minimal, the hardliners would tolerate the reform movement and its various apparatuses. However, once change appeared to be possible thanks to popular support, the conservatives resorted to utilizing their power institutionalized by the **Constitution of the Islamic Republic** to remove the threat to their monopoly of power. The closing of *Salaam* and *Sobh-i Emruz* is just one example among many in this reactionary process. *See also* NEWSPAPERS.

RELIGIONS. The primary religion of Iran today is **Islam**. Twelver Shi'ism is the state religion. The vast majority of Iranians are of the **Shiah** persuasion, though there are also a considerable number of Sunni Muslims. Other than Islam, a number of other religions are represented. **Zoroastrianism**, an ancient Persian religion and the state religion of the **Sassanian Dynasty**, still has a presence in Iran and an influence far beyond its numbers. In some ways, all Persians can identify with Zoroastrianism as a uniquely Persian phenomenon. Another ancient religious community in Iran is the **Jews** who have deep roots extending back to the **Achaemenid Dynasty**, and who attained special status under **Cyrus the Great**.

Other religious minorities found in Iran today came later. **Christians in Iran** are found in a number of locations in separate communal groupings. **Armenians** are the largest of these groups. There are also Protestants of several denominations, Catholics, and Assyrians. Finally, **Bahaism** exists in Iran, having originated there in the 19th century with the **Babi Movement**. None of the religious minorities today are entirely at ease with their circumstances under the **Islamic Republic of Iran**. Most, however, have maintained a degree of autonomy and have learned to coexist. Not so the Bahai community which is relentlessly persecuted, both officially and unofficially. It is the only religious minority that is unrecognized by the state.

REVOLUTIONARY COUNCIL. In the post-revolutionary scramble for political power, **Ayatollah Ruhollah Khomeini** and his supporters worked to consolidate popular support for a constitutionally implemented Islamic government. The Revolutionary Council was formed shortly after Khomeini's return to

Iran in February 1979 as the Islamic component of a two-prong power structure which included the more secular **Provisional Government** headed by **Mehdi Bazargan**.

The **Shapur Bakhtiar** government, left in place upon the departure of **Muhammad Reza Shah** from Iran, was snubbed by Khomeini. Soon after the formation of the Revolutionary Council, Khomeini asked it to name a prime minister to succeed Bakhtiar. The Council chose Bazargan, himself a member of the Council. In his capacity as head of the government, however, he wielded little power. Operating, in essence, as a replacement for the **Majlis** of the existing constitution, the Revolutionary Council quickly evolved as the real power center of the post-revolutionary period. It was responsible for overseeing the **Revolutionary Guards** and Revolutionary Courts, though these bodies operated semi-autonomously with moderate control exercised by the **Islamic Republican Party**.

The Revolutionary Council was a key instrument of fundamentalist clerical control during the transitional period to constitutional Islamic government. This was true both during and after the Bazargan Provisional Government. Indeed, when Bazargan resigned in the wake of the November 1979 U.S. Embassy takeover in **Tehran** and holding of **American hostages**, the Revolutionary Council became the official government. This situation prevailed well into 1980 until the constitution of the **Islamic Republic of Iran** was ratified and a new president and Majlis were elected and able to form a new government.

The 15 original Council members were appointed by Khomeini and included a few non-clerics, the liberal **Abol Hasan Bani-Sadr** being the most notable because of his later falling out with the radical clerics who followed the Khomeini line on the Council. Of the remaining appointees, Bazargan and **Ibrahim Yazdi** were members of the **Liberation Movement of Iran** and considered moderate modernists. **Sadeq Qotbzadeh** and Bani-Sadr were in the radical modernist camp. The majority of members, however, were fundamental clerical populists closely associated with the revolutionary Islamic ideology of Khomeini. Among these, Khomeini selected four of his most reliable disciples, **Ayatollah Muhammad Hussein Beheshti**,

Muhammad Javad Bahonar, **Ayatollah Morteza Mottahari**, and **Ali Akbar Hashemi-Rafsanjani** for Council positions. The only independent clerical member was **Ayatollah Mahmud Taleqani** who quickly became disillusioned, however, and was virtually a non-participant in the group's activities. The domination by fundamentalist clerics was reflected in the nature of legislation emanating from the Council which revised electoral laws to favor Islamic candidates. It was also evident when the Council closed the universities in the summer of 1979 because they served as hotbeds of secular opposition which called for democratic pluralism.

In fall 1980, the Revolutionary Council was dissolved after a constitutional Islamic government was fully established under the provisions of the new **Constitution of the Islamic Republic of Iran**. *See also* ISLAMIC REVOLUTION.

REVOLUTIONARY GUARDS. The Revolutionary Guards, also known as the *Pasdaran*, evolved from the imperative of the exiled **Ayatollah Ruhollah Khomeini** to all Muslims to fight against the corruption of **Muhammad Reza Shah**'s government. Originally, a loose collection of informal groups came into existence led by prominent local clerics. These could be described collectively as a religiously oriented militia. They arose almost spontaneously from among the members of various mosques and urban religious associations to support and sustain the efforts of the Islamic revolutionary movement.

Following the revolution in 1979, the founding members of the guard became the "core" of a more highly organized and disciplined group who served as the armed retainers of the revolutionary committees. They played a key role in subduing centrifugal forces which erupted in the aftermath of the establishment of the new **Islamic Republic**, most notably the Kurdish uprising. This military experience, along with the support of the government and the Iranian people, turned a loosely-knit band of "religious soldiers" into a powerful, formidable military force in Iran.

A force of 6,000 in 1979, the Revolutionary Guards grew in size and importance with the outbreak of the **Iran-Iraq War**.

The Revolutionary Guards existed separately from the regular armed forces, despite sporadic attempts to integrate them. Throughout the war there was an uneasy relationship between the two forces. The Revolutionary Guards had the advantage of political purity in accord with the dominant religious ideology of the Islamic Republic. They also fought tenaciously in the war, further enhancing their influence. However, despite emerging from the war larger and more powerful, the future is uncertain. As the Islamic Republic has increasingly institutionalized itself, pressures have built to eliminate the Revolutionary Guards as an armed entity separate from the regular military establishment, a situation that continues to prevail. *See also* BASIJ.

REZA SHAH (Ruled 1925-1941). No single person had a greater impact on the pages of early 20th century Iranian history than Reza Shah. Armed with a vision of Iran, free of foreign influence and competitive in world markets, he single-handedly pulled his developing nation into the modern world.

Reza Shah was born on 16 March, 1878, in the village of Alasht in the **Caspian Sea** province of Mazandaran. As a youth he joined the Persian Cossack Brigade, rose through the ranks to become minister of war, and initiated the 21 February, 1921, coup that overthrew the faltering **Qajar Dynasty**. In 1925, he was proclaimed the new Shah and established the **Pahlavi Dynasty**, which endured until overthrown by the **Islamic Revolution** in 1979.

Iran experienced radical cultural and economic shifts under the stringent leadership of Reza Shah. The Iranian army grew in size and strength, becoming a force capable of maintaining domestic order and deterring foreign aggression. For decades, Iran's **economy** and strategic geographical location had been exploited by foreign powers, and attempts were made by Reza Shah to eradicate all foreign influences. The government assumed complete control of the economy, adopted strict regulations regarding foreign **trade**, and devised policies aimed at the rapid industrialization and modernization of the country. Among the most notable achievements of his reign was the construction of the **Trans-Iranian Railway** in the 1930s with no foreign financial participation.

Not all of Reza Shah's innovations were beneficial for or acceptable to the population-at-large. His disregard for Islamic custom alienated a considerable segment of the Muslim community. Islamic law gave way to civil law and bureaucrats replaced clergy as the more influential force in the formulation of national policies. Improvements in agricultural technology were ignored as government programs focused on industrialization. Reza Shah acquired an immense personal fortune through misappropriation of public funds. Despite the flaws in his administration, he is credited with initiating and implementing changes that enabled Iran to cope with the realities of the 20th century and remain an independent entity.

Reza Shah's downfall came during World War II when both Great Britain and the Soviet Union invaded and occupied Iran despite its neutral status. Reza Shah abdicated in favor of his son, **Muhammad Reza Shah**, and fled first to Mauritius and then to South Africa where he died in exile in 1944.

REZAIYEH. *See* URMIEH.

ROOSEVELT, KERMIT (1916-2000). Kermit Roosevelt, grandson of President Theodore Roosevelt, began American government service during World War II in the Office of Strategic Services. Following the war, he joined the Central Intelligence Agency (CIA), specializing in Middle Eastern affairs.

As the head of CIA operations in the Middle East, Roosevelt served as field commander for the American intervention (Operation Ajax) which resulted in the overthrow of Prime Minister **Muhammad Mossadeq** and the return of **Muhammad Reza Shah** to power in 1953. He wrote a book entitled *Countercoup: The Struggle for Control of Iran* detailing his and the U.S. government's role in bringing the Shah back to the throne. Roosevelt maintained close ties to the **Pahlavi** regime, and his personal connections made him a key link between officials in Washington and **Tehran**. Even as the political situation in Iran deteriorated in the 1970s, Roosevelt continued to support the monarchy and recommended positive action on the Shah's behalf to the U.S. government.

RUDAKI (858-941). The poet Abu Abdollah Ja'far ibn Muhammad, known as Rudaki, was born in the Persian village of Rudak in **Khorasan**, near present-day Samarkand, Uzbekistan. Regarded as the first major Persian poet, Rudaki was the first to begin writing in the "New Persian" (Farsi) of the ninth century, a modified form of middle **Persian language** (Pahlavi) written in Arabic script. Thus, he is generally considered to be the father of Persian **poetry**. Rudaki's works are known for their simplicity and lack of Arabic and Quranic quotation, as well as for straightforward themes of time, age, death, love, and happiness.

Rudaki was known as a proficient singer and musician and was summoned to the court of Samanid ruler Nasr ibn Ahmad (913-943) where his art prospered as court poet. It is said that during his time at court, Rudaki composed a ballad, which upon recitation inspired the prince to halt his siege of Herat, Afghanistan and return to Bukhara. Rudaki is best known for his Persian translation from the Arabic of "Kalilah va Dimnah," a collection of Indian fables, also completed during his time at court. He is credited with over 100,000 couplets, of which only 1,000 survive.

The poet fell out of the court's favor in 937; some say it was because he professed religions not approved by the monarchy. After this he fell into poverty and died in 941 in his birthplace, Rudak.

Historians argue about Rudaki's talent, some asserting that the poet was born blind and used only his remaining senses as his means of observation. Others argue that poetry as rich in history and description as Rudaki's could not have been composed by a man blind since birth. Still other historians claim that near the end of his life, the poet became disenchanted with the court and refused to write empty praises—causing the ruler to order him blinded by hot iron rods. Whatever the truth may be, all would agree that Rudaki was a great poet who left an enduring mark on the Persian literary heritage. *See also* LITERATURE.

RUMI (1207-1273). Jalal al-Din Rumi was born in Balkh in the province of **Khorasan** in 1207. Rumi was raised in the **Sufi** tradition, which would become the predominant theme in the body of **literature** he produced. He engaged in 10 years of disciplined Sufi **education** and study and earned an exalted position among Islamic mystics. During the course of his study he was the disciple of many Sufi spiritualists, the most influential being Shams al-Din of **Tabriz**, who would have a great impact on Rumi's lyrical ghazals.

As a Sufi mystical leader, he devoted his life to spreading the glory of Divine Love and acquired his own following of disciples whom he guided along the Sufi path. In the course of his dedicated work with these aspiring Sufis, he founded the Mevlevi order of mysticism, the famous "whirling dervishes."

Considered to be the greatest Persian mystical poet, Rumi is one of the most well-known and closely studied Islamic mystics in Western academia. The majority of Rumi's works have been translated into English by the British Islamic scholars R.A. Nicholson and A.J. Arberry, and translations of Rumi's **poetry** continue to pour forth.

His work is infused with Sufi teachings, yet Rumi did not strictly adhere to the rigid structure of traditional Persian mystical literature. He developed a new style which allowed a freer use of allegorical images in the teachings and anecdotes he used to illuminate Sufi doctrine and to spread his spiritual message.

His most famous work is entitled *Masnavi-ye Ma'navi*. This massive composition, referred to by Islamic scholars as the "Quran of the **Persian language**," is an orthodox book grounded in Islamic theology, which seeks to lead aspiring Sufis along the path to sainthood. In the *Masnavi*, a collection of 27,500 couplets, Rumi infused Quranic verses with the deepest philosophical insights and ethical teachings of **Islam**, which widely influenced Muslim mystical thought and literature. Rumi also delved into and expounded on the origins of science in the "beyond," and conferred a spiritual legitimacy on such diverse topics as astronomy and jurisprudence.

Besides the *Masnavi*, Rumi also wrote a group of lyric love poems in the ghazal, or ode, form. These poems were composed spontaneously while Rumi was in the passionate state induced by the mystical dance of the whirling dervishes. Less didactic than the couplets of the *Masnavi*, the ghazals celebrate love, both earthly and divine, in a musical style.

-S-

SA'DI (1184-1292). Sa'di, a native of **Shiraz**, traveled widely throughout the Middle Eastern region and incorporated many of his experiences into his writing. He was a prolific poet, renowned and appreciated for his lucid style and use of simple language. His works were among the earliest of Persian **literature** to be translated into various foreign languages. They were widely available in Europe and won favorable recognition in the 17th and 18th centuries from the likes of Voltaire, Emerson, and Franklin.

Though his work is highly idealistic, it is tempered by a worldly, practical philosophy. Utilizing a wide range of human motives from greed to selflessness, his poems reveal the torment he experienced due to the conflict caused by his religious training when pitted against the harsh reality he encountered in his travels. Though Sa'di took refuge in **Sufi** mysticism, he remained dissatisfied, unable to accept the awareness of the capricious nature of Fortune which caused the good to suffer while the evil flourished.

His didactic works—*Bustan* (*The Scented Garden*) and *Gulistan* (*The Rose Garden*)—are considered exemplary samples of the genre. Sa'di reveals his mastery at bringing a scene to life. His poetic works have been widely translated into other languages and, though his lyricism is distorted in translation, the essence of his words is still maintained. His work is still widely quoted in Persia today, to enhance an argument or to color a story, much as Shakespeare's works are used by English-speaking people. Sa'di has been classified as one of the greatest of the Persian poets, sharing that distinction with the likes of **Rumi** and **Hafez**. *See also* POETRY.

SA'EDI, GHOLAM HUSSEIN (1935-1985). Gholam Hussein Sa'edi was one of Iran's premiere writers of the 1960s and 1970s, becoming a champion for the cause of the poor and oppressed of Iran amidst the **Muhammad Reza Shah** regime. Born in **Tabriz** in 1935 into an **Azerbaijan** Turkish family that valued **education**, Sa'edi would follow his family's tradition of advanced learning, eventually completing his training as a psychiatrist at **Tehran University** medical school. Through his psychiatric practice, he exemplified the concern for the poor expressed in his writing: Instead of charging patients based on market forces, Sa'edi charged patients based on what they could afford to pay.

Sa'edi is known not for his psychiatry, however, but rather for his prolific, popular, and celebrated writing. He began writing at a young age in the 1950s and would become prominent by the late 1960s and early 1970s for his short stories, plays, screenplays, and even a novel. Through his fiction—much of it written under the pseudonym Gowhar Morad—Sa'edi committed himself to expressing the plight of the poor, both rural and urban, whom he viewed as being victimized by a consolidation of Iran's wealth into the ruling and technocratic classes. Sa'edi believed the Pahlavi regime's forced modernization and "Westernization" of Iran allowed the small elite classes to exploit the rest of Iran's people, which was detrimental to both Iranian culture and the Iranian psyche. Not only were the poor being controlled by fear and superstitious religious beliefs, but even the upper classes were being consumed by an anguishing idleness brought about by the more decadent aspects of Western culture the Pahlavis seemed to emphasize. Sa'edi's writing stresses this conflict of classes and cultures, often going so far as to portray his lower-class protagonists as having no choice but to resort to violent means of opposition to an exploitive system.

Sa'edi's treatment of these issues in his fictional and academic writing brought him much fame during the 1960s and 1970s. In fact, Sa'edi was perhaps the most prolific and beloved Iranian playwright of his time, as well as an avid author and academic in other areas. In addition to nine short story collections, Sa'edi is credited with writing 21 plays, seven translations, and the novel, *The Cannon*. He also published the critical journal *Alefba* beginning in 1973. Among his better-known plays are *Workoholics in the Trenches* (1974) and *The Honeymoon* (1978).

Sa'edi was also acclaimed for his work in **cinema**. One of the tales in his short story collection entitled *The Mourners of Bayal* was rewritten by Sa'edi as a screenplay and resulted in a celebrated film directed by **Daryush Mehrjui**. The film, *Gav* (*The Cow*), even won honors at the prestigious Venice Film Festival in 1971. Sa'edi and Mehrjui collaborated again on a film, *The Cyclist*, based on one of Sa'edi's works, a story in the collection of stories published first in the early 1970s under the title *The Grave and the Cradle*.

The combination of his popularity and the often revolutionary slant to his writing led the government, through **SAVAK**, to harass Sa'edi. Nearly 20 arrests in the early 1970s culminated in 1974 with Sa'edi receiving a prison sentence of 13 years. Although he was released in 1975, Sa'edi left the country for several years, spending time in exile in the United States and England. He did return home in 1978, only to meet with similar opposition to his art, which continued with the emergence of the **Islamic Republic**. Sa'edi once again became an Iranian exile, this time settling in Paris. In Paris, Sa'edi continued to create new works, including screenplays as well as critical essays. He also began to publish new volumes of his journal *Alefba*, which had ceased producing in the 1970s after only six volumes due to persistent censorship and his regular arrests. However, Sa'edi's health deteriorated, possibly exacerbated by his forced separation from his home. He died in Paris in 1985. *See also* LITERATURE.

SAFAVID DYNASTY (1501-1736). The root of the Safavid Dynasty lies in the 14th century Zahediyeh Sufi Order, which prospered in **Azerbaijan**. This religious order was transformed by their leader Safi al-Din into a more political body, the *Safaviyeh*, as a response to the dire circumstances in northwest Iran/Azerbaijan caused by the Mongol invasion. The group had consistently expanded its membership and political power by attracting local warlords and engaging in political marriages.

Many more converts were drawn to the cause by the **Shiah** allegiance to the **Hidden Imam**. As the end of the 15th century approached the religious movement had transformed into a powerful military force able to exert control over Iran and its surrounding areas.

During this time, the Sunni Ottomans had expanded throughout the region and had maintained a policy of persecuting Shiah. In response, the *Safaviyeh* religio-political movement declared independence, while embracing soldiers fleeing persecution, and named 15-year-old Ismail, a descendant of Safi al-Din, as Shah. The army of the new Shah began battling for control of Iran, first by taking the city of **Tabriz** in 1501. Capturing the most important administrative center of Azerbaijan marked the beginning of the Safavid Dynasty. By 1510, Ismail's army had not only succeeded in thwarting the Ottomans on all fronts, but had expanded the Safavid territory to include **Hamadan**, **Shiraz**, **Kerman,** Najaf, **Kerbala**, Baghdad, **Khorasan**, and Herat.

With the region under his control, Twelver Shi'ism, previously foreign to the people of the area, was designated as the mandatory state religion. Shah Ismail instituted a practice of enforcing Shi'ism by penalty of death, either killing or exiling Sunni ulama and replacing them with imported Shiah religious leaders. These leaders were then given land and wealth in return for allegiance, creating a class of government-controlled aristocrats. Ismail also funded religious schools and promoted Shiah shrines.

Sunni followers were not the only victims of persecution as soon Shi'ites with different views came under scrutiny. Even the very **Sufism** that spawned the Safavid rule now began to be seen as anti-establishment. Mainstream Twelver Shiah thought gradually supplanted the more revolutionary thrust of the *Safaviyeh* political order. Widespread popular support of the new faith led to a great patronage of religious schools and institutions, allowing the philosophy and theological development of the Imami Shiah to prosper under Safavid rule.

While Ismail's armies were successful in capturing the area, the Ottoman pressure grew strong enough to require the following Shah, Tahmasb I, to move the empire's capital from Tabriz to the more interior Qazvin in 1548, 24 years after Ismail's death. Later, **Shah Abbas the Great**, perhaps the most renowned Safavid Shah, moved the capital to **Isfahan** where the empire embraced a more Persian spirit and the Safavid Dynasty flourished.

Shah Abbas the Great came to power in 1587 and in only a few years had declared peace with the Ottomans, turning over portions of territory in northwestern Iran. With fewer military conflicts to maintain, the new Shah proceeded to develop a trained, officer-paid military with the assistance of **Robert Sherley** of England, a force more in step with European and Ottoman forces. Once functioning, Shah Abbas returned his forces to battle with the Ottomans, as well as the Portuguese and Uzbeks. At the height of his power, the Safavid Empire included all of Iran, Iraq, Armenia, Azerbaijan, and Georgia and parts of Turkmenistan, Uzbekistan, Afghanistan, and Pakistan.

The force which fueled the growth and increasing success of the empire was the ideal economic situation of the region. The Safavid Empire encompassed the main crossroads for **trade** between Europe, Central Asia, and India and included the Silk Road, which had been revived during the 16th century. Abbas embraced trade with Europe and used European desire for local carpets, silk, and other textiles, as well as pearls, animals, and animal hair, to fund the immense growth of his expanded empire. This exchange also allowed the Safavids to import luxuries from India such as spices, metals, sugar, and coffee. Expanded trade ties enabled the folk production of traditional carpets, pottery, and handicrafts to become organized into legitimate widespread industries, many of which are essential to modern-day Iran.

Economic growth allowed the Safavid Shahs to fund and encourage the development of some of the most still-revered Iranian arts including tilework, painting, and textiles. The Safavid rulers themselves were known as poets and painters and encouraged patronage of the arts as a means of furthering imagery of previous Iranian rulers, therefore legitimizing the Safavid rule. Regardless of the motives, the climate became favorable to artistic development and creativity. It was during this time that Reza Abbasi first introduced **women**, youths, and lovers to Persian painting, creating what would become known as the Isfahan School. Illumination and calligraphy flourished as seen in the illumination of such manuscripts as the *Shahnameh*. Isfahan particularly became home not only to artists of the canvas and page, but to architects and philosophers of nature and Shiah theology.

As the 17th century unfolded, the Safavid rulers not only had the Ottomans to contend with, but also the new Russian Muscovy that had deposed of the Golden Horde and expanded to Safavid borders, as well as the Indian Mughal Dynasty that had expanded through Afghanistan and into Iranian territory. At the same time, the prospering trade routes that had supported the empire's growth began shifting south, from India around the Arabian Peninsula then north through the Red Sea to Europe. With the military success under Abbas I, the Safavid forces had become complacent and corrupt, unable to gain funding for growth or to efficiently ward off invaders at the borders.

With following rulers growing increasingly ineffectual, the end of Shah Abbas' rule in 1666 marked the start of the Safavid decline. With frontiers constantly under attack, the ninth Safavid Shah, Soltan Hossein attempted to force conversion of Afghan subjects in the eastern part of the empire from Sunni to Shiah **Islam** in hopes of once again consolidating the empire. The attempt was met by the revolt of Afghan chiefs who eventually defeated the local army, spurring a larger attack by a chief's son who led an army across Iran, captured Isfahan, and named a new "Shah."

After nearly 15 years of Afghan rule, a former slave of a vassal state of the empire, **Nader Shah Afshar**, led an army against the Afghans and claimed Iran. Nader Shah held effective power as regent of the child Shah Abbas II. Nader Shah named himself Shah in 1736 only to be assassinated 10 years later. Following the assassination, infant Ismail III, grandson of the last true Safavid ruler, was named Shah by military leader **Karim Khan Zand** in an attempt to bolster the legitimacy of the burgeoning **Zand Dynasty**. Though not a true Safavid rule, the reign of Ismail III came to a final end in 1760, when Karim Khan took over power of the empire.

SAHABI, EZZATOLLAH (1930-). Ezzatollah Sahabi was born in **Tehran**, the son of **Yadollah Sahabi**, a prominent figure in Iranian nationalist movements. Ezzatollah quickly followed in his father's footsteps, becoming well educated and politically active. Like his father, he could be classified politically as a liberal nationalist, much in the school of other followers of **Muhammad Mossadeq**.

Ezzatollah obtained a master's degree in electromechanical engineering from **Tehran University** and while studying there became an active member of the Faculty of Engineering Muslim Student Association (MSA). In fact, he edited two of the Association's publications for several years during the later 1940s and early 1950s. These publications were first the *Forugh-i Elm (The Light of Science)* and then *Ganj-i Shayegan (The Bountiful Treasure)*. The aim of the MSA was to advocate for the reform of society on the basis of Islamic law and practice. Many of the MSA members became active in the **National Front** in 1951 during the oil nationalization crisis. Ezzatollah remained politically active within the **National Resistance Movement** after the 1953 coup which toppled Mossadeq. Because of this, throughout the later 1950s Ezzatollah spent considerable time in and out of prison. In fact, because of his political activism, both before and after the **Islamic Revolution**, Ezzatollah spent over 12 years in jail.

In 1961, Ezzatollah, along with his father, were two of the founding members of the **Liberation Movement of Iran (LMI)**. In 1963, as a result of **Muhammad Reza Shah**'s crackdown following huge riots across the country, caused in part by the arrest of the rising **Ayatollah Ruhollah Khomeini**, Ezzatollah was again sentenced to do time in jail for his political affiliation and activism.

After the collapse of the Shah's regime in 1979, most of the leadership of the LMI, including Ezzatollah's father, were appointed to Cabinet positions in the **Mehdi Bazargan**-led **Provisional Government**. Most resigned from their party affiliation at the behest of Khomeini which effectively left the leadership of the LMI in the hands of Ezzatollah through most of 1979. He himself took a Cabinet position as minister without portfolio in charge of the Plan and Budget Organization in September of that year. Though allied with Bazargan, with whom he had close political and family ties, Ezzatollah was considerably more radical. He leaned more heavily towards the Islamic forces. This did not, however, prevent him from later clashing with the more extremist elements of the **Islamic Republic** which resulted in his eventual imprisonment by those very same elements.

During the debate over what shape the new constitution should take, Ezzatollah was the only member of the LMI to be elected to join the 73 members of the **Assembly of Experts**. Clerical interests, who managed to enshrine the concept of *Velayat-i Faqih* into the new Constitution, controlled the Assembly of Experts. Ezzatollah bravely spoke out against the idea of a *Faqih* and said that making religious authority subject to criticism normally directed at political authority would spell "the beginning of the decline of **Islam**." In essence, according to his argumentation, religion and religious figures would, in the eyes of the people, lose respect. They would become sullied from the mundane nature of political office, and dissastisfaction from the people was sure to come. In retrospect, some would argue decades later that his point was well taken.

In 1980, after the fall of the Provisional Government, Ezzatollah was elected to the **Majlis** representing Tehran. He attempted to distance himself from the LMI because of the political mood of the time. Even so, he failed to be reelected and served only until 1984. Though he may not have always been a member of the LMI after 1980, it is certain that he retained close ties by blood and by ideology, and remained politically active in liberal nationalist causes. Because of his opposition to the stranglehold of religious authorities he still finds himself at odds with the regime and periodically in jail. For a time, Ezzatollah was editor of publications such as the now banned *Iran-i Farda* (*Iran of Tomorrow*). For supposedly insulting Ayatollah Khomeini (within *Iran-i Farda*) and after his attendance at the **Berlin Conference** in April 2000, viewed by religious authorities as insulting to Islamic values, he was arrested for acting against national security and spreading propaganda. Though he was released on bail for a time in August of that year, he was again arrested and charged with various crimes. While in prison, he was held largely incommunicado and in solitary confinement. During this time, the then ailing Ezzatollah had several heart attacks.

Despite repeated efforts by the conservatives to keep Ezzatollah in prison, and thus out of sight, by 2005 he was once again free and quite outspoken, as always. Still, indicative of his political courage and convictions, Ezzatollah has had the dubious distinction of having served a great many years in prison under two very differently based autocratic regimes, an apt metaphor for the failure of liberal democracy in Iran.

SAHABI, YADOLLAH (1906-2002). Yadollah Sahabi was born in **Tehran**. He received his **education** in a variety of schools including the **Dar al-Fonun**. In 1928, he was admitted into Teachers Training College. He graduated first in his class in 1931. A year later, he began studying geology at the University of Lille in France on a government scholarship. He received his doctorate in geology in 1936. After returning from France he obtained a job teaching at **Tehran University** where he remained for 26 years.

Yadollah Sahabi was a religious modernist. His secular **education** as a geologist, coupled with his devout religious belief, led Yadollah to attempt to reconcile Charles Darwin's theories with the Quran. In his effort, he published a book entitled *Evolution from the Viewpoint of the Quran*, which brought criticism from traditional clergy.

Yadollah became acquainted with **Mehdi Bazargan** in 1931. As a close friend of Bazargan, and political activist in opposition to the government of **Muhammad Reza Shah** in 1961, Yadollah helped found the **Liberation Movement of Iran (LMI)**. The LMI existed as a smaller party that worked with the **National Front**. Within the LMI, Yadollah served on the Executive Committee along with Mehdi Bazargan, **Ayatollah Mahmud Taleqani**, and Rahim Ata'i. In 1963, many members of the LMI were arrested for plotting against the constitutional monarchy of the Shah, and were consequently given jail sentences.

Yadollah remained active in opposition to the Shah. In 1977, he joined the 29-member "founding council" of the Iranian Committee for the Defense of Freedom and Human Rights (ICDFHR), which set up its offices next to the **Husseiniyehi Ershad** Institute. The attempts of the ICDFHR to address civil rights violations proved problematic and brought the organization into opposition with elements of the government and the traditionalist clergy.

In the later 1970s, the **Islamic Revolution** took place and the Shah was ousted. In 1979, the short-lived **Provisional Government** of Mehdi Bazargan was formed. Within the Provisional Government Yadollah served as minister for revolutionary projects.

After the fall of the Provisional Government, ultra-conservative religious authorities gained control of most of Iranian society. Yadollah continued to work with the LMI, which now found itself, yet again, in the role of opposition. Though not officially recognized as a party, it was allowed to function, and has endorsed presidential candidates such as Yadollah himself and **Ibrahim Yazdi**.

Yadollah lost favor with the clerical right, but his nationalist credentials were so extensive and so impeccable that he remained a respected political leader by friend and foe alike. His funeral drew 30,000 people including a virtual "who's who" list of politicians across the political spectrum.

SALES, MEHDI AKHAVAN (1928-1990). Mehdi Akhavan Sales, also known by his pen name, M. Omid, was one of the most influential poets of the 20th century Iranian movement known as "New **Poetry**." Born in **Mashhad** in **Khorasan** Province, Sales spent most of his early life in his birthplace, receiving his **education** through secondary school there. Though best known for his poetry criticizing foreign influences, especially Arabic and Western, on Iranian culture, his early poetry showed little sign of this later development. It was likely his first move to **Tehran** in 1948 and his subsequent involvement in social movements, including the **Tudeh**, that awakened the critical tone that pervaded his most famous poetry.

Like many others of his period, Sales came to deplore the overarching influence of Arabic culture and **Islam** on Iranian culture. He looked to pre-Islamic Iran, in particular **Zoroastrianism** and the socialist precursor movement of Mazdak (sixth century A.D.) as models for regaining a true Iranian heritage. He also respected the work of **Abol Qasem Ferdowsi**, in particular the epic *Shanameh*, which detailed the myths and culture of ancient Iran. Sales emphasized the importance of remembering these truly Iranian myths over the Islamic myths that permeated Persian **literature** and art since the Arabic conquest of Iran. Sales also greatly criticized the more recent Western influences that he viewed as equally detrimental to the preservation of Iranian culture. Despite these views, he did not believe an abrupt change, for instance eschewing the Arabic script, would be beneficial either. Something that drastic, he thought, would cause the culture to lose its roots in the past altogether—both Arabic and Iranian. This was one of his main fears about the perceived replacement of Iranian culture by Western modes.

Not only did the subject matter of Sales' poetry reflect these ideas, but his revolutionary poetic style did so as well. Though influenced by the earlier revolutions in New Poetry, or free verse, by **Nima Yushij**, Sales chose to use the new form not only to open up his own writing, but to break away from forms he believed were Arabic in origin. His particular style, while perhaps not as free as Nima's work, became highly influential on subsequent generations of Iranian poets. Where Sales' work utilized elements of the old style, he justified such usage by claiming he felt they were Iranian, and not Arabic, in origin.

Sales' criticisms of contemporary Iranian culture brought him into conflict several times with the government. During his early years in Tehran, Sales participated in the anti-governmental riots during the early 1950s in the tumult that led to **Muhammad Mossadeq**'s rise to power. However, with the fall of Mossadeq's government, Sales found himself imprisoned for a short time for participation in the riots and his Tudeh party affiliation. He not only was persecuted for his physical acts, but later also for the views expressed in his work alone. Collections of poetry such as *The Ending of Shahnameh* and *From the Avesta*, which criticized modern Iranian society while glorifying pre-Islamic Iranian myths and Zoroastrian religion, led to further action against him, culminating in another short stint in prison in 1967. Ironically, following this, Sales worked for the Iranian Ministry of Education and even the National Iranian Radio and Television Organization. He continued to write at a progressively slower pace, and finally died in 1990. He was buried in the old city of Tus (outside his hometown of Mashhad), near the final resting place of his respected Ferdowsi.

SANJABI, KARIM (1904-1995). Karim Sanjabi was born in the **KermanShah** area. His father was Sardar Naser Sanjabi, a leader in the Kurdish tribe of Sanjabi in KermanShah. The Sanjabi were traditionally in opposition to **Reza Shah**. In 1917, the British attacked his tribe and, for a time, his family sought refuge in Baghdad. The British held his father and other tribal leaders captive during World War I. After a couple of years, Sanjabi returned to **Tehran** to pursue his **education**. Ultimately, he obtained a law degree from **Tehran University** in 1928. In 1929, he was sent to France by the government to pursue a doctorate in law. In 1935 he obtained his doctorate and returned to teach law at Tehran University where he taught for many years. In 1946, he became vice president of the Law College in Tehran.

Karim Sanjabi took part in opposition movements as one of the founders of the Iran Party, in the early 1940s the most significant secular nationalist group, and the **National Front**, as a supporter of **Muhammad Mossadeq**. In 1949, Sanjabi took part in protests against rigged elections to the 16th **Majlis** along with Mossadeq. When Mossadeq's nationalist government formed in 1951, Sanjabi served as his minister of education and was active within the Iranian delegation that presented the case for the nationalism of the Iranian **oil** industry in international forums. In the Central Intelligence Agency (CIA) sponsored coup of 1953, the Mossadeq government collapsed. The sudden upheaval marked the temporary exodus of many activists and Mossadeq supporters, including Sanjabi, from the political scene in Iran.

In the later 1970s, just prior to the **Islamic Revolution**, opposition to **Muhammad Reza Shah** once again grew. In 1977,

Sanjabi participated in the revival of the National Front (or Second National Front) as well as the Iranian Committee for the Defense of Freedom and Human Rights (ICDFHR). In 1978, in an effort to gain nationalistic support, the Shah offered the position of prime minister to Sanjabi. At the time, the government of the Shah had lost its legitimacy, with many nationalists politically lining up behind the opposition politics of **Ayatollah Ruhollah Khomeini**. In the later part of 1978, Sanjabi traveled to France, where Khomeini resided, and accepted his leadership.

After the success of the Islamic Revolution, **Mehdi Bazargan** formed a **Provisional Government**. For a few short months, Karim Sanjabi filled the position of foreign minister, but resigned because of internal strife within the government caused by multiple centers of power, including the **Revolutionary Council**. Frustrated, he again left Iranian politics and was forced to flee the country in 1982. Sanjabi fled to the United States where he died at the age of 90 in Carbondale, Illinois on 4 July, 1995.

SASSANIAN DYNASTY. The Sassanian Dynasty was founded in 224 A.D. by Ardashir who claimed descent from the rulers of the **Achaemenid Dynasty**. Supplanting the **Parthian Dynasty**, the Sassanian Empire had three capitals, but the main one was the city of Shapur in the province of Fars. The language of the dynasty was Middle Persian, written in Pahlavi script, the precursor to Farsi, the modern **Persian language**.

There were three great kings of the Sassanian Dynasty, the first being Ardashir who founded the dynasty, and the second being Shapur I. Shapur I ruled from 241 until 271. During his reign he captured the Roman Emeror Valerian in battle and held him prisoner until he died. Shapur II came to the throne in 310 and ruled for 69 years. During his reign he waged three wars with Rome. Khosrow I (the Just) ruled from 531 until 579 and was the third great king. Considered by many to be the greatest king of the dynasty, he was able to read Greek and encouraged learning. He divided the empire into four administrative districts, issued a fixed land tax based on a survey of the empire, gave aid to **agriculture**, and carried out irrigation projects. He brought prosperity to the country and tolerated Christianity.

Zoroastrianism was the state religion throughout the dynasty, though other religions were tolerated. The architecture of the period consists of palaces, fire temples, fortresses, dams and bridges, city plans, and special memorials. A lot of these buildings still stand to this day in fair condition. The main building materials were stone and fired brick. Walls were often covered in plaster and incised plaster decoration was used. Characteristic of the period was the carving of huge reliefs on rock faces which are scattered at various places throughout Iran. Also very well known are the silver dishes and bowls created during the period, many of which are in the Hermitage Museum in St. Petersburg, Russia.

The dynasty came to an end when Yazdigird III (632-651) was defeated and killed by Arab forces that had converted to **Islam**. He was buried in Merv and the remaining dynastic family fled to China. The death of Yazdigird III in 651 marked the end of the Sassanian Dynasty and the beginning of Muslim influence in Iran. Sassanian influence, however, lasted far beyond the end of the dynasty in that Sassanian motifs can be found in Islamic art and architecture. Also, branches of the dynasty continued in the form of local rulers, long after the advent of the Islamic period in Iranian history.

SAVAK (SAZMAN-I AMNIYYAT VA ETTELE'AT-I KESHVAR). SAVAK was the acronym for the notorious secret police agency organized in 1957 at the request of **Muhammad Reza Shah**. With the technical assistance of the United States and Israel, an organization which combined the characteristics and functions of the American Federal Bureau of Investigation (FBI) and the Central Intelligence Agency (CIA) emerged. Under the leadership of Teimur Bakhtiar, the original mission of SAVAK was to control the press and monitor anti-government activities, but the role of SAVAK quickly expanded into other areas. SAVAK eventually consisted of eight departments, the most important of which dealt with the collection of information regarding foreign intelligence and domestic political activity.

Referred to as the "iron fist of the Shah," it soon became the most despised and feared government agency, particularly after General Ne'matollah Naseri was appointed to head SAVAK in 1965, a position he held throughout the turbulent period preceding the **Islamic Revolution**.

Concentrating on political opposition groups, such as the **National Front** and **Tudeh**, SAVAK used brutal and coercive tactics to blunt the impact of their influence. In the early 1960s, targeting the intelligentsia and working class, SAVAK expanded its networks into established **trade** unions through the Labor Ministry. This enabled SAVAK to scrutinize all recruits into civil service or industrial jobs and, as well, applicants for university positions, both students and faculty. By the mid-1960s, the organization had some 5,300 full-time agents and an unknown number of part-time informers. SAVAK never managed to eliminate political opponents of the Shah's regime, but its activities took on nearly epic proportions amongst the Iranian populace as agents were perceived to be everywhere.

In the mid-1970s, negative reports from international agencies began to appear regarding the activities of SAVAK. Reports of torture of political prisoners, disruption of Muslim services, confiscation of religious property, and the imprisonment of religious leaders forced the Shah to curtail the more overt activities of SAVAK. SAVAK also came under attack from within, as members of underground guerilla opposition groups began to infiltrate and undermine its operations just prior to the collapse of the **Pahlavi Dynasty** in the wake of the Islamic Revolution. SAVAK ceased to function with the departure of the Shah in January 1979, and was officially abolished on 6 February, 1979.

An interesting footnote to the history of SAVAK is the emergence early on in the **Islamic Republic** of a similar organization entitled SAVAMA (Sazman-i Etteleat va Amniyyat-i Mihan). This security organization, soon to become as hated as its predecessor, followed like lines of suppressing opposition to the state. The similarity is hardly surprising given that a few key individuals with prior SAVAK experience helped establish SAVAMA. Most notable of these was the turncoat boyhood friend of Muhammad Reza Shah, former long-term Deputy Chief of SAVAK, **Hussein Fardust**.

SAYYAD, PARVIZ (1939-). Parviz Sayyad, one of Iran's earliest television stars, is known not only as a popular actor, but also as an accomplished playwright and filmmaker. Born in Lahijan, Sayyad came to be involved in the early days of Iran's National Television. Throughout the 1960s, he starred in many plays adapted for television; he also starred in Iran's first television series, *Amir Arsalan*, co-starring alongside Mary Apick, with whom Sayyad would have a lifelong professional partnership. Perhaps Sayyad's most popular character was Samad, a character in another television series, *Sarkar Ostovar*. Samad would be the vehicle for his directorial debut with the film *Samad and the Flying Carpet* (1970).

Prior to the formation of the **Islamic Republic**, Parviz Sayyad achieved acclaim as one of the "New Wave" of Iranian filmmakers. One of the final films Sayyad made in Iran was *Dead End* (1976). However, because the 1977 Moscow Film Festival awarded *Dead End* star Mary Apick the Best Actress Award, the **Pahlavi** regime banned the film in line with anti-Soviet doctrine. The Islamic Republic would also reassert the ban, but only because the lead actresses appeared without veils.

After the **Islamic Revolution**, Sayyad left Iran for the United States. While there, he worked on a Ph.D. at the City University of New York (CUNY). He also wrote and/or produced a number of plays and films, including the highly regarded film *The Mission* (1984), which made a successful round of the film festival circuit, winning the 1983 Jury Grand Prize at the Locarno Film Festival. Finally settling in Los Angeles, Parviz Sayyad continues to work in **cinema** and theater, while also being a vocal critic of the Islamic Republic.

SHAH ABBAS THE GREAT (1571-1629). Shah Abbas I, or Abbas the Great, ruled the **Safavid** Empire from 1587 to 1629. Though he would inherit a heavily troubled empire, imperiled by powerful enemies, internal strife, and an ineffectual military, his reforms and sometimes ruthless stabilization measures brought security and prosperity to the Safavids. Thus, he is still remembered in Iran as worthy of the title "the Great."

After deposing his father, Shah Muhammad Khudabandeh, at age 16 (with the help of an ambitious governor), Abbas immediately set to reforming the army and dealing with **Turkoman** tribal unrest. Not only did he reorganize existing military units by identifying and eliminating elements which might prove disloyal, but he also formed new cavalry and musketeer units to supplant any loss of military power caused by the reorganization. These new units, known as *qullar*, were primarily made up of Muslim converts from the periphery of the empire. This reformed army would not only aid Abbas's heavy-handed crushing of the Turkoman revolt, but also in the reexpansion of Safavid borders. Lands taken by the Ottomans and the Uzbeks fell back under Safavid control thanks to Abbas's efforts.

In an age normally characterized by an Islamic world made insular due to conflict between Sunni Ottomans and **Shiah** Safavids, Shah Abbas I capitalized on the increasing European presence in the Middle East. Maintaining diplomatic contacts with the emerging powers of Europe, Abbas parlayed his ties with England into military aid, resulting in the capture of Hormoz from the Portugese. There he established the port which would become the important Bandar Abbas.

Despite his harsh methods of achieving stabilization and reclaiming Safavid glory, Shah Abbas the Great's enduring legacy became his cultural contributions to Iran. In addition to improvements to the infrastructure of his kingdom, Abbas also enriched the cities of Iran with great public works and architectural achievements, especially in his capital of **Isfahan**. Standing out amongst his many improvements to the city are the Loftallah Mosque and the grand Imperial Mosque, which is still recognized as a great world achievement. He also reinvigorated many other cities, some of which had suffered under wars with and control by Safavid enemies. With these lasting stamps of his powerful reign and the resurgence of the Safavids, Shah Abbas the Great is still remembered as one of the most significant of all Iranian monarchs.

SHAHNAMEH. The Iranian epic, *Shahnameh*, written in the early 11th century by **Abol Qasem Ferdowsi**, is a monumental work that gloriously recounts the history of Persia from creation to the Islamic conquest. Though Ferdowsi did not create the many myths and legends included in the work, he is responsible for compiling and transforming them into the 50,000 rhyming couplets that compose the *Shahnameh*. The book's immense scope, complex and colorful characters, and varying themes combine to produce a world-renowned literary masterpiece.

The *Shahnameh* is an intense exploration into the lives of the ancient Persians, detailing their values, beliefs, customs, and lifestyles. It is a blend of legend and history written in emotional, lofty language, exaggerated by the generous use of similes and metaphors. Ferdowsi's characters abound with energy and conflict—heroic and powerful, but overwhelmingly human. Their experiences abound with emotional dilemmas and confrontations with the forces of good and evil. The richness of characterization invites the reader to share the triumphs—or failures—of the protagonist.

In addition to its literary merits, the *Shahnameh* is valued by the Iranians as a symbol of their heritage, a patriotic tribute to the glories of ancient Persian civilizations and their contributions to the world. It has been influential in terms of art, culture, and literary precedent, while contributing to a strong nationalistic attitude among the Persian people. *See also* SHAHNAMEH, CHARACTERS OF.

SHAHNAMEH, CHARACTERS OF. The characters of the *Shahnameh* are drawn larger-than-life with both good and evil represented. The characters and their stories are a mixture of myth and history. As a result, the fantastic and the plausible are not an uncommon juxtaposition. The following brief sketches describe the major characters and events which determined **Abol Qasem Ferdowsi**'s interpretation of Iran's glorious civilization. *See also* DAMAVAND, MOUNT.

BIZHAN AND MANIZHEH

In the midst of the fierce and bloody rivalry between the kingdoms of Iran and Turan, the Romeo and Juliet romance of two young lovers emerged. Bizhan was the noble son of Giv, warrior and faithful courtier to the Shah of Iran. Seeking pleasure, and spurred by the malevolent Gorgin, Bizhan wandered from Iran into the kingdom of Turan. He came to the attention of Manizheh, the daughter of Afrasiyab, the king of Turan, and the princess fell in love with Bizhan from a distance. She had Bizhan drugged and taken to the palace. Upon awakening and seeing Manizheh, Bizhan returned her ardor. The rage of Afrasiyab, when informed of his daughter's treachery, caused blood to pour from his eyes. He cast Bizhan into a pit covered with a rock so massive that ten soldiers could not move it, and expelled Manizheh from the palace. She was forced to beg and accept menial tasks to provide bread to feed herself and her lover. However, when word of Bizhan's imprisonment reached Iran, the Shah dispatched the great warrior Rostam to Turan. Following a bloody skirmish with Afrasiyab, Rostam lifted the massive rock covering Bizhan's prison and hurled it into the forests of China. Rostam reunited the lovers and escorted them to Iran where they married and lived forevermore under the protection of the Shah.

ESFANDIYAR

Esfandiyar was the king of Kabul during the time of Rostam's ascendancy. As a vassal of Rostam, he felt wronged by the amount of tribute demanded from his Kabul valley. Shaghad, the brother of Rostam, took advantage of the king's dissatisfaction with Rostam's rule, and hatched a plot to end his brother's life. The plan called for Esfandiyar to openly renounce Rostam and for Shaghad to inform Rostam of the king's traitorous speeches to bring him to Kabul and into a trap. Rostam returned to Kabul, and though Rostam allowed a pardon for Esfandiyar's treachery, Shaghad carried through and killed his brother.

FARIDUN

Zahhak's rule was ended by a rebellion led by Kava, the blacksmith, and Faridun, the noble. Faridun killed the evil, oppressive Zahhak and became king of Iran. He later divided his kingdom among his three sons: Salm, Tur, and Iraj. Iraj was selected to rule Iran from the Golden Throne, and his jealous brothers killed him. Manuchehr, the grandson of Iraj, returned to avenge his grandfather's murder, initiating the Iran-Turan War in the process.

JAMSHID

Jamshid was the son of Tahmuras, and the first great king of Iran. During his mythical reign of 700 years, he laid the foundations of Iranian civilization, providing clothing, weapons, an organized society, and the great city of Balkh for his people. In later years, seeing all he had accomplished, he was overcome by arrogance and angered God by declaring himself the "Creator of the World." This led to the withdrawal of divine support, without which Jamshid was weakened, and vulnerable to the invasion of the evil king Zahhak, who eventually overthrew Jamshid and assumed power.

Jamshid sought sanctuary in Zabulistan. The daughter of King Gureng of Zabulistan was informed by her magician nurse that she was destined to fall in love and marry a man named Jamshid. The two met and fulfilled their destiny. However, Jamshid's true identity was inadvertently revealed, and King Gureng planned to return him to Iran and collect the reward offered by Zahhak for his capture. The king was dissuaded from this course by his daughter, but Jamshid, fearing for his life, fled Zabulistan and wandered through China and India. He was eventually captured and Zahhak ordered his execution. When the news of his death reached Zabulistan, Jamshid's lover poisoned herself.

KAVUS

Kavus was the king of Persia during the lifetime of Rostam. Kavus was a weak monarch given to foolish and headstrong actions. His son, Siyavush, turned his back on his father and country, defecting to Turan, where Afrasiyab, the Turanian ruler, eventually executed him. Kai Khosrow, son of Siyavush and grandson of Kavus, later avenged his father's death by defeating and beheading the evil Afrasiyab.

KHOSROW AND SHIRIN

Less idyllic than the romance of Bizhan and Manizheh is the story of Khosrow and Shirin, youthful lovers parted by fate as Khosrow became king and wandered about the world seeking battle. Later reunited with Shirin, the old love was rekindled, and Khosrow overcame the objections of his princes as to Shirin's respectability and suitability for a king, and married her. Shirin was fiercely jealous of Khosrow and poisoned his first wife, Maryam, daughter of Caesar, in order that she herself could occupy the Golden Chamber. Khosrow's tyranny caused his army to revolt, and he was killed in the ensuing battle. Shirin was claimed by the victorious Shiruy, Khosrow's son. Shirin, however, chose to poison herself and die in Khosrow's burial chamber rather than submit to Shiruy's advances.

ROSTAM

Rostam was the son of Zal and the greatest hero of Persia. He was a fierce soldier of imposing physical size and strength. From an early age, he was noted for his character, loyalty, and wisdom. He rode the great stallion, Rakhsh, who accompanied Rostam on all his ventures. He married the beautiful Tahmineh, the daughter of the prince of Samangan. Rostam spent only one night with his bride, before leaving for Zabulistan. That brief union produced a son named Sohrab, who was kept apart from his father by Tahmineh in fear that Rostam would take him from her. In a tragic episode, father and son met as opponents on the battlefield and Rostam mortally wounded Sohrab, before realizing that the young warrior was his son. Rostam was himself the victim of a plot between his brother Shaghad and King Esfandiyar of Kabul. Lured to the king's territory by false tales, Rostam was murdered by his brother, but in his last moments managed to kill Shaghad with a well-placed arrow.

SOHRAB

Sohrab was the son of Rostam, raised by his mother Tahmineh as a Turanian. He was an imposing physical specimen, as fierce and noble a warrior as his father. Tragically, he was killed by his own father in a classic battle, with Rostam unaware that his opponent was his son. In his dying breath, Sohrab informed Rostam that he was his son.

TUR

Tur was the son of Faridun, the king of Iran. When his father divided his kingdom among his three sons, Tur's legacy was Turan, which would become the mythical kingdom representing the evil force in the struggle between good and evil. Tur and Salm murdered their brother Iraj, and his death established the bitter rivalry between Iran and Turan. Following the murder of Tur by Iraj's grandson Manuchehr, the new king of Turan, Afrasiyab, renewed campaigns into Iran, particularly during the period of weak kings.

ZAHHAK

Zahhak was the son of the benevolent King Merdas, and a noble youth of great courage and character. After succumbing to the temptation of the Devil, he killed his father and became an evil tyrant who terrorized his people. He wore the mark of the Devil in the form of serpents growing from each shoulder, nourished on the brains of the kingdom's youth. He met his death at the hands of Faridun, the noble.

ZAL

Zal was born to the warrior Sam, the steadfast courtier to Manuchehr. The infant Zal was abandoned in the **Alborz Mountains** when his father discovered that he was an albino. Zal was rescued by the magical bird, Simorgh, who nested on Mt. Damavand. Simorgh cared for the boy through childhood. Many years later, Sam discovered that his son was alive and they were reunited. Zal accompanied his father to Kabul where he met the beautiful Rudabeh, the daughter of Mehrab Shah, a relative of Zahhak. Zal and Rudabeh fell in love and married in a **Zoroastrian** ceremony. Their son, Rostam, was destined to become the greatest of all Persian warriors and heroes.

SHAHSEVAN. The Shahsevan came into being during the 17th century in **Azerbaijan** under **Shah Abbas the Great**, as a multitribal militia organization, or confederacy, with personal loyalty sworn to the Shah. The members were mostly Turkish in origin and spoke a Turkish language. The militia group was used to deter and extinguish rebellions of other tribal groups.

The people became **Shiah** nomads, dominating the Moghan Steppe and known for their numbers and artistry. Travelers to Iran during this time remark upon meeting with Shahsevan leaders and seeing the *Tatar* nomads who carried their homes with them. John Cook, visiting during the coronation of **Nader Shah**, wrote about seeing "upwards of a hundred thousand tents" encamped there during the event.

In the early 1800s, Russian forces invaded the Shahsevan area forcing them to either relocate permanently or become Russian citizens. In 1828, the new Russian border was drawn cutting off the nomads from Moghan, where more than two-thirds of their winter land was located. After this point, the term *Shahsevan* is used almost entirely to describe those nomads who fought against the Russians, the Meshkin group. Those who became Russian citizens abandoned the name after settling as they were no longer acting under authority of the Shah.

The Shahsevan on the Iranian side of the new border with Russia continued to exist as a tribal federation and remained largely nomadic. Many were forced to settle by the draconian centralization and Persianization policy of **Reza Shah** in the 1920s and 1930s with disastrous results in the cold winters of highland Azerbaijan. After the abdication of Reza Shah in 1941 a significant number of Shahsevan returned to a nomadic way of life. They have maintained that existence to the present day, though small in number (approximately 50,000) and influence compared to their glorious past during the time of the **Safavid Dynasty**.

SHAMLU, AHMAD (1925-2000). The poet Ahmad Shamlu, also known by his pen name A. Bamdad, is known for his role in transforming contemporary Persian **poetry** from its ornate and adorned 19th century status to the accessible, more straightforward, voice of Iran that exists today. Shamlu is also known for voicing his political opposition to the oppression of free speech found in Iran during his lifetime, as well as for bringing the written word to the people of Iran as a publisher, editor, and translator. His career and life have been said to parallel the social and political flow of his country in all of its turbulence and perseverance during the 20th century.

Shamlu was born in **Tehran** and spent much of his childhood in poverty and misery between Tehran, Khash, **Zahedan**, and **Mashhad**. During his childhood, Shamlu developed a deep yearning for music after overhearing a neighbor playing Chopin. Due to economic circumstances, Shamlu could not quench his thirst for music and turned instead to reading. It was this zealous reading that opened the world to Shamlu, from national politics to poetry and prose, and led eventually to his jailing in 1943 for his first experience in political activism. In 1945, shortly after his release, Shamlu was arrested again, this time with his father, an army officer, by the separatist local government of **Azerbaijan**. The father and son were kept waiting for hours in front of a firing squad before an order was sent for their release.

Shamlu married for the first time in 1947 and fathered four children. During this time, Shamlu began his first publication, a magazine titled *Sokhan-i Nou*, which was closed down after only five issues. Shamlu independently published seven issues of the magazine *Rowzaneh* before being appointed editor of *Khandaniha* magazine. During this time, Shamlu saw several collections of his poetry published. In 1952, Shamlu edited an anti-Shah paper called *Ateshbar*. A year later, a new collection of his poetry was burned in a raid on the printer leaving only one copy, which still exists in a private collection. After the 19 August, 1953 overthrow of **Muhammad Mossadeq**'s government, Shamlu was forced into hiding for six months before being arrested and jailed for 13 months.

After his release, Shamlu began translating literary works from authors outside Iran into Farsi for Iranian readers. His abundant poetry continued to be published, including collections called *Garden of Mirrors*, *Fresh Air*, and *Moments and Ever*. After a second marriage and divorce, Shamlu edited *Ketab-i Hafteh*, a literary, artistic, and scientific weekly which set a standard for the Iranian press. Soon after, Shamlu married his third wife Aida, the inspiration for his collections *Aida in the Mirror* and *Aida, Tree, Dagger, and Memory*.

In 1965, Shamlu began work on *Ketab-i Kucheh*, or *Book of the Street*, an epic encyclopedia of folklore that had twice before been lost in police raids. Shamlu continued compiling collections, translating foreign **literature**, writing books of verse for children, and editing magazines prolifically for the next 10 years. In 1969, like many of his publications, the magazine *Khusheh* was closed down, this time by the Shah's secret police, **SAVAK**.

In 1976, Shamlu became the Director of the Research Center at Bu'Ali University and was invited by Princeton University to lecture in the United States, where he also participated in the World Festival of Poetry in Austin, Texas. The following year, Shamlu left Iran in protest of government oppression and travelled to the U.S. and London before skeptically returning to Iran after the **Islamic Revolution**.

Shamlu continued producing more collections, children's verse, and literary publications, as well as a translation of Langston Hughes' poetry collection, *Negro*. Shamlu also continued to travel the world, sharing his poetry in Germany, Sweden, the U.S., and elsewhere. In 1990, Shamlu delivered a notable speech at the University of California, Berkeley, asking for a more egalitarian approach to Iranian history and mythology, which caused a bitter debate.

Shamlu fell ill five years later and underwent three major operations by 1997, including the amputation of his lower right leg. Collections of Shamlu's work continued to be published, as well as several volumes of his *Book of the Street*, until his death on 24 July, 2000, at the age of 74.

Ahmad Shamlu is remembered as the poet who not only fought for the written word in Iran, but who popularized the stagnating art of poetry among the young of revolutionary Iran. It is said that the writing of famed Persian poets such as **Rumi** and **Hafez** had become inaccessible by the Iranian masses, and Shamlu in the simplistic tradition of the Iranian poet **Nima Yushij** allowed common Iranians a voice. *See also* LITERATURE.

SHARI'ATI, ALI (1933-1977). Ali Shari'ati is considered the most important intellectual of the Islamic revolutionary movement in contemporary Iran. He was born in 1933 in a small village in **Khorasan** and educated in **Mashhad** where his father, a militant Muslim, taught Islamic history. With his father's encouragement he began to participate in religiously oriented political discussion at a young age. Shari'ati left Iran in 1959 to pursue sociology and Islamic studies at the Sorbonne in France and became an active member of the Iranian Student Confederation, an Islamically oriented organization opposed to the rule of **Muhammad Reza Shah**. It was during this period that he became acquainted with the work of various revolutionary philosophers and began to formulate his own ideas for **Islam**'s transformation into a religion that would appeal to modern intellectuals without alienating the more traditional middle classes and the religious masses.

Shari'ati's message was immediately embraced by other young intellectuals who shared a common background and deepseated grievances against the **Pahlavi** regime. He borrowed from Marxist theory to provide the framework needed for understanding the structure of modern societies, but rejected its overall goals. He believed that true Islam, in particular the **Shiah** sect, was a revolutionary movement unlike the conservative doctrine preached by the traditional religious scholars. Shari'ati saw Islam as a dynamic force which spoke the language of the masses and would inspire revolt against the Shah, the aristocracy, and imperialism. He spurned nationalism (especially that of pre-Islamic Iran) as an instrument used by the elite to suppress the masses and legitimize the current monarchy. Shari'ati believed that Islam redefined would enable Iran to accept Western technology and social science within its own cultural framework, i.e., the ability to modernize without Westernizing. His innovative theory thus combined social revolution, cultural innovation, and cultural self-assertion within an Islamic-based frame, a radical layman's religion disassociated from traditional clerical influences. The influence of Shari'ati was critical in shaping the revolutionary religious philosophy of the intellectual left, a significant component of the **Islamic Revolution**.

During the development and refinement of his theory, Shari'ati held various teaching positions in Iran, including a university appointment in Mashhad. Beginning in 1967, he lectured at the **Husseiniyeh-i Er-shad**, a religious center in **Tehran**, sharing his message with thousands of students before the Husseiniyeh was closed by **SAVAK** in late 1972.

The written legacy of Shari'ati consists primarily of the numerous lectures he delivered. A considerable number of these have been collected into a work which has been translated into English and entitled, *On the Sociology of Islam*.

Shari'ati was arrested in 1974 and imprisoned until 1975. He was held under house arrest for two more years. After his release in 1977, he left Iran and settled in London. In June, 1977, Shari'ati died in England. Though no firm evidence was forthcoming, popular belief in Iran held that his death involved the complicity of SAVAK. His untimely death denied him the opportunity to witness the downfall of the Pahlavi Dynasty and the revival of Islamic government in Iran. *See also* MOTTAHARI, AYATOLLAH MORTEZA.

SHARI'AT-MADARI, AYATOLLAH MUHAMMAD KAZEM (1899-1986). During the later years of **Muhammad Reza Shah**'s reign, Ayatollah Shari'at-Madari was the senior cleric in the important religious city of **Qum**. While **Ayatollah Ruhollah Khomeini** was in exile, Shari'at-Madari was a highly popular and influential religious figure in Iran. When Khomeini returned, Shari'at-Madari's popularity was a hindrance to Khomeini and his new regime. Shari'at-Madari was in opposition to Khomeini, disagreeing with him on key matters such as the role of the clergy vis-à-vis the state, in particular the concept of *Velayat-i Faqih*, and the structure of the new Islamic Constitution. Shari'at-Madari was uneasy with the idea of direct clerical political entanglement. The clash of religio-political views between Shari'at-Madari and Khomeini eventually led to confrontation and the dissolution of Shari'at-Madari's power.

Shari'at-Madari derived much of his support from the Azeri Turks. He was himself a native of **Azerbaijan** and, thus, had a significant regional power base. He also drew national support from the Westernized business community and secular political parties. He wanted a more democratic **Islamic Republic** than Khomeini intended. Along with a group of merchants and middle-class politicians, Shari'at-Madari helped found the Muslim People's Republican Party (MPRP). The MPRP emphasized collective leadership, criticized the unruly behavior of the revolutionary committees, and called for cooperation with the secular parties and freedom of the media. This party clashed heavily with Khomeini's **Islamic Republican Party (IRP)**. After Shari'at-Madari's followers seized the television station in **Tabriz** in December 1979, to broadcast their grievances against the new **Constitution of the Islamic Republic of Iran**, the Khomeini forces mounted a counterattack and succeeded in overwhelming the MPRP and its sympathizers on Shari'at-Madari's home turf. Soon thereafter, the MPRP was dissolved with the acquiescence of Shari'at-Madari. Though for several years more Khomeini continued to respect the right of his rival to dissent, Shari'at-Madari was politically crippled. Thus, he was unable to serve as a political counterweight to the forces of revolutionary religious radicalism as had been hoped by many secular moderates.

In spring of 1982, seizing upon the charge by former Foreign Minister **Sadeq Qotbzadeh** in his confession of a plot against Khomeini that Shari'at-Madari had prior knowledge and remained silent, the Khomeini regime launched a vicious propaganda campaign against Shari'at-Madari. It was rumored that Shari'at-Madari had suggested negotiations with the Shah's government as the monarchy was on the verge of collapse, that he had approved martial law in the latter days of the Shah's reign, and that he described himself as an opponent of Khomeini. The apolitical Center for Islamic Study and Publications that Shari'at-Madari had organized in Qum was shut down. In short order, Shari'at-Madari was accused of treason, stripped of his title of Grand **Ayatollah**, demoted from status as a source of religious guidance, and placed under house arrest in Qum where he remained until his death in 1986.

SHARIF-EMAMI, JA'FAR (1909-1998). Sharif-Emami was a Swedish-trained engineer and a politically powerful, though unassuming member of **Muhammad Reza Shah**'s inner circle of courtiers. Considered one of the three innermost advisors and confidants of the Shah, Sharif-Emami was neither as ruthless nor astute as the other two, **Asadollah Alam** and **Manuchehr Eqbal**. His interests seemingly leaned more towards politics as an instrument of financial gain rather than an exercise in power.

In response to a fraying **economy**, to pressure from opposition groups and election irregularities, Sharif-Emami replaced Eqbal as prime minister in September 1960. He introduced plans for economic recovery which included restrictions on imports and tight controls on foreign exchange. The new **Majlis** elections were only slightly less problematic than the nullified elections they replaced and continuing unrest rocked the country under the premiership of Sharif-Emami. His tenure was short and marked by internal opposition from the **National Front**, **bazaar** merchants, and intellectuals. External pressure from the United States also added cause for his replacement by the more reform-minded **Ali Amini** in May 1961.

Sharif-Emami remained active in state affairs. He served as chairman of the Pahlavi Foundation, and was president of the Majlis Senate when, in response to pressure from Islamic opposition groups, he replaced **Jamshid Amuzegar** as prime minister in August 1978. He hoped to form a government of national reconciliation, but Sharif-Emami was not the ideal choice for this appointment, since he was perceived as one of the more corrupt members of the **Pahlavi** regime. In order to stem mounting social unrest, he abolished the unpopular ShahanShahi **calendar**, closed gambling casinos and liquor stores, and granted freedom of speech, assembly, and press. These efforts were referred to by **Ayatollah Ruhollah Khomeini** and his supporters as "ruses" which lessened their conciliatory effect.

In early September, Sharif-Emami gave permission for a limited, peaceful demonstration which evolved into the largest protest movement of the revolutionary period. The disorder led to the declaration of martial law, a move which resulted in the infamous 8 September **Black Friday** massacre, generally acknowledged as the point of no return in the events leading up to the collapse of the Pahlavi Dynasty. General strikes erupted throughout Iran. In another conciliation attempt, Sharif-Emami released a large number of anti-Pahlavi ulama and their supporters imprisoned in 1975 and set up the Ministry of Religious Affairs. The strikes and demonstrations continued unabated.

In early October, as a retaliatory measure, the prime minister persuaded the Iraqi government to expel Khomeini, in the hope that distance from his support network would weaken the cleric's influence in Iran. This move backfired as Khomeini used his time in exile in France to consolidate his position and utilized the superior communication systems available there.

As the political situation continued to deteriorate, the Shah instituted a military government, replacing Sharif-Emami with the commander of the Imperial Guard, General Gholam Reza Azhari in November 1978. Sharif-Emami died in exile in New York on 16 June, 1998. *See also* ISLAMIC REVOLUTION.

SHATT AL-ARAB. The Shatt al-Arab is the river formed by the confluence of the Tigris and Euphrates Rivers, flowing through Iraq. A short distance before being joined by the **Karun River**, which flows from Iran, the Shatt al-Arab forms the common border of Iran and Iraq for a distance of approximately 89 kilometers until it flows into the Persian Gulf. The entire length of the Shatt al-Arab is approximately 209 kilometers, and it has long been an important route of commerce. The strategic location of the waterway has made it an object of political controversy since the days of Ottoman rule, and control has become a prize in the present-day nationalist power rivalry between Iran and Iraq.

In 1847, the second Treaty of Erzerum established the exact location of the border between Ottoman-controlled Iraq and Persia, which included the question of control of the Shatt al-Arab. The terms of the treaty isolated Persia's main port of **Khorramshahr** (today renamed Khuninshahr) in favor of open access via the Shatt al-Arab to the Ottoman port of Basra. Following the post-World War I dismantling of the Ottoman Empire, an independent Iraq declared sovereignty over the Shatt al-Arab in

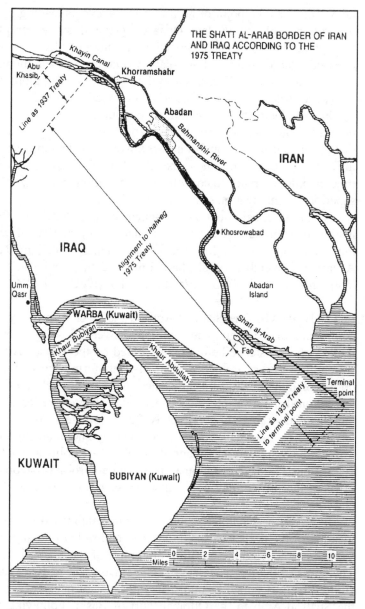

Figure 5

1932. Iran appealed the move through international channels, but later withdrew its request from the League of Nations. In 1937, the Iran-Iraq Frontier Treaty was bilaterally negotiated and Iran was granted access to its ports (**Abadan** and Khorramshahr) on the waterway, while Iraq retained political control and navigation rights. The definition of the boundary remained the low water mark on the Iranian side, which continued to place the shipping channel in Iraqi territory.

Major changes in the economic structure of Iran through the next four decades heightened the importance of the Shatt al-Arab. The booming **oil** production in **Khuzistan Province** required increased shipping access to the Persian Gulf. Iran began a systematic program to encourage rebellion in Iraq in order to pressure Baghdad to negotiate a new treaty regarding navigation rights and ownership of the Shatt al- Arab. In 1975, the Algerian Accords (not to be confused with the namesake **Algerian Accords** between the **Islamic Republic** and the United States in the wake of the **American Hostage crisis**) drew a mid-river boundary, and Iran gained unlimited access to its cities on the waterway. Though diplomatically negotiated, Iraq never fully recognized the legitimacy of the 1975 agreement since Iran had unilaterally abrogated the previous agreement in 1969 and seized what it interpreted to be in its interest by force.

The internal disorder experienced by Iran following the **Islamic Revolution** motivated Iraq to invade Khuzistan Province in 1980. The intent was to regain total control of the Shatt al-Arab along with some disputed border areas. This incursion marked the beginning of the long and bitter **Iran-Iraq War** and caused the closing of the Shatt al-Arab for the duration of the hostilities. Though a cease-fire based upon the 1987 UN Security Council Resolution 598 (Text of Resolution in Appendix D) ended the war in 1988, no formal peace settlement was agreed upon and the Shatt al-Arab remained closed for years. Its status reverted to the terms of the 1975 agreement. While reopened, the future of the Shatt al-Arab remains uncertain and depends on the progress of diplomatic relations between Iran and Iraq.

SHERLEY BROTHERS. In 1597, the British Crown sent two brothers, Anthony and Robert Sherley, as emissaries to the **Safavid** Persian Court. Robert is recognized as the first in a long line of European advisers who would influence Iranian policies. Anthony kept meticulous accounts of the events of the reign of **Shah Abbas the Great** and these documents have provided valuable information about Persian political activity in the 17th century.

The Sherley brothers are credited with the attempt to provide assistance for the Persians against Ottoman expansion into **Azerbaijan**, Armenia, and Georgia. Shah Abbas drafted both Anthony and Robert to accompany Persian embassies to European courts for the purpose of enlisting aid. Though they were unsuccessful in preventing the Ottoman takeover of Iranian territory, they did enhance the country's military capabilities with the successful completion of a cannon foundry. They also attempted to initiate **trade** relationships with Europe, though only with limited success.

SHIAH. The state religion of Iran today is Twelver Shi'ism, one of several branches of Shi'ism that split off as a separate sect from Sunni **Islam**. The origins of the split involved a difference of opinion over rightful leadership of the community of believers after the death of the prophet Muhammad. The Shiah believed that the successor to Muhammad should have been **Imam Ali** and then through his bloodline in succeeding generations. Conception of leadership based on the principle of election by consensus proved to be the majority and a caliph was selected accordingly. From the beginning and to the present day, the Shiah have been in the minority within the Islamic world. Indeed, the out-of-power minority status molded the early development of Shi'ism which quickly took on the characteristics of a revolutionary movement. The Shiah opposed the status quo, struggling against the perceived illegitimate power of the Sunni usurper. The penultimate sacrifice in this regard was the martyrdom of **Imam Hussein** on the plains of **Kerbala**, an occasion commemorated yearly by the Shiah in the mourning ceremonies of the month of Moharram in the Muslim A.H. **calendar**. A reenactment of Imam Hussein's ordeal takes place each year among the Shiah, culminating in the *Taziyeh* performances on the 10th of Moharram.

Shi'ism split into various sub-sects over time, each following a different bloodline tracing back through Imam Hussein to his father, Imam Ali. Of the four major Shiah branches, one followed a line of 12 Imams, the 12th Imam disappearing, or going into hiding, and dubbed the **Hidden Imam**. It is this branch that became the state religion of Iran in 1501 with the advent of the **Safavid Dynasty**.

Twelver Shi'ism has remained the official state religion from the Safavid period to the present day. The vast majority of the Iranian population in the 21st century is Twelver Shiah. It is of little surprise then that Shiah thought and theology play such a vital role in Iranian society. The **Islamic Revolution** and resultant **Constitution of the Islamic Republic of Iran** were ideologically driven by Shiah scholars. The influence was of such extent that a full understanding of the political dynamics of Iran today demands an acquaintance with the basic precepts of Shiah Islam. *See also* AYATOLLAH; FAQIH; KHOMEINI, AYATOLLAH RUHOLLAH; VELAYAT-I FAQIH.

SHIRAZ. The city of Shiraz is located in a high mountain valley of the **Zagros Mountains** and is 935 kilometers south of **Tehran**. Despite its southerly latitude, due to its elevation of 1,800 meters above sea level, it has a relatively mild climate allowing for its magnificent gardens. The pleasantly temperate climate has long made the city a vacation destination of southern Iran and the northern Persian Gulf states of the Arabian Peninsula. The current population of Shiraz is just under 1.1 million (1996 census).

Shiraz was an important town during the **Achaemenian** period, located only 50 kilometers south of the powerful capital of **Persepolis**. It was not, however, developed as a city until 684 after the fall of the **Sassanians** to the **Arabs**. It has served as the capital of Iran at various times in the past, the last being when **Karim Khan Zand** (ruled 1750-1779), the first ruler of the **Zand Dynasty**, made it his capital. It has served as the capital of the Fars province since the seventh century.

While Shiraz was spared from destruction during the Mongol invasion, it began to decline in the latter years of the **Safavid Dynasty**, after the Afghan raids of the 18th century, several earthquakes, and insurrections. In 1747 when **Nader Shah** was assassinated, most of the city's historical buildings were destroyed. When Karim Khan Zand made it his capital he rebuilt many of the buildings. His titled name adorns two of the notable places in the city, the Vakil Mosque, an important building in the religious life of the city as well as architecturally, and the Vakil **Bazaar**. The bazaar is a colorful place enhanced in certain seasons by the influx of nomadic **Qashqai** tribesmen and the brightly colored clothing of the tribal **women**. Shiraz is the chief market town of the Qashqai.

Shiraz is home to the third most visited pilgrimage site in Iran, the Shrine of Shah Chiraq. It is also the hometown of the important poets **Hafez** (1320-1391) and **Sa'di** (1184-1292), both of whom have their tombs located in the city. These are situated in beautiful gardens and are places of steady visitation and great veneration, reflecting the poetic propensity of Iranians. It is often commented of Shiraz, the city of "roses and poets," that it is the virtual capital of Persian **poetry**. Other attractions of the city include a number of fine old homes and associated garden estates, including the *Bagh-i Eram*, now belonging to Shiraz University and used as a reception hall and a museum, and the *Narengestan*. The latter, a nicely restored home and garden belonging to a prominent Shiraz family of the 19th century, became the home of the Asia Institute and base of operations of the important art historian, Arthur Upham Pope. There are also many local shrines in the city.

Another claim to fame of Shiraz is as an important university town. Formed in 1945, Shiraz University (formerly **Pahlavi University**) is a well-developed school which was lavishly spent on by the former **Pahlavi Dynasty**. Under contract with the University of Pennsylvania, there was a concerted attempt to establish a model American-style institute of higher **education**.

With its many charms and attractions, few would dispute that Shiraz is one of the most pleasant cities in Iran.

SHUSTER, MORGAN (1877-1960). Shuster was an American financier, lawyer, and publisher who worked for several government agencies in Cuba and the Phillipines before being assigned to Persia in 1911. He was invited at the insistence of the **Majlis** and invested with considerable powers as treasurer-general. His work involved the reorganization of Persia's financial structure in order to control the overwhelming economic difficulties confronting the country. Iran was essentially bankrupt due to the incompetence of the later **Qajar** monarchs and the machinations of the British and Russians. Shuster quickly became enmeshed in conflicts between British and Russian interests in Persia and was forced from his post in 1911, the same year as his appointment. His book, *The Strangling of Persia*, describes his experiences. *See also* SULTAN AHMAD SHAH.

SOROUSH, ABDOL KARIM (1945-). Known as an Islamic Reformist, Soroush's published works center on religious perception and practice, with a particular focus on **Islam** and its compatibility with democracy. Soroush has authored dozens of essays and books and has had a profound influence on modernistic interpretations of Islam.

Born in **Tehran**, where he was educated through primary and secondary schools, he specialized in mathematics. Upon graduation, Soroush passed Iran's nationwide university entrance exams in both physics and pharmacology, opting for the latter. After finishing his studies he spent two years of compulsory service in the military followed by 15 months of medical service in Bushehr as the director of the Laboratory for Food, Products, Toiletries and Sanitary Materials. After returning to Tehran and working for a short period at the Laboratory for Medicine Control, Soroush left for study in England where he entered a postgraduate program in analytical chemistry at the University of London. Upon completion, Soroush spent an additional five and a half years in the city, studying history and philosophy of science at Chelsea College.

It was in England that Soroush first became familiar with political activism and awareness, the focus of his activities being a Muslim students' center in west London frequently visited by

Muslim leaders. Soroush began speaking at local events where-upon his speeches would be published in booklet and pamphlet form. His first published work, appearing in Iran while Soroush remained in London, was based on a series of speeches entitled *Dialectical Antagonism*, an attempt to curtail the leftist ideology appearing in Soroush's activist peers. At the same time Soroush had begun work on his second book, *The Restless Nature of the World*, which outlined the Islamic foundations of monotheism and resurrection. This text was well received and approved by both **Ayatollah Morteza Mottahari** and **Ayatollah Ruhollah Khomeini**.

Shortly after the **Islamic Revolution** began in Iran, Soroush returned to Tehran where he attended the city's Teacher Training College and became the director of the Islamic Culture Group. A year later all universities had been closed and Ayatollah Khomeini named Soroush to a group of seven called the Cultural Revolution Institute. The group's goal was to initiate the reopen-ing of the universities with reformed curriculum. The resulting purges of faculty members deemed unsuitable for the official interpretation of Islamic values plunged Soroush into contro-versy. To the present day, he remains tainted in the eyes of many for his role in the political restructuring of universities in Iran. In 1983, Soroush resigned from the Cultural Revolution Institute and has since held no official positions in Iran, though he has served occasionally as an advisor.

Toward the end of the decade, Soroush became increasingly outspoken on the role played by the clergy within Iran's political sphere and began writing his criticism in a magazine called *Ki-yan*. The magazine, co-founded by Soroush, became extremely visible as a source of religious intellectualism and continued to publish the author's most contentious works, only to be shut down in 1998. Soroush's many articles, speeches, and lectures had become widely available during this time and with the clo-sure of *Kiyan* came censorship of Soroush's works and harass-ment and interruption at his public lectures by hardline groups.

In 2000, Soroush became a visiting professor at Harvard University where he taught Islam and democracy, philosophy of Islamic law, and Quranic studies. Soroush has also lectured as a scholar-in-residence at Yale University, Princeton University, and Wissenschaftskolleg in Berlin. The essential thoughts of Sorough are available in an English translation published by Oxford University Press entitled *Reason, Freedom, and Democracy in Islam.*

Soroush's main ideas concerning Islam and democracy have been an important contribution to both religious and political studies, though he is most often credited with theories of reform for Islam and Islamic philosophy. Soroush, who has been called the Martin Luther of Islam, argues that religion, and the practice and knowledge thereof, are two distinct facets. He stresses in his works that while religion is perfect, the practice of it and the perception of its teaching can be fatally flawed, urging modern Muslims to allow flexibility to religion, as he sees change as a natural part of the history of religion. Soroush extends this thought to democracy in much of his writing, proposing that Islam and the freedom inherent to democracy are entirely compatible in that each Muslim should see Islam as a fluctuating, growing religion with freedom of interpretation. He emphasizes that while sacred texts do not change, their interpretation can, and should, change according to current conditions. This thought is considered a volatile philosophy as it undermines the Muslim clergy's stronghold over interpretation in the public sphere, as embodied in the **Islamic Republic of Iran**.

Recognition of Soroush's intellectual impact on the religious philosophy of Islam in the late 20th and early 21st centuries is widespread. An indication of such recognition is his being named as one of the 100 top most influential thinkers of the 20th century by *Time* magazine.

STUDENT DORMITORY ATTACKS. During the summer of 1999, great tension permeated Iranian society. Politicians and clergy dedicated to pro-democratic, pro-civil rights change had emerged as a powerful force, and with the 1997 election of **Muhammad Khatami**, this reformist camp had achieved a powerful foothold into the politics of the **Islamic Republic**. However, most of the government—at this time including the **Majlis**—was still controlled by more conservative forces, and as such the popular will to reform embodied in Khatami could not reach fruition. With the combination of the Majlis passing a bill limiting freedom of the press and the closing of the popular **reformist newspaper** *Salaam* in the early summer, many reformists were angered, not least of which were their ranks amongst university students.

On the evening of 8 July, 1999, pro-reform students at **Tehran University** staged a protest around their dormitories. The situation became heated as Iranian security forces arrived, and reformist and hardline slogans between the two groups began to fill the night. Representatives from Khatami's government arrived on the scene to attempt to quell the situation, and by the early morning hours of 9 July, they had seemingly eased tensions enough that the students returned to their dorms. However, once the government officials left the scene, the security forces attacked the students in their dormitories. Though reports vary on the figures, at least one student was killed and many more were injured. Additionally, the forces ransacked the rooms, destroying or damaging much student and university property.

In the aftermath of the attacks, student protests increased, with the activists making demands including the release of the bodies of those slain in the attacks (students claimed there were multiple deaths), the removal of hardliner police chief Hedayat Lotfian, and an admission of wrongdoing by Supreme Leader **Ayatollah Ali Khamene'i**. Initially, reformist elements within the government supported the students, but as the protests became protracted, the views and demands expressed by the students became too extreme to support without becoming subject to conservative retribution. President Khatami was forced into a temporary silence as the students became more radical. Even so, conservatives used the student unrest to lambaste Khatami's reform agenda as inciting revolt.

Security forces, now including the **Basij**, battled with protestors as many demonstrations became riots, although these forces may have purposefully provoked violent reactions. Khamene'i did meet with student leaders to denounce the actions of the police, but he also insisted that foreign elements were involved in instigating the student unrest, a view hardliners would repeat throughout the crisis and beyond. On the other hand, reformist newspapers such as **Sa'id Hajjerian**'s *Sobh-i Emruz* publicized and criticized the attacks on the dormitories, which encouraged initial popular support for the students. However, this support was more sympathetic to the brutalized students than for their demands, which tended to limit the spread of the demonstrations to college campuses only.

After about a week, the worst mass uprising since the **Islamic Revolution** subsided. Although some security officers faced reprimands or even jail time, police chief Lotfian was never removed. In fact, the demands of the students were generally left to fade away. However, four of the leaders of the revolt received death sentences later in the year after a series of closed-door trials. In the years following the uprising, the anniversary date was often the occasion for renewed protests, though never on the scale of the original protest. If anything, the yearly observance of the attack and student uprising reflects a continuing frustration among Iran's massive youth population. Until the Islamic Republic addresses the factors underlying this discontent, 9 July will likely continue to be an uneasy time for the foreseeable future.

STUDENTS FOLLOWING THE IMAM'S LINE. A plan that started with a 24-year-old engineering student at **Tehran University** ended with 300 Iranian students holding 52 Americans hostage in the American embassy in Tehran in 1979. The leaders of the student group, which would become known as the "Students Following the Imam's Line," planned a protest of American support for the reign of **Muhammad Reza Shah** and American interference in Iranian policy. The plan included the storming of the embassy and demanding action.

According to one of the masterminds of the event, engineering student **Ibrahim Asgharzadeh**, the students had no plan in mind other than the initial occupation of the facility. After days of monitoring embassy security from nearby rooftops, 300 preselected students were marched to the embassy during the morning of 4 November. With the help of bolt cutters hidden under the chadors of female students, they stormed the gates and climbed the walls, overpowering the few U.S. Marine guards. Asghar-zadeh has said that the student's main fear was that the siege would be squelched by revolutionary leader **Ayatollah Ruhollah Khomeini** before the estimated three- to seven-day occupation was completed. However, their act quickly became a focus of public opinion, the embassy was labeled a "nest of spies," and many thousands of supporters of the **Islamic Revolution** swarmed the site. At this point, events engulfed the Students Following the Imam's Line and those in charge lost control of the decision making, which led to the holding of **American Hostages in Iran** for 444 days of embassy occupation.

Following the release of the hostages, the Students Following the Imam's Line found themselves revered as revolutionaries and in line for appointments in the revolutionary government, many serving in high-level positions within the government until Khomeini's death in 1989. However, changes in leadership brought into power clerics who were in disagreement with the former students, which forced a number of them to leave public service. Some of these spoke out publicly against the new leadership and criticized what they saw as faults in the government of the **Islamic Republic**. Asgharzadeh was removed from his post in the parliament and **Abbas Abdi**, another key planner in the embassy siege, was tried and imprisoned for some months. Years later, Abdi saw his popular newspaper *Salaam* closed by the conservative courts for speaking out in opposition.

Under the more moderate government of President **Muhammad Khatami**, a number of the once-revered former hostage-takers emerged back into political life in Iran. **Massoumeh Ebtekar** (dubbed "Mary" by Western media), who acted as the spokesperson for the Students Following the Imam's Line throughout the hostage crisis in 1979, was named vice president by Khatami in 1997. Others are active in the Iranian government, as well as in the reform movement. Some have come to unapologetic terms with their actions in 1979 and some have even expressed support for resolving the conflict and healing diplomatic relations with the United States. Abbas Abdi was the boldest example of this when in 1999 he traveled to Paris for a reconciliatory meeting with former American hostage Barry Rosen.

Though little came of the meeting on a large scale, it is evidence that the Students Following the Imam's Line have matured along with their beliefs. With respect to **U.S.-Iranian Relations**, the meeting has also served as an important symbolic step in a gradual process which might eventually lead to a rapprochement.

SUFISM. Sufism is the mystical, ascetic element of the Islamic religion which evolved in the ninth century in response to the perceived loss of spirituality. To a Sufi, becoming one with God (Allah) is the ultimate reality and all efforts are directed toward the unlimited horizons of the spiritual world. Acceptance of the exterior guide of law (Sharia) is the beginning of the interior path (*tariqa*), an individual spiritual discipline which a Sufi must follow in order to shed the material trappings of this world and find communion with God. Sufism has many characteristics in common with the Christian monastic orders of Western religions such as poverty and mortification of the flesh. In contrast, it does not support celibacy nor make distinctions between clerical and lay members. It emphasizes the love of God and teaches that God and the Sufis have a special relationship which transcends all aspects of life into spiritual events.

In the 10th and 11th centuries, Sufism spread rapidly as Muslims were attracted to its mystical practices and hopeful promises. Brotherhoods developed throughout Iran, the most popular being the "whirling dervishes" founded by the great mystic poet **Rumi**. Sufis later became the great missionaries and preachers of **Islam** in Asia and Africa. From the beginning, the Sufis were scorned by the established clergy. After the movement was established and the Sufi message began to spread, persecution and suppression by mainstream Sunni and **Shiah** Muslims became widespread. An element of superstition and ignorance crept in and corrupted the mystic purity of Sufi belief. Though this led to a decline in its popular status the essential elements of the movement were sustained. Iran has, from the inception of Sufism, always been an important center of Sufi practice and belief. A strong Sufi influence is found in Persian **literature** and Persian **poetry**, revealed in a strong mystical content beneath the literal meaning of the writings.

SULLIVAN, WILLIAM H. (1922-). William Sullivan was a career diplomat who entered the American foreign service in 1947. He served in various positions as a member of the State Department before his assignment as ambassador to Iran in 1977. Sullivan was at first favorably impressed with the regime of **Muhammad Reza Shah** and sent positive assessments to Washington regarding the strength and stability of the Iranian government. His opinion began to change after several months in **Tehran**, and though he was late to grasp the volatility of the internal situation, he began to communicate with Washington regarding his misgivings. Sullivan's reports were ignored or discounted, and he began to realize the depth of the U.S. government's misperceptions about the political situation in Iran. The **Huyser Mission**, in early 1979, presented a positive assessment of the Shah's military strength as a counterbalance to the revolutionary movement, and Sullivan's dissenting opinion was ignored. The United States was caught unprepared when shortly thereafter the Shah was forced to flee the country and the Islamic revolutionaries seized control of the government. Ambassador Sullivan wrote of his experiences in a 1981 book entitled *Mission to Iran*.

SULTAN AHMAD SHAH (Ruled 1909-1925). Sultan Ahmad Shah came to the Persian throne at 12 years of age after his father, **Muhammad Ali Shah**, fled to the Russian Legation in July 1909, and was forced from the throne by the Constitutionalists. Due to his age, he was appointed with a regent and never actively ruled despite a 16-year reign. His era began on an optimistic note with the opening of the Second **Majlis** and the institution of overdue reforms. These included financial reforms that resulted from the recruitment of a team of American financial experts under the leadership of **Morgan Shuster**. However, internal division and the pressure of world events coincident to World War I destroyed any semblance of central order. Weak and ineffective Ahmad Shah remained largely a bystander to a number of tumultuous events, including the Russian ultimatum to the Persian government in November 1911, which led to the dismissal of the Shuster Mission and the dissolution of the Second Majlis.

Much of Iran was occupied by Ottoman, British, or Russian forces during the course of World War I, and the end of the war did not improve the deteriorating political situation. Eventually, Colonel Reza Khan, who headed the only effective military force in the country, the Cossack Brigade, marched on **Tehran** in February 1921. This coup d'etat was ostensibly designed to save the monarchy. However, Reza Khan actively and gradually consolidated his hold on power. In 1923, Ahmad Shah left for Europe, never to return. He was deposed in October 1925, and soon thereafter Reza Khan was elected **Reza Shah** by a compliant Constituent Assembly. This event marked the end of the **Qajar Dynasty** and the beginning of the **Pahlavi Dynasty**.

SUSA. In the tradition of **Achaemenid** rulers, the capital of the Persian Empire was not one set location. According to Greek accounts, the Persian kings maintained palaces throughout the empire, in Babylon, Ecbatana (present-day **Hamadan**), Pasargadae, **Persepolis**, and Susa. During the reign of **Darius**, Susa became the principal capital, chosen because of its accessibility to the other major cities of the empire and its proximity to the original Iranian homeland. Susa was well protected by surrounding mountains and had fertile soil. The ancients claimed that grain could grow one hundred or sometimes two hundred fold.

A great deal of Susa's wealth came from **trade** in and around the Persian Gulf. The major rivers of the Persian Empire, the Euphrates, the Tigris, the Choaspes, and the Eulaeus, ran different courses than they did later in history. In the fifth and fourth centuries B.C., these rivers flowed into a marshy lake northwest of the current convergence at the **Shatt al-Arab**. This allowed various exits to the Persian Gulf and navigation was not as limited as it is today. Susa was situated 62 miles up the Tigris while Babylon was 375 miles up the Euphrates, making Susa the more favorable city for trade.

Susa had historically been a cultural center before it also became a political center of the Persian Empire, serving as the principal city of the Elamites in ancient times. Artifacts found among the ruins of the city have provided excellent archaeological records from which the history of the Elamites was reconstructed. The craftsmanship of the original artisans, the grand potters of the Elamites, was refined and preserved throughout the centuries. Incorporating these cultural traditions, Darius constructed his own grand palaces and temples on the site of the Elamite ruins. His interest in culture and the recording of his accomplishments has made Susa a center for archaeologists seeking to unravel the ancient history of the Persians. *See also* CYRUS THE GREAT.

-T-

TABRIZ. The city of Tabriz, its name derived from the words "*tap riz*" meaning "heat flow" due to surrounding hot springs, is located in the northwestern section of Iran, and is the capital of the East **Azerbaijan** Province. Located near Lake **Urumieh** in the foothills of Mt. Sahand, it has an elevation of approximately 1,372 meters above sea level. Its population of just under 1,200,000 people (according to the 1996 census) makes Tabriz the fourth-largest city in Iran. The main spoken language in Tabriz is Azeri Turkish, reflective of the city's Azerbaijani character.

In its early history, Tabriz was known as Tauris and was the capital of Atropatene, the realm of one of Alexander the Great's generals. During the third century, it became the capital of Armenia under King Tiridates III. Throughout the centuries, Tabriz would change hands on numerous occasions. It became the capital of a Mongol dynasty in the 13th and 14th centuries, and then passed into **Turkoman** hands in the 14th century. With the emergence of the **Safavid Dynasty** in 1501, Tabriz became its administrative center until the capital was moved to Qazvin in 1548. Though its geographical position made it prone to earthquakes which periodically destroyed much of the city, it also proved to be an ideal strategic and administrative location, explaining the number of times it has been made capital by various groups.

During the **Qajar Dynasty**, Tabriz regained a level of prominence it had lost after the Safavids moved the capital. With the opening of **trade** with Europe, Tabriz became an economic center as a trade hub between interior Iran and Europe. With its renewed commercial prominence, Tabriz became the seat of the Qajar Crown Prince. It was during the Qajar Dynasty in 1850 that the Bab, the leader of the **Babi Movement**, was executed along with thousands of his followers in Tabriz.

It was also in Tabriz that an uprising began during the **Constitutional Revolution of 1906**. Upset over **Muhammad Ali Shah**'s efforts—including the bombardment of the **Majlis** in **Tehran**—to render the 1906 Constitution and its democratic institutions ineffective, constitutionalists rose up in protest, an uprising which would spread throughout Iran. By 1909, Tabriz was blockaded by the Shah's forces. A force led by Sattar Khan broke the Tabriz blockade, albeit at great cost. It was during this offensive that the American missionary **Howard Baskerville** died in his efforts to aid the constitutionalists.

Throughout the 20th century, Tabriz remained important strategically and geopolitically. During World War II, the USSR. occupied the city to protect transportation links into Iran that allowed United States war materials to get to the Soviet Union. Though the Allied Forces agreed to withdraw from Iran after the war, the Soviets remained and installed a puppet government in Azerbaijan with Tabriz as its capital. This led to the **Azerbaijan Crisis**. With the United States taking the lead, and involvement of the newly formed United Nations, eventually the Soviets withdrew. The city reverted to Iranian control. Into the 21st century, Tabriz remains, consistent with its historical role, one of the most important cities of the Iranian state.

TAHEREH QURRAT AL-AYN (1814-1852). Born in Qazvin into a family of well-respected ulama, Fatima Zarrin Taj Baraghani— later to be called both Qurrat al-Ayn ("the solace of the eye") by the Shaikhi leader Rashti, and Tahereh ("the pure") by the Bab— became one of the most important figures in **Babism**, which was the precursor to **Bahaism**. Given an extensive **education**, Tahereh impressed all, even her ulama father, with her scholastic ability. However, Tahereh could not avoid tradition, and was married to her cousin, Mulla Muhammad Baraghani at age 14.

In 1828, Tahereh and her husband left for **Kerbala**, where Mulla Muhammad intended to study **Islam**. Tahereh had several children, and lived with her family in Kerbala for 13 years. During that time she discovered Shaykhi teachings. Tensions between the couple grew as Tahereh became more enmeshed in Shaykhism. Soon after returning to Qazvin in 1841, Tahereh left her family and returned to Kerbala.

Once Ali Muhammad Shirazi proclaimed himself the Bab ("the gate"), the nature of the Shaykhi movement changed. Tahereh converted to Babism and became one of its guiding intellectual forces. Her insistence that the Bab's appearance abrogated sharia enraged many, even members of the Babi Movement itself. She did not observe ritual prayer, and sometimes even appeared unveiled—often for startling effect. At one point, to show her possible revelatory position, Tahereh claimed she was imbued with the spirit of Fatima (the Prophet Muhammad's daughter), and simply by her gaze could cleanse the unclean. Despite opposition within the Babi ranks, the Bab himself showed his favor towards Tahereh and her views, giving her the moniker Tahereh in response to allegations of her immorality.

She taught first in Kerbala, and later in Baghdad; word of Tahereh's actions spread. Her family in Qazvin became worried for their reputation as Tahereh's unshrouding was leading to questions of her morality. Family members sent by her father arrived in Baghdad while Tahereh was under house arrest, and procured her release to bring her home. However, her message continued to spread, gaining converts, and opposition, even en route to Qazvin. While in Qazvin, tension between the **Shiah** ulama and the Babis led to the assassination of Tahereh's uncle—who was also the father of her abandoned husband—for his derision of the Babi. Though the assassin turned himself in after a backlash against the Babi ensued, many held captive were not released; some were even executed.

Tahereh escaped, and fled to **Khorasan** where the Babi were called to meet to discuss future action. There, Tahereh's argument of the eschewing of *sharia* and of action won out after the leader of the opposing view, Quddus, converted to Tahereh's message. Following a time of violence, and subsequent hiding,

Tahereh was finally captured in 1849. She was held under house arrest in the home of the mayor of **Tehran** until a failed Babi attempt on **Naser al-Din Shah**'s life in 1852 led to the decision to execute Tahereh. She was strangled in the night, and her body was thrown into a well. *See also* WOMEN.

TALEQANI, AYATOLLAH MAHMUD (1911-1979). Born in Taleqan, Mahmud Taleqani became one of the most influential clerics behind the 1979 **Islamic Revolution**. He studied religion at **Qum** where he was a fellow student of **Ayatollah Ruhollah Khomeini**. He later went on to become a teacher in **Tehran**.

After the abdication of **Reza Shah** in 1941, Taleqani formed the Islamic Society, which began as meetings for the purpose of interpreting the Quran, but expanded to encompass discussions on religious modernism. It was through the Islamic Society that the close collaboration of Taleqani and **Mehdi Bazargan** began, a collaboration that was to extend into the Islamic Revolution and last until the death of Taleqani in 1979. These two became founding members of the important political grouping, **Liberation Movement of Iran**, which was first organized in 1961. Taleqani was also affiliated with the **National Resistance Movement (NRM)** that various Mossadeqists formed to keep the Nationalist Movement alive after the toppling of the **Muhammad Mossadeq** government in 1953.

Preparatory to the Islamic Revolution, Taleqani was a member of the exiled Khomeini's support network in Iran and used his writing and speaking abilities to spur the revolutionary movement. He went on to become one of the seven core figures of Khomeini's **Revolutionary Council**.Taleqani authored a book, translated into English as *Society and Economics in Islam*. In his book he explained practical applications of Islamic principles regarding distribution of resources, inheritance, and land reform. The Islamic viewpoint he espoused on economics heavily influenced the policies of the new revolutionary regime.

A key link in the broad-based coalition that brought about the Islamic Revolution, Taleqani consistently strived to bridge secular and religious elements. In particular, he was important in connecting those secular nationalists who had religious inclinations and leftist Islamic groups, with the more dominant radical ulama coalesced around Khomeini. Some, in fact, have argued that it was the untimely death of Taleqani in September 1979 that destroyed the last hope for collaboration among groups with widely disparate interpretations of Islamic government and assured the capture of the Islamic Revolution by religious extremists. *See also* ISLAMIC REPUBLIC.

TAZIYEH. The *Taziyeh* is a dramatic presentation of one of the key events in the formation of the **Shiah** branch of **Islam**. The word *Taziyeh* in Arabic means "mourning," which in this case refers to the commemoration of the tragic events that occurred in **Kerbala**. The *Taziyeh*, or passion play, presents a reenactment of the murders of **Imam Hussein** and his family, who were direct descendants of **Imam Ali**.

The events portrayed by the *Taziyeh* take place in Iraq around 680 A.D., and visually establish the tragedy surrounding the origin of Shiism as a separate sect of Islam. The most compelling aspect of the drama is the emotional reaction generated throughout the audience. Many viewers burst into tears and become otherwise physically engaged throughout the *Taziyeh*.

There are few performances that equal the heightened realism and what appear to be violent actions that occur throughout the *Taziyeh*. The reaction of audiences throughout this play often focuses on the brutal scenes, which dramatically depict the murders of Hussein and his family. The violence of these scenes sometimes creates violence of its own amongst audiences, as they view the murder of their beloved religious leader being reenacted. Such strong emotional reactions were also frequently tied throughout history to struggles against tyranny, the political status quo sometimes being identified with the murderers of Imam Hussein and his family. It is not unheard of that the actor playing the evil part of Yazid, the reigning Caliph who ordered the charge against Imam Hussein, is attacked by the audience and, on occasion, wounded or killed. Such is the power of the emotions kindled by the tragedy of Hussein.

Another interesting facet of the *Taziyeh* is the location of the drama in relationship to the audience. The stage is centrally set, but actions occur throughout and around the audience, which often requires the direct participation of the audience. It resembles, thusly, the concept of theater in the round. The set depicts the emptiness of the Kerbala desert; props and costumes are minimal and symbolic, and protagonists and antagonists are divided by color, while the antagonists recite their parts and protagonists sing their portion of the *Taziyeh*.

Since there is no set script and the play is interactive, there can be considerable variation in its performance depending on such factors as where it is performed and local interpretations. The plays are conducted during the first 10 days of the month of Moharram (the first month of the Islamic **calendar**). The culminating play is the depiction of the martyrdom of Hussein, which is performed on the 10th day of Moharram.

During the rule of **Reza Shah** in the 1930s until the **Islamic Revolution** of the 1970s the *Taziyeh* was restricted. The **Pahlavi** Shahs believed that the reenactment of the play hindered modernization. Nor were the political implications lost on the secularizing monarchs. Religious emotions run high during the first 10 days of Moharram and can readily be translated into political channels. Indeed, perhaps the final blow to the rule of **Muhammad Reza Shah** was dealt in December 1978 with the defiance exhibited during Moharram when literally millions of Iranians filled the streets of **Tehran** in the face of martial law. It was only after **Ayatollah Ruhollah Khomeini** became supreme religious ruler of Iran, that the *Taziyeh* was officially reintroduced as an important part of Iranian culture.

TEHRAN. Tehran is Iran's largest city. Tehran is also the capital of Iran, and has been since 1788. It is, as well, the capital of Tehran Province. The city population is approximately seven million within a 1,200 square kilometer area, which includes the extensive suburban areas of the city. The province has a population of nearly 12 million. Most of the inhabitants are Muslims and **Persian language** is most generally spoken. Azeri Turkish is also widely spoken, by some estimates by as many as one-fourth of the population.

Tehran is located 100 kilometers south of the **Caspian Sea** on the slopes of the **Alborz Mountains**. The elevation of the city is 1,200 meters above sea level. Due to its altitude, Tehran experiences four distinct seasons with pleasant but brief springs and autumns, frigid winters, and very warm summers. A 50 degree centigrade (122 degree Fahrenheit) swing in temperature from winter to summer is not uncommon. The high central **Iranian Plateau** is to the south of Tehran, the most adjacent portion of which is the Dasht-i Kavir.

The name Tehran is dervided from the Old Persian *"teh"* meaning "warm" and *"ran"* meaning "place." **Rayy**, now essentially a suburb of Tehran, was the far more important historical town prior to its destruction by the Mongols in 1220. Parts of the ancient city of Rayy can still be found in the southern part of Tehran.

During the **Pahlavi Dynasty**, modernization and industrialization took place with Tehran experiencing a building boom, partly due to the thriving **oil** sector. After the overthrow of **Muhammad Reza Shah** in 1979, the economic status of Tehran suffered due to the **Iran-Iraq War**, lack of investment, and internal strife. Modernization and growth took an upward turn under the presidency of **Muhammad Khatami** during the 1990s. The increase of motor traffic and the increase of the use of fossil fuel by **industry** have brought about the rapid decline of air quality. Tehran has been cited as one of the cities with the worst traffic congestion in the world in world travelers' lists. Tehran is home to more than 50 percent of Iran's industry. The manufacturing industry includes electrical equipment, textiles, sugar, chinaware, pottery, pharmaceuticals, and an assembly plant for motor vehicles.

Tehran has three paved roads that go northward and one road that goes west; two roads run south and one road runs east. There is an Iranian State Railway that has lines going in all directions from Tehran and the trans-Europe railway system that links Tehran to Turkey. Ten kilometers west of central Tehran is Mehrabad, which houses an international airport. The **National Iranian Oil Company** located in Tehran administers the crude-**oil** industry.

Given the relative newness of Tehran, there are few histori-cal sites of note. Perhaps the most notable is the famous Peacock Throne found in the Gulistan Palace, dating back to the period of **Nader Shah**. There are a number of important museums in Te-hran, in particular an archaeological museum and an ethno-graphical museum. As well, several of the Shah's palaces have been turned under the **Islamic Republic** into museums, the Sa'adabad Palace and the Niavaran Palace, with the intent of displaying the extravagant opulence of the Pahlavi Dynasty.

Beyond its role as a political and administrative center, Te-hran is also a center of **education**. The highest concentration of educational institutions exists in Tehran including the largest and oldest modern state university in the country, **Tehran Univer-sity**.

The more modern area of the town is found to the north of the city, with the older area of the town and **bazaar** to the south of the city. The bazaar, which is large in size, is the leading cen-ter for the sale and export of carpets. Since most of the increase of growth of Tehran has been post-World War II, it has the feel of a modern city. Most architecture is new, with many 10- to 18-story buildings. Significant recent building additions have been a stadium capable of holding 100,000 people and a new interna-tional airport.

TEHRAN CONFERENCE. From 28 November to 1 December, 1943, U.S. President Franklin Roosevelt, British Prime Minister Winston Churchill, and Soviet Premiere Joseph Stalin met for the first time in **Tehran**. In the Conference, the Allied leaders set forth their plan for the execution of the war against the Axis powers, and laid the groundwork for the later Yalta Conference.

Two important declarations came out of the Conference, the first being the Declaration of the Three Powers. In this declara-tion, the Allies pledged mutual cooperation in war and peace. They further committed themselves to the destruction of the German Army and Navy, as well as their ability to make war. They also committed themselves to the destruction of tyranny, slavery, and intolerance.

The second important declaration to come out of the Conference was the Declaration of the Three Powers Regarding Iran. In this declaration, the Three Powers recognized the role Iran played in the prosecution of the war against the Axis Powers; promised economic assistance to the government of Iran both during and after the war; and promised to maintain the independence, sovereignty, and territorial integrity of Iran. This declaration was important due to the fact that, at the time, the Soviet Army occupied the northern part of Iran and the Iranian government feared the Soviets would not leave the nation at the war's conclusion. The Soviets did, in fact, try to maintain their occupation of the northern part of Iran; however, they were forced to withdraw in May of 1946 when Great Britain and the United States pressured them to honor the terms of the Declaration.

Due to U.S. participation in the Conference, the United States replaced Germany as the "neutral" power that ensured that neither the USSR. nor Great Britain gained too much power in Iran. Eventually, however, by the 1950s, the U.S. had supplanted Great Britain as the chief rival for influence in Iran, counterbalancing the Russians. In essence, the Cold War replaced the Great Game with respect to superpower sparring over Iran. U.S. intervention in the early 1950s leading to the collapse of the **Muhammad Mossadeq** government and the restoration of **Muhammad Reza Shah** to the throne was a landmark in this shift. This eventuality helped set the stage for the anti-Americanism leading up to the **Islamic Revolution** of 1979.

It is interesting to note that the Conference was held in Tehran without the permission of the Iranian government, though Iran was considered an ally in the war against Adolf Hitler. Furthermore, due to a fear there might be an attempt to assassinate Roosevelt during the conference, the president of the United States resided in the Soviet Embassy during the Conference. *See also* AZERBAIJAN CRISIS; U.S.-IRANIAN RELATIONS AFTER THE ISLAMIC REVOLUTION.

TEHRAN TREATY OF 1814. The **Tehran** Treaty was fourth in a quick succession of treaties between Persia and Great Britain early in the 19th century. It was negotiated on behalf of the British government by Sir Henry Ellis and James Morier and signed on 25 November, 1814. The Treaty became the basis for relations between Persia and Great Britain for the next half-century. It was a revision of the **Definitive Treaty of 1812**, particularly in those clauses which bound Britain to aid Persia in the event its sovereignty was violated. With the defeat of Napoleon in Europe, the British were less interested in aiding **Fath Ali Shah**. This watered-down version of the Definitive Treaty of 1812 still offered British military assistance or an annual war subsidy along with weapons if Persia was attacked by a foreign state, but did not extend the fullness of military aid that had been forthcoming while hostilites were continuing between Persia and Russia. This was a disappointment since Persia still considered itself threatened by Russia, even after the **Treaty of Gulistan** in 1813 which ended the long, drawn-out first Irano-Russian War. After the treaty was signed, Britain withdrew the majority of its military presence from Persia and delayed subsidy payments and arms shipments. Eventually, Britain bought its way entirely out of the entangling clauses by agreeing to pay an indemnity to Persia to mollify the harsh terms of the 1828 **Treaty of Turkman-chai** which ended the second Irano-Russian War. *See also* ABBAS MIRZA; QAJAR DYNASTY.

TEHRAN UNIVERSITY. Tehran University was established in 1935 with programs in arts, science, medicine, law, and engineering. The areas of theology, fine arts, and **agriculture** were later additions. The predominately secular university opened its doors to **women** in 1937 as part of the educational reform program of **Reza Shah**. By the early 1960s, the curriculum equaled that of other major world universities. In 1967, the Administrative Council was formed to make the school independent financially and administratively. Enrollment had swelled to 20,000 students by the early 1970s, and 17 distinct faculties composed the university by the mid-1970s.

On 21 January 1962, Tehran University was the scene of an unprovoked attack by government troops on unarmed students holding a political demonstration against the regime of **Muhammad Reza Shah**. The sheer brutality of the attack deepened the anti-government stance of many Iranian students. The relationship of the university with the government was often strained. On the one hand, the government needed the universities, Tehran University being the largest and most important, to provide the talent and skills necessary for economic development. On the other hand, many of the political and social ideas circulating in the university environment were anathema to the regime.

Large numbers of Tehran University students were active in the revolutionary movement that brought the **Pahlavi Dynasty** to an end. In the early days of the **Provisional Government**, the university was the site of occasional significant political announcements, particularly in the course of the mass prayer sessions held on campus each Friday. However, when the religio-political views of **Ayatollah Ruhollah Khomeini** prevailed nationally, increasing distrust occurred between the government and the intellectual class, heavily represented by Tehran University and its sister institutions of higher **education**. The **student dormitory attacks** at Tehran University during the "liberalization" period of the 1990s (after the election of President **Muhammad Khatami**) served as notice of the continuing uneasy relationship between government and universities. *See also* MELLI UNIVERSITY; PAHLAVI UNIVERSITY.

TOBACCO REVOLT. The seeds for the Tobacco Revolt were sown in 1890 when **Naser al-Din Shah** granted Britain's Major Gerald Talbot a 50-year concession on the production, sale, and export of the nation's entire tobacco crop. The granting of monopolistic concessions to foreign interests was not new, but previous concessions had involved undeveloped resources. The tobacco **industry** in Iran was flourishing. The producers and merchants were incensed by the idea that the products they had grown and the businesses they owned would now be under the influence of foreigners.

The strong negative feelings of the public were played on by the ulama who had been dissatisfied with foreign intervention in national affairs for many years. Supported by Russia, the clergy spearheaded a drive to have the concession revoked. The population responded en masse, and an alliance was formed across all social classes. Demonstrations and protests were widespread. The Shah, unaccustomed to massive organized opposition, responded by having the protesters arrested. These skirmishes continued until the end of 1891 when an influential member of the ulama called for a boycott of tobacco products until the concession was revoked.

The response was universal and the Shah was forced to cancel the concession and pay 500,000 pounds as compensation to Talbot's Imperial Tobacco Corporation. Ironically, the money was loaned to the Iranian government by the British Imperial Bank of Iran. This was the first of many loans which heightened Russian and British economic penetration and influence in Iran.

The Tobacco Revolt marked the beginning of popular defiance by Iranians against the economically damaging transactions being negotiated between the government and foreign powers. In this sense, it was an important precursor to the **Constitutional Revolution of 1906**. *See also* QAJAR DYNASTY.

TRADE. Trade is important to the Iranian **economy**. In 2004, imports to Iran were valued at $31.3 billion and consisted of industrial raw materials and intermediate goods, capital goods, foodstuffs and other consumer goods, technical services, and military supplies. Significant import partners and their percentages of Iran's total imports include the following: Germany, 12.8; France, 8.3; Italy, 7.7; China, 7.2; the United Arab Emirates, 7.2; South Korea, 6.1; and Russia, 5.4 percent. Notably lacking is the United States which has minimal economic interaction with Iran dating back to the **Islamic Revolution**, the holding of **American Hostages in Iran**, and the resulting economic sanctions. These sanctions are largely in effect to the present day over a quarter of a century later.

The value of exports in 2004 was $38.79 billion, exceeding the value of imports by more than $7 billion. This disparity has prevailed for a number of years and Iran accumulated by 2005 a positive foreign exchange balance of over $50 billion. Exports consist mainly of **oil**, natural gas, minerals, chemical and petrochemical products, fruits, nuts, caviar, and carpets. Chief export partners by percentage of total exports in 2004 include the following: Japan, 18.4; China, 9.7; Italy, 6; South Africa, 5.8; South Korea, 5.4; Taiwan, 4.6; Turkey, 4.4; and the Netherlands, 4 percent.

While other sectors of the economy do play a role in Iranian export trade, most particularly **agriculture** and handicrafts (carpets), the natural resources dominate. Mineral exports, led by copper, are substantial, but pale in comparison to the amount and value of fossil fuel exports, especially oil. Fossil fuels account for the vast majority of export trade, some 80 percent, and provide a disproportionate amount of the national income. In the foreseeable future, Iranian trade will continue to be dominated by the oil and natural gas industries.

TRANS-IRANIAN RAILWAY. The Trans-Iranian Railway, planned and constructed during the reign of **Reza Shah**, began operations in 1938 after 11 years of construction. It ran 865 miles—from the new port of Bandar Shahpur on the Persian Gulf, through **Tehran**, to Bandar Shah on the **Caspian Sea**. The Shah had shunned foreign loans in order to avoid outside influence, and financed the construction costs with revenues from state-owned **industry** and inflated taxes on commodities, especially sugar and tea. Though non-Iranians were hired to work on the project, they were generally assigned subordinate positions, and job seekers from smaller countries were favored over those from Great Britain and Russia in order to minimize the pervasive influence of those two countries.

The project cost $150 million to complete. New **oil** revenues became available to help offset the cost. The railway increased military effectiveness, enhanced government control in the rural areas, and spurred the domestic **economy**. The Trans-Iranian Railway was viewed as a symbol of the Shah's "new Iran," an important asset to his progressive modernization and nationalistic programs.

Due to the strategic location of the railway, concern among the Allies regarding Reza Shah's presumed sympathies with Germany prompted Russia and Britain to occupy Iran from 1941 until the end of World War II. The invasion of neutral Iran by the

Allied powers led directly to the abdication of Reza Shah in 1941, and to his replacement on the throne by his young son, **Muhammad Reza Shah**. The physical presence of the Allied powers secured the rail lines for the shipment of American lend-lease military supplies being sent to Russia via the Persian Gulf. This event marked the first large-scale American presence in Iran, and set the stage for the substitution of American for British influence in Iran after the war.

Expansion of the railway continued following the war. Lines were constructed connecting once remote areas in the far provinces with Tehran, and in 1971 a line was completed which allowed passengers to travel from Iran to Europe by train via the Turkish Rail System. Into the 1980s, the Trans-Iranian Railway transported almost four million passengers per year and carried more than 50 million tons of freight annually, remaining the single most important communication route in Iran, and it continues this importance to the present day. *See also* RAILROADS.

TRANSPORTATION. The transportation system in Iran is better than many third-world countries, but less developed than more economically advanced countries. Compared with first world countries, for instance, Iran has a very low number of airports and helipads. It has a total of 305 airports with only 127 of the railways being paved. It possesses only 40 airports total that have runways of over 3,047 meters. There are only 13 heliports in the entire country. There is a state-owned airline, **Iran Air**, which covers the country.

Iran does, however, possess a high number of **oil** and natural gas pipelines due to its reliance upon the revenue of such products for its economic success. It has 17,000 kilometers of gas pipeline, 570 kilometers of liquid petroleum gas pipeline, 8,256 kilometers of oil pipeline, and 7,817 kilometers of refined oil pipeline.

The rugged geography of Iran has made the development of transportation facilities a formidable task. Furthermore, Iran as a country started rather late in developing transportation infrastructure as a matter of state policy due to political factors. There have been major strides in developing a railroad network, not begun until the 1930s under **Reza Shah** and a process that continues to the present day. The building of the **Trans-Iranian Railway** has been a major factor in Iranian transportation and, given the difficulties overcome to build it through mountainous terrain, the railway was also a major engineering feat. Iranian state railways today cover much of the country (See Appendix map of Iranian **railroads**).

Iran only has 850 kilometers of waterways. This distance exists solely on the **Karun River** and Lake **Urmieh**. The number of merchant ships registered in Iran is 144. The majority of these ships are cargo and oil transportation vessels.

Roadways are also limited within Iran. There are (as of 2004) a total of 167,157 kilometers of highway. Only 94,109 kilometers of these are paved highway. The **Islamic Republic** made an attempt, particularly in the early post-**Islamic Revolution** years, to facilitate rural road construction. Nonetheless, the Iranian road network remains thin.

TREATY OF ERZERUM (1847). *See* SHATT AL-ARAB.

TREATY OF FINKENSTEIN (1807). The Treaty of Finkenstein was signed in Poland (Prussia) by Napoleon and a representative of the **Qajar** king **Fath Ali Shah**, on 4 May, 1807. It sealed a new alliance between Persia and France and largely came about due to the refusal of the British to aid the Persian forces against Czarist Russia's expansion into Persia's Caucasian provinces. Persia declared war on Great Britain and ended relations with her former ally. In this new treaty, the Shah guaranteed passage for French expeditionary forces through Persia to India. Engaged at the time of signing in a campaign against Russia, Napoleon had even larger ambitions to invade British India and Persia was seen as a stepping stone. Under the terms of the treaty the French sent a military and commercial mission to **Tehran**, led by General Gardane. Gardane was to begin training Persian soldiers and officers for combat against Russian forces in Georgia and to establish munition factories. His efforts were undermined when the very same year (1807) France signed the Treaty of Tilsit with Russia which, in light of the primary Persian interest of military help against Russia, destroyed the Franco-Persian Alliance. This event reopened the door for British influence in Persia. *See also* PRELIMINARY TREATY OF FRIENDSHIP AND ALLIANCE.

TREATY OF GULISTAN (1813). The signing of the Treaty of Gulistan on 13 October, 1813 temporarily ended the long hostilities between Russia and Persia which dated back to the attempts of **Agha Muhammad Khan Qajar** to reestablish Persian hegemony in the Caucasus. The defeat of Napoleon in Russia in 1812 had allowed greater allocation of Russian resources to the Caucasus, and led to a series of military defeats which prompted Persia to seek a negotiated settlement. The Treaty was negotiated with British mediation and the conditions were notably unfavorable for Persia. By its terms, Persia lost five of its Caucasian provinces and granted sole naval supremacy to Russia in the **Caspian Sea**, leaving Persia's northern border vulnerable to future Russian invasion. Advantageous commercial arrangements regarding tariffs and **trade** regulation were also granted to Russia. Several clauses in the Treaty proved to be troublesome, particularly one in which Russia promised recognition and support to the "legitimate" heir to the Persian throne and another which realigned the border between the two countries. Both were vague enough to promise future misinterpretation and encourage Russian interference in the internal affairs of Iran.

　　Clearly, both sides regarded the Treaty of Gulistan as more a truce than a treaty—an interruption rather than a decisive ending to the ongoing conflict between the two countries. Continuing incidents led to the resumption of hostilities once again years later. The result was a disastrous defeat for Persia, concluding with the **Treaty of Turkmanchai** in 1828. *See also* FATH ALI SHAH; QAJAR DYNASTY.

TREATY OF TURKMANCHAI (1828). The Treaty of Turkmanchai was signed between the Russian Empire and Persia on 21 February, 1828. It ended hostilities that had broken out a second time between the two countries in 1826. Persian forces were overwhelmingly defeated, and disastrous terms were dictated which set the course for relations between Russia and Iran for nearly a century. John MacDonald, British envoy in **Tabriz**, and his assistant, John McNeill, played an intermediary role by arranging a cease-fire and the eventual withdrawal of Russian expeditionary forces in **Azerbaijan**. All prisoners of war were to be returned, and Russian defectors were not to be permitted to serve in Persian military units near the new Russian-Iranian frontier. Extra-territorial rights were granted to Russian subjects, rights later granted to the subjects of other European powers. Significant tariff and economic benefits for Russia were negotiated. Exclusive navigation rights were granted to Russia in the **Caspian Sea**. As part of the Treaty, Persia lost all territory north of the Aras River and was forced to pay a massive war indemnity, an impossibility for the state of the **economy** which existed in Persia.

To mollify the harsh financial terms, the British stepped in and granted 200,000 pounds sterling to Persia, purportedly under the terms of the **Tehran Treaty of 1814**. This Treaty did not, however, apply in this case since Persia initiated the hostilities with Russia. The British thus leveraged the odious financial burden dictated by Russia in the Treaty of Turkmanchai to change the terms of the very agreement under which they provided the means to reduce the indemnity Persia was obligated to pay to Russia. Persia agreed to nullify that part of the agreement formalized in the Tehran Treaty of 1814 with Britain which obliged the British to provide military aid to Persia if attacked. The British government saw no real benefit mediating the conflicts between the Persians and the Russians and used this opportunity to abandon their prior obligations.

Ironically, the harshness of the terms of the Treaty of Turkmanchai contributed significantly to a reawakening of British concern over the extension of rival European Power influence in the affairs of Persia, a concern which had originally been caused by the extension of French influence and had been addressed in earlier treaties between Persia and Britain. The Treaty of Turkmanchai signaled the substitution of Russia for France as the chief contender for foreign influence at the Persian Court. It also established the continuing framework for Great Power interactions with Persia for the remainder of the 19th and well into the 20th century. *See also* DEFINITIVE TREATY OF 1812; QAJAR DYNASTY; TREATY OF GULISTAN.

TRIBES. Tribalism in Iran developed as a political, economic, and social organizing structure during the course of conquests and the migrations onto the **Iranian Plateau** of diverse populations through the millennia.

Many of these "immigrants" still identify themselves primarily as tribesmembers, considering themselves to be "citizens" of a particular tribe rather than citizens of the Iranian nation-state. A number of tribes inhabit trans-border regions which encompass tribal territory and disregard nation-state political boundaries which are often seen as arbitrary. The rugged and mountainous geography of the Iranian Plateau has contributed to the multiplication of distinct tribes and tribal groupings and their continued existence. In addition, the continuing tradition of hereditary tribal chiefs as head of "state" contributes to the maintenance of tribal insularity.

Twentieth-century government reform programs such as land redistribution and the nationalization of forests and pasturelands, along with national construction projects such as roads and dams, have economically damaged and linguistically, and geographically fragmented some tribal groups. Though many discrete tribal/ethnic groups remain, the distinct physical and cultural differences have softened through long contact with others.

Listed on the previous two pages are the most significant tribal population groups found in Iran today, along with their locale, estimated population and characteristics such as language, religion, and economic base. These are the **Afshar**, **Arabs**, **Bakhtiari**, **Baluchi**, **Kurds**, **Qashqai**, **Shahsevan**, **Lurs**, and the **Turkoman**. There are also smaller tribal/ethnic groups, too numerous to mention, scattered throughout the country. Tribes account for approximately 15 percent of the total population of the Iranian nation-state. Because of the nomadic nature of most of the tribes, accurate population figures are impossible to compile.

MAJOR TRIBAL GROUPS OF IRAN

TRIBE	LOCALE	EST. POP	% OF TOTAL
AFSHAR	Kerman Province Western Iran	90,000.	2%
ARABS	Khuzistan Persian Gulf Coast	1,000,000	3.0%
BAKHTIARI	Khuzistan Central Zagros Esfahan	250,000	.5%
BALUCHI	Baluchistan	500,000	1.0%
KURDS	Kurdistan	4,000,000 Bakhtaran W. Azerbaijan	7.0%
LURS	Luristan	500,000	1.0%
QASHQAI	Fars Khuzistan	250,000	.5%
SHAHSEVAN	Azerbaijan	50,000	.1%
TURKOMAN	Eastern Caspian Coastal Plain	1,000,000	2.0%

MAJOR TRIBAL GROUPS OF IRAN

LANGUAGE	RELIGION	ECONOMIC BASE
Turkish	Shiah Muslim	Nomadic pastoralists
Arabic	Sunni/Shiah Muslim	Farmers Nomadic pastoralists
Bakhtiari	Shiah Muslim	Farmers Nomadic pastoralists
Baluchi	Sunni Muslim	Nomadic pastoralists
Kurdish	Sunni Muslim	Farmers Nomadic pastoralists
Luri	Shiah Muslim	Semi-nomadic pastoralists
Qashqai	Shiah	MuslimFarmers Semi-nomadic pastoralists Weavers
Turkish	Shiah Muslim	Nomadic pastoralists
Turkomani	Sunni Muslim	Carpetmakers Horsebreeders Farmers

Table 2
Note: Population figures based on 1996 census estimate.

Major Tribal Groups

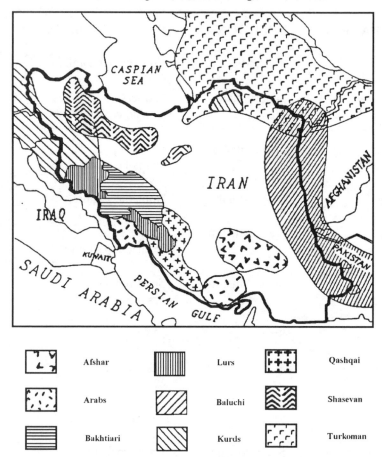

	Afshar		Lurs		Qashqai
	Arabs		Baluchi		Shasevan
	Bakhtiari		Kurds		Turkoman

Figure 6

The figures indicated, while drawn from the most recent demographic information, are estimates that have been collected from widely varying sources. *See also* ALBORZ MOUNTAINS; BALUCHISTAN; KHUZISTAN; ZAGROS MOUNTAINS.

TUDEH PARTY. The Tudeh (Masses) Party is Iran's Communist organization which was heavily influenced and supported by the former Soviet Union and East German regimes. Forerunners were the Persian Social Democratic Party (1904) and the Iranian Justice Party (1917). In 1941, Marxist intellectuals developed the modern ideological platform and began overt activities throughout the country.

The Tudeh was responsible for the 1949 assassination attempt on **Muhammad Reza Shah** and strongly supported the nationalistic policies of **Muhammad Mossadeq** during his tenure. The party also used this period (1951-1953) to exploit the revolutionary mood of Iran to its advantage. When the Shah returned in 1953, the Tudeh Party became the target of government reprisals and was forced to operate covertly. Bolstered by foreign support, the party encouraged the formation of radical movements, particularly among Iranian students in Western universities. Dissident leftist movements within Iran were never directly identified with the Tudeh although their goals were obviously parallel.

Following the 1979 **Islamic Revolution**, the party realigned its image, replacing its basic anti-**Islam** stance in order to conform with the clerical influence in the new government. Tolerated by the regime, the Tudeh began a well-organized propaganda campaign designed to capitalize on the internal disarray which marked the post-revolutionary period. This revitalized version of the party alarmed the government of the **Islamic Republic**, and in 1983 the Tudeh was dissolved by the Islamic regime. Party leaders were executed as "instruments of Soviet foreign policy" and the remaining membership was once again forced underground.

With the dissolution of the Soviet Union and the reunification of East and West Germany, the international support system of the party has eroded tremendously, casting doubt on the future of Tudeh influence in Iranian political affairs. *See also* NATIONAL FRONT.

TURKOMAN. The Turkoman of Iran originated from the immigration of Turko-Mongolian **tribes** from the area of inner Asia. Most came during the Seljuk period of the 11th century, though there is evidence of much earlier migration into the large frontier zone referred to as the **Khorasan**-Central Asian frontier. Overall, there are nine Turkoman tribes spread throughout the geographical region of Khorasan, all of which speak an Eastern Oghuz-Turkish dialect, the same language spoken in the Republic of Turmenistan.

While not all Turkoman tribes are present in Iran, several including the Yomut, live in the fertile Gorgan plains to the east of the **Caspian Sea** near Iran's border with Turmenistan. In the past, many tribes crossed state borders freely until groups were divided permanently among Russia, Afghanistan, and Iran in 1885.

The Turkoman, unlike some of the tribes of Iran such as the **Shahsevan** or **Afshar**, have a common ethnicity as well as a tribal form of social and political organization. This has not necessarily led to a well-developed national minority consciousness or a movement demanding regional autonomy within the Iranian state, as happened, for instance, amongst the **Kurds**. Such a consciousness has occasionally surfaced, as it did in response to the land reform efforts of **Muhammad Reza Shah** in the 1960s as part of the **White Revolution**. For the most part, however, the Turkoman have remained politically quiescent throughout the 20th century and into the 21st century. A notable exception was the disturbances that took place in the Gorgan area in 1979 after the **Islamic Revolution**. These were mainly over issues of land tenure and ownership, however, rather than any organized movement towards autonomy.

The Turkoman are the second-largest Turkish-speaking population in Iran, their numbers estimated at over a quarter million. The majority are Sunni Muslim, following the Hanafi branch of Islamic law.

TWELVER SHI'ISM. *See* HIDDEN IMAM; IMAM ALI; IMAM HUSSEIN.

-U-

URMIEH. Urmieh is the provincial capital of Western **Azerbaijan** in the extreme northwest of Iran. It lies about 1,300 meters (4,290 feet) above sea level. Urmieh has 435,200 inhabitants (according to a 1996 census) with diverse ethnic and religious backgrounds. There are **Christians** from a variety of sects, most significantly the Chaldean Assyrians, and Muslims of Persian, Kurdish, and Turkish ethnicity, living in Urmieh. Around 1900, Christians respresented about half the population in Urmieh, but now represent a much smaller percentage.

According to legend, Urmieh is the birthplace of Zoroaster and the burial site of one of the Three Magi. Local Christians believe that the city was visited by the Three Wise Men on the way to Bethlehem.

Due to the large Assyrian population, the city has hosted many Christian missions. In 1835, a mission representing the **American Board of Commissioners for Foreign Missions** was seated in Urmieh. **Justin Perkins** was the first American Protestant missionary to Iran, joined quickly by a medical missionary by the name of **Asahel Grant**. This Protestant inroad was followed by missions representing the French Lazarists in 1840, the British Anglicans in 1844, and a Russian Orthodox mission in 1902. The U.S. Presbyterian Church founded their own organization in Urmieh in 1870, the **Iran Mission**, which expanded the Protestant missionary thrust beyond the local Assyrian community to **Armenians** and Muslims.

The name of the city has changed several times. Known in historical times as Urmieh, it was called Rezaiyeh in the years 1930 to 1988 when the name was changed back to Urmieh. The city itself is surrounded by a wall and a ditch which can be flooded. There are extensive gardens and orchards in and around the city as it is situated in a fertile area of **agriculture**. The export of fruit and tobacco and a rug-making industry are important economic pillars. Of architectural significance is the Friday Mosque which dates to the Seljuk Period and is located in the **bazaar**. Urmieh has a covered bazaar which is reminiscent of the

Isfahan bazaar in the pattern of its traditional lines. It is built with domed vaults which have circular openings to provide ventilation and light.

Urmieh is located just 19 kilometers west from the largest body of water in Iran, Lake Urmieh (or Lake Rezaiyeh, which it is still often termed), which is about the size of the Great Salt Lake in Utah, but even saltier. The lake is so full of salt that it cannot support fish or other usual forms of life, and so salty that it never freezes despite a frigid winter climate. Flats around the lake contain a salty mud that is used to treat skin diseases and rheumatoid disorders. This is a prevalent practice in modern times and there are historical references to such treatment dating back to ancient times.

U.S.-IRANIAN RELATIONS AFTER THE ISLAMIC REVO-LUTION. From the mid 20th century, anti-American sentiment among the masses in Iran had been growing, but was checked by the efforts of the pro-Western king, **Muhammad Reza Shah** and **SAVAK**. The United States considered Iran a strategic, "stable" force in the Middle East, and the **Pahlavi** regime enjoyed the associated advantages of being America's bulwark against forces such as communism or anti-Israeli sentiments.

However, following the **Islamic Revolution** of 1979, which was steeped in anti-Americanism, the relations between the two countries rapidly deteriorated. Early in the revolution, the U.S. did attempt to maintain diplomatic relations with the more moderate **Provisional Government** of **Mehdi Bazargan**, and later of **Abol Hasan Bani-Sadr**, but paranoia amongst the more radical elements of the revolution elicited fear that these overtures to the government were a prelude to another incident like the overthrow of the **Muhammad Mossadeq** government in 1953, and the subsequent return of the Shah to power. With the capture of the U.S. embassy in Tehran in response to the Shah's admittance to the U.S. for cancer treatment, student captors (**Students Following the Imam's Line**) found intelligence documents alluding to contact between the Central Intelligence Agency and the Bazargan and Bani-Sadr administrations, further denigrating the moderates' stance with the **Ayatollah Ruhollah Khomeini** camp.

With the hostage crisis and the ouster or marginzalization of some Iranian moderates and liberals from the new **Islamic Republic**'s government, Washington and **Tehran** officially discontinued diplomatic recognition of one another. The United States also initiated a long series of economic sanctions against Iran, including the freezing of Iranian assets within American jurisdiction. To reach a resolution to the hostage crisis, Iran and the U.S. worked through Algeria as an intermediary in negotiations. Though not agreeing to all of the Iranian students' terms for release, the **Algerian Accords** was reached. In exchange for the hostages' release, the U.S. agreed, among other things, not to interfere in Iranian interests, to lift the freeze on assets, and to recover the Pahlavi family assets. After 444 days in captivity, the hostages were released only hours after Ronald Reagan's 1981 inauguration as a snub to the administration of Jimmy Carter.

During the **Iran-Iraq War** that dominated the 1980s, the United States, fearing an Iranian victory, began in 1983 to support Saddam Hussein's regime in Iraq after several years of neutrality. Iraq was no longer considered by America to be supportive of international terrorism, and soon found financial and intelligence aid from the U.S. forthcoming. This further entrenched an attitude of anti-Americanism in Iran. It seemed to Iranians that America would even support oppressive regimes to undermine the Islamic Republic. Since both superpowers, the U.S. and the USSR., had converged in supporting Iraq, Iran eventually felt coerced into a cease-fire, which occurred in 1988.

Ironically, at the same time, secret negotiations took place in 1985-1986 between Iran and members of the U.S. National Security Council. These officials, backed by President Reagan and the CIA, sought to acquire Iranian aid in recovering hostages held by Lebanese groups, in exchange for spare parts and weaponry, which Iran needed for its war effort. Though the mission was fraught with American ignorance—and controversy after it became public as the **Iran-Contra Arms Affair** in late 1986—it did mark a point at which, with the approval of both the American president (Reagan) and the Iranian *Faqih* (Khomeini), the two nations were able to approach some degree of direct communication.

Following the death of Khomeini in 1989, the Iranian dialogue began to include discussions of U.S.-Iranian relations, which had before been, at best, politically suicidal, and at worst, grounds for imprisonment in Iran. Even Iranian President **Ali Akbar Hashemi-Rafsanjani** discussed the concept. However, most discussions were tempered with the requirement that the United States must first show its good intentions before any true diplomatic intercourse could begin. The United States, from an Iranian perspective, certainly did not meet these requirements. Iranians were especially angered at what America called "dual-containment," which was aimed at keeping both Iran and Iraq from becoming a powerful entity. They also resented the continuing, albeit mostly ineffective, unilateral sanctions the United States enacted and imposed on Iran throughout the 1990s.

President **Muhammad Khatami**'s landslide election in 1997 breathed new life into the possibility of renewed diplomatic relations between Washington and Tehran. He urged the country to choose aspects of Western civilization that could help advance Iran and **Islam**, while eschewing the decadent, culturally degrading aspects of the West. Though discourse still took the stance that the United States had to make the first move, it became even more open, even in the midst of still strong conservative opposition, especially from the office of the *Faqih*, Supreme Leader **Ali Khamene'i**.

Even as Iran seemed on occasion to "leave the door open" to talks with the United States, America continued to seemingly act with belligerence towards the Islamic Republic. Following the terrorist attacks on New York and Washington on 11 September, 2001, both the U.S. and Iran sought to combat the brand of terrorism responsible. However, President George W. Bush, in his 2002 State of the Union Address, labeled Iran as part of an "Axis of Evil" with Iraq and North Korea, which rekindled much ire and paranoia towards America among Iranians. In addition, the Bush administration regularly expressed support of dissidents in Iran, strengthening the conservative elements of the Islamic Republic in their opposition to the more pragmatic and progressive elements in the Iranian government. These types of blunders and misunderstandings on both sides continue to typify the relationship between the two countries which still refuse to officially recognize one another, two and a half decades after the establishment of the Islamic Republic. *See also* BENJAMIN, SAMUEL GREEN WHEELER; ROOSEVELT, KERMIT; TEHRAN CONFERENCE.

-V-

VELAYAT-I FAQIH. *Velayat-i Faqih* refers to government by the Islamic jurist-scholar. This doctrine, which legitimizes the absolute authority of a supreme jurist, became a central issue in the formation of a constitution for the new **Islamic Republic. Ayatollah Ruhollah Khomeini** had expounded this theocratic political theory in his book of the same name and believed that an Islamic society must be guided by its principles, including the inseparability of church and state. He insisted on articles in the new **Constitution of the Islamic Republic of Iran** which provided for rule by a supreme jurist, or *Faqih*, until the return of the **Hidden Imam**. The concept was incorporated into the new constitution, though not without resistance on the part of those, including a considerable number of religious scholars, who feared that this position would concentrate unlimited power in one person, which in the wrong hands would be catastrophic. The views of Khomeini prevailed and he became the first supreme jurist of the new Islamic government. Subsequent history in the Islamic Republic has demonstrated the contentious nature of the concept of *Velayat-i Faqih*. There continue to be significant political differences in society over whether sovereignty lay with God or with the people. *See also* KHAMEIN'I, AYATOLLAH ALI; SOROUSH, ABDOLKARIM.

-W-

WHITE REVOLUTION. The White Revolution was a consolidated group of reforms initiated by **Muhammad Reza Shah** on

26 January, 1963, in order to broaden his power base. At the end of the 1950s, the majority of Iranians were among the poorest people in the world, even though Iran enjoyed great income from its **oil** production. Furthermore, the Iranian people lacked basic civil and political liberties. The Shah had a truly narrow power base: the military, the landlords, and the bureaucrats.

The United States began to apply pressure on Iran to introduce political, social, and economic reforms. The American government was particularly alarmed over the economic situation in Iran. Despite the millions of dollars flowing into the country from oil revenue and American aid, the **economy** was near bankruptcy. The U.S. attempt to stir reform was motivated largely by the desire to protect Western interests in the Persian Gulf. The American government offered the Shah $35 million in economic assistance, if he would appoint **Ali Amini** to the position of prime minister. The U.S. hoped that the pro-Western Amini, who was an economist, former Iranian ambassador to Washington, and had ties with the John F. Kennedy administration, would be able to implement the reform policies that they demanded.

In 1961, Amini was named prime minister and quickly instituted reforms. As a reluctant choice of the Shah, Amini was crippled from the start. Not only did the Shah perceive Amini as a threat, but the ulama also had reason to oppose him. They did not want to lose the large land holdings held in religious endowment (*vaqf*) which the proposed reform program of Amini would have entailed. Pressure from both the Shah and the ulama caused the Amini government to step down after only 14 months.

Once the Shah consolidated control, he took over Amini's reforms and turned them into his White Revolution. The reforms were supposed to initiate massive changes within Iran, without bloodshed, hence the term "White Revolution." The White Revolution called for social, political, and economic "democracy." There was also a call for social justice and economic and political independence from the West. Some areas of reform were successful to varying degrees, though there was no movement toward political democracy. The Shah did little to change the traditional political structure.

The reforms of the White Revolution did redefine the Iranian industrial and agrarian sectors. The heart of the reforms was the Third Five Year Plan that called for speedy development of **agriculture**, **industry**, and the social sectors. With the Land Reform Law of January 1962, the government purchased 16,000 villages, or approximately 19.5 percent of Iran's farmland, from landlords and gave control of plots to 743,406 peasant families. The landlords were restricted from owning more than one village. Furthermore, the government established collectives to guide the new farmers and give them assistance. Unfortunately, this program failed miserably due to the desire of the government to retain a strangling centralized control and the failure to fund it properly. Economically, the Third Plan was successful in that it increased Gross National Product (GNP) growth by 12.7 percent, 2.7 percent higher than expected. Many new factories were built and industrial employment increased dramatically. And, as part of the more independent stance it was trying to carve out, Iran normalized relations with the Soviet Union and declared that no foreign military bases would be built on her soil.

However, the Shah ran into similar problems with the ulama as had Amini. The Land Reform Law included religiously endowed land and the ulama saw this as an attack upon an important resource base of their traditional power. Some ulama began to attack the White Revolution and cause public protest which erupted violently in June, 1963. This is when the first direct clash between the Shah and the **Ayatollah Ruhollah Khomeini** occurred, an event which led to Khomeini's exile in Iraq.

The offical name of the White Revolution was the Revolution of the People and the Shah. But, "the People" never adopted the Revolution as their own. It was always perceived for what it was, an imposition from above.

Ultimately, the White Revolution failed, not as an economic plan, but in the imbalances it caused as rapid development in the economic sector found no parallel in the political sphere and resulted in major social disruptions. *See also* LITERACY CORPS.

WILBER, DONALD N. (1907-1997). Donald Wilber was a specialist in Iranian history and a recognized expert on Iranian architecture. He served in the Office of Strategic Services (OSS) in Iran during World War II and as a consultant to the Central Intelligence Agency (CIA) from 1947-1969. Wilber was one of the American participants in **Kermit Roosevelt**'s CIA intervention operation (Operation Ajax), which ousted Prime Minister **Muhammad Mossadeq** in 1953 and restored **Muhammad Reza Shah** to the throne.

A prolific and influential author, Wilber has written numerous books on Iran. These include a general history entitled *Iran: Past and Present*, which has been released through nine editions, and several highly regarded books on Iranian gardens and architecture. He was a dedicated supporter of the **Pahlavi Dynasty** and his writing largely ignored or misinterpreted the social and political problems in Iran, even during the turbulent events of the 1960s.

WOMEN. The core of women's history in Iran begins in the 19th century and evolves along with Iran's political landscape into the current women's movement. Dozens of Iranian women have made an impact in the modern world on religion, politics, and status beginning with the 1814 birth of Fatima, a daughter of a well-known religious leader in Ghazvin. At the age of 14, Fatima, who had been well educated in various fields including language, **literature**, and religion, was married to a prominent religious leader. During time spent in Iraq with her husband, Fatima became familiar with the **Babi Movement** which alienated her from her family and husband. Concern with the egalitarian treatment of women allowed Fatima an outlet and she began participating in public debates, often unveiled. This habit caused even her fellow Babi's to recoil and often caused her to move to another city.

Fatima's outspoken vigor for her cause led to the creation of the first women's organization in Iran, a group of prominent women who began meeting regularly and spreading their beliefs throughout the country. Fatima, known by this time as **Tahereh Qurrat al-Ayn**, took a leading role, gaining the support of several royal women. In 1848, Tahireh attended a gathering of now exiled Babi leaders where she tore off her veil and demanded liberation of women. Even though the leadership was torn, her action caused her arrest and exile. In 1852, after escape and re-capture in **Tehran**, Tahereh was executed along with other Babi leaders, after an abortive Babi assassination attempt on the life of the **Qajar** Shah.

The actions of the Babi women's groups, and the **Bahai** groups that would follow them were progressive for their day though their sectarian qualities stunted their growth and abilities. Nevertheless, the way was paved by Tahereh for women such as Taj Saltaneh, daughter of **Naser al-Din Shah**, who criticized the failure of Iran's social and political institutions, admonishing the disgraceful state of women and the practice of veiling. Royal Servant Bibi Khanom Astarabadi composed a pamphlet called "The Shortcomings of Men" in which she attacked a popular training text for women as derogatory, insisting that the author only understood complete subjugation of women.

Women became a political force in Iran during such events as the **Tobacco Revolt** where masses of women took to the streets in demonstration. As the **Constitutional Movement** swept Iran in the early 1900s, women began rejecting foreign goods in favor of domestic cloth and other items, and began sell-ing their jewelry and offering their dowries toward funds to es-tablish the national bank. However, neither the Constitution of 1906 nor any subsequent law granted women equal rights and opportunities, only reinforcing the common conception that women and their **education** should focus only on home life, child rearing, and preserving the honor of the family. And, fam-ily law remained determined by Islamic Law (Sharia).

Iranian women began to organize officially in the early 1900s using education of women as their primary focus. Chris-tian missionary groups had been operating girls' schools in Iran since 1838, though Muslim students were barred until the 1870s. In January 1907, a conference of women in Tehran resolved to establish schools for girls and to abolish dowries, using the money instead for female education. The attendees began to es-tablish schools in their homes and other available structures, though they met with severe opposition and frequent threats from political and religious realms. However, by 1913, the nine existing women's societies in Iran were educating nearly 2,500 students in 63 schools in Tehran. These schools allowed for the first generation of formally educated and prominent women in Iran and women's societies flourished. In 1918, the first girls' school was opened in **Isfahan** by a publisher named Sadigeh Dawlatabadi, who was later among the first women to appear in public unveiled. In only a few years, girls' schools were opened in all major Iranian cities. Though some were burned and all were under constant threat, the schools managed to endure.

Women were beginning to express themselves in print by publishing magazines. Dawlatabadi was the third women to become a publisher, after the example set by Navabeh Safavi in 1912 with her publication *Jahan-i Zanan (Women's World)*. In 1920, Fakher Afaghi Parsa, mother of the first woman minister of Iran, published a magazine from **Mashhad** which prompted violent opposition from religious groups forcing her to escape into exile. By the 1930s, however, 14 women's magazines would be in distribution, discussing women's rights, veiling, and education.

In 1926 **Reza Shah** came to power bringing changes and reform to Iranian life, and especially for women. After Sadigeh Dawlatabadi's public appearance in European clothing the same year, the attire was approved by the new government. At this time it was decided that all government employees were to dress in Western attire at work and federal taxes were removed from ladies hat's. Four years later, a civil code was approved allowing women to request divorce under appropriate conditions and the legal marriage age was raised to 15. Though this code was secular in origin, the family law itself remained under Islamic Law.

The Oriental Feminine Congress was held in Tehran in 1932, where Iranian women demanded voting privileges, equal pay for women, a ban on polygamy, and compulsory education for both boys and girls. The demands met much resistance from the traditional societal majority, though the progressive attempt was encouraged by the **Pahlavi** government. Four years later, veiling was officially banned and a national education system was formed to include both boys and girls. The same year 12 female students were admitted to **Tehran University**, becoming the first women to attend.

Dozens of women's organizations and societies were established and active throughout Iran by the mid-20th century. In 1951, Mehrangiz Dawlatshahi and Safeyeh Firuz formed *Rah-i Nou (The New Way)*, the first Iranian human rights group, and demanded voting rights. As with previous demands, religious opposition squelched the movement. Finally in 1963, women were granted the right to vote and to be voted into office. Five years later divorce was referred to family courts, progress was made with divorce law, the marriage age was raised to 18, and polygamy was restricted by requiring the first wife's consent. Shortly thereafter, abortion, though never legalized, lost its severe penalties making it more accessible. Reforms began that would allow for family planning as a means of population control, and as a response to a call for new employment, women were permitted to sit as judges and to volunteer for military service as "soldiers" of either knowledge or health, acting as village teachers or doctors.

The **Women's Organization of Iran** (WOI) was founded in 1966 with the blessing and a high level of support from the government. The intent of the WOI was to provide social services to women and it was headed by the sister of the ruling monarch, Princess Ashraf Pahlavi. The women's rights activist, **Mahnaz Afkhami**, served as secretary-general of the WOI and also served as minister of state for women's affairs in the cabinet-level position established to look after women's issues in the late Pahlavi era.

As the **Islamic Revolution** approached, the variance in women's behavior and how they responded to changes of status of women in Iran was highly influenced by their economic conditions. Upper and secular middle-class women frequently worked outside the home as professionals, while traditional middle-class women worked only out of necessity. Lower-class women, unless extremely traditional, often worked outside the home as their income was essential to the family. By 1977, two million women were present in the Iranian workforce, 190,000 of whom were professionals with university degrees.

Women of all backgrounds were active participants in the Islamic Revolution. Many came from the ranks of the professional middle class. It was this group where education and political understanding brought nationalist sympathy and resentment for the image of **Muhammad Reza Shah** as a pawn of the United States. More substantial, however, were the large numbers of traditional lower-class women who responded to the call of religious leader **Ayatollah Ruhollah Khomeini**. Female student **Massoumeh Ebtekar**, acting as the spokesperson for the **Students Following the Imam's Line** who took the American embassy hostage in November 1979, became a familiar face of the revolution in the U.S. Their participation in the toppling of the Shah compelled the new government to see women's participation in social and political affairs as legitimate and necessary, though at the same time the revolutionary government held strict traditional beliefs that kept Iranian women tied to traditional roles.

After the revolution, the power shifted away from the secular upper class to the traditional middle class that defended a segregated society and a traditional woman's role. Laws that had reflected progress in women's rights were repealed and new laws were enacted that supported more traditional roles, thereby restricting women's rights, using the reasoning that laws contradictory to Islamic Law should be revoked. Among the new laws was compulsory veiling of the hair and skin (excepting only the face and hands), a ban on women judges, reduction of women's military service to only clerical work, a revocation of family planning and population control policies, and a reduction in the marriage age to 13, which also left complete rights of determining marriage to the father or paternal grandfather.

While the segregation of society forced many women to work in facilities serving women only, some in power foresaw resistance and future protest and moved toward what would be called the "moderate" view. This view is touted by some as progress, but condemned by others as a pacifier. However, the 1997 landside election of President **Muhammad Khatami**, due in part to the support of women voters urging progress, proved that women in Iran are active, as they have been for the past century in determining the fate of their country's policy and future.

Currently, and regardless of policy, women are ever present in Iranian academia, business, and politics. In 2000, 53 percent of all candidates sitting for university entrance exams were women and during the same year over half of the students accepted to attend were women. Access to higher education has allowed women to excel in the workforce where, between 1998 and 2000, nearly 1,000 women either earned executive positions or retained such positions. During the presidency of Khatami, three women served as advisors, two-thirds of government ministries had a woman as either director general or deputy director, and Massoumeh Ebtekar, the student revolutionary, was named vice president in 1997.

The arts have become a platform for Iranian women to speak out to their country and the global community concerning their lives and conditions. Many Iranian women have found success in **poetry**, fiction, and visual arts. The number of significant women contributors to the field of literature is remarkable. To mention only a few of the 20th century, one can point to **Parvin E'tesami**, **Simin Behbahani**, **Simin Daneshvar**, and **Forugh Farrokhzad**.

Of particular note in more recent times is the emergence of women film directors. While the contemporary Iranian film **industry** itself is intensely political, several women filmmakers have found in it a voice, as well as international acclaim. In 2000, 19-year-old **Samira Makhmalbaf** became the youngest prize winner in the history of the Cannes Film Festival for her second film, *Blackboards*. At the award ceremony, Makhmalbaf broke even more ground by speaking on the prospect of democracy and women's equality in Iran. Director **Rakhshan Bani-Etemad** uses her documentaries and films, including *Nargess* and *Lady in May*, to confront taboo issues of crime, divorce, and polygamy in Iranian life. As the Islamic Revolution becomes more distant, **cinema** is playing a more important role in communicating the role of women in Iran and the relationship between the revolution and progress. For example, the **Ja'far**

Panahi film *The Circle* is a bold fictional account of female life in Iran from motherhood to prostitution.

Attorney and women's rights activist **Mehrangiz Kar** sees exposing these taboo subjects as a way of eliminating the control of religious traditionalism in Iran. Kar feels that those conservative clerics holding key positions see women's rights and freedoms as an acceptance of unnecessary modernity and "Western permissiveness." "To them," she says, "modernizing models using such 'western' concepts as freedom, equality and individualism amount to a challenge in defiance of **Islam** . . . The most powerful opponent of human rights of women in Iran is a mentality that attacks these values in the guise of religion and in the name of religiosity." Iranian women have indeed come a long way. And, whatever the ruling system may be in Iran, women will continue to make their voice, and presence, known. *See also* ZAN NEWSPAPER; ZANAN MAGAZINE.

WOMEN'S ORGANIZATION OF IRAN (WOI). The **Women**'s Organization of Iran was formed in 1966 at the behest of **Muhammad Reza Shah** to oversee the efforts of various women's groups in Iran. Its charter designated the organization as a nonpolitical body whose aim was to provide a variety of social services to women of the lower classes.

The most significant contribution of the WOI was the creation of a network of Family Welfare Centers throughout the country. Women were able to receive vocational training, legal counsel, literacy instruction, health care, and child-care facilitation. By 1977, there were 94 centers providing these services.

The non-political status of the WOI changed in 1975 with the adoption of a one-party political system. The core membership based in **Tehran** became a strong lobbying group, and was influential in the passage of legislation legalizing abortion in 1977. Their position was weakened by the need to conceal the reforms they initiated from conservative Muslims. As a result, many women never became aware of the benefits accorded them by the new laws.

Internal criticism of the WOI centered on its elite governing structure and its reliance on government funding. Local-level ideas and opinions tended to be subordinated, thanks to leadership positions that mostly revolved among a pro-government, wealthy elite. Indeed, the single president of the WOI from its beginning was Princess Ashraf **Pahlavi**, sister of the Shah. Many perceived the organization as a vehicle used by the Pahlavi regime to impress the West with its progressive attitudes towards women's rights. Others felt that with the failure to inform women of their new rights or to initiate programs to implement reform, it did little to change the position of women in Iranian society. The organization dissolved under the impact of the **Islamic Revolution**. *See also* AFKHAMI, MAHNAZ; WOMEN.

-Y-

YARSHATER, EHSAN (1920-). Ehsan Yarshater was born in **Hamadan**. He studied Persian **literature** at **Tehran University** from which he received a doctorate in 1947. He received an M.A. degree in 1953 in Iranian linguistics at the University of London, and with an intervening stint of teaching ancient languages at Tehran University, a Ph.D. in 1960. In 1961, he took up a teaching post at Columbia University where he has remained to the present day.

Though long retired from teaching, Yashater has remained active in the field of Iranian studies, and has for many years been a tireless contributor and promoter of Iranian studies. He has been a prolific scholar writing a large number of highly regarded articles and books. The work he is most associated with, however, is the massive undertaking he conceived and has prepared for over three decades, the *Encyclopedia Iranica*. Begun in the early 1970s and still incomplete, this many volumed work is the ultimate guide in the field of Iranian studies. Fascicles continue to appear under the auspices of the Center for Iranian Studies, which Yashater founded at Columbia University in 1966. Few would question the importance of this work as the most reliable scholarly reference work on Iran and, once completed, it is likely to hold a place of high regard for the indefinite future.

A major contributor to the field of Iranian Studies, Yashater will long be remembered both for the high integrity of his scholarship and for his guidance and encouragement of several generations of Iranian scholars.

YAZDI, IBRAHIM (1931-). Ibrahim Yazdi became politically active as a student leader in the **National Resistance Movement**, a successor to the **National Front** of the 1950s, in which **Mehdi Bazargan** played a prominent role. Yazdi participated in political rallies and protests as part of the National Resistance Movement. In 1962, he moved to the United States for graduate study where he remained until 1979, first as a student and later as an assistant professor in the Baylor College of Medicine. While a doctoral student at Baylor he helped organize, and became an active member of, the Islamic Student Society in North America, serving as **Ayatollah Ruhollah Khomeini**'s key representative in the United States. It was with Yazdi's encouragement that Khomeini moved to Paris while in exile, in order to focus worldwide attention on the Iranian situation and to ensure reliable communications with his network in Iran.

Though Yazdi was a secular politician, he had strong credentials as an Islamic activist and developed a close relationship with Khomeini. In 1979, he returned to Iran to participate in the establishment of the new Islamic order. He was a member of Khomeini's **Revolutionary Council** in **Tehran** and worked closely with Prime Minister Bazargan during the transition to Islamic government. Yazdi served as a foreign minister in the **Provisional Government**, and promoted normal diplomatic relations with the United States, within the framework of Iranian independence and autonomy.

Yazdi was involved in a politically sensitive meeting in Algiers on 1 November, 1979, between U.S. National Security Advisor Zbigniew Brzezinski and Prime Minister Bazargan. Along with Bazargan, he was accused of collaboration with an enemy government and ultimately resigned from his position after the takeover of the American Embassy and the ensuing **American Hostage** affair. Eventually, disillusioned with the increasing prominence and assumption of power by the **Islamic Republi-**

can **Party (IRP)** within the Islamic government, Yazdi joined in opposition to the IRP, working with Bazargan and **Abol Hasan Bani-Sadr** in what proved to be a vain effort toward moderating the flood of fundamentalist Islamic radicalism which ultimately took control of the Revolution. *See also* ISLAMIC REPUBLIC OF IRAN.

YUSHIJ, NIMA (1896-1960). Nima Yushij, born Ali Esfandiyari, is commonly regarded as one of the most important innovators of modern Persian **poetry**. Nima grew up in Yush, a small village in Mazandaran Province where his father was a farmer. Nima often had the chance to listen to campfire tales of nomadic life from shepherds and farm workers. His mother was an educated woman who instilled in him a love of classical Iranian poetry from such luminaries as **Nezami** and **Hafez**.

After being a somewhat unruly student at the local school, Nima traveled to **Tehran** where, at 12 years old, he began studies at the St. Louis Catholic School. Though he was equally disinterested in the general schooling at St. Louis, Nima did fall under the tutelage of one of his teachers, the respected poet Nezam Vafa. While Nima's poetic output increased as he practiced in the classical forms under Vafa, his new experiences in the urban center of Tehran were creating a disjunction with his earlier rural life. Much in the same way his actual life shifted to the more modern ways of the dynamic city, his poetry would also see a radical shift away from the traditional.

By the early 1920s, Nima's poetry began to break away from the classical forms. Instead of restricting his poetry to a set form, he allowed the subject matter to dictate the flow of words. Much like **Ali Akbar Dehkhoda** had revolutionized Iranian prose around the same period, Nima also allowed colloquialisms (many from the dialect of his childhood home) and vernacular language not usually seen in Persian **literature** to flourish in his work. Symbolism was a hallmark of his revolutionary style, borrowed from European modes that had already been in use for some time. Nima's verse, this New Poetry, was also used as a method of addressing social issues. To Nima, social commitment was of major importance to poetry in the modern era.

Though great criticism followed Nima's work, he advocated his New Poetry, as it came to be known, as a necessary break from the triteness and decadence of **Qajar** era poetry which still had its major adherents in the mainstream. Nima espoused New Poetry in the hope that others would follow his lead, which they did, including **Nader Naderpour**, **Mehdi Akhavan Sales**, and **Forugh Farrokhzad** among others.

Nima's poetry fit the trend of Persianism and modernization that dominated the early and mid-20th century, and especially during the **Pahlavi Dynasty**. However, his social commitment drove him towards the political left, even towards Marxism. Much of his most important work was published in the flood of leftist publications to appear after the creation of the **Tudeh** party.

Nima Yushij's impact was so important, and so influential on the overall nature of Iranian poetry, that by the time of his death in 1960, he was regarded as no less than the originator of modern Persian verse. His legacy would live on, and even take on a renewed vigor after the new challenge of the **Islamic Revolution** came about, antagonistic as it has been with its reversion to Arabism (Arabic being the language of God), and thus antithetical to the Persianism inherent in New Poetry.

-Z-

ZAGROS MOUNTAINS. The Zagros Mountains originate in Turkey and run northwest to southeast through central Iran, linking with the **Alborz Mountains** in the north to form the **Iranian Plateau**. The mountain range is one of the most developed and imposing in the Middle East with elevations to 4,267 meters, dominating the western portion of Iran. Both the **Karun** and Kharkeh Rivers flow through the Zagros, the waters of which ultimately empty into the Persian Gulf via the **Shatt al-Arab**. Many other small rivers and streams originate in the mountains, but evaporate in the extremely dry atmosphere of the plateau region. The range presents a formidable barrier to moisture from the Persian Gulf reaching the interior, contributing to the formation of the vast arid region in central Iran.

The terrain of the Zagros Mountain system consists of enormous domes, jagged peaks, deep gorges, and fertile valleys. Settlements are found at all elevations, usually situated near water courses. Pastoralism dominates in the higher regions, where a variety of **tribes**, including **Kurds**, **Bakhtiari**, and **Lurs**, tend herds of goats and sheep. The valleys are suited for a more settled agricultural lifestyle and farmers produce cash crops of cereals, fruits, and vegetables. Copper mining, along with marble and alabaster quarrying, provide additional economic resources.

The populations of the Zagros region have periodically been subjected to catastrophic earthquakes. Formed primarily by the action of two earth plates pushing against one another and creating folds, much of the Zagros is inherently unstable. Despite this instability of the land, such large and historical cities as **Shiraz** and **Tabriz** have flourished in the foothills of the mountains. Other major cities either in or on the fringes of the Zagros are **Isfahan**, **Kashan**, **Hamadan**, **KermanShah**, and **Urmieh**.

ZAHEDAN. The city of Zahedan, capital of the Sistan and Baluchistan Province, is located in southeastern Iran near the borders of Afghanistan and Pakistan, east of the Dasht-i Lut. Formerly called *"Dozd-ab,"* meaning "bandit's water place," the city was known for being a meeting place for robbers and criminals. Regarded as a poorer city, it was not until the 20th century that Zahedan began to develop. Named as the provincial center in the 1930s while still a small village, the population began to grow dramatically from 17,500 in 1956 to 93,000 20 years later. After the 1979 invasion of Afghanistan by the Soviet Union, during the 1980s, Zahedan expanded even more by taking in Afghan refugees to reach a population of over 281,000 by 1986. Zahedan's population reached 419,518 10 years later.

Zahedan has historically served as a gateway to the east and southeast of Iran. Modern Zahedan is linked by highways to **Tehran**, **Mashhad**, Bandar Beheshti on the Gulf of Oman, and to the Pakistani city of Quetta. A rail line connects the city to Quetta, while another line to **Kerman**, in central Iran, is under construction. An airport suitable for international travel also services Zahedan.

Zahedan is home to many small- to medium-sized industries including textiles, ceramics, milled rice, bricks, and reed mats and baskets. The best known products of the city are woven and hand-knotted rugs. Many of these items can be purchased at the central "Rasouli **Bazaar**," frequented by the local **Baluchi tribes**.

Ninety-six kilometers south of the city lies Taftan, an active volcano with dual summits at over 4,000 meters. Taftan saw its last lava flow on 25 April, 1993, reaching 96 kilometers down slope. This area, long known as a tribal residence, was identified in 2002 as possessing examples of residences carved into the mountainside dating 70,000 to 100,000 years old. These structures are currently under preservation through Iran's Cultural Heritage Organization.

ZAN NEWSPAPER. In July 1998, Fa'ezeh Hashemi, daughter of **Ali Akbar Hashemi-Rafsanjani**, launched *Zan (Woman)* newspaper, the first daily publication permitted on **women**'s issues in Iran. Hashemi was also a member of the **Majlis**, and a supporter of the recently elected President **Muhammad Khatami**, which made her unpopular amongst the anti-reform establishment.

Problems began for the magazine later that year after it presented a story claiming that the chief of police security had been present during an assault on reformists and Khatami cabinet members **Abdollah Nouri** and **Ata'ollah Mohajerani**. Hashemi was fined, and *Zan* was banned for two weeks.

In April 1999, *Zan* published a **Now Ruz** (New Year) message from **Muhammad Reza Shah**'s wife, the former Empress Farah **Pahlavi**, as well as a cartoon that lampooned the Islamic "blood money" prescription. The Revolutionary Courts, which Hashemi claimed had no jurisdiction over the paper, banned *Zan* as un-Islamic and anti-Revolutionary. Fa'ezeh Hashemi maintained this was just part of a continuing effort by conservatives threatened by the reformist trend to discredit and eliminate the reformists. The ban remained in effect, and thus *Zan* never resumed publication, yet another victim of the triumph of fundamentalist over reformist interpretations of the Islamic conception of society in the **Islamic Republic**.

ZANAN MAGAZINE. Beginning its run in 1991, *Zanan* magazine set out to tackle **women**'s issues within the **Islamic Republic**. Its publisher, Shahla Sherkat, sought to fight for the rights of women within the confines of **Islam**. She required the staff to abide by Islamic standards, including the chador, which has alienated some secular feminists in Iran. Also, while pushing the limits of what is allowable in the Iranian press, *Zanan* generally stops short of going over the line, perhaps contributing to *Zanan*'s longevity without being closed by the courts.

However, *Zanan* has not been without criticism from both the conservative and liberal elements within Iranian society. Conservatives cite the magazine as deemphasizing the good qualities of a proper family life while emphasizing rare instances of true domestic problems. Liberals have said that the magazine is too conservative in its strict observance of **Islam**, and many Iranian feminists avoid and even distrust the magazine and its publisher. The magazine has also been criticized for exploiting its position among women by shrouding political agendas in women's issues.

Though *Zanan* itself has continued without having been shut down, Shahla Sherkat has been reprimanded. In 2000, Sherkat attended a conference in Berlin, Germany which the Iranian courts deemed anti-Islamic. Also, particular to Sherkat, the courts were displeased with her statements denouncing a requirement for the chador, while at the same time encouraging it through belief and her own actions. Though the courts were displeased with her statements at the **Berlin Conference**, they were not focusing exclusively on Sherkat, as many Iranian activists in attendance were brought before the courts, and ultimately received fines and sentences. In early 2001, the courts fined her the equivalent of $3,000, and sentenced her to four months imprisonment. Sherkat appealed, and continued to publish her magazine. As of 2006, it continues to be published.

ZAND DYNASTY. *See* KARIM KHAN ZAND.

ZOROASTRIANISM. Zoroastrianism was introduced in 590 B.C. by the prophet Zarathushtra, and has since played an important role in Iranian history, particularly during the **Achaemenid** and **Sassanian** Periods. Not much is known about Zarathushtra, but it is believed that he was born in Iran and rose to prominence by converting Prince Vishtaspa to this new religion. According to legend, Ahura Mazda—the supreme god exemplifying wisdom, purity, goodness, and light—revealed the truths of Zoroastrianism to Zarathushtra. These revelations were recorded in the Avesta, the sacred Zoroastrian text containing 72 chapters of hymns, codes, and rituals. Only portions of the book have been preserved.

Zoroastrianism is a dualistic religion, seen as the bridge between the ancient polytheistic cults and the Islamic religion of today. Considered to be the earliest of the "revealed" religions, its tenets are based on the conflict between the forces of good, represented by Ahura Mazda, and those of the evil spirit Ahriman. Their struggle is shared by the people who worship them. Individuals are constantly challenged to choose between the two, with the reward of heaven and the punishment of hell awaiting the choices made. Fire is a symbol of justice, immortality, and the purity of Ahura Mazda. Although Zoroastrianism is belief centered, rituals involving fire, water, and recitations of the Gathas (the earliest Zoroastrian Scriptures) are performed in sacred temples by the magis, or priests.

Unable to oppose the spread of Christianity and **Islam**, most Zoroastrians fled to India beginning in the 10th century. They formed the Parsi community which still exists today. Besides the Parsis of India, small practicing communities are also found in Sri Lanka and Iran. In 1976, it was estimated that the world's Zoroastrian population numbered 130,000.

Although the practice of Zoroastrianism is confined to isolated groups, it is valued by most Iranians for its contribution to Iranian culture and nationalism. Its ideals have penetrated all aspects of Iranian culture—spiritual, political, artistic, and moral. Because Zoroastrianism is entirely Iranian in origin, much nationalistic pride surrounds it and the ideas it represents.

ZURKHANEH. The Zurkhaneh, translated as "House of Strength," can best be described as a combination of gymnasium, martial arts studio, dance accommodation, and spiritual center all unified into one remarkable art. It is a representation of a long and winding culture and an expression of the Iranian people. Men perform a combination of calisthenics, acrobatics, weight lifting, and dance to the mantra of the **Shahnameh** of **Abol Qasem Ferdowsi**, the chanting of poetic verses, and the beating of a drum as a prelude to wrestling competitions. Many times they perform for the public, and they are involved heavily in community activities. The members wear leather short pants for their exercises and membership is restricted to men only.

Although the origins are unclear, the oldest Zurkhaneh that still exists was built during the **Safavid Dynasty**. Some believe it is safe to assume the art existed long before this period because of the repeated appearance of athletic tales in 13th century **literature**. Still others trace its origins as early as the ninth century A.D.

The Zurkhaneh melds a feeling of brotherhood among its members, who vary in social class. Each member contributes according to his resources, and the idea of social distinction is abandoned so that they may serve the community in an honorable way. The Zurkhaneh remains a hierarchy by honoring the more experienced veteran members, who prove themselves to be not only physically superior, but also morally advanced.

Whereas the martial art itself is called "ancient sport" and the literal meaning of the term Zurkhaneh refers to the building where these activities take place, in popular usage, the latter term refers to both. The building is often dome shaped. The ground level is a sunken arena and usually composed of a clay floor with several levels above it. It is surrounded by dressing rooms, rest areas, and chambers. The entire building is considered sacred. The upper levels are used for spectators. Also located above the arena is the *Sardam*, a decorative seat of the mentor. The mentor, or *murshid*, is the lead athlete or coach, and is responsible for the administrative duties.

During the 20th century, the Zurkhaneh was considered a safe haven where those in need could go for help, an extension of the principle of *bast*. In the **Pahlavi** period there are instances of the Zurkhaneh being inserted into the political process as a ready source of a strong-armed street crowd. The most famous instance of such activity involved a man known as Sha'ban the Brainless, a huge man who was easily bought and called upon for crowd manipulation. For the most part, however, the Zurkhaneh maintained its ancient role as helper and defender of the needy. Today, the Zurkhaneh still exists on a more limited basis, and is frequently combined with a more Western type of gymnasium. According to some observers, this has contributed greatly to the Iranian success in wrestling at the Olympics. In general, in today's Iran the Western-style gymnasium is slowly replacing the Zurkhaneh.

APPENDIX A

BASIC FACTS

Official Name: Islamic Republic of Iran
Area: 1,648,000 sq. km (636,296 sq. mi)
Area—World Rank: 18
Population: 60,055,488 (1996)
Population—World Rank: 20
Capital: Tehran
Boundaries: Total land boundaries 5440 km (3378 mi) total sea boundaries (includes Caspian Sea) 3180 km (1975 mi); Afghanistan 936 km (581 mi); Armenia 35 km (22 mi); Azerbaijan 611 km (380 mi); Iraq 1458 km (906 mi); Pakistan 909 km (565 mi); Turkey 499 km (310 mi); Turkmenistan 992 km (616 mi).
Coastline: 2440 km; note—Iran also borders the Caspian Sea (740 km).
Highest Point: Mount Damavand, 5671 m (18,607 ft).
Lowest Point: Caspian Sea 28 m (92 ft) below sea level.
Land Use: 10% arable; 27% permanent pastures; 1% permanent crops; 7% forest and woodland; 55% other.

Source: *Encyclopedia of the World's Nations*. Kurian, George Thomas. New York: Facts on File, 2002.

APPENDIX B

PROVINCES: AREA AND POPULATIONS

Province	Capital	Area sq km	Population 1996
Ardabil	Ardabil	17,881	1,168,011
Azerbaijan, East	Tabriz	47,830	3,325,540
Azerbaijan, West	Urmieh	39,487	2,496,320
Bushehr	Bushehr	23,191	743,675
Chahar Mahal and Bakhtiari	Shahr-i-Kord	16,201	761,168
Isfahan	Isfahan	107,027	3,923,255
Fars	Shiraz	122,416	3,817,036
Gilan	Rasht	14,106	2,241,896
Gulistan	Gorgan	20,891	1,426,288
Hamadan	Hamadan	19,547	1,677,957
Hormozgan	Bandar-i Abbas	71,193	1,062,155
Ilam	Ilam	20,151	487,886
Kerman	Kerman	181,814	2,004,328
Kermanshah	Kermanshah	24,641	1,778,596
Khuzistan	Ahwaz	63,238	3,746,772
Kuhgiluyeh and Boyer Ahmad	Yasuj	15,563	544,356
Kurdistan	Sanandaj	29,151	1,346,383
Luristan	Khorramabad	28,392	1,584,434
Markazi	Arak	29,406	1,228,812
Mazandaran	Sari	23,064	2,602,008
North Khorasan	Bojnurd	——	*676,333

Qazvin	Qazvin	15,502	968,257
Qum	Qum	11,237	853,044
Razavi-Khorasan	Mashhad	*247,622	*4,991,818
Semnan	Semnan	96,816	501,447
Sistan and Baluchestan	Zahedan	178,431	1,722,579
South Khorasan	Birjand	——	*319,878
Tehran	Tehran	18,637	10,343,965
Yazd	Yazd	73,467	750,769
Zanjan	Zanjan	21,841	900,890

Population according to 1996 census, * indicates estimated figures. Source: Turner, Barry, ed. *The Statesman's Yearbook, 2005*. New York: Palgrave Macmillan, 2004.

APPENDIX C

PRINCIPAL TOWNS AND POPULATIONS

Tehran	6,758,845
Mashhad	1,887,405
Isfahan	1,266,072
Tabriz	1,191,043
Shiraz	1,053,025
Karaj	940,968
Ahwaz	804,980
Qum	777,677
Bakhtaran	692,986
Urmieh	435,200
Zahedan	419,518
Rasht	417,748
Hamadan	401,281
Kerman	384,991
Arak	380,755
Ardabil	340,386
Yazd	326,776
Qazvin	291,117
Zanjan	296,295
Sanandaj	277,808
Bandar-i Abbas	273,578
Khorramabad	272,815
Islamshahr	265,450
Borujerd	217,804
Abadan	206,073

Dezful 202,639
Khuninshah.. 105,636

Population according to 1996 census.

Source: *The Statesman's Yearbook, 2005.* Turner, Barry, ed. New York: Palgrave Macmillan, 2004.

APPENDIX D

TEXT OF UN SECURITY COUNCIL RESOLUTION 598

The following resolution was issued by the United Nations in July, 1987 as the framework for promoting a cease-fire in the Iran-Iraq War, at that point in its seventh year of duration. *See also* IRAN-IRAQ WAR; SHATT AL-ARAB.

THE SECURITY COUNCIL,
   REAFFIRMING its Resolution 585 (1986),
   DEEPLY CONCERNED that, despite its calls for a cease-fire, the conflict between Iran and Iraq continues unabated, with further heavy loss of human life and material destruction,
   DEPLORING the initiation and continuation of the conflict,
   DEPLORING also the bombing of purely civilian population centers, attacks on neutral shipping or civilian aircraft, the violation of international humanitarian law and other laws of armed conflict, and in particular, the use of chemical weapons contrary to obligations under the 1925 Geneva Protocol,
   DEEPLY CONCERNED that further escalation and widening of the conflict may take place,
   DETERMINED to bring to an end all military actions between Iran and Iraq,
   CONVINCED that a comprehensive, just, honorable and durable settlement should be achieved between Iran and Iraq,
   RECALLING the provisions of the Charter of the United Nations, and in particular the obligation of all member states to

settle their international disputes by peaceful means in such a manner that international peace and security and justice are not endangered,

DETERMINING that there exists a breach of the peace as regards the conflict between Iran and Iraq,

ACTING under Articles 39 and 40 of the Charter of the United Nations,

1. DEMANDS that, as a first step towards a negotiated settlement, Iran and Iraq observe an immediate cease-fire, discontinue all military actions on land, at sea and in the air, and withdraw all forces to the internationally recognized boundaries without delay;

2. REQUESTS the Secretary General to dispatch a team of United Nations observers to verify, confirm and supervise the cease-fire and withdrawal and further requests the Secretary General to make the necessary arrangements in consultation with the parties and to submit a report thereon to the Security Council;

3. URGES that prisoners of war be released and repatriated without delay after the cessation of active hostilities in accordance with the Third Geneva convention of 12 August 1949;

4. CALLS UPON Iran and Iraq to cooperate with the Secretary General in implementing the resolution and in mediation efforts to achieve a comprehensive, just and honorable settlement, acceptable to both sides, of all outstanding issues, in accordance with principles contained in the Charter of the United Nations;

5. CALLS UPON all other states to exercise the utmost restraint and to refrain from any act which may lead to further escalation and widening of the conflict, and thus to facilitate the implementation of the present resolution;

6. REQUESTS the Secretary General to explore, in consultation with Iran and Iraq, the question of entrusting an impartial body with inquiring into responsibility for the conflict and to report to the Security Council as soon as possible;

7. RECOGNIZES the magnitude of the damage inflicted during the conflict and the need for reconstruction efforts, with appropriate international assistance, once the conflict is ended

and, in this regard, requests the Secretary General to assign a team of experts to study the question of reconstruction and to report to the Security Council;

8. FURTHER REQUESTS the Secretary General to examine, in consultation with Iran and Iraq and with other states of the region, measures to enhance the security and stability of the region;

9. REQUESTS the Secretary General to keep the Security Council informed on the implementation of this resolution;

10. DECIDES to meet again as necessary to consider further steps to ensure compliance with this resolution.

APPENDIX E

IRANIAN STATESMEN: 1787-2005

RULING MONARCHS

QAJAR SHAHS

Agha Muhammad Khan Qajar	1787-1797
Fath Ali Shah	1797-1834
Muhammad Mirza Shah	1834-1848
Naser al-Din Shah	1848-1896
Mozaffar al-Din Shah	1896-1907
Muhammad Ali Shah	1907-1909
Sultan Ahmad Shah	1909-1925

PAHLAVI SHAHS

Reza Shah	1925-1941
Muhammed Reza Shah	1941-1979

POST-CONSTITUTIONAL PRIME MINISTERS

QAJAR PERIOD

Moshir al-Dowleh	1906
Naser al-Molk	1907-1908
Sepahdar-i Azam	1909-1911

Samsam al-Saltaneh	1911-1914
Mostowfi al-Mamalik	1914
Moshir al-Dowleh	1915
Mirza Farman Farmayan	1915
Mostowfi al-Mamalik	1915-1917
Ala al-Saltaneh	1917
Ain al-Dowleh	1917
Mostowfi al-Mamalik	1917-1918
Samsam al-Saltaneh	1918
Vishu al-Dowleh	1918-1920
Moshir al-Dowleh	1920-1921
Sardar-i Sipah Fathu'llah Gilani	1921
Mostowfi al-Mamalik	1921
Sardar-i Sepah Fathu'llah Gilani	1921
Sayyid Zia al-Din Tabatabai	1921
Ahmad Qavam	1921
Moshir al-Dowleh	1922
Ahmad Qavam	1922-1923
Mostowfi al-Mamalik	1923
Moshir al-Dowleh	1923
Reza Khan	1923-1925

PAHLAVI PERIOD

Reza Shah Era

Muhammad Ali Foroughi	1925-1926
Mostowfi al-Mamalik	1926-1927
Medhi Quli Hedayat	1928-1933
Muhammad Ali Foroughi	1933-1935
Mahmud Jam	1935-1939
Dr. Matin Daftari	1939-1940
Ali Mansur	1940-1941

Muhammad Reza Shah Era

Muhammad Ali Foroughi	1941

Ali Soheily	1942
Ahmad Qavam	1942-1943
Muhammad Sa'ed	1944
Morteza Quli Bayat	1944-1945
Ibrahim Hakimi	1945
Mohsen Sadr	1945
Ibrahim Hakimi	1945-1946
Ahmad Qavam	1946-1947
Ibrahim Hakimi	1947-1948
Muhammad Sa'ed	1948
Abdol Hussein Hajir	1948-1949
Ali Mansur	1949-1950
Ali Razmara	1950-1951
Muhammad Mossadeq	*1951-1953
Fazlollah Zahedi	1953-1955
Hussein Ala	1955-1956
Manuchehr Eqbal	1957-1960
Ja'far Sharif-Emami	1960-1961
Ali Amini	1961-1962
Asadollah Alam	1962-1964
Hasan Ali Mansur	1964-1965
Amir Abbas Hoveida	1965-1977
Jamshid Amuzegar	1977-1978
Ja'far Sharif-Emami	1978
Gholam Reza Azhari	1978
Shapur Bakhtiar	1978-1979

*Ahmad Qavam served as prime minister for four days in 1952.

ISLAMIC REPUBLIC: HEADS OF STATE

SUPREME LEADERS

Ayatollah Ruhollah Khomeini	1979-1989
Ayatollah Ali Khamene'i	1989-

PRESIDENTS

Abol Hasan Bani-Sadr	1980-1981
Muhammad Ali Raja'i	1981
Ali Khamene'i	1981-1989
Ali Akbar Hashemi-Rafsanjani	1989-1997
Muhammad Khatami	1997-2005
Mahmud Ahmadinejad	2005-

PRIME MINISTERS

Mehdi Bazargan	1979
Muhammad Ali Raja'i	1980-1981
Muhammad Javad Bahonar	1981
Muhammad Madavi-Kani	*1981
Mir Hussein Musavi	**1981-1989

*Appointed interim minister August-October.
**Office of prime minister abolished July 1989.

APPENDIX F

IRANIAN GOVERNMENT STRUCTURE

Supreme Leader: Highest ranking official in the country. He appoints the Head of the Judiciary, six of the members of the powerful Guardian Council, and the commanders of all the armed forces.

President: The second-highest ranking official in the country. He is head of the executive branch of power and is responsible for ensuring the Constitution is implemented.

Armed Forces Commanders: Appointed by the Supreme Leader.

Head of Judiciary: He nominates the six lay members of the Guardian Council. The Head of the Judiciary is appointed by, and reports to, the Supreme Leader.

Expediency Council: The Council is an advisory body for the Supreme Leader with an arbitrating power in disputes over legislation between the Parliament and the Guardian Council. The Supreme Leader appoints its members.

Guardian Council: The Council consists of six theologians appointed by the Supreme Leader and six jurists nominated by the Head of the Judiciary and approved by Parliament. The council has to approve all bills passed by Parliament and make sure they conform to the constitution and Islamic Law. Additionally, the Council screens candidates, with the power of approval or resection, for the elected positions of President, Parliament, and the Assembly of Experts.

Parliament: The Parliament (Majlis) has the power to introduce and pass laws, as well as to summon and impeach ministers or the president. However, all Majlis bills have to be approved by the Guardian Council.

Cabinet: Members of the Cabinet, or Council of Ministers, are chosen by the President and approved by Parliament.

Assembly of Experts: Publicly elected, they appoint the Supreme Leader, monitor his performance, and can remove him if he is deemed incapable of fulfilling his duties. Only clerics can join the Assembly and candidates for election are scrutinized by the Guardian Council.

APPENDIX G

INSTITUTIONAL RELATIONSHIPS
OF GOVERNMENT

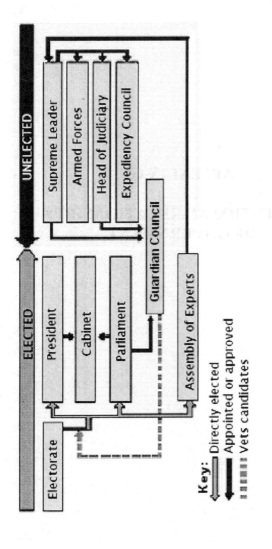

UNELECTED

Supreme Leader

Armed Forces

Head of Judiciary

Expediency Council

ELECTED

President

Cabinet

Parliament

Guardian Council

Assembly of Experts

Electorate

Key: Directly elected
         Appointed or approved
         Vets candidates

BIBLIOGRAPHY

The works which appear in this bibliography are intended to provide a substantive listing of major works in English on all aspects of Iranian history and culture. There is, of necessity, a certain degree of arbitrariness. Not everything could be included. However, if successful, this bibliography will be both suggestive of further reading and comprehensive to the extent of providing the reader with a sound listing of important and relevant works on the listed subject matter. Since many works could easily be placed in multiple categories I had to choose which was the most relevant category, often a difficult choice. Nonetheless, I adhered to the principle that a book would only appear once. The only exception to that rule is in listings for the multivolume *Cambridge History of Iran* which appears under the category of "Reference Works" in a generic reference to the set, and then again under the appropriate historical category for each individual volume. Other principles upon which the bibliography is based are as follows:

1) All works are in English. This, of course, leaves out many important books in other languages. However, there is a sufficient body of literature on Iran in English to build a sizable and topically inclusive bibliography.

2) The singular subject of works is Iran. The lone exception is the reference work *The Encyclopedia of Islam*. In a few categories, "Sufism" for instance, there are some more general books. But, in all categories, unless there is considerable information relating to Iran or a clear focus on Iran, general works are rare and only included with considered reluctance.

3) Only books or monographs are included. Edited books containing articles are included if the entire focus of the work is on Iran. Generally, edited works that only deal partially with Iran are excluded, as are books that are divided into sections with only one dealing with Iran.

In the periodical literature, there are literally thousands of valuable articles and essays dealing with one aspect or another of Iranian culture and history. To have included these here would have expanded the bibliography beyond reasonable bounds. In any event, the works cited in the lead-off "Bibliographies" category will direct the curious to the more extensive body of literature which would encompass articles and essays. One exception to the above rule, though many of these might well be considered monographs, is the inclusion of catalogues of art and carpet exhibitions which contribute unique material not readily found elsewhere.

4) In categorizing, consideration was given to achieving some degree of balance. In certain categories, a large number of books could well be included, but some were categorized elsewhere or excluded altogether. The latter case only occurred when the subject matter was fully covered in other works cited. In other categories, a few works of questionable stand-alone value are included because of a unique perspective or a paucity of material in that particular category.

Within the limitation of space, the overall goal in biblio-graphic selection was to provide reasonably comprehensive guidance on further reading and research on specific subject matters. Many difficult choices of number and subject category had to be made. I apologize for exclusions that cannot be adequately explained on the basis of the above principles and working guidelines. Any such oversights are unintentional.

The bibliography of this second edition has been considerably enlarged thanks to the large number of books that have been published on Iran in the decade of the 1990s and in the 21st century and into the year 2006. The expansion of bibliography proceeded along the same lines of principle as iterated above. A number of new categories have been added. For instance, the categories on "Historiography and Intellectual History," "Exilic Literature," and "Film and Photography" are new. These new categories are a reflection of the number of books that have appeared illuminating such topics, sufficient in number to warrant a separate category.

The sheer number of books in the English language alone published since the Iranian Revolution of 1979 is remarkable. Furthermore, though there are numerous books of a political nature, the interest is clearly not just in politics. Works on religion, philosophy, mysticism, geography, economics, art and architecture, language, painting, and the literature of all genres and periods abound. In one area, film, there were very few works existent a decade ago. Now there are nearly a dozen.

BIBLIOGRAPHY CONTENTS

I. GENERAL

1. BIBLIOGRAPHIES

Ahadi, Shahram. *New Persian Language and Linguistics: A Selected Bibliography up to 2001.* Wiesbaden, Germany: Harrassowitz, 2002.

Bartsch, William H. and Julian Bharier. *The Economy of Iran, 1940-1970: A Bibliography.* Durham, England: University of Durham, 1971.

Behn, Wolfgang. *The Iranian Opposition in Exile: An Annotated Bibliography of Publications from 1341/1962 to 1357/1979 with*

Selective Locations. Wiesbaden, Germany: Harrassowitz in Komm, 1979.

―――. *Islamic Revolution or Revolutionary Islam in Iran: A Selected Bibliography.* Berlin: Adiyok, 1980.

―――. *Twenty Years of Iranian Power Struggle: A Bibliography of 951 Political Periodicals from 1341/1962 to 1360/1981 with Selective Locations.* Berlin: Adiyok, 1982.

Diba, Farhad. *A Persian Bibliography.* London: TNR Productions, 1981.

Ehlers, Eckart. *Iran: A Bibliographic Research Survey.* Munich, Germany: K.G. Saur, 1980.

Elwell-Sutton, Laurence P. *Bibliographical Guide to Iran.* Sussex, England: Harvester Press, 1983.

Farman, Hafez F. *Iran: A Selected and Annotated Bibliography.* New York: Greenwood Press, 1968.

Ghani, Cyrus. *Iran and the West: A Critical Bibliography.* New York: Kegan Paul International, 1987.

Gitisetan, Dariush. *Iran: Politics and Government Under the Pahlavis, An Annotated Bibliography.* Metuchen, NJ: Scarecrow Press, 1985.

Iranian Culture Foundation. *A Bibliography of Iran: A Catalogue of Books and Articles on Iranian Subjects, Mainly in European Languages.* Vols. 1 and 2. Tehran: Iranian Culture Foundation, 1971.

Navabpour, Reza. *Iran.* World Bibliographical Series, Volume 81. Oxford, England: CLIO Press, 1988.

Okazaki, Shoko and Kinji Eura. *Bibliography on Qajar Persia.* Osaka, Japan: Osaka University of Foreign Studies, 1985.

Pearson, J.D. *A Bibliography of Pre-Islamic Persia.* London: Mansell, 1975.

Saba, Mohsen. *English Bibliography of Iran.* Tehran: Bank Melli Iran Press, 1965.

Storey, Charles A. *Persian Literature: A Bio-Bibliographical Survey.* London: Luzac, 1927-.

Tabataba'i, Hossein Modarresi. *An Introduction to Shi'i Law: A Bibliographical Study.* London: Ithaca Press, 1984.

Wilson, Sir Arnold T. *A Bibliography of Persia.* Oxford, England: Clarendon Press, 1930.

2. REFERENCE WORKS

Boardman, John, N.G.L. Hammond, and David M. Lewis. *The Cambridge Ancient History.* Volume 4, *Persia, Greece and the Western Mediterranean.* Cambridge: Cambridge University Press, 1997.

The Cambridge History of Iran. 7 Vols. Cambridge, England: Cambridge University Press, 1968-1991.

Encyclopedia Iranica. Edited by Ehsan Yar-Shater. London: Routledge & Kegan Paul, 1982-.

The Encyclopedia of Islam. Edited by M. Th. Houtsma, A.J. Wensinck et al. Leiden: E.J. Brill, 1911-1938. New Edition, 1960.

Jarman, Robert L. and R.M. Burrell, eds. *Iran: Political Diaries 1881-1965.* 14 Vols. London: Archive Editions, 1997.

Naficy, Hamid (compiled by). *Iran Media Index.* Westport, Connecticut: Greenwood Press, 1984.

Nasr, Seyyed Hossein, Ahmad Mostofi, and Abbas Zaryab. *Historical Atlas of Iran.* Tehran: Tehran University Press, 1971.

Sahab, Abbas (compiled by). *Atlas of Geographical Maps and Historical Documents on the Persian Gulf.* Tehran: Sahab Geographic and Drafting Institute, 1971.

3. GUIDES AND YEARBOOKS

Behnam, Farjam and Karan Behrooz, eds. *Iran Almanac: The Book of Facts.* 22nd Edition. Tehran: Echo of Iran, 2003.

Elwell-Sutton, L.P. *A Guide to Iranian Area Study.* Ann Arbor, Michigan: J.W. Edwards, 1952.

Facts and Figures About Iran. Tehran: Bank Markazi Iran, 1968.

Iran Yearbook. Tehran: Kayhan Newspaper Group, 1977.

Nyrop, Richard, ed. *Iran, A Country Study.* Washington, DC: U.S. Government Printing Office, 1978.

Smith, Harvey H. et al. *Area Handbook for Iran.* Washington, DC: U.S. Government Printing Office, 1971.

4. DESCRIPTION AND TRAVEL

Adams, Rev. Isaac. *Persia by a Persian.* London: E. Stock, 1906.

Bird, Christiane. *Neither East Nor West: One Woman's Journey through the Islamic Republic of Iran.* New York: Pocket Books, 2001.

Brancaforte, Elio Christoph. *Visions of Persia: Mapping the Travels of*

Adam Olearius. Cambridge, MA: Harvard University Press, 2003.

Byron, Robert. *The Road to Oxiana.* London: Picador, 1981.

Jackson, A.V. Williams. *Persia, Past and Present: A Book of Travel and Research.* New York: The Macmillan Company, 1906.

Matheson, Sylvia. *Persia: An Archaeological Guide.* London: Faber, 1972.

Molavi, Afshin. *The Soul of Iran: A Nation's Journey to Freedom.* New York: W.W. Norton, 2005.

Namikawa, Banri. *Iran.* Tokyo: Kodansha International, 1973.

Payne, Robert. *Journey to Persia.* London: Heinemann, 1951.

Stevens, Sir Roger. *The Land of the Great Sophy.* London: Methuen and Co., 1962.

Wearing, Alison. *Honeymoon in Purdah: An Iranian Journey.* New York: Picador, 2000.

II. HISTORY

1. GENERAL

Arberry, Arthur J., ed. *The Legacy of Persia.* Oxford, England: Clarendon Press, 1953.

Armajani, Yahya. *Iran.* Englewood Cliffs, NJ: Prentice-Hall, 1972.

Bausani, Alessandro. *The Persians from the Earliest Days to the Twentieth Century.* Translated by J.B. Donne. New York: St. Martin's Press, 1971.

Boyle, James A., ed. *Persia: History and Heritage.* London: Allen and Unwin, 1978.

Chelkowski, Peter J., ed. *Iran: Continuity and Variety.* New York: New York University Press, 1971.

Clawson, Patrick and Michael Rubin. *Eternal Iran: Continuity and Chaos.* New York: Palgrave Macmillan, 2005.

Daniel, Elton. *The History of Iran.* Westport, CT: Greenwood, 2000.

Ebadi, Shirin. *History and Documentation of Human Rights in Iran.* Persian Studies Series, Number 18. Translated by N. Fathi. New York: Bibliotheca Press, 2000.

Foran, John. *A Century of Revolution: Social Movements in Iran.* Minneapolis: University of Minnesota Press, 1994.

Fraser, James Baillie. *An Historical and Descriptive Account of Persia.* Edinburgh: Oliver and Boyd, 1834.

Garthwaite, Gene. *The Persians.* Oxford: Blackwell, 2005.

Groseclose, Elgin E. *Introduction to Iran.* New York: Oxford

University Press, 1947.

Haas, William S. *Iran*. New York: Columbia University Press, 1946.

Hovannisian, Richard G. and Georges Sabagh, eds. *The Persian Presence in the Islamic World*. New York: Cambridge University Press, 1998.

Katouzian, Homa. *Iranian History: The Dialectic of State and Society*. New York: Routledge Curzon, 2003.

Keddie, Nikki R. and Rudi Matthee, eds. *Iran and the Surrounding World: Interactions in Culture and Cultural Politics*. Seattle: University of Washington Press, 2002.

Ladjevardian, Reza. *From Ancient Persia to Contemporary Iran: Selected Historical Milestones*. Washington, DC: Mage Publishers, 1999.

Limbert, John W. *Iran: At War with History*. Boulder, CO: Westview Press, 1987.

Mackey, Sandra. *The Iranians: Persia, Islam, and the Soul of a Nation*. New York: Plume Books, 1998.

Malcolm, Sir John. *The History of Persia, From the Most Early Period to the Present Time*. 2 Vols. London: James Moyes, 1815.

Marashi, Mehdi, Ed. *Persian Studies in North America: Studies in Honor of Mohammad Ali Jazayery*. Bethesda, MD: Iranbooks, 1994.

Markham, Clements R. *A General Sketch of the History of Persia*. London: Longmans, 1874.

Matthee, Rudi and Beth Baron, eds. *Iran and Beyond, Essays in Middle Eastern History in Honor of Nikki R. Keddie*. Costa Mesa, CA: Mazda, 2000.

Ross, Sir E. Denison. *The Persians*. Oxford, England: Clarendon Press, 1931.

Sykes, Sir Percy. *A History of Persia*. 2 Vols. London: Macmillan and Co., 1915.

Wilber, Donald N. *Iran: Past and Present*. Princeton: Princeton University Press, 1976.

Wilson, Lt. Col. Sir Arnold T. *Persia*. London: E. Benn, 1932.

2. PRE-ISLAMIC

Allen, Lindsay. *The Persian Empire*. Chicago: University of Chicago Press, 2005.

Bengston, Hermann et al. *The Greeks and the Persians: From the Sixth to the Fourth Centuries*. London: Weidenfeld & Nicolson, 1968.

Bulsara, Sohrab Jamshedjee. *The Laws of the Ancient Persians as Found in the "Matikan e Hazar Datastan."* or *"The Digest of a Thousand Points of Law."* Mumbai: K.R. Cama Oriental Institute, 1999.

Cameron, George G. *History of Early Iran.* Chicago: University of Chicago Press, 1936.

Cook, J.M. *The Persian Empire.* New York: Schocken Books, 1983.

Culican, William. *The Medes and the Persians.* New York: Praeger, 1965.

Curtis, John E. and Nigel Tallis. *Forgotten Empire: The World of Ancient Persia.* Berkeley: University of California Press, 2005.

Curtis, Vesta Sarkhosh and Sarah Stewart, eds. *Birth of the Persian Empire.* New York: Palgrave Macmillan, 2005.

Dandamaev, Muhammad A. *Iranians in Achaemenid Babylonia.* Columbia Lectures on Iranian Studies, No. 6. Costa Mesa, CA and New York: Mazda Publishers in association with Bibliotheca Persica, 1992.

Dandamaev, Muhammad A. and Vladimir G. Lukonin. *The Culture and Social Institutions of Ancient Iran.* Cambridge, England: Cambridge University Press, 1989.

Dodgeon, Michael H. and Samuel N.C. Lieu. *The Roman Eastern Frontier and the Persian Wars (AD 226-363): A Documentary History.* London: Routledge, 1994.

Dusinberre, Elspeth. *Aspects of Empire in Achaemenid Sardis.* Cambridge, England: Cambridge University Press, 2002.

Frye, Richard. *The Heritage of Persia.* London: Weidenfeld & Nicolson, 1962.

Gershevitch, Ilya, ed. *The Cambridge History of Iran.* Vol. 2. *The Median and Achaemenian Period.* Cambridge, England: Cambridge University Press, 1985.

Ghirshman, Roman. *Iran: Parthians and Sassanians.* London: Thames and Hudson, 1962.

Gnoli, Ghearardo. *Zoroaster in History.* New York: Bibliotheca Persica, 2000.

Greatrex, Geoffrey and Samuel N.C. Lieu. *The Roman Eastern Frontier and the Persian Wars, Pt. 2 (AD 363-630): A Narrative Sourcebook.* London: Routledge, 2002.

Herodotus. *The History of Herodotus.* Translated by George Rawlinson. New York: Tudor, 1956.

Huart, Clement I. *Ancient Persia and Iranian Civilization.* Translated by M.R. Dobie. 1927. Reprint. New York: Barnes & Noble, 1972.

Olmstead, Albert T. *History of the Persian Empire.* Chicago: University of Chicago Press, 1948.

Rawlinson, George. *Parthia.* London: T. Fisher Unwin, 1893.

————. *The Seventh Great Oriental Monarchy.* New York: Dodd, Mead & Co., 1875.

Rogers, Robert W. *A History of Ancient Persia.* New York: Charles Scribner's Sons, 1929.

Sekunda, Nick and Angus McBride. *Seleucid and Ptolemaic Reformed Armies 168-145 BC.* Stockport: Montvert, 1995.

Shaul, Shaked. *From Zoroastrian Iran to Islam.* Brookfield, VT: Variorum, 1995.

Sherwin-White, Susan and Amelie Kurt. *From Samarkhand to Sardis: A New Approach to the Seleucid Empire.* Hellenistic Culture and Society Series, No. 13. Berkeley, California: University of California Press, 1993.

de Souza, Philip. *The Greek and Persian Wars, 499-386 BC.* Oxford: Osprey, 2003.

Tadgell, Christopher. *Imperial Form: From Achaemenid Iran to Augustan Rome.* New York: Whitney Library of Design, 1998.

Tafazzoli, Ahmad. *Sasanian Society.* Winona Lake, IN: Bibliotheca Persica Press, 2000.

Wheeler, Mortimer. *Flames Over Persepolis.* New York: Reynal & Company, 1968.

Wiesehofer, Josef. *Ancient Persia.* London: I.B. Tauris, 2001.

Yar-Shater, Ehsan, ed. *The Cambridge History of Iran.* Vol. 3, *The Seleucid, Parthian and Sasanian Periods*, 2 Vols. Cambridge, England: Cambridge University Press, 1983.

Xenophone. *The Persian Expedition.* Translated by Rex Warner. Harmondsworth, England: Penguin Books, 1967.

3. IRAN IN THE AGE OF ISLAM TO 1501

Bosworth, Clifford Edmund. *The Ghaznavids: Their Empire in Afghanistan and Eastern Iran 994-1040.* Edinburgh: Edinburgh University Press, 1963.

————. *The History of the Saffavids of Sistan and the Maliks of Nimrus (247/861 to 949/1542-3).* Costa Mesa, CA: Mazda Publishers in Association with Bibliotheca Persica, 1994.

————, ed. *Iran and Islam.* Edinburgh: Edinburgh University Press, 1971.

————. *The Medieval History of Iran, Afghanistan and Central Asia.*

London: Variorum Reprints, 1977.

Boyle, John Andrew, ed. *The Cambridge History of Iran*. Vol. 5. *The Saljuq and the Mongol Periods*. Cambridge, England: Cambridge University Press, 1968.

Frye, Richard N., ed. *The Cambridge History of Iran.* ·Vol. 4. *The Period from the Arab Invasion to the Saljuqs*. Cambridge, England: Cambridge University Press, 1975.

―――. *The Golden Age of Persia: The Arabs in the East*. London: Weidenfeld and Nicholson, 1975.

―――. *Islamic Iran and Central Asia (7th-12th Centuries)*. London: Variorum Reprints, 1979.

Kolbas, Judith G. *The Mongols in Iran: Chingiz Khan to Uljayta 1220-1309*. New York: RoutledgeCurzon, 2005.

Lambton, Ann K.S. *Continuity and Change in Medieval Persia: Aspects of Administrative, Economic and Social History, 11th - 14th Century*. London: I.B. Tauris, 1988.

Morgan, David. *Medieval Persia 1040-1797*. New York: Longman, 1988.

Siddiqi, Amir Hasan. *Caliphate and Kingship in Medieval Persia*. Lahore, Pakistan: Shaikh Muhammad Ashraf, 1942.

Woods, John. *The Aqquyunlu: Clan, Confederation, Empire*. Minneapolis: Bibliotheca Islamica, 1976.

4. THE SAFAVIDS AND IRAN TO THE LATE EIGHTEENTH CENTURY

Abisaab, Rula Jurdi. *Converting Persia: Religion and Power in the Safavid Empire*. London: I.B. Tauris, 2004.

Babaie, Sussan. *Slaves of the Shah: New Elites of the Safavid*. New York: I.B. Taurus, 2004.

Chardin, Sir John. *Sir John Chardin's Travels in Persia*. London: The Argonaut Press, 1927.

Erewants'i, Abraham and George A. Bournoutian. *History of the Wars: 1721-1738*. Costa Mesa, CA: Mazda Publishers, 1999.

Floor, William. *Safavid Government Institutions*. Costa Mesa, CA: Mazda Publishers, 2001.

Jackson, Peter and Laurence Lockhart, eds. *The Cambridge History of Iran*. Vol. 6. *The Timurid and Safavid Periods*. Cambridge, England: Cambridge University Press, 1986.

Kondo, Noubaki, ed. *Persian Documents: Social History of Iran and Turan in the Fifteenth to Nineteeth Centuries*. London:

RoutledgeCurzon, 2003.

Krusinski, Judasz Tadeusz. *The History of the Revolution of Persia.* London: J. Pemberton, 1729.

Lockhart, Laurence. *The Fall of the Safavi Dynasty and the Afghan Occupation of Persia.* Cambridge, England: Cambridge University Press, 1958.

———. *Nadir Shah: A Critical Study Based Upon Contemporary Sources.* London: Luzac, 1938.

Matthee, Rudi. *The Pursuit of Pleasure: Drugs and Stimulants in Iranian History, 1500-1900.* Princeton: Princeton University Press, 2004.

Mazzaoui, Michel M. *The Origins of the Safawids: Shi'ism, Sufism, and the Gulat.* Wiesbaden, Germany: F. Steiner, 1972.

Minorsky, Vladimir. *Iranica. Twenty Articles.* Vol. 775. Publications of the University of Tehran. Hertford, Herts, England: Stephen Austin & Sons, 1964.

Monshi, Eskandar Beg. *History of Shah 'Abbas the Great.* 2 Vols. Translated by Roger M. Savory. Boulder, CO: Westview Press, 1978.

Newman, Andrew J. *Society and Culture in the Early Modern Middle East: Studies on Iran in the Safavid Period.* Boston: Brill, 2003.

Perry, John R. *Karim Khan Zand: A History of Iran, 1747-1779.* Chicago: University of Chicago Press, 1979.

Reid, James J. *Studies in Safavid Mind, Society and Culture.* Costa Mesa, CA: Mazda, 2000.

Rumlu, Hasan. *The Ahsanu't-Tawarikh (A Chronicle of the Early Safavids).* Translated by C.N. Seddon. Baroda, India: Oriental Institute, 1934.

Sarwar, Ghulam. *History of Shah Isma'il Safawi.* Aligarh, India: Sarwar, 1939.

Savory, Roger. *Iran under the Safavids.* Cambridge, England: Cambridge University Press, 1980.

Tucker, Ernest. *Nadir Shah's Quest for Legitimacy in Post-Safavid Iran.* Gainesville, FL: University Press of Flordia, 2006.

5. MODERN IRAN

a) *The Qajar Period*

Algar, Hamid. *Religion and State in Iran, 1785-1906: The Role of the Ulama in the Qajar Period.* Berkeley: University of California

Press, 1969.

Amanat, Abbas. *Pivot of the Universe: Nasir al-Din Shah Qajar and the Iranian Monarchy, 1831-1869.* Berkeley: University of California Press, 1997.

Arnold, Arthur. *Through Persia by Caravan.* New York: Harper & Brothers, 1877.

Avery, Peter, Gavin Hambly and Charles Melville, eds. *The Cambridge History of Iran.* Vol. 7. *From Nadir Shah to the Islamic Republic.* Cambridge, England: Cambridge University Press, 1991.

Bakhash, Shaul. *Iran: Monarchy, Bureaucracy and Reform under the Qajars (1858-1896).* London: Ithaca Press, 1978.

Bayat, Mangol. *Mysticism and Dissent: Socioreligious Thought in Qajar Iran.* Syracuse, NY: Syracuse University Press, 1982.

————. *Iran's First Revolution: Shi'ism and the Constitutional Revolution of 1905-1909.* New York: Oxford University Press, 1991.

Benjamin, S.G.W. *Persia and the Persians.* London: J. Murray, 1887.

Berberian, Houri. *The Love for Freedom Has No Fatherland: Armenians and the Iranian Constitution Revolution of 1905-1911.* Boulder, CO: Westview, 2000.

Bosworth, Edmund and Carole Hillenbrand, eds. *Qajar Iran: Political, Social and Cultural Change, 1800-1925.* Edinburgh: Edinburgh University Press, 1983.

Bournoutian, George A. *The Khanate of Erevan Under Qajar Rule 1795-1828.* Persian Studies Series, No. 13. Costa Mesa, CA: Mazda Publishers in Association with Bibliotheca Persica, 1992.

Browne, Edward G. *The Persian Revolution of 1905-1909.* 1910. Reprint. London: Frank Cass & Co., 1966.

Brydges-Jones, Sir Harford. *An Account of the Transactions of His Majesty's Mission to the Court of Persia, in the Years 1807-1811.* London: J. Bohn, 1834.

Curzon, Lord George N. *Persia and the Persian Question.* 2 Vols. London: Longmans Green & Co., 1892.

Fasa'i, Hasan. *History of Persia under Qajar Rule.* Translated by Heribert Busse. New York: Columbia University Press, 1972.

Gleave, R., ed. *Religion and Society in Qajar Iran.* London: CurzonRoutledge, 2004.

Hairi, Abdul-Hadi. *Shi'ism and Constitutionalism in Iran.* Leiden: E.J. Brill, 1977.

Katouzian, Homa. *State and Society in Iran: The Eclipse of the Qajars and the Emergence of the Pahlavis.* London: I.B. Tauris, 2000.

Keddie, Nikki R. *Religion and Rebellion in Iran: The Tobacco Protest of 1891-1892.* London: Frank Cass, 1966.

Kedourie, Elie and Sylvia Haim, eds. *Towards A Modern Iran.* London: F. Cass, 1980.

Kelly, Laurence. *Diplomacy and Murder in Tehran: Alexander Griboyedov and Imperial Russia's Mission to the Shah of Persia.* London: I.B. Taurus, 2001.

Lambton, Ann K.S. *Qajar Persia.* London: I.B. Tauris, 1988.

Martin, Vanessa. *Islam and Modernism: The Iranian Revolution of 1906.* Syracuse, NY: Syracuse University Press, 1989.

———. *The Qajar Pact: Bargaining, Protest and the State in 19th Century Persia.* New York: I.B. Tauris, 2005.

Nashat, Guity. *The Origins of Modern Reform in Iran, 1870-1880.* Urbana, IL: University of Illinois Press, 1982.

Shuster, W. Morgan. *The Strangling of Persia.* New York: Century Co., 1912.

Stack, Edward. *Six Months in Persia.* London: S. Low, Marston, Searle, & Rivington, 1882.

Sykes, Christopher. *Wassmuss: "The German Lawrence."* New York: Longmans, Green and Co., 1936.

Sykes, Ella C. *Persia and Its People.* London: Methuen and Co., 1910.

Sykes, Sir Percy Molesworth. *Ten Thousand Miles in Persia or Eight Years in Iran.* London: J. Murray, 1902.

Watson, Robert Grant. *A History of Persia From the Beginning of the Nineteenth Century to the Year 1858.* London: Smith, Elder & Co., 1866.

Wills, Charles James. *In the Land of the Lion and Sun.* London: MacMillan and Company, 1883.

Zahedi, Dariush. *The Iranian Revolution, Then and Now: Indicators of Regime Instability.* Boulder, CO: Westview, 2000.

b) *The Pahlavi Period*

Amirie, Abbas and Hamilton A. Twitchell, eds. *Iran in the 1980's.* Tehran: Institute for International Political and Economic Studies, 1978.

Amirsadeghi, Hossein and R.W. Ferrier, eds. *Twentieth-Century Iran.* New York: Holmes & Meier, 1977.

Amuzegar, Jahangir. *The Dynamics of the Iranian Revolution: The Pahlavi's Triumph and Tragedy.* Albany: State University of New York Press, 1991.

Atabaki, Touraj and Erik J. Zurcher. *Men of Order: Authoritarian Modernization under Ataturk and Reza Shah.* New York: I.B. Taurus, 2004.

Avery, Peter. *Modern Iran.* New York: Praeger, 1965.

Azimi, Fakhreddin. *Iran: The Crisis of Democracy, 1941-1953.* London: I.B. Tauris, 1989.

Banani, Amin. *The Modernization of Iran, 1921-1941.* Stanford, CA: Stanford University Press, 1961.

Bayne, Edward A. *Persian Kingship in Transition.* New York: American Universities Field Staff, 1968.

Cronin, Stephanie, ed. *The Making of Modern Iran: State and Society under Reza Shah, 1921-1941.* New York: RoutledgeCurzon, 2003.

Forbis, William H. *The Fall of the Peacock Throne: The Story of Iran.* New York: McGraw-Hill, 1980.

Gasiorowski, Mark J. and Malcolm Byrne, eds. *Mohammad Mosaddeq and the 1953 Coup in Iran.* Syracuse, NY: Syracuse University Press, 2004.

Halliday, Fred. *Iran: Dictatorship and Development.* New York: Penguin Books, 1979.

Heiss, Mary Ann. *Empire and Nationhood: The United States, Great Britain, and Iranian Oil, 1950-1954.* New York: Columbia University Press, 1997.

Jacqz, Jane W., ed. *Iran: Past, Present and Future.* New York: Aspen Institute for Humanistic Studies, 1976.

Kamrava, Mehran. *Revolution in Iran: The Roots of Turmoil.* New York: Routledge, 1990.

Kapuscinski, Ryszard. *Shah of Shahs.* Brand, William R. and Katarzyna Mroczkowska-Brand, trans. San Diego: Harcourt Brace Jovanovich, 1985.

Karanjia, Rustom Khurshedji. *The Mind of a Monarch.* London: Allen & Unwin, 1977.

Katouzian, Homa. *Musaddiq and the Struggle for Power in Iran.* London: I.B. Tauris, 1990.

Keddie, Nikki R. *Roots of Revolution: An Interpretive History of Modern Iran.* New Haven: Yale University Press, 1981.

Lenczowski, George, ed. *Iran under the Pahlavis.* Stanford, CA: Hoover Institution Press, 1978.

Parsons, Sir Anthony. *The Pride and the Fall: Iran 1974-1979.* London: Jonathan Cape, 1984.

Roosevelt, Kermit. *Countercoup: The Struggle for Control of Iran.* New York: McGraw-Hill, 1981.

Saikal, Amin. *The Rise and Fall of the Shah.* Princeton, NJ: Princeton University Press, 1980.

Schulz, Ann Tibbits. *Buying Security: Iran Under the Monarchy.* Boulder, CO: Westview Press, 1989.

Sheean, Vincent. *The New Persia.* New York: The Century Co., 1927.

Treverton, Gregory F. and James Klocke. *The Fall of the Shah of Iran.* Washington, DC: Distributed by the Institute for the Study of Diplomacy, School of Foreign Service, Georgetown University, 1994.

Upton, Joseph M. *The History of Modern Iran: An Interpretation.* Cambridge, MA: Harvard University Press, 1960.

Wilber, Donald Newton. *Contemporary Iran.* New York: Praeger, 1963.

Yar-Shater, Ehsan, ed. *Iran Faces the Seventies.* New York: Praeger, 1971.

Zabih, Sepehr. *The Mossadegh Era: Roots of the Iranian Revolution.* Chicago: Lake View Press, 1982.

c) *The Islamic Revolution and Republic*

Abrahamian, Ervand. *The Iranian Mojahedin.* New Haven, CT: Yale University Press, 1989.

————. *Khomeinism: Essays on the Islamic Republic.* Berkeley, CA: University of California Press, 1993.

Afkhami, Gholam R. *The Iranian Revolution: Thanatos on a National Scale.* Washington, DC: Middle East Institute, 1985.

Afshar, Haleh, ed. *Iran: A Revolution in Turmoil.* London: Macmillan & Co., 1985.

Algar, Hamid. *The Islamic Revolution in Iran.* Edited by Kalim Siddiqui. London: Open Press, 1980.

Amirahmadi, Hooshang and Manoucher Parvin, eds. *Post-Revolutionary Iran.* Boulder, CO: Westview Press, 1988.

Amjad, Mohammed. *Iran: From Royal Dictatorship to Theocracy.* New York: Greenwood Press, 1989.

Arjomand, Said Amir. *The Turban for the Crown: The Islamic Revolution in Iran.* New York: Oxford University Press, 1988.

Bakhash, Shaul. *The Reign of the Ayatollahs.* London: Allen & Unwin, 1986.

Banisadr, Abolhassan. *Islamic Government.* Translated by M.R. Ghanoonparvar. Lexington, Kentucky: Mazda Publishers, 1981.

Bashiriyeh, Hossein. *The State and Revolution in Iran, 1962-1982.*

London: Croom Helm, 1984.

Benard, Cheryl and Zalmay Khalilzad. *"The Government of God":* *Iran's Islamic Republic.* New York: Columbia University Press, 1984.

Carlsen, Robin Wordsworth. *The Imam and His Islamic Revolution.* Victoria, British Columbia: Snowman Press, 1982.

Clawson, Patrick L. *Iran under Khatami: A Political, Economic, and Military Assessment.* Washington D.C.: Washington Institute for Near East Policy, 1998.

Dabashi, Hamid. *Theology of Discontent: The Foundations of the Islamic Revolution in Iran.* New York: New York University Press, 1993.

Farhi, Farideh. *States and Urban Based Revolutions: Iran and Nicaragua.* Urbana, IL: University of Illinois Press, 1990.

Fischer, Michael M.J. *Iran: From Religious Dispute to Revolution.* Cambridge, MA: Harvard University Press, 1980.

Ganji, Manouchehr. *Defying the Iranian Revolution: From a Minister to the Shah to a Leader of Resistance.* Westport, CT: Praeger Publishers, 2002.

Green, Jerrold D. *Revolution in Iran: The Politics of Countermobilization.* New York: Praeger, 1982.

Heikal, Mohamed. *The Return of the Ayatollah: The Iranian Revolution from Mossadeq to Khomeini.* London: Andre Deutsch, 1981.

Hiro, Dilip. *Iran under the Ayatollahs.* London: Routledge and Kegan Paul, 1985.

Hoogland, Eric. *Twenty Years of Islamic Revolution: Political and Social Transition in Iran Since 1979.* Contemporary Issues in the Middle East Series. Syracuse, NY: Syracuse University Press, 2002.

Hunter, Shireen T. *Iran After Khomeini.* The Washington Papers, No. 156. Published with the Center for Strategic and International Studies. New York: Praeger, 1992.

Jabbari, Ahmad and Robert Olson, eds. *Iran: Essays on a Revolution in the Making.* Lexington, KY: Mazda Publishers, 1981.

Katzman, Kenneth. *The Warriors of Islam: Iran's Revolutionary Guard.* Boulder, CO: Westview Press, 1993.

Keddie, Nikki R. and Eric Hoogland, eds. *The Iranian Revolution and the Islamic Republic.* Washington, DC: Middle East Institute, 1982.

Koury, Enver M. and Charles G. MacDonald, eds. *Revolution in Iran: A Reappraisal.* Hyattsville, MD: Institute of Middle Eastern and

North African Affairs, 1982.

Kurzman, Charles. *The Unthinkable Revolution in Iran.* Cambridge, MA: Harvard University Press, 2004.

McDaniel, Tim. *Autocracy, Modernization, and Revolution in Russia and Iran.* Princeton, NJ: Princeton University Press, 1991.

Milani, Mohsen M. *The Making of Iran's Islamic Revolution.* Boulder, CO: Westview Press, 1988.

Onat, Hasan. *Shi'ism in the Twentieth Century, and the Islamic Revolution of Iran.* Ankara: Research Foundation for Public Services, 1996.

Parsa, Misagh. *Social Origins of the Iranian Revolution.* New Brunswick, NJ: Rutgers University Press, 1989.

Peress, Gilles and Ghulam Husayn Sa'idi. *Telex Iran: In the Name of Revolution.* Zurich: Scalo, 1997.

Ram, Haggay. *Myth and Mobilization in Revolutionary Iran: The Use of the Friday Congregational Sermon.* Lanham, MD: University Publishing Associates, 1994.

Ramazani, R.K., ed. *Iran's Revolution: The Search for Consensus.* Bloomington, IN: Indiana University Press, 1990.

Reed, Fred A. *Persian Postcards: Iran after Khomeini.* Vancouver, Canada: Talonbooks, 1994.

Salehi, M.M. *Insurgency Through Culture and Revolution: The Islamic Revolution of Iran.* New York: Praeger, 1988.

Sarraf, Tahmoores. *Cry of a Nation: The Saga of the Iranian Revolution.* New York: Peter Lang Publishing, Inc., 1990.

Simpson, John. *Inside Iran: Life under Khomeini's Regime.* New York: St. Martin's Press, 1988.

Sreberny, Annabelle and Ali Mohammadi. *Small Media, Big Revolution: Communication, Culture, and the Iranian Revolution.* Minneapolis: University of Minnesota Press, 1994.

Stempel, John. *Inside the Iranian Revolution.* Bloomington, IN: Indiana University Press, 1981.

Taheri, Amir. *The Spirit of Allah: Khomeini and the Islamic Revolution.* London: Hutchinson, 1985.

Wright, Robin. *In the Name of God: The Khomeini Decade.* New York: Simon and Schuster, Inc., 1989.

6. BIOGRAPHIES AND MEMOIRS

Akbari Joochy, Bemanjan. *Lion and Sword.* London: Minerva Press, 2001.

Alam, Asadollah. *The Shah and I: The Confidential Diary of Iran's Royal Court, 1969-1977.* Translated by Alinaghi Alikhani and Nicholas Vincent. Edited by Alinaghi Alikhani. London: I.B. Tauris, 1991.

Alavi, Bozorg. *The Prison Papers of Bozorg Alavi.* Translated by Donne Raffat. Syracuse, NY: Syracuse University Press, 1985.

Algar, Hamid. *Mirza Malkum Khan: A Biographical Study of Iranian Modernism.* Berkeley, CA: University of California Press, 1977.

Arfa, Hassan. *Under Five Shahs: An Autobiography.* London: J. Murray, 1964.

Baniameri, Siamack. *The Iranican Dream.* College Station, TX: Virtualwormbook.com Publishing, Inc., 2005.

Bani-Sadr, Abol Hassan. *My Turn to Speak: Iran, the Revolution and Secret Deals with the U.S.* Translated by William Ford. McLean, VA: Brassey's (U.S.) Inc., 1991.

Banisadr, Masoud. *Masoud: Memoirs of an Iranian Rebel.* London: Saqi, 2004.

Behnam, Mariam. *Zelzelah: A Woman before Her Time.* Dubai: Motivate, 1994.

Bell, Gertrude. *Persian Pictures.* London: Benn, 1928.

de Bellaigue, Christopher. *In the Rose Garden of the Martyrs: A Memoir of Iran.* London: Harper Collins, 2004.

Blanch, Lesley. *Farah, Shahbanou of Iran, Queen of Persia.* London: Collins, 1978.

Browne, Edward Granville. *A Year Amongst the Persians.* London: Adam and Charles Black, 1893.

Dashti, Sayeh. *Stranger in Paradise: A Memoir.* Tehran: Ghalam-e-Ashena, 2000.

Diba, Farhad. *Mohammed Mossadegh: A Political Biography.* London: Croom Helm, 1986.

Ebadi, Shirin. *Iran Awakening: From Prison to Peace Prize: One Woman's Struggle at the Crossroads of History.* Toronto, Canada: Alfred A. Knopf, 2006.

Farmanfarma'iyan, Manuchihr and Roxane Farmanfarmaian. *Blood and Oil: Memoirs of a Persian Prince.* New York: Random House, 1997.

Frye, Richard N. *Greater Iran: A 20th-Century Odyssey.* Costa Mesa, CA: Mazda Publishers, 2005.

Ghani, Cyrus. *Iran and the Rise of Reza Shah: From Qajar Collapse to Pahlavi Rule.* London: I.B. Taurus, 2000.

———, ed. *Man of Many Worlds: Diaries and Memoirs of Dr. Ghasem*

Ghani. Washington, D.C.: Mage Publishers, 2006.

Guppy, Shusha. *The Blindfold Horse: Memories of a Persian Childhood*. London: I.B. Tauris and Co., 2004.

Hall, Melvin. *Journey to the End of an Era*. New York: Scribner's Sons, 1947.

Harnack, Curtis. *Persian Lions, Persian Lambs*. Ames, IA: Iowa State University, 1981.

Harney, Desmond. *The Priest and The King: An Eyewitness Account of The Iranian Revolution*. London: I.B. Tauris, 1998.

Helms, Cynthia. *An Ambassador's Wife in Iran*. New York: Dodd Mead, 1981.

Hoveyda, Fereydoun. *The Fall of the Shah*. Translated by Roger Liddell. London: Weidenfeld and Nicolson, 1980.

Huyser, Gen. Robert E. *Mission to Tehran*. New York: Harper and Row, 1986.

Johanyak, Debra. *Behind the Veil: An American Woman's Memoir of the 1979 Iran Hostage Crisis*. Akron, Oh: University of Akron Press, 2006.

Katouzian, Homa, ed. *Musaddiq's Memoirs: The End of the British Empire in Iran*. London: Jebhe, 1988.

Kordi, Gohar. *Mahi's Story*. London: Women's Press, 1995.

Ladjevardi, Habib, ed. *Memoirs of Ali Amini, Prime Minister of Iran (1961-62)*. Bethesda, MD: Iranbooks, 1995.

―――. ed. *Memoirs of Prince Hamid Kadjar: Son of the Last Qajar Crown Prince*. Bethesda, MD: Iranbooks, 1996.

Milani, Abbas. *The Persian Sphinx: Amir Abbas Hovyeda and the Riddle of the Iranian Revolution*. Washington, DC: Mage Publishers, 2000.

Moin, Baqer. *Khomeini: Life of an Ayatollah*. London: I.B. Taurus, 1999.

Najafi, Najmeh. *Persia is My Heart*. New York: Harper, 1953.

Naraqi, Ehsan. *From Palace to Prison: Inside the Iranian Revolution*. Translated by Nilou Mobasser. Chicago: Ivan R. Dee, 1994.

Pahlavi, Farah Shahbanou. *My Thousand and One Days: An Autobiography*. Translated by Felice Harcourt. London: W.H. Allen, 1978.

Pahlavi, Mohammad Reza Shah. *Answer to History*. New York: Stein and Day, 1980.

―――. *Mission for My Country*. New York: McGraw-Hill, 1961.

―――. *The White Revolution of Iran*. Tehran: Imperial Pahlavi Library, 1967.

Precht, Henry. *A Diplomat's Progress: Ten Tales of Diplomatic Adventure in and around the Middle East.* Savannah, GA: Williams and Company, 2005.

Radji, Parviz C. *In the Service of the Peacock Throne.* London: Hamish Hamilton, 1983.

Rahnema, Ali. *An Islamic Utopian: A Political Biography of Ali Shariati.* London: I.B. Taurus, 2000.

Ramazani, Nesta. *The Dance of the Rose and the Nightingale.* Syracuse, NY: Syracuse Univerity Press, 2002.

Sabri-Tabrizi, Gholam-Reza. *Iran: A Child's Story, A Man's Experience.* New York: International Publishers, 1989.

Shawcross, William. *The Shah's Last Ride.* New York: Simon & Schuster Inc., 1988.

Sheil, Lady Mary Leonora. *Glimpses of Life and Manners in Persia.* London: J. Murray, 1856.

Sullivan, William H. *Mission to Iran.* New York: W.W. Norton, 1981.

de Villiers, Gerard et al. *The Imperial Shah: An Informal Biography.* Translated by June P. Wilson and Walter B. Michaels. Boston: Little, Brown, 1976.

Wilber, Donald Newton. *Riza Shah Pahlavi: The Resurrection and Reconstruction of Iran.* Hicksville, NY: Exposition Press, 1975.

Wynn, Antony. *Our Man in Persia: The Life of Sir Percy Sykes—Explorer, Consul, Soldier, Spy.* London: Plantagenet, 2001.

Zonis, Marvin. *Majestic Failure: The Fall of the Shah.* Chicago: University of Chicago Press, 1991.

7. CITY AND REGIONAL

Adamec, Ludwig W. *Historical Gazeteer of Iran: Abadan and Southwestern Iran.* Vol. 3. Graz, Austria: Akademische Druck-u. Verlagsanstalt, 1989.

———. *Historical Gazeteer of Iran: Meshed and Northeastern Iran.* Vol. 2. Graz, Austria: Akademische Druck-u. Verlagsanstalt, 1981.

———. *Historical Gazeteer of Iran: Tehran and Northwestern Iran.* Vol. 1. Graz, Austria: Akademische Druck-u. Verlagsanstalt, 1976.

Arberry, Arthur J. *Shiraz: Persian City of Saints and Poets.* Norman, OK: University of Oklahoma Press, 1960.

Atabaki, Touraj. *Azerbaijan: Ethnicity and the Struggle for Power in Iran.* London: I.B. Taurus, 2000.

Blunt, Wilfred and Wim Swaan. *Isfahan, Pearl of Persia.* London: Elek Books, 1964.

Clarke, John. *The Iranian City of Shiraz.* Durham, England: University of Durham, 1963.

Clarke, John and Brian D. Clark. *Kermanshah: An Iranian Provincial City.* Durham, England: University of Durham, 1969.

Connel, John, ed. *Semnan: Persian City and Region.* London: University College London, 1970.

Costello, V.F. *Kashan: A City and Region of Iran.* London: Bowker, 1976.

Eagleton, Williams, Jr. *The Kurdish Republic of 1946.* London: Oxford University Press, 1963.

Frye, Richard Nelson. *Bukhara: The Medieval Achievement.* Costa Mesa, CA: Mazda Publishers, 1996.

Gaube, Heinz. *Iranian Cities.* New York: New York University Press, 1979.

Kazembeyki, Mohammad Ali. *Society, Politics and Economics in Mazandaran, Iran 1848-1914.* London: Curzon Press, 2001.

Lockhart, Laurence. *Persian Cities.* London: Luzac and Company, Ltd., 1960.

Rabino, H.L. *Mazandaran and Astarabad.* Gibb Memorial, New Series, vii. London: Luzac, 1928.

Wilson, Sir Arnold T. *S. W. Persia.* London: Oxford University Press, 1941.

8. HISTORIOGRAPHY AND INTELLECTUAL HISTORY

Afary, Janet and Kevin B. Anderson. *Foucault and the Iranian Revolution: Gender and the Seductions of Islamism.* Chicago: University of Chicago Press, 2005.

Boroujerdi, Mehrdad. *Iranian Intellectuals and the West: The Tormented Triumph of Nativism.* Syracuse: Syracuse University Press, 1996.

Gheissari, Ali. *Iranian Intellectuals in the 20th Century.* Austin: University of Texas Press, 1998.

Hosseini, Ali Reza Agha. *The Failure of Transformism in Contemporary Iran, 1921-1979: The Role of Iranian Intellectuals in Constituting Political Identities.* Colchester, England: University of Essex, 2003.

Jahanbegloo, Ramin, ed. *Iran: Between Tradition and Modernity.* New York: Lexington Books, 2004.

Kashani-Sabet, Firoozeh. *Frontier Fictions: Shaping the Iranian Nation, 1804-1946.* Princeton: Princeton University Press, 1999.

Meisami, Julie Scott. *Persian Historiography*. Edinburgh: University of Edinburgh Press, 1999.

Milani, Abbas. *Lost Wisdom: Rethinking Modernity in Iran.* Washington, DC: Mage Publishers, 2004.

Mirsepassi, Ali. *Intellectual Discourse and the Politics of Modernization: Negotiating Modernity in Iran.* New York: Cambridge University Press, 2000.

Najmabadi, Afsaneh. *The Story of the Daughters of Quchan: Gender and National Memory in Iranian History*. Syracuse, NY: Syracuse University Press, 1998.

Quinn, Sholeh A. *A Historical Writing During the Reign of Shah Abbas: Ideology, Imitation and Legitimacy in Safavid Chronciles.* Salt Lake City: The University of Utah Press, 2000.

Tavakoli-Targhi, Mohamad. *Refashioning Iran: Orientalism, Occidentalism, and Historiography*. Houndmills: Palgrave, 2001.

Vahdat, Farzin. *God and Juggernaut: Iran's Intellectual Encounter with Modernity*. Syracuse, NY: Syracuse University Press, 2002.

Vaziri, Mostafa. *Iran as an Imagined Nation: The Construction of National Identity*. New York: Paragon Press, 1993.

III. POLITICS AND GOVERNMENT

1. DOMESTIC

Abdo, Geneive and Jonathan Lyons. *Answering Only To God: Faith and Freedom in Twenty-First Century Iran*. New York: Henry Holt and Company, 2003.

Abrahamian, Ervand. *Iran Between Two Revolutions.* Princeton, NJ: Princeton University Press, 1982.

Akhavi, Shahrough. *Religion and Politics in Contemporary Iran.* Albany: State University of New York Press, 1980.

Behnam, M. Reza. *Cultural Foundations of Iranian Politics.* Salt Lake City: University of Utah Press, 1986.

Bill, James Alban. *The Politics of Iran: Groups, Classes, and Modernization.* Columbus, OH: Charles E. Merrill, 1972.

Binder, Leonard. *Iran: Political Development in a Changing Society.* Berkeley, CA: University of California Press, 1962.

Bonine, Michael and Nikki Keddie, eds. *Modern Iran: The Dialectics of Continuity and Change.* Albany: State University of New York Press, 1981.

Brumberg, Daniel. *Reinventing Khomeini: The Struggle for Reform in Iran.* Chicago: University of Chicago Press, 2001.

Chaqueri, Cosroe. *Origins of Social Democracy in Modern Iran.* Seattle: University of Washington Press, 2001.

Chehabi, H.E. *Iranian Politics and Religious Modernism: The Liberation Movement of Iran under the Shah and Khomeini.* Ithaca, NY: Cornell University Press, 1990.

Clawson, Patrick L. et al. *Iran Under Khatami: A Political, Economic, and Military Assessment.* Washington, DC: The Washington Institute for Near East Policy, 1998.

Constitution of the Islamic Republic of Iran. Translated by Hamid Algar. Berkeley, CA: Mizan Press, 1980.

Cottam, Richard W. *Nationalism in Iran.* Pittsburgh: University of Pittsburgh Press, 1979.

Cronin, Stephanie, ed. *Reformers and Revolutionaries in Modern Iran: New Perspectives on the Iranian Left.* London: RoutledgeCurzon, 2004.

Dorraj, Manochehr. *From Zarathustra to Khomeini: Populism and Dissent in Iran.* Boulder, CO: Lynne Rienner Publishers, Inc., 1990.

Farsoun, Samih K. and Mehrdad Mashayekhi, eds. *Iran: Political Culture in the Islamic Republic.* London: Routledge, 1992.

Gheissari, Ali and Vali Nasr. *Democracy in Iran: History and the Quest for Liberty.* New York: Oxford University Press, 2006.

Ghods, M. Reza. *Iran in the Twentieth Century: A Political History.* Boulder, CO: Lynne Rienner Publishers, Inc., 1989.

Horowitz, Shale Asher and Schnabel, Albrecht. *Human Rights and Societies in Transition: Causes, Consequences, Responses.* Tokyo: United Nations University Press, 2004.

Human Rights Watch. *Iran: Like the Dead in Their Coffins: Torture, Detention, and the Crushing of Dissent in Iran.* New York: Human Rights Watch, 2004.

Hussain, Asaf. *Islamic Iran: Revolution and Counter-Revolution.* New York: St. Martin's Press, 1985.

The Iranian Constitution with Amendments. Translated by Ali Pasha Saleh. New York: Oceana Publications, 1971.

Kamali, Masoud. *Revolutionary Iran: Civil Society and State in the Modernization Process.* Brookfield, VT: Ashgate, 1998.

Kamrava, Mehran. *The Political History of Modern Iran: From Tribalism to Theocracy.* Westport, CT: Praeger, 1992.

Katzman, Kenneth. *Iran: Arms and Weapons of Mass Destruction Sup-*

pliers. Washington, DC: Congressional Research Service, The Library of Congress, 2003.

Keddie, Nikki R., ed. *Iran: Religion, Politics, and Society: Collected Essays.* London: F. Cass, 1980.

Khatami, Muhammad and Alidad Mafinezam. *Hope and Challenge: The Iranian President Speaks.* Kinghamton, NY: Institute of Global Cultural Studies, 1997.

Khomeini, Ayatollah Ruhollah. *A Clarification of Questions: An Unabridged Translation of Resaleh Towzih al-Masael.* Translated by J. Boroujerdi. Boulder, CO: Westview Press, 1984.

Khomeini, Ayatollah Ruhollah. *Islamic Government.* New York: Manor Books, 1979.

Laylaz, Saeed. *The Era of Construction: A Narration of Eight Years of Construction During the Presidency of Ayatollah Hashemi Rafsanjani, 1989-1997.* Tehran: Nashr-e-Kelid, 1997.

Malek-Ahmadi, Farshad. *Trapped by History: 100 Years of Struggle for Constitutionalism and Democracy in Iran.* New York: RoutledgeCurzon, 2003.

Marlowe, John. *Iran: A Short Political Guide.* London: Pall Mall Press, 1963.

Menashri, David. *Iran: A Decade of War and Revolution.* New York: Holmes & Meier, 1990.

Moaddel, Mansoor. *Class, Politics, and Ideology in the Iranian Revolution.* New York: Columbia University Press, 1993.

Mohammadi, Ali. Ed. *Iran Encountering Globalization: Problems and Prosspects.* New York, NY: RoutledgeCurzon, 2003.

Moslem, Mehdi. *Factional Politics in Post-Khomeini Iran.* Syracuse, NY: Syracuse University Press, 2002.

Mottale, Morris Mehrdad. *Iran: The Political Sociology of the Islamic Revolution.* Lanham, MD: University Press of America, 1995.

Omid, Homa. *Islam and the Post-Revolutionary State in Iran.* New York: St. Martin's Press, 1994.

Schahgaldian, Nikola. *The Clerical Establishment in Iran.* Santa Monica, CA: Rand Corporation, 1989.

Schirazi, Asghar. *The Constitution of Iran: Politics and State in the Islamic Republic.* Translated by John O'kane. London: I.B. Tauris, 1997.

Sciolino, Elaine. *Persian Mirrors: the elusive face of Iran.* New York: Free Press, 2000.

Siavoshi, Sussan. *Liberal Nationalism in Iran: The Failure of a Movement.* Boulder, CO: Westview Press, 1990.

Taghavi, Seyed Mohammad Ali. *Flourishing of Islamic Reformism in Iran: Political Islamic Groups in Iran (1941-61)*. New York: Routledge Curzon, 2005.

Wright, Robin. *The Last Great Revolution: Turmoil and Transformation in Iran*. New York, Alfred A. Knopf, 2000.

Zabih, Sepehr. *The Communist Movement in Iran*. Berkeley, CA: University of California Press, 1966.

———. *The Left in Contemporary Iran*. Beckenham, England: Croom Helm, 1986.

Zonis, Marvin. *The Political Elite of Iran*. Princeton, NJ: Princeton University Press, 1971.

2. FOREIGN RELATIONS

a) *General*

Buckley, Richard. *Iran and the West: A Failure to Communicate*. Cheltenham, England: Understanding Global Issues, 1997.

Chaqueri, Cosroe. *The Russo-Caucasian Origins of the Iranian Left: Social Democracy in Modern Iran*. Richmond, Surrey: Curzon Press, 2001.

Chubin, Shahram and Sepehr Zabih. *The Foreign Relations of Iran: A Developing State in a Zone of Great-Power Conflict*. Berkeley, CA: University of California Press, 1974.

Ehteshami, Anoushiravan and Mansour Varasteh, eds. *Iran and the International Community*. London: Routledge, 1991.

Esposito, John L., ed. *The Iranian Revolution: Its Global Impact*. Miami: Florida International University Press, 1990.

Fatemi, N. *Diplomatic History of Persia, 1917-1923*. New York: Russell F. Moore, 1952.

Fuller, Graham E. *The "Center of the Universe": The Geopolitics of Iran*. Boulder, CO: Westview Press, 1991.

Hamzavi, A.H. *Persia and the Powers: An Account of Diplomatic Relations, 1941-1946*. London: Hutchinson & Company, 1946.

Hunter, Shireen T. *Iran and the World: Continuity in a Revolutionary Decade*. Bloomington, IN: Indiana University Press, 1990.

Iran's Nuclear Programme: A Collection of Documents. London: The Stationary Office, 2005.

Menashri, David, ed. *The Iranian Revolution and the Muslim World*. Boulder, CO: Westview Press, 1990.

Miroshnikov, L.I. *Iran in World War I*. Moscow: Nauka Publishing

House, 1964.

Okata, Frank E. *Is Iran Ripe for a New Revolution*. Monterey, CA: Naval Postgraduate School.

Pearson, John H. *Can the World Stand a Nuclear Iran?* Carlisle Barracks, PA: U.S. Army War College, 2005.

Ramazani, Rouhollah. *The Foreign Policy of Iran: A Developing Nation in World Affairs 1500-1941.* Charlottesville, VA: University Press of Virginia, 1966.

————. *Iran's Foreign Policy 1941-1973: A Study of Foreign Policy in Modernizing Nations.* Charlottesville, VA: University Press of Virginia, 1975.

Reppa, Robert B. *Israel and Iran: Bilateral Relationships and Effect on the Indian Ocean Basin.* New York: Praeger, 1974.

Rezun, Miron, ed. *Iran at the Crossroads: Global Relations in a Turbulent Decade.* Boulder, CO: Westview Press, 1990.

Singh, K.R. *Iran, Quest for Security.* New Delhi: Vikas, 1980.

Skrine, Sir Clarmont. *World War in Iran.* London: Constable & Company, 1962.

Sobhani, Sohrab. *The Pragmatic Entente: Israeli-Iranian Relations, 1948-1988.* New York: Praeger, 1989.

b) *European*

Adamiyat, Fereydoun. *Bahrein Islands, A Legal and Diplomatic Study of the British-Iranian Controversy.* New York: Praeger, 1955.

Amini, Iradj. *Napoleon and Persia: Franco-Persian Relations under the First Empire.* Richmond, Surrey: Curzon, 1999.

Bonakdarian, Mansour. *Britain and the Iranian Constitutional Revolution of 1906-1911: Foreign Policy, Imperialism, and Dissent.* Syracuse, NY: Syracuse University Press, 2005.

Bullard, Reader. *Letters from Tehran: A British Ambassador in World War II, Persia.* Edited by E.C. Hodgkin. London: I.B. Taurus, 1991.

Ingram, Edward. *Britain's Persian Connection, 1798-1828: Prelude to the Great Game in Asia.* New York: Oxford University Press, 1992.

Greaves, Rose Louise. *Persia and the Defense of India, 1884-1892.* London: Athlone Press, 1959.

Kazemzadeh, Firuz. *Russia and Britain in Persia, 1864-1914.* New Haven: Yale University Press, 1968.

Martin, Bradford G. *German-Persian Diplomatic Relations: 1873-*

1912. The Hague: Mouton & Company, 1959.

Mohammadi, Ali and Anoushiravan Ehteshami. *Iran and Eurasia.* Reading: Ithaca, 2000.

Olson, William J. *Anglo-Iranian Relations during World War I.* London: F. Cass, 1984.

Wright, Denis. *The English Amongst the Persians during the Qajar Period, 1787-1921.* London: Heinemann, 1977.

————. *The Persians Amongst the English: Episodes in Anglo-Persian Relations.* London: I.B. Tauris, 1985.

c) *Superpower*

Alexander, Yonah and Allan Nanes, eds. *The United States and Iran: A Documentary History.* Frederick, MD: University Publications of America, 1980.

Ansari, Ali. *Confronting Iran: The Failure of American Foreign Policy and the Next Great Crisis in the Middle East.* Boulder, CO: Basic Books, 2006.

Askari, Hossein. *Case Studies of U.S. Economic Sanctions: The Chinese, Cuban, and Iranian Experience.* Westport, CT: Praeger, 2003.

Atkin, Muriel. *Russia and Iran.* Minneapolis: University of Minnesota Press, 1980.

Beeman, William O. *The "Great Satan" vs. the "Mad Mullahs": How the United States and Iran Demonize Each Other.* Westport, CT: Praeger Publishers, 2005.

Bill, James A. *The Eagle and the Lion: The Tragedy of American-Iranian Relations.* New Haven: Yale University Press, 1988.

Chase, Gary M. *The Impact of U.S. Foreign Policy on the Structure of Iran's Government.* Monterey, CA: Naval Postgraduate School, 2003.

Cordesman, Anthony H. and Ahmed S. Hashim. *Iran: Dilemmas of Dual Containment.* Boulder, CO: Westview Press, 1997.

Corsi, Jerome R. *Atomic Iran: How the Terrorist Regime Bought the Bomb and American Politicians.* Nashville, TN: WND Books, 2005.

Cottam, Richard W. *Iran and the United States: A Cold War Case Study.* Pittsburgh: University of Pittsburgh Press, 1988.

Cumings, Bruce, Ervand Abrahamian and Moshe Ma'oz. *Inventing the Axis of Evil: The Truth about North Korea, Iran, and Syria.* New York: New Press, 2004.

Dorman, William A. and Mansour Farhang. *The U.S. Press and Iran: Foreign Policy and the Journalism of Deference.* Berkeley, CA: University of California Press, 1987.

Entner, Marvin L. *Russo-Persian Commercial Relations, 1828-1914.* Gainesville, FL: University of Florida Press, 1965.

Fatemi, Faramarz S. *The U.S.S.R. in Iran.* South Brunswick, NJ: A.S. Barnes, 1980.

Fawcett, Louise L'Estrange. *Iran and the Cold War: The Azerbaijan Crisis of 1946.* Cambridge, England: Cambridge University Press, 1992.

Gallagher, Daniel J. *Should the U.S. Policy Towards Iran Change?* Carlisle Barracks, PA: U.S. Army War College, 2005.

Gasiorowski, Mark J. *U.S. Foreign Policy and the Shah: Building a Client State in Iran.* Ithaca, NY: Cornell University Press, 1991.

Gold, Fern R. and Melvin Conant. *Access to Oil: The United States Relationships with Saudi Arabia and Iran.* Honolulu, HW: University Press of the Pacific, 2003.

Grayson, Benson Lee. *United States-Iranian Relations.* Washington, DC: University Press of America, 1981.

Harris, David. *The Crisis: The President, the Prophet, and the Shah-1979 and the Coming of Militant Islam.* New York: Little, Brown and Company, 2004.

Heikal, Mohamed. *Iran, the Untold Story: An Insider's Account of America's Iranian Adventure and Its Consequences for the Future.* New York: Pantheon Books, 1982.

Heravi, Mehdi. *Iranian-American Diplomacy.* Brooklyn, NY: T. Gaus Sons, 1969.

Ioannides, Christos P. *America's Iran: Injury and Catharsis.* Lanham, MD: University Press of America, 1984.

Katzman, Kenneth. *Iran: U.S. Concerns and Policy.* Washington, DC: Congressional Research Service, Library of Congress, 2004.

Keddie, Nikki R. and Mark J. Gasiorowski, eds. *Neither East nor West: Iran, the Soviet Union, and the United States.* New Haven: Yale University Press, 1990.

Kinzer, Stephen. *All the Shah's Men: An American Coup and the Roots of Middle East Terror.* Hoboken, NJ: John Wiley and Sons, 2003.

Ledeen, Michael. *Debacle, the American Failure in Iran.* New York: Alfred A. Knopf, 1981.

Lenczowski, George. *Russia and the West in Iran, 1918-1948: A Study in Big Power Rivalry.* Ithaca, NY: Cornell University Press, 1949.

Lennon, Alexander T. and Eiss, Camille. *Reshaping Rogue States:*

Preemption, Regime Change, and U.S. Policy Toward Iran, Iraq, and North Korea. Cambridge, MA: MIT Press, 2004.

Martin, Al. *The Conspirators: Secrets of an Iran-Contra Insider.* Pray, MT: National Liberty Press, 2001.

McDaniel, Robert A. *The Shuster Mission and the Persian Constitutional Revolution.* Minneapolis: Bibliotheca Islamica, 1974.

Miglietta, John P. *American Alliance Policy in the Middle East, 1945-1992: Iran, Israel, and Saudi Arabia.* Lanham, MD: Lexington Books, 2002.

Millspaugh, Arthur C. *The American Task in Persia.* New York: Arno Press, 1973.

———. *Americans in Persia.* New York: Da Capo Press, 1946.

Peimani, Hooman. *Iran and the United States: The Rise of the West Asian Regional Grouping.* Westport, CT: Praeger, 1999.

Pollack, Kenneth M. *The Persian Puzzle: the Conflict between Iran and America.* New York: Random House, 2004.

Rafizadeh, Mansur: *Witness: From the Shah to the Secret Arms Deal, an Insider's Account of U.S. Involvement in Iran.* New York: William Morrow & Co., 1987.

Ramazani, Rouhollah K. *The United States and Iran: The Patterns of Influence.* New York: Praeger, 1982.

Rubin, Barry. *Paved with Good Intentions: The American Experience and Iran.* Oxford, England: Oxford University Press, 1980.

Russillo, Victor L. *Reassessing U.S. Policy Toward Iran.* Carlisle Barracks, PA: U.S. Army War College, 2003.

Saleh, Ali Pasha. *Cultural Ties Between Iran and the United States.* Tehran: Sherkat-e-Chapkhaneh Bistopanj-e-Shahrivar, 1976.

Seliktar, Ofira. *Failing the Crystal Ball Test: The Carter Administration and the Fundamentalist Revolution in Iran.* Westport, CT: Praeger, 2000.

Sick, Gary. *All Fall Down: America's Tragic Encounter with Iran.* New York: Random House, 1985.

Sicker, Martin. *The Bear and the Lion: Soviet Imperialism and Iran.* New York: Praeger, 1988.

Sokolski, Henry D. and Patrick Clawson. *Checking Iran's Nuclear Ambitions.* Carlisle Barracks, PA: Strategic Studies Institute, U.S. Army War College, 2004.

Walsh, Lawrence E. *Firewall: The Iran-Contra Conspiracy and Cover-Up.* New York: Norton, 1997.

Wroe, Ann. *Lives, Lies and the Iran-Contra Affair.* London: I.B.

Taurus, 1991.

Yeselson, Abraham. *United States-Persian Diplomatic Relations, 1833-1921.* New Brunswick, NJ: Rutgers University Press, 1956.

Yodfat, Aryeh Y. *The Soviet Union and Revolutionary Iran.* London: Croom Helm, 1984.

d) *American Hostage Crisis*

Bowden, Mark. *Guests of the Ayatollah: The First Battle in America's War with Militant Islam.* New York: Atlantic Monthly Press, 2006.

Christopher, Warren. *American Hostages in Iran: Conduct of a Crisis.* New Haven: Yale University Press, 1985.

Daughtery, William. *In the Shadow of the Ayatollah: A CIA Hostage in Iran.* Annapolis, MD: Naval Institute Press, 2001.

Farber, David. *The Iran Hostage Crisis and America's First Encounter with Radical Islam.* Princeton, NJ: Princeton University Press, 2005.

Follet, Ken. *On Wings of Eagles.* New York: William Morrow and Company, 1983.

Kennedy, Moorehead. *The Ayatollah in the Cathederal: Reflections of a Hostage.* New York: Hill and Wang, 1986.

Koob, Kathryn. *Guest of the Revolution.* Nashville, TN: Thomas Nelson Publishers, 1982.

Kyle, James H. *The Guts to Try: The Untold Story of the Iran Hostage Rescue Mission by the On-Scene Desert Commander.* New York: Orion Books, 1990.

Laingen, Bruce. *Yellow Ribbon.* Washington, DC: Brassey's (U.S.), 1992.

Lillich, Richard B., ed. *The Iran-United States Claims Tribunal; 1981-1983.* Charlottesville, VA: University Press of Virginia, 1984.

McFadden, Robert, Joseph Treaster, Maurice Carroll et al. *No Hiding Place: The New York Times Inside Report on the Hostage Crisis.* New York: Times Books, 1981.

McManus, Doyle. *Free at Last.* New York: New American Library, 1981.

Rosen, Barbara and Barry Rosen (with George Feifer). *The Destined Hour.* Garden City, NY: Doubleday, 1982.

Ryan, Paul B. *The Iranian Rescue Mission: Why It Failed.* Annapolis, MD: Naval Institute Press, 1985.

Salinger, Pierre. *America Held Hostage: The Secret Negotiations.* Garden City, NY: Doubleday, 1981.

Sick, Gary. *October Surprise: America's Hostages in Iran and the Election of Ronald Reagan.* New York: Times Books, 1991.

Sickman, Rocky. *Iranian Hostage: A Personal Diary.* Topeka, KS: Crawford Press, 1982.

Wells, Tim. *444 Days: The Hostages Remember.* New York: Harcourt, Brace, Jovanovich, 1985.

3. REGIONAL POLITICS

a) *General*

Amirahmadi, Hooshang and Nader Entessar, eds. *Iran and the Arab World.* New York: St. Martins Press, 1993.

Aqayi, Bahman. *The Law & Politics of the Caspian Sea in the Twenty-First Century: The Positions and Views of Russia, Kazakhstan, Azerbaijan, Turkmenistan, with Special Reference to Iran.* Bethesda, MD: Ibex Publishers, 2003.

Bilgin, Veli. *Turkish-Israeli Entente: The Impact of Turkish-Israeli Alignment on Turkish-Iranian Relations.* Ankara: Department of International Relations of Bilkent University, 2004.

Davar, Firoze Cowasji. *Iran and India Through the Ages.* New York: Asia Publishing House, 1962.

———. *Iran in Iraq: How Much Influence?* Amman: International Crisis Group, 2005.

Furtig, Henner. *Iran's Rivalry with Saudi Arabia Between the Gulf Wars.* Reading, UK: Garnet Publishing Ltd., 2002.

Marschall, Christin. *Iran's Persian Gulf Policy: From Khomeini to Khatami.* New York: RoutledgeCurzon, 2003.

Menashri, David, ed. *The Iranian Revolution and the Muslim World.* Boulder, CO: Westview Press, 1990.

Mirfendereski, Guive. *A Diplomatic History of the Caspian Sea: Treaties, Diaries, and Other Stories.* With a Foreword by H.E. Chehabi. New York: Palgrave, 2001.

Natali, Denise. *The Kurds and the State: Evolving National Identity in Iraq, Turkey, and Iran.* Syracuse, NY: Syracuse University Press, 2005.

———. *Neighbors Not Friends: Iraq and Iran after the Gulf Wars.* New York: Routledge, 2001.

Olson, Robert. *The Kurdish Question and Turkish-Iranian Relations From World War I to 1998.* Costa Mesa, CA: Mazda Publishers, 1998.

————.*Turkey-Iran Relations, 1979-2004: Revolution, Ideology, War, Coups and Geopolitics.* Costa Mesa, CA: Mazda Publishers, 2004.

Pasha, A.K. *India, Iran and the GCC States: Political Strategy and Foreign Policy.* New Delhi: Manas Publications, 2000.

Peimani, Hooman. *The Caspian Pipeline Dilemma: Political Games and Economic Losses.* Westport, CT: Praeger, 2001.

————. *Regional Security and the Future of Central Asia: The Competition of Iran, Turkey, and Russia.* Westport, CT: Praeger, 1998.

Perkovich, George. *Iran is not an Island: A Strategy to Mobilize the Neighbors.* Washington, DC: Carnegie Endowment for International Peace, 2005.

Reppa, Robert B. *Israel and Iran: Bilateral Relationships and Effect on the Indian Ocean Basin.* New York: Praeger, 1974.

Shoham, Dany. *Chemical and Biological Weapons in the Arab Countries and Iran: An Existential Threat to Israel?* Shaarei Tikva, Israel: ACPR Publishers, 2001.

Shojakhani, Mohsen and M.R. Rikhtegran. *Indo-Iranian Thought: A World Heritage.* Delhi: Renaissance Publishing House, 1995.

Sobhani, Sohrab. *The Pragmatic Entente: Israeli-Iranian Relations, 1948-1988.* New York: Praeger, 1989.

Souresrafil, Behrouz. *Khomeini and Israel.* England: I Researchers Inc., 1988.

Sweiner, Myron and Ali Banuazizi. *The Politics of Social Transformation in Afghanistan, Iran, and Pakistan.* Syracuse, NY: Syracuse University Press, 1994.

Zimmerman, Doran. *Tangled Skein or Gordian Knot: Iran and Syria as State Supporters of Political Violence Movements in Lebanon and in the Palestinian Territories.* Zurich: Forschungsstelle fur Sicherheitspolitik der ETH Zurich, 2004.

b) *Persian Gulf*

Amin, Sayed Hassan. *International and Legal Problems of the Gulf.* Boulder, CO: Westview Press, 1981.

Amirahmadi, Hooshang and Nader Entessar, eds. *Reconstruction and Regional Diplomacy in the Persian Gulf.* London: Routledge, 1992.

Amirie, Abbas, ed. *The Persian Gulf and the Indian Ocean in International Politics.* Tehran: Institute for International Political and Economic Studies, 1976.

Amirsadeghi, Hossein, ed. *The Security of the Persian Gulf.* London:

Croom Helm, 1981.

Burrell, R.M. *The Persian Gulf.* Washington Papers, No. 1. New York: Library Press, 1972.

Cordesman, Anthony H. *Iran and Iraq: The Threat from the Northern Gulf.* Boulder, CO: Westview Press, 1994.

Ramazani, Rouhollah K. *The Persian Gulf: Iran's Role.* Charlottesville, VA: University Press of Virginia, 1972.

al-Saud, Faisal bin Salman. *Iran, Saudi Arabia and the Gulf: The Transformation of Great Power Politics.* London: I.B. Tauris, 2003.

Smith, Barbara. *Iran and Iraq: Prospects and Policies.* Enstone: Ditchley Foundation, 1999.

Wilson, Arnold T. *The Persian Gulf.* Oxford, England: Oxford University Press, 1928.

c) *Iran-Iraq War*

Abdulghani, Jasim M. *Iran and Iraq: The Years of Crisis.* Baltimore, MD: The Johns Hopkins University Press, 1984.

El Azhary, M.S., ed. *The Iran-Iraq War: An Historical, Economic, and Political Analysis.* New York: St. Martin's Press, 1984.

Chubin, Shahram and Charles Tripp. *Iran and Iraq at War.* Boulder, CO: Westview Press, 1988.

Cordesman, Anthony H. *The Iran-Iraq War and Western Security, 1984-1987.* London: Jane's Publishing, 1987.

Davis, Charles, ed. *After the War: Iran, Iraq and the Arab Gulf.* Chichester, West Sussex, United Kingdom: Carden Publications, 1990.

Grummon, Stephen R. *The Iran-Iraq War: Islam Embattled.* The Washington Papers, No. 92. New York: Praeger, 1982.

Hiro, Dilip. *The Longest War.* New York: Routledge, 1991.

Ismael, Tareq Y. *Iraq and Iran: Roots of Conflict.* Syracuse, NY: Syracuse University Press, 1982.

Joyner, Christopher C. *The Persian Gulf War: Lessons for Strategy, Law, and Diplomacy.* Westport, CT: Greenwood Press, 1990.

Karsh, Efraim, ed. *The Iran-Iraq War: Impact and Implications.* London: The MacMillan Press, 1989.

Khadduri, Majid. *The Gulf War: The Origins and Implications of the Iraq-Iran Conflict.* New York: Oxford University Press, 1988.

Pelletiere, Stephen C. *The Iran-Iraq War: Chaos in a Vacuum.* New York: Praeger, 1992.

Potter, Lawrence G. and Gary G. Sick. *Iran, Iraq, and the Legacies of War.* New York: Palgrave, 2004.

Rajee, Farhang, ed. *Iranian Perspectives on the Iran-Iraq War.* Gainsville, FL: University Press of Florida, 1997.

————. *The Iran-Iraq War: The Politics of Aggression.* Gainesville, FL: University Press of Florida, 1993.

Sole, Joseph T. *Realism and Balance of Power: The Iran-Iraq Conflict.* 2004.

Tahir-Kheli, Shirin and Shaheen Ayubi, eds. *The Iran-Iraq War: New Weapons, Old Conflicts.* New York: Praeger, 1983.

Trab Zemzemi, Abdel-Majid. *The Iraq-Iran War: Islam and Nationalisms.* San Clemente, CA: United States Publishing Company, 1986.

IV. RELIGION, THEOLOGY, AND PHILOSOPHY

1. PRE-ISLAMIC RELIGIONS

Abd-ru-shin. *Zoroaster: Life and Work of the Forerunner in Persia; Received in the Proximity of Abd-ru-shin Through the Special Gift of One Called for the Purpose.* Gambier, OH: Grail Foundation Press, 1996.

Amighi, Janet Kestenberg. *The Zoroastrians of Iran: Conversion, Assimilation, or Persistence.* New York: AMS Press, 1990.

Asmussen, Jes Peter. *Manichaean Literature.* Delmar, NY: Scholars' Facsimiles & Reprints, 1975.

Bailey, H.W. *Zoroastrian Problems in the Ninth-Century Books.* Oxford, England: Clarendon Press, 1971.

Bausani, Alessandro. *Religion in Iran: From Zoroaster to Baha'ullah.* Translated by J.M. Marchesi. New York: Bibliotheca Persica Press, 2000.

Boyce, Mary. *A History of Zoroastrianism.* Vol. 1. *The Early Period.* Leiden: E.J. Brill, 1975.

————. *A History of Zoroastrianism.* Vol. 2. *Under the Achaemenians.* Leiden: E.J. Brill, 1982.

————. *A Persian Stronghold of Zoroastrianism.* Oxford, England: Clarendon Press, 1977.

————. *Textual Sources for the Study of Zoroastrianism.* Manchester, England: Manchester University Press, 1984.

————. *Zoroastrianism: Its Antiquity and Constant Vigour.* Costa Mesa, CA: Mazda Publishers in association with Bibliotheca

Persica, 1992.

———. *Zoroastrians: Their Religious Beliefs and Practices.* Oxford, England: Clarendon Press, 1979.

Boyce, Mary and Frantz Grenet. *A History of Zoroastrianism.* Vol. 3. *Zoroastrianism under Macedonian and Roman Rule.* Leiden: E.J. Brill, 1989.

Burkitt, F.C. *The Religion of the Manichees.* Cambridge, England: The University Press, 1925.

Choksy, Jamsheed K. *Evil, Good, and Gender Facets of the Feminine in Zoroastrian Religious History.* Toronto Studies in Religion, Vol. 28. New York: Peter Lang, 2002.

Cumont, Franz. *The Mysteries of Mithra.* Translated by Thomas J. McCormack. Chicago: The Open Court Publishing Company, 1963.

Curtis, John E. and Nigel Tallis, eds. *Forgotten Empire: The World of Ancient Persia.* Berkeley, CA: University of California Press, 2005.

Darmesteter, J. and L.H. Mills, trans. *The Zend-Avesta.* 3 Vols. Oxford, England: Clarendon Press, 1880-1887.

Dhalla, M.N. *History of Zoroastrianism.* New York: Oxford University Press, 1938.

———. *Zoroastrian Theology: From the Earliest Times to the Present Day.* New York: AMS Press, 1972.

Duchesne-Guillemin, Jacques. *The Hymns of Zarathustra.* Translated by Mrs. M. Henning. Boston: Beacon Press, 1963.

———. *Symbols and Values in Zoroastrianism: Their Survival and Renewal.* New York: Harper and Row, 1966.

———. *The Western Response to Zoroaster.* Oxford, England: Clarendon Press, 1958.

Foltz, Richard C. *Spirituality in the Land of the Noble: How Iran Shaped the World's Religions.* Oxford, England: Oneworld, 2004.

Herzfeld, Ernst E. *Zoroaster and His World.* 2 Vols. Princeton, NJ: Princeton University Press, 1947.

Insler, S. *The Gathas of Zarathustra.* Leiden: E.J. Brill, 1975.

Irani, D.J. *The Divine Songs of Zorathustra.* London: George Allen & Unwin, 1924.

Jackson, A.V. Williams. *Avesta Reader.* Stuttgart, Germany: W. Kohlhammer, 1893.

———. *Researches in Manichaeism.* New York: Columbia University Press, 1932.

———. *Zoroaster: The Prophet of Ancient Iran.* New York: The

MacMillan Co., 1899.

————. *Zoroastrian Studies.* New York: Columbia University Press, 1928.

Kanga, M.F., ed. *Avesta Reader.* Pune, India: Vaidika Samsodhana Mandala, 1988.

Krlwaczek, Paul. *In Search of Zarathustra: Across Iran and Central Asia to Find the World's First Prophet.* New York: Vintage Departures/Vintage Books, 2004.

Laing, S. *A Modern Zoroastrian.* London: F.V. White, 1887.

Malandra, W. *An Introduction to Ancient Iranian Religion.* Minneapolis: University of Minnesota Press, 1983.

Mikalson, Jon D. *Herodotus and Religion in the Persian Wars.* Chapel Hill, NC: University of North Carolina Press, 2003.

Moreen, Vera Basch. *In Queen Esther's Garden: an Anthology of Judeo-Persian Literature.* New Haven: Yale University Press, 2000.

Moulton, J.H. *Early Zoroastrianism.* London: Williams and Norgate, 1913.

Patterson, Leonard. *Mithraism and Christianity.* Cambridge, England: Cambridge University Press, 1921.

Pavry, Jal Dastur Cursetji. *The Zoroastrian Doctrine of a Future Life: From Death to the Individual Judgment.* New York: Columbia University Press, 1926.

Phythian-Adams, W.J. *Mithraism.* London: Constable, 1915.

Reichelt, Hans. *Avesta Reader.* Strassburg: K.J. Truebner, 1911.

Rose, Jenny. *The Image of Zoroaster: The Persian Mage Through European Eyes.* New York: Bibliotheca Press, 2000.

Sanjana, Rastamji E.D.P. *Zarathushtra and Zarathushtrianism in the Avesta.* Leipzig: O. Harrosowitz, 1906.

Settegast, Mary. *When Zarathustra Spoke: The Reformation of Neolithic Culture and Religion.* Costa Mesa, CA: Mazda Publishers, 2005.

Widengren, George. *Mani and Manichaeism.* Translated by Charles Kessler. London: Weidenfeld and Nicolson, 1965.

Zaehner, R.C. *The Dawn and Twilight of Zoroastrianism.* New York: G.P. Putnam's Sons, 1961.

————. *The Teachings of the Magi.* London: Allen & Unwin, 1956.

————. *Zurvan, A Zoroastrian Dilemma.* Oxford, England: Clarendon Press, 1955.

2. ISLAM IN IRAN

a) *Historical Shi'ism*

Aghaie, Kamran Scot. *The Martyrs of Karbala: Shi'i Symbols and Rituals in Modern Iran.* Seattle: University of Washington Press, 2004.
Arjomand, Said Amir, ed. *Authority and Political Culture in Shi'ism.* Albany: State University of New York Press, 1988.
Bill, James A. and John Alden Williams. *Roman Catholics and Shi'i Muslims: Prayer, Passion and Politics.* Chapel Hill, NC: University of North Carolina Press, 2002.
Brunner, Rainer and Ende Werner, eds. *The Twelver Shia in Modern Times: Religious Culture and Political History.* Social, Economic and Political Studies of the Middle East and Asia, Vol. 72. Leiden: Brill, 2001.
Clarke, Lynda, ed. *Shi'ite Heritage: Essays on Classical and Modern Traditions.* Binghamton, NY: Global Publications, 2001.
Cole, Juan. *Sacred Space and Holy War: The Politics, Culture and History of Shi'ite Islam.* London: I.B. Taurus, 2002.
Daftary, Farhad. *The Isma'ilis: Their History and Doctrines.* Cambridge, England: Cambridge University Press, 1990.
Donaldson, Dwight M. *The Shi'ite Religion.* London: Luzac and Company, 1933.
Halm, Heinz. *Shi'a Islam: From Religion to Revolution.* Princeton, NJ: Markus Wiener Publishers, 1997.
Hussain, Jassim M. *The Occultation of the Twelfth Imam.* London: Muhammadi Trust, 1982.
Jafri, S.H.M. *The Origins and Early Development of Shi'a Islam.* London: Longman, 1979.
Jamal, Nadia Eboo. *Surviving the Mongols: Nizari Quhistani and the Continuity of Ismaili Tradition in Persia.* London: I.B. Taurus, 2002.
Kohlberg, Etan. *Shi'ism.* Willston, VT: Ashgate, 2003.
Momen, Moojan. *An Introduction to Shi'i Islam.* New Haven: Yale University Press, 1985.
Nasr, Seyyed Hossein. *The Islamic Intellectual Tradition in Persia.* Richmond, Surrey: Curzon, 1996.
———. *Shi'ism: Doctrines, Thought, and Spirituality.* Albany: State University of New York Press, 1988.

Nasr, Seyyed Hossein, Hamid Dabashi and Seyyed Vali Reza Nasr, eds. *Expectations of the Millennium: Shi'ism in History.* Albany: State University of New York Press, 1989.

Newman, Andrew J. *The Formative Period of Twelver Shi'ism: Hadith as Discourse Between Qum and Baghdad.* London: Curzon Press, 2000.

Petrushevsky, I.P. *Islam in Iran.* Translated by Hubert Evans. Albany: State University of New York Press, 1985.

Pinault, David. *The Shiites: Ritual and Popular Piety in a Muslim Community.* New York: St. Martin's Press, 1993.

Sachedina, Abdulaziz A. *Islamic Messianism: The Idea of the Mahdi in Twelver Shi'ism.* Albany: State University of New York Press, 1981.

Tabataba'i, Allamah Seyyid Muhammad Husayn. *Shi'ite Islam.* Translated and edited by S.H. Nasr. London: George Allen and Unwin, 1975.

———. *A Shiite Anthology.* Translated by William C. Chittick. Albany: State University of New York Press, 1981.

Turner, Colin. *Islam Without Allah? The Rise of Religious Externalism in Safavid Iran.* London: Curzon Press, 2001.

Walbridge, Linda S. *The Most Learned of the Shi'a: The Institution of the Marja' Taqlid.* New York: Oxford University Press, 2001.

b) *Philosophical Shi'ism*

Chittick, William C. *The Heart of Islamic Philosophy: The Quest for Self-Knowledge in the Teachings of Afdal al-Din Kashani.* Oxford, England: Oxford University Press.

Corbin, Henry. *Spiritual Body and Celestial Earth: From Mazdean Iran to Shi'ite Iran.* Translated by N. Pearson. Princeton, NJ: Princeton University Press, 1977.

Dahlen, Ashk. *Deciphering the Meaning of Revealed Law: The Soroushian Paradigm in Shi'i Epistemolgy.* Uppsala: Acta Universiatis Upsaliensis, 2001.

Faghfoory, Mohammad H., ed. *Beacon of Knowledge: Essays in Honor of Seyyed Hossein Nasr.* Louisville, KY: Fons Vitae, 2003.

Iqbal, Sir Muhammad. *The Development of Metaphysics in Persia.* London: Luzac, 1908.

Keshavjee, Rafique. *Mysticism and the Plurality of Meaning: The Case of the Ismailis of Rural Iran.* London: I.B. Taurus, 1998.

Khusraw, Nasr-i. *Knowledge and Liberation: A Treatise on*

Philosophical Theology. Translated by Faqir Muhammad Hunza'i. London: I.B. Taurus, 1998.

Lewis, Edwin Hahn, et al, eds. *The Philosophy of Seyyed Hossein Nasr.* Chicago: Open Court, 2001.

Moris, Zailan, ed. *Knowledge is Light: Essays in Honor of Seyyed Hossein Nasr.* Chicago: Kazi Publications, 1999.

Morris, James W. *The Wisdom of the Throne: An Introduction to the Philosophy of Mulla Sadra.* Princeton, NJ: Princeton University Press, 1981.

Nasr, Seyyed Hossein. *Sadr al-Din Shirazi and his Transcendent Theosophy.* Tehran: Imperial Iranian Academy of Philosophy, 1978.

Nasr, Seyyed Hossein and Mehdi Amirazavi, eds. *An Anthology of Philosophy in Persia,* 2 Vols. Oxford, England: Oxford University Press, 1999-2001.

———. *Three Muslim Sages.* Cambridge, MA: Harvard University Press, 1964.

Rahman, Fazlur. *The Philosophy of Mulla Sadra.* Albany: State University of New York Press, 1975.

Renard, John. *All the King's Falcons: Rumi on Prophets and Revelation.* Albany: State University of New York Press, 1994.

Sabzavari, Hadi Ibn Mahdi. *The Metaphysics of Sabzavari.* Translated by Mehdi Mohaghegh and Toshihiko Izutsu. Delmar, NY: Caravan Books, 1977.

Sachedina, Abdulaziz Abdulhussein. *The Just Ruler in Shi'ite Islam: The Comprehensive Authority of the Jurist in Imamite Jurisprudence.* New York: Oxford University Press, 1988.

Sadri, Mahmoud and Ahmad Sadri, trans. eds. *Reason, Freedom, and Democracy in Islam: Essential Writings of Abdolkarim Soroush.* New York: Oxford University Press, 2000.

Tusi, Nasir al-Din. *Contemplation and Action: The Spiritual Autobiography of a Muslim Scholar.* Translated by S.J. Badakhchani. London: I.B. Taurus, 1998.

Walbridge, John. *The Science of Mystic Lights: Qutb al-Din al-Shirazi and the Illuminationist Tradition in Islamic Philosophy.* Cambridge, MA: Harvard University Press, 1972.

Walker, Paul E. *Early Philosophical Shi'ism: The Ismaili Neoplatonism of Abu Ya'qub al-Sijistani.* New York: Cambridge University Press, 1993.

c) *Sufism*

Attar, Farid al-Din. *Muslim Saints and Mystics*. Translated by A. J. Arberry. Chicago: University of Chicago Press, 1966.

Bakhtiar, Laleh. *Sufi: Expressions of the Mystic Quest*. London: Thames and Hudson, 1976.

de Bruijn, J.T.P. *Persian Sufi Poetry: An Introduction to the Mystical Use of Classical Poems*. Richmond, Surrey: Curzon Press, 1997.

Burckhardt, Titus. *An Introduction to Sufism: The Mystical Dimension of Islam*. Translated by Donald MacLeod Matheson. Wellingborough, Northamptonshire, England: Crucible, 1990.

————. *The Sufi Doctrine of Rumi: An Introduction*. Tehran: Aryamehr University, 1974.

Chittick, William C. *The Sufi Path of Knowledge: Ibn al-Arabis' Metaphysics of Imagination*. Albany: State University of New York Press, 1989.

————. *The Sufi Path of Love: The Spiritual Teachings of Rumi*. Albany: State University of New York Press, 1983.

————. *Sufism: A Short Introduction*. Oxford, England: Oneworld, 2000.

Corbin, Henry. *Creative Imagination in the Sufism of Ibn Arabi*. Translated by Ralph Manheim. Princeton, NJ: Princeton University Press, 1969.

Davis, F. Hadland. *The Persian Mystics: Jalalu'd Din Rumi*. New York: E.P. Dutton, 1908.

————. *The Persian Mystics: Jami*. New York: E.P. Dutton, 1908.

Ernst, Carl W. *Ruzbihan Baqli: Mysticism and the Rhetoric of Sainthood in Persian Sufism*. Curzon Sufi Series. Richmond, Surrey: Curzon, 1996.

————. *Words of Ecstacy in Sufism*. Albany: State University Press of New York, 1985.

Iqbal, Afzal. *The Life and Work of Jalul-ud-din Rumi*. London: Octagon Press, 1983.

Jamnia, Mohammad Ali and Mojdeh Bayat. *Under the Sufi's Cloak: Stories of Abu Sa'id and His Mystical Teachings*. Beltsville, MD: Writers' Inc. International, 1995.

Lewisohn, Leonard, ed. *The Legacy of Medieval Persian Sufism*. London: Khaniqahi Nimatullahi Publications, 1992.

Moayyad, Heshmat and Lewis, Franklin. *The Colossal Elephant and His Spiritual Feats: Shaykh Ahmad-e Jam: The Life and Legend of a Popular Sufi Saint of 12th Century Iran.* Costa Mesa, CA: Mazda Publishers, 2004.

Moris, Zailan. *Revelation, Intellectual Intuition and Reason in the Philosophy of Mulla Sadra.* New York: RoutledgeCurzon, 2003.

Nasr, Seyyed Hossein. *Sufi Essays.* London: George Allen and Unwin, Ltd., 1972.

Nicholson, Reynold Alleyne. *The Idea of Personality in Sufism.* Lahore, Pakistan: M. Ashraf, 1964.

Razi, Abd Allah Ibn Muhammad Najm al-Din. *The Path of God's Bondsmen from Origin to Return: A Sufi Compendium.* Translated by Hamid Algar. Delmar, NY: Caravan Books, 1982.

Ridgeon, Lloyd. *Persian Metaphysics and Mysticism: Selected Works of 'Aziz Nasafi.* London: Curzon Press, 2001.

Schimmel, Annemarie. *As Through a Veil: Mystical Poetry in Islam.* New York: Columbia University Press, 1982.

————. *I am Wind, you are Fire: The Life and Work of Rumi.* Boston: Shambhala, 1992.

————. *Mystical Dimensions of Islam.* Chapel Hill, NC: University of North Carolina Press, 1975.

————. *The Triumphal Sun: A Study of the Works of Jalaloddin Rumi.* London: Fine Books, 1978.

Tabataba'i, 'Allamah Syyed Muhammad Husayn. *Lubb-i Lubab dar sayr wa Suluk-i ulul albab: Kernal of a Kernal: A Shi'a Approach to Sufism.* Trans. Mohammad H. Faghfoory. New York: State University of New York Press, 2003.

Vitray-Meyerovitch, Eva de. *Rumi and Sufism.* Translated by Simone Fattal. Sausalito, CA: Post-Apollo Press, 1987.

d) *Avicenna*

Corbin, Henry. *Avicenna and the Visionary Recital.* Princeton, NJ: Princeton University Press, 1960.

Goodman, L.E. *Avicenna.* New York: Routledge, 1992.

Heath, Peter. *Allegory and Philosophy in Avicenna (Ibn Sina), with a Translation of the Book of the Prophet Muhammad's Ascent to Heaven.* Philadelphia: University of Pennsylvania Press, 1992.

Inati, Shams C. *Ibn Sina and Mysticism: Remarks and Admonitions.* London: Degan Paul International, 1996.

McGinnis, Jon. *Interpreting Avicenna: Science and Philosophy in Medieval Islam, Proceedings of the Second Conference of the Avicenna Study Group.* Leiden: Brill, 2004.

Morewedge, Parviz. *The Metaphysica of Avicenna (Ibn Sina).* New York: Columbia University Press, 1973.

Wisnovsky, Robert, ed. *Aspects of Avicenna.* Princeton, NJ: Markus Wiener Publishers, 2001.

3. BABISM AND BAHAISM

Amanat, Abbas. *Resurrection and Renewal: The Making of the Babi Movement in Iran, 1844-1850.* Ithaca, NY: Cornell University Press, 1989.

Balyuzi, H.M. *The Bab: The Herald of the Day of Days.* Oxford, England: George Ronald, 1973.

———. *Baha'u'llah: The King of Glory.* Oxford, England: George Ronald, 1980.

———. *Edward Granville Browne and the Baha'i Faith.* Oxford, England: George Ronald, 1970.

Brown, Keven and Eberhard von Kitzing. *Evolution and Baha'i Belief: Abdu'l-Baha's Response to Nineteenth Century Darwinism.* Studies in Babi and Baha'i Religions, Vol. 12. Los Angeles: Kalimat Press, 2001.

Browne, Edward Granville, comp. *Materials for the Study of the Babi Religion.* Cambridge, England: Cambridge University Press, 1918.

Cole, Juan R. and Moojan Momen, eds. *From Iran East and West: Studies in Babi and Baha'i History.* Vol. 2. Los Angeles: Kalimat Press, 1984.

Esslemont, John E. *Baha'u'llah and the New Era.* 5th Edition. Wilmette, IL: Baha'i Publishing Trust, 1980.

Gulpaygani, Mirza Abu'l-Fadl. *The Brilliant Proof.* Los Angeles: Kalimat Press, 1998.

Husain, Hamadani. *The Tarikh-i Jadid, or New History of Mirza Ali Muhammad the Bab.* Translated and edited by Edward G. Browne. Cambridge, England: Cambridge University Press, 1893.

MacEoin, Denis. *The Sources of Babi Doctrine and History.* Leiden: E.J. Brill, 1992.

Momen, Moojan, ed. *The Babi and Baha'i Religions, 1844-1944: Some Contemporary Western Accounts.* Oxford, England: George Ronald, 1981.

———, ed. *Studies in Babi and Baha'i History,* Vol. 1. Los Angeles: Kalimat Press, 1982.

Nabil, Muhammad Zarandi. *The Dawn Breakers: Nabil's Narrative of the Early Days of the Baha'i Revelation.* Translated and edited by

Shoghi Effendi. Wilmette, IL: Baha'i Publishing Trust, 1932.

Smith, Peter. *The Babi and Baha'i Religions: From Messianic Shi'ism to a World Religion*. Cambridge, England: Cambridge University Press, 1987.

———, ed. *In Iran: Studies in Babi and Baha'i History*. Vol. 3. Los Angeles: Kalimat Press, 1986.

4. CHRISTIANITY

Anonymous. *A Chronicle of the Carmelites in Persia and the Papal Mission of the XVIIth and XVIIIth Centuries*. London: Eyre and Spottiswoode, 1939.

Buck, Christopher. *Paradise and Paradigm: Key Symbols in Persian Christianity and Baha'i Faith*. Albany: State University of New York Press, 1999.

Coan, Frederick G. *Yesterdays in Persia and Kurdistan*. Claremont, CA: Saunders Studio Press, 1939.

Cochran, Joseph G. *The Persian Flower: A Memoir of Judith Grant Perkins of Oroomiah, Persia*. Boston: John P. Jeweet and Co., 1853.

Dehqani-Tafti, H.B. *The Hard Awakening*. New York: Seabury Press, 1981.

Elder, John. *History of the American Presbyterian Mission to Iran, 1834-1960*. Tehran: Church Council of Iran, n.d.

Laurie, Thomas. *Dr. Grant and The Mountain Nestorians*. Boston: Gould and Lincoln, 1853.

Perkins, Justin. *A Residence of Eight Years in Persia*. New York: M.W. Dodd, 1843.

Presbyterian Church in the U.S.A. *Iran Mission: A Century of Mission Work in Iran (Persia), 1834-1934*. Beirut: The American Press, 1936.

Roberts, Paul William. *Journey of the Magi: In Search of the Birth of Jesus*. Toronto: Stoddart, 1995.

Waterfield, Robin E. *Christians in Persia: Assyrians, Armenians, Roman Catholics, and Protestants*. London: George Allen and Unwin, 1973.

Wishard, John G. *Twenty Years in Persia*. New York: Fleming H. Revell Co., 1908.

Yamauchi, Edwin M. *Persia and the Bible*. Grand Rapids, MI: Baker Book House, 1990.

5. JUDAISM

Albertz, Rainer and Bob Becking. *Yahwism after the Exile: Perspectives on Israelite Religion in the Persian Era.* Assen, The Netherlands: Royal Van Gorcum, 2003.

Berquist, Jon L. *Judaism in Persia's Shadow, A Social and Historical Approach.* Minneapolis: Fortress Press, 1995.

Levy, Habib. *Comprehensive History of the Jews of Iran: The Outset of the Diaspora.* Edited by Hooshang Ebrami. Translated by George W. Maschke. Costa Mesa, CA: Mazda Publishers, 1999.

Loeb, Laurence D. *Outcast: Jewish Life in Southern Iran.* New York: Gordon and Breach, 1977.

Moreen, Vera B., ed. *Iranian Jewry During the Afghan Invasion.* Stuttgart, Germany: Franz Steiner Verlag, 1990.

Netzer, Amnon, ed. *Padyavand.* Vol.1. Costa Mesa, CA: Mazda Publishers, 1996.

————. *Padyavand.* Vol.2. Costa Mesa, CA: Mazda Publishers, 1997.

————. *Padyavand.* Vol.3. Costa Mesa, CA: Mazda Publishers, 1999.

Sarshar, Homa and Houman Sarshar, eds. *The History of Contemporary Iranian Jews.* Vol. 4. Beverly Hills, CA: Center for Iranian Jewish Oral History, 2001.

V. PERSO-ISLAMIC POLITICAL AND SOCIAL THOUGHT

1. RELIGION AND POLITICS

Arjomand, Said Amir. *The Shadow of God and the Hidden Imam: Religion, Political Order, and Societal Change in Shi'ite Iran from the Beginning to 1890.* Chicago: The University of Chicago Press, 1984.

Cole, Juan R.I. and Nikki R. Keddie, eds. *Shi'ism and Social Protest.* New Haven: Yale University Press, 1986.

Davari, Mahmood T. *The Political Thought of Ayatollah Murtaza Mutahhari.* New York: RoutledgeCurzon, 2005.

Enayat, Hamid. *Modern Islamic Political Thought.* Austin, TX: The University of Texas Press, 1982.

Fischer, Michael M.J. and Mehdi Abedi. *Debating Muslims: Cultural Dialogues in Postmodernity and Tradition.* Madison, WI: The

University of Wisconsin Press, 1990.

Keddie, Nikki R., ed. *Religion and Politics in Iran: Shi'ism from Quietism to Revolution*. New Haven: Yale University Press, 1983.

Khomeini, Imam. *Islam and Revolution: Writings and Declarations*. Translated by Hamid Algar. London: Routledge & Kegan Paul, 1985.

Lambton, Ann K.S. *Islamic Society in Persia*. London: School of Oriental and African Studies, University of London, 1954.

————. *Theory and Practice in Medieval Persian Government*. London: Variorum Reprints, 1980.

Mahmood, Sohail. *Islamic Fundamentalism in Pakistan, Egypt and Iran*. Lahore, Pakistan: Vanguard, 1995.

Martin, Vanessa. *Creating an Islamic State: Khomeini and the Making of a New Iran*. London: I.B. Taurus, 2000.

Moaddel, Mansoor and Kamran Talatoff. *Contemporary Debates in Islam: An Anthology of Modernist and Fundamentalist Thought*. New York: St. Martin's Press, 2000.

Mosteshar, Cherry. *Unveiled: Love and Death among the Ayatollahs*. London: Coronet, 1995.

Mottahedeh, Roy. *The Mantle of the Prophet: Religion and Politics in Iran*. New York: Simon and Schuster, 1985.

Mutahhari, Ayatullah Murtaza. *Fundamentals of Islamic Thought: God, Man and the Universe*. Translated by R. Campbell. Berkeley, CA: Mizan Press, 1985.

————. *Social and Historical Change: An Islamic Perspective*. Translated by R. Campbell. Berkeley, CA: Mizan Press, 1986.

Omid, Homa. *Islam and the Post-Revolutionary State in Iran*. New York: St. Martin's Press, 1994.

Rahnema, Ali. *An Islamic Utopian: A Political Biography of Ali Shari'ati*. London: I.B. Tauris, 1998.

Rajaee, Farhang. *Islamic Values and World View: Khomeini on Man, the State and International Politics*. Lanham, MD: University Press of America, 1983.

Ridgeon, Lloyd. *Religion and Politics in Modern Iran: A Reader*. New York: I.B. Tauris, 2005.

Sabet, Amr G.E. *Islam, Iran, and the Western Discourse: Behind the Veil*. Amsterdam: Research Center for International Political Economy and Foreign Policy Analysis (RECIPE), 1995.

Shari'ati, Ali. *Marxism and Other Western Fallacies: An Islamic Critique*. Translated by R. Campbell. Berkeley, CA: Mizan Press, 1980.

———. *On the Sociology of Islam.* Translated by Hamid Algar. Berkeley, CA: Mizan Press, 1979.

Taleghani, Ayatullah Sayyid Mahmud. *Society and Economics in Islam.* Translated by R. Campbell. Berkeley, CA: Mizan Press, 1982.

2. MIRRORS FOR PRINCES, ADMINISTRATIVE MANUALS AND ETHICAL WORKS

Anonymous. *Tadhkirat Al-Muluk: A Manual of Safavid Administration.* Translated and edited by V. Minorsky. London: Luzac & Co., 1943.

Anushiravani, Alireza. *The Sea of Precious Virtues (Bahr al-Fava'id): A Medieval Islamic Mirror for Princes.* Translated by Julie Scott Meisami. Salt Lake City: University of Utah Press, 1991.

Ibn Isfandiyar, Muhammad Ibn al-Hasan. *The Letter of Tansar.* Translated by M. Boyce. Rome: Instituto Italiano per il Medio ed Estremo Oriente, 1968.

Kai Ka'us, Ibn Iskandar. *A Mirror for Princes: The Qabusnameh of Kai Ka'us Ibn Iskandar.* Translated by Reuben Levy. New York: E.P. Dutton, 1951.

Nasir-i Khusraw. *Make a Shield from Wisdom: Selected Verses from Nasir-i Khusraw's Divan.* Translated and edited by Annemarie Schimmel. London: Kegan Paul International, 1993.

Nezam al-Mulk. *The Book of Government or Rules for Kings.* Translated by Hubert Drake. London: Routledge & Kegan Paul, 1960.

Nizami, Arudi. *The Chahar Maqala ("Four Discourses").* Translated by Edward Granville Browne. Hertford, England: S. Austin and Sons, 1899.

al-Tusi, Nasir al-Din Muhammad Ibn Muhammad. *The Nasirean Ethics.* Translated and edited by G.M. Wickens. London: Allen and Unwin, 1964.

VI. SOCIETY AND CULTURE

1. ANTHROPOLOGY, ETHNOLOGY AND SOCIOLOGY

Adelkhah, Fariba. *Being Modern in Iran.* Translated by Johnathon Derrick. New York: Columbia University Press, 2000.

Arasteh, A. Reza. *Faces of Persian Youth: A Sociological Study.* Leiden: E.J. Brill, 1970.
———. *Man and Society in Iran.* Leiden: E.J. Brill, 1964.
Bulliet, Richard W. *The Patricians of Nishapur: A Study in Medieval Islamic Social History.* Cambridge, MA: Harvard University Press, 1972.
Campbell, Elizabeth Yoel. *Yesterday's Children: Growing Up in Persia.* Traralgon, Australia: LV Printers, 1996.
Fazeli, Nematollah. *Politics of Culture in Iran: Anthropology, Politics, and Society in the Twentieth Century.* New York: Routledge, 2006.
Field, Henry. *Contributions to the Anthropology of Iran.* 2 Vols. Chicago: Field Museum of Natural History, 1939.
Foran, John. *Fragile Resistance: Social Transformation in Iran from 1500 to the Revolution.* Boulder, CO: Westview Press, 1993.
Friedl, Erika. *Women of Deh Koh: Lives in an Iranian Village.* Washington, DC: Smithsonian Institute Press, 1989.
Loffler, Rheinhold. *Islam in Practice: Religious Belief in a Persian Village.* Albany: State University of New York Press, 1988.
Mahdi, Ali Akbar and Abdolali Lahsaeizadeh. *Sociology in Iran.* Bethesda, MD: Jahan Book Company, 1992.
Prigmore, Charles S. *Social Work in Iran Since the White Revolution.* Tuscaloosa, AL: University of Alabama Press, 1976.
Rahimieh, Nasrin. *Missing Persians: Discovering Voices in Iranian Cultural History.* Gender, Culture, and Politics in the Middle East Series. New York: Syracuse University Press, 2001.
Rejali, Darius M. *Torture and Modernity: Self, Society, and State in Modern Iran.* Boulder, CO: Westview Press, 1994.
Shepherd, Kevin R.D. *Minds and Sociocultures: An Analysis of Religious and Dissenting Movements.* Cambridge: Philosophical Press, 1995.
Varzi, Roxanne. *Warring Souls.* Durham, NC: Duke University Press, 2006.
Yaghmaian, Behzad. *Social Change in Iran: An Eyewitness Account of Dissent, Defiance, and New Movements for Rights.* Albany: State University of New York Press, 2002.

2. DEMOGRAPHY, MIGRATION AND IMMIGRATION

Bahrambeygui, H. *Tehran: An Urban Analysis.* Tehran: Sahab Books Institute, 1977.

Carter, Charles E. *The Emergence of Yehud in the Persian Period: A Social and Demographic Study.* Sheffield, England: Sheffield Academic, 1999.

Fata, Soraya and Raha Fafii. *Strength in Numbers: The Relative Concentration of Iranian Americans across the United States: Iran Census Report.* Washington, DC: National Iranian American Council, 2003.

Fathi, Asghar. *Iranian Refugees and Exiles Since Khomeini.* Costa Mesa, CA: Mazda Publishers, 1991.

Hemmasi, Mohammad. *Migration in Iran: A Quantitative Approach.* Tehran: Pahlavi University Publications, 1974.

Kamalkhani, Zahra. *Iranian Immigrants and Refugees in Norway.* Bergen, Norway: Migration Project Studies, 1988.

Kazemi, Farhad. *Poverty and Revolution in Iran: The Migrant Poor, Urban Marginality and Politics.* New York: New York University Press, 1981.

Kelly, Ron and Jonathan Friedlander, eds. *Irangeles: Iranians in Los Angeles.* Berkeley, CA: University of California Press, 1993.

McLachlan, K.S. and F. Ershad. *Internal Migration in Iran.* London: University of London, 1989.

Mehryar, Amir H. *Demographic and Health Survey of Iran, 2000: A Summary of Main Findings.* Tehran, Iran: Ministry of Science, Research & Technology, Population Studies and Research Center for Asia and the Pacific, 2003.

Momeni, Jamshid A., ed. *The Population of Iran: A Selection of Readings.* Honolulu: East-West Population Institute, East-West Center, 1977.

National Census of Population and Housing (1966). Tehran: Statistical Center of Iran, 1967.

Shaffer, Brenda. *Borders and Brethren: Iran and the Challenge of Azerbaijani Identity.* Cambridge, MA: MIT Press, 2002.

3. EDUCATION AND HEALTH

Arasteh, Reza. *Education and Social Awakening in Iran.* Leiden: E.J. Brill, 1962.

Ebrahimnejad, Hormoz. *Medicine, Public Health and the Qajar State: Patterns of Medical Modernization in Nineteenth-Century Iran.* Leiden: Brill, 2004.

Ekhtiar, Maryam. *Modern Science, Education and Reform in Qajar Iran: The Dar al-Funun.* Richmond, Surrey: Curzon Press, 2001.

Elgood, Cyril. *A Medical History of Persia and the Eastern Caliphate.* Amsterdam: Apa-Philo Press, 1979.

———. *Medicine in Persia.* New York: Paul B. Hoeber, 1934.

———. *Safavid Medical Practice or the Practice of Medicine, Surgery and Gynaecology in Persia Between 1500 A.D. and 1750 A.D.* London: Luzac, 1970.

Harnwell, Gaylord P. *Educational Voyaging in Iran.* Philadelphia: University of Pennsylvania Press, 1962.

Hendershot, Clarence. *Politics, Polemics and Pedagogs: A Study of United States Technical Assistance in Education to Iran, Including Negotiations, Political Considerations in Iran and the United States, Programming, Methods, Problems, Results, and Evaluation.* New York: Vantage Press, 1975.

Khalilidehkordi, Bahman. *Epidemiology of Childhood Diarrhoea in Iran.* Liverpool: University of Liverpool, 2004.

Mehryar, Amir H. and Hassan Eini Zinab. *Teenage Marriage, Pregnancy, Contraception, and Fertility in the Islamic Republic of Iran.* Tehran, Iran: Ministry of Science, Research & Technology, Population Studies and Research Center for Asia and the Pacific, 2003.

Menashri, David. *Education and the Making of Modern Iran.* Ithaca, NY: Cornell University Press, 1992.

Overseas Liaison Committee. *An Analysis of U.S.-Iranian Cooperation in Higher Education.* Washington, DC: American Council on Education, 1976.

Pliskin, Karen L. *Silent Boundaries: Cultural Constraints on Sickness and Diagnosis of Iranians in Israel.* New Haven: Yale University Press, 1987.

Ringer, Monica M. *Education, Religion, and the Discourse of Cultural Reform in Qajar Iran.* Costa Mesa, CA: Mazda Publishers, Inc., 2001.

Sabahi, Farian. *The Literacy Corps in Pahlavi Iran, 1963-1979: Political, Social, and Literary Implications.* Lugano, Switzerland: Editrice Sapiens, 2002.

Sadiq, Issa Khan. *Modern Persia and Her Educational System.* New York: Columbia University, 1931.

Shavarini, Mitra K. and Wendy R. Robison. *Women and Education in Iran and Afghanistan: An Annotated Bibliography of Sources in English, 1975-2003.* Lanham, MD: Scarecrow Press, 2005.

Slocum J.B. *Iran: A Study of the Educational System.* Washington, DC: World Education Series, 1970.

4. BELIEFS, CUSTOMS AND FOLKLORE

Curtis, Vesta Sarkhosh. *Persian Myths*. Austin, TX: The University of Texas Press, 1993.

Donaldson, Bess Allen. *The Wild Rue: A Study of Muhammadan Majic and Folklore in Iran*. London: Luzac, 1938.

Edwards, A. Cecil. *A Persian Caravan*. New York: Harper, 1928.

Hekmat, Forough-es-Saltaneh. *Folk Tales of Ancient Persia*. Delmar, NY: Caravan Books, 1974.

Hinnells, John R. *Persian Mythology*. London: Hamlyn, 1973.

Masse, Henri. *Persian Beliefs and Customs*. New Haven, CT: Human Relations Area Files, 1954.

Nakosteen, Mehdi Khan. *In the Land of the Lion and the Sun: The Country, Customs and Culture of My People*. Denver, CO: The World Press, 1937.

Suratgar, Olive. *I Sing in the Wilderness: An Intimate Account of Persia and the Persians*. London: E. Stanford, 1951.

Wills, C.J. *Persia as It Is: Being Sketches of Modern Persian Life and Character*. London: Sampson, Low, Marston, Searle and Rivington, 1888.

Wilson, S.G. *Persian Life and Customs*. New York: F.H. Revell, 1895.

Yasavuli, Javad. *The Fabulous Land of Iran: Colourful and Vigorous Folklore: With Over 411 Photos in Colour*. Tehran: Farhang-Sara (Yassavoli), 1994.

5. TRIBES AND TRIBALISM

Arfa, Hassan. *The Kurds: An Historical and Political Study*. London: Oxford University Press, 1966.

Barth, Fredrik. *Nomads of South Persia: The Basseri Tribe of the Khamseh Confederacy*. London: George Allen and Unwin, 1961.

———. *Principles of Social Organization in Southern Kurdistan*. Oslo, Norway: Brodrene Jorgensen A.S., 1953.

Beck, Lois. *Nomad: A Year in the Life of a Qashqa'i Tribesman in Iran*. London: I.B. Tauris, 1991.

Bradburd, Daniel. *Ambiguous Relations: Kin, Class, and Conflict among Komachi Pastoralists*. Washington, DC: Smithsonian Institution Press, 1990.

van Bruinessen, Martin. *Kurds and Identity Politics*. London: I.B. Taurus, 2003.

Cooper, Merian C. *Grass*. New York: G.P. Putnam's Sons, 1925.

Cronin, Vincent. *The Last Migration.* London: Hart-Davis, 1957.

Entessar, Nader. *Kurdish Ethnonationalism.* Boulder, CO: Lynne Rienner Publishers, 1992.

Garthwaite, Gene. *Khans and Shahs: The Bakhtiari in Iran.* Cambridge, England: Cambridge University Press, 1982.

Jahani, Carina, Agnes Korn and Gunilla Gren-Eklund, eds. *The Baloch and their Neighbors, Ethnic and Linguistic Contact in Balochistan in Historical and Modern Times.* Wiesbaden, Germany: Reichert Verlag, 2003.

Koohi-Kamali, Farideh. *The Political Development of the Kurds in Iran: Pastoral Nationalism.* New York: Palgrave-Macmillan, 2003.

Oberling, Pierre. *The Qashqa'i Nomads of Fars.* The Hague: Mouton, 1974.

Reid, James J. *Tribalism and Society in Islamic Iran, 1500-1629.* Malibu, CA: Undena Publications, 1983.

Tapper, Richard, ed. *The Conflict of Tribe and State in Iran and Afghanistan.* London: Croom Helm, 1983.

Ullens de Schooten, Marie. *Lords of the Mountains: Southern Persia and the Kashkai Tribe.* London: Chatto & Windus, 1956.

Vali, Abbas. *Modernity and the Stateless: The Kurdish Question in Iran.* London: I.B. Taurus, 2002.

6. WOMEN

Afkhami, Mahnaz and Erika Friedl, eds. *In the Eye of the Storm: Women in Post-Revolutionary Iran.* Syracuse, NY: Syracuse University Press, 1994.

Amanat, Abbas, ed. *Crowning Anguish: Memoirs of a Persian Princess from the Harem to Modernity, 1884-1914.* Washington, DC: Mage Publishers, 1993.

Amin, Cameron Michael. *The Making of the Modern Iranian Woman: Gender, State Policy, and Popular Culture, 1865-1946.* Gainesville, FL: University of Florida Press, 2002.

Ansari, Sarah and Vanessa Martin. *Women, Religion and Culture in Iran.* London: Curzon Press, 2001.

Azari, Farah, ed. *Women of Iran: The Conflict with Fundamentalist Islam.* London: Ithaca Press, 1983.

Bamdad, Badr ol-Moluk. *From Darkness into Light: Women's Emancipation in Iran.* Translated and edited by F.R.C. Bagley. Hicksville, NY: Exposition Press, 1977.

Beck, Lois and Guity Nashat, eds. *Women in Iran from 1800 to the Islamic Republic.* Urbana, IL.: University of Illinois Press, 2004.

Farman-Farmaian, Sattereh. *Daughter of Persia: A Woman's Journey from Her Father's Harem through the Islamic Revolution.* New York: Crown Publishers, 1992.

Fathi, Asghar, ed. *Women and the Family in Iran.* Leiden: E.J. Brill, 1985.

Howard, Jane. *Inside Iran: Women's Lives.* Washington DC: Mage Publishers, 2002.

Isfandiyari, Halah. *Reconstructed Lives: Women and Iran's Islamic Revolution.* Washington, DC: Baltimore, MD: Woodrow Wilson Center Press; John Hopkins University Press, 1997.

Kazemzadeh, Masoud. *Islamic Fundamentalism, Feminism, and Gender Inequality in Iran under Khomeini.* Lanham, MD: University Press of America, 2002.

Kermani, Touba and S. Golmenzerji. *Holy Presence: The Twenty-Year Activities of Women in the Islamic Republic of Iran.* Tehran: Al-huda International, 1999.

Milani, Farzaneh. *Veils and Words: The Emerging Voices of Iranian Women Writers.* Syracuse, NY: Syracuse University Press, 1992.

Moallem, Minoo. *Between Warrior Brother and Veiled Sister: Islamic Fundamentalism and the Politics of Patriarchy in Iran.* Berkeley, CA: University of California Press, 2005.

Moghissi, Haideh. *Populism and Feminism in Iran: Women's Struggle in a Male-Defined Revolutionary Movement.* New York: St. Martin's Press, 1996.

Nafisi, Azar. *Reading Lolita in Tehran: A Memoir in Books.* New York: Random House, 2003.

Najmabadi, Afsaneh. *Women with Mustaches and Men without Beards: Gender and Sexual Anxieties of Iranian Modernity.* Berkeley, CA: University of California Press, 2005.

———, ed. *Women's Autobiographies in Contemporary Iran.* Cambridge, MA: Harvard University Press, 1990.

Nashat, Guity, ed. *Women and Revolution in Iran.* Boulder, CO: Westview Press, 1983.

Paidar, Parvin. *Women and the Political Process in Twentieth-Century Iran.* New York: Cambridge University Press, 1997.

Rice, Clara C. *Persian Women and Their Ways.* Philadelphia: J.P. Lippincott, 1923.

Sanasarian, Eliz. *The Women's Rights Movement, and Represssion from 1900 to Khomeini.* New York: Praeger, 1982.

Shahidian, Hammed. *Resistance in the Islamic Republic: Emerging Voices in the Iranian Women's Movement.* Westport, CT: Greenwood Press, 2002.

———. *Women in Iran: Gender Politics in the Islamic Republic.* Westport, CT: Greenwood Press, 2002.

Sullivan, Soraya Paknazar, comp. and trans. *Stories by Iranian Women Since the Revolution.* Austin, Texas: The University of Texas Press, 1991.

Tabari, Azar and Nahid Yeganeh, eds. *In the Shadow of Islam: The Women's Movement in Iran.* London: Zed Press, 1982.

7. COOKERY

Batmanglij, Najmieh. *New Food of Life: Ancient Persian and Modern Iranian Cooking and Ceremonies.* Washington, DC: Mage Publishers, 1992.

———. *Persian Cooking for a Healthy Kitchen.* Washington, DC: Mage Publishers, 1994.

———. *A Taste of Persia: An Introduction to Persian Cooking.* Washington, DC: Mage Publishers, 1999.

Ghanoonparvar, M.R. *Persian Cuisine: Traditional Foods.* Lexington, KY: Mazda Publishers, 1982.

———. *Persian Cuisine: Regional and Modern Foods.* Lexington, KY: Mazda Publishers, 1984.

Hekmat, Forough-es-Saltaneh. *The Art of Persian Cooking.* Tehran: Ebn-e-Sina Publishers, 1961.

Mazda, Maideh. *In a Persian Kitchen.* Tokyo, Japan: Charles E. Tuttle Company, 1960.

Ramazani, Nesta. *Persian Cooking: A Table of Exotic Delights.* New York: Quadrangle, 1974.

Shaida, Margaret. *The Legendary Cuisine of Persia.* Northampton, MA: Interlink Publishing, 2006.

VII. LANGUAGE AND LITERATURE

1. DICTIONARIES AND GLOSSARIES

Amuzegar, Hooshang. *A Dictionary of Common Persian and English Verbs: With Synonyms and Examples.* Bethesda, MD: IBEX Publishers, Inc., 2005.

Aryanpur-Kashani, Abbas and Manoochehr Aryanpur-Kashani. *The Combined New Persian-English and English-Persian Dictionary.* New York: Media Link International, Inc., 1986.

Boyle, John A. *A Practical Dictionary of the Persian Language.* London: Luzac, 1949.

Cannon, Garland and Kaye S. Alan. *The Persian Contributions to the English Language: A Historical Dictionary.* Wiesbaden: Harrassowitz Verlag, 2001.

Gilani, Dariush B. *An English-Persian Dictionary.* Bethesda, MD: IBEX Publishing, 1999.

Hayyim, S. *New English-Persian Dictionary.* 2 Vols. Tehran: Beroukhim, 1929-1931.

———. *New Persian-English Dictionary.* 2 Vols. Tehran: Beroukhim, 1934-1936.

———. *The Larger English-Persian Dictionary.* 2 Vols. Tehran: Beroukhim, 1941-1943.

Hillmann, Michael Craig. *Basic Tajik(i) Word List.* Springfield, VA: Dunwoody Press, 2003.

Kasraie, Asadollah and Hassan Kasraie. *Persian and English Glossary for Humanities and Social Sciences.* Burnsville, NC: Celo Valley Books, 1991.

Lambton, Ann K.S. *Persian Vocabulary.* Cambridge, England: Cambridge University Press, 1954.

Shahryari, Parviz, ed. *A Dictionary of Scientific Terms.* Tehran: Franklin Book Programs, 1970.

Steingass, Francis J. *A Comprehensive Persian-English Diction-ary.* London: Routledge and Kegan Paul, 1957.

Turner, Colin. *A Thematic Dictionary of Modern Persian.* London: Routledge Curzon, 2004.

2. LANGUAGE LEARNING AND LINGUISTICS

Abrahams, Simin. *Modern Persian: A Course Book.* London: RoutledgeCurzon, 2005.

Ayman, Lily. *A Persian Reader, Book One.* Bethesda, MD: Iranbooks, 1993.

Beeman, William O. *Language, Status, and Power in Iran.* Bloomington, Indiana: Indiana University Press, 1986.

Boyle, John Andrew. *Grammar of Modern Persian.* Wiesbaden, Germany: Otto Harrassowitz, 1966.

Brunner, Christopher J. *A Syntax of Western Middle Iranian.* Delmar,

NY: Caravan Books, 1977.

Elwell-Sutton, L.P. *Elementary Persian Grammar*. Cambridge, England: Cambridge University Press, 1983.

Ghanoonparvar, M.R. *Reading Chubak*. Costa Mesa, CA: Mazda Publishers, 2005.

———. *Translating the Garden*. Austin, Texas: University of Texas Press, 2002.

Ghanoonparvar, M.R. and F. Givehchian. *Persian for Beginners*. Lexington, KY: Mazda Publishers, 1985.

Habibian, Simin K., ed. *1001 Persian-English Proverbs: Learning Language and Culture through Commonly Used Sayings*. Bethesda, MD: IBEX Publishers, 2000.

Hanaway, William L. and Brian Spooner. *Reading Nasta'liq: Persian and Urdu Hands from 1500 to the Present*. Costa Mesa, CA: Mazda Publishers, 1995.

Hawker, C.L., ed. *Simple Colloquial Persian*. London: Lowe and Brydone, 1937.

Hillman, Michael Craig. *Persian Vocabulary Acquisition*. 2nd Edition. Springfield, VA: Dunwoody Press, 2003.

———. *Reading Iran, Reading Iranians*. 2nd Edition. Springfield, VA: Dunwoody Press, 2003.

———. *Tajiki Textbook and Reader*. 2nd Edition. Springfield, VA: Dunwoody Press, 2003.

Janani, Carina. *Language in Society: Eight Sociolinguistics Essays on Baluchi*. Uppsala: Uppsala University Press, 2000.

Kamshad, Hassan. *A Modern Persian Prose Reader*. Cambridge, England: Cambridge University Press, 1968.

Kent, Roland G. *Old Persian: Grammar, Texts, Lexicon*. New Haven: American Oriental Society, 1950.

Lambton, Ann K.S. *Persian Grammar*. Cambridge, England: Cambridge University Press, 1966.

Lazard, Gilbert. *A Grammar of Contemporary Persian*. Translated by Shirley A. Lyon. Costa Mesa, CA: Mazda Publishers, 1992.

Mace, John. *Persian Grammar: For Reference and Revision*. London: RoutledgeCurzon, 2003.

Mahmoudi, Jalil. *Reading and Writing Persian*. Salt Lake City: University of Utah Press, 1967.

Marashi, Mehdi. *Let's Read Persian*. Salt Lake City: The University of Utah, 1973.

McCarus, Ernest N. *A Kurdish Grammar*. New York: American Council of Learned Societies, 1958.

Meskoob, Shahrokh. *Iranian Nationality and the Persian Language.* Translated by Michael Hillmann. Edited by John Perry. Washington, DC: Mage Publishers, 1992.

Moshiri, Leila. *Colloquial Persian.* London: Routledge, 1988.

Perry, John R. *A Tajik Persian Reference Grammar.* Leiden: Brill, 2005.

Skalmowski, Wojciech and Alois van Tongerloo. *Iranica Selecta: Studies in Honour of Professor Wojciech Skalmowski on the Occasion of His Seventieth Birthday.* Turnhout: Brepols, 2003.

Stilo, Donald, Kamran Talattof, and Jerome Clinton. *Modern Persian: Spoken and Written.* Vols. 1 and 2. New Haven CT: Yale University Press, 2005.

Thackston, Wheeler M. *An Introduction to Persian.* Revised Third Edition. Bethesda, MD: Iranbooks, 1993.

Windfuhr, Gernot, ed. *Iranian Languages.* London: Routledge-Curzon, 2003.

Windfuhr, Gernot L., William Beeman et al. *Intermediate Persian.* Vols. 1 and 2. Ann Arbor, MI: Department of Near Eastern Studies, University of Michigan, 1979.

Yar-Shater, Ehsan. *A Grammar of Southern Tati.* The Hague: Mouton Publishers, 1969.

3. LITERATURE—GENERAL

Akbar, Fatollah. *The Eye of the Ant: Persian Proverbs and Poems.* Bethesda, MD: Iranbooks, 1995.

Browne, Edward G. *A Literary History of Persia.* 4 Vols. 2nd Edition. Cambridge, England: The University Press, 1928-1929.

Ghanoonparvar, M.R. *In a Persian Mirror: Images of the West and Westerners in Iranian Fiction.* Austin, Texas: The University of Texas Press, 1993.

Green, John. *Iranian Short Story Authors: A Bio-Bibliographic Survey.* Costa Mesa, CA: Mazda Publishers, 1989.

Hillmann, Michael C. *Persian Culture: A Persianist View.* Lanham, MD: University Press of America, 1990.

Javadi, Hasan. *Persian Literary Influence on English Literature.* Piedmont, CA: Jahan Book Company, 1987.

———. *Satire in Persian Literature.* Rutherford, NJ: Farleigh Dickinson University Press, 1988.

Levy, Reuben. *Introduction to Persian Literature.* New York: Columbia University Press, 1969.

Melville, Charles, ed. *History and Literature in Iran*. Cambridge, England: British Academic Press and Centre of Middle Eastern Studies, Cambridge University, 1990.

Morrison, G., ed. *History of Persian Literature from theBeginn ing of the Islamic Period to the Present Day*. Leiden: E.J. Brill, 1981.

Parsinejad, Iraj. *A History of Literary Criticism in Iran (1866-1951): Literary Criticism in the Works of Enlightened Thinkers of Iran, Akhundzadeh, Kermani, Malkam, Talebof, Maraghe'i, Kasravi and Hedayat*. Bethesda, MD: IBEX Publishers, 2003.

Ravani'pur, Muniru, Hirad Dinavari, and M.R. Ghanoonparvar. *Kanizu: Stories*. Costa Mesa, CA: Mazda Publishers, 2004.

Ricks, Thomas, ed. *Critical Perspectives on Modern Persian Literature*. Washington, DC: Three Continents Press, 1984.

Rypka, Jan. *History of Iranian Literature*. Edited by Karl Jahn. Dordrecht, Holland: D. Reidel, 1968.

Shahideh, Laleh. *The Power of Iranian Narratives: A Thousand Years of Healing*. Lanham, MD: University Press of America, 2004.

Storey, C.A. *Persian Literature: A Bio-Bibliographical Survey*. 5 Vols. Richmond, Surrey: Curzon Press, 2002.

Talattof, Kamran. *The Politics of Writing in Iran: A History of Modern Persian Literature*. Syracuse, NY: Syracuse University Press, 2000.

Yamamoto, Kumiko. *The Oral Background of Persian Epics: Storytelling and Poetry*. Boston, MA: Brill, 2003.

Yarshater, Ehsan, ed. *Persian Literature*. New York: The Persian Heritage Foundation; Bibliotheca Persica, 1988.

Yohannan, John. *Persian Literature in England and America*. Delmar, NY: Caravan Books, 1977.

4. CLASSICAL LITERATURE

a) *General*

Arberry, A.J. *Classical Persian Literature*. Richmond, Surrey: Curzon Press, 1993.

'Attar, Farid al-Din. *The Conference of Birds: The Selected Sufi Poetry of Farid ud-Din Attar*. Edited by Raficq Abdulla. New York: Interlink Books, 2003.

Barnham, Henry D. *Tales of Nasreddin Khoja: 181 Mulla Nasreddin Stories*. Bethesda, MD: IBEX, 1999.

Blondel Saad, Joya. *The Image of Arabs in Modern Persian Literature*.

Lanham, MD: University of Washington Press, 1999.

Clinton, Jerome W. *The Divan of Manuchihri Damghani: A Critical Study*. Minneapolis: Bibliotheca Islamica, 1972.

Cowen, Jill Sanchia. *Kalila Wa Dimna: An Animal Allegory of the Mongol Court*. New York: Oxford University Press, 1989.

Curtis, Vesta Sarkhosh and Sheila R. Canby. *Persian Love Poetry*. Northampton: Interlink Books, 2006.

Davidson, Olga M., ed. *Comparative Literature and Classical Persian Poetics: Seven Essays*. Costa Mesa, CA: Mazda Publishers, 2000.

Davis, Dick. trans. *Borrowed Ware: Medieval Persian Epigrams*. Washington, DC: Mage Publishers, 1997.

Elwell-Sutton, L.P. *The Persian Metres*. Cambridge, England: Cambridge University Press, 1976.

Farzad, Mas'ud. *Persian Poetic Metres*. Leiden: E.J. Brill, 1967.

Ganjavi, Nizami. *The Poetry of Nizami Ganjavi: Knowledge, Love and Rhetoric*. Edited by Kamran Talattof and Jerome W. Clinton. New York: Palgrave, 2000.

Guppy, Shusha. *The Secret of Laughter: Magical Tales from Classical Persia*. New York: I.B. Tauris, 2005.

Hagg, Tomas. *The Virgin and Her Lover: Fragments of an Ancient Greek Novel and a Persian Epic Poem*. Leiden: Brill, 2003.

Hovannissian, Richard, ed. *Armenian Van/Vaspurakan*. Costa Mesa, CA: Mazda, 2000.

Hunsberger, Alice. *Nasir Khusraw: The Ruby of Badakhshan, A Portrait of the Persian Poet, Traveler and Philosopher*. Ismaili Heritage Series, 4. London: I.B. Taurus, 2000.

Losensky, Paul E. *Welcoming Fighani: Imitation and Poetic Individuality in the Safavid-Mughal Ghazal*. Costa Mesa, CA: Mazda Publishers, 1998.

Mabey, Juliet. *Rumi: A Spiritual Treasury*. Oxford: Oneworld Publications, 2000.

Meisami, Julie Scott. *Medieval Persian Court Poetry*. Princeton, NJ: Princeton University Press, 1987.

―――. *Structure and Meaning in Medieval Arabic and Persian Poetry*. London: RoutledgeCurzon, 2003.

Nasir-i Khusraw. *Make a Shield from Wisdom: Selected Verses from Nasir-i Khusraw's Divan*. Edited by Annemarie Schimmel. London: Kegan Paul International, 1993.

―――. *Naser-e Khosraw's Book of Travels*. Translated by W.M. Thackston. Albany, NY: Bibliotheca Persica, 1986.

Sharma, Sunil. *Amir Khusraw: The Poet of Sultans and Sufis*. Oxford,

England: Oneworld Publications, 2005.

Talatoff, Kamaran and Jerome Clinton, eds. *The Poetry of Nizami Ganjavi.* New York: Palgrave, 2000.

Thisen, Finn. *A Manual of Classical Persian Prosody.* Wiesbaden, Germany: Otto Harrassowitz, 1982.

Zakani, Obeid. *The Story of the Cat and Mice.* Translated by Abbas Aryanpur Kashani. Tehran: Taban Press, 1971.

b) *Ferdowsi*

Davis, Dick. *Epic and Sedition: The Case of Ferdowsi's Shahnameh.* Fayetteville, AR: University of Arkansas Press, 1992.

Davidson, Olga. *Poet and hero in the Persian Book of Kings.* Ithaca, NY.: Cornell University Press, 1994.

————, trans. *Stories from the Shahnameh of Ferdowsi.* Vols. 1-3. Washington, DC: Mage Publishers, 1998-2004.

The Epic of the Kings: Shah-nama, The National Epic of Persia. Translated by Reuben Levy. Chicago: University of Chicago Press, 1967.

The Legend of Seyavash. Translated by Dick Davis. Harmonds-worth, Middlesex, England: Penguin Books, 1992.

Robinson, R.W. *The Persian Book of Kings: An Epitome of the Shahnama of Firdowsi.* New York: RoutledgeCurzon, 2002.

Shahbazi, A. Shapur. *Ferdowsi: A Critical Biography.* Costa Mesa, CA: Mazda Publishers, 1991.

The Shahnameh (Book of Kings). 3 Vols. Edited by Djalal Khalighi-Motlaq. New York: Bibliotheca Persica, 1987, 1990, 1992.

The Shahnameh of Firdausi. 9 Vols. Translated by Arthur George and Edmond Warner. London: Kegan Paul, 1905-1925.

Suhrab and Rustam: A Poem from the Shah Namah of Firdausi. Translated by James Atkinson. 1914. Reprint. Delmar, NY: Scholar's Facsimiles and Reprints, 1972.

The Tragedy of Sohrab and Rostam. Translated by Jerome W. Clinton. Seattle: University of Washington Press, 1987.

Wilkinson, J.V.S. *The Shah-Nameh of Firdausi: The Book of Persian Kings.* London: India Society, 1931.

c) *Hafez*

Crowe, Thomas Rain. *In Winesellers Street: Renderings of Hafez.* Bethesda, MD: IBEX Publishers, 1998.

The Divan-i-Hafiz. Translated by H. Wilberforce Clarke. Bethesda, MD: IBEX Publishers, 1998.

The Gift: Poems by the Great Sufi Master. Translated by Daniel James Ladinsky. New York: Arkana, 1999.

The Green Sea of Heavn: Fifty Ghazals from the Diwan of Hafiz. Translated by Elizabeth T. Gray, Jr. Introduction by Daryush Shayegan. Ashland, OR: White Cloud Press, 1995.

Hafez: Dance of Life. Translated by Michael Boylan. Washington, DC: Mage Press, 1988.

Hafez: Fifty Poems. Edited by Arthur J. Arberry. Cambridge, England: Cambridge University Press, 1953.

Hillmann, Michael C. *Unity in the Ghazals of Hafez.* Minneapolis: Bibliotheca Islamica, 1976.

Odes of Hafez: Political Horoscope. Translated by Abbas Aryanpur. Lexington, KY: Mazda Publishers, 1984.

Poems from the Divan of Hafiz. Translated by Gertrude Lowthian Bell. London: William Heinemann, Ltd., 1897.

The Subject Tonight is Love: 60 Wild and Sweet Poems. Translated by Daniel James Ladinsky. New York: Penguin Compass, 2003.

d) *Khayyam*

Aminrazavi, Mehdi. *The Wine of Wisdom: The Life, Poetry and Philosophy of Omar Khayyam.* Oxford, England: Oneworld Publications, 2005.

Dashti, Ali. *In Search of Omar Khayyam.* Translated by L.P. Elwell-Sutton. London: George Allen and Unwin, 1971.

FitzGerald's Rubaiyat. Centennial Edition. Edited by Carl J. Weber. Waterville, ME: Colby College Press, 1959.

A New Selection from the Rubaiyat of Omar Khayyam. Edited by John Charles Edward Bowen. Warminster, England: Aris and Phillips, 1976.

The Romance of the Rubaiyat. Edward FitzGerald's First Edition. Translated by Edward FitzGerald. With an introduction by A.J. Arberry. Richmond, Surrey: Curzon Press, 2001.

Ruba'iyat of Omar Khayyam. Translated by Ahmad Saidi. Berkeley, CA: Asian Humanities Press, 1991.

The Ruba'iyat of Omar Khayyam. Translated by A.J. Arberry. London: Walker, 1949.

Ruba'iyat of Omar Khayyam. Translated by Edward FitzGerald. London: A. & C. Black, 1909.

The Ruba'iyat of Omar Khayyam. Translated by Peter Avery and John Heath-Stubbs. Harmondsworth, Middlesex, England: Penguin Books, 1981.

The Ruba'iyat of Umar Khayyam. Translated by Parichehr Kasra. Delmar, NY: Scholar's Facsimiles and Reprints, 1975.

e) *Rumi*

Discourses of Rumi. Translated by A.J. Arberry. London: John Murray, 1961.

Love is a Stranger: Selected Lyric Poetry of Jelaluddin Rumi. Translated by Edmund Helminski. Putney, VT: Threshold Books, 1993.

The Essential Rumi. Translated by Coleman Barks, Reynold Nicholson, A.J. Arberry, and John Moyne. San Francisco, CA: Harper, 2004.

The Masnavi, Book One. Translated by J.A. Mojaddedi. Oxford, England: Oxford University Press, 2004.

The Mathnawi of Jalaluddin Rumi. 6 Vols. Translated by Reynold Alleyne Nicholson. 1926. Reprint. London: Luzac, 1982.

Mystical Poems of Rumi: First Selection, Poems 1-200. Translated by A.J. Arberry. Chicago: University of Chicago Press, 1968.

Mystical Poems of Rumi: Second Selection, Poems 201-400. Translated by A.J. Arberry. Boulder, CO: Westview Press, 1979.

Open Secret: Versions of Rumi. Translated by John Moyne and Coleman Barks. Putney, VT: Threshold Books, 1984.

The Ruins of the Heart: Selected Lyric Poetry of Jelaluddin Rumi. Translated by Edmund Helminski. Putney, VT: Threshold Books, 1981.

Rumi, Jalal al-Din. *The Illuminated Rumi.* Translated by Coleman Barks, Illustrated by Michael Green. New York: Broadway Books, 1997.

Rumi, Jalal Al-Din. *Rumi: A Spiritual Treasure.* Oxford: Oneworld Publications, 2000.

Selected Poems from the Divani Shamsi Tabriz. Translated by Reynold A. Nicholson. Cambridge, England: Cambridge University Press, 1952.

Tales from the Masnavi. Translated by A.J. Arberry. London: Allen and Unwin, 1961.

This Longing: Poetry, Teaching Stories, and Selected Letters of Rumi. Translated by John Moyne and Coleman Barks. Brattleboro, VT: Threshold Books, 1988.

f) *Sa'di*

The Bustan. Translated by G.M. Wickens. Tehran: Sepehr Print House, 1985.

Bustan of Sadi. Translated by A. Hart Edwards. Lahore, Pakistan: M. Ashraf, 1950.

The Gulistan or Rose Garden of Sa'di. Translated by Edward Rehatsek. London: George Allen and Unwin, 1964.

Kings and Beggars. Translated by A.J. Arberry. London: Luzac, 1945.

Morals Pointed and Tales Adorned: The Bustan of Sadi. Translated by G.M. Wickens. Toronto: University of Toronto Press, 1974.

Yohannan, John D. *The Poet Sa'di: A Persian Humanist.* Lanham, MD: University Press of America, 1987.

5. MODERN LITERATURE

a) *Anthologies*

Bagley, F.R.C., ed. *Sadeq Chubak: An Anthology.* Delmar, NY: Caravan Books, 1982.

Basmenji, Kaveh, ed. *Afsaneh: Short Stories by Iranian Women.* London: Saqi, 2005.

Hillmann, Michael C., ed. *Iranian Society: An Anthology of Writings by Jalal Al-e Ahmad.* Lexington, KY: Mazda Publishers, 1982.

———. *Literature East and West: Major Voices in Contemporary Persian Literature. Vol.20.* Austin, TX: Oriental-Western Literay Relations Group of the Modern Language Association, 1976 (Published 1980).

Moayyad, Heshmat, ed. *Stories from Iran: A Chicago Anthology, 1921-1991.* Washington, DC: Mage Publishers, 1991.

Mozaffari, Nahid, ed. *Strange Times, My Dear: The PEN Anthology of Contemporary Iranian Literature.* New York: Arcade Publishing, 2005.

Ricks, Thomas M., ed. *The Literary Review: An International Journal of Contemporary Writing.* Vol. 18, No. 11, Fall, 1974. Rutherford, NJ: *The Literary Review,* 1974.

Siavosh, Danesh, ed. *An Anthology of Persian Prose.* Tehran: Vahid Publishing Company, 1971.

Southgate, Minoo S., ed. *An Anthology of Persian Prose.* Washington, DC: Three Continents Press, 1980.

Yar-Shater, Ehsan, ed. *Sadeq Hedayat: An Anthology.* Boulder, CO:

Westview Press, 1979.

b) *Fiction—Novels and Short Stories*

Al-e Ahmad, Jalal. *By the Pen.* Translated by M.R. Ghanoon-parvar. Austin, TX: Center for Middle Eastern Studies, The University of Texas, 1988.

Amirshahi, Mahshid. *Suri and Co.: Tales of a Persian Teenager.* Translated by J.E. Knorzer. Austin, TX: Center for Middle Eastern Studies at The University of Texas at Austin, 1995.

Daneshvar, Simin. *Daneshvar's Playhouse.* Translated by Maryam Mafi. Washington, DC: Mage Publishers, 1990.

———. *Savushun.* Translated By M.R. Ghanoonparvar. Washington, DC: Mage Publishers, 1994.

———. *Sutra and Other Stories.* Translated by Hasan Javadi and Amin Neshati. Washington, DC: Mage Publishers, 1994.

Esfandiary, Fereidoun. *The Day of Sacrifice.* London: William Heinemann Ltd., 1960.

———. *Identity Card.* New York: Grove Press, 1966.

Fassih, Ismail. *Sorraya in a Coma.* London: Zed Books, 1985.

Firouz, Anahita. *In the Walled Garden: A Novel.* New York: Little, Brown, 2002.

Green, John and Farzin Yazdanfar, eds. *A Walnut Sapling on Masih's Grave and other Short Stories by Iranian Women.* Portsmouth, NH: Heinemann, 1992.

Hedayat, Sadegh. *The Blind Owl.* Translated by D.P. Costello. New York: Grove Press, 1969.

———. *Haji Agha: Portrait of an Iranian Confidence Man.* Translated by G.M. Wickens. Austin, TX: Center for Middle Eastern Studies, The University of Texas, 1979.

Irani, Manuchehr. *King of the Benighted.* Translated by Abbas Milani. Washington, DC: Mage Publishers, 1990.

Modarressi, Taghi. *The Pilgrim's Rules of Etiquette.* New York: Doubleday, 1989.

Parsipur, Shahrnush. *Women Without Men: A Novella.* Translated by Kamran Talattof and Jocelyn Sharlet. Syracuse, NY: Syracuse University Press, 1998.

Parvin, Manoucher. *Avicenna and I: The Journey of Spirits.* Costa Mesa, CA: Mazda Publishers, 1996.

———. *Cry for My Revolution, Iran.* Costa Mesa, CA: Mazda Publishers, 1987.

———. *Dardedel: Rumi, Hafez and Love in New York.* Sag Harbor, NY: The Permanent Press, 2003.

Pezeshkzad, Iraj. *My Uncle Napoleon.* Translated by Dick Davis. Washington, DC: Mage Publishers, 1996.

Rachlin, Nahid. *Foreigner.* New York: W.W. Norton, 1978.

———. *Married to a Stranger.* San Francisco: City Lights, 1993.

———. *Veils: Short Stories.* San Francisco: City Lights, 1992.

Raffat, Donne. *The Caspian Circle: A Novel.* Boston: Houghton Mifflin, 1978.

Ravanipur, Moniru. *Satan's Stories.* Edited by M.R. Ghanoonparvar. Translated by Persis Karim et al. Austin, TX: University of Texas Press, 1996.

Taraqqi, Goli. *Winter Sleep.* Translated by Francine T. Mahak. Costa Mesa, CA: Mazda Publishers, 1994.

c) *Poetry*

Behbahani, Simin. *A Cup of Sin: Selected Poems.* Translated by Farzaneh Milani and Kaveh Safa. Syracuse, NY: Syracuse University Press, 1999.

Browne, Edward G. *The Press and Poetry of Modern Persia.* Cambridge, England: The University Press, 1914.

E'tesami, Parvin. *A Nightingale's Lament: Selections from the Poems and Fables of Parvin E'tesami.* Translated by Heshmat Moayyad and A. Margaret Arent Madelung. Lexington, KY: Mazda Publishers, 1985.

Farrokhzad, Furugh. *Another Birth: Selected Poems of Forugh Farrokhzad.* Translated by Hasan Javadi and Susan Sallee. Emeryville, CA: Albany Press, 1981.

———. *Bride of Acacias.* Translated by Jascha Kessler and Amin Banani. Delmar, NY: Caravan Books, 1982.

Hillmann, Michael. *A Lonely Woman: Forugh Farrokhzad and Her Poetry.* Washington, DC: Mage Publishers, 1987.

Ishaque, Mohammad. *Modern Persian Poetry.* Calcutta, India: Mohammad Israil, 1943.

Karimi-Hakkak, Ahmad, ed. *An Anthology of Modern Persian Poetry.* Boulder, CO: Westview Press, 1978.

Karimi-Hakkak, Ahmad and Kamran Talattof, eds. *Essays on Nima Yushij: Animating Modernism in Persian Poetry.* Leiden: Brill, 2004.

Naderpour, Nader. *False Dawn: Persian Poems (1951-1984).*

Translated by Michael C. Hillmann. Austin, TX: *World Literature Annual, Literature East and West.* Department of Oriental and African Languages and Literatures, The University of Texas at Austin, 1986.

Papan-Matin, Firoozeh. *The Love Poems of Shamlu.* Bethesda, MD: Ibex Publishers, Inc., 2005.

Rahman, Munibur. *Post-Revolution Persian Verse.* Aligarh, India: Institute of Islamic Studies, Muslim University, 1955.

Tikku, Girdhari with Alireza Anushiravani. *A Conversation with Modern Persian Poets.* Costa Mesa, CA: Mazda Publishers, 2004.

d) *Essays, Satire, Social and Literary Criticism*

Al-e Ahmad, Jalal. *Gharbzadegi (Westruckness).* Translated by John Green and Ahmad Alizadeh. Lexington, KY: Mazda Publishers, 1982.

———. *Occidentosis: A Plague from the ,West.* Translated by R. Campbell. Berkeley, CA: Mizan Press, 1983.

———. *Plagued by the West (Gharbzadegi).* Translated by Paul Sprachman. Delmar, NY: Caravan Books, 1982.

Bashiri, Iraj. *The Fiction of Sadeq Hedayat.* Lexington, KY: Mazda Publishers, 1984.

———. *Hedayat's Ivory Tower: Structural Analysis of the Blind Owl.* Minneapolis: Manor House, 1974.

Beard, Michael. *Hedayat's Blind Owl as a Western Novel.* Princeton, NJ: Princeton University Press, 1990.

Behrangi, Samad. *The Little Black Fish and Other Modern Persian Stories.* Translated by Mary and Eric Hooglund. Washington, DC: Three Continents Press, 1976.

Ghanoonparvar, Mohammad Reza. *Prophets of Doom: Literature as a Socio-Political Phenomenon in Modern Iran.* Lanham, MD: University Press of America, 1984.

Haidari, Javad, ed. *Iran.* New York: *Review of National Literatures.* Vol. II, No. 1, 1971.

Hillmann, Michael C. *Hedayat's "The Blind Owl" Forty Years Aft- ter.* Austin, TX: Center for Middle Eastern Studies, The University of Texas, 1978.

———, ed. *Literature and Society in Iran.* Boston: *Iranian Studies,* Vol. 15, Nos. 1-4, 1982.

———, ed. *Sociology of the Iranian Writer.* Boston: *Iranian Studies* , Vol. 18, Nos. 2-4, 1985.

Jamalzadeh, Mohammad Ali. *Once Upon a Time.* Translated by Heshmat Moayyad and Paul Sprachman. New York: Bibliotheca Persica, 1985.

Kamshad, H. *Modern Persian Prose Literature.* Cambridge, England: Cambridge University Press, 1966.

Katouzian, Homa. *Sadeq Hedayat: The Life and Legend of an Iranian Writer.* London: I.B. Tauris, 1991.

6. DRAMA

Aghaie, Kamran Scot. *The Women of Karbala: Ritual Performance and Symbolic Discourses in Modern Shi'i Islam.* Austin: University of Texas Press, 2005.

Chelkowski, Peter J., ed. *Ta'ziyeh: Ritual and Drama in Iran.* New York: New York University Press, 1979.

Floor, Willem. *The History of Theater in Iran.* Washington, DC: Mage Publishers, 2005.

Forough, Mehdi. *A Comparative Study of Abraham's Sacrifice in Persian Passion Plays and Western Mystery Plays.* Tehran: Ministry of Culture and Arts Press, 1973.

Ghanoonparvar, M.R. and John Green, eds. *Iranian Drama: An Anthology.* Costa Mesa, CA: Mazda Publishers, 1989.

Kapuscinski, Gisele, trans. *Modern Persian Drama: An Anthology.* Lanham, MD: University Press of America, 1987.

Malekpour, Jamshid. *The Islamic Drama.* Portland, OR: Frank Cass, 2004.

Pelly, Sir Lewis. *The Miracle Play of Hasan and Husain.* 2 Vols. London: W.H. Allen, 1879.

Riggio, Milla Cozart, ed. *Ta'ziyeh: Ritual and Popular Beliefs in Iran.* Hartford, CT: Trinity College, 1988.

Sayyad, Parviz. *Theater of the Diaspora: Two Plays: The Ass and the Rex Cinema Trial.* Edited by Hamid Dabashi. Costa Mesa, CA: Mazda Publishers, 1993.

VIII. ECONOMICS

1. NATIONAL ECONOMY

a) *Historical and Developmental*

Ali, Mohammad, ed. *Iran Encountering Globalization: Problems and Prospects.* New York: RoutledgeCurzon, 2003.

Amuzegar, Jahangir. *Iran: An Economic Profile.* Washington, DC: Middle East Institute, 1977.

———. *Technical Assistance in Theory and Practice: The Case of Iran.* New York: Praeger, 1966.

Amuzegar, Jahangir and M. Ali Fekrat. *Iran: Economic Development under Dualistic Conditions.* Chicago: University of Chicago Press, 1971.

Baldwin, George B. *Planning and Development in Iran.* Baltimore, MD: The Johns Hopkins University Press, 1967.

Bharier, Julian. *Economic Development in Iran, 1900-1970.* London: Oxford University Press, 1971.

Graham, Robert. *Iran: The Illusion of Power.* London: Croom Helm, 1978.

Issawi, Charles. *The Economic History of Iran, 1800-1914.* Chicago: University of Chicago Press, 1971.

Jacobs, Norman. *The Sociology of Development: Iran as an Asian Case Study.* New York: Praeger, 1966.

Looney, Robert. *A Development Strategy for Iran through the 1980s.* New York: Praeger, 1977.

———. *The Economic Development of Iran: A Recent Survey with Projections to 1981.* New York: Praeger, 1973.

Mani, Sunil. *A National System of Innovation in the Making: An Analysis of the Role of Government with Respect to Promoting Domestic Innovations in the Manufacturing Sector in Iran.* Maastricht, The Netherlands: United Nations University, Institute for New Technologies, 2004.

McCabe, Ina Baghdiantz. *The Shah's Silk for Europe's Silver: The Eurasian Trade of the Julfa Armenians in Safavid Iran and India (1530-1750).* University of Pennsylvania Armenian Texts and Studies, No. 15. Atlanta: Scholars Press, 1999.

Razavi, Hossein and Firuz Vakil. *The Political Environment of Economic Planning in Iran, 1971-1983: From Monarchy to Islamic Republic.* Boulder, CO: Westview Press, 1984.

Shahnavaz, Shahbaz. *Britain and the Opening up of South-West Persia, 1880-1914.* New York: RoutledgeCurzon, 2005.

b) *Finance, Industry, Commerce and Labor*

Amanat, Abbas, ed. *Cities and Trade: Consul Abbot on the Economy and Society of Iran 1847-1866.* London: Ithaca Press, 1983.

Bayat, Asaf. *Workers and Revolution in Iran: A Third World Experience of Workers' Control.* London: Zed Books, 1986.

Benedick, Richard Elliot. *Industrial Finance in Iran: A Study of Financial Practice in an Underdeveloped Economy.* Boston: Division of Research. Graduate School of Business Administration, Harvard University, 1964.

Bostock, F. and G. Jones. *Planning and Power in Iran.* London: Frank Cass, 1989.

Floor, Willem. *Industrialization in Iran, 1900-1941.* Durham, England: University of Durham, 1984.

————. *Labour Unions, Law and Conditions in Iran (1900-1941).* Durham, England: University of Durham, 1985.

Hafsi, Taieb and Mehdi, Farashahi. *Strategic Management in Highly Constrained Environments: The Case of Textile Firms in Iran.* Montreal: HEC Montreal, 2003.

Johnson, Gail Cook. *High Level Manpower in Iran: From Hidden Conflict to Crisis.* New York: Praeger, 1980.

Jones, G. *Banking and Empire in Iran: The History of the British Bank of the Middle East.* Cambridge, England: Cambridge University Press, 1986.

Ladjevardi, Habib. *Labour Unions and Autocracy in Iran.* Syracuse, NY: Syracuse University Press, 1985.

Mobasser, Samad. *The Seed Industry in Iran.* Aleppo, Syria: WANA Seed Network Secretariat, 2003.

Vaghefi, Mohammad Reza. *Entrepreneurs of Iran: The Role of Business Leaders in the Development of Iran.* Palo Alto, CA: Altoan Press, 1975.

Vakil, Firuz. *Determining Iran's Financial Surplus 1352-1371: Some Management Concepts.* Tehran: The Institute for International Political and Economic Studies, 1975.

c) *Agriculture and Land Tenure*

Amid, Mohammad Javad. *Agriculture, Poverty and Reform in Iran.*

London: Routledge, 1990.

Aresvik, Oddvar. *The Agricultural Development of Iran.* New York: Praeger, 1976.

Farazmand, Ali. *The State, Bureaucracy, and Revolution in Iran: Agrarian Reform and Politics.* New York: Praeger, 1989.

Hooglund, Eric. *Reform and Revolution in Rural Iran.* Austin, TX: The University of Texas Press, 1982.

Lambton, A.K.S. *Landlord and Peasant in Persia.* Oxford, England: Oxford University Press, 1953.

———. *The Persian Land Reform, 1962-1966.* Oxford, England: Clarendon Press, 1969.

McLachlan, Keith. *The Neglected Garden: The Politics and Ecology of Agriculture in Iran.* London: I.B. Tauris, 1988.

Najmabadi, Afsaneh. *Land Reform and Social Change in Iran.* Salt Lake City: University of Utah Press, 1987.

Nattagh, M. *Agriculture and Rural Development in Iran, 1962-1978.* London: Middle East and North African Studies Press, Ltd., 1986.

Schirazi, Asghar. *Islamic Development Policy: The Agrarian Question in Iran.* Translated by P.J. Ziess-Lawrence. Boulder, CO: Lynne Rienner Publishers, 1993.

2. POLITICAL ECONOMY

Amid, Mohammad Javad and Amjad Hadjikhani. *Trade, Industrialization and the Firm in Iran: The Impact of Government Policy on Business.* London: I.B. Tauris, 2005.

Amirahmadi, Hooshang. *Revolution and Economic Transition: The Iranian Experience.* Albany: State University of New York Press, 1990.

Amuzegar, Jahangir. *Iran's Economy under the Islamic Republic.* London: I.B. Taurus, 1997.

Bina, Cyrus and Hamid Zangeneh, eds. *Modern Capitalism and Islamic Ideology in Iran.* New York: St. Martin's Press, 1992.

Hakimian, Hassan. *Labor Transfer and Economic Development: Theoretical Perspectives and Case Studies from Iran.* Herefordshire, England: Harvester Wheatsheaf, 1990.

Hulbert, Mark. *Interlock: The Untold Story of the American Banks, Oil Interest, and the Shah's Money, Debts and the Astounding Connections Between Them.* New York: Richardson and Snyder, 1982.

Jazani, Bizhan. *Capitalism and Revolution in Iran.* London: Zed Press,

1980.

Katouzian, Homa. *The Political Economy of Modern Iran: Despotism and Pseudo-Modernism, 1926-1979.* New York: New York University Press, 1981.

Looney, R.E. *Economic Origins of the Iranian Revolution.* New York: Pergamon Press, 1982.

Malek, M.M.H. *The Political Economy of Iran under the Shah.* London: Croom Helms, 1986.

Rahnema, Ali and Farhad Nomani. *The Secular Miracle: Religion, Politics and Economic Policy in Iran.* London: Zed Books, 1990.

Robinson, Debbie. *Privatisation & Public Private Partnership: Review 2002/2003.* Colchester, United Kingdom: Euromoney, 2003.

Vali, Abbas. *Pre-Capitalist Iran: A Theoretical History.* New York: New York University Press, 1993.

3. OIL

Bahgat, Gawdat. *American Oil Diplomacy in the Persian Gulf and the Caspian Sea.* Gainesville, FL: University Press of Florida, 2003.

Bill, James A. and W. Roger Lewis, eds. *Mussadiq, Iranian Nationalism and Oil.* Austin, TX: The University of Texas Press, 1988.

Elm, Mostafa. *Oil, Power and Principle: Iran's Oil Nationalization and Its Aftermath.* Syracuse, NY: Syracuse University Press, 1992.

Elwell-Sutton, L.P. *Persian Oil: A Study in Power Politics.* London: Laurence and Wishart, Ltd., 1955.

Fatemi, Nasrollah S. *Oil Diplomacy: Powderkeg in Iran.* New York: Whittier Books, 1954.

Fesharaki, Fereidun. *Development of the Iranian Oil Industry: International and Domestic Aspects.* New York: Praeger, 1976.

Karshenas, Massoud. *Oil, State and Industrialization in Iran.* Cambridge, England: Cambridge University Press, 1990.

Koussari, Shahrokh. *The Iranian Oil Gas Report.* London: SMI Publishing, 1999.

Motamen, Homa. *Expenditure of Oil Revenue: An Optimal Control Approach with Application to the Iranian Economy.* New York: St. Martin's Press, 1979.

Salehi-Isfahani, Djavad. *Government Subsidies and Demand for Petroleum Products in Iran.* Oxford, England: Oxford Institute for Energy Studies, 1996.

Williamson, John W. *In a Persian Oil Field: A Study in Scientific and*

Industrial Development. London: E. Benn, 1927.

IX. THE ARTS

1. GENERAL

Ackerman, Phyllis. *Guide to the Exhibition of Persian Art.* New York: The Ivanis Institute, 1940.

Belloni, Gianguido. *Iranian Art.* London: Pall Mall Press, 1969.

Canby, Sheila R. *Safavid Art and Architecture.* London: The British Museum Press, 2002.

Daneshvari, Abbas and Jay Gluck. *Survey of Persian Art: From Prehistoric Times to the Present.* Costa Mesa, CA: Mazda Publishers, 2005.

Ettinghausen, Richard and Ehsan Yar-Shater, eds. *Highlights of Persian Art.* Boulder, CO: Westview Press, 1979.

Ferrier, R.W., ed. *The Arts of Persia.* New Haven: Yale University Press, 1989.

Godard, Andre. *The Art of Iran.* Translated by Michael Heron. London: George Allen and Unwin, 1965.

Golombek, Lisa and Maria Subtelny, eds. *Timurid Art and Culture: Iran and Central Asia in the Fifteenth Century.* Leiden: E.J. Brill, 1992.

Hillenbrand, Robert. *The Art of the Saljuqs in Iran and Anatolia: Proceedings of a Symposium held in Edinburgh in 1982.* Costa Mesa, CA: Mazda Publishers, 1994.

Lentz, Thomas W. and Glenn D. Lowry. *Timur and the Princely Vision: Persian Art and Culture in the 15th Century.* Washington, DC: Smithsonian Press, 1989.

Mahboubian, Houshang, Haideh Sahim and Geoffrey Wilkinson. *Treasures of the Mountains: The Art of the Medes.* London: Houshang Mahboubian, 1995.

O'Kane, Bernard. *Studies in Persian Art and Architecture.* Cairo, Egypt: American University in Cairo Press, 1995.

Pope, Arthur Upham. *An Introduction to Persian Art since the Seventh Century A.D.* 1931. Reprint. Westport, CT: Greenwood Press, 1972.

Pope, Arthur Upham and Phyllis Ackerman, eds. *A Survey of Persian Art from Prehistoric Times to the Present.* 6 Vols. London: Oxford University Press, 1938-1939.

Porada, Edith and Richard Ettinghausen. *7000 Years of Iranian Art.*

Washington, DC: Smithsonian Publications, 1964.

Ross, Sir E. Denison, ed. *Persian Art*. London: Luzac and Company, 1930.

Roxburgh, David J. *The Persian Album, 1400-1600: From Dispersal to Collection*. New Haven: Yale University Press, 2005.

————. *Prefacing the Image: The Writing of Art History in Sixteenth-Century Iran*. Leiden: Brill, 2001.

Simpson, Marianna Shreve. *Persian Poetry, Painting & Patronage: Illustrations in a Sixteenth-Century Masterpiece*. Washington, DC: Freer Gallery, 1997.

Sims, Eleanor. *Peerless Images: Persian Painting and Its Sources*. New Haven: Yale University Press, 2002.

Thackston, W.M. *A Century of Princes: Sources of Timurid History and Art*. Cambridge, MA: Aqa Khan Program, 1989.

2. VISUAL ARTS

a) *General*

Binyon, Laurence, James Wilkinson and Basil Gray. *Persian Miniature Painting*. London: Oxford University Press, 1933.

Brend, Barbara. *Perspectives on Persian Painting: Illustrations to Amir Khusrau's Khamsah*. London: RoutledgeCurzon, 2003.

Canby, Sheila R. *Persian Painting*. Northampton, MA: Interlink Publishing, 2006.

Chelkowski, Peter and Hamid Dabashi. *Staging a Revolution: The Art of Persuasion in the Islamic Republic of Iran*. London: Booth-Clibborn Editions, 2000.

Dickson, Martin and Stuart Cary Welch. *The Houghton Shannameh*. 2 Vols. Cambridge, MA: Harvard University Press, 1981.

Falk, S.J. *Qajar Paintings: Persian Oil Paintings of the 18th and 19th Centuries*. London: Faber and Faber, 1972.

Floor, Willem. *Wall Paintings in Qajar Iran*. Costa Mesa, CA: Mazda Publishers, 2005.

Grabar, Oleg. *Mostly Miniatures: An Introduction to Persian Painting*. Princeton, NJ: Princeton University Press, 2000.

Grabar, Oleg and Sheila Blair. *Epic Images and Contemporary History: The Illustrations of the Great Mongol Shahnama*. Chicago: University of Chicago Press, 1980.

Gray, Basil. *Persian Painting*. New York: Skira, 1961.

Hillenbrand, Robert. *Imperial Images of Persian Painting*. Edinburgh:

Scottish Arts Council Gallery, 1977.

Khazaie, Mohammad. *The Arabesque Motif in Early Islamic Persian art: origin, form and meaning.* London: BookExtra, 1999.

Kubickova, Vera. *Persian Miniatures.* Translated by R. Finlayson-Samsour. London: Spring Books, 1959.

Martin, F.R. *The Miniature Painting and Painters of Persia, India and Turkey, from the 8th to the 18th Century.* 2 Vols. Delhi: B.R. Publishing Corporation, 1912.

Mohasses, Ardeshir. *Closed Circuit History.* Washington, DC: Mage Publishers, 1994.

———. *Life in Iran: The Library of Congress Drawings.* Washington, DC: Mage Publishers, 1994.

O'Kane, Bernard. *Early Persian Painting: "Kalila wa Dimna" Manuscripts of the Late 14th Century.* London: I.B. Taurus, 2003.

Raby, Julian. *Qajar Portraits: Figure Paintings from Nineteenth Century Persia.* London: I.B. Tauris, 2001.

Robinson, B.W. *Persian Drawings from the 14th through the 19th Century.* New York: Shorewood Publishers, 1965.

———. *Persian Paintings in the Collection of Royal Asiatic Society.* Richmond, Surrey: Curzon Press, 1998.

Sims, Eleanor, Boris I. Marshak and Ernst J. Grube. *Peerless Images: Persian Painting and Its Sources.* New Haven, CT: Yale University Press, 2002.

Soudavar, Abolala. *Art of the Persian Courts: Selections from the Art and History Trust Collection.* New York: Rizzoli International Publications, 1992.

Swietochowski, Marie L. *Persian Drawings in the Metropolitan Museum of Art.* New York: Metropolitan Museum, 1989.

Titley, Norah M. *Persian Painting and Its Influence on the Arts of Turkey and India.* London: British Library, 1983.

Welch, Anthony. *Artists for the Shah: Late Sixteenth-Century Painting at the Imperial Court of Iran.* New Haven: Yale University Press, 1976.

Welch, Stuart Cary. *A King's Book of Kings: The Shah-Nameh of Shah Tahmasp.* New York: The Metropolitan Museum of Art, 1972.

———. *Persian Painting: Five Royal Safavid Manuscripts of the Sixteenth Century.* New York: George Braziller, 1976.

Welch, Stuart Cary, Kimberly Masteller, Mary McWilliams, et. al. *From Mind, Heart, and Hand: Persian, Turkish, and Indian Drawings from the Stuart Cary Welch Collection.* New Haven: Yale University Press, 2004.

b) *Film and Photography*

Ahmadi, Mohammed and Mohsen Makhmalbaf. *Gabbeh: Film Script and Photographs*. Tehran: Ney Publishing House, 1997.

Andrew, Geoff. *10*. London: BFI Publishing, 2005.

Bohrer, Frederick N. *Sevruguin and the Persian Image: Photographs of Iran, 1870-1930*. Seattle: University of Washington Press, 1999.

Damandan, Parisa. *Portrait Photographs From Isfahan: Faces in Transition, 1920-1950*. London: Saqi Press, 2004.

Egan, Eric. *The Films of Makhmalbaf: Cinema, Politics and Culture in Iran*. Washington, DC: Mage Publishers, 2005.

Elena, Alberto. *The Cinema of Abbas Kiarostami*. London: Saqi, Iran Heritage Foundation, 2005.

Fischer, Michael M.J. *Mute Dreams, Blind Owls, and Dispersed Knowledges: Persian Poesis in the Transnational Circuitry*. Durham, NC: Duke University Press, 2004.

Issari, Mohammad Ali. *Cinema in Iran, 1900-1979*. Metuchen, NJ: The Scarecrow Press, 1989.

Maghsoudlou, Bahman. *Iranian Cinema*. New York: Kevorkian Center for Near Eastern Studies, New York University, 1987.

Milani, Farzaneh. *Shirin Neshat*. Milan: Art Books International, 2001.

Ridgeon, Lloyd V.J. *Makhmalbaf's Broken Mirror: The Socio-Political Significance of Modern Iranian Cinema*. Durham, UK: University of Durham, Centre for Middle Eastern and Islamic Studies, 2000.

Saeed-Vafa, Mehrnaz and Jonathan Rosenbaum. *Abbas Kiarostami*. Urbana, IL: University of Illinois Press, 2003.

Scarce, Jennifer. *Isfahan in Camera: 19th Century Persia through the Photographs of Ernst Hoeltzer*. London: Art and Archaeology Research Papers, 1976.

Tapper, Richard. *The New Iranian Cinema: Politics, Representa-ion and Identity*. London: I.B. Taurus, 2002.

3. BUILDING ARTS

'Arab, Ghulam Husayn. *Churches of Iran*. Esfahan: Rasaneh Kaj, 1998.

Ardalan, Nader and Laleh Bakhtiar. *The Sense of Unity: The Sufi Tradition in Persian Architecture*. Chicago: University of Chicago Press, 1973.

Daneshvari, Abbas. *Medieval Tomb Towers of Iran: An Iconographical Study*. Lexington, KY: Mazda Publishers, 1986.

Eshragh, Abol-Hamid, ed. *Masterpieces of Iranian Architecture*.

Tehran: Ministry of Development and Housing, 1970.

Grabar, Oleg. *The Great Mosque of Isfahan.* London: I.B. Tauris, 1990.

Hutt, Anthony and Leonard Harrow. *Iran I.* London: Scorpion Publications, 1977.

Jodidio, Philip. *Iran, Architecture for Changing Societies: An International Seminar.* Turin: U. Allemandi for Aga Khan Award for Architecture, 2004.

Khansari, Mehdi and Minouch Yavari. *The Persian Bazaar: Veiled Space of Desire.* Washington, DC: Mage Publishers, 1993.

Khansari, Mehdi, M.R. Moghtader and Minouch Yavari. *The Persian Garden: Echoes of Paradise.* Washington DC: Mage Publishers, 2004.

Perrot, Georges and Charles Chipiez. *History of Art in Persia.* London: Chapman and Hall, 1892.

Pope, Arthur Upham. *Introducing Persian Architecture.* London: Oxford University Press, 1969.

———. *Persian Architecture.* London: Thames and Hudson, 1965.

Vaux, John H. *Domes of Paradise.* Los Angeles, CA: Eqbal Printing & Publishing, 1994.

Wilber, Donald N. *The Architecture of Islamic Iran: The Il Khanid Period.* Princeton, NJ: Princeton University Press, 1955.

———. *Persian Gardens and Pavilions.* Rutland, VT: C.E. Tuttle, 1962.

Willey, Peter. *Eagle's Nest: Ismaili Castles in Iran and Syria.* London: I.B. Taurus, 2004.

4. TEXTILE ARTS

Arastoo, Dr. Seyed Morteza. *The Essence of Persian Carpets: Woven in Oriental History.* Kyoto, Japan: Kyoto Shoin, 1994.

Aschenbrenner, Erich. *Persian Rugs and Carpets.* Tehran: Farhang-Sara Yassavoli, 1996.

Beattie, May. *Carpets of Central Persia.* Northampton, MA: Interlink Publishing, 2006.

Bier, Carol. *The Persian Velvets at Rosenborg.* Copenhagen: De Danske Kongers Kronologiske Samling, 1995.

Bier, Carol, ed. *Woven from the Soul, Spun from the Heart, Textile Arts of Safavid and Qajar Iran, 16th-19th Centuries.* Washington, DC: Textile Museum, 1987.

Biggs, Robert D., ed. *Discoveries from Kurdish Looms.* Evanston, IL: Northwestern University, 1983.

Eagleton, William. *An Introduction to Kurdish Rugs and Other Weavings.* New York: Interlink Books, 1988.

Edwards, A. Cecil. *The Persian Carpet.* London: Duckworth, 1953.

Floor, Willem. *The Persian Textile Industry in Historical Perspective.* Paris: L'Harmattan, 1999.

de Franchis, Amedeo and John T. Wertime. *Lori and Bakhtiyari Flatweaves.* Tehran: Tehran Rug Society, 1976.

Gans-Ruedin, E. *Iranian Carpets: Art, Craft and History.* London: Thames and Hudson, 1978.

Helfgott, Leonard M. *Ties That Bind: A Social History of the Iranian Carpet.* Washington, DC: Smithsonian Institution Press, 1994.

Hilliard, Elizabeth. *Kilims: Decorating with Tribal Rugs.* San Francisco, CA: Soma Books, 1999.

Housego, Jenny. *Tribal Rugs: An Introduction to the Weavings of the Tribes of Iran.* London: Scorpion Publications, 1978.

Konieczny, M.G. *Textiles of Baluchistan.* London: British Museum Publications, 1979.

Mackie, L.W. and J. Thompson, eds. *Turkmen Tribal Carpets and Traditions.* Washington, DC: Textile Museum, 1980.

Murphy, Brian. *The Root of Wild Madder: Chasing the History, Mystery, and Lore of the Persian Carpet.* New York: Simon Schuster, 2005.

Opie, James. *Tribal Rugs of Southern Persia.* Portland, OR: James Opie Oriental Rugs, Inc., 1981.

Petsopoulos, Yanni. *Kilims: The Art of Tapestry Weaving in Anatolia, the Caucasus and Persia.* London: Thames and Hudson, 1979.

Reath, Nancy Andrews and Eleanor B. Sachs. *Persian Textiles and Their Techniques from the Sixth to the Eighteenth Centuries, Including a System for General Textile Classification.* London: H. Milford, Oxford University Press, 1937.

Schlamminger, Karl and Peter Lamborn Wilson. *Weaver of Tales: Persian Picture Rugs.* Munich, Germany: Verlag Georg D.W. Callwey, 1980.

Stanzer, Wilfried. *Kordi: Lives, Rugs, Flatweaves of the Kurds in Khorasan.* Vienna: Adil Besim, 1988.

Tanavoli, Parviz. *Bread and Salt: Iranian Tribal Spreads and Salt Bags.* Translated by Shirin Samii. Tehran: Ketab Sara Company, 1991.

———. *Lion Rugs: The Lion in the Art and Culture of Iran.* New York: Transbooks, 1985.

———. *Shahsevan: Iranian Rugs and Textiles.* New York: Rizzoli,

1985.

Vogelsang-Eastwood, Gillian and L.A.F. Barjesteh van Waalwijk van Doorn. *An Introduction to Qajar Era Dress*. Rotterdam: Barjesteh van Wallwijk van Doorn & Co's Uitgeversmaatschappij, 2002.

5. MUSIC

During, Jean. *The Spirit of Sounds: The Unique Art of Ostad Elahi (1895-1974)*. Cranbury, NJ: Cornwall Books, 2003.

During, Jean, Zia Mirabdolbaghi and Dariush Safvat. *The Art of Persian Music*. Washington, DC: Mage Publishers, 1991

Fallahzadeh, Mehrdad. *Persian Writing on Music: A Study of Persian Musical Literature from 1000 to 1500 AD*. Acta Universitatis Upsaliensis. Studia Iranica Upsaliensia 8. Uppsala, Sweden: Uppsala Univeritetsbibliotek, 2005.

Farhat, Hormoz. *The Dastgah Concept in Persian Music*. Cambridge, England: Cambridge University Press, 2004.

Gerson-Kiwi, Edith. *The Persian Doctrine of Dastgah-Composition: A Phenomenological Study in the Musical Modes*. Tel Aviv, Israel: Israel Music Institute, 1963.

Miller, Lloyd. *Music and Song in Persia*. Richmond, Surrey: Curzon Press, 1999.

Nettl, Bruno. *The Radif of Persian Music: Studies of Structure and Culture Context*. Champaign, IL: Elephant and Cat, 1987.

Nettl, Bruno and Bela Foltin, Jr. *Daramad of Chahargah: A Study in the Performance Practice of Persian Music*. Detroit, MI: Information Coordination, 1972.

Notes to the System of Traditional Persian Music: The Dastgah. Book One: Abu 'Ata. Costa Mesa, CA: Mazda Publishers, 1988.

Wright, O. *A Modal System of Arab and Persian Music*. Oxford, England: Oxford University Press, 1978.

Zonis, Ella. *Classical Persian Music: An Introduction*. Cambridge, MA: Harvard University Press, 1973.

6. CRAFTS AND CRAFTMANSHIP

a) *Metalwork, Jewelry, and Numismatics*

Allan, James W. *Persian Metal Technology, 700-1300 A.D.* London: Ithaca Press, 1979.

Borgomale, Rabino di. *Coins, Medals and Seals of the Shahs of Iran,*

1500-1941. Hertford, England: S. Austin and Sons, Ltd., 1945.

Dhamija, Jasleen. *Living Tradition of Iran's Crafts.* New Delhi, India: Vikas, 1979.

Gluck, Jay and Sumi, eds. *A Survey of Persian Handicraft.* Tehran: Bank Melli Iran, 1977.

Meen, V.B. and A.D. Tushingham. *Crown Jewels of Iran.* Toronto: University of Toronto Press, 1968.

Melikian-Chirvani, Assadullah Souren. *Islamic Metalwork from the Iranian World: 8th-18th Centuries.* London: Her Majesty's Stationery Office, 1982.

Moorey, P.R.S. *Ancient Bronzes from Luristan.* London: British Museum Publications, 1974.

Poole, Reginald S. *The Coins of the Shahs of Persia.* Tehran: Imperial Organization for Social Services, 1976.

Tanavoli, Parviz and John T. Wertime. *Locks from Iran: Pre-Islamic to Twentieth Century.* Washington, DC: Smithsonian Institution, 1976.

Weeks, Lloyd R. *Early Metallurgy of the Persian Gulf: Technology, Trade, and the Bronze Age World.* Boston: Brill, 2003.

Wulff, Hans E. *The Traditional Crafts of Persia: Their Development, Technology, and Influence on Eastern and Western Civilizations.* Cambridge, MA: Massachusetts Institute of Technology Press, 1966.

b) *Ceramics*

Carboni, Stefano and Tomoko Masuya. *Persian Tiles.* New York: Metropolitan Museum of Art, 1993.

Fukai, Shinji. *Ceramics of Ancient Persia.* New York: Weatherhill, 1981.

Kiani, M.Y. *Iranian Pottery.* Tehran: Prime Ministry of Iran, 1978.

Mason, Robert B. *Shine Like the Sun: Lustre-Painted and Associated Pottery from the Medival Middle East.* Costa Mesa, CA: Mazda Publishers in Association with Royal Ontario Museum, 2004.

Mitsukuni, Yoshida. *In Search of Persian Pottery.* New York: Weatherhill, 1981.

Watson, Oliver. *Persian Lustre Ware.* London: Faber, 1985.

Wilkinson, Charles K. *Iranian Ceramics.* New York: H.N. Abrams, 1963.

X. SCIENTIFIC AND LEGAL

1. ARCHAEOLOGY

Boardman, John. *Persia and the West: An Archaeological Investigation of the Genesis of Achaemenid Art.* New York: Thames and Hudson, 2000.

Carter, Elizabeth and Ken Deaver. *Excavations at Anshan (Tal-e Malyan): The Middle Elaite Period.* Philadelphia: University Museum of Archaeology and Anthropology, 1996.

Delougaz, Pinhas, Helene J. Kantor and Abbas Alizadeh. *Chogha Mish. 1961-1971, Part 1: Text, Part 2: Plates.* Vol. 1, Chicago: Oriental Institute of the University of Chicago, 1996.

Ghirshman, Roman. *Iran: From the Earliest Times to the Islamic Conquest.* Baltimore, MD: Penguin Books, 1954.

Goff, Clare. *An Archaeologist in the Making: Six Seasons in Iran.* London: Constable, 1980.

Haerinck, E., B. Overlaet and Berghe, Louis Vanden. *The Iron Age III Graveyard at War: Kabud, Pusht-i Kuh, Luristan.* Leuven: Peeters, 2004.

Herrmann, Georgina. *The Iranian Revival.* Oxford, England: Elsevier-Phaidon, 1977.

Herzfeld, Ernst. *Iran in the Ancient East.* London: Oxford University Press, 1941.

Hole, Frank. *The Archaeology of Western Iran: Settlement and Society from Prehistory to the Islamic Conquest.* Washington, DC: Smithsonian Institution Press, 1987.

Lukonin, Vladamir G. *Persia II.* Translated by James Hogarth. New York: World Publishing Co., 1967.

Miller, Naomi F. and Kamyar Abdi, eds. *Yeki Bud, Yeki Nabud: Essays on the Archaeology of Iran in Honor of William M. Sumner.* Los Angeles: Cotsen Institute of Archaeology in association with the American Institute of Iranian Studies and the University of Pennsylvania Museum of Archaeology and Anthropology, 2003.

Negahban, Ezat O. *Marlik: The Complete Excavation Report.* Philadelphia: University Museum, 1996.

——. *Preliminary Report on Marlik Excavation.* Tehran: University of Tehran, 1964.

——. *Weapons from Marlik.* Berlin: D. Reimer, 1995.

Schmidt, Erich F. *Flights over Ancient Cities of Iran.* Chicago: University of Chicago Press, 1940.

Stein, Sir Aurel. *Archaeological Reconnaissances in N.W. India and S.E. Iran.* London: MacMillan Co., 1937.

————. *Old Routes of Western Iran.* London: MacMillan and Co., 1978.

Stronach, David. *Pasargadae.* Oxford, England: Clarendon Press, 1978.

Watson, Patty Jo. *Archaeological Ethnography in Western Iran.* Tucson, AZ: University of Arizona Press, 1979.

Wilber, Donald N. *Persepolis: The Archaeology of Parsa, Seat of Persian Kings.* 2nd Edition. Revised. Princeton, NJ: The Darwin Press, 1989.

2. GEOGRAPHY

Akhani, Hossein. *The Illustrated Flora of Golestan National Park, Iran.* Tehran: Tehran University Publications, 2005.

Ambraseys, N.N. and C.P. Melville. *A History of Persian Earthquakes.* Cambridge, England: Cambridge University Press, 1982.

Barthold, W. *An Historical Geography of Iran.* Translated by Svat Soucek. Edited by C.E. Bosworth. Princeton, NJ: Princeton University Press, 1984.

Bonine, Michael Edward. *Yazd and Its Hinterland: A Central Place of Dominance in the Central Iranian Plateau.* Marburg, Germany: Selbstverlag des Geographischen Institutes der Universitat Marburg, 1980.

English, Paul W. *City and Village in Iran.* Madison, WI: University of Wisconsin Press, 1966.

Goldsmid, F.J. et al. *Eastern Persia: An Account of the Journeys of the Persian Boundary Commission, 1870-72.* 2 Vols. London: Macmillan and Company, 1876.

Kheirabadi, Masoud. *Iranian Cities: Formation and Development.* Austin, TX: The University of Texas Press, 1991.

Kinnier, Sir John MacDonald. *A Geographical Memoir of the Persian Empire.* London: J. Murray, 1813.

Mansoori, Jamshid. *The Hamoun Wildlife Refuge.* Heidelberg, Germany: M. Kasparek, 1994.

Mujtahidzadah, Piruz. *The Amirs of the Borderlands: And Eastern Iranian Borders.* London: Urosevic Foundation, 1995.

Oberlander, T.M. *The Zagros Streams.* Syracuse, NY: Syracuse University Press, 1965.

Sahab, Abbas. *Map of Iran: River Basins.* Tehran: Sahab Geographic and Drafting Institute, 1963.

3. LAW

Abrahamian, Ervand. *Tortured Confessions: Prisons and Public Recantations in Modern Iran.* Berkeley: University of California Press, 1999.

Afkhami, Mahnaz, ed. *Women and the Law in Iran (1967-1978).* Bethesda, MD: Foundation for Iranian Studies, 1994.

al-Aziz, Khalid. *The Shatt al-Arab River Dispute in Terms of Law.* Baghdad: Iraqi Ministry of Information, 1972.

Delaney, William F. *Labor Law and Practice in Iran.* Washington, DC: U.S. Department of Labor, Bureau of Labor Statistics, 1964.

Fahim, K., J. Habibion and F. Vittor. *English-Persian Dictionary of Legal and Commercial Terms.* Leiden: E.J. Brill, 1989.

Ford, Alan W. *The Anglo-Iranian Oil Dispute of 1951-1952: A Study of the Role of Law in the Relations of States.* Berkeley: University of California Press, 1954.

Haeri, Shahla. *Law of Desire: Temporary Marriage in Shi'i Iran.* Syracuse, NY: Syracuse University Press, 1989.

Mir-Hosseini, Ziba. *Marriage on Trial: A Study of Islamic Family Law: Iran and Morocco Compared.* London: I.B. Tauris, 2000.

Nagavi, Seyyed Ali Reza, ed. *Family Laws of Iran.* Islamabad, Pakistan: Islamic Research Institute, 1971.

Saney, Parviz. *Law and Population Growth in Iran.* Medford, MA: Fletcher School of Law and Diplomacy, Tufts University, 1974.

Westberg, John A. *International Transactions and Claims Involving Government Parties: Case Law of the Iran-United States Claims Tribunal.* Washington, DC: International Law Institute, 1991.

XI. IRANIAN IMMIGRANTS AND THE EXILE COMMUNITY

1. EXILE COMMUNITY STUDIES

Ahlberg, Nora. *No Five Fingers Are Alike: What Exiled Kurdish Women in Therapy Told Me.* Portland, OR: Solum Forlag, 2000.

Ansari, Maboud. *Of the Iranian Community in America: A Case Study of Dual Marginality, Continuity and Change.* New York: Fardis Press, 1992..

Mortazavi, Houman. *Project Misplaced: The Rise and Fall of Simon Ordoubadi*. Los Angeles: Art Project Catalogue, 2004.

Naficy, Hamid. *The Making of Exile Cultures: Iranian Television in Los Angeles*. Minneapolis: University of Minnesota Press, 1993.

Spellman, Kathryn. *Religion and Nation: Iranian Local and Transnational Networks in Britain*. New York: Berghahan Books, 2004.

Sullivan, Zohre T. *Exiled Memories: Stories of Iranian Diaspora*. Philadelphia: Temple University Press, 2001.

2. IMMIGRANT AND EXILIC LITERATURE

Karim, Persis M. *Let Me Tell You Where I've Been: New Writing by Women of the Iranian Diaspora*. Fayetteville: University of Arkansas Press, 2006.

Raffat, Donne. *The Folly of Speaking: The Seventh Tale*. Costa Mesa, CA: Mazda Publishers, 2000.

Swinburn, Anna Woodward. *The Scent of Rosewater: A New Zealand Bride in Iran*. Christchurch, New Zealand: Shoal Bay Press, 1998.

Vatanabadi, S. and M. Khorrami, eds. *Another Sea, Another Shore: Stories of Iranian Migration*. Northampton, MA: Interlink Publishing, 2006.

3. MEMOIRS

Asayesh, Gelareh. *Saffron Sky: A Life Between Iran and America*. Boston: Beacon Press, 1999.

Bahrampour, Tara. *To See and See Again: A Life in Iran and America*. Berkeley: University of California Press, 2000.

Hakakian, Roya. *Journey from the Land of No*. New York: Crown Publishers, 2004.

Latifi, Afschineh and Pablo F. Finjves. *Even After All This Time: A Story of Love, Revolution and Leaving Iran*. New York: Regan Books, 2005.

Milani, Abbas. *Tales of Two Cities*. Washington, DC: Mage Publishers, 1996.

Moaveni, Azadeh. *Lipstick Jihad*. New York: Public Affairs, 2005.

Pahlavi, Princess Ashraf. *Faces in a Mirror: Memoirs from Exile*. Englewood Cliffs, NJ: Prentice-Hall, 1980.

XII. POPULAR PUBLICATIONS

1. COFFEE TABLE AND PICTORIAL BOOKS

Beny, Roloff. *Iran: Elements of Destiny.* Antwerp: Mercatorfonds, 1978.

———. *Persia: Bridge of Turquoise.* London: Thames and Hudson, 1975.

Boulanger, Robert. *Iran.* Paris: Hachette, 1956.

Costa, A. *Persia.* New York: Praeger, 1958.

Ghirshman, Roman, Vladamir Minorsky and Ramesh Sanghvi. *Persia: The Immortal Kingdom.* London: Orient Commerce Establishment, 1971.

Kasraian, N. *Isfahan.* Tehran: Sekeh Press, 1992.

Morath, Inge. *From Persia to Iran: An Historical Journey.* New York: Viking Press, 1960.

Namikawa, Banri. *The Legacy of Cyrus the Great: On the Occasion of the Celebration of the 2500th Anniversary of the Founding of the Persian Empire.* Tokyo: Tokyo International Publishers, 1971.

Kisra'iyan, Nasr Allah and Ziba 'Arshi. *Abyanah.* Tehran: Agah, 2001.

Teta, Jon A. *Iran (Persia) in Pictures.* New York: Sterling Publishing Co., 1968.

Wood, Roger, James Morris and Denis Wright. *Persia.* London: Thames and Hudson, 1969.

Woolley, Al E. *Persia/Iran: A Pictorial Treasury of Twenty-Five Centuries.* New York: Amphoto, 1965.

2. MISCELLANEOUS

Alavi, Nasrin. *We Are Iran.* Brooklyn, NY: Soft Skull Press, 2005.

Badakhshani, S.J., ed. and trans. *Omar Khayyam the Mathematician.* New York: Bilbiotheca Persica, 2000.

Doctor, Raiomond and Karl F. Geldner,. *The Avesta: A Lexico-Statistical Analysis (Direct and Reverse Indexes, Hapax Legomena and Frequency Counts).* Louvain: Peeters, 2004.

Farrokh, Rokn od Din. *History of Books and the Imperial Libraries of Iran.* Translated by Abutaleb Saremi. Tehran: Ministry of Culture and Art, 1968.

Kelsey, Alice Geer. *Once the Mullah.* Leicester, England: Brockhampton Press, 1957.

Mazahiri, Hushang. *The Foreigners Buried in Isfahan, Iran.* Isfahan:

Ghazal, 2004.

Morier, James. *The Adventures of Hajji Baba of Isfahan.* 1824. Reprint. London: Oxford University Press, 1959.

O'Donnell, Terence. *Garden of the Brave in War.* New Haven, CT: Ticknor and Fields, 1980.

Satrapi, Marjane. *Persepolis.* New York: Pantheon Books, 2003.

———. *Persepolis 2: The Story of a Return.* New York: Pantheon Books, 2004.

Smith, Anthony. *Blind White Fish in Persia.* London: George Allen and Unwin, 1953.

Soudavar, Abolala. *The Aura of Kings: Legitimacy and Divine Sanction in Iranian Kingship.* Costa Mesa, CA: Mazda Publishers, 2003.

Vaughan, Leo. *The Jokeman.* London: Eyre and Spottiswoode, 1962.

Za'imi, Khosrow. *Calligraphy from Iran.* London: Commonwealth Institute, 1976.

INDEX

473

ABOUT THE AUTHOR

John H. Lorentz holds an undergraduate degree from Miami University, a master's degree in Middle Eastern Studies from Harvard University, and a Ph.D. from Princeton University. He has resided for over five years in the Middle East, mostly in Iran. He first encountered the country as a Peace Corps Volunteer in Iran Group I. He has worked as a consultant on Middle East affairs and as Executive Director of American Aid for Afghans, in addition to a 35-year academic career as a teacher and administrator at several universities. In addition to having attained several awards for distinguished teaching at the local and state-wide levels, Dr. Lorentz is also renowned as a film producer. He is currently teaching at Shawnee State University in Ohio where he is a professor of history and also serving as Director of the Center for International Programs and Activities.